THE INTERNATIONAL MAIL-ORDER SHOPPING GUIDE

Patricia Wogen Wathey

A SPECTRUM BOOK

PRENTICE-HALL, INC., Englewood Cliffs, New Jersey 07632

Library of Congress Cataloging in Publication Data

Wathey, Patricia Wogen.
    The international mail-order shopping guide.

    "A Spectrum Book."
    Includes index.
    1. Mail-order business—Directories. 2. Catalogs,
Commercial—Directories. I. Title.
HF5466.W38 1984   381'.14'025   84–8390
ISBN 0–13–473083–6
ISBN 0–13–473075–5 (pbk.)

10 9 8 7 6 5 4 3 2 1

ISBN 0-13-473083-6

ISBN 0-13-473075-5 {PBK.}

This book is available at a special discount when ordered in
bulk quantities. Contact Prentice-Hall, Inc., General
Publishing Division, Special Sales, Englewood Cliffs, N.J. 07632.

Editorial/production supervision: Peter Jordan and Marlys Lehmann
Cover design: Hal Siegel
Manufacturing buyer: Pat Mahoney

Prentice-Hall International, Inc., *London*
Prentice-Hall of Australia Pty. Limited, *Sydney*
Prentice-Hall Canada Inc., *Toronto*
Prentice-Hall of India Private Limited, *New Delhi*
Prentice-Hall of Japan, Inc., *Tokyo*
Prentice-Hall of Southeast Asia Pte. Ltd., *Singapore*
Whitehall Books Limited, *Wellington, New Zealand*
Editora Prentice-Hall do Brasil Ltda., *Rio de Janeiro*

To Jim, Brigham, and Brittany

CONTENTS

INTRODUCTION

Welcome to the exciting world of mail-order shopping! No matter what you're searching for, there's a catalog for you. This book offers more than 2200 mail-order catalogs to shop from conveniently—at home! *The International Mail-Order Shopping Guide* is loaded with helpful shopping tips and information on your rights as a mail-order shopper.

If you are ordering from out of state, ordering from your armchair saves time, money, gas, and sales tax. Shopping by mail is an easy way to comparison shop, find goods for specialized interests, discover hard-to-find items, order replacement parts, and find the unusual. Often you can buy items for less from the many discount stores listed in the book. Why pay more?

Catalog shopping offers every product imaginable (and some so imaginative I chose not to list them in the book). Beginning with antiques and ending with the unusual, the catalog offerings are extensive. There are the latest electronic gadgets for the home or office, and epicurean edibles and cooking utensils no kitchen klutz should be without. There are elegant fashions for men and women—with many catalogs featuring special sizes.

A creative gift-giver might select a $25,000 alligator briefcase featuring 18-karat gold locks. A romantic might ask *the* question spelled in solid milk chocolate letters. You might pamper yourself by soaring in your own hot air balloon, buying a computerized fishing reel, or buying an estate on a private island in the Caribbean. There's no shortage of unusual products available by mail: apple trees bearing three-pound fruit, mail order brides, Christmas trees, your portrait in chocolate, and your name in neon lights.

There are terrific bargains if you know where to shop by mail. Cameras from New York are competitively priced with Japan's. There are discount prices on many items including 50% off sterling silver and china, 25% to 50% off lingerie, 30% to 50% off major brand appliances, vacuum cleaners, typewriters, telephones, answering machines, and video recorders.

The selection of mail-order goods is greater than you'll be able to find locally. One catalog features 500 varieties of daffodil bulbs; another offers mahogany, teak and exotic veneers and reproduction furniture kits. There are china from England, hand carved creches from Germany, sweaters from Ireland, Florentine leather goods from Italy, and art reproductions from American museums.

The mail-order industry is enjoying phenomenal growth. This year an estimated 5 billion catalogs will be mailed (half the number beginning in October for the Christmas shopping season). There's no cure for catalogomania save to enjoy it. This book is full of helpful suggestions to make mail-order shopping a fun and exciting experience for you. Even veteran mail-order shoppers may learn a few things. If you know a company that should be listed, or have a mail-order shopping experience to share with me, my address is listed in the *Guide*. Happy mail-order shopping!

HOW TO FIND A PRODUCT OR COMPANY

To find a product, review the Table of Contents, which lists catalog categories. Some catalogs feature such a wide variety of products that it created a problem in organizing the book. The Index should be a big help. Located in the usual place, it lists products alphabetically. Each chapter begins with *see also*—helpful directions to other chapters where you might find similar products. But the fun of this book is really in the browsing. You'll be amazed at all that is offered by mail order!

HOW TO ORDER A CATALOG

Catalog Form

Most companies produce a price list, brochure, or catalog. These can vary from a computer printout of stock available to glamorous, glossy catalogs with color photographs. Some companies will respond only if you enclose a self-addressed stamped envelope (SASE). When requesting information from a company, be sure to state which items you are interested in because many companies produce more than one catalog or brochure.

Paying for the Catalog

Many catalogs are free; others charge from 25¢ to $5. For catalogs that cost more than $1, it is not advisable to pay by personal check because you will have to wait weeks for your check to clear. You should pay by money order, or risk sending cash through the mail. (It's a no-no to send cash through the mail, but grandparents send it in birthday cards and it is a convenient way to order catalogs.) For fees under $1, simply tape the coins to a piece of cardboard. Some catalog fees are refundable, which means that the company will deduct the price of the catalog from your first order. Since the catalog printing schedules vary, you may have to wait some time if you have ordered between printings. The majority of mail-order catalogs are mailed in the fall for Christmas shopping, so that is a good time to order a current copy.

Ordering Overseas Catalogs

Foreign catalogs can be paid for by U.S. dollars, international money orders, or International Reply Coupons (IRCs). IRCs are available from the Post Office and currently sell for 65¢ (U.S.). They are the equivalent of one unit of surface postage and are a good method of catalog payments for under $1, or to supply return postage when requesting information. Remember: U.S. postage stamps cannot be used as return postage from overseas. Most overseas companies will accept U.S. dollar bills as catalog fees, but if the catalog fee is substantial you are safer ordering an international money order. Catalogs will either arrive by surface mail in about six weeks, or by air mail in one week.

HOW TO ORDER A PRODUCT

Order Blank

Order from the latest catalog published, because inventory and prices change frequently, and observe the minimum order requirements. Every order form usually states *print clearly,* and every order department always receives a fair share of orders they can't decipher. *Consumer Reports* magazine stated that sometimes as many as fifteen to twenty percent of a company's orders can't be processed due to errors on the order forms. There are usually minimum order requirements for charge card orders indicated on the order blanks, and they vary from $5 to $45.

Method of Payment

Methods of payment include:

AE American Express
BD Bank Draft, or Foreign Draft. This can be bought at the bank and mailed immediately. It is an excellent means of overseas payment. Fees for the service vary from one bank to the next, but are minimal.
CB Carte Blanche
DC Diners Club
MC MasterCard, often accepted overseas
V Visa, often accepted overseas
MO Money Order, or International Money Order. Money orders are used within the United States. International money orders are used when orders are sent and received overseas. They are the equivalent of cash, do not take time to clear, and are one of the simplest methods of paying for overseas orders. They are available from the Post Office or bank; for orders from $1 to $400, the Post Office charges from $1.30 to $1.80; the bank usually offers a larger limit and slightly higher fee.
PC Personal Check. This is used frequently for payment of goods within the U.S. It is generally a slower method because companies will usually wait three weeks for the check to clear. If an overseas company will accept a personal check (and that is rare), add $3 for the currency conversion fee.
C.O.D. Cash on Delivery.

Price Quote

Why pay more? Comparison shop and save. The catalogs, newspapers, and local merchants offer an excellent opportunity to compare products and find the very best price. Some companies listed do not produce catalogs, brochures, or price lists. They may be discount stores with prices changing frequently, or companies carrying one-of-a-kind merchandise. Call them or write them, stating the brand name, model or style number, and other pertinent information such as color, size, or fabric swatch number. Keep your request to a few items and, if you are writing, be sure to enclose a SASE. Once you decide on a product, act quickly because a price quote has a short life.

Toll Free Numbers

All telephone numbers with the area code 800 are free to out-of-state U.S. callers. There are two types of toll-free telephone services. If you're lucky, the company you're dealing with has a phone service staffed by their own employees who are knowledgeable about store merchandise and store policies. This is a great service, offering immediate information on product availability, substitutions, and even (occasionally) sale items. The other toll-free service is a telemarketing service, taking orders for many companies simultaneously. Both services are great—you can order as quickly as a phone call at your convenience. And, for those insomniacs, some toll-free phone services take orders twenty-four hours a day. When placing an order by phone, have your catalog, order blank, and credit card ready. These are trained professionals taking your order, frequently double checking your information to reduce the chance of order errors.

Overseas Orders

Some overseas catalogs list their product prices in their own currency. Since currency rates change daily and vary from one bank to another, supplying a conversion chart in the book would not be helpful. It is, however, relatively easy to find this information. In the financial section of most newspapers there is a list of more than twenty countries and their foreign exchange rates. It is not always accurate, however, because the newspaper lists the wholesale exchange rate; it should be used only for making estimations. The international department of your local bank will quote exact rates, as will Deak-Perrera at 29 Broadway, New York, New York 10006. Or call Deak-Perrera toll-free at (800) 221-5700. Exchange rates are surprisingly simple to work with. For example, if there is a dress you would like to buy from Sweden priced at 898 kronor, take the example exchange rate of .1271 and multiply it by the price in krona: $.1271 \times 898 = \$114.14$ U.S. Duty is not as high as people usually think. It is applied to the transaction value of goods according to the country of origin and type of product. When you receive your package, a tag wil be attached to the outside wrapper showing the tariff item number, rate of duty, and amount of duty to be paid on the package. You will pay the Post Office both the duty and the postage due. The twelve-page pamphlet, "U.S. Customs International Mail Imports," is available from the Department of Treasury, U.S. Customs Service, Washington, D.C. 20229. It is an excellent reference guide to the most frequently asked questions on customs. A chart of the U.S. customs charges is provided in the appendixes (unless you're planning to order only antiques and truffles, which are duty free). There is also a handy comparative chart on European and American clothing sizes listed in the appendixes.

RECEIVING YOUR ORDER

It's estimated that more than 90 percent of packages are sent by United Parcel Service (UPS—the guys in the brown trucks). The good part is that they automatically insure each package up to $100 without charge and are generally less expensive than the United States Postal Service. The bad part is they do not deliver to a post office box, so you must include a street address. United States Postal Service (USPS) does not automatically insure packages but will provide insurance for a small fee.

If a problem occurs, write the company first. A few companies even offer a toll-free consumer service telephone number. Late delivery or no delivery seem to be two of the biggest complaints. The Federal Trade Commission's (FTC) 30-day rule states that the company must ship your merchandise within thirty days. And if there is going to be a delay in shipment, the company must contact you with the options of either waiting, or canceling your order and receiving a refund. The thirty days starts when they receive your completed prepaid order, so be patient. If your order was paid by check they must provide a refund within seven working days; for charge card orders the company must credit your account within one billing cycle. The FTC 30-day rule does not apply to purchases made over the telephone.

If the company cannot resolve the matter in a reasonable amount of time, there are several agencies to which you can send copies of your transactions and register your complaint. The Chief Postal Inspector, U.S. Postal Service, Washington, D.C. 20260, will notify the company of your complaint. They're pretty effective, too: they can withhold the company's mail! The Federal Trade Commission, Washington, D.C. 20580, cannot handle individual disputes, but the FTC will compile patterns of practices and recommend action to be taken by the Commission. The Direct Marketing Association, Mail Order Action Line, 6 East 43rd Street, New York, New York 10017, and your local Better Business Bureau will write letters to the company on your behalf.

Return policies vary from one company to the next. Quite a few companies offer a no-questions-asked money-back guarantee, but read the company statement before ordering. Save copies of all transactions: forms of payment, letters, and ordering information. Before returning a product, write the company stating the reasons for the return and wait for their instructions. Returned goods should always be sent insured and (preferably) in the original boxes.

AVOIDING PROBLEMS

If you are just starting out in mail order shopping, start small. Make a purchase with an amount of money you're comfortable with, from a business you recognize or was recommended to you. Once you've gained some experience and confidence, there are thousands of companies to shop from and enjoy. A helpful pamphlet, called *A Consumer's Directory of Postal Services and Products,* is available from the United States Postal Service, Washington, D.C. 20260. Also, *Know Before You Go* is an excellent pamphlet, available from the Department of Treasury, U.S. Customs Service, Washington D.C. 20229.

Even if you are a seasoned mail-order shopper, keep a record of your orders. In the back of your calendar or in a special notebook, design a record sheet including: the name and address of the company, title and date of the catalog, name of the item, product number and catalog page number the item appears on, price, shipping and extra charges, date sent, form of payment, and date received. It may seem like a lot of paperwork at first, but when you have orders going out and coming in, it's imperative. Also, keep copies of checks, order blanks, letters, and the original catalog.

When your package arrives, unwrap it carefully. Save all the packing material and the original box until you're satisfied that you've received what you ordered, that it's the right color, that it fits, it works, and it is everything you dreamed it would be.

OVERSEAS READERS

Many of the mail-order shopping tips described earlier apply to overseas readers. American companies prefer to be paid in U.S. dollars for both their catalogs and products. Stock up on U.S. dollar bills for ordering catalogs—most U.S. companies are either reluctant to use or unaware of IRCs. Each catalog listing indicates which forms of payment are acceptable. Certainly your credit cards, (international) money orders, and bank drafts are acceptable, but not your personal checks.

I'm always searching for new mail-order companies. If you know of a company that should be listed, or just want to share some information, send a SASE to:

Patricia Wogen Wathey
P.O. Box 19569
Portland, Oregon 97219

ANTIQUES

A. Goto
1-23-9 Higashi Shibuyaku
Tokyo, Japan
Price list, free U.S. and overseas.
Requested photographs $1 U.S. and
    overseas. Minimum order $30. BD,
    MO.
A. Goto does not have a catalog, but for
$1 U.S. will include photographs
accompanied by a price list for his
Chinese and Japanese antiques. Most
pieces date from 1850 to 1900. Netsuke
(small carved figures) of ivory, black
coral, amber, stag horn, and porcelain
vary in price from about $15 to $60.
There are also cloisonne, Ojime beads,
snuff boxes, and wood block prints.

Antique Imports Unlimited
P.O. Box 2345 Dept. PH
Carson City, NV 89701
(702) 882-0520
Variety of price lists, $1; overseas $2.
    MC, V, MO, PC.
Antique Imports specializes in antique
jewelry but also deals in European
antiquities, old legal documents and
antique maps, prints and paintings. The
jewelry price list is about twenty-two
pages and provides detailed descriptions
on each item. Antique Imports sells to
many antique retailers.

Billard's Old Telephones
21710 Regnart Rd.
Cupertino, CA 95014
(408) 252-2104
16-page catalog, $1 refundable U.S. and
    overseas. MO, PC.
Billard's sells old oak and brass
telephones and carries a complete stock
of restoration repair parts for most
phones made from 1882 to 1940. There
are parts for the old Kellogg oak crank
phone, Western Electric, and many
others.

Charles & Philippe Boucaud
25 Rue du Bac
Paris 75007 France
261 26-07
30-page catalog, $3 U.S. and overseas.
    MO, PC.
Charles & Philippe Boucaud's firm is
over 100 years old and is internationally
known as a dealer in antique pewter.

Christie's
502 Park Avenue
New York, NY 10022
(212) 546-1000
Subscription information on over 24
    catalogs free U.S. and overseas.
Christie's provides a portfolio on how to
subscribe to their beautifully illustrated
catalogs and an excellent leaflet on how
to buy and sell at Christie's auctions.
There are over twenty-five catalog
categories: paintings, drawings and
prints, decorative arts and furniture,
books and stamps, and special
categories such as guns, wines and
photographic images. Subscription
prices range from $18 to $100 for the
Impressionist and Modern paintings
catalog and are issued on a twelve-
month basis. Catalogs arrive three to
four weeks before the sale. Following
the sale, Christie's sends subscribers a
list of prices realized so that specific
prices of Borh items and market trends
can be tracked.

Christopher Sykes Antiques
The Old Parsonage
Woburn, Milton Keynes
MK17 9QL England
052 525 259
35-page brochure, $7 U.S. and overseas.
    Minimum order $30. MC, PC.
Christopher Sykes is the largest
"stockist" in Great Britain of antique
and unusual vintage corkscrews. They
usually carry over 300 different designs

of corkscrews ranging in price from $8 to $450 each. Since 1966.

Collins Antiques
Corner House, Church Street
Wheathampstead, Hertsfordshire
AL4 8AP England
20-page catalog, $2; overseas free. V, MO, PC.
Collins Antiques is located in Wheathampstead, a village about twenty-five miles north of London in the valley of the Lea. In their 15,000-square-foot showroom they carry a comprehensive stock of late eighteenth- and ninteenth-century furniture. They have a wide range of antiques mostly in mahogany and oak. The catalog displays photographs, prices, descriptions and circa of each item.

Dale C. Anderson Co.
32 Taylor St.
Hampton, NH 03842
(603) 926-5863
30-page catalog, $6; overseas $15. MC, V, MO, PC.
Dale C. Anderson publishes a catalog about every two months of American military and patriotic antiques dated usually 19th century or earlier. The catalog recently included antique firearms, edged weapons, uniforms, headgear, accoutrements, Indian and Western material, photographs, books and documents. There are many items available relating to the Civil War, Indian War periods, WWI and WWII.

East Coast Casino Antiques
98 Main Street
Fishkill, NY 12524
(914) 896-9492
80-page catalog, $4; overseas $6. MC, V, MO, PC.
A great selection of rare and early gambling antiquities. From porcelain dice to wheels of fortune, from decorator chip racks to Samuel Hart card decks. There are also antique cheating devices such as the Jacob's ladder ($1,850), which was concealed in the sharper's clothing and would hold out several cards when turned on by arm pressure. The Jacob's ladder was unique in featuring a locking device so the sharper

could move freely without any chance of the hold-out operating at an inopportune moment.

Eugene & Ellen Reno
Box 191
Lawrence, MA 01842
(603) 898-7426
8-page price list, $3; overseas $6. MO, PC.
Since 1940, Eugene and Ellen Reno have supplied antique glass, china, and miscellaneous small antique items.

Harriet Wynter, Ltd.
50 Redcliffe Road
London SW10 9NJ England
352 6494
24-page (some color) catalog, free U.S. and overseas. MO, PC.
Harriet Wynter offers an excellent selection of antique scientific instruments including sextants, marine barometers from the mid-eighteenth century, and a variety of microscopes and telescopes. There are trumpets (pre-electric hearing aids) in many elaborate styles.

Iron Horse Antiques, Inc.
RD #2
Poultney, VT 05764
(802) 287-4050
16-page catalog, $1.50 U.S. and overseas. MC, V, MO, PC.
The Iron Horse Antiques features antique hand tools and related books. They also produce a monthly newsletter, *The Fine Tool Journal,* with a subscription rate of $10.

John F. Rinaldi
Dock Square Box 765
Kennebunkport, ME 04046
(207) 967-3218
20-page catalog, $2; overseas $5. BD, MO, PC.
Rinaldi's sells nautical antiques, marine paintings, and whaling items. A spyglass, signed "J. P. Cutts & Son Opticians to her majesty. Sheffield & London," extends to over thirty-eight inches and is priced at $390. There are surveyor's compasses, levels, telescopes, protractors, octants, and timing glasses.

Keith Harding
93 Hornsey Road
London N7 6D5 England
607 6181
10-page catalog, $10; overseas $5. AE,
DC, MC, V, MO, PC.
Keith Harding is internationally
recognized as a leading authority on the
restoration of antique music boxes and
clocks. He also sells antique clocks, from
small carriage clocks to tall grandfather
clocks, and music boxes.

The Leopard's Head, Ltd.
P.O. Box 3517
San Francisco, CA 94119
(415) 771-1680
50-page catalog, $7 U.S. and overseas.
AE, MC, V, MO, PC.
The Leopard's Head offers fine antique
silver and specializes in antique English
sterling flatware. They actually took
their name from the earliest mark to be
struck on English silver—the leopards
head, symbolizing the purity (and thus
the quality) of the metalwares.

The Magnificent Doll
P.O. Box 1981
Centerville, MA 02632
8-page brochure, free U.S. and overseas.
AE, MC, V, MO, PC.
The Magnificent Doll offers antique
dolls, such as the pretty bisque-head
German dolls which sell for about $350
to $450, American dolls for about $500
to $5,000, and fine French dolls from
$1,500 to $15,000. They also publish a
twelve-issue newsletter, *The Doll
Investment newsletter,* for a
subscription rate of $27 U.S. and $35
overseas.

Nancy Neale Typecraft
Box 40J
Roslyn, NY 11576
(516) 621-7130
6-page brochure, free U.S. and overseas.
Minimum order $15. MO, PC.
Nancy Neale's hobby of collecting
antique woodtypes of all sizes, shapes
and designs is now a successful
business. The woodtypes range in size
from one-inch to twenty-two inches
high and were previously used for
printing posters and handbills. They are

now used as decorations, collages,
hangings, crafts, and as collector's
items.

Neal's Antiques
23 Waldo Ave.
Bloomfield, NJ 07003
(201) 748-8046
7-page brochure, $2 U.S. and overseas.
MO, PC.
Neal's carries antique phonographs and
parts. There are original Edisons,
Victors, Columbias, as well as others.
Neal Gerichten also operates a machine
shop, can make parts for phonographs
that are unavailable today, and service
and refinish antique phonographs.

N. Flayderman & Co.
RD #2
New Milford, CT 06776
(203) 354-5567
144-page catalog, $5; overseas $10. MO,
PC.
N. Flayderman is probably the best
known antique arms dealer and
authority. There are antique firearms of
all kinds, powder flashes and horns,
military guns, swords, helmets, Bowie
knives, and many books on guns.

Phillips Fine Art Auctioneers
406 East 79th Street
New York, NY 10021
(212) 570-4830
Subscription information on specific
catalogs, free U.S. and overseas.
In England since 1796, Phillips has been
a fine arts auctioneer and appraiser.
They now have offices throughout the
United Kingdom and Europe, and in
New York and Boston. Write for specific
catalogs on fine paintings, art nouveau,
jewelry, oriental art, and books.

Sotheby Parke Bernet
1334 York Ave.
New York, NY 10021
(212) 472-3400
Subscription information on over 30
catalogs, free U.S. and overseas.
Sotheby's was founded in London in
1744 and is the world's leading fine art
auction firm. They auction fine
paintings, furniture, and works of art as
well as books, coins, and jewelry.
Whether you're interested in buying or

selling a single object or a collection, Sotheby's maintains twelve locations in North America and forty offices worldwide. Each catalog is a complete guide for each auction and arrives well in advance of the sale date. With a subscription you also receive Sotheby's informative ten-issue newsletter and a list of final prices following each auction. Subscription rates for catalogs range from $15 to $95, or you can purchase all categories for a total of $1,370.

Souvenir and Unusual Spoons
1802 Chestnut Street
Philadelphia, PA 19103
(215) 563-7369
4-page price list, $2 U.S. Does not sell
   overseas. AE, MC, V.
Antique sterling spoons, souvenir spoons, and unusually designed spoons from around the turn of the century are offered. They also carry some china and glass.

Spink & Son, Ltd.
5–7 King Street, St. James
London SW1Y 6QS England
930 7888
22-page color *Octagon* catalog, free U.S.
   and overseas. AE, MO, PC.
Spink and Son are prestigious antique dealers for the serious collectors. Although their catalog, *Octagon,* is free on request (published two to three times a year for regular customers), the prices of the items listed in a recent issue ranged from $1,275 for a St. Louis dahlia antique paperweight to over $80,000 for a Dominic Serres oil painting, and there were a few paintings listed without prices. The *Numismatic Circular* is printed ten times a year and is available on a subscription basis.

Strike One (Islington) Ltd.
51 Camden Passage
London N1 8EA England
226 9709
4-page brochure, free U.S. and overseas.
   AE, DC, MC, V, MO, PC.

Strike One sells antique clocks, watches and barometers. They say they can supply every type of English antique clock from 1680 to 1840.

Tobin Fraley Studios
3246 Ettie St. #12
Oakland, CA 94608
(415) 654-3031
Price list, 50¢ U.S. and overseas. MO, PC.
Tobin Fraley sells carousel horses and menagerie animals of all types, sizes, and prices ranging in condition from original factory paint to fully restored or simply stripped. They also offer supplies for displaying and restoring animals, and books on carousel history. Mr. Fraley is working on a new catalog; it will be ready by the time you request it.

Vi & Si's Antiques, Ltd.
8970 Main St.
Clarence, NY 14031
(716) 634-4488
Price list, $3; overseas $5. MC, V, MO,
   PC.
All types of mechanical and automated music players are carried here. There are music boxes, organettes, phonographs, cylinder phonographs, nickelodeons, and reproducing pianos. Piano rolls, Edison Diamond Disc Records, and small size 78-rpm records are also available, as well as catalogs and magazines related to mechanical music.

Wurtsboro Wholesale Antiques, Inc.
P.O. Box 386
Sullivan Street
Wurtsboro, NY 12790
(914) 888-4411
17-page catalog, $2 U.S. Does not sell
   overseas. MC, V, MO, PC.
Wurtsboro specializes in country antiques such as wooden hanging racks, iron utensils, brass candlesticks, and copper decorative items. There are many interesting items fireplace bellows, brass dippers, spinning wheels, butter churns, and copper plates. They also sell antique and estate jewelry, ranging in price from $100 to $10,000.

ART

SEE ALSO
- Antiques
- Collectibles
- Crafts
- Gifts
- Handcrafts

ORIGINAL ART

Ancient World Arts
50 West 76 St.
New York, NY 10023
(212) 724-9455
12-page brochure, $5; overseas $10. AE, MC, V, MO, PC.
Ancient World Art offers archeological relics from ancient cultures such as Egypt, Greece, Rome, Persia, Mexico, and South America. There are pottery, jewelry, figurines, coins, and glass thousands of years old. They also sell fine reproductions of jewelry and handpainted papyrus paintings. Prices range from $25 to thousands of dollars.

Cartoodles
6000 Independence Road
Racine, WI 53406
6-page brochure, free. PC.
Claudia Rohling offers a selection of 5 × 7 in. color cartoons which can be personalized by cleverly adding a name to the humorous cartoon scene. Cartoons illustrate many occupations, sports (all the usual plus exercise lady and beach vacationer), and children in their bedrooms surrounded by toys. Each cartoon is in full color and framed in pine for $15 postpaid.

G. Cramer
38 Javastraat
2585 AP The Hague
Holland
070 63 07 58
Catalog, $30 U.S. and overseas.
For the serious art collector, G. Cramer offers Oude Kunst (old art). There is a fine selection of valuable old master paintings, mainly of the Dutch Golden Age (17th century).

Goffman Fine Art
P.O. Box 350 A
Blue Bell, PA 19422
(215) 643-6310
36-page color catalog, free U.S. and overseas. MO, PC.
Goffman's specializes in paintings by American illustrators. They offer a large selection of original works by Norman Rockwell, Maxfield Parrish, J. C. Leyendecker, Howard Pyle, N. C. Wyeth, and other important illustrators.

Lucien Goldschmidt, Inc.
1117 Madison Ave.
New York, NY 10028
(212) 879-0070
50-page catalog, $5 U.S. and overseas. MO, PC.
There are continental and European original prints, drawings, and illustrated books dating from 1500 to

1950. There are "prints by old and modern masters from Dürer to Matisse."

Nature's Nest Gallery
101 Coyote Circle, Rt. 6
Golden, CO 80403
(303) 582-5466
10-page color catalog, free U.S.
Nature's Nest offers quality original wildlife art by several national artists James E. Faulkner, Michael J. Riddet, Pamela Davis King, Gary Hoffman, and Rick Smith. They also produce and market many fine prints and reproductions.

Old Hall Gallery Limited
Crown Lodge
Drown Road, Morden
Surrey SM4 5BY England
01 540 9918
6-page brochure $1.50; overseas $1. BD.
Oil paintings, mostly of the eighteenth and nineteenth century, are offered by Old Hall Gallery.

Paul Prouté
74 Rue de Seine
Paris 75006 France
326 89 80
96-page catalog, $15. MO, PC.
Paul Prouté offers an extensive selection of original drawings and prints from the fifteenth through the twentieth centuries. Since 1876.

Post Oak Fine Art Distributors
1980 Post Oak Blvd. Suite J
Houston, TX 77056
(173) 627-7024
12-page color catalog. AE, MC, V.
All prints offered by Post Oak are original, limited edition works, hand-signed and numbered by the artists. Post Oak offers works by contemporary artists: Elizabeth Franzheim, Ivan Theimer, Slavko Kopäc, and others. Prices range from about $250 to $600.

Robert Koch
P.O. Box 5249
Berkeley, CA 94705
(415) 4421-0122
56-page catalog.

Robert Koch presents a fine collection of nineteenth and twentieth century photography from America, France, and Britain. They offer some rare works, including the signed print, *Carcassone,* by the nineteenth century French master Gustave Le Gray, and vintage Cuzco photographs of *Indians in Peru,* by Irving Penn.

Silhouette Studio
52 Woodhouse Ave.
Wallingford, CT 06492
(203) 269-2687
No catalog available.
Natalie Garvin cuts charming silhouettes from clear profile-view snapshots. She cuts two silhouettes of each customer (on folded paper) and mounts the three-inch figure on a 5×7 in. card for $8.50. It takes about two weeks for her to complete your order.

Yoseido Gallery
5–5–15 Ginza
Chuo-Ku
Tokyo, Japan
120-page (some color) catalog, $8 surface, $12 air mail U.S. and overseas. MO, PC.
Over 200 Japanese artists exhibit their work at the Yoseido Gallery. These limited edition prints include woodblock prints, lithographs, etchings, serigraphs, aquatints, mezzotints, engravings, and stencil-dyed prints. Prices range from $30 to $420.

PRINTS AND REPRODUCTIONS

Art Poster Company
22255 Greenfield Rd. #142
Southfield, MI 48075
(313) 559-1230
48-page color catalog, $2 U.S. and overseas. DC, MC, V, MO, PC.
Art Poster offers a vast selection of contemporary graphics, silk screens, botanicals, classical posters, pop art, orientals, children's art, and photographic posters. They also provide custom framing services. The catalog photography and the layout make the catalog alone an enjoyable experience to review.

Chapman Studios Inc.
2800 Hedberg Drive
Minnetonka, MN 55343
(612) 544-6622
2-page brochure free U.S. and overseas.
  MC, V.
Loyal Chapman has humorously
created prints of fictitious golf holes,
called *18 Infamous Golf Holes.* He
combines the geographical splendor of
famous landmarks (Victoria Falls,
Redwood Forest and the Grand Canyon)
with the whimsical impossibility of a
golf hole. There are single prints of
eighteen holes which sell for $11.95, or
you can buy *The 19th Hole,* a composite
rendering of each of the eighteen golf
holes in a scenic landscape.

Collector's Guild, Ltd.
601 W. 26th St.
New York, NY 10001
(212) 741-0400
38-page color catalog, free U.S. and
  overseas. AE, DC, MC, V, MO, PC.
Collector's Guild sells prints, posters and
limited editions—all framed and at very
reasonable prices. There are over 150
framed pictures of various styles and
quite a few lithographs priced under
$50.

The Crossroads of Sports, Inc.
5 East 47th Street
New York, NY 10017
(212) 755-6100
48-page color catalog, $1 U.S. Does not
  sell overseas. AE, MC, V, MO, PC.
Fine sporting paintings, prints,
etchings, and decorative items such as
carvings, decoys, china, and glassware.
Started in 1938, it is one of the oldest
galleries of sporting art in the
country.

Decor Prints
227 Main Street
P.O. Box 502
Noel, MO 64854
(417) 475-6367
16-page color catalog, $2 refundable U.S.
  Does not sell overseas. MO, PC, C.O.D.
Over 200 nostalgic prints of all types,
including antique reproductions and
prints of old masters. Priced from $4 to
$6.

Hansen Planetarium Publications
15 South State Street
Salt Lake City, UT 84111
(801) 535-7007
75-page color catalog, $2 U.S. and
  overseas. MC, V, MO, PC.
The Hansen Planetarium offers terrific,
full color astronomical posters from
some of the world's greatest
observatories Kitt Peak National
Observatory, Cerro Tololo Inter-
American Observatory, and Sacramento
Peak Observatory. There are also maps,
charts, slides, postcards, and booklets
available.

Icart Vendor Gallery
7956 Beverly Blvd.
Los Angeles, CA 90048
(213) 653-3190
16-page color catalog, $5; overseas $10
  refundable. AE, MC, V, MO, PC.
There are over 150 different art nouveau
and art deco images illustrated in fine
quality prints. They have an extensive
collection by Louis Icart in both original
etchings and reproductions. There are
also prints by Maxfield Parrish, Mucha,
Lautrec, Nelle, and other important
artists. Prices range from $7 to $50.

Incredible Edibles
146 Everson St.
San Francisco, CA 94131
(800) 752-8840
California (415) 333-5151
20-page color catalog, free. AE, MC, V,
  MO, PC.
A series of fantasy fun pictures created
by Ed Pardee, called Incredible Edibles,
are guaranteed conversation pieces.
They are whimsical photographs of real
food that has been sculpted into
surprisingly new forms. There are
walnuts cracked to display brussel
sprouts in their centers. A halved potato
shows the unmistakable bright green of
a kiwi fruit instead of the pure white
potato. They are available in color
lithographs or original photographs,
framed or unframed.

Marilyn Pink
817 North La Cienega Blvd.
Los Angeles, CA 90069
(213) 657-5810

56-page catalog, $6.50 U.S. and overseas. MO, PC.

Marilyn Pink's inventory comprises a wide range of drawings and prints from the fifteenth through the twentieth centuries, including a few contemporary artists such as Ralph Gilbert and Loretta Kramer. In addition to the master prints and drawings of pastels and water colors, their collection also has historical, botanical, genre, and Currier and Ives prints. From time to time they also feature California artists and sculptors.

Murray's Pottery
802 Kings Highway
Brooklyn, NY 11223
(212) 376-6002
123-page catalog, $2 U.S. Does not sell overseas. MO, PC.

Murray's offers a large collection of sculpture reproductions, many priced just under $50. Each piece is cast in Durastone or Sculptureglas and is finished to match the original treasure. An individual history card accompanies each piece of sculpture, detailing its significance.

Museum Editions New York, Ltd.
105 Hudson St.
New York, NY 10013
(800) 221-9576
32-page color catalog, $4 U.S. and overseas refundable. MC, V, MO, PC.

Museum Editions began in 1980 as the distributor for the Guggenheim Museum in New York. Today, they publish and distribute many fine art images from artists and cultural organizations. They often offer free poster coupons and special monthly discounts, making posters a most affordable way of decorating with quality artwork. Prices range from $6 to $40 and include such favorites as *Watermelon* by Simmons, *Vegetable Alphabet* by Henders, and *End of the Rainbow* by Scollard.

The National Gallery of Art
Publications Department
Trafalgar Square
London WC2N 5DN England
01 839 1912

16-page color catalog, $1.80 U.S. and overseas. Prices in $U.S. MC, V, MO, PC.

London's National Gallery of Art produces a great catalog of print reproductions using the finest technical developments in color photography and printing. The catalog lists reproduction prints by school of painting, and includes American, British, Dutch, Flemish, French, German, Italian, Spanish, Twentieth Century, and graphics. Large color reproductions range from $5 to $10, plaques are $3.50, and framed prints range from $15 to $85.

Nina Hunter
P.O. Box 1306
Murray Hill Station
New York, NY 10156
(212) 532-0628
12-page brochure free. MC, PC.

Nina Hunter's original lithographic prints are a collection of delicate drawings, titled *The Garden Collection*. There are twelve beautiful botanical prints to choose from, ranging in price from $8 to $20 each.

Pace Posters
115 East 23rd St.
New York, NY 10010
(212) 673-8240
9-color pages, PC.

There are art museum posters (*Save Our Planet*), ecology posters (*America: The Third Country*), bicentennial posters, and Pace edition posters by Dubuffet, Picasso, Trova, and others. Prices range from $10 to $40.

Pomegranate
Box 748
Corte Madera, CA 94925
48-page catalog, $2 U.S. and overseas. MC, V, MO, PC.

Contemporary and fine art posters, postcards, note cards, and calendars are available.

Poster Originals Limited
924 Madison Ave.
New York, NY 10028
(212) 816-0422
110-page color catalog $7.50 U.S. and overseas. AE, MC, V, MO, PC.

Poster Originals started in 1967 publishing and distributing American and European fine art posters. They offer over 500 posters, plus matting and framing services. Their table of contents lists their various catagories American art posters, Glaser/Chwast, Linder, Pitigliani, 1972 Olympics, European art posters, Folon, Musées de France, Nouvelles Images Editions, Polish Circus and Zoo posters, Botanicals, Billboards, and Amnesty International. Prices range from $15 to $40.

Poster Pals
1003 Crest Circle
Cincinnati, OH 45208
(513) 871-5057
4-page color brochure, $1 U.S. Does not sell overseas. MC, V, MO, PC.
John Brady offers colorful old woodcut circus posters in verticals, half-sheets, and full sheets measuring 28 × 42 in. These bright and boldly colored clowns, lions, tigers, and circus extravaganzas can be framed or just tacked up as posters. They range from $5.95 to $19.95. They are even available in billboard sizes 84 × 84 in. and 84 × 126 in. Do you have a wall (or ceiling) that you would like to cover with *Leaping Lion* for about $60?

The Print Mint
1147 Greenleaf Ave.
Wilmette, IL 60091
(312) 256-4140
16-page catalog, free U.S. and overseas. AE, MC, V, MO, PC.
Over 15,000 prints including etchings, engravings, limited editions, woodcuts, children's, and ethnic. They have also expanded into Eskimo and Chinese ceramics.

The Silver Image Gallery
92 So. Washington St.
Seattle, WA 98104
(206) 623-8116
20-page catalog, $2 refundable U.S. and overseas. MC, V, MO, PC.
The Silver Image claims to carry the largest selection of photographic posters available in the U.S. They offer a selection of over 130 images from over 100 different artists, printed in both black and white and in color. Some of their popular posters include Edward Curtis, Ansel Adams, Bruce Barnbaum, Imogen Cunningham, Lilo Raymond and Edward Weston.

Triton Gallery
323 West 45th St.
New York, NY 10036
(212) 765-2472
4-page color brochure, 50¢ U.S. and overseas. AE, MC, V, MO, PC.
Triton Gallery features current and past theatrical posters which can be collected or framed and hung as decorative art. There are Broadway show posters for *Cats, La Cage Aux Folles, 42nd Street, Annie, Chicago,* and others. They offer original broadway showcards priced from $10 to $100, archives (out of print posters reproduced) for $45, and posters (from sizes 23 × 46 in. to 42 × 84 in.) from $4 to $20.

Turtle Bay Galleries
P.O. Box 115
Darien, CT 06820
(03) 853-7876
6-page color brochure, $2 U.S. and overseas. MC, V, MO, PC.
Primitive American scenes and cats by Bruce Butte, Annie and Bruce Wallace. These charming limited editions are signed and numbered by the artist. There are six to ten new prints issued per year in four-color lithography editions of 500 to 1,000. They are priced from $8.95 to $35.00.

ART SUPPLIES

A. I. Friedman, Inc.
25 West 45th St.
New York, NY 10036
(212) 575-0200
352-page catalog, free U.S. and overseas. There's a complete supply of art and drafting materials, from furniture and art cases to colors and mediums, and from drawing instruments to brushes. You can find most any art supply at Friedman's.

Aiko's Art Materials Import, Inc.
714 N. Wabash Ave.
Chicago, Il 60611
(312) 943-0745
20-page catalog, $1.50; overseas $2.
  Sample book of Japanese papers $15;
  overseas $18. MO, PC.
Aiko's is a combination artist's supply
shop, gallery, gift and card shop. It offers
over 500 types of paper. They range from
French and Swedish marbled papers,
Gampi, Mingei and Chiyogami paper, to
handmade Japanese mulberry paper
and exotic Egyptian papyrus. Aiko's
carries over 100 different brushes made
mostly in Japan from soft hairs of horse,
badger, sheep, and deer.

Arthur Brown & Bro., Inc.
2 West 46 St.
New York, NY 10036
(212) 575-5555
226-page *Art Materials* catalog $3;
  overseas $6. 40-page *Pen* catalog.
  Minimum order $50. AE, DC, MC, V,
  MO, PC.
Art Brown carries over 22,000 different
products for the artist, draftsman,
graphic designer, and office, including
craft and fine art printing supplies.
Supplies are shipped within twenty-four
hours of receiving the order. Since 1924.

The Art Store
4300 West 190th St.
P.O. Box 2826
Torrance, CA 90509-9970
(800) 821-5514
(800) 243-3423
42-page catalog, free U.S. MC, V, MO,
  PC.

ASF Sales
1340 Tomahawk Drive
Maumee, OH 43537
(800) 537-0944
Ohio (419) 893-8785
2-page brochure, free. AE, MC, V, MO,
  PC.
ASF manufactures aluminum section
picture frames in lengths from 5 to 79
inches. Standard, canvas, radius, and
shadow box designs are available in
anodized silver, gold, pewter, copper
brown, black, satin silver, and satin gold
finishes. Price for a standard 6 × 20 in.

frame is about $5.80 and includes all
assembly hardware, two hangers, and
eight springs.

Barnwood Frames
11115 Rendezvous
San Antonio, TX 78216
(512) 344-0438
Price list, free U.S. Does not sell
  overseas. MO, PC.
Lee Grauke, owner, uses old and
weathered wood to make rustic picture
frames. He makes any size from 5 × 7
in. to 28 × 36 in., and the prices range
from $7.95 to $15.45. There are also
double frames (frame around a frame)
which give pictures depth by designing
the first frame flat and the second one
perpendicular to it.

Beard's Frame Shoppes
6639 S. W. Macadam Ave.
Portland, OR 97201
(800) 245-6464
(800) 245-6639
23-page color catalog, free U.S. AE, MC,
  V, MO, PC.
Beard's offers both do-it-yourself metal
sectional frames and finished frames in
a good selection of styles and sizes.
There are hand-cut beveled mats,
double matting, and clear box acrylic
frames. Framing supplies (tools, cutters,
hangers, etc.) are available as well as
brushes, oils, pastels, and Winsor &
Newton mediums and varnishes.

The Calligraphy Studio
P.O. Box 24-FP
Orangeburg, NY 10962
(914) 359-5754
12-page catalog, $1.50; overseas $2. MC,
  V, MO, PC.
The Calligraphy Studio offers
calligraphy, hand-lettering, and art
supplies for the beginner and
professional. They offer four basic kits
for the beginner for $6 each, containing
practice sheets, an ink-contained
beginner-size pen, and easy-to-follow
instructions. These are great gift ideas.
There are also pens, papers, labels,
stickers, bookplates, fun certificates, and
a beautiful family tree chart for $3.50.

Crown Art Products
75 East 13 Street
New York, NY 10003
(212) 673-0150
30-page catalog, $1; overseas $2.50. MC,
V, MO, PC.
Crown Art is probably best known as
manufacturers and distributors of silk
screen supplies and kits. They also sell
metal frames at very competitive prices.

Custom Picture Frame
1031 Bay Blvd.
Chula Vista, CA 92011
(800) 854-6606
California (619) 427-8540
18 color pages, free U.S. Minimum order
$50. MC, V, MO, PC.
Custom picture frames are available in
a wide selection of materials and styles.

Dick Blick
P.O. Box 1267
Galesburg, IL 61401
(309) 343-6181
480-page *art materials* catalog, 334-
page *graphic arts materials* catalog,
free; overseas $5. MC, V, MO, PC.
Dick Blick sells a complete line of art
and craft supplies ranging from pre-
school level to professional studio
products. Started in 1911, they now have
their headquarters in Galesburg and
retail stores in three locations. Dick
Blick has an excellent reputation for
quality products and service—"Blick
ships quick."

Falkiner Fine Papers, Ltd.
117 Long Acre
London WC2E 9PA England
01 240 2339
14-page catalog, $1 U.S. and overseas.
AE, MC, V, MO, PC.
Falkiner's is well known for their
selection of papers for artists and
craftsmen, including painters,
printmakers, book binders,
calligraphers, and restorers. They also
offer stationery.

Graphik Dimensions Ltd.
41–23 Haight St.
Flushing, NY 11355
(800) 221-0262
New York (212) 463-3500

32-page color catalog. PC.
Graphik Dimensions carries frames,
matboard, oils, pastels, watercolors,
sketch books, drawing pencils, brushes,
canvases, presentation cases, and easels.
Frames are available in blackshadow
aluminum, sectional aluminum, and by
Rainbow and Precious Metals. Wood
frames are available in a variety of
styles including Nordic, Masterpiece,
Oriental, Oak, Designer Oak, Teak, and
in pre-assembled and sectional.

Jerry's Artarama Inc.
117 S. Second St.
New Hyde Park, NY 11040
(800) 221-2323
New York (212) 343-4545
128-page catalog, $1; overseas $2
Jerry's offers hundreds of materials for
the artist and graphic artist, from
beginner to professional, at discounts of
20% to 50% below retail price.

MaSaDa Frame & Molding Corp.
6002 Fort Hamilton Parkway
Brooklyn, NY 11219
(212) 851-1999
Price list, free U.S. Minimum order $30.
PC.
MaSaDa wholesales aluminum section
frames in five color choices (silver, gold,
copper, black and pewter), in both
standard size and canvas size. Sections
are available in lengths from 5 to 48 in.
The price for a 16 × 20 in. frame is about
$4.80 and includes free spring clips,
hangers, and hardware. There is a
minimum order of $30, so you might
want to join forces with a friend.

New England Frameworks
RFD #1
Wilton, NH 03086
(603) 878-1633
16-page catalog, self-addressed stamped
envelope; overseas $1. Minimum order
$15. AE, MC, V, MO, PC.
New England Frameworks
manufactures unique round frames for
displaying collector's plates.

New York Central Art Supply Co.
62 3rd Ave.
New York, NY 10003
(800) 242-2408
New York (212) 473-7705

60-page *Fine paper* catalog, 26-page *Print making* catalog, 38-page *Artists' Color Canvas & Easel* catalog, 225-page *General* catalog. Each catalog, U.S. and overseas, is $2 except the large *General* catalog, which is $3. Minimum order $10. AE, DC, MC, V, MO, PC.

The *General* catalog includes over 10,000 items and is a virtual encyclopedia for all artists, designers, architects, draftsmen, sculptors, audio visual display and graphic artists. The *Print making* supply catalog contains supplies for etchings, lithography, silkscreen, batik, marbling, and rubbing from manufacturers of fine printmaking supplies. The *Color Canvas & Easel* catalog lists an extensive supply of oils, acrylics, watercolors, egg temperas, dry pigments, and painting mediums, as well as easels for school or professional use.

Noisy Crow Artisans
99 Beechwood Hills
Newport News, VA 23602
(804) 877-2228
1-page flyer with samples, free U.S. and overseas, Minimum order $2.

Noisy Crow specializes in handmade decorative papers also known as marbled, stained, or vat-dyed. The method Noisy Crow uses to produce these beautiful one-of-a-kind papers is similar to Turkish paper produced in the late sixteenth and seventeenth centuries. Sheets of marbled paper (12 × 18 in.) start at $5 each. They also offer note pads, note cards, sketch books, and guest books, and they welcome inquiries for custom made items.

Pearl Paint Co.
308 Canal St.
New York, NY 10013
(212) 431-7932
30-page catalog, $1 U.S. Does not sell overseas. AE, MC, V, MO, PC.

Pearl Paint is considered to be one of the largest sources of artist materials in the world, and offers its vast selection at discounts of 20% to 50% below retail prices. They have a larger 250-page catalog that has "everything" listed.

Polyart Products
1199 East 12th St.
Oakland, CA 94606
(415) 451-1048
12-page brochure, $2 U.S. Does not sell overseas. MC, V, MO, PC.

Polyart manufactures and sells Polyart, an acrylic artist's paint very popular in schools. Available in pint jars in twelve colors, there are excellent discounts for large orders. The brochure and price list is sent free to art teachers who request catalogs on school letterhead stationery.

Sax Arts & Crafts
P.O. Box 2002
Milwaukee, WI 53201
(414) 272-4900
380-page (some color) catalog, $3 U.S.; free to schools, educators and institutions. Does not sell overseas. Minimum order $10. MC, V, MO, PC.

Their products range from fine arts supplies to materials for camp and recreational activities. They offer a complete line of supplies and equipment for painting, drawing, graphics, ceramics, sculpture, art metals, weaving, mosaics, basketry, and textile decoration. Their slogan probably says it best: complete one-stop shopping for "everything your art desires."

Stu-Art
2045 Grand Ave.
Baldwin, NY 11510
(800) 645-2855
New York (516) 546-5151
16-page brochure and samples, free U.S. Does not sell overseas. Minimum order $15. MC, V, MO, PC.

Stu-Art manufactures and distributes five different series of mats including the Redi-mat series, featuring a single mat with a double mat look. Prices are listed at about 40% to 60% below retail price. There are thirty sizes and sixteen colors available in one series alone. There are lightweight economy mats, custom hand-cut beveled edged mats, and top-of-the-line Nielsen aluminum metal frame sections.

BEAUTY & HEALTH

SEE ALSO
- Clothing
- Food and Drink
- Gifts
- Large Department Stores and Mail Order
- Houses

COSMETICS

Amica Cosmetics
736 Parkside Ave.
Brooklyn, NY 11226
(212) 856-2222
24-page color catalog, free U.S. and
   overseas. MC, MO, PC.
Cosmetic products from Amica,
Personal Choice, Aime, and European
companies (Wolo and Swiss Skin Spa)
are offered by Amica Cosmetics. There
are varicose vein cover, sparkle nail
enamel, whitening toothpaste, and the
latest shades in lipstick. Who needs
anything more?

Beautiful Visions, Inc.
810 S. Hicksville Rd.
C.S. 4001
Hicksville, NY 11802
48-page color catalog, free U.S. Does not
   sell overseas. MC, V, MO, PC.
Discounts up to 40% to 75% below retail
on famous name brand cosmetics
L'Oreal, Vidal Sassoon, Jovan, Elizabeth
Arden, Revlon, Coty, and Anita of
Denmark. Great values on "specials."
(Recently they offered a six piece
makeup brush set for $2.95.)

Beauty Buy Book
65 East South Water
Chicago, IL 60601
(312) 977-3740
40-page color catalog, price unavailable.
   Does not sell overseas. AE, MC, V, MO,
   PC.
There are over 200 brand name cosmetic
and accessory items at savings of up to
90% from regular retail: Elizabeth
Arden, Charles of the Ritz, Max Factor,
Jovan, Helena Rubinstein, and Rive
Gauche. Orlane Emulsion B21 ($7.95 for
1.7 oz.) and Charles of the Ritz
Wholesome Makeup ($2.95 for 2 oz.) are
both good buys. One page was recently
devoted to 98¢ limited quantity items. A
great catalog.

Beauty By Spector
Dept. IMSG
McKeesport, PA 15134-0512
(412) 673-3259
5-10 page brochure, usually free U.S.
   and overseas. MC, V, MO, PC.
Popular synthetic and 100% human hair
wigs, wiglets, cascades and falls are
offered at 50% below retail prices. Skin
and hair care products, cosmetics and
fragrances, as well as jewelry—baubles

---

and bangles no jewelry box should be without.

Boyd's Madison Avenue
655 Madison Ave.
New York, NY 10021
(212) 838-6558
32-page catalog, $2; overseas price unavailable. Minimum order $10. AE, DC, MC, V, MO, PC.
Boyd's sells hard-to-find imported toiletries and cosmetics as well as products from their own line. Maybe you've been longing for a badger bristle toothbrush, or perhaps a wild boar bristle hair brush?

Cathay of Bournemouth Ltd.
32 Cleveland Rd.
Bournemouth BH1 4QG England
0202 37178
68-page color catalog, $4 U.S. and overseas. V, MO, PC.
Cathay is the largest retail herbalist in Great Britain and carries a fine selection of creams, balms, unguents and bath-time luxuries. They manufacture and retail over 90 specialized cosmetics under their exclusive label. There are many delightful explanations and directions for using these products: Asian Fruits Tooth Paste, Spring Breeze Deodorant Balm, Comely Oil, and Friction Massage Cream.

Ella Bache
8 West 36th St.
New York, NY 10018
(212) 279-0842

Ella Bache
8 Rue De La Paix
Paris 75002 France
32-page brochure, $2; small booklets, free U.S. Overseas readers contact the Paris address.
Skin care is the specialty of Ella Bache. Skin creams, cleansers, moisturizers and cold and hot wax depilatories are available. The brochure begins with a brief description of each skin type and the recommended treatment. A daily skin care regime utilizing their products is listed. The last portion of the brochure is brief descriptions of each product and application procedures.

Gold Medal Hair Products, Co.
1 Bennington Ave.
Freeport, NY 11520
(516) 378-6900
40-page (some color) catalog, price unavailable U.S. and overseas. MC, V, MO, PC.
Here is an excellent selection of wigs and hair care products for blacks. Over fifty wigs and wiglets for men and women. Hair care accessories include shampoos, curling irons, combs, brushes, hair coloring and pressing compounds.

Homebody, Inc.
8521 Melrose Ave.
Los Angeles, CA 90069
(213) 659-2917
4-page brochure, $1 U.S.
Homebody carries a full range of pre-scented and unscented moisture lotions, cream scrubs, shampoos, bath gels, soaps, and massage products. Over seventy different perfume oils are sold as scents, or for you to mix with any of their unscented products. "Rain" perfume oil ($6.95 for 4 fl. oz.) is a soft and fresh fragrance, while "China Rain" is a muskier oil.

La Costa Products International
La Costa Hotel and Spa
2251 Las Palmas Drive
Carlsbad, CA 92008
(800) 854-6666
California (collect) (619) 438-1434
48-page color catalog, $2 U.S. and overseas. AE, CB, DC, MC, V, MO, PC.
Most of the personal care products developed and manufactured by La Costa Products International are for the exclusive use of the renowned La Costa Hotel and Spa in La Costa, California. The complete La Costa men's line in elegant black containers offers products for total skin care. Women may choose from many healthy sounding products: Vitamin EDA, Lemon Peel Masque, Collagen moisturizing lotions, and Lustre Eye Smoothing Oil. For years the luxurious La Costa Spa has been making people look and feel better. This catalog is the next best thing to going there.

Oleda Unlimited, Inc.
1 E. 44th St.
New York, NY 10017
(212) 697-9408
28-page catalog, free U.S. and overseas.
  MC, V, MO, PC.
This catalog is full of many pictures of
youthful-looking Oleda Baker, President
of Oleda Unlimited. She offers mud
packs, facial tonics, vitamins, brown
spot removers, and wheat germ skin-
feeders, all to give that "age-less" look
to your skin.

Paula Young
321 Manley St.
W. Bridgewater, MA 02379
(800) 343-9695
32-page catalog, free. Does not sell
  overseas. Minimum order $10. MC, V,
  MO, PC.
More than twenty different high quality
Eva Gabor wig styles are available in
twenty-eight natural-looking colors.
Few stores can offer so many different
styles and colors of wigs. Most orders are
shipped the day after receipt and all
offer an unconditional guarantee.
Started in 1979, this catalog was the
winner of "Best Catalog" in cosmetics
classification (1983), chosen by the
Maxwell Sroge Company.

FRAGRANCES

Catherine
6 Rue de Castiglione
Paris 75001 France
4-page price list, free U.S. and overseas.
  AE, V, MO, PC.
Catherine's boutique in Paris carries
most brands of French perfumes and
cosmetics: Orlane, Lancome, Chanel,
Dior, Stendhal, Yves St. Laurent, and
Germaine Monteil. She also carries fine
Rigaud candles, bags, signature scarves
and ties, and French umbrellas. Buying
French perfumes from France can save
you up to 30% off U.S. retail prices even
after postage and duty.

Country Garden Perfume Factory
68 Wheeler Rd.
P.O. Box 278
Hollis, NH 03049
(603) 465-7475

9-page brochure, 40¢ U.S. Does not sell
  overseas.
Country Garden fragrances are locally
made by Elaine Edwards and sold in
their own handmade, glass-stoppered
bottles. Natural extracts and oils are
blended to create amber, lilac, rose, and
ylang ylang water. The price range is
$15 to $20 for 2 ounces.

Crabtree & Evelyn
Box 167
Woodstock, CT 06281
(203) 928-2766
48-page color toiletries catalog, $3 U.S.
  and overseas. Minimum order $7.50.
  PC.
Crabtree & Evelyn was founded over ten
years ago with the aim of producing
naturally based toiletries and
traditional foods. They offer toiletries in
an assortment of fragrances: lavender,
millefleurs, sandalwood, carnation, lily
of the valley, and others. Their antique
packaging assures these gifts will be
well received.

Essential Products Co., Inc.
90 Water St.
New York, NY 10005
(212) 344-4288
3-page price list, free U.S. and overseas.
  MO, PC.
Why buy expensive original perfume
when you can buy interpretations of
those fragrances under the trademark
of Naudet? Currently, Yves Saint
Laurent's Opium perfume costs about
$150 per ounce; Naudet's version is $17.
Over forty-two ladies' perfume
interpretations and thirteen men's
colognes are available.

Grillot
10 Rue Cambon
Paris 75001 France
206 7635
Price list, free U.S. and overseas. MO,
  PC.
Many French perfumes and toilet
waters, and bags by Lancel, are offered
by Grillot of France.

J. Floris, Ltd.
89 Jermyn St.
London, SW1Y 6JH England
01 930 4136

20-page color catalog, $1 U.S. and overseas. AE, DC, MC, V, MO, PC.
Perfumes were a novelty in 1730, when Juan Famenias Floris set up his sign in the fashionable quarter of St. James. The family has continued through the years to offer a unique selection of English flower fragrances in perfumes, colognes, bath essences, sachets, talcum powders, and soaps. Perfumes include florissa, jasmine, lily of the valley, malmaison (carnation), ormonde, red rose, sandalwood, and stephanotis. Men will find a collection of powders, soaps, lotions, and shaving accessories.

J. W. Chunn
Société Benal
43 Rue Richer
Paris 75009 France
1 824 4206
Price list, free U.S. and overseas. MO, PC.
J. W. Chunn carries all the leading brands of French perfumes, complete with bath line when available. They also carry gift items, but they are not listed on the price list. Prices and exchange rates fluctuate daily, so comparisons are not always accurate. J. W. Chunn's prices are competitive with Catherine's and occasionally slightly lower.

Key West Fragrance & Cosmetic Factory, Inc.
524 Front St.
Key West, FL 33040
(305) 294-5592
Color catalog, free U.S.
The inner leaf gel of the aloe barbadensis plant is the moisturizing fluid that Key West Fragrance uses in a variety of preparations to heal and moisturize the skin. Long known for its healing abilities when applied to cuts and minor burns, even Egypt's Queen Nefertiti is said to have used aloe as a cosmetic. This sharp catalog offers a full line of cosmetics and fragrances for men and women, reasonably priced.

Norfolk Lavender
Caley Mill, Heacham
Kings Lynn, Norfolk
PE31 7JE England
0485 70384

Norfolk Lavender
J. W. Lowry Imports
21 Collamore Terrace
West Orange, NJ 07052
(201) 736-2261
8-page brochure and price list, free U.S. and overseas. V, PC.
Founded in 1932, Norfolk Lavender grows approximately 100 acres of lavender. They are the largest growers and distillers of lavender in Britain. Visitors are welcome in the Cottage Tea Room in July and August to see the lavender harvest underway. Specially designed harvesters cut the lavender at full bloom; it is then taken either to be dried or distilled. At Caley Mill the lavender soaps, perfumes, talcs, lotions, and men's colognes are hand prepared and packaged. Americans can buy from J. W. Lowry Imports, listed above.

Penhaligon's
41 Wellington St.
Covent Garden
London WC2 England
01 836 2150 12-page color catalog, $3 U.S.; price unavailable overseas. AE, DC, MC, V, MO, PC.
Penhaligon's perfumes were well known in the courts of Europe in the 1800s and are still supplied to many of them today, using the original formulas of the founder, William Henry Penhaligon. In Covent Garden, at 41 Wellington Street, customers may watch through glass partitions as perfumes are compounded in large vats, then are matured and filtered before being bottled and labeled. Blenheim and Hammam bouquet fragrances are available to gentlemen in after shave, shampoos, soaps and talcum powder. Penhaligon's candles, scented in Hammam and English fern, are sold in traditional old English stoneware jars.

Taylor of London
166 Sloane St.
London SW1X 9QF England
01 235 4653
8-page color catalog, $1 U.S. and overseas. AE, DC, MC, V, MO, PC.
The floral perfumes, after shaves, and bath scents have been created for many of the crowned heads of Europe for

nearly a hundred years by Taylor of London. The traditional fragrances are still made by hand, using the same quality ingredients. Potpourri fragrances include Old English, Royal Rose, Freesia, and Victorian Spice. In distinguished-looking chunky bottles are gentlemen's after shave fragrances of Eau de Portugal and Florida water. The wonderful scented drawer lining paper could also be used in your suitcases.

Tuli-Latus Perfumes, Ltd.
136–56 39th Ave. Suite 450
Flushing, NY 11354
(212) 746-9337
4-page brochure, free U.S. Does not sell
   overseas. AE, DC, MC, V, MO, PC.
Never believe that old saying, "all good perfumes must come from Paris." Tuli-Latus offers, in simple bottling and packaging, inexpensive renditions of famous high-priced fragrances. Here are some of their prices: (1 oz.) perfume versions of Opium ($22), Shalimar ($18), Private Collection ($22), and Oscar de la Renta ($22). Why pay more?

HEALTH

AARP Pharmacy Service, Inc.
510 King St. Suite 420
Alexandria, VA 22314
(703) 684-0268
40-page color brochure, free U.S.
   Limited sales overseas. MO, PC.
The American Association of Retired Persons provides low-cost prescriptions, vitamins, and health care products delivered postage paid. This pharmacy service operates out of 10 regional mail operation centers nationwide.

Adam & Eve
Box 800
Carrboro, NC 27510
(919) 929-2143
48-page color catalog, $2 U.S. Does not
   sell overseas. MC, V, MO, PC.
Adam & Eve offers sexy lingerie for men and women, contraceptives, and a wide variety of sex books and sexual aids. Started in 1970, by providing mail order contraceptives the company is today a

multimillion dollar mail order company.

A. J. Masuen, Co.
11 Central Ave. NW
Le Mars, IA 51031
(712) 546-4563
48-page catalog, free U.S. and overseas.
   Minimum order $10. MO, PC.
First aid kits and supplies at "close to wholesale prices." First aid kits start at $5.95 for a good car traveling model, and go up to $115 for an industrial kit.

Allergy Products
Box 393
Bronxville, NY 10708
(914) 779-2400
24-page catalog, free U.S. MC, V, MO,
   PC.
Household products to help minimize irritants contributing to allergy sufferers. Children with allergy symptoms may be helped by non-allergenic and non-toxic plush toy animals, crib sheet sets, and pillows. Many will benefit from a wide variety of filtration air cleaners, non-allergenic household products, beauty aids, and skin care products.

American Foundation for the Blind
15 W. 16th St.
New York, NY 10011
(212) 620-2165
40-page catalog, free U.S. and overseas.
   AE, MC, V, MO, PC.
An extensive offering of products for people with vision problems is featured in this catalog. Since 1921, American Foundation for the Blind has purchased and adapted appliances to offer a variety of talking products, including calculators, clocks and bathroom scales. Quartz braille watches, tools, and measuring instruments are available. Games for all ages include Scrabble, puzzles, backgammon, dominoes, cards, checkers, and raised-line drawing kits.

American Health Service, Inc.
1206 Golf Rd.
Waukegan, IL 60087
(312) 662-4700
32-page newsalog, free. Does not sell
   overseas. MC, V, MO, PC.

Specializing in the sale of replacement hearing aids to current hearing aid users, particularly senior citizens, American Health Service offers over 400 models of hearing aids made by more than twenty leading manufacturers. With today's economy and the limited income of many senior citizens, the 30% to 50% discount off regular retail price is most welcome.

Barth's of Long Island
270 W. Merrick Rd.
Valley Stream, NY 11580
(516) 8800
48-page catalog, free U.S. and overseas. MC, V, MO, PC.
Barth's was started by a pharmacist and his wife over thirty-five years ago. They were interested in helping people gain, maintain, or improve their health naturally. Using the finest quality natural vitamins, formulas, health and beauty aids, Barth's offers a huge selection of health supplements, from vitamin A to zinc.

Better Sleep, Inc.
57 Industrial Rd.
Berkley Heights, NJ 07922
(201) 464-2200
Catalog, free U.S.
This catalog offers aids and practical suggestions for improved sleep, comfort, and convalescent care: blanket supports for the feet, sculptured pillows and cushions for the arms, back and neck.

Dental Alternatives, Inc.
3141 Ann St.
Baldwin, NY 11510
(516) 378-7585
Brochure, free U.S. and overseas. MC, V, MO, PC.
Emergency Dental Kit has all the emergency items you need to temporarily repair a broken denture or lost filling until you can get to your dentist. The Kit includes temporary cement and filling, toothache drops, denture repair, cotton, wax, mixing dish and spatula, gauze and tweezers. The Deluxe Kit is priced at $19.95, and the Mini Kit is $10.95.

Dyna-Med, Inc.
6200 Yarrow Drive
Carlsbad, CA 92008
106-page catalog, $1 U.S. and overseas. AE, DC, MC, V, MO, PC.
Emergency care products to assist the sick and injured: splints, first aid kits, stretchers, blanket, and training manikins.

Freeda Vitamins, Inc.
36 East 41st St.
New York, NY 10017
(212) 685-4980
36-page catalog, free U.S. Limited sales overseas. MC, V, MO, PC.
Over 200 vitamin and nutrient formulas are manufactured in Freeda Vitamins plant. Special formulas—eliminating sugar, starch, coal tar dyes, sulphiting agents, artificial colors, salt fillers and preservatives—are used. These supplements appear to be well tolerated by people with sensitivities to certain foods and chemicals. Because swallowing pills is a problem for some people, Freeda also offers new miniaturized tablets. Since 1928.

Harbor Aquatics
575 W. 6th St.
San Pedro, CA 90731
(213) 832-1185
4-page brochure, free U.S. and overseas. MC, V, MO, PC.
Harbor Aquatics makes prescription sport goggles, including masks for skin divers, swimming, motorcycle and ski goggles. "You're missing half the fun under water if you can't see clearly," says Harbor Aquatics. You'll need to send them a copy of your prescription for glasses plus your inter-pupillary measurement (the distance from the center of one eye to the center of the other eye). If that sounds like too much trouble, send them your glasses—if you can spare them that long. They bond your special correction to the faceplate of your goggle or one you've selected from their line.

Haussman's Pharmacy, Inc.
534–536 W. Girard Ave.
Philadelphia, PA 19123
(215) 627-2143

20-page catalog, free U.S. and overseas. MO, PC.

Haussman's specializes in filling difficult and unusual prescriptions. Many items are obtained from other countries and not available in this area. You'll find extensive lists of imported and domestic herbs and spices. A selective staff is equipped to receive and ship overseas orders. Herbs and spices can be powdered and packed in capsules on request.

Health Savings Center
33 Bell St. Dept. A
Valley Stream, NY 11582
(800) 645-2978
32-page newsalog, free U.S. MC, V, PC.

L & H Vitamins, Inc.
38–01 35th Ave.
Long Island City, NY 11181
(800) 221-1152
(212) 937-7400
64-page newsalog, free U.S. Does not sell overseas. MC, V, MO, PC.

There are 100 nationally advertised brands of vitamins, all at 20% off the manufacturer's list price. By taking a smaller unit sale profit and marketing to a larger and growing clientele, L & H Vitamins passes on to you a substantial savings on vitamins and health care products. Take time to compare these prices.

Prescription Delivery System
136 S. York Rd.
Hatboro, PA 19040
(800) 441-8976
Pennsylvania (215) 674-1565
10-page brochure, price unavailable.

Does not sell overseas. MC, V, MO, PC. Prescription Delivery Systems stocks over 50,000 drugs at comparably low prices. Unfortunately their brochure listings are somewhat limited, making comparison shopping difficult. They do encourage use of the toll free number, so check with them on your next prescription. Ordering is made simple; mail in your prescription and you will be billed, plus postage. Orders over $100 require pre-payment.

Pharmaceutical Services
127 West Markey Rd.
Belton, MO 64012
(816) 331-0700
6-page price list, free U.S. Does not sell overseas. MO, PC.

85 percent of Pharmaceutical Services orders are for prescriptions and the balance are for vitamins, antacids, first aid supplies, health and beauty aids. A recent price list showed good savings on Tetracycline, Benadryl and Dilantin. If you can have your doctor write your prescription for generic drugs you'll save close to 50%. On the price list, the generic products are shaded to show the comparison between generic and brand names.

Prism Optical, Inc.
10992 NW 7th Ave.
N. Miami, FL 33168
(305) 754-5894
Men's, women's, and children's quality eyeglasses are available at discount prices. Fashion and designer frames, and all types of prescription lenses, at discounts of up to 30% to 50% off retail prices.

Royal National Institute for the Blind
224 Great Portland St.
London W1N 6AA England
01-388 1266
65-page catalog, price unavailable.

RNIB, founded in 1868, offers a large supply of aids for the blind or sight-impaired. There are tools for carpenters, gardeners, musicians, and typists. There are many maps, measuring instruments, games, puzzles, and writing aids. A special overseas price list is available with ordering instructions.

Science Products
Box A
Southeastern, PA 19399
(800) 233-3121
Pennsylvania (800) 233-3121
48-page newsalog, free U.S. and overseas. MC, V, MO, PC.

Science Products provides aids, materials, and consultation for the vision-impaired. Many newly developed instruments and equipment are available for the vision-impaired while at work, school, or play. There an electronic calculator with a braille printout, audible volleyball, talking computers, scratch-and-sniff cards, clocks, and musical greeting cards.

Self-Care Guide
149 Marion Dr.
West Orange, NJ 07052
(201) 325-9205
24-page catalog, $1 U.S. Does not sell overseas. MC, V, MO, PC.
Self-Care Guide features aids for mobility for the physically handicapped. There are also health care products aimed at safety, convenience, and greater individual independence.

Sunburst Biorganics
838 Merrick Rd.
Baldwin, NY 11510
(516) 623-8478
48-page catalog, free; overseas $1.50. MC, V, MO, PC.
A complete line of natural vitamins, minerals, cosmetics, appliances, and dietary supplements at a savings of up to 70% off retail prices. All Sunburst supplements are made without sugar, starch, salt, and preservatives.

U.S. Health Club, Inc.
Box 293
Yonkers, NY 10702
70-page catalog, free U.S. Does not sell overseas. MC, V, MO, PC.
This firm sells a complete line of natural vitamins and supplements. Health

books, natural cosmetics, health foods, and digestive aids are also available. Since 1957.

Western Natural Products
511 Mission St.
P.O. Box 284-IM
South Pasadena, CA 91030
(213) 441-3447
16-page catalog, free U.S., Canada and Mexico; overseas .50¢. Small handling charge for orders under $10. MC, V, MO, PC.
Full line of vitamins and supplements from natural sources, including an exclusive line of shampoos, lotions, and creams. Children's chewable cherry-flavored vitamins, sweetened with fructose, are very reasonably priced.

The Xandria Collection
Lawrence Research Group
P.O. Box 31039
San Francisco, CA 94131
(415) 863-2266
35-page catalog, free U.S. Does not sell overseas. MC, V, MO, PC.
The Xandria Collection of sex paraphernalia is presented in a professional, almost clinical manner. There is every imaginable sexual aid offered, as well as an extensive list of guides and books on sex. All merchandise is shipped in a plain wrapper and the company states customers' names are never sold or rented to other companies.

BOOKS

SEE ALSO
- Antiques
- Collectibles

GENERAL

American Indian Books & Relics
P.O. Box 683
Athens, AL 35611
(205) 881-6727
4-page price list, free U.S. and overseas.
  MO, PC.
Books on American Indian artifacts and
Civil War relics.

Appalachian Literature and Music
104 Center St.
Berea, KY 40403
80-page catalog, $3 U.S. Does not sell
  overseas. MC, V, MO, PC.
This company specializes in books and
music relating to Appalachian history
and culture. The catalog is divided into
special categories: Appalachian culture
(traditional and contemporary),
Appalachian studies, autobiography,
literature, book and record shop,
photography, regional issues, travel and
children's literature.

Arco Publishing, Inc.
215 Park Avenue South
New York, NY 10003
(212) 777-6300
80-page catalog, free U.S. and overseas.
  Minimum order $25. MO.
Arco is a publisher of many special
interest publications whose categories
include consumer books, test
preparation and educational reviews,
education and guidance books, health
and nutrition, horse books, pets and
crafts, and many others.

Barnes & Noble Bookstore
126 Fifth Ave.
New York, NY 10011
(212) 675-5500
72-page catalog, free U.S. Does not sell
  overseas. AE, MC, V.
Barnes & Noble sells hardcover and
paperbacks on almost every subject
available. They specialize in selling
publisher's overstocks at discount prices
up to 80% and 90%. They run sections
in the catalog headed "any book on these
pages $3.98 or less," and pages of
paperback titles on inventory clearance
sales of 50% off list price.

Book Call
59 Elm St.
New Canaan, CT 06040
(800) 255-2665
(203) 966-5470
33-page catalog, U.S. and overseas. AE,
  MC, V, PC.
Book Call will gift wrap, enclose an
elegant gift card, and mail a gift book
anywhere in the world. There are over
150 of the latest titles reviewed by top
magazines and newspapers.

Brunner/Mazel
19 Union Square West
New York, NY 10003
8-page brochure, free U.S. and overseas.
  AE, MC, V, MO, PC.
Brunner/Mazel is both publisher and
dealer of books mainly for mental
health professionals, though some titles
are also for general interest. They have
a number of titles in the areas of
psychotherapy, psychoanalysis, and
hypnotherapy.

Blackwell's
Broad St.
Oxford OX1 3BQ England
0865 244944
Variety of catalogs available, free U.S.
  and overseas. MC, V, MO, PC.
Blackwell's is primarily an academic
bookshop and is trusted with orders
from many of the world's major
universities and research institutes.
They stock over 180,000 titles in over
thirteen subject areas, including music,
rare books, sheet music, and records.
Specialists in their subjects maintain
these stocks, supported by experts in
freighting and packing.

Bookmart
P.O. Box 101
Sand Hill Rd.
Gardiner, NY 12525–0101
(914) 255-5141
2-page brochure, free U.S. and overseas.
Bookmart is a purchasing service for
books and educational materials.
Whether you need a single best-selling
book, complete technical library, or an
overview of current material in a
specialty field, Bookmart can supply it.
Their brochure states, "We thoroughly
research, evaluate, recommend,
purchase and distribute books,
periodicals, tapes, cassettes and audio-
visual materials (in English) to fill every
conceivable educational, professional
and cultural need."

Consumer Information Catalog
Pueblo, CO 81009
16-page catalog, free U.S. and overseas.
  MO, PC.
The Consumer Information Catalog is
actually a quarterly listing of more than

200 free or moderately priced federal
publications. Single copies of the catalog
are available free, and bulk copies are
free to educators, libraries, and other
non-profit groups. There are booklets on
a variety of subjects, including
automobiles, children, employment and
education, food, gardening, health,
housing, money management, travel,
and other hobbies. It is such a
worthwhile publication that it is cited
here—for lack of a more appropriate
place in the book.

Discount Books By Mail
P.O. Box 22011
Seattle, WA 98122
(206) 323-5962
22-page catalog, free U.S. MC, V, MO,
  PC.
Discount Books by Mail lists about 200
new and popular books at a discount of
20% off retail bookstore prices. Their
categories are varied: fiction and
nonfiction, reference, sports and
recreation, humor, computers, love and
sex, gardening, parents, and children's
classics.

Folio Books Ltd.
202 Great Suffolk St.
London SEI IPR England
01 407 7411
Catalog, free U.S. and overseas.
Folio Books operates as part publisher
and part book club. Unlike other book
clubs, you order a minimum of four
books in advance each year from a
selection of over 130 titles. They also
offer handsomely bound Folio Special
Publications. The books are mostly
classics with some fiction, poetry, and
drama.

Gambler's Book Club Press
630 South 11th St.
Las Vegas, NV 89101
(702) 382-7555
20-page newsalog, free U.S. and
  overseas. MC, V, MO, PC.
Gambler's Book Club has the largest
selection of gambling books, many of
which are out of print, along with a
large selection of used books (some more
than 100 years old). The newsalog offers
more than 1,000 books with

approximately twenty new titles listed every six weeks. The catalog has fifteen subcategories of gambling listed, including thoroughbred racing, casino games, poker, novels, card games, and sociology and psychology of gambling. And wouldn't you know, the store is owned by John Luckman. (That's his real name.)

The Good Book Guide
P.O. Box 400
Havelock Terrace
London SW8 4AU England
01 622 1262
The Good Book Guide is a unique, independent consumer guide to good books published in Great Britain. Books covering every conceivable topic are selected or rejected by the Guide's panel of professional book reviewers, and *only* the most worthwhile and interesting books are then reviewed in the Guide. It is not just a listing of the latest best-sellers, but an excellent selection of books, both fiction and nonfiction. You do not have to commit yourself to the purchase of any books; they are simply bringing interesting books to your attention and making them available to you through a helpful mail order department. The Good Book Guide was honored with the *Queen's Award for Export Achievement,* which is very rarely granted to publishers.

Gotham Book Mart
41 West 47th St.
New York, NY 10036
(212) 719-4448
20-page catalog, .50¢ U.S. and overseas. Minimum order $10. AE, MC, V, MO, PC.
Gotham Book Mart issues specialized catalogs in various categories. Their catalogs list current, new, and forthcoming titles, and often a selection of out-of-print titles. Be sure when you write that you ask for the specific subject area you're interested in.

Hatchards
187 Piccadilly
London W1V 9DA England
01 439 9921
20-page catalog, free U.S. and overseas. AE, DC, MC, V, MO, PC.
Hatchards is London's oldest bookshop and sells books to members of the royal family. Their catalog lists over 300 hardbound and paperback books. And Hatchards will gladly supply any book currently in print in Great Britain if you should not find it listed.

Heffers Booksellers
20 Trinity St.
Cambridge CB2 3NG England
0223 358351
Many catalogs, all free U.S. and overseas. Prices in British pounds. MO, PC.
Heffers was founded in 1876, and currently operates six bookshops in Cambridge. Heffers provides a check list, with topics ranging from Archaeology to Zoology, and fifty-nine subjects in between. You simply indicate those subjects which interest you and they in return will send you catalogs and announcements of the new books in those categories. A few catalog examples include 128-page *History of Art and Design,* 56-page *Literature,* 64-page *Architecture,* 66-page *Agriculture & Veterinary Studies,* and 46-page *Evolution.*

Kroch's and Brentano's
29 S. Wabash Ave.
Chicago, IL 60603
(312) 332-7500
42-page catalog, free U.S. Does not sell overseas. Minimum order $5. AE, MC, V, MO, PC.
Kroch's and Brentano's was founded in 1907 by Adolf Kroch and has grown to a chain of seventeen stores. In addition to a fine selection of books there are many gift items for the whole family: imported pens, picture frames, stuffed animals, jigsaw puzzles ("Nails" will either drive you insane or blind you), and board games.

Prentice-Hall, Inc.
Englewood Cliffs, NJ 07632
(201) 592-2000
380-page catalog, free U.S. and overseas.
Prentice-Hall is a publisher offering thousands of their titles, cloth and

paperbound, in this large catalog. Their range is extensive and sure to satisfy many reader's interests: business, children's books, cookbooks, history, public relations, music, photography, science, education, and travel.

Publisher's Central Bureau
1 Champion Ave.
Avenel, NJ 07131
66-page catalog, free. AE, MC, V, MO, PC.
Chances are you are probably already on the mailing list of Publishers Central Bureau. But just in case you have missed them, or they have missed you, this is one of the leading discount mail order companies for books and records. Covering virtually every category (and with many popular titles) the cover of the catalog claims "huge savings of up to 85% by mail."

The Science Fiction Shop
56 Eighth Ave.
New York, NY 10014
(212) 741-0270
8-page price list, free; overseas $1.
   Minimum order $10. MC, V, MO, PC.
The most complete stock of English language fantasy and science fiction books and magazines. Especially helpful are two of their own titles: *A Reader's Guide to Science Fiction,* and *A Reader's Guide to Fantasy,* both published by Avon Books.

Strand Bookstore, Inc.
828 Broadway
New York, NY 10003
(212) 473-1452
Strand sells newly published books at 50% off list price, used and out-of-print books, rare books, and books on art. They are undoubtedly the largest out-of-print book dealer in the U.S. The store is enormous and has a staff of over 100 people. They offer a variety of catalogs. Write for the subject area of your choice: *Strand Specials, Review Specials Half-Price* (these are reviewer hardcover copies and a great buy), *Art Books,* and *Rare and Unusual Art Books.*

Underground Homes
PO Box 1346
Portsmouth, OH 45662
(614) 354-7708
4-page brochure, free U.S. and overseas. MC, V, PC.
Underground Homes lists over forty books available on earth-sheltered homes. There are books on underground housing plans and designs, building codes, estimating the cost of building, how-to-build, and survival.

Womansplace Bookstore
425 S. Mill Ave.
Tempe, AZ 85281
40-page catalog, $1; overseas $2. MC, V, MO, PC.
Womansplace Bookstore specializes in feminist literature. Titles include *You Can't Keep A Good Woman Down* and *Ambitious Woman.* There are many other titles expressing the growing female spirit, as well as books on nonsexist children's books, fiction, poetry, parenting, birthing psychology, and gay lifestyles.

ANTIQUES AND COLLECTIBLES

Harlin House, Ltd.
P.O. Box 1199
New Milford, CT 06776
(800) 824-7888
(800) 824-7919
40-page newsalog, $1.50; overseas $4.
   Minimum order $15 by phone. MC, V, MO, PC.
The Harlin House catalog contains over 1,000 reference books and price guides on every conceivable collecting category: porcelain, pottery, paper dolls, Hummel figures, furniture, wicker, baskets, quilts, postcards, baseball cards, pewter, autographs, bottles, salt dips and shakers, decoys, and much more.
Printed four times annually, each issue adds the best and latest books published on antiques and collectibles.

Hotchkiss House
18 Hearthstone Rd.
Pittsford, NY 14534
(716) 381-4735

10-page newsalog, free U.S. and
overseas. MO, PC.
Hotchkiss House is the largest mail
order antique book business in the U.S.
James Panosian, owner, sells to private
customers, 350 bookstores, and over
1,000 libraries and museums in the U.S.
and overseas. Within forty-eight hours
of receiving them, Panosian fills and
ships orders for books on Chinese
porcelain, unusual thimbles, old
records, country pine furniture, doll
collecting, silver, and jewelry.

Lamplighter Books
101–103 Main St.
Leon, IA 50144
12-page newsalog, free U.S. and
overseas. MC, V, MO, PC.
Started in 1964, Lamplighters carries a
large selection of books on antiques and
collectibles.

The Reference Rack
Box 445
Orefield, PA 18069
(215) 395-0004
20-page price list, free U.S. and overseas.
MO, PC.
Betty and Tim Johnston stock over 2,000
different books on antiques and
collectibles; half of them appear in the
catalog. With each publication new
titles are rotated in, so be sure to write
requesting a specific title if you don't see
it. Many of their books are works
published by museums, authors, private
companies, or foreign publishers.

The Vestal Press
P.O. Box 97
Vestal, NY 13850
(607) 797-4872
64-page catalog, $2 refundable U.S. and
overseas. AE, MC, V, MO, PC.
Books, publications, and records
primarily in the field of technical
antiquarian hobbies: theater pipe
organs, steam equipment, old cars,
carousels, antique radios, gambling
machines, wooden boats, and jukeboxes.
Started twenty-one years ago with the
publication of their first book, *Player
Piano Treasury,* today they still
specialize in supplying technical and

historical information to mechanical
music hobbyists.

ANTIQUARIAN

Arthur H. Minters
84 University Place
New York, NY 10003
(212) 989-0593
32-page catalog, $2; overseas $4.
Subscription rates for six annual
printings $12; overseas $24. MC, V,
MO, PC.
Rare twentieth-century art and
architecture books, and books on
photography, fine and decorative arts.
Since 1957.

B. M. Israel
N. Z. Voorburgwal 264
Amsterdam 1012 RS Netherlands
020 247040
100-page catalog, $5 U.S. and overseas.
AE, MO, PC.
B. M. Israel offers an extensive
collection of rare books, specializing in
the field of medicine and sciences. Since
1898.

Goodspeed's Book Shop, Inc.
7 Beacon St.
Boston, MA 02108
(617) 523-5970
Goodspeed's, founded in 1898, has
collections of rare books on Americana,
English and American literature, early
printing, autographs, and engravings.
They also have sections of old books on
art, architecture, ships and the sea,
natural history, biography, and the
social sciences. They publish many
catalogs varying in size from eight to
128 pages. It is probably best that you
write, stating your special interest(s),
and they will send their catalogs.

Hampton Books
Rt. 1 Box 202
Newberry, SC 29108
(803) 276-6870
26-page *Aerospace History* catalog, $2
U.S. and overseas. 120-page *Cinema 13*
catalog, $3 U.S. and overseas. MO, PC.
Hampton Books has built collections of
certain kinds of antiquarian books

written in many languages, plus prints and photographs. The Aerospace History collection, they claim, is the largest of its kind in the U.S. *Cinema 13* catalog is a collection of books on movie history, theory, and related subjects of photography, television, and radio.

Henry Sotheran, Ltd.
2, 3, 4 & 5 Sackville St.
Piccadilly
London W1X 2DP England
01 734 1150
30-page catalog, $1 U.S. and overseas.
  AE, DC, V, MO, PC.
Sotheran's of Sackville Street is one of London's oldest and most famous bookshops. Fine old books have been Sotheran's speciality since 1761. Charles Dickens was a regular customer during his lifetime; after his death his library was purchased by Sotheran's. They offer an excellent selection of English handcolored engravings mainly from the 19th century: Natural History, English Sporting Prints, Topographical Views, and Military and Naval Subjects.

J. N. Bartfield Books
45 West 57th St.
New York, NY 10019
(212) 753-1830
96-page catalog, $3; overseas, $5. MO, PC.
Bartfield's offers an extensive collection of leather-bound sets and single-volume books by famous authors. They also carry fore-edge paintings, color plate books, atlases, and old books before 1865. Franklin Mint Library books are sold by subscription ($35 each plus postage). Amidst all those fine leather-bound, gilt-edged books, Bartfield does claim to have one paperback—his mail order catalog.

Paul Breman, Ltd.
1 Rosslyn Hill
London NW3 5UL England
01 435 7730
48-page catalog, free U.S. and overseas.
  BD, MO, PC.
Paul Breman's specializes in illustrated antiquarian books in a variety of categories: architecture, landscape,

perspective, photography, bridge building, English fortification, and decorative prints—to name a few. Since 1961.

ART

Abbeville Press
505 Park Ave.
New York, NY 10022
(212) 888-1969
48-page catalog, free U.S. and overseas.
  AE, MC, V, MO.
An excellent collection of current titles in fine art books. A 25% discount is available on the purchase of five books, 40% discount if ten books are ordered. Abbeville's Modern Masters series includes books on Willem de Kooning (abstract expressionism), Roy Lichtenstein (popular imagery), Jackson Pollock, George Segal, and Andy Warhol, which sell for about $30 clothbound and $17 paperback. Other titles include *Canova, Early Sea Charts, Kandinsky, Mary Cassatt,* and *Sargent Castles in Spain.*

Morgan & Morgan, Inc.
145 Palisade St.
Dobbs Ferry, NY 10522
(914) 693-9303
16-page catalog, prices unavailable U.S. and overseas. PC.
Morgan & Morgan are publishers of photography and related arts. Some of their titles include *The Keepers of Light, New American Nudes, 101 Experiments in Photography,* and *Rising Goddess.*

Nancy Scheck
3300 Netherland Ave.
Riverdale, NY 10463
(212) 543-7521
14-page catalog, free U.S. and overseas.
  MO, PC.
Nancy Scheck runs a small and personal business supplying art reference books: art, photography, sculpture, drawings and graphics, and all periods of American art.

Rizzoli International Publications
712 Fifth Ave.
New York, NY 10019
(212) 397-3785

40-page (some color) catalog, $1
    overseas $1.50 AE, DC, MC, V, MO, PC.
Founded in 1975, Rizzoli is a publisher
of fine arts books. They bring out sixty
to seventy new books each year in art,
architecture, music, photography,
antiques, decorative arts, and fashion
books. They won an award from the
American Institute of Architects in 1982
for excellence in publishing, and they
are frequently reviewed in book review
media (*Library Journal, Art in America,*
and *Choice*).

Wittenborn Art Books
1018 Madison Ave.
New York, NY 10021
20-page catalog, free U.S. and overseas.
    MC, V, MO, PC.
Books on the fine arts, architecture,
photography, furniture, porcelain,
prints, and sculpture are offered by
Wittenborn. Their bookstore is the type
you could easily lose yourself in for
hours. The catalog (price list by
category, without descriptions), though
extensive, cannot compare to browsing
through the bookshop in person.

BOOKS ON TAPE

Caedmon
1995 Broadway
New York, NY 10023
(800) 223-0420
New York (212) 580-3400
30-page color catalog, free U.S. and
    overseas. MC, V, MO, PC.
Caedmon is the world's foremost
producer of spoken-word recordings in
LP or cassette format. The Chronicles
of Narnia, Winnie the Pooh, Robert
Frost Reads, and Breakfast of
Champions are just some of the works.
Prices for each tape start at $8.50. The
catalog is conveniently arranged by
category of interest and within each
category there is an alphabetical list of
titles. The categories include prose,
novels, science fiction, fairy tales,
children's classics, theater, and
Shakespeare recordings. *Time*
magazine called Caedmon "the thinking
man's CB;" travelling parents with

children have called it "nothing short
of paradise."

Listen for Pleasure
417 Center St.
Lewiston, NY 14092
(800) 962-5200
New York, NY 252-1144
8-page (some color) brochure, free U.S.
    MC, V, MO, PC.
Listen for Pleasure sells books recorded
on cassette tapes. They offer a good
selection of books the whole family will
enjoy, with prices ranging from $13.95
to $19.95. Now you can listen to the
bestsellers while gardening, puttering
in the work shop, driving in the car, or
house cleaning.

CHILDREN'S

Baker Book Services
Little Mead, Alford Road, Cranleigh
Surrey GU6 8NU England
0483 275444
4-page newsletter, one-year subscription
    $10; overseas $5. Printed four times a
    year. MC, V, MO, PC.
Baker Book Services is a division of the
renowned Children's Book Center in
London. The newsletter describes about
seventy of the 500 or more newly
published children's books which they
have reviewed in the last quarter. In
addition to this excellent service there
are three booklets available in a series
called *Reading for Enjoyment,*
recommending books for ages 0–6, 7–11,
and 12 and up. It's superb.

Bank Street College Bookstore
610 West 112th St.
New York, NY 10025
(212) 663-7200
10-page brochure, free U.S. and
    overseas. MO, PC.
Juvenile books and literature for
parents and teachers. The bookstore is
owned and operated by the Bank Street
College of Education and the many
books reflect the College's educational
philosophy. Bank Street publications
include *Education Before Five*, $6.50, a
comprehensive handbook on preschool
educational theory and practice, and *A*

Big Bite of the World, $6.95, a collection of poems, stories and plays by children, plus practical tips to help them grow in creativity through writing.

Bellerophon Books
36 Anacapa St.
Santa Barbara, CA 93101
(805) 965-7034
4-page color catalog, self-addressed stamped envelope U.S.; overseas 2 IRCs. MO, PC.
Bellerophon Books sells many intricate "coloring books", which appeal to people of all ages. Some books (*Ancient China, Greece, Egypt, Japan,* and *Ancient Ireland*) are meant primarily to be colored. Others include lots of text: *Great Composers, Myths and Legends of Indians of the Southwest.* Using a master set of felt tip pens, the finished products have the vivid color qualities of stained glass art work or water color mastery. Most are priced around $3.

Children's Book and Music Center
P.O. Box 1130
Santa Monica, CA 90406–1130
(213) 829-0215
96-page catalog, $1; overseas $3.50. MC, V, MO, PC.
Children's Book and Music Center is a unique source of phonograph records and books for use by children, teachers, and parents. They currently occupy a 7,000-square-foot showroom where you can actually listen to the records before you buy. And browse. And browse. They carry about 25,000 various titles from all the major publishers and from many individual authors who self-publish. This is definitely a "don't miss" catalog.

The Green Tiger Press
P.O. Box 3000
La Jolla, CA 92038
(619) 238-1001
80-page catalog, $3.95; overseas $4.95. AE, MC, V, MO, PC.
Delghtful children's books, many illustrated in the old hand-tipped method, creating beautifully textured works of art. *Teddy Bears' Picnic, Hanimals,* and *If You're Afraid of the Dark, Remember the Night Rainbow,* are a few of the titles to choose from.

"We stress those qualities that the child exemplifies—the freshness of vision, the spontaneity, the hunger for mystery and adventure."

Heffers Booksellers
20 Trinity St.
Cambridge CB2 2NG England
0223 358351
Many catalogs, all free U.S. and overseas. Prices in British pounds. MO, PC.
The Children's Book catalog is possibly the finest collection of English-language books to be found. Heffers (founded in 1876) supplies libraries, institutions, and individuals with their book requirements throughout the world. See Heffers listing in the general book section.

Learn Me Bookstore
642 Grand Ave.
St. Paul, MN 55105
(612) 291-7888
50-page catalog, $3 U.S. and overseas. Minimum order $20. MC, V, PC.
Learn Me Bookstore is an exciting catalog filled with well-selected children's books, games, records, and parenting and teaching materials. It has grown since 1973 to include many special-need materials to use with children, including subjects of family changes, disabilities, and sexuality.

Nursery Books
4430 School Way
Castro Valley, CA 94546
(415) 538-4249
24-page catalog, $1 U.S. and overseas. MC, V, MO, PC.
Nursery Books offers a good selection of books for all ages of children. There are vinyl, board, or cloth books for babies (from four to six months old) from the U.S., England, Germany and Denmark, For toddlers there are books by Richard Scarry, Dick Bruna, and Dr. Seuss. There are picture books, "hands-on" activity books, and music books.

Parent Child Press
P.O. Box 767
Altoona, PA 16603
(814) 946-5213

14-page catalog, free U.S. MC, V, MO,
PC.
All the materials listed in this catalog
were designed for Montessorians by a
fellow Montessori teacher, Aline Wolf.
There are many books, art postcards,
and posters available for teachers and
parents. *The World of the Child* is a
modern fable retelling an imaginary
tale which Maria Montessori, early
childhood educator, used in many of her
lectures.

Spoken Arts, Inc.
PO Box 289
New Rochelle, NY 10802
(914) 636-5482
Spoken Arts is a multi-media company
offering cassette and record filmstrips
for children of all ages. Mostly sold to
schools, there are some excellent sound
filmstrips that start at about $32. There
are hundreds of masters ranging from
Shakespeare to Yeats, from Edgar Allan
Poe to Langston Hughes, from
Cinderella to Peter Rabbit and Mrs.
Tiggy-Winkle, and from Grimm and
Andersen to Louisa May Alcott.

COOKBOOKS

Cooks Books
34 Marine Dr.
Rottingdean, Brighton
Sussex BN2 7HQ England
0273 32707
48-page catalog, free U.S. and overseas.
   Prices in British pounds. MO, PC.
Cooks Books sells many out-of-print,
secondhand, and antiquarian books on
food, cookery, wine, herbs, etiquette, and
related subjects. The catalog lists the
books alphabetically by author and
provides a very brief description. Some
books are as recent as last year, and
some date back to the early 1500s. Prices
range from one pound to 1,000 pounds.

Jessica's Biscuit Cookbook
Box 301
Newtonville, MA 02160
(800) 225-4264
Massachusetts (617) 965-0530
64-page color catalog, $1; overseas $2.
   MC, V, PC.

Hundreds of titles of exciting new
cookbooks as well as familiar favorites.
Many of the cookbooks are listed with
photographs of their cover and all have
excellent descriptions. *The Art of Food
Processor Cooking,* by Freiman ($6.98),
and Charles Viron's *French Country
Cookbook* ($8.98) are both good buys.

Sil Maria
Box 433, Route 22
Peru, NY 12972
(514) 483-1609
8-page brochure, free; overseas $5.
   Written in French, prices in $ U.S. MC,
   V, MO, PC.
Sil Maria offers a large selection of
books on cooking and wine in French.
Each book is reviewed in French and
prices are in $ U.S. Cookbooks by
Lenotre and Girardet have been very
popular.

The Wine and Food Library
1207 W. Madison
Ann Arbor, MI 48103
(313) 663-4894
30-page catalog, $2 U.S. and overseas.
   MO, PC.
The Wine and Food Library is really a
unique service. They stock about 10,000
volumes of old, rare, interesting,
unusual, and out-of-print books on all
matters culinary, gastronomic, and
oenological. It is a small, personal
enterprise run by Jan Longone. She both
buys and sells single books and
collections, and offers a free
international search service if your
request is not currently available. The
titles and dates are impressive: 1879
Godey's Lady's Receipts, and a 1681
British Pressure Cooker Cookbook.

CRAFT BOOKS

Books for Embroidery
96 Roundwood Rd.
Newton, MA 02164
(617) 969-0942
24-page price list, $1 U.S. and overseas.
   MO, PC.
Bette Feinstein offers old and new, rare,
out-of-print, and imported books on

embroidery. There is a 40% to 90% discount on prices of special selections.

The Unicorn
Box 645
Rockville, MD 20851
(301) 881-4770
20-page newsalog, $1 U.S. and overseas.
  Minimum order $7.50. MC, V, MO, PC.
The Unicorn offers a large selection of sewing and needlework craft books. Some are published privately (or by museums) and some are collected from around the world. The catalog categories include embroidery, weaving, spinning, dyeing, appliqué-quilting, smocking, knitting, and crochet.

GARDENING BOOKS

Brooklyn Botanic Garden
1000 Washington Ave.
Brooklyn, NY 11225
(212) 622-4433
4-page brochure, free U.S. and overseas.
  MOC, PC.
The brochure lists gardening handbooks in numerous categories: gardening practices, indoor gardening, bonsai, herbs, specialty plants, trees and shrubs. The Brooklyn Botanic Garden also offers an extensive gardening book series; each publication is a concise, well-illustrated manual of 64 to 104 pages, with ideas to use in any garden. Priced at $2.25, they are a good buy.

ISBS Timber Press
P.O. Box 1632
Beaverton, OR 97075
(503) 292-2606
20-page brochure, free U.S. and
  overseas. MC, V, MO, PC.
Books on gardening, horticulture and forestry. In horticultural publishing, they offer excellent books for everyone from plant propagators to the homeowner wanting to enhance his or her yard. These books should appeal to those horticulturists and gardeners who want definitive, in-depth information on topics from general to specific. *The Complete Book of Roses,* $50, is a study of the rose from prehistoric times to

1981. *Rhododendron Species,* Volume 1, $60, is written by the worldwide authority on this family of plants, J. J. Davidian.

Landsmans Bookshop, Ltd.
Buckenhill, Bromyard,
Herefordshire England
0885 83420
126-page catalog, $1 U.S. and overseas.
  MO, PC.
Landsmans specializes in horticultural and agricultural books, and allied subjects such as beekeeping, forestry, fur-bearing animals, irrigation, and botany. Loaded with book sources on every imaginable topic, there is even an interesting subsection devoted to computers in agriculture and horticulture.

HISTORICAL

The Filter Press
P.O. Box 5
Palmer Lake, CO 80133-0005
(303) 481-2523
2-page price list, self-addressed stamped
  envelope U.S. MO, PC.
Paperback books on the west and southwest, ranging from 24–200 pages. Most are original publications; some are reprints of classic works long out of print and unavailable.

HOBBY

American Reprints Co.
2200 Eldridge Ave.
P.O. Box 6011
Bellingham, WA 98227
(206) 647-0107
32-page catalog, $1 U.S. and overseas.
  MC, V, MO, PC.
American Reprints sells horological books including history, price lists, and identification of clocks and watches. Since 1962.

Heraldry Today
10 Beauchamp Place
London SW3 England
01 584-1656

36-page catalog, free U.S. and overseas.
MO, PC.
Heraldry Today sells many new and old books, antiquarian and sewn-by-hand, on heraldry, genealogy, and biography. Located on Beauchamp Place in smart Knightsbridge, just around the corner from Harrods. Their large stock of books is available in many languages. They will undertake genealogical searches and research coats of arms.

Lewis Davenport Ltd.
51 Great Russell St.
London WC1B 3BA England
01 405 8524
300-page catalog, $9 U.S. and overseas.
MO, PC.
Lewis Davenport offers the most comprehensive book catalog on magic, conjuring, illusion, juggling, and ventriloquism. The company was formed in 1891 by the grandfather of one of the present directors, Mrs. Betty Davenport. The company has invented many magical effects and is well known as a publisher of books on magic and card magic.

Speleobooks
Box 333
Wilbraham, MA 01095
(413) 596-9516
24-page catalog, free U.S. and overseas.
MC, V, MO, PC.
This is an unusual catalog of old and new books on speleology (the study of caves). Actually Emily Davis Mobley, owner, sells many items—including art, kites, dolls and rubber stamps—on the theme of bats and caves. Ms. Mobley says, "I am the largest volume new book dealer in this field in the country." Indeed, she does appear to have cornered this market.

INTERNATIONAL

China Books and Periodicals, Inc.
2929 24th St.
San Francisco, CA 94110
(415) 282-2994
32-page catalog, $1 U.S. and overseas.
MC, V, MO, PC.

Books in English imported from the Peoples Republic of China on history, art, travel, current affairs, literature, children's books, and learning the Chinese language. China Books was one of the first companies to engage in trade with China—their catalog is excellent. The children's books, starting around $1.95, are especially colorful and charming.

European Publishers Representatives, Inc.
11-03 46th Ave.
Long Island City, NY 11101
(212) 937-4606
6-page brochure, $1 U.S. Does not sell overseas. MO, PC.
European Publishers Representatives are U.S. importers and distributors of European and Australian newspapers, magazines, periodicals, and paperback books. They offer visually beautiful magazines in specialized fields of fashion, interior decoration, and photography. Some of their titles include *Officiel, Match, Linea, Jours de France, Le Monde, Epoca, Zoom, L'Express,* and *Sunday London Times.* The catalog indicates the language of the text.

The French and Spanish Book Corp.
115 Fifth Ave.
New York, NY 10003
(212) 673-7400
Four catalogs: 88-page *The Best in Books in Spanish* catalog, 158-page *Spanish Literature* catalog, 86-page *New French Books* catalog, 346-page *French Books* catalog, each $2.95; overseas $6.95 each. Minimum order $10. AE, DC, MC, V, MO, PC.
The French and Spanish Book store has a huge selection of French and Spanish books. They are imported from France, Belgium, Switzerland, Canada, Spain, Latin and Central America. They sell to schools, universities, and individuals. A 10% to 50% price discount is available, depending on titles and quantities ordered.

Motilal Books, Ltd.
52 Crown Rd. Wheatley
Oxford OX9 1UL England
0865 3478

10-page catalog, $1 refundable U.S. and overseas. Minimum order $35 or 25 British pounds. MO, PC.

Motilal Books are specialized dealers of Indian-published books in the English language, on all subjects. Stocks of the major titles are substantially less expensive here than in other shops. Their expertise in obtaining Indian material and their knowledge of the Indian book market is based on twenty-five years of experience.

Overseas Publishers' Representatives
47 West 34th St.
New York, NY 10001
(212) 564-3954

OPR is a subscription service for specialized international publications on fashion, trade, technical and scientific periodicals. Their customers include corporations, small companies, government agencies and individuals. *Made in Europe* is a publication that would appeal to manufacturers of giftware, leather goods, toys, jewelry, or to people generally interested in the latest products from Europe. The annual subscription rate is $40.

Unicorn Limited, Inc.
P.O. Box 778
Morgantown, WV 26505
(304) 292-2811

16-page newsalog, free U.S. and overseas. MC, V, MO, PC.

The Unicorn Limited is actually a company with three divisions, all dedicated to providing books and gift items about Scotland. The Scotpress prints (and reprints) classic Scottish books, with emphasis on genealogical and family history. The Scottish Merchant is a newspaper ($10 subscription yearly rate) devoted to Scots-Americans.

METAPHYSICAL

DeVorss & Company
P.O. Box 550
Marina Del Rey, CA 90294–0550

DeVorss stocks over 3,000 titles of metaphysical, inspirational, self-help and New Age books. Founded in 1929, DeVorss has continued to expand on the categories it handles: astrology, healing, ESP, yoga, UFOs, and nutrition. You can find popular titles, including *The Game of Life and How to Play It,* by Florence Shinn, and *Key to Yourself,* by Venice Bloodworth.

Fountain of Light
7877 Jefferson Hwy.
Baton Rouge, LA 70809
(504) 927 2385

100-page catalog, free U.S. and overseas. MC, V, MO, PC.

An expansive listing of books on the metaphysical. Subtopics include astrology, dreams, hypnosis, palmistry, handwriting analysis, numerology, tarot, ESP, meditation, Eastern thought and healing.

Samuel Weiser, Inc.
P.O. Box 612
York Beach, ME 03910
(207) 363-4394

40-page catalog, free U.S. and overseas. MO, PC.

Samuel Weiser's has been described in articles in leading magazines as one of the largest bookstores specializing in the occult. The books cover a variety of metaphysical and occult topics including astrology, tarot, Buddhism, tai-chi, kabbalah, Tibetan studies, magic and witchcraft. Titles include *Foundations of Tibetan Mysticism,* by Govinda, *Finding the Third Eye,* by Alder, and *The Book of Thoth,* by Crowley.

MILITARY

Fairfield Specialty Book Co.
P.O. Box 1199
New Milford, CT 06805
(800) 824-7888
(800) 824-7919

56-page newsalog, $1.50; overseas $4. MC, V, MO, PC.

An excellent reference catalog for books, videotapes, records and other specialty merchandise relating to military or guns. The table of contents varies from month to month offering a good selection of topics: Napoleonic Wars, badges and medals, military history, aircraft, war games, modern guns, police and law enforcement, and more.

MYSTERY

Marjon Books
16 Mannering Gardens
Westcliff-On-Sea
Essex SSO OBQ England
0702 347119
14-page catalog, free U.S. and overseas. MO, PC.
Marjon sells first editions, new and used, of detective, crime, and mystery thriller books. They also carry a good selection of quality paperback books, particularly first printings of Penguin editions. Their stock in Agatha Christie books is excellent. Advice is also given in suggesting other authors you might find interesting. Personal callers are always offered a cup of tea—and some have been known to stay for dinner, says M. E. Cooper.

Murder Ink
271 W. 87th St.
New York, NY 10024
(212) 362-8905
4-page newsletter-brochure, self-addressed stamped envelope U.S.; overseas 2 IRCs. MO, PC.
Murder Ink sells in print and out-of-print paperback and hardcover mystery books. They also carry books relating to mysteries, mystery writers, and mystery writing. Mystery theme records, games, notepaper, cards and bookplates are also available. If there is a specific book you're looking for, Carol Brener will keep your request on file (either a title, author, or type of mystery) and notify you when she has found something for you.

The Mysterious Bookshop
129 W. 56th St.
New York, NY 10019
(212) 765-0900

6-page brochure, self-addressed stamped envelope U.S.; overseas 2 IRCs. Minimum order $10. AE, DC, MC, V, MO, PC.
This interesting mystery book brochure is divided into various categories: The 1983 Edgar Awards, The Reference Shelf, New Titles, New in Paperback, Sherlockian Items, and Special Sale. The Crime Collectors Club is not your usual book club; here members receive a first edition, inscribed by the author, at no increase over the published price of the book. A refundable $20 deposit and postage is required.

NATURAL HISTORY

John Johnson
Natural History Books
R. D. 2
N. Bennington, VT 05257
(802) 442-6738
30-page catalog, price unavailable U.S. and overseas.
The catalog lists hundreds of books (without reviews) in categories: general natural history, botany, cryptograms, birds, fish, reptiles, amphibians and invertebrates, marine and freshwater biology.

Wheldon and Wesley, Ltd.
Lytton Lodge, Codicote
Hitchin
Herts SG4 8TE England
0438 820370
112-page catalog, free by surface U.S.; overseas free. MO, PC.
An extensive offering of old and new books on natural history. They emphasize zoology, geology, palaeontology, and botany. They also have books on marine and freshwater biology, travel, and local natural history and historical works. They say, "Our principal strength lies in our expertise backed up by an immense store of information . . . and we hope that the service we offer is second to none."

PERFORMING ARTS

Da Capo Press, Inc.
233 Spring St.
New York, NY 10013
(212) 620-8000
52-page catalog, U.S. and overseas. AE,
 DC, MC, V, PC.
Da Capo's catalog offers a good selection
of books in the areas of music and dance
and the visual arts, including
architecture and decorative art, graphic
arts, and photography. They also carry
a number of titles on theater and film.

Drama Book Publishers
821 Broadway
New York, NY 10003
(212) 228-3400
64-page catalog, free U.S. and overseas.
 MO, PC.
Drama Book Publishers offers over 400
titles of books they have published on
the performing arts. There are how-to
books that deal with voice, producing
theater, film, and design. There are
books on costumes, lighting, and
makeup. Some of the Broadway plays
and musicals they have published are
Hello Dolly, Bye Bye Birdie, and
Carnival. They also publish texts for the
academic and professional theater
community. They sell to individuals and
stores worldwide.

Marga Schoeller Bucherstube
Knesebeckstr. 33
D 1000 Berlin 12
West Germany
030 881 11 12
20-page catalog, free U.S. and overseas.
 MO, PC.
Books written in both German and
English on the performing arts: film,
theater, ballet, and music. Founded in
1929 by the late Marga Schoeller, it is
now run as a cooperative and specializes
in books on film.

REFERENCE

The Dictionary Store
115 Fifth Ave.
New York, NY 10003
(212) 673-7400

200-page catalog, $4.95; overseas $8.95.
 Minimum order $10. AE, DC, MC, V,
 MO, PC.

Reference Book Center, Inc.
175 Fifth Ave.
New York, NY 10010
(212) 677-2160
16-page price list, 75¢ U.S. and overseas.
 MO, PC.
Reference Book Center provides an
extensive list of reference books,
dictionaries, reference sets, and
encyclopedias from a wide variety of
publishers. Titles include *Morris
Dictionary of Word and Phrase Origins,
New Encyclopedia of Sports, All the
Years of American Popular Music, The
Oxford Dictionary of English
Etymology,* and many more.

RELIGIOUS

Augsburg Publishing House
426 So. 5th St.
P.O. Box 1209
Minneapolis, MN 55440
(612) 330-3300
196-page catalog, free U.S. and overseas.
 Minimum order $10. MO, PC.
Augsburg sells religious books and
church supplies. There are educational
resources, Bibles and testaments,
Christian education, enrichment books,
church and school supplies, and art.
There is also a section on worship
resources and music.

Concordia Publishing House
3558 S. Jefferson Ave.
St. Louis, MO 63118
(314) 325-3040
335-page catalog, free U.S. and overseas.
 MO, PC.
Concordia publishes religious
materials: adult books, children's
theological curriculum, and music.

Reiner Publications
Swengel, PA 17880
(717) 922-3213
2-page price list, free U.S. and overseas.
 MO, PC.
Reiner Publications stocks over 60,000
new and used religious books,

particularly those dealing with the Protestant Reformation. Approximately 150 of the titles are out-of-print works republished by Reiner. Owner Donald Reiner doubles as the town's postmaster, operating both businesses inside a former church complete with stained glass windows and steeple.

SPORTS

The Anglers Art
R. D. 9, Box 204
Carlisle, PA 17013
(717) 243-9721
4-page newsletter, free U.S. and
  overseas. MC, V, MO, PC.
The Anglers Art produces an interesting newsletter for fly fisher enthusiasts. There are a few newsy articles, but the majority of the newsletter is devoted to listing new and old books on fly fishing. Over 90% of their orders are sent out the same day as they are received. They also handle a few limited edition prints on fly fishing.

Pegasos Press
535 Cordova Rd., Suite 163
Santa Fe, NM 87501
48-page newsalog, MC, V, MO, PC.
A wide range of books for the equestrian: reference, riding, schooling and training, horse health, horse management, racing and breeding. There are also many books on the different breeds of horses; *A World of Horses* $35, is a beautifully color-illustrated book presenting the horse in many roles throughout history.

Soccer for Americans
Box 836
Manhattan Beach, CA 90266
(213) 372-9000
4-page brochure, free. PC.
Books on soccer for coaches, referees, players, and spectators. *Soccer, A Guide for Parents,* $3.95, is an excellent book for parents who are seeking advice on how to buy equipment and want to learn the rudiments of the game right along with their children.

TRANSPORTATION

Aero Publishers, Inc.
329 West Aviation Rd.
Fallbrook, CA 92028
(800) 854-6550
California (619) 728-8456
32-page catalog, free U.S. and overseas.
  Minimum order $25. MC, V, MO, PC.
Aero Publishers claim to be the world's largest publisher of aviation and space books. Their catalog shows over 200 books on all phases of aviation and space with excellent book descriptions. There are books on pilot training, reference manuals, famous military and civil airplanes, World War I and II aviation, antique aircraft, modeling, racing planes, missiles, and space flight.

Armchair Sailor Bookstore
Lee's Wharf
Newport, RI 02840
(401) 847-4252
220-page catalog, $4; overseas $8. AE,
  MC, V, MO, PC.
Armchair offers over 6,000 marine books. They also carry charts, nautical instruments, maritime posters, cassettes, and records. There are books on racing techniques by Gary Jobson and Ted Turner. There are seafaring chronicles of single-handed voyages, stories of survival at sea, and many books on maritime history. America's Cup enthusiasts would enjoy the trio: *Enterprise to Endeavor,* plus *America's Cup Fever, An Inside View of Cup Competition Including the 1980 Defense,* plus *The America's Cup: An Informal History.*

Aviation Book Company
1640 Victory Blvd.
Glendale, CA 91201
(213) 240-1771
48-page catalog, $1; overseas $2. MC, V,
  MO, PC.
The Aviation Book Company stocks approximately 1,500 different titles of new aeronautical books from many publishers. They also carry a select line of pilot supplies and sundry aviation items like calendars, aircraft posters, and aviation gifts. Most orders are shipped within forty-eight hours.

Carbook
181 Glen Ave.
Sea Cliff, NY 11579
(516) 676-8043
24-page catalog, free U.S. AE, MC, V,
    MO, PC.
Brief but informative descriptions on an
extensive variety of books on cars. The
catalog is categorized by make of car,
starting with Alfa Romeo and ending
with Volvo. Other categories include
technical areas such as fuel systems,
brakes and suspension, and restoration.

Chater and Scott, Ltd.
8 South St.
Isleworth, Middlesex
TW7 7BG England
01 568 9750
10-page catalog, free U.S. and overseas.
    MC, V, MO, PC.
Chater and Scott sells new and old books
and magazines on cars and motorcycles.
They stock many back issues of
motoring magazines. "Any books or
magazines not available from our vast
stock are carefully noted and supplied
when available."

International Marine Publishing Co.
21 Elm St.
Camden, ME 04843
16-page newslog, free in U.S. and
    overseas. MC, V, MO, PC.
International Marine carries over 500
nautical books and 100 art prints on
marine subjects selected from all over
the world. They emphasize boat
building and design but also list other
categories: New Titles, About Boats,
Boat Maintenance, Commercial
Fishing, Cook Books (*The Cruising
Cook,* $15.95, sounds great), Cruising
Guides, Cruising Stories, Marine
Reference, Maritime History,
Marlinspike Seamanship, Navigation,
Racing, and Underwater.

Motor Books
33 St. Martins Court
London WC2N 4AL England
01 836 5376
Catalog, free U.S. and overseas. MC, V,
    MO, PC.
Books on transportation: motor, railway,
aviation and naval. Since 1957.

Motorbooks International
P.O. Box 2
Osceola, WI 54020
(800) 826-6600
(715) 294-3345
50-page *Aviation* catalog, 120-page
    Motorbook catalog, $2 U.S. and
    overseas. AE, MC, V, MO, PC.
Started in 1968, Motorbooks offers a
large source of books on automotive and
aviation books. For enthusiasts in either
area, they can supply books from the
most common to the most obscure. Some
of their titles include: *New Observer's
Book of Aircraft, X-Plans, B-24 Liberator
at War, Corvette Buyer's Guide,* and
Delorean: Stainless Steel Illusion.

Owen Davis Bookseller
200 W. Harrison St.
Oak Park, IL 60304
(312) 848-1186
12-page catalog, free U.S. and overseas.
    MO, PC.
New and used books related to
transportation history, especially of
railroads and steamships: history,
economics, technology, timetables,
annual reports, and travel brochures.

TRAVEL AND MAPS

Varna Enterprises
P.O. Box 2216
Van Nuys, CA 91404
(213) 786-0841
2-page brochure, free U.S. Does not sell
    overseas. MO, PC.
Varna Enterprises offers a collection of
maps of the Old West. These maps
would appeal to adventurists looking to
explore California's old ghost towns and
mining camps in sites called Bogus
Thunder, Helltown Camp, and Three
Dollar Bar. There is a map for historians
of pioneer trails from 1541 to 1867,
showing rivers, creeks, mines, forts, and
famous trails from the Great Lakes to
the West Coast.

Wayfarer Books
P.O. Box 1121
Davenport, IA 52805
(319) 355-3902

24-page catalog, free U.S. and overseas. MO, PC.

Travel and outdoor books and maps. The catalog is subtitled "a catalog of unique and unusual travel guides." In addition to the well-known guides by Fielding, Sunset, Zellers, AAA, and others, Tom and Judy Betts offer something special. A catalog section, titled Exploring Unusual Places, offers many unusual guides: *Travelers Guide to Running in Major American Cities, Amusement Parks of America, Exploring Caves: A Guide to the Underground Wilderness,* and *Nooks and Crannies: An Unusual Walking Tour Guide to New York City.*

Wide World Books and Maps
401 N. E, 45th St.
Seattle, WA 98105
(206) 634-3453
12-page catalog, $1 U.S. and overseas. MC, V, MO, PC.

Travel books, guides, and maps on most countries. They also carry foreign language dictionaries and phrase books, picture books, and posters. You can also find travel accessories, such as currency convertors and money belts.

CLOTHING

SEE ALSO
- College and Prep School Gift Shops
- Crafts—Sewing
- Department Stores and Major Mail Order Houses
- Gifts
- Handcrafts
- Sports and Recreation

MEN AND WOMEN

Adam York
Unique Merchandising Mart
Building 6
Hanover, PA 17333
(800) 621-5800
Illinois (800) 972-5858
60-page color catalog, $1 U.S. and
overseas. AE, DC, MC, V, MO, PC.

Bay Country Shop
419 Dorchester Ave.
Cambridge, MD 21613
(301) 228-87
8-page color catalog, free U.S. AE, MC,
V, PC.
Bay Country Shop sells clothing and gift
items, all embroidered or painted with
ducks, geese, pheasants, and quail
characteristic of Maryland's renowned
Eastern Shore. Shetland sweaters,
bookends, ties, men's slacks, and serving
trays—all for the wildlife lover.

Bemidji Woolen Mills
P.O. Box 277
Bemidji, MN 56601
(218) 751-5166
24-page color catalog, free U.S. Does not
sell overseas. MC, V, MO, PC.
These are high quality woolen goods,
many items manufactured in the

Bemidji Woolen Mills. Popular men and
women's Jac Coat ($35) and the Alaskan
White Mountain Coat ($62) are both 85%
wool, 15% nylon, and warm! There are
also wool blankets, throw rugs, and wool
shirts.

Bill Tosetti's
17632 Chatsworth St.
Granada Hills, CA 91344
(213) 363-2192
32-page color catalog, free U.S. Does not
sell overseas.
Bill Tosetti's is "The Pendleton
Specialist." A nice selection of shirts,
slacks, jackets, sweaters, and coats, all
in the traditional good taste of
Pendleton, are featured.

Blair
220 Hickory St.
Warren, PA 16366
(800) 458-2000
Pennsylvania (814) 723-3600
68-page color catalog, free U.S. Does not
sell overseas. MC, V, MO, PC.
Blair is the trademark of New Process
Company, one of the nation's largest
firms that mail orders low-to medium-
priced men's and women's clothing.
Their line is extensive—men's slacks,
suits, outerwear, underwear, and shoes;
women's coordinated separates,

sportswear, dresses, pantsuits, lingerie, and outerwear. A women's polyester knit two-piece pants suit is about $20, and available in half sizes up to 24½. There are fashionable dresses under $30, and two-piece wash-and-wear men's suits for $75.

British Isles Collection
Route 16
North Conway, NH 03860
(617) 338-0099
32-page color catalog, free U.S. Does not sell overseas. AE, DC, MC, V, MO, PC.
Traditional clothing from the British Isles. This company's theme is "natural materials worked by craftsmen in the British Isles [that] result in a product of enduring quality, long to be appreciated." This includes genuine Wellington-style boots @ $475, twill trousers @ $69, and a lovely knitted Irish linen dress for $195.

Brown's of Bermuda
Front St.
Hamilton, Bermuda 5–31
(809) 295-2928
16-page color catalog, free U.S. and overseas. AE, MC, V, MO, PC.
Brown's of Bermuda specializes in fine 100% British woolens including Pringle of Scotland, Braemar International, and tartan goods. Knitwear for men, women, and children in Shetland, lambswool, and cashmere. They also carry Harris Tweed jackets, velvet blazers, and Irish knits.

Cable Car Clothiers
150 Post St.
San Francisco, CA 94108
(415) 397-4740
64-page color catalog, free U.S. and overseas. AE, DC, MC, V, MO, PC.

Camp Beverly Hills
9615 Brighton Way Suite 210
Beverly Hills, CA 90210
(213) 858-3925
16-page color catalog, $1 U.S. and overseas. AE, MC, V, MO, PC.
From Southern California comes Camp Beverly Hills, featuring trendy activewear and military-inspired

sportswear for men and women. There are lots of sweatshirts and T-shirt styles, many with the Camp Beverly Hills logo, in great colors.

Castlemoor
Castle St.
Bampton Tiverton
Devon EX16 9NS England
0398 31530
16-page color catalog, $1; overseas, free. AE, MC, V, MO, PC.
Fine clothing using British wool, grown and manufactured in the United Kingdom. Mostly good-looking sweaters for men and women, but also sheepskin car seat covers, blankets, and a snuggly soft fleece pram cover.

Cotton Dreams
Box 1261
Sebastian, FL 32958
(305) 589-7011
50-page catalog, free U.S. and overseas. MC, V, MO, PC.
Cotton Dreams specializes in natural fiber (100% cotton) clothing for the entire family. They have an especially nice selection of children's clothes: sunsuits, overalls, creepers, longjohns, underalls, smocks, sweaters, and terry robes. Prices seem quite low—many of the children's short sets are about $8, men's chambray shirts are $19.50, and girl's overalls $11,75.

Dallas Alice
1047 Taft St.
Rockville, MD 20850
(301) 424-1640
12-page color catalog, $1 U.S. and overseas. MC, V, MO, PC.
T-shirts and sweatshirts are screen-printed with many delightful character themes: Teddy Bears, Pierrots (french pantomime), cartoon character Cathy, and (ever-popular with pre-schoolers) dinosaurs. Prices range from about $6.95 for children's T-shirts to about $18 for an adult sweatshirt.

David Morgan
P.O. Box 70190
Seattle, WA 98107
(206) 282-3300

80-page catalog, 25¢; overseas $1. MC, V,
MO, PC.
David Morgan sells Akubra felt hats
from Australia, in many different
shapes, colors and trims. They sell for
about $50. He also sells traditional
natural fiber clothing: cotton Celtic
cable-knit sweaters, moleskin and
hickory shirts.

Denny Andrews
Clock House Workshop, Coleshill
Near Swindon, Wiltshire
SN6 7PT England
0793 762476
Denny Andrews imports clothes from
India. The Kurtas, roomy vests, and
pajama trousers are mainly in white.
There are Rajasthani (gathered skirts
with a drawstring waist), with colored
borders designed in blue and red
patterns. Prices range from $7.50 to $34.

Deva Natural Clothes
Box SG
Burkittsville, MD 21718
(301) 473-4900
12-page catalog with swatches, free U.S.
and overseas. MC, V, MO, PC.
Deva Natural Clothes is a network of
friends and neighbors who function in
a classical cottage industry, fashioning
a line of pure cotton clothes for men and
women. Each garment is made from
start to finish by one sewer, who then
sews her name into it. The garments
have simple and graceful lines;
drawstring shorts $10, wrap skirts $20,
kimono $35, cotton tights $10, socks for
$2.50 to $3.50 a pair, and cotton pullover
sweaters $25.

Dunham's of Maine
64 Main St.
Waterville, ME 04901
(207) 872-5501
32-page color catalog, free U.S. and
overseas. AE, DC, MC, V, MO, PC.
Traditional, classic quality apparel for
men and women. There's a wonderful
selection of tailored suits, ladies' oxford
shirts and coordinated ties, Top-siders
and argyle socks for the preppy look.
Dunham's is one of the finest mail order
firms in the country and mails three
million catalogs annually.

Especially Maine
Kennebunkport, ME 04046
(207) 985-3749
24-page catalog, free U.S. and overseas.
AE, DC, MC, V, MO, PC.
Especially Maine specializes in fine
natural clothing and gifts indigenous to
Maine. Strawberry Bermuda bags are
$30, a twenty-four-inch wreath of
freshly gathered balsam boughs for
Christmas is $18.95, cotton sweaters and
Maine slipper socks are $20.

Fashion Able
Box 5
Rocky Hill, NJ 08553
(609) 921-2563
8-page newsalog, 50¢ U.S. Does not sell
overseas. MC, V, MO, PC.
A terrific catalog of clothing and aids
for the elderly and handicapped:
playing card holder and shuffler, self-
opening scissors, front-zippered slip,
raised toilet seat that fits all bowls,
dressing and eating aids, and many
more useful items.

French Creek Sheep and Wool
Route 345 R. D. #1
Elverson, PA 19520
(800) 345-4091
Pennsylvania (215) 286-5700
48-page color catalog, $2 U.S. and
overseas. AE, MC, V, MO, PC.
French Creek Sheep and Wool Company
is a limited production company
dedicated to the design and
craftmanship of natural fiber garments.
Elegant Shearling coats: the Stokesay,
$650, is double-breasted with a
slimming waist and a half-belt in back;
the Biarritz, $750, is a great little jacket
made from Pyrenean Lamb and features
long silky and curly fleece. There are
greasewool raglan pullovers,
Brindletweed sweaters, and fashionable
sweater coats and sweater dresses. Eric
Glaxenburg, owner, says "at French
Creek we are concerned with value
rather than price; it is our goal, always,
to make things best, not just better."
They certainly have.

Garnet Hill
Box PH
Franconia, NH 03580
(603) 823-5545

60-page catalog, $1 U.S. and overseas.
AE, DC, MC, V, MO, PC.
Garnet Hill, "The Natural Fibers"
catalog, offers wonderfully soft bedding
and clothing for the whole family. Their
100% cotton flannel sheets are available
in twelve solid colors and priced at $23
each. There are lovely wool and cotton
blankets and a wide selection of cotton
or wool long underwear, tights, socks,
flannel clothing, and cotton turtlenecks
for men, women, and children.

Gohn Bros.
Box 111
Middlebury, IN 46540
(219) 825-2400
8-page price list, free U.S. Does not sell
overseas. MO, PC.
Gohn Bros. sells clothes and dry goods
products directed towards the Amish
trade. Their prices for high quality basic
clothing are about 30% below regular
retail prices. The pants are broadfall
style in grey and blue. There are union
suits and coats made with hooks and
eyes, or snaps, with no outside pockets.
There is also a large selection of yard
goods. Since 1900.

Goodthings Collective
One Cottage St.
P.O. Box 751
Easthampton, MA 01027
(413) 527-6403
36-page catalog, free U.S. Does not sell
overseas. MC, V, MO, PC.
Goodthings offers natural fiber clothing
and bedding. Cotton is the primary
fabric in most items, also wool and wool
blends. There are cotton flannel sheets,
cotton shower curtains, Lotus Duvet
down comforters and cotton Chinese
shoes.

Haband Company
265 N. 9th St.
Paterson, NJ 07530
(201) 942-2600
24-page color catalog, free U.S. Does not
sell overseas. MC, V, MO, PC.
Haband's is well known for their men's
and women's clothing at low prices. Two
pairs of ladies' orlon knit slacks for

$24.95 are available in sizes petite and
average (8 to 20), tall (14 to 20), and
petite and average (34 to 42). Dresses are
about $24.95, robes $19.95, in sizes up to
46 and 48. Men's knit slacks in dacron
polyester are priced at two pairs for
$21.95.

Health Harvest
P.O. Box 427
Fairfax, CA 94930
(415) 459-5699
4-page brochure, free. PC.
Health Harvest sells novelty T-shirts.
There are zany T-shirts featuring
anatomically correct drawings of the
human skeleton and the musculature of
the torso (front and back, so that when
the T-shirt is worn untucked the gluteus
maximus covers the real set). There is
a Digestion and a Pregnancy T-shirt
showing a term fetus in utero. The
Doctor T-shirt features a drawing of the
lab coat—pockets full of stethoscope,
otoscope, sphygmomanometer, etc. A
Dentist T-shirt is also available. Price
range is from $8.50 to $10.

H. T. C. Inc.
2091 South Main St.
Pittsford, MI 49271
(517) 523-2167
4-page brochure, free U.S. Does not sell
overseas. MO, PC.
H. T. C. manufactures men's, women's,
and children's insulated coats and
outerwear—and sells direct to you, by
mail order, at about 30% below retail
price. There are ladies' nylon coats
(insulated with Dupont Dacron Holofil)
in six styles, sixteen colors, and sizes 8
to 22. They are priced from $26.95 to
$39.95. Snowmobile suits are available
in sizes S to XXXL, and priced from
$42.95 to $89.95.

Jos. A. Bank Clothiers
123 Market Place
Baltimore, MD 21202
(301) 837-1700
96-page color catalog, free U.S. and
overseas. AE, MC, V, MO, PC.
Jos. A. Bank sells a complete line of
men's and women's tailored clothing
and accessories. "Our clothing is

restrained and understated in cut, tailored with care from exceptional fabrics, and proves itself for years to come," says the catalog.

Kevin & Howlin, Ltd.
31 Nassau St.
Dublin 2 Ireland
770257
6-page brochure, free U.S. and overseas. MC, V, MO.
Kevin & Howlin is a small retail shop offering Donegal handwoven tweeds for men and women. Hundreds of lengths of tweeds are available, as well as ready-made jackets and suits.

Lands' End
Lands' End Lane
Dodgeville, WI 53533
(800) 356-4444
Wisconsin (608) 935-2788
112-page color catalog, free U.S. AE, MC, V, MO, PC.
Traditional sportswear for men and women. Casual and dressy sweaters, slacks, outerwear, sportshirts, soft luggage, sailing gear, accessories, and a nice selection of flannel sheets are featured.

Loden-Frey
Verkaufshaus GmbH & Co.
Maffeistrabe 7–9
8000 Munich 2 West Germany
23693-233
28-page color catalog, free U.S. and overseas. Prices in German marks. MO.
Established in 1842, this firm is famous for developing the Loden fabric and bringing it into the fashion scene in the forms of Loden coats and fine suits. Sheared wool combined with mohair, camel's hair, alpaca, and thistles specially imported from France provide Loden cloth with some of its special and unique properties. Known for their durability under abrasion and weather resistance, garments made from Loden last longer than those made from other fabrics. Loden can be obtained in the classic colors of gray, dark green, and brown as well as high fashion hues popular today. The catalog has some glamorous photographs of Loden capes,

coats, and suits for men and women. They also feature a few traditional national costumes.

Moffat Woollens, Ltd.
Middleton Mill 87 Bongate
Jedburgh, Roxburghshire
TD8 6DU Scotland
0835 62583
16-page color catalog, free U.S. and overseas. AE, DC, MC, V, MO, PC.
Moffat offers a fine quality range of Scottish knitwear in lambswool, shetland, merino, and cashmere. Kilted skirts are available in ready-made and made-to-measure. There are suits in wool tweed, worsted, and mixed fibers. They also carry Cheviot sheepskin jackets, gloves, and mittens. Since 1940.

Nandi Naturals
P.O. Box 2719-SG
Petaluma, CA 94953
(707) 763-0888
8-page brochure, $1 refundable U.S.
  Does not sell overseas. MC, V, MO, PC.
Pure cotton, natural fiber clothing for men and women: shirts, skirts and drawstring pants.

Norm Thompson
P.O. Box 3999
Portland, OR 97208
(800) 547-1160
80-page color catalog, free U.S. Does not sell overseas. AE, DC, MC, V, MO, PC.
The cover of Norm Thompson's says "Escape From the Ordinary." There is page after page of some very fine clothing, accessories, gifts, and food items. A lady's camel hair suit (also sold as separates), sizes 6 to 16, is very reasonably priced at $320, and a good-looking 100% cashmere sport coat in navy, natural, or grey is priced at $395. There are Gurkha leather purses and bags, Bally court shoes by Allen Edmonds, and beautiful Shearling coats.

On The Rise
2282 Four Oaks Grange Rd.
Eugene, OR 97405
(503) 687-0119
On the Rise is a nonprofit organization making fashionable custom-made clothing for the individual measure-

ments and needs of the physically handicapped. Write for their brochure.

Richman Co.
2627 Piner Rd.
Santa Rosa, CA 95401
(707) 526-4909
12-page brochure, free U.S. and
   overseas. MO, PC.
Richman's offers 100% cotton clothing, available in sizes infant through adult XL. "We try to provide products for families with a natural lifestyle and for people that have problems with allergies to synthetic fabrics. All of our clothing is brightly colored and also comes in white for those with dye sensitivities," say the Richmans.

Royal British Legion
Cambrian Factory
Llanwrtyd Wells
Powys LD5 4SD Wales
05913 211
6-page brochure, free U.S. and overseas.
   MC, V, MO, PC.
Royal British Legion manufactures Welsh wool from state to cloth. Fine garments are woven or knitted into suits, travel rugs, and hats.

R. Watson Hogg, Ltd.
Auchterarder Perthshire
PH3 1BS Scotland
076-H6-2151
12-page color catalog, free U.S. and
   overseas. AE, DC, MC, V, MO, PC.
R. Watson Hogg is well known for their excellent selection of cashmere knitwear, jackets, and coats. Many garments are made to their own designs and specifications. Located near the famous Gleneagles Hotel, their clientele is the rich and famous.

Saint Laurie, Ltd.
84 5th Ave.
New York, NY 10011
(800) 221-8660
(212) 242-2530
40-page color catalog, free U.S. Swatch
   brochure $5 U.S. Limited overseas
   sales. AE, DC, MC, V, MO, PC.
Saint Laurie specializes in men's and women's business apparel, suits, sportcoats, slacks, skirts, and overcoats.

As manufacturers selling direct to you by mail order, they offer savings of 30% to 50% off regular retail prices. Their suits are tailored in New York, using old world standards of hand cutting, sewing, and pressing. These same suits can be found in the finest specialty stores in the country under the store label. Each garment is fully lined, and the winter line features finely spun worsteds for suiting, and scottish tweeds, pure camel hair, and blazer cloth for sportcoatings.

The Sporting Life
P.O. Box 9136
5302 Eisenhower Ave.
Alexandria, VA 22304
(703) 823-1500
32-page color catalog, free U.S. Limited
   overseas sales. AE, MC, V, MO, PC.
The Sporting Life features classic clothing for men and women.

Strength Garment Ltd.
No. 130B, Deck 1
Cheung Chau Gallery
Ocean Terminal
Kowloon, Hong Kong
K-661703
32-page brochure with swatches, free
   U.S. and overseas. MO, PC.
Custom-made coats, jackets, rain coats, ski jackets, and nylon and polyester cotton materials.

Top to Toe
3 Alderney Rd.
Croftlands, Dewsbury
West Yorkshire, England
0924 464304
3-page price list and swatches, $2 U.S.
   and overseas. MO, PC.
Top to Toe specializes in made-to-measure garments for men and women who are not stock size. They have made trousers in up to a 63-inch waist and a 44-inch inside leg seam (presumably not for the same person). There are slacks, jackets, skirts, suits, and waistcoats with about forty different materials to choose from. Discounts are available when more than one garment is ordered (even if it is for a friend or other family member).

Victory Shirt Company
345 Madison Ave.
New York, NY 10017
(212) 687-6375
8-page catalog, $1 U.S. and overseas. AE,
  DC, MC, V, MO, PC.
Mary Sprague is quite the success story
with her shirt manufacturing and retail
business. Victory manufactures men
and women's shirts in sizes 14 × 32 to
18½ × 36 for men, and sizes 4 through
16 for women. Both straight and button-
down collars as well as button and
french cuffs are featured in a wide
range of fabrics for men. The tailored
women's line ($25–$35) features classic,
round, ruffled, and button-down styles.
Victory also offers a nice selection of
handmade men's ties, and silk ties in
nice styles for women. Alterations and
hand monogramming are also
available.

VRGS
2239 East 55th St.
Cleveland, OH 44103
(216) 431-7800
25-page catalog, $2 U.S. and overseas.
  MO, PC.
VRGS features clothing and aids for the
handicapped. VRGS manufactures a
line of ready-made clothing for men and
women. Garments have velcro
fasteners, generously cut sleeves, low
wide pockets, and double-stitched
seams. Many styles have back or front
openings.

MOSTLY MEN

Ascot Chang Co., Ltd.
2/F Block D
41 Man Yue St.
Hung Hom, Kowloon
Hong Kong
3 644384
2-page brochure with swatches, free
  U.S. and overseas. MO, PC.
Ascot Chang is well known for custom-
making classic-styled shirts, pajamas,
robes, and shorts. Shirts start at $40,
undershorts at $21, and pajamas at $81.
If you're wary of venturing into buying
custom-made shirts—rather than
sending measurements, mail them one

of your old shirts. Ascot Chang is a most
reputable firm. Started in 1954.

Baker Street Shirtmakers
281 Centennial Ave.
Piscataway, NJ 08854
(800) 528-6050
(800) 352-0458
"Creators of classic shirts at affordable
prices," says the catalog. There are
classic shirts, ties, and accessories.
Long-sleeved Oxford button-downs and
cotton poplin dress shirts are both about
$19. Exact sleeve lengths up to 36 in. are
available in dress shirts only.

Brooks Brothers
346 Madison Ave.
New York, NY 10017
(212) 682-8800
40-page catalog, $2 U.S. and overseas.
  Minimum overseas order $20. AE, DC,
  MC, V, MO, PC.
Conservative men's clothing—always in
good taste. Brooks Brothers is an
American tradition in clothing and is
famous for the exclusive Brooks
Brothers suit. Their popular
herringbone tweed sport jacket is priced
at about $290. Oxford shirts for about
$31 and shetland pullover sweaters
about $47.50.

Bullock & Jones
340 Post St.
San Francisco, CA 94108
(800) 227-3050
(415) 392-4243
34-page color catalog, free U.S. AE, CB,
  DC, MC, V, MO, PC.
Bullock & Jones is one of San Francisco's
finest men's clothiers. They offer
imported cashmere pea coats from Italy,
rainwear from Burberrys of England,
and fine apparel with their own
exclusive label.

Chipp
Custom Tailors and Furnishers
14 East 44th St.
New York, NY 10017
(212) 687-0850
8-page color brochure, free U.S. and
  overseas. AE, DC, MC, V, MO, PC.
Chipp is a small family-owned business.
"We think of ourselves as a conservative,

traditional store—but, we have a sense of humor." There are Oxford button-down shirts with contrasting collars, and batiste lightweight cotton shirts for warm weather. Much of their sportswear *is* whimsical, and they are quite well known for their novelty club figure ties: Little Black Book Tie ($14) features handpainted phone numbers (you designate which ones) printed upside down for easy reference, and a tie with the repeating diagonal acronym IITYWTMWYBMAD ("If I Tell You What This Means Will You Buy Me A Drink?") is priced at $13.50. The Jock Tie (unmistakable athletic supporters printed on a navy colored tie), for $13.50, is another popular one.

Harvie and Hudson, Ltd.
77–96–97 Jermyn St.
London SW1Y 6NP England
01 930 3949
6-page color brochure, free U.S. and
   overseas.
Harvie and Hudson specialize in custom-made shirts. Shirting fabrics from the finest cotton poplin are designed, colored, and hand-sewn in the traditional way. There is a minimum order of four shirts.

Henry Poole and Company
15 Savile Row
London W1X 1AE England
01 734 5985
No Catalog available.
Located on Savile Row, the heart of the English tailoring industry, Henry Pooles caters to the successful and prominent members of society. Suits are made from the finest British woolens including Huddersfield worsteds, tweeds from the lowlands of Scotland, Harris and Shetland Isles, and mohair worsteds for cool summer wear. Twice yearly representatives tour the U.S. and Europe for tailoring appointments for overseas clients. Write to them if you're interested in more information.

H. Huntsman & Sons, Ltd.
11 Savile Row
London W1X 2PS England
01 734-7441

All replies answered, including
   swatches when appropriate, U.S. and
   overseas. AE, DC, MC, V, MO, PC.
H. Huntsman have been tailors to royalty since 1820. They can supply either bespoke (custom) or ready-to-wear men's suits, jackets, overcoats, trousers, blazers, sport coats, tuxedos, and shirts featuring exclusive fabrics and fine handwork.

Huntington Clothiers
1285 Alum Creek
Columbus, OH 43209
(614) 237-5695
48-page (some color) catalog, free U.S.
   Does not sell overseas. AE, DC, MC,
   MO, PC.
Traditional men's and women's apparel, including shirtings, clothing and accessories. Huntington's manufactures about 70% of its products and sells direct to the consumer at prices about 30% lower than retail prices. There are many shirts to choose from, including button-down Oxfords (100% cotton or easy care 60/40 reverse blend), solids, university stripes, graph checks, tattersalls, madras, and tartan plaids. There are also casual slacks, shorts, and jackets.

Hutton's
117 Washington Ave.
North Haven, CT 06473
(203) 239-3702
16-page color catalog, free U.S. and
   overseas. AE, MC, V, MO, PC.
National brand-name men's sportswear: polar fleece jacket by Woolrich ($47), Haggar's gabardine stretch slacks ($20), Van Heusen's dress shirts (3 for $35), jeans by Levi's, and jackets from Mighty Mac of Gloucester.

Imperial Wear
48 W. 48th St.
New York, NY 10036
(212) 541-8220
32-page (some color) catalog, free U.S.
   and overseas. AE, DC, MC, V, MO, PC.
Menswear for extra-tall and extra-large men with extra-large bank accounts. Now extra-large men can choose fine suits from labels by Halston, Oleg Cassini, Givenchy, Rafael, Lanvin, Cardin, and Chaps by Ralph Lauren.

There are raincoats by London Fog and Christian Dior, and jackets by Zero King and Lakeland. Shirts by Cyril Bartlett, Damon, Adolfo, Pierre Cardin, and Gant. There are also velour warmups, robes, and twenty styles of shoes. Shoe sizes up to 15 and widths of D and EEE are available. Shirt sizes in 20-inch neck and 38-inch sleeve lengths. Suit sizes are available from 46 to 56 portly to extra long.

International Male
2800 Midway Dr.
P.O. Box 85043
San Diego, CA 92138
(619) 226-8751
52-page color catalog, $2 refundable U.S. and overseas. AE, MC, V, MO, PC.
In an era of conservative and traditional men's clothing, Gene Burkard has broken the mold. He offers exciting, even daring men's sportswear with a decided international flair. Shortcut shorts are European in design for freedom of wear; scoop neck tops and capped sleeve shirts are worn with just one button buttoned above the waist. Mesh polo shirts, sculptured sweaters, racing bikinis, and terrific-looking workout gear make this one exciting catalog.

The James River Traders
James River Landing
Hampton, VA 23631
(804) 827-6000
52-page color catalog, free U.S. AE, MC, V.
Good-looking menswear includes country classics: cotton turtlenecks (two for $11), polo shirts ($15), shetland sweaters ($45), and Oxford button-down shirts ($18). There are sport jackets in tweed, corduroy and suede, and many styles of athletic wear.

J. Press
262 York St.
New Haven, CT 06511
24-page catalog, prices unavailable. AE, MC, V, PC, C.O.D.
Traditional men's clothing. Wool suits, tuxedos, sport jackets, trousers, outercoats, sweaters, shirts and ties.

King Size Co.
24 Forse St.
Brockton, MA 02402
(800) 343-9678
(617) 580-0500
King Size is an excellent source of clothing for tall, extra-tall, or big men. Five pages are devoted to athletic workout clothes, socks, and running shoes. There are casual slacks, jeans, twills and corduroys, sportcoats, and all-weather jackets. Shirts by Arrow and undergarments by Jockey are available. For the sportsmen there are oversized sleeping bags, hunter's coveralls, and insulated bib ski overalls. Ten pages are devoted to shoes, boots, golf shoes, and slippers for sizes up to 16 and EEE widths.

Kreeger and Sons
16 West 46th St.
New York, NY 10109
(212) 575-7825
8-page color brochure, free U.S. AE, MC, V, MO, PC.
Kreeger and Sons features outdoors clothes: flannel-lined chino pants, 100% cotton turtlenecks, and safari jackets by Willis and Geiger.

Milton's Clothing Cupboard
163 East Franklin St.
Chapel Hill, NC 27514
(919) 968-4408
8-page brochure, free U.S. and overseas. AE, MC, V, MO, PC.
Milton's features suits, sport coats, trousers, shirts, neckwear, and better sweaters including shetlands, lambswool and merino wools, at very good prices. Crew neck cable shetland sweaters for about $23, V-neck lambswool sweaters $23, Milton's own Oxford button-down shirts (in a 60/40 poly blend) are $18.

Paul Stuart
Madison Avenue at 45th St.
New York, NY 10017
(212) 682-0320
40-page color catalog, $2; overseas $3. AE, DC, MC, V, MO, PC.
"Clothing defined by tradition, quiet and confident yet interpreted with flair and elan." There are shirts, ties, shoes,

sweaters, and suits—everything for a well-balanced wardrobe. The Southwick tailored, tan plaid suit ($485), is an Italian blend of silk and wool worsted. The two-button suit jacket has side vents and an outside ticket pocket. The pleated trousers feature an extension waistband with no belt loops.

Sam's Tailor
TST P.O. Box 95392
Hong Kong
16-page catalog, with swatches, free U.S.
  and overseas. BD, MO.
Custom-made men's shirts. Over 100 swatches, fifteen collar styles, seven cuff styles, and four pocket styles to choose from. Prices range from $17 to $20.

Sussex Clothes
302 Fifth Ave.
New York, NY 10001
(212) 260-1910
4-page brochure with swatches, $2
  refundable U.S. Does not sell overseas.
  AE, MC, V, MO, PC.
Sussex is a manufacturer of men's suits and sport coats at discounts of 50% off retail prices. Pants sizes in regular to extra long, and coat sizes 36 to 50. A summer tweed sport jacket, 50% silk and 50% wool, is about $169. A 100% camel's hair sportcoat is about $198.

MOSTLY WOMEN

A. B. Lambdin
2050–E Carroll Ave.
Chamblee, GA 30341
(800) 554-9231
(404) 451-1057
32-page color catalog, free U.S. and
  overseas. AE, DC, MC, V, MO, PC.
A. B. Lambdin is a relatively new company and a big success. They carry apparel for active women. Sportswear ideal for a cruise or summer holiday. Conservative maillots to teeny bikinis, exotic full-length sundresses, strapless terry dresses, poolside loungewear, tennis and golf dresses.

Access
450 Endo Blvd.
Garden City, NY 11530
(800) 526-0359

New Jersey (800) 932-0878
38-page color catalog, AE, MC, V, MO,
  PC.
Access is a catalog designed for the working woman. The catalog offers great dresses, coordinates, and accessories to pull a complete wardrobe together. They also sell organizing aids for the desk and office to make life simpler, and a nice selection of gifts for men. Still need more assistance to help balance your hectic schedule? Access offers a preferred customer program ($15 membership fee) for extra service, such as discount coupons, weekly specials, and shopping assistance through a toll-free number.

Ambassador International
711 W. Broadway
Tempe, AZ 85282
(602) 968-4411
56-page color catalog, $2 U.S. Does not
  sell overseas. AE, DC, MC, V, MO, PC.

Ann Taylor
P.O. Box 805
New Haven, CT 06503
(800) 228-5600
(800) 642-8777
18-page color catalog, U.S. and overseas.
  AE, MC, V, MO, PC.
Ann Taylor features Donegal tweeds, sweaters, and knitwear in current fashions with the influence of Scotland.

Avon Fashions
Avon Lane
Newport News, VA 23630
64-page color catalog, free U.S. AE, MC,
  V, MO, PC.
You didn't know Avon sells clothes? You bet, and at great prices. Bathing suits from $14.99 to $22.95, terry wrappers $16.99, playsuits, jump suits, casual dresses, tops, pants, and shorts.

Bedford Fair
157 Kisco Ave.
Mt. Kisco, NY 10549
(914) 666-6400
48-page color catalog. AE, MC, V, MO,
  PC.
Women's fashions at reasonable prices. Classic dresses for the career-minded

range from $29 to $45, shirtdresses from $29.99, and casual coordinates in many attractive styles.

Betsey Johnson
Box 455 Canal Street Station
New York, NY 10013
9-page catalog, free U.S. AE, MC, V, MO, PC.
There are slim-skirted dresses with dolman sleeves, and Beatnik sweaters á la 50's, cinched-waist dresses with petticoats, and off-the-shoulder dresses—all by Betsey.

Career Guild
6412 Vapor Lane
Niles, IL 60648
(800) 228-5000
36-page color catalog, $5 membership fee. Does not sell overseas. AE, MC, V, MO, PC.
Career Guild offers coordinated, updated fashions designed for the working woman who has to "dress up" for the office and her busy lifestyle. The catalog features versatile blazers, jackets, skirts, and blouses as a guide to coordinating an efficient and versatile working wardrobe within a reasonable budget. The membership fee entitles you to 25% discounts on all items, newsletters, and seasonal catalogs.

Carroll Reed
Mill St.
Conway, NH 03866
(603) 447-2511
64-page color catalog, free U.S. and overseas. AE, MC, V, MO, PC.
Carroll Reed features classic clothing from New England, mostly for women—Bermuda bags, monogrammed shirts, sweaters, blouses and jumpers, and casual coordinates.

Chelsea Collection
Unique Merchandising Mart
Building 18
Hanover, PA 17333
(800) 621-5800
40-page color catalog, $2 U.S. and overseas. AE, DC, MC, V, MO, PC.

Chico Fabric Designs
Box 152 Cohasset Stage
Chico, CA 95926
(916) 342-9178
2-page price list, free U.S. and overseas. MO, PC.
Practical women's chino pants ($28) are also available with flannel lining ($38). They're good for working, gardening, and activities requiring durable clothing.

Colette Modes, Ltd.
66 South Great Georges St.
Dublin 2 Ireland
752188
Color brochure, free U.S. AE, DC, V, MO, PC.
There are women's handwoven tweed coats and suits in classic styles, in sizes from 10 to 18. Some lines are available in size 20.

Esprit
950 Tennessee St.
San Francisco, CA 94107
(800) 437-7748
36-page color catalog, $2 U.S. Does not sell overseas. AE, DC, MC, V, MO, PC.
Esprit's collection of colorful fashions has a delightful European look—very different from the usual mail order clothes catalogs. The styles range from sporty to dressy. There are many accessories pictured throughout the catalog that coordinate with these fun fashions.

Exactitude
91 Stillman St.
San Francisco, CA 94107
(415) 543-5190
13-page brochure and fabric swatches, $2 U.S. and overseas. MO, PC.
Exactitude offers a lovely selection of women's executive dress shirts and blouses featuring proportioned sleeve lengths in short, regular, and long in sizes 4 through 14. These classic suit blouses are made in cotton, silk, and cotton-linen. The terrific, wrinkle resistant Executive Travel Shirt is a cotton-poly blend. Their exclusive styles are priced from $34 to $74 and discounts are available on purchases of two or more shirts.

Fashion Galaxy
Unique Merchandising Mart
Building 26
Hanover, PA 17333
(800) 621-5800
32-page color catalog, $1 U.S. and
  overseas. AE, DC, MC, V, MO, PC.
Fashionable dresses from $28.95 to
$39.95 for everyday, work, or evening
wear.

FBS
659 Main St.
New Rochelle, NY 10801
(800) 228-5200
80-page color catalog, free. AE, MC, V,
  MO, PC.
Sophisticated women's wear in the
latest fashions. An anthracite jumpsuit
in the leather look ($105), turtleneck
mini dress ($70), soft slouchy suede
boots ($46–$62), chic blouses, and
cocktail wear are offered in the FBS
catalog.

Gidding Jenny
18 West Fourth St.
Cincinnati, OH 45202
(800) 543-7237
Ohio (800) 582-7282
40-page color catalog. AE, CB, DC,
  MC, V.

Gudrun Sjödén
Erstagatan 20
11632 Stockholm Sweden
08 404517
14-page color catalog, free U.S. and
  overseas. AE, V.
Gudrun and Bjorn Sjödén make good-
looking casual clothes in popular
Scandinavian designs. The natural
materials and colors mix and match in
a variety of trendy fashions. Skirts,
blouses, trousers, sweaters, jackets,
socks, belts, and purses. A very
interesting catalog.

Halls of Hanover
Unique Merchandising Mart
Building 56
Hanover, PA 17333
40-page color catalog, $2 U.S. and
  overseas. AE, DC, MC, V, MO, PC.
Halls offers stylish dresses, velveteen
jackets, sophisticated city suits, and
dramatic blouses for fashion-conscious

women. There are also accessories for
your home and lovely gift items: satin
artwork pillows, brass key keepers, wine
goblets, and vases.

Hayashi Kimono Co.
Izui, Building 3F
6–3–6 Ginza
Chuo-Ku Toyko
Japan
03 571 1528
18-page color brochure, free U.S. and
  overseas. MO.
Hayashi's offers over 100 styles of
traditional japanese kimonos in silk,
polyester, and cotton-and-polyster
blends in beautiful colors. There are
also happicoats for men, women, and
children. Accessories to the kimono
include obis, obi materials, zoris and
getas (thonged shoes), and tabis (socks
worn with getas).

Heather Valley
Brunstane Road
Edinburgh, EH15 2QL Scotland
031 669-6161
32-page color catalog, free U.S. and
  overseas. AE, DC, V, PC.
Quality clothing in classic designs for
the mature woman. Heather Valley is
known for their fine tweeds and
knitwear. The catalog is especially
suitable for wardrobe planning as many
of the garments are color coordinated
in versatile combinations.

Honeybee
2745 Philmont Ave.
Huntingdon Valley, PA 19006
(800) 523-6534
(800) 354-8080
64-page color catalog, $1 U.S. Does not
  sell overseas. AE, MC, V, MO, PC.
Honeybee offers the latest in designer
fashions for women in sizes 4–14.
Exciting clothes by Ralph Lauren, Liz
Claiborne, Jill Stuart, Robert Krugman,
and Ann Klein. There are soft knit
dresses, romantic blouses, and suedes
shown in many styles.

The Ingram Collection
214 West 39th St.
P.O. Box 711
New York, NY 10018
(800) 23-5679

32-page color catalog, $2; overseas $4.
AE, DC, MC, V, MO, PC.
The Ingram Collection, started in 1982, has enjoyed success in offering fashionable women's wear and accessories. Dresses are priced around $170 and suits about $275. There is an excellent selection of dresses and many jackets, skirts, blouses, and sweaters.

J. D. Matthew & Co.
P.O. Box 1118
Bristol, CT 06010
(203) 589-4453
8 pages, free U.S. Does not sell overseas.
MC, V, MO, PC.
Shetland sweaters, Bermuda Bags, and monogrammed turtleneck sweaters are offered by J. D. Matthew & Co.

J. Jill
Stockbridge Rd.
Great Barrington, MA 01230
32-page color catalog, free U.S. and overseas. AE, MC, V, MO, PC.
Aunt Abigail's country clothes collection is designed here, made from only natural fibers: cotton, wool, and silk. J. Jill is a very successful mail order business.

Johnny Appleseed's
50 Dodge St.
Beverly, MA 01915
(800) 255-0786
(615) 922-2040
48-page color catalog, free U.S. Does not sell overseas. AE, MC, V, MO, PC.
Johnny Appleseed's specializes in quality casual clothing for the mature woman—dresses, sportswear, footwear, outerwear, and bathing suits.

Kinloch Anderson
John Knox House
45 High St.
Edinburgh EH1 1SR Scotland
031 556 6961
12-page color catalog, free U.S. and overseas. AE, DC, MC, V, MO, PC.
Kinloch Anderson is a fifth generation family company and is a respected manufacturer and retailer of fine clothing—in tartans and tweeds

for ladies and Highland dress for men.

Knight's, Ltd.
1226 Ambassador Blvd.
St. Louis, MO 63132
(314) 993-1516
72-page color catalog. AE, DC, CB, V, MC.
Knight's sells a nice selection of better dresses and a few coordinates. Interspersed throughout the catalog are accessories, many shoes, household and kitchen gifts.

La Shack
19 The Plaza
Locust Valley, NY 11560
(800) 645-3524
New York (516) 671-1091
32-page color catalog, free U.S. and overseas. AE, MC, V, MO, PC.
Elegant dresses, dressy sportswear, and clothes for entertaining.

Laura Ashley
55 Triangle Blvd.
Carlstadt, NJ 07072
34-page color catalog, 16-page color *Bridal Collection* catalog $4 U.S. Does not sell overseas. AE, MC, V, MO, PC.
Laura Ashley was founded in 1953 as a retail home furnishers shop. Today there are over 100 shops worldwide (30 in the U.S. alone). They are renowned for garments of 100% natural fibers, exclusively designed by internationally famous designers. The catalog features romantic period dresses, many in the distinctive Laura Ashley print fabrics. Their nostalgic wedding gowns are exquisite.

Les Première Editions
Unique Merchandizing Mart
Building 12
Hanover, PA 17333
(800) 621-5800
40-page color catalog, $2 U.S. and overseas. AE, MC, V, MO, PC.
Career clothes, evening fashion, loungewear, lingerie, and accessories at moderate prices.

Lew Magram
250 West 54th St.
New York, NY 10019
(800) 228-5000
72-page color catalog, free U.S. AE, CB,
    DC, MC, V, MO, PC.
Lew Magram features great women's
fashions, from casual weekender outfits
to career and dressy designs.

Lilly Pulitzer
1101 Clare Ave.
West Palm Beach, FL 33401
(305) 832-0687
32-page color catalog, free U.S. and
    overseas. AE, MC, V, MO, PC.
Lilly Pulitzer fabrics are distinctive
floral prints in pinks, greens, and bright
citrus colors. The garments are sporty
and conservative—terrific for resort or
vacation wear. Dresses are priced
around $85. There are also golf outfits,
bathing suits, and a few sun hats.

Mark Fore & Strike
P.O. Box 640
Del Ray Beach, FL 33444
(800) 327-3627
Florida (305) 276-0366
24-page color catalog. AE, DC, MC, V,
    PC.
Classic clothing for at-home,
entertaining, or casual fun. There are
beachwear, loungewear, dresses, and
coordinates.

Peachtree Report
Palo Verde at 33rd Dept. ABG5
Tuscon, AZ 85726
(602) 747-5000
38-page color catalog, $1 U.S. and
    overseas. AE, DC, MC, V, MO, PC.
Peachtree Report brings you the best in
the new season's fashion, shoes, and
accessories for play, work, leisure, and
comfort. There are also original gift and
decor items.

Pennsylvania Station
Unique Merchandising Mart
Building 14
Hanover, PA 17333
(800) 621-5800
Illinois (800) 972-5858

38-page color catalog, $2 U.S. and
    overseas. AE, DC, MC, V, MO, PC.

Pin Linni Prints
23 Chapel St.
Camelford, Cornwall
England
0840 212733
8-page color catalog, $1 U.S. and
    overseas. V.
Pin Linni Prints are uniquely handprinted and-designed clothing. Most
garments are made of a polycotton blend
which makes them machine washable
and easy to care for. There are dresses,
skirts, blouses, and jumpers mostly in
shades of blue, fawn, green, and pink
with their distinctive border prints.

Pitlochry Knitwear Co.
Scottish Woollens House
P.O. Box 8
East Kilbride G74 5QZ Scotland
0 3552 42080
10-page color catalog, free U.S. and
    overseas. AE, DC, MC, V, MO, PC.
Pitlochry features a beautifully
coordinated range of tartans, tweeds,
and knitwear in popular shades such as
dusty blue, mauve, beige, and soft grey.

Putumayo
149 Wooster St.
New York, NY 10012
(212) 982-0775
16-page color catalog, $1; overseas $4.
    AE, MC, V, MO, PC.
Putumayo offers unique (though
limited) mixtures of handwoven fabrics
in interesting styles collected from all
over the world. There's quite a collection
of colorful sashes and shawls.

Roamanes and Paterson
Waverly Mills
Langhom Dumfrieshire
Scotland
32-page color catalog, free U.S. and
    overseas. AE, DC, MC, V, MO, PC.
Roamanes and Paterson offers Scottish
Tweeds, tartans, and knitwear of high
quality and good value. Roamanes and
Paterson was established in 1808 and
has traded on Princes Street in
Edinburgh for over 150 years.

Royal Silk, Ltd.
Royal Silk Plaza
45 East Madison Ave.
Clifton, NJ 07011
(201) 727-4100
32-page color *Silk Blouse* catalog, 15-page color *Silk Dress* catalog, 15-page *Silk Night-Life* catalog. $1 U.S. and overseas. AE, DC, MC, V, MO, PC.
Royal Silk offers their own label silk and silk blend dresses, blouses, and evening wear at great prices through their three catalogs. Pure silk blouses range from $27 to $55, pure silk crepe de chine dresses are priced $48 to $62, pure silk and angora sweaters are priced $30 to $60, and their evening collection ranges from $50 to $120.

Shopping International
Palo Verde at 33rd Dept. AEY3
P.O. Box 27600
Tuscon, AZ 85726
48-page color catalog, $1 refundable U.S. and overseas. AE, DC, MC, V, MO, PC.
Shopping International features fashions and jewelry from around the world. Some of the fashions are made just for them.

Sara Fermi
25 Gwyder St.
Cambridge CB1 2LG England
0223 312048
6-page brochure, $1; overseas free. MC, V, MO, PC.
Sara Fermi's clothing collection consists of seven to ten handmade garments of natural fiber (wool, cotton, and silk), in ageless styles and often based on historic models. Usually one garment will incorporate handwork such as smocking or embroidery. "Ingrid" is an embroidered shirt derived from styles of the old Swedish midsummer Festival shirt, with puffed sleeves edged in guipure lace, and priced at about $70.

Serendipity
Palo Verde at 33rd
P.O. Box 27500
Tuscon, AZ 85726
(602) 747-5000

44-page color catalog, $2 U.S. and overseas. AE, DC, MC, V, MO, PC.
Fashions, shoes, and accessories in some great styles make Serendipity one of the more popular catalogs. There's also a nice selection of gifts for a simple thank you or for that special someone.

Talbots
175 Beal St.
Hingham, MA 02043
(617) 749-7600
60-page color catalog, $2 U.S. and overseas. AE, DC, MC, V, MO, PC.
Classic and traditional clothing with emphasis on investment dressing in a variety of ageless styles.

The Tog Shop
Liester Square
Americus, GA 31710
(912) 924-3800
128-page color catalog, free U.S. Does not sell overseas. AE, DC, MC, V, MO, PC.
Suits, dresses, skirts, blouses, and sleepwear in traditional styles by brand-name clothiers.

Trade Exchange (Ceylon) Limited
72 Chatham Street
Colombo 1, Sri Lanka
4-page color brochure, $2; overseas free. AE, BD.
The Trade Exchange manufactures and exports simple traditional kaftans handmade from beautiful batik fabrics. They are made from 100% cotton voile and poplin and are inexpensively priced from $9.50 to $12.50. Also available though not pictured are batik cushion covers, table cloths, bedspreads, and batik fabric by the meter.

The Very Thing
P.O. Box 7427
Charlottesville, VA 22906
(800) 336-4051
Virginia (703) 456-8177
32-page color catalog, free U.S. and overseas. AE, MC, V, MO, PC.
The Very Thing features smartly styled traditional women's clothing, sizes 4 to 20. Mostly dresses, plus some tennis, beachwear and sleepwear.

Water Witch
Box 329-G
Main St.
Castine, ME 04421
(207) 326-4884
12-page color catalog, $1; overseas $1.50
AE, MC, V, MO, PC.
Unusual women's clothes (dresses, jackets, and vests) made from imported cottons and Viyellas. The cottons are Dutch Wax Batiks, including the famous Escher print, as well as Dutch Java prints. The fabrics vary from paisleys and pinstripes to the vibrant earthiness of the Java-inspired prints. Dresses range in price from $75 to $165.

Willow Ridge
135 Kisco Ave.
Mt. Kisco, NY 10549
(914) 666-8500
36-page color catalog. AE, MC, V, MO, PC.
Dresses for the office or about town, suits, dressy dresses, and conservative casuals at very good prices.

SPECIAL WOMEN'S SIZES

Beloff's
192 W. Main St.
Meriden, CT 06450
(800) 243-3966
(203) 634-1419
16-page color catalog, free U.S. and overseas. MC, V, MO, PC.
The catalog cover says, "Livelier fashions for larger women." Better-tailored quality sportswear: coats, dresses, shoes, lingerie, robes, and accessories for larger-sized women are featured. Sizes 16 to 20 and 14½ to 16½.

Lady Annabelle
P.O. Box 1490
Boston, MA 02205
10-page catalog, free U.S. AE, MC, V, MO, PC.
Lady Annabelle's collection is full of lacy lingerie. There are elegant bras in sizes up to 44DD, delicately designed teddies in sizes up to 48, and daring

bikinis in sizes up to 4X. There are also bra-slips, stockings, camisoles, pettipants, and briefs.

Lane Bryant
2300 Southeastern Ave.
Indianapolis, IN 46207-7201
103-page color catalog, free U.S. MC, V, MO, PC.
Lane Bryant is one of the foremost companies featuring fashionable clothes for women's sizes 32 through 60, half sizes 12½ through 34½, and misses' sizes 14 through 28. They have an especially good selection of boots (in widths up to WW) and winter coats.

Nancy's Choice
2300 Southeastern Ave.
P.O. Box 7201
Indianapolis, IN 46207
60-page color catalog, free. MC, V, MO, PC.
Good-looking fashions in large sizes for the career woman: dresses, suits, coats, shoes, and sportswear. In misses' sizes 10 to 20, women's 36 to 46, and half sizes 14½ to 16½.

Old Pueblo Traders
Palo Verde at 33rd Dept. ARE1
Tuscon, AZ 85726
(602) 747-5000
48-page color catalog, $1 U.S. and overseas. AE, DC, MC, V, MO, PC.
Old Pueblo Traders features fashionable clothes in special sizes. They carry misses' sizes 8 to 18, half sizes 14½ to 26½, petite sizes 2 to 18, plus shoes in up to WW widths.

Piaffe
1500 Broadway
New York, NY 10036
(212) 869-3320
16-page color catalog, $2 U.S. and overseas. AE, DC, MC, V, MO, PC.
Piaffe offers a full line of better quality merchandise for the small woman—5' 4" and under, and wearing sizes 0, 2, 4, and 6. There are sports and active wear, dresses, suits, coats, lingerie, and some accessories.

Regalia
Palo Verde at 33rd
P.O. Box 27800 Dept. ACR6
Tuscon, AZ 85726
(602) 747 5000
Catalog, $1 refundable U.S. and
  overseas. AE, DC, MC, V, MO, PC.
Regalia fashions are an attractive mix
of style and proportion in half and
women's sizes, selected misses' sizes,
plus shoes up to WW widths.

Roaman's
1500 Broadway
New York, NY 10036
(212) 930-9802
120-page color catalog, free U.S. Does
  not sell overseas. AE, MC, V, MO, PC.
Roaman's offers an excellent line of
clothing and shoes, all specially styled
and sized to fit the larger figure. They
carry dresses, sportswear, coats,
lingerie, sleepwear, foundations,
hoisery, and accessories. Their selection
is superb and their prices very
reasonable.

Shelly's Tall American Beauties
747 Towne Ave.
Los Angeles, CA 90021
(213) 627-8255
24-page color catalog. MC, V, PC.
Shelly's operates 59 retail stores in the
U.S. for tall figures. They feature a full
line of suits, dresses, coats, and
sportswear specifically tailored for a
true tall fit. Dresses range from $64 to
$129, suits from $98 to $137, and velour
jogging suits for about $78.

Tailored Petites
1051 Hummel Ave.
Lemoyne, PA 17043
(800) 228-2028
(800) 642-8300
24-page color catalog, free U.S. CB, MC,
  V, MO, PC.
From casual and dressy to coordinates
and suits, Tailored Petites offers a great
line of clothes for the shorter woman
in sizes 0 to 16.

Tall Collection
2300 Southeastern Ave.
P.O. Box 7201
Indianapolis, IN 46207-7201

A good selection of dresses, sportswear,
shoes, lingerie, coats, and suits
proportioned for the figure over 5′ 6″ tall,
and in shoes to size 12AA.

Unique Petite
Palo Verde at 33rd Dept. ANM2
P.O. Box 27800
Tuscon, AZ 85726
(601) 748-8600
32-page color catalog, $1 U.S. and
  overseas. AE, DC, MC, V, MO, PC.
This catalog is filled with fashions,
shoes, and accessories expressly
designed for petite women. Sizes 2 to 16
are available.

MATERNITY

Baby Love
P.O. Box 127
Laguna Beach, CA 92652
(714) 494-5415
3-page brochure and swatches, free U.S.
  and overseas. MO, PC.
Marilyn Johnson makes attractive tops
and dresses designed for easy access and
closure while breast feeding your baby.
There's no need to unbutton or pull up
clothing—velcro openers make it
comfortable and convenient. Swatches
show a variety of attractive prints, and
dresses are priced at about $28, with tops
about $16.

Deerlick Springs
P.O. Box 56-IM
Douglas City, CA 96024
(916) 623-2957
24-page catalog, $1 U.S. and overseas.
  MC, V, MO, PC.
Deerlick Springs offers only natural
fiber clothing and accessories for
pregnant and/or nursing women, and
children up to size six. There are dresses
(from about $24 to $43), blouses (about
$29), and lovely nursing nighties (from
about $25 to $42). There are also
overalls, maternity pants (Blooming
Britches), and skirts.

5th Avenue Maternity
518 Union St.
Seattle, WA 98101
(800) 426-3569
Washington (206) 426-3569

12-page color catalog, $2 U.S. and
   overseas. AE, MC, V, MO, PC.
12-page color catalog, $2 U.S. and
overseas. AE, MC, V, MO, PC.
5th Avenue Maternity's shop is located
in Seattle, Washington. By popular
demand, they recently expanded into
the direct marketing field with a great
catalog. It features a fun and colorful
maternity wardrobe to be enjoyed
during and after pregnancy. The styles
are sophisticated yet simply styled. They
offer a career collection, day and
evening dresses, casual fashions,
swimwear, coats and jackets, and
sleepwear. They're priced from $20 to
$178 and are available in sizes 4
to 18.

Lady Madonna
36 East 31st St.
New York, NY 10016
(212) 685-4555
16-page color catalog, free U.S. MC, V,
   MO, PC.
Lady Madonna has a great catalog of
maternity wear for the office, party, and
fast-paced life. There are comfortable
sportswear and swimwear, too. Write to
their main office in New York to obtain
a copy of their super catalog.

Mother's Work
P.O. Box 40121
Philadelphia, PA 19106
(215) 625-9259
20 color sheets and swatches, $3 U.S. and
   overseas. MC, V, MO, PC.
Mother's Work has a great line of
business suits and dresses for the
pregnant executive (finally!). For years
there has been little to choose from in
maternity wear for career women. This
catalog includes the maternity Business
Suit (about $230), a 100% wool tailored
jacket with matching jumper. Less
expensive and terrific looking is the all-
occasion suit ensemble $124, a matching
wool-looking polyester jacket and
jumper with coordinating paisley
silquessa blouse. There are many
fabrics to mix for shirts and jumpers.
The basic shirtdress is about $57, and
basic dresses are priced from $29 to $56.
There is also lingerie and sleepwear.

Reborn Maternity
1449 3rd Ave.
New York, NY 10028
(212) 737-8877
16-page color catalog, $1 U.S. and
   overseas. AE, MC, V, MO, PC.
Fashionable maternity clothes at prices
10% to 50% below retail prices. There
are great-looking cotton blend jogging
outfits for about $29, and a crisp red-and-
white striped 100% cotton pinafore for
$68. There are nine bold and bright
swimsuits to choose from, plus
coordinates, sportswear, and casual
dresses. Don't miss this catalog.

CHILDREN

Biobottoms
57 Grant Ave.
Petaluma, CA 94952
(707) 778-7945
2-page brochure, free U.S. and overseas.
   MC, V, MO, PC.
Jan Cooper and Anita Diamondstein
present, from Japan Biobottoms, diaper
covers made of 100% wool felt. They
form a natural absorbent barrier to keep
bed and clothes dry. They claim that
babies are rash-free because fresh air
can circulate freely. The cloth diaper is
folded inside the biobottoms, which
close with velcro fasteners (eliminating
the need for pins). Soft fabric bindings
prevent leakage at leg openings. They
are machine washable and available in
five sizes at $10 each. (A minimum of
four Biobottoms will do the job.)

Brights Creek
Bay Point Place
Hampton, VA 23653
(804) 827-1703
32-page color catalog, free U.S. AE, MC,
PC
Brights Creek features cute and colorful
children's clothes in sizes infant
through 14. Their prices seem most
reasonable. A darling sailor dress of
blue-and-white chambray stripes with
double-sailor collar and short puff
sleeves is only $17. It is also available
for $17 in a matching boys sailor suit
in sizes 2–4T. There are rompers, stylish
jeans, party dresses, and school
coordinates.

Clothkits
24 High Street, Lewes
East Sussex BN7 2LB England
07 916 77111

Charing Cross Kits
Box 798822
Meredith, NH 03253
(603) 279-8449
40-page color catalog, $1 U.S. and
    overseas. MC, V, MO, PC.
Charing Cross, the American affiliate of
the English company Clothkits, sells
lovely unique silk-screened clothing
sewing kits for children, sizes 0 to 8.
They offer lovely dresses, pinafores,
dungarees, and jackets. Their ready-to-
wear knit sweaters and heavy tights are
available in four solid colors and
coordinate nicely with the outfits. They
also offer striped sweaters, hats, scarves,
and gloves that mix and match. For
infants there are some cozy-looking
(machine-washable) velour playsuit
sewing kits, too.

Cotton Cookie
P.O. Box 569-I
Woodacre, CA 94930
(415) 488-0705
16-page catalog, free U.S. and overseas.
    MC, V, MO, PC.
Cotton Cookie features a variety of
colorful children's clothes made
exclusively of 100% natural fibers—
cotton, wool, and sheepskin. From
newborn to size 5, there are infant
wrappers ($13), cotton twill pants ($9),
T-shirts and shirts ($5), playsuits,
sweatshirts and underclothes. Most of
the clothes are described as pre-shrunk
except where noted.

Cottontails
1325 43rd St.
Los Alamos, NM 87544
(505) 662-4558
6-page color brochure, $1; overseas $2.
    MC, V, MO, PC.
Cottontails is a cottage industry, making
quality children's clothing from
newborn to size ten. European-styled
jumpers, overalls, and dresses are
intended to grow with the child;
hemlines on dresses are pleated, so they
can be let out, and straps on jumpers

and overalls are longer than necessary
so they can be lengthened. Prices are
most reasonable.

Espirit
950 Tennessee St.
San Francisco, CA 94107
(800) 437-7748
16-page color catalog, $2 U.S. Does not
    sell overseas. AE, DC, MC, V, MO, PC.
Terrific! Now Espirit has produced a
catalog of children's wear in sizes 7 to
14 and pre-teen sizes 7 to 14. You'll find
the same fun "European look" casual
clothes, in splashy colors, that have been
so popular with the grownups.

Hopscotch
251 Brixton Rd.
London SW9 England
01 274 7260
4-page color brochure, $1 U.S. and
    overseas. MC, V, MO, PC.
Hopscotch features children's clothes in
pre-cut kits with sewing instructions,
thread, and all the notions. The easy-
care fabrics are from France and the
styles are simple and fashionable. The
clothes can be made on a standard
sewing machine and require limited
sewing experience. There is a good
selection of boy's clothing (that's rare!)
including corduroy trousers, a duvet
waistcoat, a warm quilted jacket, and
zip-front dungarees (great for children
learning to dress themselves). For girls
there are versatile pinafores, cute
knickerbockers, and generously
gathered day dresses (for about $10.50)
in check or floral prints.

The Kids Stop
1730 Butter Rd.
Dover, PA 17315
(800) 528-6050
16-page color catalog, free U.S. MC, V,
    MO, PC.
Brightly colored children's clothes from
newborn to size 14 are offered by Kids
Stop at great prices. Monogrammed
acrylic cardigan sweaters from $6.60 to
$9.00, and poly/cotton ruffled turtleneck
shirts start at $4.50. This is a great
catalog for planning a back-to-school
wardrobe as many of the outfits are mix
and match. There's a good selection of

baby crawlers, overalls, and elasticized knit pants (up to 2-year-old size for $5.66). Don't miss this catalog.

The Kids Warehouse, Ltd.
Brownell Hollow Rd.
Eagle Bridge, NY 12057
(518) 677-8214
16-page catalog, $1 U.S. and overseas. MC, V, MO, PC.
The Kids Warehouse specializes in durable children's clothes from natural fibers: Oshkosh overalls, chamois shirts and lumber jackets. They also manufacture some unique items: mother-daughter sun dresses, a lumberjack prairie dress for women and children. You just can't beat Oshkosh's hotliners ($30)—they are basic blue denim bib overalls, fully lined in cozy plaid flannel and matching flannel shirt.

Laughing Bear Batik
P.O. Box 732
Woodstock, NY 12498
(914) 679-7650
5-page (some color) brochure, $1 U.S. and overseas. PC.
All Laughing Bear children's clothing is original handmade batik in a variety of vivid color combinations. The children's clothes, mostly shirts with some infant sets, are all 100% cotton. The designs are delightful: pegasus, cat, lion, unicorn, hearts and stars, dinosaurs and bunnies. The color combinations are terrific—sky blue and magenta, light purple and dark purple, green on turquoise, to name a few. Infant shirts are about $10; children's long-sleeve shirts start at around $12.50.

Proud Parent
900½ South Main St.
Fairfield, IA 52556
(515) 472-6907
2-page color brochure, free U.S. Does not sell overseas. MC, V, MO, PC.
Proud Parent features children's natural fiber clothing made of 100% pure cotton. There are colorful turtlenecks (in solids and prints), overalls, and a hooded sweater. There are darling striped wool sweaters and

coordinating pants sets. Sizes range from six mos. to size 4.

Richard Hanten for Children
6137 N. Scottsdale Rd.
Scottsdale, AZ 85253
(602) 991-8222
6-page brochure, free U.S. AE, MC, V, MO, PC.
Richard Hanten sells fine traditional children's clothing, sizes 6 mos. to 14. Many feature bright appliqués and monograms.

The Young Idea
9 Kingsbury
Aylesbury, Bucks
HP20 2JA England
88068
32-page (some color) catalog, free U.S. and overseas. MC, V, MO, PC.
Young Idea has some terrific bargains on Ladybird overstocks, current Ladybird, and their own children's garment label, Young Idea. They carry sizes 2 to 15. They mail order world-wide to customers fond of the Ladybird line.

Youngland
30 N. W. 23rd Place
Portland, OR 97210
(503) 227-1414
32-page color catalog. MC, V, MO, PC.
Top name-brand children clothes in sizes infant through 14. There are dresses by Yves St. Laurent, Petite Elegance, and Florence Eiseman. There are also fashions by Crazy Horse, Gant Thompson, Perry Ellis, and Lacoste.

KNITWEAR

Alice in Wonderland Creations
Rt. 1 Box 405
Millstone, WV 25261
(304) 354-7531
12-page catalog, $1; overseas $2. MO, PC.
From the black sheep raised on the Stough's farm, Alice and Lee shear, wash, card, spin and knit the wool. These naturally colored sweaters will not fade, and the natural oils allowed to remain in the wool make the finished garments water-repellent and dirt-

resistant. Each hand-knit garment by Alice, is one-of-a-kind. Adult-sized pullover sweaters start at about $82. They also create ponchos and shawls, scarves, hats and blankets.

Art Needlework Industries
7 St. Michael's Mansions
Ship Street, Oxford
England
247 556
20-page catalog, $4.50; overseas $6. AE, MO, PC.
Heinz Kiewe is a world-renowned expert in the knitting craft. He is a researcher, writer, and lecturer on the subject of knitwear, but he is also in touch with today's style trends. Knitting kits for Aran, Icelandic, mohair, and Shetland sweaters (and hats) are available.

Avoca Handweavers
Ballinacor House
Church Road
Ballybrack, County Dublin
Ireland
01 855816
14-page color catalog, $3 U.S. and overseas. AE, DC, MC, V, MO, PC.
Hand-weavers and hand-knitters of natural fabrics since 1723. The Wicklow Jacket ($40) is a popular hand-knitted combination of Aran and Astrakhan wools, with zipper and built-in pockets. They also feature coats, cloaks, men's sport jackets, shawls, stoles, scarves, and carriage rugs.

Cleo, Ltd.
18 Kildare St.
Dublin 2 Ireland
353 1 761421
6-page color brochure with swatches, $2 U.S. and overseas. MO, PC.
Cleo offers an excellent selection of Aran sweaters, hand-knit in an intricate and distinctive pattern by women of the Aran Islands of Ireland. The natural oils left in the sweaters gives them an oatmeal-to-cream shade and provides waterproofing properties, making them ideal for skiing or yachting. Pullovers start at about $73. They use buttons that are entirely handmade from either ceramic, wood, or marble. Coats, caps,

suits, and vests are also available. There is even a romantic full-length Munster cloak suitable for evening wear.

Daphne Imports
7 Norden Lane
Huntington Station, NY 11746
(800) 228-5000
32-page color catalog, free U.S. AE, CB, DC, MC, V.
Daphne offers an elegant collection of Icelandic knitwear of Alafoss, Icewool, and Lopi. All coats and jackets are shipped with a complimentary brush that removes surface soil and conditions the mohair-like finish of these lovely Icewool garments. There are a few elegantly designed lightweight knit coats, and a terrific selection of children's sweaters, mittens and scarves. For après ski there are comfortable sweaters, vests, and zippered jackets for men and women.

The Dublin Woollen Company, Ltd.
Metal Bridge Corner
Dublin 1 Ireland
775014
10-page brochure, free U.S. and overseas. AE, DC, MC, V, MO, PC.
The Dublin Woollen Company undoubtedly sells the largest selection of Irish knitwear, crafts, and tweeds— and at very competitive prices. Aran crew neck sweaters start at $52. There are tweed skirts and jackets, cashmere and lambswool sweaters, Gaeltarra nordic sweaters, and linen crochet dresses.

Guernsey Knitwear
6 The Bridge, St. Sampson
Guernsey, Channel Isles
Great Britain
0481 44487
4-page (some color) brochure with swatches, free U.S. and overseas. MC, V, MO, PC.
Both Guernsey and Jersey garments are made in the age-old traditional fashion of countless generations of the fisher folk of the Channel Islands. The Guernsey is the older of the two sweaters, and is still the better known in the fishing villages of the British Isles and Australia. Both are made from

heavy 5-ply worsted wool with a very tight knit, which makes it a durable and "shower-proof" woollen. The design has neither a front or back; it is simply put on as it is picked up. Prices start at about $24.

Helen McGroarty
7 Grafton Arcade
Dublin Ireland
01 777508
10-page color brochure, free U.S. and overseas. V, MO, PC.
Helen McGroarty sells Aran hand-knit sweaters, caps, and scarves. There is a nice selection of children's sweaters, and Helen McGroaty's prices are most competitive with others listed here.

Icemart
P.O. Box 23
Keflavik International Airport
Keflavik, Iceland 235
92 2790
35-page color catalog, $1 U.S. and overseas. AE, DC, MC, MO, PC.
The collection you'll find in this catalog is a carefully selected offering of the most popular items available from Iceland. From the famous one-of-a-kind sweaters, hand-knitted from Lopi, to beautiful knitted evening dresses. There is fine lava-ceramic ware, silver jewelry from contemporary artists, and soft woven blankets. Iceland's most sought-after products are woolen goods— ponchos and sweater jackets, in many styles and gorgeous natural colors. Prices are most reasonable. Don't miss this catalog.

Irish Cottage Industries
44 Dawson St.
Dublin 2 Ireland
713039
6-page (some color) brochure, $1 U.S. and overseas. AE, DC, MC, PC.
"All pure wool and knitted garments in traditional Aran designs." They also offer a large selection of tweeds, purses, table mats, blankets, cushions, scarves and hats.

Kennedy's of Ardara
Ardara, County Donegal
Ireland

16-page brochure, $3 U.S. AE, DC, MC, V, MO, PC.
Kennedy's of Ardara employs 900 cottage knitters working year round to supply traditional Irish knit goods. "On the label of each sweater you'll see the name of the knitter who personally made your sweater. It may be Sally Maloney or Peggy O'Donnell—these are not factory workers but the wives and daughters of Donegal fishermen and farmers working in their own thatched cottages . . ." Kennedy's claims to be Ireland's largest manufacturers and exporters of traditional handknits.

Landau
114 Landau St.
P.O. Box 671
Princeton, NJ 08540
(800) 257-9445
New Jersey (800) 792-8333
28-page color catalog. CB, DC, MC, V.
Landau sells traditional Icelandic handknits of 100% pure Icelandic wool. Many of the styles are exclusively designed for Landau. There are lovely sweaters, jackets, and coats in white and shades of grey, light blue, and light brown. Classic Icelandic sweaters remain a popular 1,100-year-old tradition. There are knitted gloves, mittens, hats, scarves, leg warmers, and Shearling slippers.

Le Tricoteur and Co., Ltd.
Pitronnerie Road Estate
St. Peter Port
Guernsey, Channel Islands
Great Britain
0481 26214
Le Tricoteur are manufacturers of the hand-knit, all-wool fisherman's sweater called a traditional Guernsey. Made of specially prepared weather-resistant worsted wool, they date back to the reign of Elizabeth I, when knitted stockings were an important export item. (Mary Queen of Scots is said to have been executed in a pair of Guernsey stockings.) Guernsey sweaters are available in ten colors and in sizes for children, women, and men.

Millhaven Knitting Services
Knowstone, South Molton
North Devon EX36 4RT England
1-page brochure, free U.S. and overseas.
  PC.
Norman E. Lord runs a small business
dedicated to the customer's personal
attention. They will create a pattern and
hand-knit or crochet any garment for
you, personally. You provide them with
a picture or sketch and your
measurements. For price quotations
send $3 U.S., 50p British, or five
International Reply Coupons. If you
have an old favorite that has shrunk (or
that you've out-grown), they will match
the pattern and use English yarn to
make you a new one.

Monaghan's
15/17 Grafton Arcade
Dublin 2 Ireland
01 770823
16-page color catalog, free U.S. and
  overseas. AE, DC, V, MO, PC.
Monaghan's offers a wide selection of
cashmere and 100% wool sweaters.
Name brands include Pringle of
Scotland, Glenmac, Barric, Glen Abbey,
Lyle and Scott, Alan Paine, and Aran.

Muileann Beag a'Chrotail, Ltd.
Camus Chros, Isle of Skye
Scotland IV43 8QR
6-page color brochure, free surface, $1
  air mail; overseas free. MC, V, MO, PC.
There are beautiful hand-knitted
sweaters based on traditional Hebridean
patterns using three types of wools:
Shetland, Harris and Gotland. While
Shetland is universally well known, the
latter two are not. Harris wool is rough,
but very warm and durable, and is used
in the Crofter sweater. Gotland wool
comes from a Swedish breed of sheep
raised in Skye, and is a soft and silky
wool. Prices range from about $30
to $40.

Oomingmak
604 H Street
Anchorage, AK 99501
(907) 272-9225
10-page brochure, free U.S. and
  overseas. AE, MC, V, MO.
Oomingmak features hand-knitted
items from Qiviut wool. Every spring
Alaskan musk oxen shed their soft
underwool, Qiviut (ki-vee-ute). After the
wool goes to a cooperative spinning mill,
the yarn is mailed to over 150 knitters
who work at home in isolated villages.
They produce luxuriously soft scarves,
hats, stoles, smoke rings (called Pelatuk
and worn as a cowl), and tunics.
Warmth, lightness, and the special
softness make Qiviut garments
cherished possessions.

The Peruvian Connection
Canaan Division
Tanganoxie, KS 66086
(800) 255-6429
Kansas (913) 845-2450
48-page color catalog, $2 U.S. and
  overseas. AE, MC, V, MO, PC.
The Peruvian Connection is a small
specialty import company offering
exclusive designer alpaca sweaters, all
handmade in Peru. The lovely Jasmine
Stitch pullover ($139) is an intricate
stitch in lightweight natural-colored
alpaca. Alpaca crew neck sweaters ($99)
are available in primary solid colors for
both men and women. This is also a good
source for Peruvian cotton turtleneck
jerseys ($24) in thirteen colors.

Rammagerdin
Hafnarstraeti 19
P.O. Box 751
Reykjavik 121 Iceland
91 11122
24-page color catalog, $1; overseas free.
  AE, DC, MC, V, MO, PC.
Rammagerdin of Reykjavik started
offering Icelandic woolen wear in 1950.
Today they operate three shops in
Reykjavik's largest hotels and a large
downtown store. They offer beautiful
machine-and hand-knitted garments for
men, women, and children in very
attractive styles.

Reekies, Ltd.
The Old Coach House
Grasmere, Cumbria
LA22 9SL England
09665
4-page price list, $1 refundable; overseas
  free. AE, DC, MC, V, MO, PC.

Reekie is well known for their fine hand-woven materials, hand-knit woolen sweaters, mohair blankets, scarves, stoles, and garments.

Royal Hand-Knits
1 Hammerichsgade
Copenhagen, Denmark 1611
01 117578
24-page color catalog, $1; overseas free. AE, DC, MC, V, MO, PC.
Royal Hand-knits sells colorful Scandinavian sweaters good for skiing, après-ski, or any casual occasion. There are traditional sweaters, ponchos, jackets, and even a few silk-lined Icelandic wool jackets. Pullover Scandinavian sweaters start at about $69.

Sweater Market
15 Frederiksberggade
1459 Copenhagen, Denmark
02 152773
11-page color brochure, $1; overseas free. AE, DC, VC, V, MO, PC.
Hand-knit sweaters and jackets from Denmark and Iceland in classic, chic, and sporty styles. Most of their sweaters incorporate beautiful blends of color. The Sweater Market is located on the Pedestrian Mall, near the Town Hall Square, and is great for browsing and shopping.

Una O'Neill
30 Oakley Park
Blackrock, County Dublin
Ireland
01 8862723
4-page brochure, free U.S. and overseas. V, MO, PC.
Una O'Neill employs over 1,000 Irish knitters to provide an excellent selection of hand-knit Aran sweaters for men, women, and children. They are famous for their top quality garments: tams, hats, mittens and scarves. They also make Aran coats and dresses to measure.

W. S. Robertson, Ltd.
41 Bank St.
Galashiels, Scotland
0896 2152

20-page color brochure, $5; overseas free. MO, PC.
W. S. Robertson's has one of the largest selections of classic knitwear by Pringle. There are sweaters in luxurious cashmere, soft lambswool, lamaine and Shetland wool in good-looking styles and colors for men and women. A singleweight cashmere ladies' pullover is about $79.

UNDERGARMENTS

A. Rosenthal
92 Orchard St.
New York, NY 10002
(212) 473-5428
12-page brochure, $1 U.S. Does not sell overseas. MC, V, MO, PC.
A. Rosenthal carries over seventy famous name brands of intimate apparel, including Maidenform's Sweet Nothing bras and bikinis, and Vassarette's Frankly Feminine bras and undergarments. They stock the most popular styles and sizes, and sell at about 20% to 50% below retail prices.

Charles Weiss & Sons
38 Orchard St.
New York, NY 10002
(212) 226-1717
36-page catalog, free U.S. Does not sell overseas. AE, MC, V, MO, PC.
Top name-brand lingerie and bras at 25% to 50% below retail prices. Maidenform, Vassarette, Warner, Christian Dior, Pierre Cardin, Formfit, Playtex, and others.

Damart
1811 Woodbury Ave.
Portsmouth, NH 03805
(603) 431-4700
48-page color catalog, free U.S. Does not sell overseas. AE, MC, V, MO, PC.
Damart Thermolactyl underwear is sold in many styles for men and women. Slips, turtlenecks, shirts, long and mid-length panties and nightshirts.

D & A Merchandise Co.
22 Orchard St.
New York, NY 10002
(212) 925-4766

2-page brochure, free U.S. Does not sell overseas.
Lingerie and sleepwear at 25% below retail prices. Men's underwear, socks, robes; women's foundations, lingerie, sleepwear, hosiery, socks; and boys' underwear.

Frederick's of Hollywood
P.O. Box 229
Hollywood, CA 90078
(213) 466-5151
64-page catalog. Prices unavailable. AE, MC, V.
This catalog is famous for sexy lingerie. There is lingerie to hold you in, push you up, and build you up where you may be lacking. There are push-up bras, falsies, panties with padded derriéres, micro bikinis in the sheerest of laces, nighties, cocktail bras (cups that adhere to the breasts, eliminating straps of any kind), and many more special items.

Funn
P.O. Box 102
Steyning, West Sussex, England
0903 892-841
2-page price list, $1 U.S. and overseas. MO.
100% pure silk stockings with seams or seam-free ($108 per dozen), cotton stockings ($54 per dozen), and wool stockings ($99 per dozen) in a wide choice of colors.

Intimate Boutique
901 W. Dundee
P.O. Box F
Wheeling, IL 60035
(800) 323-6153
Illinois (312) 537-8560
16-page color catalog, $1 U.S. Does not sell overseas. AE, MC, V, MO, PC.
Brand-name women's lingerie, swimwear, and beach accessories are offered at competitive prices. Full length terry wraparound robe ($36), full-length nightgown by Olga ($39). There are bras, girdles and slips, too.

Intimates
Unique Merchandising Mart
Building 22
Hanover, PA 17333
(800) 621-5800

31-page color catalog, $2 U.S. and overseas. AE, CB, DC, MC, V, MO, PC.
Intimates features elegant peignoirs, silk hosiery, lacy bras and panties, marabou-covered slippers and fashionable body briefs.

Intimique
Winterbrook Way
Meredith, NH 03253
(603) 279-7071
48-page color catalog, free U.S. Does not sell overseas. AE, CB, DC, MC, V, MO, PC.
Intimique features better designer intimate apparel and loungewear. Channel-quilted jacket and pajama set by Periphery ($95), Bouson Cami and French Pant by Lily of France ($43), and other satin and lace (and alluring) designs by Christian Dior, Bill Tice, Eve Stillman, Ralph Montenero and others.

J. Simister Design
P.O. Box 10
Tamworth, Staffs England
0827-52327
20-page brochure, free U.S. and overseas. PC.
J. Simister's brochure shows line drawings of her pure silk lingerie and sleepwear creations. They are trimmed with traditional Nottingham laces (some are 50 years old) and are made to customer's specifications.

L'eggs Brands, Inc.
Box 6000
Rural Hall, NC 27098
32-page color catalog, free U.S. MC, V, PC.
Big savings are available on all L'eggs brand hosiery, slips, bras, socks, and underwear for men and women.

Linda's Hosiery Outlet, Inc.
311 Trindale Rd.
High Point, NC 27263
(919) 431-2568
10-page price list free U.S. Does not sell overseas. MC, V, MO, PC.

The Lingerie Shop
8230 Forsyth
Clayton, MO 63105
(314) 721-7982

Brochure, self-addressed stamped
envelope, U.S. Does not sell overseas.
MC, V, MO, PC.

Louis Chock
74 Orchard St.
New York, NY 10002
(212) 473-1929
50-page catalog, $1 U.S. Does not sell
overseas. MO, PC.
Louis Chock carries top name brands of
men's, ladies', and children's underwear
and hosiery at prices 25% below retail
prices. Men's underwear brands by
B.V.D., Duofold, Hanes, Jockey, and
Munsingwear. Men's hosiery by
Burlington, Interwoven, Christian Dior
and Supp-hose. Children's and infant's
underwear and pajamas by Carters.

Mendel Weiss
91 Orchard St.
New York, NY 10002
(212) 925-6815
Write or call for a price quote. MC, V,
MO, PC.
Women's lingerie, bras, girdles, robes,
housecoats at prices 25% to 33% below
retail prices.

National Wholesale Company
400 National Blvd.
Lexington, NC 27292
(704) 246-5904
48-page color catalog, free U.S. and
overseas. AE, MC, V, MO, PC.
Over twenty-one styles of panty hose
(sheer, support, control top, surgical
hose (knee-high, ankle-high, thigh-
highs), bras, panties, slips, support
undergarments, sleepwear, loungewear,
men's underwear and socks. Priced at
30% to 50% below retail price.

Private Moments
Dept. 700
P.O. Box 60308
Los Angeles, CA 90060
(800) 323-1717
(213) 465-2220
32-page color catalog. AE, MC, V, MO,
PC.
Glamorous women's lingerie, bras,
panties, camisoles, teddies, nightgowns
and robes.

The Red Flannel Factory
73 S. Main
Cedar Springs, MI 49319
(616) 696-9240
10-page catalog with swatches, free U.S.
and overseas. MC, V, MO, PC.
Traditional red flannel sleepwear and
underwear for the whole family. For
children there are traditional one-piece
long johns with front buttons and drop
bottoms. For women there are many
styles of red flannel nightgowns,
sleepshirts, pajamas, long johns, and
robes. For men there are long johns,
robes, nightshirts, shirts, and vests. Get
each family member a red flannel
sleeper for Christmas.

St. Michele
212 Fifth Ave. Suite 412
New York, NY 10001
4-page color brochure.
  Very lacy and daring lingerie is
  featured in St. Michele's catalog.

Victoria's Secret
P.O. Box 31442
San Francisco, CA 94115
(800) 821 0001
(800) 821-1021
36-page color catalog, $3 U.S. Does not
sell overseas. AE, MC, V, MO, PC.
Women's lingerie in romantic lacy
creations are offered, many created
exclusively for Victoria's Secret. There
are beautiful sleeping gowns, silky
robes, demi-cup underwire bras, lacy
bikinis, and garter belts. So many pretty
styles—it might be hard to choose.

SPORTSWEAR

The Best Choice
P.O. Box 13
Hershey, PA 17033
(717) 533-8339
48-page color catalog, free U.S. and
overseas. AE, DC, MC, V, MO, PC.
Brand-name tennis and running
sportswear and athletic shoes for men,
women, and children are sold at
discounts of 15% to 15% off retail prices.
Running shoes by Adidas, Nike, New
Balance, Saucony, Brooks, Reebok,

Tiger, LeCoq, and Ectonic are available in men's and women's hard-to-find sizes, too. Running outerwear from Sub 4, Bill Rodgers, Head, and Brooks are featured.

Bob Hinman Outfitters
1217 W. Glen
Peoria, IL 61614
(309) 691-8132
32-page color catalog, free U.S. and
  overseas. MC, V, MO, PC.
Bob Hinman's is renowned for high quality outdoor gear, and clothing especially for hunting and camping.

Capezio Dance-Theater Shop
755 7th Ave.
New York, NY 10019
(212) 245-213-
65-page color catalog, $1.50 U.S. and
  overseas. AE, MC, V, MO, PC.
Capezio is the "professional shop in the heart of the dance theater world." They sell footwear (from ballet, tap, jazz and ballroom, to square dance shoes), legwear, bodywear, and accessories for dance, theater and recreation. There's a terrific variety of dance sneakers, and leotards in splashy colors.

Casco Bay Trading Post
Freeport, ME 04032
(800) 722-6066
24-page color catalog, free U.S. AE, DC,
  MC, V, MO, PC.
Casco Bay features natural Shearling sheepskin slippers, popular insulated duck shoes, and many warm and comfortable clothing items. Lambskin mittens, "acorn" slipper socks, cotton sweaters, and plaid flannel shirts.

C. C. Filson
205 Maritime Bldg.
911 Western Ave.
Seattle, WA 98104
(206) 624-4437
16-page color catalog, free U.S. Does not
  sell overseas. MC, V, MO, PC, C.O.D.
Quality outdoor wear, favorites among foresters, loggers, sportsmen, farmers, cattlemen and outdoorsmen. From Filson's "Forestry Cloth Cruiser and Pants" (known as the outdoorsman's tuxedo) to Mackinaws, trail pants,

logger coats, and cruiser vests in safety orange.

Cutter Bill Western World
5818 L. B. J. Freeway
Dallas, TX 75240
(214) 239-3742
31-page catalog, free U.S. and overseas.
  AE, DC, MC, V, MO, PC.

Early Winters
110 Prefontaine Place South
Seattle, WA 98104
(206) 624-5599
76-page color catalog, free U.S. and
  overseas. AE, DC, MC, V, MO, PC.
Early Winters designs and sells Gore-Tex parkas, cozy bunting jackets, outerwear, jogging suits, and other clothes for outdoor enthusiasts. There are classic rag wool sweaters and jackets insulated with Silver Lining and Thinsulate. Waterproof bags come in many sizes and colors to keep your personal items dry.

Eddie Bauer
15010 NE 36th St.
Redmond, WA 98052
(206) 882-6100
100-page color catalog, free U.S. Does
  not sell overseas. AE, MC, V, MO, PC.
Eddie Bauer designed and patented the first goosedown jacket in 1936. Today Eddie Bauer manufactures and retails many goosedown products, some exclusive with them. The catalog is loaded with excellent quality outdoor clothing and equipment for men, women, and children. Flannel shirts, sweaters, goosedown parkas, outdoor wear, sleeping bags, camping accessories, shoes and boots are offered.

Eisner Bros.
76 Orchard St.
New York, NY 10002
(212) 431-8800
20-page catalog, free U.S. and overseas.
  Minimum order one dozen garments.
  MO.
You can order imprinted active sportswear with your favorite team's logo, jackets, hats, warmups, sweatshirts, team jerseys, ladies'

front placket tennis shirts and halter tops.

The Finals
21 Minisink Ave.
Port Jervis, NY 12771
(914) 856-4456
24-page catalog, free U.S. and overseas. AE, MC, V, MO, PC.
Athletic swim suits in twenty different team colors at 30% to 50% below retail prices.

Force 10
4304 West Jefferson Blvd.
Los Angeles, CA 90016
(213) 734-9702
16-page color catalog, $1 U.S. and overseas. MC, V, MO, PC.
Force 10 manufactures high quality outerwear, parkas, jackets and vests for men, women and children, constructed from fine materials—Gore-Tex, Ramar, and Thinsulate.

Fun Wear Brands, Inc.
141 E. Elkhorn Ave.
Box 2800
Estes Park, CO 80517
(303) 586-3361
32-page catalog, free U.S. and overseas. AE, DC, MC, V, MO, PC.
Men's and women's Levis, moccasins, boots, shirts, and hats with the flavor of the west and rugged outdoors are sold by Fun Wear Brands.

Greaves Sports, Ltd.
23 Gordon St.
Glasgow, Scotland
041 221 4531
24-page color catalog, free U.S. Prices in Scottish pounds. AE, DC, MC, V, MO, PC.
The smaller summer catalog features clothing and equipment for tennis, running, golf, cricket and lawn bowling. (Yes. If you've been searching for cricket shoes, they carry Winit Warwickshires.) The larger sports catalog is an extensive price list of clothing and equipment for most all sports.

Just Bikinis
4120 Birch St.
Newport Beach, CA 92660
(714) 752-6771

40-page color catalog, $2 U.S. and overseas. AE, MC, V, MO, PC.
Just Bikinis sells bikini tops and bottoms separately so you may choose a style and size that fits your figure. Tops are in sizes A, B, C, D, and DD, and bottoms in sizes 5,7,9,11, and 13. Made of lycra spandex, they are available in five solid color and three printed fabrics. One page features a very helpful style guide which enables you to mix and match the different styles on a photographed model.

L. L. Bean
Freeport, ME 04033
(207) 865-311
128-page color catalog, free. AE, MC, V, MO, PC.
Leon Leonwood Bean started a little business on Main Street in 1912 and sold funny-looking rubber-bottomed hunting boots he designed himself and sold by mail across the U.S. Today L. L. Bean is a *giant* mail order business—and still markets successfully (very successfully) those boots, as well as chamois shirts, parkas and jackets, sleeping bags, long underwear, tents, camping gear, flannel shirts, and sweaters.

J. Crew
18 Lincoln Place
Garfield, NJ 07026
(800) 562-0258
New Jersey (201) 471-7084
40-page color catalog, free U.S. Does not sell overseas. AE, MC, V, MO, PC.
J. Crew's catalog displays traditional active weekend apparel for men and women in imaginative sporty scenes on or at the river's edge. There are placketed and ribbed-neck jerseys (like those worn by racing crews for daily practices) in nine different colors. Shetland, lambswool, lightweight cable and cotton crew sweaters, rugby wear, and elastic waist pants and shorts in twill or corduroy.

Herbert Dancewear
902 Broadway
New York, NY 10010
(212) 677-7606
22-page color catalog. PC.

Leotards, skirts, tights, warmers, gymtards, and shoes for ballet, pointe, tap, jazz, gymnastics, and acrobatics are sold from Herbert Dancewear's catalog.

Highlander
1072 N. Jacoby Rd.
Akron, OH
(216) 253-9524
36-page brochure, $2.75 U.S. and
   overseas. AE, DC, MC, V, MO, PC.
Highlander offers quality golf equipment and clothing. You can order imprinted golf balls and tees, Stabilizer golf gloves, Easy Driver, and Superstick Adjustable Golf Stick.

Lewis Leathers
120 Great Portland St.
London, W1 2DL England
01 636 4314
52-page color catalog, 50¢ U.S. and
   overseas. MC, V, MO, PC.
Lewis Leathers offers a full line of motorcycle clothing for men and women: leather motorcycle jackets, racing suits, leather motorcycle boots and gloves. They also offer made-to-measure leather garments. Since 1930.

Luskey's Western Stores
101 N. Houston St.
Fort Worth, TX 76102-2080
(817) 335-5833
64-page catalog, free U.S. and overseas.
   AE, D, MC, V, MO, PC.
Luskey's is a recognized leader in designing new Western-style clothing and quality equipment, cowboy hats, boots, belts, jackets, chaps, vests, leather wallets, and jewelry. Family owned and operated since 1919.

Mountain Camper
P.O. Box 291
Seymour, TN 37865
(800) 251-1021
Tennessee (615) 573-3028
   32-page color catalog, free U.S. MC, V,
   MO, PC.
Mountain camper offers some stylish long coats made of warm goosedown. They also offer car coats, jackets and sport vests. Flannel-lined mountain parkas are great for hiking or everyday

protection against rain and wind. There's a nice selection of rugged footwear, camouflage clothing, tents, and camping equipment.

Orvis
10 River Road
Manchester, VT 05254
(802) 362-1300
102-page color catalog, free U.S. and
   overseas. Minimum order overseas
   $20. AE, MC, V, MO, PC.
Orvis' catalog cover states, "A Sporting Tradition since 1856." The clothing and gifts catalog features many casual items the outdoorsmen would appreciate: hand-blown quartz glasses, placemats, stacking tables and other bibelots painted with different game birds or hunt scenes. They even go so far as to offer Lindt Chocolate in molds of leaping bass—and a pair of mallards.

Patagonia
P.O. Box 150
Ventura, CA 93002
(805) 648-3386
50-page color catalog, free U.S. and
   overseas. AE, MC, MO, PC.
Patagonia designs some excellent inner and outerwear for a full range of outdoor, recreational clothing needs. Very popular are their bunting sweater jackets (about $53). But also look at their bunting jackets with outer water-repellent, nylon taslan shell ($86). There are Oolong shorts (great for walking), and slightly lighter weight Stand Up Shorts in four to six colors. A great catalog with exciting photography.

Saba's Western Wear
7254 E. Main St.
Scottsdale, AZ 85251
(800) 352-0458
(800) 528-6600
20-page color catalog, $1 U.S. and
   overseas. AE, MC, V, MO, PC.
Saba's offers western wear in top fashions, with lots of gorgeous leather and suede, for men and women. Women's fashions are by Karen Kane, Salaminder and Char. Hats are by

Stetson, and boots by Dan Post and Tony Lama.

Sheplers
P.O. Box 7702
Wichita, KS 67277
(800) 835-4004
Kansas (312) 943-2151
64-page color catalog, free U.S. and
  overseas. AE, MC, V, MO, PC.
Shepler's sells Western-inspired
clothing for men and women—boots,
hats, belts and buckles. There's a
good selection of dresses, blouses,
and women's Western suits. For
men there are knit shirts, Western
shirts, slacks, and many styles of
jeans.

Split-S Aviation
1050-K Pioneer Way
El Cajon, CA 92020
(619) 440-0894
16-page catalog, free U.S. and overseas.
  AE, MC, V, MO, PC.
Split-S sells pilot's flight clothing and
leather flight jackets. There are Army
Air Corps A-2 flight jackets (about $190)
made from genuine goatskin, designed
to duplicate the thousands worn by
World War II Army Air Corps aviators,
and U.S. Navy G-1 flight jackets (about
$225). The MA-1 flight jacket ($70), is
made from 100% nylon flite satin, and
is current USAF issue. Flight helmets,
goggles, and flight suits are also
available and, of course, white silk
scarves.

Sub 4
2620 Temple Heights Dr.
Oceanside, CA 92054
(800) 782-4444
California (800) 782-3687
20-page color catalog, free U.S. and
  overseas. AE, MC, V, MO, PC.
Sub-4 features some great athletic
clothes for runners and athletes. Nylon
tricot running shorts (about $13 to $14),
mesh singlets, 100% cotton long-sleeve
training shirts ($13.95), Malibu
workouts for women ($70), and 100%
Riptron Nylon training suits for cold
weather workouts ($80).

The Swim Shop
1400 8th Ave. South
P.O. Box 1402
Nashville, TN 37203
(615) 329-9746
48-page color catalog, free U.S. and
  overseas. MC, V, PC, C.O.D.
The Swim Shop supplies swimwear and
accessories for athletic teams and swim
enthusiasts. They carry all the top
names—including Speedo, Arena and
Ocean Pacific—in a great selection of
styles and colors.

Taffy's
701 Beta Dr.
Cleveland, OH 44143
(216) 461-3360
78-page color *Parade* catalog, $3. 80-
  page color *Dance and Gymnastics*
  catalog, $3. 114-page *Records and
  Books* catalog $2. Each sold in the U.S.
  and overseas. AE, MC, V, MO, PC.
Taffy's is a well-known supplier of
dance leotards, tights, legwarmers,
skirts, shoes, and accessories. Request
the specific catalog you're interested in,
the selection is outstanding.

Visions
557 Willow Rd.
P.O. Box 850
Menlo Park, CA 94025
14-page catalog, $1 U.S. Does not sell
  overseas. MO, PC.

ACCESSORIES AND LUGGAGE

Ace Leather Products
2211 Ave. U.
Brooklyn, NY 11229
(212) 891-0998
15-page color sheets, free U.S. Does not
  sell overseas. MC, V, MO, PC.
Ace Carries a large selection of brand-
name luggage (Hartman, Lark,
American Tourister, Diane Von
Furstenburg, Verdi, and Ventura), men's
and ladies' personal leather goods (Rolf,
Bosca, Christian Dior, Bally, Pierre
Cardin, and Bill Blass), and ladies
handbags. All this is offered from 30%
to 50% below retail prices.

Alan Costley
816 S.W. 10
Portland, OR 97205
(503) 222-2577
8-page color brochure, AE, MC, V.
Fine leather accessories by Alan Costley include top zipper leather portfolios by Schlesinger Bros., Becker desk organizers, men's wallets by Hugo Bosca, and Italian calfskin leather boots.

The Baggage Claim
307 S. Galena
P.O. Box 1567
Aspen, CO 81611
(303) 925-8777
32-page color catalog, free; overseas $2.
  AE, MC, V, PC.
The Baggage Claim has a nice collection of luggage, leather goods and gift items. Famous designer names include Coach, Gucci, Gold-Pfeil of Germany, and Dunhill. They feature Pegasus luggage, with tough Cordura nylon in black or red, and manufactured in America. You can have initials monogrammed free on luggage and leather goods.

Bernardo
2400 Westheimer, Suite 108 W
Houston, TX 77098
(713) 526-2686
2-page brochure, free U.S. and overseas.
  MC, V, MO, PC.
Bernardo's has a variety of American suspenders, English braces, and French bretelles with designs reflecting the antique and country influences of the 1920s and 1930s when they were so popular. Made from authentic patterns and materials (silk, cotton, buckcloth, wool, rayon, elastic, and leather), they are available in a combination of styles and colors. They range in price from about $20 to $60 for a pair of British braces made of 1½ in. elegant buckcloth.

Bri-son
P.O. Box 1235
Studio City, CA 91604
(213) 763-6070
4-page brochure, free, U.S. and overseas.
  AE, DC, MC, V, MO, PC.
Bri-son has mail ordered top grain leather wallets with replaceable plastic inserts for over 35 years. These slim-lined wallets are available in about ten styles and are manufactured in America.

Brooks Leather Designs
Rt. 1 Box 343
Pittsboro, NC 27312
(919) 542-4020
10-page color brochure, $2; overseas $3.
  MC, V, MO, PC.
Started in 1969, Stephen Brooks designs and hand-manufactures a line of top grain cowhide handbags, briefcases, business folders, and luggage with solid brass hardware. His work has been featured in magazines and galleries as well as national shows. Custom design requests are also accepted.

Creative House
100 Business Parkway
Richardson, TX 75081
(800) 527-5940
(800) 527-5941
(214) 231-3461
31-page color catalog, free U.S. AE, MC,
  V, PC.
Creative House offers more than thirty styles of leather briefcases, portfolios, and cases. Made in fine quality cowhide, there's a briefcase to match every need and personal taste.

Frank Smythson, Ltd.
54 New Bond Street
London W1Y ODE England
01 629 8558
14-page color catalog, $3; overseas, free.
  AE, DC, MO, PC.
Founded by Frank Smythson at the turn of the century to supply the carriage trade of Mayfair, today they continue to sell fine stationery, pocket and desk diaries, small leather goods, address and guest books, photograph and press clipping albums. Over 90% of the items presented are British made.

Herbert Johnson
13 Old Burlington St.
London W1X 1LA England
01 439 7397
Herbert Johnson has a fine collection of classic hats. There are town-and-

country felt hats such as the Homburg, and the Grosvenor, a formal town hat. Tweed hats, caps, and sporting headwear are also available: the Deerstalker with earflaps, the sporty Eight Piece Cap, Burlington, Hexham and Fyfe. Riding headwear includes a hunting bowler, polo caps, racing hats, and helmets. The Bermuda is a seasonal, wide-brimmed Panama straw hat and a long time favorite.

Houston Trunk Factory
P.O. Box 1425
Bellaire, TX 77401
(800) 231-6404
Texas (800) 329-4259
32-page color catalog, free U.S. and
    overseas. AE, DC, MC, V, MO, PC.
Houston Trunk Factory is one of the leading luggage and leather goods dealers in Texas with over fifteen stores in the state. They offer the luxurious Gold-Pfeil, Pegasus, Tumi, Samsonite, and Tourister lines. There are many items to fit your traveling needs—tiny travel clocks, ladies accessory bags, portable smoke alarms, travel diaries, and shaving kits.

Innovation
487 Hackensack Ave.
River Edge, NJ 07661
(800) 631-0742
New Jersey (201) 487-6000
10-page brochure, free U.S. AE, DC, MC,
    V, MO, PC.
Innovation has 15 luggage stores in America and sells top name brand luggage, portfolios and attachés, at discounts of 20% to 50% off retail prices. Use their handy 800 telephone number.

Jeff Samuel
Combe Farm, West Anstey
South Molton Devon
England
Brochure, free U.S. and overseas. MO,
    PC.
Jeff Samuel hand carves all kinds of walking sticks, crooks, thumb sticks, and rustic knob sticks with either the head or whole shape of an animal, bird, gnome, fish, or mermaid. They are entirely handmade from either ash,

hazel, holly, or thorn wood cut from the valleys around Exmoor. The wood is seasoned and polished with beeswax and should last a lifetime. Almost any carving can be done and prices, of course, vary according to the amount of work required. They start at about $15 and go up.

John Helmer
969 S. W. Broadway
Portland, OR 97205
(503) 223-4976
2-page brochure, free U.S. and overseas.
    MC, V, MO, PC.
John Helmer, haberdasher since 1921, specializes in hats from all over the world. Featured in the brochure are a Greek fisherman's hat, Basque beret, Scottish tam, and a ladies' oversize beret. The prices are most reasonable and postage paid.

The Leather Artisan
Childwold, NY 12922
(518) 359-3102
8-page brochure. MC, V, PC.
Handcrafted cowhide leather handbags range from about $30 to $66, and leather belts from $7.50 to $24.50.

Leather School
Piazza Santa Croce 16
Florence, Italy
244 533 34
16-page color catalog, free U.S. and
    overseas. MO, PC.
Fine Florentine leather goods: bags, wallets, leather-covered boxes, albums, desk sets, and luggage. These beautiful pieces are exported to sell in some of the best shops in foreign countries. The Leather School was established by the church fathers of the Santa Croce church, in Florence, to establish an apprenticeship program for the boys left in the church's care at the end of the war.

Le Sportsac
320 Fifth Ave.
New York, NY 10001

22-page color catalog, free U.S. AE, MC, V, PC.

Le Sportsac is lightweight luggage made of ripstop nylon with built-in selflock zippers and sturdy natural fiber webbings and shoulder straps. There are weekender bags, suit and dress carriers, cargo carriers, and hand bags. Le Sportsac luggage comes in twelve color choices, including a few good-looking tattersall patterns.

Linekin Bay Fabrics
37 I Silver St.
Portland, ME 04112
(207) 774-7563
18-page brochure with swatches, $2.50 U.S. and overseas. AE, MC, V, PC.

Robin Whitten owns a shop that hand weaves lovely shawls, neckties, scarves, lap robes, baby and carriage blankets, and pillows from natural fibers, including mohair, wool, cotton, and silk. Their colors are carefully designed and reflect the colors and textures of Maine. Mohair shawls are about $39, and come in thirteen shades. Handsome hand-woven ties are about $15.

Mark Cross
645 Fifth Ave.
New York, NY 10022
(800) 233-1678
48-page color catalog, free U.S. Does not sell overseas. AE, CB, DC, MC, V, MO, PC.

Mark Cross was founded in 1845 by Henry Cross of Boston. All the fine leather goods are handcrafted exclusively for Mark Cross by artisans, using the finest materials. Choice leathers of calfskin, pigskin, lizard, ostrich, lambskin and suede, and exquisite nappa leather, are combined with elegant design. Their line includes luxurious small leather accessories, handbags, attachés, desk sets, and luggage. Mark Cross is not for the small pocketbook.

North Country Leather
1 Front St.
P.O. Box 25
East Rochester, NH 03867
(603) 332-0707

6-page brochure, $2 refundable U.S. Does not sell overseas. MC, V, MO, PC.

Handbags of selected cowhide leathers and sturdy brass hardware are available at about 50% off retail price. The brochure shows drawings of about thirty styles of lined and unlined handbags, with prices ranging from about $30 to $97.

Pagano Gloves
3–5 Church St.
Johnstown, NY 12095
(518) 762-8425
34-page color catalog, $1.50; overseas $2.50. MC, V, MO, PC.

Pagano specializes in top grade deerskin leather and cowhide gloves and mittens. Over twenty styles of gloves are shown, as well as leather jackets, coats, handbags, slippers, and slip-on shoes.

Swaine Adeney Brigg & Sons, Ltd.
185 Piccadilly
London W1V OHA England
01 734 4277
20-page color catalog, $4 U.S. and overseas. AE, DC, MC, V, MO, PC.

Swaine Adeney and Brigg's is one of London's oldest and most traditional family-run businesses, established in 1750, and royal warrant holder. They offer fine gentleman's umbrellas, more than twenty different walking sticks, distinguished hats (grey ascot shell top hats and classic black bowlers), wallets, luggage, and travel accessories. There are also items for the gentlemen hunter, such as a picnic basket complete with china, fleece-lined gun slips, leather-trimmed game bags, and most important—a seatstick complete with umbrella, so you don't get all mucky.

Villari Handerkerchief Company
30 West 54 St.
New York, NY 10019
(212) 596-2991
2-page brochure, .50¢ U.S. and overseas. MO, PC.

Lia Villari makes handerkerchiefs for the bride and as gifts for members of the wedding party. The lovely handkerchiefs are made from white Irish linen and bordered with French lace, for the ladies. Men's handkerchiefs are always hand-rolled. The handkerchiefs can be personalized on request with the bride's name, monogram, or wedding date. They could also be used to commemorate a birthdate, or personalized for a special gift. The linen baby bonnet ($12.50), is designed to open up into a full-sized wedding handkerchief.

LEATHER AND FUR

Bootleg Leathers
P.O. Box 564
Plymouth, WI 53073
(414) 892-4590
12-page brochure, $1.50 U.S. and
    overseas. Minimum order $25. MC, V,
    MO, PC.
Bootleg Leathers specializes in handcrafted one-of-a-kind deerskin garments and accessories. Each garment is made to order from your specifications: leather shirts, jackets, briefcases, halter tops, sheepskin mittens, wallets, billfolds, chaps, and vests. They also will complete orders for customers who supply their own deerskins.

Cornelius Furs
72 Castlereagh Street
Sydney Australia 2000
02 232 5822
12-page color brochure, free U.S. and
    overseas. AE, DC, MC, V, MO.
Cornelius Furs is one of the top fur houses in the world. Started in 1912, they employ about 200 people in their design studio, factory, and four retail shops in Australia. Their range is extensive and includes rabbit, fox, chinchilla, and mink. A full-length Australian fox coat is about $1,800.

Custom Coat Co.
227 N. Washington St.
Berlin, WI 54923
(414) 361-0900
26-page color catalog, free U.S. Does not
    sell overseas.
Custom-made deerskin coats, jackets, and vests for men and women. The catalog shows their complete line and list prices, using either the customer's own hides or Custom Coat's stock of deerskin. If a customer sends his own deer hides, and they are insufficient to fill the order, Custom Coat supplies the balance of leather to complete the garment. They also make gloves, mittens, wallets, slippers, and golf club mitts.

The Deerskin Place
283 Akron Road
Ephrata, PA 17522
(717) 733-7624
8-page brochure, free U.S. Does not sell
    overseas. M, V, MO, PC.
Elam Fisher, owner, offers an excellent selection of quality deerskin jackets, handbags, wallets, gloves, moccasins, and slip-on shoes for men and women. The savings are about 30% to 50% off retail prices, and Mr. Fisher is always most helpful.

Deerskin Trading Post
119 Foster Street
Peabody, MA 01960
(617) 532 2260
52-page color catalog, free U.S. Does not
    sell overseas. AE, MC, V, MO, PC.
"Quality leather products for 37 years" doesn't begin to describe the variety and quality of leather goods available from Deerskin Trading Post. Fashionable full-length coats and jackets in deerskin, Shearling, suede, Australian opossum fur, and eelskin leather. There are elegant suede and leather suits, pants suits, and many lovely leather accessories.

Li Skinntrykk
Lille Ulefos
Basarhallene Domkirken
Oslo 1 Norway
035 84002
4-page color brochure, free U.S. and
    overseas.
Li Dahl has revived the ancient Norwegian handcraft of decorating sheepskin blankets with handprinted symbols. She uses similar techniques in producing unique high fashion leather goods: capes, coats, dresses and hats. Her

garments, made from the softest suede and lambskin, have been exhibited all over the world.

Mademoiselle Furs, Inc.
350 7th Ave.
New York, NY 10001
(212) 736-8620
12-page color catalog, free U.S. and
  overseas. AE, DC, MC, V, MO, PC.
"We are the mail order kings of the fur industry." The catalog is page after page of stunning furs on gorgeous women. Norwegian blue fox, rabbit, Australian red fox, Kalgan lamb, sable, and mink. Their prices are competitive and range from $49 to $40,000.

North Beach Leather
P.O. Box 99682 Dept. IM
San Francisco, CA 94109
(415) 922-5452
16-page color catalog, $3 U.S. and
  overseas. AE, MC, V, MO, PC.
North Beach Leather creates high fashion leather clothing and is a favorite clothier for show and record industry people—and has a large celebrity clientele. Most items are designed and created exclusively for North Beach. Each season they offer a very special collection of coats, jackets, dresses, and coordinates including skirts, pants, and tops. Electric blue lamb suede jumpsuit, worn belted or beautifully baggy, is about $635. The red chamois cocktail dress, with a snakeskin-trimmed neckline and snakeskin cinch belt, is about $750. There are two pages of body beautifuls modeling bathing suits: a white leather maillot and a lamb suede fringed bikini (with very little fringe). Swimsuits range from $125 to $170. Slightly wild, and very wonderful.

Pierre Furs
130 West 30th St.
New York, NY 10001
(212) 244-3790
4 pages, free.
Write for Pierre Furs' latest "style report," a series showing the latest fur fashions.

Rahikainen & Co.
PB 75
00211 Helsinki 21 Finland
6922 796
16-page color brochure, free U.S. and
  overseas. AE, DC, V, MO, PC.
Furs by Rahikainen are internationally known for their distinctive design and detail. There are beautiful full-length Finnish blue fox worked in stripes with leather, mink-lined cotton coats, and Russian squirrel coat with Kolinsky insets. They're truly beautiful.

Sickafus
Rts. 78 & 183
Strausstown, PA 19559
(215) 488-1782
16-page color catalog, .50¢; overseas $1.
  AE, MC, V.
Located on the northern tip of Pennsylvania Dutch country, Sickafus stocks a good variety of sheepskin products: men's bomber jackets (starting at about $199), closed and open seam jackets, vests, and ladies' long fitted coats. They also have ladies' leather blazers, snuggly sheepskin slippers, auto seat covers, and hats.

Skinny's Down Under
P.O. Box 88067
Seattle, WA 98188
(800) 426-4626
16-page color catalog, free U.S. and
  overseas. MC, V, MO, PC.
Skinny's Down Under has a luxurious line of Australian sheepskin and Shearling products. The soft Shearling aviator jacket is popular, made of warm double-faced sheepskin with knit cuffs and waistband ($250). There are cozy-looking slippers in many styles, car seatcovers, baby stroller liners and, of course, sheepskin throw rugs.

Specialty Leathers of California
388 Orange Show Lane
San Bernardino, CA 92408
(714) 884-2216
4-page brochure, $1 U.S. and overseas.
  MC, V, MO, PC.
Men's and women's calfskin leather coats and jackets. They also have some suede and cabretta garments. All at

discount prices—45% to 65% off retail prices. Women's fitted blazer with satin and acetate lining is about $129, men's lined sport coat about $139.

SHOES

Alan McAfee, Ltd.
5 Cork Street
London W1X 1PB England
734 7301
6-page color brochure, $1; overseas free. AE, DC, MC, V, MO, PC.
Finest quality men's shoes available by fittings, from stock or made to order. Alan McAfee's shoes have been previously sold by Saks Fifth Avenue, Nieman Marcus, Marshall Field, and others. Prices range from $44 to $108. There is a choice of styles and leathers, including turtle and ostrich.

Bostonian
111 N. Forney Ave.
Hanover, PA 17331
(800) 345-8500
Color catalog, free U.S. MC, V, MO, PC.
Bostonian has over 100,000 men's shoes in stock, in sizes 6 to 15 and widths from A to EEE.

Chester Beard Shoes
2716 Colby
Everett, WA 98201
(206) 259-2716
6-page brochure, free U.S. and overseas. MC, V, MO, PC.

Church's English Shoes, Ltd.
428 Madison Ave.
New York, NY 10017
(212) 755-4313
32-page color brochure, free. U.S. and overseas.
Church's tradition for making fine shoes was established in 1873 in England. Prices range from $150 to $1,300 for a pair of alligator leather shoes. (Sorry, not available in size 12½.)

Cosmo Pedics
Unique Merchandising Mart
Building 16
Hanover, PA 17333
(800) 621-5800
32-page color catalog, free U.S. and overseas. AE, DC, MC, V, MO, PC.

Danner Shoe Manufacturer Co.
5188 S. E. International Way
Milwaukee, OR 97222
(503) 653-2920
12-page color catalog, free U.S. Does not sell overseas. MC, V, MO, PC.
Danner is well known for their outstanding boots: lightweight, long-wearing, watertight, stylish yet practical. There are many styles of boots to choose from: outdoor, walking, hiking, hunting, logging, work boots, and great casual boots. Danner Lights, made with leather and breathable Gore-Tex, are quite popular and sell for about $104.

Hanover Shoe
111 N. Forney Ave.
Hanover, PA 17331
(800) 345-8500
(717) 632-7575
40-page color catalog, free U.S. Does not sell overseas. AE, CB, DC, MC, V, MO, PC.
High quality footwear for men and women at reasonable prices. Started in 1899.

Hershey Custom Shoe Co.
RFD #3 Box 7390
Farmington, ME 04938
(207) 778-4303
4-page brochure, free U.S. and overseas. MO, PC.
Bart Hershey owns probably the only custom-made running shoe manufacturing company. Bart personally makes each shoe and can accommodate a large variety of cushioning components to suit the individual runner's need. Priced at $150 a pair.

Hill Brothers, Inc.
99 Ninth St.
Lynchburg, VA 24504
(804) 528-1000
48-page color catalog, free U.S. Does not sell overseas. AE, MC, V, MO, PC.
Hill Brothers offers a great selection of women's shoes in hard-to-find sizes,

Most of their shoes are made in their own factory. Dress and casual shoes, sandals, boots, and slippers are offered year round. Sizes 5 to 12 and widths AAAA to D, E and EE.

Imprints
Unique Merchandising Mart
Building 20
Hanover, PA 17333
(800) 621-5800
16-page color catalog, free U.S. and
  overseas. AE, CB, DC, MC, V, PC.
Women's shoes in popular sizes.

John Lobb Bootmaker
9 St. James Street
London SW1A 1EF England
01 930 3664
John Lobb's prestigious firm has been bootmaker to more than one British King, to European royalty, and other distinguished gentry. Should you require "the best" in handmade-to-measure boots, or men's and women's shoes, John Lobb's will send you a portfolio showing you available ready-made styles, or an appointment card for a representative to fit you on his next trip to this country. They tour about twice yearly.

Kow Hoo Shoe Co.
23 Hennessy Rd.
Wanchai, Hong Kong
5 276 147
Price list, free U.S. and overseas. PC.
Custom-made leather shoes and boots for men and women. Prices range from $45 to $52 for calfskin, suede, and patent leather. They also offer snakeskin, kangaroo, kid, lizard, lizardgator, sea turtle, ostrich, and French baby alligator leathers.

Lawson Hill Leather and Shoe Co.
61 A Emery St.
Sanford, ME 04073
(207) 324-0161
24-page color catalog, free; overseas $1.
  MC, V, MO, PC.
American name-brand women's shoes in many sizes and widths. There are sandals, boots, slippers, pumps, and casuals in some styles and colors not readily found in retail stores. In sizes 3

to 12 and widths AAAA to EEE. You have a full thirty-one days to wear the shoes and, if not satisfied, return for full refund or exchange.

Lee Kee Boot and Shoemaker, Ltd.
65 Peking Rd.
Kowloon, Hong Kong
4-page price list, free U.S. and overseas.
  BD, MO, PC.
Custom-made men's and women's shoes, golf shoes, jodhpur boots, riding boots, cowboy boots, and lowboots in all the usual leathers. Softer leather, suede and patent leather shoes are priced at about $60. In addition to the more unusual leathers, they offer an extended variety including wild boar, sharkskin, antelope, gnu, sea lion, and elephant.

Merrill's Westgate Shoes
99 Westgate Dr.
Brockton, MA 02403
(617) 586-1509
24-page catalog, free U.S. and overseas.
  MC, V.
American-made, brand-name women's shoes in hard-to-find sizes, from slims to extra wides. Unworn shoes are refunded if returned within two weeks.

Mooney & Gilbert
31 West 57th St.
New York, NY 10019
(212) 355-6674
12-page catalog, free U.S. Does not sell
  overseas. MC, V, MO, PC.
Established in 1942 to provide shoes for women in hard-to-fit extra, extra narrow widths and narrow-fitting heels. Sizes range from 6 to 12 in widths from AAAAAA to B. Styles include elegant dress shoes, casuals, tailored shoes, boots, sport shoes, and tennis sneakers in popular styles. Returns within ten days are gladly refunded.

National Odd Shoe Exchange
R. R. 4
Indianola, IA 50125
(515) 961 5125
The National Odd Shoe Exchange is a service organization to help foot-handicapped people whose feet are not the same size, or people with only one foot. The exchange brings together

people with similar shoe problems to help them in exchanging shoes with those of opposite shoe sizes. They offer a list of 14,000 participating customers, and names of shoe manufacturing companies that donate their mismates. Lifetime membership registration fee is $32.50, of which $25.00 is a lifetime registration and $7.50 is the annual dues. Send for their newsletter and brochure.

Nierman's Tall Girl Shoes
17 N. State. St. Suite 1202
Chicago, IL 60602
(312) 346-9797
16-page color catalog, free; overseas $1.
  AE, MC, V, MO, PC.
Nierman's carries a complete line of footwear for tall women in hard-to-find sizes. Everything includes shoes, golf shoes, boots, and highly styled hosiery. They even have a nice selection of nursing shoes.

Peter Limmer and Sons
Box 88 Rte. 16A
Intervale, NH 03845
(603) 356-5378
6-page brochure, free U.S. Does not sell
  overseas. MO, PC.
Peter Limmer offers custom-made boots for hiking and backpacking. They are made of full grain, Swiss chrome-tanned, water-repellent black cowhide leather. The upper is made of only one piece and has one inside side seam, which provides less potential for leakage and tearing. The Limmer Hiking Boot sells for $150.

The Shoe Bazaar
159 S. Central Ave.
Hartsdale, NY 10530
(914) 997-0313
16-page color catalog, MC, V, MO, PC.
Women's name-brand shoes, boots, slippers, and purses.

Slipper House
1450 Ala Moana Blvd. #1200
Honolulu, HI 96814
(808) 949-0155
5-page brochure, free U.S. and overseas.
  AE, MC, V, MO, PC.

Slippers and sandals made in Hawaii. Prices range from $8.50 to $34, with over forty styles to choose from: thongs, Japanese getas, wedgies, goza mat slippers, Holo holo slippers, and more.

Sofwear
1811 San Jacinto
Houston, TX 77002
(713) 650-0916
45-page color catalog, AE, MC, V, PC.
Hundreds of styles of fashionable women's shoes at reasonable prices.

Syd Kushner
1204 Arch St.
Philadelphia, PA 19107
(215) 665-1538
32-page catalog, free U.S. Does not sell
  overseas. AE, DC, MC, V, MO, PC.
Syd Kushner offers current styles of hard-to-find women's wide width shoes at very good prices. Sizes 5 to 12 in widths C to EEE. Over eleven styles of boots, elegant dress shoes, pumps, casuals, loafers, and slip-ons.

Todd's
5 S. Wagash
Chicago, IL 60603
(312) 372-1335
24-page color catalog, free U.S. and
  overseas. MC, V, MO, PC.
Good-looking boots: Chukka, cowboy, ranch, hiking, sidewinders, workboots, logger's boots, and snaker's. They have an excellent selection (a separate catalog devoted to them) of moccasins, from infant sizes to adult men's and women's.

Village Shoemaker
Freeport, ME 04032
(207) 865-6463
32-page mostly color catalog. MC, V, PC.
Casual men's and women's shoes and moccasins.

W. C. Russell Moccasin Co.
285 S. W. Franklin
Berlin, WI 54923
(414) 361-2252
32-page color catalog. MC, V, MO, PC.
Men's boots, casual shoes, and moccasins.

UNIFORMS

Algy Costumes & Uniforms
440 N. E. First Ave.
Hallandale, FL 33009
(305) 457-8100
50-page color catalog, free U.S. and
  overseas. MC, V, MO, PC.
Uniforms for Majorettes, drill teams,
and color guards. There are also dance
costumes and supplies for ballet, tap,
and baton.

Bencone Uniforms
121 Carver Ave.
Westwood, NJ 07675
32-page color catalog, free U.S. Does not
  sell overseas. AE, MC, V, MO, PC.
A full line of professional medical and
dental uniforms. Lab coats, shoes, and
hosiery.

Eastern Wear-Guard
P.O. Box 400
Hingham, MA 02043
(800) 343-4406
52-page color catalog, free U.S. AE, MC,
  V, MO, PC.
Work clothes and industrial uniforms.

I. Buss & Co.
738 Broadway
New York, NY 10003
(212) 242-3338
20-page catalog, free U.S. Does not sell
  overseas. AE, MC, V, MO.
Authentic military surplus clothing,
mostly European (English, French, and
Italian). They have rain slickers, French
army raincoats, British drill pants, bush
jackets, jungle fatigue jackets, khaki
pants, Swiss army bags, and much more.

Industrial Uniform Co.
906 E. Waterman
Wichita, KS 67202
(800) 835-2834
(316) 264-2871
32-page catalog, free U.S. Does not sell
  overseas. MC, V, MO, PC.
Industrial uniforms in many styles—
hats, smocks, aprons and jackets.

Hundreds of in-stock emblems are also
available.

Laurence Corner
62-64 Hampstead Rd.
London NW1 2NU England
01 388 6811
30-page catalog, free U.S. and overseas.
  AE, DC, MC, V, MO, PC.
Government surplus clothing and
offbeat fashions. There are costumes,
theatrical wear, expedition and safari
wear, and a great deal of miscellany.

Ruvel & Co., Inc.
3037 North Clark
Chicago, IL 60657
(312) 248-1922
64-page catalog, $3; overseas $2. MO, PC.
Ruvel sells army and navy surplus,
military and commercial sporting
goods. There are camouflage fatigues,
army and navy jackets and coats, hats,
camping equipment, binoculars,
holsters, helmets, gas masks, and more.

Sara Glove Company, Inc.
16 Cherry Ave.
P.O. Box 4069
Waterbury, CT 06704
(203) 574-4090
36-page catalog, $1; overseas free.
  Minimum order $25. MC, V, MO, PC.
Industrial safety products including
gloves, coveralls, first aid kits, hard hats,
eye protection, and earmuffs.

U.S. Cavalry Store, Inc.
1375 North Wilson Rd.
Radcliff, KY 40160
(502) 351-1164
100-page color catalog, $3; overseas $6.
  AE, MC, V, MO.
Military uniforms and equipment are
either genuine issue or manufactured to
government specifications. There are
surplus, martial arts uniforms,
camouflage and hunting gear, survival
foods, and supplies for the hunter and
outdoorsmen.

COLLECTIBLES

SEE ALSO
- Antiques
- Art
- College and Prep School Gift Shops
- Crafts
- Gifts
- Handcrafts

GENERAL

Alingh Dimensional Images, Inc.
2705 70th
Des Moines, IA 50322
(515) 276-7703
12-page brochure, $1; overseas free. MO,
PC.
Alingh offers memorabilia of movie and
television, comic strips, western
legends, and Marilyn Monroe.

Antique Electronic Supply
1725 W. University Suite 2
Tempe, AZ 85281
(602) 894-9503
16-page catalog, $1 U.S. Does not sell
overseas. MC, V, MO, PC.
Antique Electronic Supply specializes in
obsolete tubes and parts for the radio
collector hobbyist. There are over 2,000
tube types in stock, including many
antique and unusual types. They also
carry books on antique radios and
phonograph collecting.

Avalon Forge
409 Gun Rd.
Baltimore, MD 21227
(301) 242-8431
40-page catalog, $1; overseas $2.
  Minimum order $15. MO, PC.
Avalon Forge makes quality
reproductions of items in use in
eighteenth-century America. Each item

is well researched and documented and
includes cookware, leather goods,
woodenware, brassware, military goods,
tools, and items made from cow
horns.

Cinema City
P.O. Box 1012
Muskegon, MI 49441
(616) 722-7760
24-page catalog, $1 U.S. and overseas.
Cinema City offers original movie
memorabilia including posters, stills,
lobby cards, press kits, pressbooks, and
unusual movie promotional items.
Their items date back to the 1920s as
well as the recently released big hits.

Commemorative Imports
5901 Omaha Ave. N.
Box 21
Stillwater, MN 55082
(612) 439-6993
8-page brochure, free U.S. Does not sell
  overseas. AE, MC, V, MO, PC.
Limited edition collector's plates
including Shulamuth Wulfing,
Hummel, Bareuther, and the Rockwell
Society.

The Dance Mart
Box 48 Homecrest Station
Brookly, NY 11229
(212) 627-0477

16-page brochure, self addressed
    stamped envelope U.S.; overseas 1
    International Reply Coupon. MO, PC.
Collectibles of the dance theater
including ballet scores, autographs, and
original works of art (including costume
sketches and paintings). There are
many books on dance, current and out-
of-print.

Down's Collector's Showcase
2200 S. 114th Street
Milwaukee, WI 53227
(414) 327-3300
56-page color catalog, $1 U.S. Does not
    sell overseas. AE, CB, DC, MC, V, MO,
    PC.
Down's is one of America's largest
suppliers of Limited Edition Collector's
plates. They also carry bells, thimbles,
spoons, eggs, music boxes, and dolls.

Elizabeth Edge Studios
5060 West Lake Rd.
Canandaigua, NY 14424
(716) 396-2656
8-page color brochure, free U.S. and
    overseas. MC, V, MO, PC.
Elizabeth Edge sells reproductions of
cast-iron handpainted mechanical
banks that were originally made in the
late 1800s. The Punch and Judy bank
($76.45) of 1882 is designed so Punch
takes a whack at Judy when she deposits
a coin.

Front Row Photos
P.O. Box 484-F
Nesconset, NY 11767
36-page catalog, $2; overseas $5.
    Minimum order $5. MO, PC.
Front Row Photos offers photos, buttons,
and collectibles of Rock Stars. There are
hundreds of descriptions of Rock Stars
in concert. Glossy photos are available
in 8 × 10 in. and 3½ × 5¼ in. sizes.

Gimbel & Sons Country Store
36 Commercial St.
P.O. Box 57
Boothbay Harbor, ME 04538
(207) 633-5088
32-page color catalog, free U.S. MC, V,
    PC.
Gimbel & Sons offers many collectibles
including porcelain dolls dressed in

authentic Bavarian dress, thimbles and
display cases, Wedgewood Queensware,
bisque dolls, figurines, and plates.

The Great Americana Store
17 Russell Woods Rd.
Great Neck, NY 11021
(516) 466-4555
24-page catalog, .75¢ U.S. Does not sell
    overseas. MC, V.
The Great Americana Store sells
original or high quality replicas of
nostalgic items from America's past:
Burma Shave signs, real gumball
machines, authentic reproductions of
advertising signs, and thermometers.

Hake's Americana & Collectibles
P.O. Box 1444
York, PA 17405
(717) 848-1333
96-page catalog sample copy $2;
    overseas $3. Annual subscription $8;
    overseas $15. MC, V, MO, PC.
Hake's offers over 2,000 collectibles (in
over 100 collecting categories) for sale
to the highest mail or telephone bidder.
All catalog items are illustrated,
accurately described, and have an
estimated value. Bidders submit their
bids over a three-week period and, on
the closing date, may call to learn the
bidding results. Most of the items are
one-of-a-kind, and they specialize in
1930s Disney items, toys, radios,
premiums, cowboy heroes, and 1950s
television collectibles.

The Hamilton Group
9550 Regency Square Blvd.
Jacksonville, FL 32211
(904) 723-6020
Brochure, free U.S. and overseas. AE,
    DC, MC, V, MO, PC.
The Hamilton Group is a large direct
mail marketer of limited edition
collector's plates, figurines, bells, steins,
pewter, Chokin, and terra cotta. Prices
range from $20 to $240. The Hamilton
Group introduces between ten and
twelve new products each year.

Hughes'
2410 North Hill Dr.
Williamsport, PA 17701
(717) 326-1045

20-page brochure, $1; overseas $2. MO, PC.

Hughes' sells old and rare American and British newspapers from 1644 through the Civil War period. Also, eighteenth-century magazines and some colonial documents.

James H. Crawley Records
246 Church St.
London N9 9HQ England
01 807 7760
40-page catalog, $8; Europe $4, Far East $8.50.
James H. Crawley buys and sell 78-rpm gramophone records, deleted LPs, and music memorabilia such as photos and autographs. Since 1950.

John and Jo Withers
Eaton House
14 Station Road, Madeley
Teleford TF7 5AY England
0952 585131
6-page color brochure, $1.50; overseas $1. MO.
John and Jo Withers individually hand paint enamel boxes, thimbles, and miniature paintings. The brochure contains photographs of their most recent work. They sell through art galleries and upscale retail shops. They accept commissioned work, such as an exclusive enamel of your house (or pet) with an appropriate inscription. Two-inch diameter enamel boxes with silver-plated bezel are priced at about $40.

Kendal Playing Card Sales
3 Oakbank House
Skelsmergh Kendal
Cumbria LA8 9AJ England
14-page price list, free surface mail, 50¢ airmail; overseas free. MO, PC.
Kendal buys and sells unusual playing cards, old and new, from all over the world. They carry over 250 different types of playing cards. There are bridge cards featuring history, folklore, and art. There are cards of national and regional games from India, Japan, and China. Tarot cards, books on cards, and reprints of famous historical cards are also sold.

Liberty Gifts
2324 Liberty St.
Trenton, NJ 08629
(800) 257-5147
(800) 792-8844
130-page color catalog, free U.S. and overseas. AE, MC, V, MO, PC.
Liberty catalog states, "The World's Largest 'Hummel' retailer." They do have many pages of Hummel figurines, including the complete nineteen-piece nativity set for $1,188. There are also music boxes by Schmid-Anri, and a fine collection of Norman Rockwell figurines.

Navy Arms Company
689 Bergen Blvd.
Ridgefield, NJ 07657
(201) 945-2500
32-page catalog, $2 U.S. and overseas. Minimum order $25. AE, MC, V, MO.
Navy Arms sells replica firearms representing the eras from the Revolutionary War to the turn of the twentieth century. All firearms are technically functional.

The Nostalgia Factory
Brick Market Place
Newport, RI 02840
(401) 849-3441
4-page price list, $1; overseas $2. AE, DC, MC, V, MO, PC.
The Nostalgia Factory carries a selection of twentieth-century U.S. memorabilia. There are original political buttons, advertising graphics, old signs and posters. There are also old cigar boxes, and orange and fruit crate labels.

The Old Train Shop
3 New Bridge St.
Exeter, Devon
England
31548
Computer print-out of items in stock, 2 International Reply Coupons U.S. and overseas. MC, V, MO.
The Old Train specializes in old metal toys, especially Meccano Ltd. products from 1902 to 1979, including Dinky Toys, Hornby O Gauge railways, and Hornby Duplo up to 1964. They also carry Lesney Matchbox toys, "Modes of Yesteryear"

from 1956 to date, obsolete Corgi Toys, and Bing and Bassett-Lowke.

Palmetto Collectibles
RT. 1 Hwy. 321
Norway, SC 29113
(803) 263-4730
100-page catalog, $3.25; overseas $3.25 surface, $5 air mail. Minimum order $35. MO, PC.
Palmetto offers collectibles of Coca-Cola and breweriana. There are posters, trays, mirrors, bottles, and knives with the slogans and trademark of Coca-Cola.

Shopping Service Gifts
The Thimble Specialists
63 Cranbourne Gardens
London NW11 OJB England
01 455-1815
12-page brochure $3 U.S. and overseas. AE, MC, V, MO, PC.
Shopping Service Gifts is the largest direct marketing thimble firm in Great Britain. They offer thimbles collected from around the world, mini bells, mini tankards and candle-snuffers.

Thimble Collectors Guild
The Bell Tower
New Lanark ML11 7BR England
14-page brochure, free U.S. and overseas. AE, MC, V, MO, PC.
The Thimble Collectors Guild was established in 1982 by Scotland Direct Limited. They offer many thimbles, including Spode and Wedgewood, and many lovely British commemorative thimbles.

Thurston Moore Country, Ltd.
P.O. Box 1829
Montrose, CO 80142
(303) 249-8363
24-page newsalog, free U.S. and overseas. MC, V, PC.
Thurston Moore has a large collection of country music products. There are books, including *The Stars of Country Music* ($14.95) and *The Encyclopedia of Folk Country and Western Music* ($50). There are sheet music, posters, hard-to-find records, personality key chains, postcards, and personalized dollar bills.

AUTOGRAPHS

Charles Hamilton Galleries
200 West 57th St.
New York, NY 10019
(212) 245-7313
44-page catalog, U.S. and overseas. MO, PC.
Charles Hamilton Galleries is a major dealer of autographs. The catalog contains descriptions of letters and documents, and their signatures. There are many celebrities', movie stars', political leaders', and presidents' autographs for sale.

La Scala Autographs
P.O. Box 268
Plainsboro, NJ 08536
110-page catalog, free U.S. and overseas. MC, V, MO, PC.
La Scala specializes in autographs of operatic, musical, theatrical, and cinematic performers, plus composers and writers.

Walter R. Benjamin Autographs
Box 255
Schribner Hollow Rd.
Hunter, NY 12442
(518) 263-4133
24-page catalog subscription, $10; overseas $20.
Benjamin's deals in original letters and manuscripts of Presidents, musicians, authors, American Revolutionary figures, Civil War figures, and notable foreign persons, with emphasis on the content of the letters.

COINS AND STAMPS

Colonial Coins
909 Travis
Houston, TX 77002
(713) 654-0052
62-page newsalog, free U.S. AE, MC, V.

H. E. Harris & Co., Inc.
Box O
Boston, MA 02117
(617) 269-5200

48-page catalog, free U.S. Does not sell
overseas. Minimum order $10. AE,
MC, V, MO, PC.
H. E. Harris publishes their own line of
stamp albums, both world-wide and
American. They offer an extensive line
of stamp packets, stamp collecting
accessories, and first day covers.

Littleton Stamp & Coin Co., Inc.
253 Union St.
Littleton, NH 03561
(603) 444-5386
128-page U.S. stamp catalog, 56-page
U.S. coin and banknote catalog, free
U.S. Does not sell overseas. AE, DC,
MC, V, MO, PC.
Founded in 1945 by Maynard Sundman,
it remains today a family business
providing U.S. coins and stamps for
collectors.

Midland Stamp Co.
P.O. Box 22308
Memphis, TN 38122
(901) 452-8701
20-page catalog, free U.S. and overseas.
MO, PC.
Midland offers postage stamps and
picture postcards for collectors and
dealers. Since 1964.

Paramount Coin Corporation
600 Union Rd.
Englewood, OH 45322
(513) 836-8641
20-page catalog, free U.S. and overseas.
AE, MC, V, MO, PC.
Paramount specializes in rare coin sales
and purchases as well as modern issue
coinage offerings.

Unicover Corporation
One Unicover Center
Cheyenne, WY 82202–0001
(307) 634-5911
40-page catalog, free U.S. and overseas.
AE, DC, MC, V, PC.
Unicover Corporation imports stamps
and first day covers from 160 countries
worldwide, and exports to various
countries. Each first day cover includes
a cachet and historical information, and
often includes an album to store or
display the product.

United States Stamp Co., Inc.
368 Bush St.
San Francisco, CA 94104
(415) 421-7398
67-page catalog, free U.S. and overseas.
AE, MC, V, MO, PC.
Since 1939, United States Stamp
Company has been supplying stamps
and supplies for collectors. They carry
accessories, albums, and a worldwide
stock of stamps.

Village Coin Shop
P.O. Box 207
Plaistow, NH 03865
(603) 382-5492
32-page catalog, free U.S. and overseas.
Minimum order $7. MC, V, MO, PC.

COMICS

Grand Book, Inc.
659 Grand St.
Brooklyn, NY 11211
(212) 384-4059
12-page catalog, $1; overseas $1.50. MO,
PC.
Grand stocks over one million collector's
comics from good to mint condition,
from the 1940s to the present. Since 1952.

Russ Cochran Publisher
P.O. Box 469
West Plains, MO 65775
(417) 256-2226
18-page some color catalog, free U.S.
MC, V, MO, PC.
Russ Cochran offers original comic art
and related collector's items, including
animation from Walt Disney Studios,
original newspaper comic art from daily
strips and Sunday pages, and original
illustrations and paintings by Carl Barks
and Frank Frazetta.

West Side Comics
107 W. 86
New York, NY 10024
(212) 724-0432
18-page brochure, .50¢; overseas $1.
Minimum order $5. MC, V, PC.
West Side offers old and new comic
books. They stock back issues of all
Marvel and DC comics, dating back to

Fantastic Four #1. There is also a large selection of Golden Age and Silver Age comics.

DOLLS AND MINIATURES

Doll House Factory Outlet
325 Division St.
Boonton, NJ 07005
(201) 335-5501
32-page booklet $2; overseas $3. AE, MC, V, MO, PC.
The Doll House Factory Outlet is one of the largest manufacturers and distributors of doll houses and miniatures. They sell at discounts of up to 75% below retail price.

The Doll House Toys
29 The Market
Covent Garden
London WC2 8RE England
01-379 7243
28-page catalog, $4; overseas $1.50.
The Doll House specializes in handmade doll houses, miniature furniture, and accessories—many made exclusively for their shop, some imported from Korea and Taiwan.

Eric Horne
54, Majorfield Rd.
Topsham Exeter
Devon Ex3 OES England
Brochure, $2 U.S. and overseas. MO.
Eric Horne handcrafts miniature handpainted wooden dolls with movable arms and legs. They range in size from an incredibly small ¼ inch to one-inch, which is the smallest fully jointed doll that bends at the elbow and knee as well. The sizes increase to two, three, four, seven and one-half, and eight and one-half inches.

Favorites From the Past
5401 Redfield Dr.
P.O. Box 888577
Atlanta, GA 30356–0577
48-page catalog, $1.50 U.S. Does not sell overseas. MC, V, MO, PC.
Hundreds of miniature furniture pieces, doll houses, and display boxes are available from Favorites of the Past.

House of Nisbet
Dunster Park
Winscombe
Avon BS25 1AG England
0934 84 2905
16-page color catalog, free U.S. and overseas. AE, DC, MC, V, MO, PC.
Peggy Nisbet makes over 100 historical portrait and costume dolls. Each doll is approximately eight to twelve inches tall. Prices range from $30 to $60.

Kimport Dolls
P.O. Box 495
Independence, MO 64501
(816) 461-0757
16-page brochure, annual subscription $3; overseas $6. MC, V, MO, PC.
Kimport is one of the oldest and largest companies in America dealing exclusively in dolls for collectors. They have been reviewed in many national magazines. They feature all types of dolls for collectors including imported foreign costume dolls, modern dolls, artist dolls, and antique dolls, books, and stands.

The Miniature Mart
1807 Octavia St.
San Francisco, CA 94109
(415) 563-8745
78-page some color catalog, $4; overseas $6. Minimum order $10. MO, PC.
The Miniature Mart offers an exquisite collection of miniature furniture and accessories, scaled one inch to one foot. 80 percent of the miniatures in the catalog are manufactured in The Miniature Mart's studio. They are famous for displaying the Maynard Manor, a forty-room miniature castle with over 8,000 individual miniatures.

Paul A. Henfield
Standard Doll Co.
23–83 31st St.
Long Island City, NY 11105
(212) 721-7787
75-page color catalog, $3; overseas $5. Minimum order $25. AE, MC, V, MO, PC.
Paul A. Henfield carries china and bisque doll kits along with the supplies and materials needed to complete them.

They carry clothes patterns, books, and doll parts. Since 1922.

Quest-Eridon Books
5 Court Place
Puyallup, WA 98371
(206) 845-0340
10-page brochure, 50¢ U.S. and overseas. Loraine Burdick offers collectibles, celebrity dolls and paper dolls, comic items, and reprints of rare paper dolls in both color and black and white. Loraine Burdick has written a number of articles and books on paper doll collecting which are also for sale.

Scientific Models
340 Snyder Ave.
Berkley Heights, NJ 07922
(201) 464-7070
16-page color catalog, $1; overseas $2. AE, MC, V, MO, PC.
Scientific models offers miniature furniture kits and accessories. They are mostly museum quality scale replicas of period furniture for doll houses, collectors, or display.

Warrick Miniatures
P.O. Box 1498
Portsmouth, NH 03801
(603) 431-7139
10-page brochure, $1; overseas $3. MC, V, MO, PC.
Warrick offers modern-day versions of the traditional gloss-painted, moveable-arm toy soldiers. They are cast in metal and sculpted with an antique toy implement. The figures range from Napoleonic soldiers to circus figurines to Santa Claus.

MAPS AND PRINTS

American Map Corporation
46–35 54th Rd.
Maspeth, NY 11378
(212) 784-0055
35-page catalog, free U.S. Minimum orders $10. MO, PC.
American Map has many U.S. and world maps. There are maps of metropolitan areas, individual state maps, city street maps, principal city maps, and many varieties of world maps.

Collectors Treasures
Hogarth House
Hight Street, Wendover
Bucks HP22 6DU England
624402
No catalog available. U.S. and overseas. AE, DC, MC, V, MO, PC.
Collectors Treasures has original antique maps from 1500 to 1880. They also have antique engravings and lithographs on many subjects. Since 1961.

Edward Stanford, Ltd.
12–14 Long Acre
Covent Garden
London WC2E 9LP England
Price list, free U.S. and overseas. MO, PC.
Edward Stanford's have been mapsellers since 1952. They offer maps, guide books, travel books, globes and atlases.

The Globe
P.O. Box A3398
Chicago, IL 60690
(312) 528-6228
40-page catalog, $1; overseas $2. BD, MO, PC.
The Globe offers rare maps, atlases, and books. Many of the maps are beautiful engravings in hand-applied color or black and white. They list many reference books on map collecting.

The Gold Bug
P.O. Box 588
Alamo, CA 94507
2-page price list, free U.S. Does not sell overseas. MO, PC.
The Gold Bug provides copies of historic maps to researchers, genealogists, and others interested in the locations of historical sites and ghost towns.

The Greater London Council
Room 225 County Hall
London SE1 7PB England
01 633 4165
4-page color brochure, free U.S. and overseas. MO, PC.
The Greater London Council offers a good selection of reproductions from the Greater London Council Archives.

There are many fine topographical maps and prints of London.

Historic Urban Plans
Box 276
Ithaca, NY 14851
(607) 273-4695
75-page catalog, $1; overseas free MO, PC.
Historic Urban Plans has over 400 facsimile map reproductions of cities of historical interest. They include plans, views, surveys, and lithographs. There are smaller souvenir series of the western hemisphere including the U.S., Canada, and the Caribbean.

Kistler Graphics
4000 Dahlia St.
Denver, CO 80216
(303) 399-2581
8-page brochure, free U.S. Does not sell overseas. MO, PC.
Kistler prints full color, raised relief maps. The U.S. 22 × 34 in. size is about $13. Maps of the world, the thirteen original colonies, and the 50 separate states are available.

The Map House
54 Beauchamp Place
London SW3 1NY England
Catalog of exhibitions. U.S. and overseas. AE, V, MO, PC.
The Map House was founded in 1907, and is now one of Europe's largest collections of original antique maps and engravings. They specialize in antique maps, published between 1480 and 1850, of all parts of the world. There are antique topographical, floral, and decorative engravings, plus antique atlases.

Postaprint
Taidsworth House, Iver Heath
Bucks SLO OPQ England
10-page price list, $1 refundable U.S. and overseas. MO, PC.

Richard Fitch
2324 Calle Halcon
Santa Fe, NM 87501
(505) 982-2939

43-page catalog, $2; overseas $4. MC, V, MO, PC.
Richard Fitch offers antique maps, prints, and books from the sixteenth through the nineteenth century, created in wood, copper, and steel engravings and lithographs. They specialize in creating a sequence of maps, showing the growth and development of a particular county, state, or country.

Richard Nicholson of Chester
25 Watergate St.
Chester CH3 7AG England
0244 26818
28-page catalog, $3; overseas free. MO, PC.
Nicholson's offers antique maps of all parts of the world, from 1540 to 1860. There are antique topographical views of many parts of the world, plus early atlases.

W. Grahm Arader III
1000 Boxwood Court
King of Prussia, PA 19406
(215) 825-6570
54-page catalog, free U.S. and overseas. W. Grahm offers an excellent collection of historical maps, books, and prints for the serious collector. There are exemplary maps of British Colonial America, American Indian portraits, and rare collotype maps of the Mississippi and Ohio valleys.

MILITARY

The Black Watch
P.O. Box 666
Van Nuys, CA 91408
(213) 701-5177
Four 120-page catalogs, $13 U.S. and overseas. MC, V, MO, PC.
The Black Watch supplies the hobbyist with everything for collecting toy soldiers and military miniatures. They supply miniatures produced worldwide, books and uniform guides, and hobby construction materials.

Collector's Armoury, Inc.
800 Slaters Lane
P.O. Box 1061
Alexandria, VA 22313
(703) 684-6111

36-page color catalog $2; overseas $4.
  AE, DC, MC, V, MO, PC.
Collector's Armoury supplies both
original and replica military
collectibles. The replica model guns
cannot be made to fire real ammunition,
though they look real. There are
Samurai swords with tempered steel
blades.

Globe Militaria
RFD 1 Box 269
Keene, NH 03431
(603) 352-1961
10-page price list, 50¢; overseas free.
  Minimum order $5. MO, PC.
Globe Militaria offers militaria, war
relics, and military books. They have a
good selection of WWII relics.

Jacques Noel Jacobsen Jr.
Collectors Antiquities
60 Manor Rd.
Staten Island, NY 10310
(212) 981-0973
64-page brochure, $3; overseas $10. MC,
  V, MO, PC.
Jacobsen's is a large dealer in soldiers',
sailors', firemen's, and policemen's
antiques and memorabilia. There are
uniforms, hats, insignias, books, and
photographs offered.

Peter Hlinka Historical Americana
P.O. Box 310
266 E. 89 St.
New York, NY 10028
(212) 369-1660
24-page brochure, 50¢; overseas $1.
Hlinka's business slogan is "a rarity
always in stock." Much of his
memorabilia is one-of-a-kind. There are
military medals, insignia, helmets,
military books, and war relics.

Soldier Shop, Inc.
1222 Madison Ave.
New York, NY 10128
(212) 535-6788
166-page catalog, $5 U.S. and overseas.
  MC, V, MO, PC.
The Soldier Shop carries everything for
military collectors. There are antique
toy soldiers, military books, military
miniatures, medals, militaria,
paintings, rare books, and prints.

Sydney B. Vernon
Box 387
Baldwin, NY 11510
(516) 536-5287
20-page catalog, 50¢; overseas $1.25.
  Minimum order $10.
Sydney B. Vernon's has military medals
and decorations from the late
eighteenth century to the present, and
from Europe, Japan and the U.S.

MUSIC BOXES

Richters
900 North Point Street
Ghirardelli Square
San Francisco, CA 94109
(415) 441-2663
40-page catalog, $1 U.S. and overseas.
  MC, V, MO, PC.
Richter's is located in the charming
Ghirardelli Square of San Francisco.
They specialize in music boxes from all
over the world. They come in many sizes
and designs, and range in price from $10
to several thousands of dollars. There
are lovely music boxes from Hummel,
Norman Rockwell, Anri, Beatrix Potter,
and many others.

The San Francisco Music Box Company
P.O. Box 26433
San Francisco, CA 94126
(415) 428-0194
48-page color catalog, free; overseas $2.
There are hundreds of music boxes from
around the world. There is Mickey
Mouse and Snow White (and the Seven
Dwarfs) for children, a beautiful Jack-
in-the-Box for baby's room, Garfield for
the young at heart, and beautiful crystal,
wood, and lacquered music boxes for
serious collectors.

World of Music Boxes
412 Main St.
Avon, NJ 07717
(201) 341-8788
32-page color catalog, $1 U.S. and
  overseas. AE, DC, MC, V, MO, PC.
The World of Music Boxes is one of the
few places featuring all music boxes
and figurines, for which you can choose
your own tune from a selection of over
700 popular and classical melodies.

There are clowns, unicorns, lacquered Orientals, figurines, and many beautiful wood-inlaid music boxes.

NATURE

Allen's Shellarama
P.O. Box 15575 Dept. IMO
Ft. Lauderdale, FL 33318
(305) 472-8542
20-page catalog, $1; overseas $2. MO, PC.
Allen's offers hundreds of seashells, craft shells, decorator shells, coral, sea life, and sea oddities. There are lovely shell jewelry items, novelties, and kits.

Butterfly Co.
51–17 Bockaway Beach Blvd.
Far Rockaway, NY 11691
(212) 945-5400
20-page catalog, free U.S. and overseas. MC, V, MO.
Butterfly offers over 800 specimens of beautiful and exotic butterflies, moths, and not-so-beautiful beetles collected from all over the world. Specimens arrive daily and the availability of specimens constantly changes. An electric blue Morpho Didius butterfly ($3 for a male—and $6 for a female!), mounted and framed, would make an interesting wall display.

Derby Lane Shell Center
10515 Gandy Blvd. Dept PH
St. Petersburg, FL 33702
(813) 576-1131
16-page color brochure, $2; overseas $4. Minimum order $10. MC, V, MO, PC.
Derby Lane sells sea shells (down by the seashore . . .) as collector items, shell craft, and craft kits. Many customers buy the shells by the pound and create their own interesting jewelry and decorator items.

Dover Scientific Co.
Box 6011
Long Island City, NY 11106
(212) 721-0136
44-page catalog, $1; overseas $2. MO, PC.
Dover supplies fine collector shells, fossils, and minerals. Since 1962 they have sold to collectors, educational institutions, decorators, and museums all over the world. There are many colorful and exotic decorator items and many hard-to-find species.

Ferguson's Marine Specialties
617 N. Fries Ave.
Wilmington, CA 90744
(213) 835-0811
15-page price list, free U.S. and overseas. MO, PC.
Ferguson's carries sea shells, sealife novelties, and carved coconut items.

Mallicks Fossils
5514 Plymouth Rd.
Baltimore, MD 21214
(301) 426-2969
110-page catalog, $4; overseas $6. Minimum order $10. MO, PC.
Mallicks is regarded as the major supplier of Earth Science materials and specimens. They offer over 13,000 species of fossils and artifacts.

Watkins & Doncaster
Four Throws, Hawkhurst
Kent England
33-page catalog, $4; overseas free BD, MO.
Watkins & Doncaster, "The Naturalists," are suppliers of insects, geological specimens, and microscopy. They also carry many tools, educational charts, and books.

PAPERWEIGHTS

The Friar's House
Bene't St.
Cambridge CB2 2QN England
0223 60275 England
6-page color brochure, free U.S. and overseas. AE, DC, MC, V, MO, PC.
The Friar's House is a family-operated firm offering an extensive variety of British and European modern glass paperweights.

George Kamm
406 W. Marion St.
P.O. Box 254
Lititz, PA 17543
(717) 626-2338

Brochure, U.S. AE, MC, V, PC.
George Kamm offers a monthly
newsletter for a subscription of $5. The
newsletter is the means for advertising
contemporary and antique
paperweights.

L. H. Selman
761 Chestnut St.
Santa Cruz, CA 95060
(800) 538-0766
(408) 427-1177
136-page color catalog, $10 refundable
    U.S. and overseas. AE, DC, MC, V, MO,
    PC.
L. H. Selman features antique
paperweights by classic French
manufacturers (Baccarat, Clichy and
Saint Louis) as well as English and
American glassworks. Selman's also
carries contemporary paperweights by
today's modern artists. The catalog
features over 240 paperweights and
provides interesting information on
the world's leading paperweight
factories.

POSTERS

Fiesta Arts
Greenvale, NY 11548
(516) 617-6888
7-page color brochure, $3; $4.50 overseas
    refundable. MO, PC.
Fiesta Arts offers eleven color opera
posters imported from the Ricordi
Company of Milan, Italy. In art nouveau
style, they celebrate such famous operas
as Madame Butterfly, Tosca, Manon,
Turandot, and Parsifal.

Miscellaneous Man Antiques
Box 1776
New Freedom, PA 17349
(717) 235-4766

80-page catalog, $3; overseas $4. MC, V,
    MO, PC.
Miscellaneous Man carries over 7,000
original posters dating from the 1880s
to the 1940s. They are probably one of
the largest dealers in original posters
and old advertising collectibles.

SPORTS

Beulah Sports, Inc.
1863 Waukeman Rd.
Glenview, IL 60025
(312) 998-5252
24-page brochure, $2 U.S. and overseas.
    MC, V, MO, PC.
Beulah carries a good selection of sports
memorabilia including baseball cards,
media guides, and programs of sporting
events. They have back issues of
magazines including *The Sporting
News* and *Sports Illustrated*.

TCMA
1000 N. Division St.
Peekskill, NY 10566
(914) 763-0161
108-page newsalog, free U.S. Does not
    sell overseas. MC, V, MO, PC.
TCMA specializes in new and old
baseball memorabilia including
baseball cards and event covers.

Wholesale Cards
Box 496
Georgetown, CT 06829
(203) 544-8288
32-page catalog, $1; overseas $2. MO, PC.
Wholesale Cards buys and sells baseball
cards, and collector's cards of other
sports including football, basketball,
hockey, and boxing.

COLLEGE &
PREP SCHOOL
GIFT SHOPS

Many colleges, universities, and prep schools offer a catalog, brochure, or price list featuring items imprinted with their school name or insignia. There are T-shirts, sweatshirts, shorts, posters, pennants, mugs and steins available from many of the schools listed below. Whether you want to start a collection of coffee mugs of the Pac 10, honor a newborn with a tiny T-shirt from an Ivy League school, or buy a cuddly stuffed mascot from your own alma mater, you'll enjoy these school gift shop catalogs. Let the bells of preppydom ring.

University of Alabama
The Crimson Collection
P.O. Box AE
University, AL 35486
(205) 348-6125
14-page color catalog, free U.S. AE, MC, V, PC.

University of Arizona
Wildcat Gifts ASUA Bookstore
Tucson, AZ 85721
6-page some color brochure, free U.S. MO, PC.

Arizona State University
The ASU Shop, Ltd.
905 South Mill Ave.
Tempe, AZ 85281
(800) 528-6050
(800) 352-0458
(602) 829-1743

4-page color brochure, free U.S. AE, MC, V, MO, PC.

Baylor University
Baylor Book Store
Box 6325
Waco, TX 76706
Price list, free MC, V, PC.

University of Bern
Institute for Physical Education and Sport
Bremgartenstr. 145
CH-3012 Bern
Switzerland

Brigham Young University
BYU Book Store
Provo, UT 84604–9989
2 pages, free U.S. PC.

Brown University
Brown University Bookstore
Campus Shop
Box 1878
Providence, RI 02912
8-page color catalog, MC, V, PC.

University of California, Berkeley
ASUC Store
Berkeley, CA 94720
(415) 642-3905
20-page color catalog, free U.S. MC, V, PC.

Clemson University
Clemson Athletic Department
Clemson Station
Clemson, SC 29632
(803) 656-2050

14-page color brochure, free U.S. MC, V, MO, PC.

Colgate University
Colgate University Bookstore
O'Conner Campus Center
Hamilton, NY 13346
(315) 824-1000
6-page brochure. MC, V, PC.

Columbia University
Columbia University Bookstore
2960 Broadway
New York, NY 10027
(212) 280-4136
Price list, free U.S. MC, V, PC.

Cornell University
Cornell Campus Store
Ithaca, NY 14853
(607) 256-4111
8-page color catalog, free U.S. AE, MC, V, MO, PC.

Dartmouth College
The Dartmouth Co-op
P.O. Box 899
Hanover, NH 03755
(603) 643-3100
2-page brochure, free U.S. AE, MC, V, PC.

Duke University
Duke University Stores
Drawer AM, Duke Station
Durham, NC 27706
(919) 684-2344
14-page color catalog, free U.S. MC, V, PC.

University of Florida
Campus Shop & Bookstore
Gainesville, FL 32611
(904) 392-0194
14-page color catalog, free U.S. MO, PC.

Fordham University
Fordham University Shop
McGinley Center
Bronx, NY 10458
1-page brochure, free U.S. PC.

University of Georgia
University Book Store
Georgia University Station
P.O. Box 2217
Athens, GA 30602

8-page color brochure, free U.S. MC, V, PC.

Georgia Tech University
Georgia Tech Bookstore
350 Ferst Drive, N. W.
Atlanta, GA 30322
(404) 894-2516
16-page color brochure, free U.S. MO, PC.

Harvard University
The Harvard Cooperative Society
1400 Massachusetts Ave.
Cambridge, MA 02238
Massachusetts (800) 792-5170
36-page color catalog, free U.S. AE, MC, V, MO, PC.

University of Hawaii
University of Hawaii Bookstore
2465 Campus Rd.
Honolulu, HI 96822
10-page color brochure, free U.S. MC, V, PC.

The Hill School (Prep)
Hill School Bookstore and Athletic
Supply Store
Pottstown, PA 19464
1-page brochure, free U.S. PC.

Hotchkiss School (Prep)
The Hotchkiss School Bookstore
Lakeville, CT 06039
Price list, free U.S. PC.

Idaho State University
University Bookstore
P.O. Box 8013
Pocatello, ID 83209–0009
Price list, free U.S. PC.

Indiana University
Indiana University Bookstore
Indiana Memorial Union
Bloomington, IN 47405
(812) 335-6823
4-page brochure, MC, V, MO, PC.

University of Iowa
Iowa Memorial Union Bookstore
Iowa City, Iowa 52242
8-page brochure, free U.S. MC, V, PC.

Johns Hopkins University
The Johns Hopkins University Book
Center
Charles and 34th Streets
Baltimore, MD 21218
(301) 338-8317
6-page color brochure, free U.S. MC, V,
PC.

University of Kentucky
University Book Store, Student Center
Lexington, KY 40506
(606) 258-4731
12-page color catalog, free U.S. PC.

Marquette University
Marquette University Bookstore
1320 West Wisconsin Ave.
Milwaukee, WI 53233
8-page brochure, free U.S. PC.

Michigan State University
MSU Bookstore
East Lansing, MI 48824–1022
18-page color catalog, free U.S. MC, V,
MO, PC.

University of Minnesota
Gopher Gifts
290 Williamson Hall
Minneapolis, MN 55455
16-page color brochure, free U.S. MO,
PC.

University of Mississippi
The Rebel Shop
P.O. Box 9
University, Mississippi 38677
(601) 232-7693
2-page color brochure, free U.S. MC, V,
PC.

University of Nebraska
University Bookstore
14th and R Street
Nebraska Union Rm 340
Lincoln, NE 68588–0460
(402) 472-2285
Catalog, free U.S. MC, V, MO, PC.

*University of North Carolina (Chapel
  Hill)*
Student Stores
Daniels Bldg. 062A
Chapel Hill, NC 27514

16-page color catalog, free U.S. MC, V,
PC.

North Dakota State University
Varsity Mart The University Store
Box 5476 State University Station
Fargo, ND 58105
(701) 237-7761
Price list, free U.S. MO, PC.

University of Notre Dame
The Hammes Notre Dame Bookstore
Notre Dame, IN 46556
16-page color catalog, free U.S. PC.

Ohio State University
OSU Bookstore Homesales Dept.
1315 Kinnear Rd.
Columbus, OH 43212
(614) 422-9400
8-page color brochure, free U.S. MC, V,
MO, PC.

University of Oregon
University of Oregon Bookstore
P.O. Box 3176
Eugene, OR 97403
(503) 686-4331
2-page color brochure, free MC, V, MO,
PC.

Oregon State University
OSU Book Stores, Inc.
P.O. Box 489
Corvallis, OR 97339
(503) 754-4323
4-page color brochure, free U.S. MC, V,
MO, PC.

Pennsylvania State University
Penn State Bookstore on Campus
Bookstore Building
University Park, PA 16802
23-page color catalog, free U.S. MC, V,
PC.

Phillips Exeter Academy (Prep)
The Exeter Bookstore
13 Spring St.
Exeter, NH 03833
6-page brochure, free U.S. PC.

Princeton University
Princeton University Store
36 University Place
Princeton, NJ 08540
(609) 921-8500

4-page color brochure, free U.S. AE, MC, V, PC.

Purdue University
University Bookstore
360 State St.
West Lafayette, IN 47906
(317) 743-9618
29-page catalog, free U.S. PC.

Rice University
Rice Campus Store
P.O. Box 1892
Houston, TX 77251
4-page color brochure, free U.S. MO, PC.

Rutgers University
Rutgers University Bookstore
One Penn Plaza
New Brunswick, NJ 08901
Price list, free U.S. MC, V, PC.

St. Mark's School (Prep)
School Store
Southborough, MA 01772
3-page brochure, free U.S. PC.

University of Southern California
USC Trojan Gifts
P.O. Box 77538
Los Angeles, CA 90007
(213) 743-7180
26-page color catalog, free U.S. MC, V, MO, PC.

Stanford University
Stanford Bookstore
Stanford, CA 94305
3 pages, free U.S. MC, V, PC.

University of Tennessee
Book and Supply Store
University Center
Knoxville, TN 37996
14-page color brochure, free U.S. MC, V, MO, PC.

Texas A & M
Texas A & M Bookstore
Drawer B-9
University Center
College Station, TX 77844
6-page color brochure, free U.S. MC, V, MO, PC.

University of California, Los Angeles
UCLA Bearwear Mail Order
ASUCLA Student's Store
308 Westwood Plaza
Los Angeles, CA 90024
(213) 206-8458
16-page color catalog, free U.S. MC, V, PC.

United States Naval Academy
Naval Academy Gift Shop
Ricketts Hall
Annapolis, MD 21402
(301) 268-3355
Price list, free U.S. PC.

Vanderbilt University
Vanderbilt University Bookstore
Nashville, TN 37240
(615) 322-2994
Price list, free U.S. MC, V, PC.

Villanova University
The University Shop
Villanova, PA 19085
3-page price list, free U.S. PC.

University of Washington
University Bookstore
4326 University Way NE
Seattle, WA 98105
(202) 634-3400
8-page color brochure, free U.S. MC, V, PC.

Washington State University
Student Book Corporation
NE 700 Thatuna
Pullman, WA 99163
(509) 332-2537
4-page color brochure, free U.S. MC, V, MO, PC.

University of Wisconsin
The University Book Store
711 State Street
Madison, WI 53703
Price list, free U.S. MC, V, PC.

Yale University
Yale Co-operative Corporation
77 Broadway
New Haven, CT 06520
(203) 772-2200

CRAFTS

SEE ALSO
- Art
- Handcrafts
- Hobby
- Tools

GENERAL

Adventures in Crafts
1321 Madison Ave.
New York, NY 10028
(212) 410-9793
18-page catalog, $2; overseas $3. MC, V,
MO, PC.
For the craftsperson there is découpage,
collage, tole painting, stenciling, wood
burning, gilding and marbleizing
supplies.

Basic Crafts, Co.
1201 Broadway
New York, NY 10001
(212) 679-3516
16-page catalog, $2; overseas $3.
   Minimum order $25. MC, V, MO.
There are supplies and equipment for
the hand bookbinder: tools (shears and
presses), gold-stamping type, leathers,
cloth, endpapers, marbling, and papermaking kits, calligraphy, and writing
supplies.

Bersted's Hobby Craft, Inc.
521 West 10th Ave.
PO Box 40
Monmouth, IL 61462
(309) 734-7011
16-page catalog, $1; overseas $2. MO, PC.
Bersted's manufactures rubber and
plastic molds. The sell hobby and craft
items (including liquid rubber) to make
your own molds, Shreddi Mix Instant
Papier Maché, Fluf-E-Kote (flocking for
velvety finishes), weaving looms,
molding plaster, and rubber and plastic
molds for plaster casting.

Better Homes and Gardens
Craft Kits Department
P.O. Box 374
Des Moines, IA 50336
(800) 247-5099
48-page color catalog, free U.S. AE, MC,
   V, PC.
This is one of the best known craft kit
catalogs. Better Homes offers hundreds
of kits—from quilts and mobiles to
appliqué kits, dolls, and latch-hook rugs.
There are many colorful needlework
projects to choose from.

Boycan's
P.O. Box 897
Sharon, PA 16146
(412) 346-5534
132-page catalog, $2 U.S. Does not sell
   overseas. Minimum order $10. PC.
Boycan's catalog includes over 10,000
supplies and over 500 craft and
needlework kits. There are kits and
supplies for almost every craft
including needlework, flower making,
doll making, tole, doll house and
accessories, macramé, dried flowers,

potpourri, basketry, party favors, holidays, Christmas, weddings, kids' crafts, ribbons, glues, paints, trims, wood items, and more.

Cambridge Brass Rubbing Center
The Wesley Church Library
King Street, Cambridge CB1 1LG
England
0223 61318
Brass rubbing is no longer permitted in many of the churches of England, but at Cambridge Brass rubbing Center you can rub from your choice of 80 different facsimile brasses. These exact replicas were made from moulds of original brass memorials on the tombs of medieval and tudor knights and ladies. By mail order you can buy finished brass rubbings with gold wax on black paper. (Not as much fun, but just as special).

The Cracker Box
River Road
Pt. Pleasant, PA 18950
(215) 297-5700
32-page color catalog, $3; overseas surface $3, air mail $5.79. MC, V, MO, PC.
These Christmas ornament kits are not your church bazaar types. These tree ornaments are made with styrofoam balls, beads, sequins, and satin—each a work of art. As the owners state, "They are lengthy, aggravating, absorbing, and probably addictive." They offer over 100 different styles of tree ornaments and range in price from $7.25 to $53.98.

The Craft Basket
Colchester, CT 06415
(800) 243-4642
56-page color catalog, free U.S. MC, V, PC.
There are hundreds of creative craft kits for all ages: needlepoint, candlewicking, cross-stitch, leather, plastic, canvas, model construction kits, stained glass, and Christmas ornaments.

Craftsman Supply House
35 Brown's Ave.
P.O. Box 13
Scottsville, NY 14546
(716) 889-3403
50-page catalog, MO, PC.
Craftsman offers a good selection of supplies for most craft projects: caning basketry, macramé, wood plaques, glue, clock movements, floral, styrofoam, paints, beads, feathers, molds, leather kits, and more.

Crafts Mfg. Co.
72 Massachusetts Ave.
Lunenberg, MA 01462
(617) 342-1717
16-page catalog, 50¢ U.S. Does not sell overseas. MO, PC, C.O.D
Crafts offers handmade reproductions of Early American tinware. They sell finished trays, sconces, lamps, and switch and door plates. The last six pages of the catalog give excellent instructions on how to paint tinware of your own design.

Discount Craft Supplies
4320 31st. Street North
St. Petersburg, FL 33714
(813) 527-4592
56-page newsalog, free U.S. Does not sell overseas. MO, PC.
Arts and Crafts supplies at discounts 30% to 50% below retail price. They offer something for everyone who is interested in arts and crafts: purse handles, wire wreaths (10 in. wreath for 59¢), plastic and ceramic beads, wiggle eyes (the 5 mm size of 30 per package is 30¢), lamp frames, music boxes, silk flowers, needlecraft supplies, and much more at great prices.

Gill Mechanical Company
P.O. Box 7247
Eugene, OR 97401
(503) 686-1606
3-page brochure, free U.S. Limited overseas sales. MO, PC.
The Tube Wringer, distributed by Gill Mechanical, is a unique tool designed to get the most out of the contents of collapsible, roll-up tubes. It's especially handy for extruding those last drops of expensive oil paints. It also gives enough support to convert tubes of caulking material into a caulking gun. It is available in three sizes, from toothpaste

and oil paint tube size to industrial size (good for the mechanic using silicones, epoxies and sealants).

Holiday Handicrafts
P.O. Box 470
Winsted, CT 06098
(203) 379-3374
40-page color catalog, $1 U.S. Does not sell overseas. AE, MC, V, MO, PC.
Holiday handicrafts sells hundreds of kits, many of them boutiquing techniques (with sequins and beads) which require little or no sewing. There are costume dolls, spangle art bead projects, needlecraft, pre-cut clothing kits, and paper dolls.

Kirchen Bros.
Box C1016
Skokie, IL 60076
Illinois (312) 676-2692
56-page color catalog, $1 U.S. Does not sell overseas. MC, V, MO, PC.
Kirchen carries one of the largest and most complete line of craft supplies and kits in the country. In addition to the many general craft supplies offered, there is quite a good selection of doll-making parts and kits.

Krastman & Associates
Box 8042
Van Nuys, CA 91409
(213) 366-1090
175-page newsalog, $1; overseas $2. MC, V, MO, PC.
Beads, doll parts, styrofoam, adhesives, ribbons, lamp frames, craft books, macramé, ceramics, wood frames, and hundreds of other items are available for the craftsperson.

Lamrite
565 Broadway
Bedford, OH 44146
(216) 232-9300
50-catalog. PC.
Lamrite's general crafts supply catalog has everything from acrylic paints and baskets to tole supplies and wood plaques. They feature a nice selection of wedding decoration supplies.

Mary Maxim
2001 Holland Ave.
Port Huron, MI 48060
(313) 987-2000
64-page color catalog. MC, V, MO, PC.
Mary Maxim is one of the better known general crafts catalog. They feature many Christmas ornament kits, needlepoint kits, beautiful latch-hook rug kits, knitting supplies, needlepoint and cross-stitch, crochet, and sweater patterns especially for children.

National Artcraft
23456 Mercantile Rd.
Beachwood, OH 44122
(216) 292-4944
384-page color catalog, $3 U.S. and overseas. MC, V, MO, PC.
National artcraft is the largest primary parts supplier in the ceramic craft field. They supply craft materials for plastercraft, tole, china painting, lapidary, and general craft and hobby markets. Their depth of offerings extends to practically all categories of crafts. They even offer over 250 tunes in a dozen different styles and sizes of musical movements.

Oldstone Enterprises
77 Summer St.
Boston, MA 02110
(617) 542-4112
4-page brochure, free U.S. and overseas. PC.
Oldstone has rubbing materials for historical markers, grave headstones, coins, plaques, manhole covers, and designs in relief. They offer rubbing wax in ten shades, and hemp paper in black and white that is lightweight but strong.

Pourette Mfg. Inc.
6910 Roosevelt Way NE
Seattle, WA 98115
(206) 525-4488
60-page catalog, $1 refundable U.S. and overseas. MC, V, MO, PC.
Pourette carries the largest selection of candle-making supplies available, and is the only distributor which manufactures its own molds in metal,

plastic, and rubber. (They also carry soap-making supplies.)

Tackle Craft
P.O. Box 280
Chippewa Falls, WI 54729
(715) 723-3645
88-page catalog, free U.S. and overseas. MO, PC.
Tackle Craft sells supplies for make-your-own fly and jig tying. Quills, deertails, calftails, hooks, corks, glues, lacquers, tools, feathers, hooks, instruction sheets and books.

Vanguard Crafts, Inc.
1701
Utica Ave.
Brooklyn, NY 11234
(212) 337-5188
52-page catalog. MC, V, PC.
Basic arts and crafts supplies for a variety of interests.

World Arts
P.O. Box 2008
Covina, CA 91722
10-page catalog, 25¢ U.S. Does not sell overseas. MO, PC.

W. Wooley Co.
Box 68
Peoria, IL 61650
31-page catalog, $2 U.S. and overseas. MC, V, PC.
W. Wooley sells plastercraft supplies, rubber mold-making kits, and candle molds. They also have a large supply of small to large ready-to-use rubber molds. Since 1917.

CANING

Cane and Basket Supply
1283 So. Cochran Ave.
Los Angeles, CA 90019
(213) 939-9644
16-page catalog, $1 U.S. Does not sell overseas. AE, MC, V, MO, PC.

Connecticut Cane and Reed Company
P.O. Box 1276
Manchester, CT 06040
(203) 646-6586

70-page brochure, 50¢ U.S. and overseas. Minimum order $5. AE. MC, V, MO, PC.

Frank's Cane and Rush Supply
7244 Heil Ave.
Huntington Beach, CA 92647
(714) 847-0707
16-page brochure, free U.S. and overseas. MC, V, MO, PC.

H. H. Perkins
10 South Bradley Rd.
Woodbridge, CT 06525
(203) 389-9501
24-page brochure, free U.S. and overseas.
H. H. Perkins offers reeds, rattan and rattan products, and other seat-weaving materials.

Newell Workshop
19 Blain Ave.
Hinsdale, IL 60521
(312) 323-7367
6-page brochure, free U.S. Does not sell overseas. MO, PC.

New Hampshire Cane and Reed Co.
65 Turnpike St.
P.O. Box 176
Suncook, NH 03275
(603) 485-5111
4-page brochure, free U.S. and overseas. MO, PC.

Peerless Rattan
222 Lake Ave.
Yonkers, NY 10701
(914) 968-4046
16-page brochure free U.S. Does not sell overseas. Minimum order $10. MO, PC.

CLOCKMAKING

Craft Products
2200 Dean St.
St. Charles, IL 60174
(312) 584-9600
100-page color catalog, $1.50; overseas $3. MC, V, MO, PC.
Craft Products carries some rather beautiful clockmaking kits and

supplies. There are about six styles of grandfather clocks, and many regulators, wall hangings, mantel and alarm clocks to choose from.

Emperor Clock Company
Emperor Industrial Park
Fairhope, AL 36532
(205) 928-2316
6-page color brochure, free U.S. and
    overseas. MC, V, MO, PC.
Emperor offers six grandfather clock kits made of solid American hardwoods, notably American black walnut, cherry, and oak.

H. DeCovnick & Son
P.O. Box 68
Alamo, CA 94507
(415) 837-1244
20-page catalog, $1 U.S. Does not sell
    overseas. AE, MC, V, MO, PC.
Clock movements, dials, battery movements, and clock parts.

Klockit
P.O. Box 629
Lake Geneva, WI 53147
(414) 248-1150
64-page color catalog, free U.S. Does not
    sell overseas. MC, V, MO, PC.
Klockit sells many terrific clock-making kits, supplies, and tools. They carry quartz movements, clock-making accessories (movements, dials, finials, brass fixtures, and hands), imported brass weight-driven movements, and hardwood clock kits. From mantel clocks and grandfathers to 400 day clock kits, the selection is very good.

Mason & Sullivan
586 Higgins Crowell Rd.
W. Yarmouth, MA 02673
(617) 775-4643
32-page color catalog, $1; overseas $3.
    AE, MC, V, MO, PC.
Mason & Sullivan have at least twenty-four types of clock kits, including a grandfather clock in the Shaker design and multi-functional hardware (knobs, hinges, finials, and locks). There are kits for building jewelry boxes and weather instrument panels, too.

Newport Enterprises
2313 W. Burbank Blvd.
Burbank, CA 91506
(800) 423-2740
California (213) 845-0555
80-page catalog, $2 U.S. Does not sell
    overseas. MC, V, MO, PC.
Clock movements, parts and accessories.

Selva Borel
P.O. Box 796
347 13th St.
Oakland, CA 94604
(415) 832-0355
65-page catalog, $2 U.S. Does not sell
    overseas. Minimum order $5. MC, V,
    MO, PC.
Selva Borel specializes in imported and domestic movements, tools, and supplies for the professional clockmaker as well as the amateur. Established in 1929, this is a third generation family-operated business.

Westwood Clocks 'N Kits
3210 Airport Way
Long Beach, CA 90806
(213) 595-4981
20-page color catalog, $1; overseas $2.
    MC, V, MO, PC.
Westwood has a large selection of clock kits—mostly grandfather clocks, with some wall and mantel clocks. All models are available assembled and finished with your choice of options.

Yankee Ingenuity
P.O. Box 26
Thompson, CT 06277
(203) 923-2061
8-page brochure $1 U.S. and overseas.
    MC, V, MO, PC.
There are battery-operated clock movements (compact, pendulum, and digital) and parts for crafts people who make handcrafted clocks.

DOLLS AND DOLLHOUSES

Colonial House of Dolls
300 S. York St.
P.O. Box 546
Mechanicsburg, PA 17055–0546
(717) 697-9089

8-page brochure, $2 U.S. MC, V, MO, PC.
Colonial House sells a complete line of
dolls and doll supplies. There are wigs,
shoes, stockings, hats, dresses, stands,
books, and patterns. The catalog is
directed towards people who make,
collect, and repair antique and modern
dolls.

Craft Products
2200 Dean St.
St. Charles, IL 60174
(312) 584-9600
68-page color catalog, $1.50; overseas $3.
  MC, V, MO, PC.
Filled with great-looking doll house kits
in many styles: turn-of-the-century farm
house, southern colonial mansion, San
Francisco, Swiss Chalet, Cape Cod,
Victorian, and ranch style. There are
miniature furniture and many home
accessories.

Den Young
63-Earith Rd.
Willingham
Cambs CB4 5LS England
0954 60015
Price list, 4 International Reply
  Coupons, U.S. and overseas. MO.
Den Young makes miniature furniture
to ½ in. scale for collectors and doll
house owners. Any special piece can be
made to order from a sized sketch or
magazine photograph. (Your own house
can be reproduced in ¾ in. scale.)

Doll & Craft World
125 8th St.
Brooklyn, NY 11215
(212) 768-0887
36-page catalog, $3 U.S. and overseas.
  AE, MC, V, MO, PC.
An excellent source for doll parts and
clothing (including patterns), and many
books on the subject.

Handcraft Designs
89 Commerce Dr.
Rockhill Industrial Park
Telford, PA 18969
(800) 523-2430
20-page color catalog, free U.S. and
  overseas. Minimum order $10 U.S.,
  overseas $25.

Handcraft designs miniature furniture
for complete room settings. There is a
fifteen-piece contemporary patio room,
a nine-piece colonial bedroom, or a four-
piece Victorian loo collection. There is
much to choose from.

House With The Blue Door
23 Portland Rd.
Kennebunk, ME 04043
(207) 985-3461
8-page brochure, $1 U.S. Does not sell
  overseas. MO, PC.
There are fifteen styles of all-wood
handcrafted doll houses made from
Baltic birch. They are sold unfinished
so that they can be decorated to your
taste. They are sold in kits (starting at
$123), or assembled (ranging from
$40 to $93). They are scaled 1 in. to 1
ft. or ½ in. to 1 ft. furniture. There are
wooden toys including a rocking horse,
train, truck, step-stool, wheelbarrow,
tote wagon, doll trunk, and toy
box.

Small Sales Co.
P.O. Box 7803
Boise, ID 83707
(208) 345-2281
48-page catalog, $3 refundable U.S. and
  overseas. MC, V, MO, PC.
Small Sales has a complete line of scale
model building and miniature supplies.
There is also an excellent textbook and
cassette-filmstrip educational program
available, providing step-by-step
demonstrations of architectural model
home construction.

FLOWER ARRANGING

Christopher Book
P.O. Box 595
W. Patterson, NJ 07424
(201) 785-4600
24-page color catalog, free U.S. Does not
  sell overseas. Minimum order $10.
  MC, V, MO, PC.
A complete line of the finest silk flowers,
house plants, hanging plants, floor
plants, and trees. Their cover features
a beautiful hanging fuchsia for $30.

Dorothy Biddle Service
US 6 at Lake Rd.
Greeley, PA 18425–9799
12-page brochure, 25¢ U.S. and overseas.
MO, PC.

Petals
1 Aqueduct Rd.
White Plains, NY 10060
(800) 431-2464
New York (914) 946-8606
24-page color catalog. AE, MC, V.
Beautiful silk flower arrangements
starting at about $19 and up.

Ran
c/o Sogetsu School
No. 2–21
Akasaka 7-Chome
Minato-ku, Tokyo 107
Japan
03 408 1126
34-page color catalog, $7 U.S. and
  overseas. Prices in Japanese yen. MO,
  PC.
Sogetsu features materials and supplies
for Ikebana (Japanese flower
arranging). There are many pages of
simple though beautiful ceramic,
plastic, bamboo, porcelain, and pottery
containers. There are also scissors,
needle-point holders, and many unusual
dried flower materials.

Silk Plants, Ltd.
P.O. Box 19896
Columbus, OH 43219
(614) 471-8178
20-page color catalog, $1 refundable U.S.
  Does not sell overseas. MC, V, MO, PC.
Silk Plants offers over 50 silk plants at
discounts of up to 50% below retail
prices. A twenty-five stemmed, thirty-
inch diameter Boston fern is priced at
$9.45; a thirty-five-inch dieffenbachia
with seven large leaves is about $14.

FOLK ART

Adele Bishop
Box 557
Manchester, VT 05254
(802) 362-3537
32-page catalog, $2.50 U.S. and overseas.
  AE, MC, V, MO, PC.

Stencils, stencil patterns, stencil
brushes, and paints are available in
Adele Bishop's catalog. Stencils made
from clear mylar plastic (instead of the
old materials of cardboard or paper)
allow reliable placement and are
durable. They provide excellent
instructions, brushes, and materials for
stenciling on many surfaces including
artificial suede, brick, nonglazed
ceramics, clothes, concrete, leather,
paper, wood, wallpaper, and metals.

E. & S. Robinson Associates
Gage Road
Wilton, NH 03086
(603) 654-9257
8-page brochure, self-addressed
  stamped envelope U.S. Does not sell
  overseas. MO, PC.
E. & S. Robinson sells authentic old
designs of early American decorative
art. The patterns cover many phases of
early American art including stencil,
tinplate, wood painting, reverse
painting on glass, and tinsel painting
patterns. This is a small family-owned
business which began when Sarah
Robinson inherited her great Uncle
William Crowell's private collection of
old designs.

Pat Virch, Inc.
1506 Lynn Ave.
Marquette, MI 49855
(906) 226-3931
12-page catalog, $1; overseas $1.50. MO,
  PC.
Pat Virch sells supplies for traditional
Norwegian rosemaling and early
American decorative art.

Peg Hall Studios
111 Clapp Rd.
Scituate, MA 02066
(617) 545-3605
4-page brochure, 25¢ U.S. Does not sell
  overseas. MO, PC.
Books and patterns on early American
decorative art.

S & C Huber, Accoutrements
82 Plants Dam Rd.
East Lyme, CT 06333
(203) 739-0772

22-page brochure, $1 U.S. Does not sell overseas. MO, PC.
S & C Huber produces and sells handmade goods of eighteenth- and nineteenth-century design. They sell supplies for making goods of that era, including papermaking supplies and how-to books on rug making and folk art, dyeing, spinning and weaving, and tin ware.

The Whole Kit & Kaboodle Co., Inc.
8 West 19th St.
New York, NY 10011
(212) 675-8892
15-page brochure, $1; overseas $3. MO, PC.
The Whole Kit and Kaboodle sells stencils under the product name "Stencil Magic." They are inexpensive clear plastic stencils, priced from $2.25 to $3.98. They also sell stencil supplies and hard and soft cover books.

JEWELRY AND LAPIDARY

Allcraft Tool and Supply Co., Inc.
100 Frank Rd.
Hicksville, NY 11801
(516) 433-1660
130-page catalog, $3 U.S. and overseas. Minimum order $15. MC, V, MO, PC.
Allcraft provides the best tools available for manufacturing jewelry, metal enameling, lost wax casting, metalsmithing, and lapidary.

Bourget Bros.
1636 11th Street
Santa Monica, CA 90404
180-page catalog, free U.S. and overseas. Minimum order $20. MC, V, MO, PC.
Bourget is one of the largest jewelry mail order supply houses. They sell jewelry tools and supplies to hobbyists and professionals manufacturing jewelry items. They carry lapidary tools, casting supplies, gemstones, tools, and much more.

California Crafts Supply
1096 N. Main St.
Orange, CA 92667
(800) 432-5199
(714) 633-8891

120-page catalog, free U.S. and overseas. Minimum order $15. MC, V, MO.
Complete supply catalog for jewelry making. Sterling silver, solders, sheet metals, settings, ring shanks, loupes, gemstones, chains, abrasive wheels, tools, welding supplies, and scales.

Clear Creek Trading Co.
P.O. Box 1250
1634 Miner St.
Idaho Springs, CO 80452
(303) 567-4987
67-page catalog, $5; overseas $6. MO.
Clear Creek has over 1,500 different styles and colors of beads, ranging from the smallest seed beads to large wooden beads. They specialize in old and unusual beads. The catalog is filled with bits of history and interesting factual information about beads—and is really fun to read.

Covington Engineering Corp.
P.O. Box 35
715 W. Colton Ave.
Redlands, CA 92373
(714) 793-6636
36-page catalog, free U.S. and overseas. MC, V, MO, PC.
Covington's has over 200 lapidary machines, tools, and accessories, many with the Covington trademark. Since 1848.

Geode Industries
108 W. Main St.
New London, IA 52645
(319) 367-2255
20-page catalog. $2; overseas $5. Minimum order $25. MC, V, MO.
Geode Industries offers gem-cutting equipment and tools for jewelry making: vibratory tumblers, bead-making and faceting machines, and ultrasonic drills.

Greiger's, Inc.
900 S. Arroyo Pwy.
Box 93070-DM
Pasadena, CA 91109
(800) 423-4181
145-page catalog, free; overseas 2 International Reply Coupons. Minimum order $5. MC, V, MO, PC.

Greiger's offers a large selection of mountings, stones, and jewelry-making supplies.

Kingsley North, Inc.
910 Brown St.
P.O. Box 196
Norway, MI 49870-0196
(800) 339-9280
(906) 563-9228
200-page catalog, free; overseas $5. Minimum order $15.
Over 6,000 tools and supplies and equipment for technicians, jewelers, draftsmen, hobbyists, and rockhounds. They offer trim and slabing saws, polishing units, burnout ovens, soldering machines, diamond blades, and setting burs. Discounts of 10% to 50% are available on certain items and quantity orders.

Kit Kraft, Inc.
12109 Ventura Pl.
Studio City, CA 91604
(213) 877-5001
12-page catalog, free U.S. Does not sell overseas. MC, V, MO, PC.
Supplies for copper enameling, jewelry making, and flower making.

Norman Greene Designs
P.O. Box 8451
Emeryville, CA 94608
(415) 652-7464
4-page brochure, $1 U.S. and overseas. MC, V, MO, PC.
Norman Greene handcrafts puzzle rings from four to ten bands in sterling silver, yellow, rose or white 14-karat gold. Prices range from $14 to $540.

W. D. Christianson
200 Napier St.
Barrie, Ontario L4M 1W8
Canada
(705) 726-8713
12-page price list free U.S. and overseas. MC, V, MO, PC.
W. D. Christianson offers a comprehensive list of mineral species in all sizes. Some are rare and unusual and in short supply, so you may want to list substitutions.

KNITTING AND WEAVING

Babouris Handicrafts
56 Adrianov St.
Athens 116 Greece
01 324 7561
2-page price list and yarn samples, $2 U.S. and overseas. Minimum order 22 lbs. of yarn. AE, MO, PC.
Handspun Greek yarn, fast-dyed, is sold in a choice of forty colors.

Brandy Creek Farm
R. R. #1
3608 Zieme Rang Nord
Valcourt, Quebec J0E 2L0
Canada
(514) 532-2300
Brandy Creek is a farm that raises prizewinning Angora goats. The Multhaupts sell the mohair as raw fleece by the pound, semi-finished for handspinning and mechanically spun for knitting and weaving.

Bartlettyarns, Inc.
Box MOSG
Harmony, ME 04942
(207) 683-2251
3-page brochure, $1 plus self-addressed stamped envelope for yarn samples, U.S. and overseas.
Bartlettyarns specializes in 100% wool knitting yarn, spun on their own spinning machine, the Bartlett Mule. Their yarn has a soft, natural homespun appearance appreciated by knitters.

Cambridge Wools, Ltd.
40 Anzac Ave.
Auckland, C. 1. New Zealand
30769
1-page price list, $1 U.S. and overseas. MO.
Cambridge Wools sells spinning and weaving wools, and handknitting wools in natural and dyed colors. They also sell Aran sweaters and sheepskins.

Cheryl Kolander
440 Blair
Eugene, OR 97402
(503) 683-2359
8-page price list with natural yarn samples, $5; overseas $6. 4-page price

list with colored yarn samples, $4; overseas $5. MO, PC.

Cheryl offers silk yarns in a wide variety of textures, lustres, spins, colors, and weights. Specify either natural or colored (or both) yarn samples when ordering price list.

Condon's Yarns
P.O. Box 129
Charlottetown, Prince Edward, C1A 7K3
Canada
Color card 50¢ U.S. and overseas. AE, MC, V, MO, PC.

Condon's has traditional woolen yarns in forty-five colors and five different weights, packaged mostly in the hank.

Contessa Yarns
Tobacco St.
P.O. Box 37
Lebanon, CT 06249
(203) 423-3479
Price list with sample yarns, $1 U.S. and overseas. MO, PC.

Weaving yarns in cotton, wool, rayon, nylon, and blends, and also silk and linen when available.

Elizabeth Zimmerman
Box 157
Babcock, WI 54413
(715) 884-2566
2-page price list, with yarn samples, $1 U.S. and overseas. MO, PC.

Elizabeth Zimmerman sells handknitting wools and books on handknitting. She also sells knitting supplies including circular needles, swifts, ball winders, and knitter's graph paper.

Falcon By Post
Balcon Mills, Bartle Lane
Bradford, West Yorkshire
BD7 4QJ England
0274 576702
80-page color catalog with more than 100 yarn samples, $2 U.S. and overseas. MC, V, MO, PC.

Falcon sells a full range of mainly British-produced yarns for hand and machine knitting and needle-point.

Forte Fibers
P.O. Box 818
Palisade, CO 81526
(303) 464-7397
Price list, free U.S. and overseas. MO, PC.

Forte offers luxury yarns and spinning fibers including cashmere and camel's hair in a variety of weights.

Handspun in Oregon Yarns
5445 S. W. 14th Ave.
Portland, OR 97201
(503) 246-3436
2-page price list and yarn samples, $1 plus self-addressed stamped envelope, U.S. Does not sell overseas. Minimum order $7. MC, V, MO, PC.

Handspun yarns popular with both knitters and weavers.

Holmfirth Wools, Ltd.
Briggate, Windhill
Shipley, West Yorkshire
BD18 2BS England
0274 586943
16-page catalog, with yarn samples, $2; overseas $1.50. BD, MC, V, MO, PC.

Their catalog includes 400 yarn samples. Yarns are available in ball or cone and range from chunky and bulky knits to extra fine in all wool, wool mixtures, and synthetics. They stock knitting supplies: needles, patterns, buttons, and knitting bags.

Leclerc Corporation
P.O. Box 491
Plattsburgh, NY 12901
(518) 561-7900
30-page catalog, $1 U.S. and overseas. MC, V, MO, PC.

Leclerc manufactures and distributes worldwide Leclerc weaving looms. Made of Canadian hard maple or birch, they offer many styles of looms: table, floor, jack-type, counter-balanced, and two- and four-harness looms.

Macomber Looms
P.O. Box 186
Beech Ridge Road
York, ME 03909
(207) 363-2808
10-page brochure, free U.S. and overseas. MO, PC.

Macomber sells AD-A-Harness looms in sixteen- to seventy-two-inch widths with computerized programming for graphic design patterns. Designed by Macomber Looms in York in conjunction with the Atari Personal Computer system, you can design and weave heirloom-quality clothing, blankets, rugs, and hangings.

Norsk Kunstvevgarn
Arnevik
N-4890 Grimstad Norway
041 462 87
Sample cards, $7 U.S. and overseas. MO, PC.
Wool yarns from Norwegian Spelsau sheep for weaving and knitting are available in tapestry, regular weaving, knitting, and rough carpet yarn weights.

Paula Simmons
Box 12
Suquamish, WA 98392
Price list, free; overseas .50¢. MO, PC.
Paula Simmons raises her own sheep, then shears, cards and spins the yarn. She offers one-ply handspun yarn in natural colors from black sheep.

The Pendleton Shop
Handweaving-Knitting-Needlepoint Shop
P.O. Box 233
Sedona, AZ 86336
(602) 282-3671
Price list, $1 U.S. and overseas. MO, PC.
The Pendleton Shop has everything for the handweaver, knitter, and canvas worker. From looms and spinning wheels to needles and ball winders.

Romni Wools and Fibres, Ltd.
3779 W. 10th Ave.
Vancouver, B.C. V6R 2G5
Canada
12-page brochure, $1; overseas $2. MO, PC.
Romni sells a large selection of spinning and weaving wools and supplies. Raw wools imported from New Zealand, plus natural and synthetic fibers.

School Products Co., Inc.
1201 Broadway
New York, NY 10001
(212) 679-3516

32-page catalog $2 U.S. Does not sell overseas. MC, V, MO, PC.
School Products nationally distributes spinning wheels, looms, and weaving supplies to schools, institutions, and individuals.

Stavros G. Kouyoumoutzakis
166 Kalokerinou Ave.
Iraklion Crete Greece
284 466
Price list, $1 U.S. and overseas.
  Minimum order 10 lbs. of wool. PC.
Stavoros Kouyoumoutzakis spins about 300 pounds of yarn a day from Greek and Australian wool in his workshop in Crete.

Straw Into Gold
3006 San Pablo Ave.
Berkeley, CA 94702
(415) 548-5247
14-page newsalog, $2; overseas $2 surface mail, $4 air mail. MC, V, MO, PC.
Straw Into Gold's newsalog of weaving supplies is conveniently divided into three sections: books and related items, fibers, and dyes and yarns. They offer an interesting opportunity to find out about sales, unusual items that won't appear in the catalog, and other tidbits by becoming an "envelope person." You send them four self-addressed stamped envelopes, and every few months Straw Into Gold will mail you new offers and news.

Trefriw Woollen Mills, Ltd.
Trefriw, Gwyneed LL27-ONQ
Wales
Woolen swatch samples, $3; overseas free MC, V, PC.
Trefriw Woollen Mills sells beautiful Welsh tapestry bedspreads (about $75 for a double bed size), tapestry and tweed yardage, clothing, handbags, and placemats.

Yarns Unlimited
Box 1161
1418 Santa Monica Mall
Santa Monica, CA 90406
(213) 395-4267
Price list, free U.S. MC, V, PC.

LEATHER

Berman Leathercraft, Inc.
145 South St.
Boston, MA 02111-2882
(800) 341-3278
(617) 426-0870
32-page color catalog, $1 U.S. and
  overseas. Minimum order $10. AE, DC,
  MC, V, MO.
Berman's is a fourth-generation, family-
run leather business. They offer hides,
dyes, hardware, tools and leather kits for
all ages.

The Hide and Leather House
101 South Coombs St.
Napa, CA 94558
(800) 453-2847
(707) 255-6160
4-page brochure, free U.S. and overseas.
  MC, V, MO, PC.
Rob Deits, owner, sells tanned leather
hides at discounts of 20% to 30% below
leather retail shops. They have a good
selection including deerskin, elkskin,
buffalo, goatskin, lambskin, cowhide,
and upholstery leather.

NEEDLEWORK

The American Needlewoman
2946 S. E. Loop 820
Fort Worth, TX 76140
(817) 293-1229
64-page color catalog, free; overseas $2.
  MC, V, MO, PC.
The latest in popular needlecraft kits,
accessories, threads, and related items.

Annie's Attic
Rte. 2 Box 212B
Big Sandy, TX 75755
(214) 636-4353
32-page color catalog, $2 U.S. and
  overseas. MC, V, MO, PC.
Hundreds of enchanting needlecraft
projects are colorfully displayed in the
Annie's Attic catalog. There are patterns
and kits for crochet, afghans, wall
hangings, toys, baby booties, and dolls.
Big Foot Boutiques ($8.90) is an Annie's
Original; it contains crochet patterns to
make seven clever footies—high top
tennies, work boots, track shoes, Mary
Janes, ski boots, tennis socks, and little
red sandals—in sizes small child to large
adult.

Cottonwood Studio, Inc.
P.O. Box 5003
Scottsdale, AZ 85261
(602) 948-3821
20-page catalog, $5 U.S. and overseas.
  AE, MC, V, MO, PC.
Cottonwood's catalog features over 100
original handpainted needlepoint
designs. This catalog would appeal to
discriminating stitchers who enjoy
working with the finest materials. They
feature designs from authentic Indian
rugs to an Oriental fireplace screen.
Christmas stockings, beautiful
southwest desert scenes, colorful
clowns, and elegant classical designs are
available. Canvas prices range from $15
to $175 for a 16 × 23 in. Navajo animal
pictorial.

Curriculum Resources, Inc.
2 Post Road Box 923
Fairfield, CT 06430
(203) 255-4538
24-page color catalog, .25¢ U.S. and
  overseas.
Curriculum Resources is a teaching
craft catalog mailed to schools and
institutions, but anyone may buy their
kits at discount prices. They offer over
1,500 needlecraft items in a twenty-four
page catalog. The pictures are
somewhat smaller than other catalogs.)
There are discounts of 10% and more.
They offer cross-stitch, crewel, quilting,
economy and designer needlepoint, and
a very large selection of latch-hook.

Eva Rosenstand
Box 775
Kennebunk, ME 04043
(207) 985-7089
76-page color catalog, $3 U.S. and
  overseas. MC, V, MO, PC.
Founded in 1957 in Copenhagen,
Denmark, Eva Rosenstand now has
stores throughout Denmark and many
agencies in Europe. Eva Rosenstand is
famous for their excellent counted
cross-stitch embroidery and Clara
Weaver designs. There are hundreds of

the finest designs offered. Don't miss this catalog.

Faye-Raye Stitcheries
P.O. Box 2155
Clinton, MS 39056
(601) 924-1567
Catalog free, U.S. Does not sell overseas. MO, PC.
As designers and publishers of needlework books, Faye-Raye offers fourteen publications—thirteen for cross-stitch and one for candlewicking with stenciling.

Foxxie Stitchery
P.O. Box 224
Ridgewood, NJ 07450
22-page catalog, $1 U.S. Does not sell overseas. MC, V, MO, PC.
Needlework supplies including over 500 books, counted cross-stitch supplies, fabrics, DMC floss, Danish Flower threads, trays, frames, spring tension hoops, and accessories are available.

Ginger Snap Station
P.O. Box 81086
Atlanta, GA 30366
(404) 455-8227
112-page color catalog, 50¢ U.S. and overseas. MC, V, MO, PC.
Ginger Snap supplies quilting, patchwork, calico, appliqué and patterns. There are 100% cotton fabrics from Yours Truly, Inc., and stitchery books from New Cross. They offer a terrific selection of quilted items, from the smallest of baby toys and Christmas ornaments to great-looking bed quilts in Dresden plate, log cabin, Mexican star, rolling star, and rail fence designs.

Jane Snead Samplers
Box 4909
Philadelphia, PA 19119
(215) 848-1577
48-page catalog, 50¢ U.S. and overseas. MC, PC.
There are over 250 embroidery sampler kits, printed on 100% imported linen, including instructions and floss.

Jane Whitmire
2353 S. Meade St.
Arlington, VA 22202
(703) 684-8036

16-page catalog, $2; overseas $3. MO, PC.
Jane Whitmire publishes a small but lovely catalog of pattern adaptations of fine historical needlework. There are a flying daemon of the ancient Paracan Indians of Peru, Persian rug patterns, and traditional Japanese Imari textile patterns—as well as modern abstracts, such as the Psychedelic Cat in light beige shading through backgrounds of gold to copper. Prices range from about $15 to $95.

Kelly's Crafts, Inc.
P.O. Box 36195
Cincinnati, OH 45236
(513) 791-0727
15-page brochure, $1.50 U.S. and overseas. MC, V, MO, PC.
Craft and needlework kits, including colorful plastic "stained glass" items to hang from windows, are sold in Kelly's Crafts catalog.

Lacis
2982 Adeline St.
Berkeley, CA 94703–2590
(415) 843-7178
16-page price list, $1; overseas $2. BD, MC, V, MO, PC.
Lacis supplies a complete line of specialty tools, materials, and books for all lace techniques including tatting, bobbin lace, needle lace, tenerife, crochet lace, knitted lace, filet lace, and smocking equipment. There are fine handcrafted crochet hooks in genuine bone and horn ($6), engraved German silver tatting shuttles ($20), and shuttles in mother-of-pearl, abalone, horn, exotic hardwoods, and 14-karat gold.

Merribee
2401 Centennial Dr.
Arlington, TX 76011
(800) 433-2924
Texas (817) 265-9142
48-page color catalog. MC, V, MO, PC.
Merribee is one of the more popular needlecraft catalogs, featuring many kits in needlepoint, candlewick, cross-stitch, punch needle, and pic 'n latch. There are many kits for tablecloths, bedspreads, and children's room accessories.

Modern Needlepoint Mounting
11 West 32nd St.
New York, NY 10001
2-page brochure, $4 U.S. and overseas.
  MO, PC.
This company is nationally known for
their craftmanship in professional
needlepoint mounting services. The
catalog displays over twenty-five
handbag frame styles and many
plaques, tennis racquet covers, and book
covers. They carry quality silk lining
materials in faille, moire, and satin in
a wide range of colors.

Needles 'N Hoops Co.
P.O. Box 165
Abington, PA 19001
22-page color catalog, U.S. and overseas.
  MC, V, MO, PC.
Needles 'N Hoops offers many printed
sampler kits, counted cross-stitch kits,
and hoops and frames. There are many
"hearth and home" samplers for
children, and traditional inscriptions.
There are printed cross-stitch quilt
squares, placemats, and guest towels.

Peacock Alley
650 Croswell SE
Grand Rapids, MI 49506
(616) 454-9898
31-page color pages, $2; overseas $4. MO,
  PC.
Peacock Alley sells original
handpainted needlepoint designs on the
finest imported canvases, using only the
best Persian wool. They display over 200
kits, including a child's chair with a
darling Christopher Robin seat cushion,
for $48.

Rainbow Gallery
13615 Victory Blvd. #245SG
Van Nuys, CA 91401
(213) 787-3542
32-page color catalog, $1; overseas $2
  MC, V, MO, PC.
Rainbow Gallery specializes in
European needlepoint. They feature
tapestries which may be worked in 10
count alone, or 20 count petit point
alone, or a combination of both.
Traditional richly colored designs
include Old Masters and medieval
tapestries as well as contemporary

subjects. Special orders are welcomed—
and they also have a search service if
you're looking for something special
they don't carry. Canvases are sold alone
or in kits with DMC tapestry wool.

Royal School of Needlework
25 Princes Gate
London SW7 England
01 589 0077
13-page color catalog, 29-page price list,
  $1.50 U.S.; overseas $2.25. MO, PC.
The Royal School of Needlework was
founded in 1872, by HRH Princess
Christina, daughter of Queen Victoria,
with the object of restoring ornamental
needlework to the high standards once
held by the decorative arts. In the Royal
School of Needlework workroom
apprentices undertake commissions;
repair and clean lace samplers, antique
embroideries and tapestries; stretch
canvases and make banners to order.
They hold exhibits and classes and
operate a retail shop. The mail order
catalog features materials and
equipment including canvases, wools,
metal threads, lace threads, frames and
books. The handpainted patterns
include many lovely historical
reproductions.

The Stitchery
Department 158A
204 Worcester St.
Wellesley, MA 02181
(800) 225-4127
(617) 237-1744
62-page color catalog, PC.
The stitchery offers over 200 kits,
predominently needlepoint with some
candlewicking, crewel and latch-hook.
There is the elegant Tabriz-style
Hunting Rug needlepoint kit (complete
for $265) and a colorful crewel-and-
candlewicked Christmas skirt
($34.95).

Virginia's Needlecraft Books
P.O. Box 1797
Buena Vista, CA 81211
4-page brochure, free U.S. and overseas.
  MO, PC.
Patterns and books for knitting, sewing,
and crocheting doll clothes.

The World in Stitches
82 South St.
Milford, NH 03055
(603) 673-6616
64-page color catalog, $1.50; overseas $3.
   Minimum order $10 MC, V, MO, PC.
The World in Stitches prides themselves on the extensive and high quality needlework supplies and kits they stock. They carry embroidery kits from over fifteen different countries, including beautiful Hungarian embroidery and Oriental embroidery done in Japanese silk and metal threads—an exacting technique, and quite beautiful.

POTTERY

Cedar Heights Clay Co.
P.O. Box 295
Oak Hill, OH 45656
(614) 682-7794
4-page brochure, free U.S. and overseas.
   MO, PC.
Cedar Heights mines and processes raw clay to varying sizes and textures. They sell ceramic clay (Goldart, Redart, and bonding clay) which is used extensively by potters for stoneware pottery.

Oak Hill Industries, Inc.
1335 N. Utah Ave.
Davenport, IA 52804
(319) 386-5937
4-page brochure, free U.S. and overseas.
   MO, PC.
Oak Hill manufactures and sells Oak Hill pottery wheels, both electric and kick wheel, in both assembled and kit forms.

Pacifica Crafts
P.O. Box 1407
Ferndale, WA 98248
(206) 384-1504
3-page brochure, free U.S. and overseas.
   MO, PC.
Electric potter's wheels priced from about $493 to $656.

Sculpture Associates, Ltd.
40 East 19th St.
New York, NY 10003
(212) 777-2400

60-page catalog, $2; overseas $5.
   Minimum order $20. AE, MC, V, MO, PC.
They offer sculptor's supplies and art materials including tools for carving stone, wax, plastic, wood, plaster, and clay. There are power tools, electric grinders, cutting machines, and welding equipment.

Soldner Pottery Equipment, Inc.
P.O. Box 428
Silt, Co 81652
(800) 525-3459
Colorado (303) 876-2935
12-page brochure, free U.S. and
   overseas. MO, PC.
Soldner sells pottery equipment designed and patented by Paul Soldner. He offers seven different pottery wheels (including two kits and a special wheel for the handicapped). He also carries two sizes of clay mixers, a 150 pound and a 300 pound capacity model.

Westwood Ceramic Supply Co.
14400 Lomitas Ave.
City of Industry, CA 91746
(213) 330-0631
180-page catalog, $3 U.S. and overseas.
   AE, DC, MC, V, MO, PC.
Westwood sells a large product line of raw materials and equipment for hobby ceramics, pottery, and mold making. Discounts are available in quantity purchases.

SEWING

Agalios L. Vrailas
7 Philellinon Str.
P.O. Box 76
Athens, Greece
01 3222659
6-page brochure with swatches, free
   U.S. and overseas. Prices in U.S.$. AE, DC, MC, V, MO, PC.
Agalios sells over twenty different handwoven silks and cottons. Silks (in 32 in. widths) range from about $30 to $46 a yard, and 100% cotton (in 56 in. widths) is about $17 a yard. The brochure is written in English, French, German, and Greek.

Altra, Inc.
5541 Central Ave.
Boulder, CO 80301
(800) 621-8103
(303) 449-2401
32-page color catalog, free U.S. MC, V,
  PC.
Altra creates top quality pre-cut sewing
kits for great-looking outerwear for
sports enthusiasts. There are kits for
nylon shell pullovers, Taslan bunting
jackets ($48.50), and pullovers ($33).
Mountain parkas with Thinsulate
insulation, snap-down vests, ski wear,
and activewear kits are in popular 100%
breathable nylon.

The Bee Lee Company
P.O. Box 36108
Dallas, TX 75235
(800) 527-5271
Texas (214) 351-2091
23-page catalog. MC, V, MO, PC.
The Bee Lee company offers "sewing
supplies with a western accent." There
are pearl snap fasteners, western trims,
western buckles, and many sewing aids.

Bo Sew Accents
P.O. Box 2289 Dept. BB
Vista, CA 92083
(619) 727-4363
64-page newsalog, free; overseas $1
  refundable. MC, V, MO, PC.
Bo Sew sells a terrific selection of sewing
and craft patterns, notions, and books.
There are patterns for soft baby pack
carriers, darling baby buntings, quilts,
and sportswear patterns for size toddlers
to adult. There are patterns from
Kappie, American School of
Needlework, The Sandbox Gang,
McCalls, Patch Press, Apple Dumplings,
and others.

Britex-By-Mail
146 Geary St.
San Francisco, CA 94108
(415) 392-2910
No catalog available. Swatch service $2.
  PC.
Britex Fabrics located just off Union
Square in San Francisco has four floors
devoted to unique fabrics imported from
all over the world, including a fine

selection of domestic and imported
wools. They do not have a catalog but
will send you a swatch request form.
You fill out what fabrics you're
interested in, what pattern you'll be
using, and your $2 fee.

The Button Shop
P.O. Box 1065
Oak Park, IL 60304
(312) 383-3875
16-page price list, free U.S. PC.
The Button Shop sells many types of
sewing supplies and notions including
zippers, threads, elastics, needles,
bobbins, velcro, scissors, tapes, pins,
hooks, buckles, interfacing, and buttons.

Cabin Fever Calicoes
Box 6256
Washington, D.C. 20015
(202) 686-0311
24-page catalog and over 200 solid color
  swatches, $2.75 U.S. and overseas.
"From the hundreds of products now
created for quiltmakers, Cabin Fever
Calicoes carefully selects those we
believe most helpful," says owner,
Eleanor Sienkiewicz. She offers books,
innovative notions, and solid color 100%
cotton fabrics.

Clothkits
24 High St., Lewes
East Sussex BN7 2LB England
07916 77111

Charing Cross Kits
Box 79882
Meredith, NH 03253
(603) 279-8449
40-page color catalog, $1 U.S. and
  overseas. MC, V, MO, PC.
Clothkits from England and Charing
Cross in the U.S. sell unique
silkscreened clothing kits for children's
sizes 0–8. The pattern-cutting lines are
stenciled on the fine English fabrics, so
there are no pattern papers to fuss with.
They offer lovely dresses, pinafores,
dungarees, and jackets. Especially nice
are the heavy ready-made knit sweaters
and leggings that coordinate with the
outfits.

Colorado Sunkits
Box 3288
Boulder, CO 80307
(303) 494-5476
10-page color catalog. MC, V, PC.
Colorado Sunkits offers complete sewing
kits for athletic running gear and tennis
outfits for men and women and children.
The kits include pre-cut fabrics,
trims, notions, and easy-to-follow
directions.

D. MacGillivray & Co.
Muir of Aird
Benbecula PA88 5NA
Scotland
4-page brochure with swatches. $4 U.S.
  and overseas. AE, MC, V, MO, PC.
D. MacGillivray has been "selling
crofter woven tweeds and knitwear all
over the world for the past 39 years."
They will send a price list, ordering
information, and swatches. Their
Harris tweeds (29-in. widths at $10 a
yard), are made from pure Scottish wool
that is spun, dyed, and finished in the
Outer Hebrides and handwoven by the
islanders in their own homes. They also
send swatches of Scots tweeds and
Donegals (both 56 in. wide at $6.40 a
yard). For an additional $6 you can
receive swatches of Scottish clan tartans
which come in 54-in. widths and range
in price from $18.80 to $20 a yard.

Daisy Kingdom
217 N. W. Davis
Portland, OR 97209
(503) 222-9033
24-page catalog, $1 U.S. and overseas.
  MC, V, MO, PC.
Daisy Kingdom designs ski wear sewing
kits for men, women and children.
These popular ski wear designs include
parkas, gaiters, ski suits, wind skirts and
pants, ski vests, cut-away overalls and
stretch pants. You can sew your own ski
wear for a great custom fit, and save
about half the cost of ready mades.
Although not listed in their catalog,
Daisy Kingdom is a goldmine of
beautiful imported trims, ribbons, and
buttons if you ever have the opportunity
to visit the store.

Dharma Trading Co.
P.O. Box 916
San Rafael, CA 94915
8-page brochure, free; overseas $3. MC,
  V, PC.
Dharma sells fabric dyes for batik, tie-
dye, and handpainting on natural
fabrics.

Eagle Mill Fabrics
Direct Discount Sales Division
Box 10
Wills Point, TX 75169
8-page brochure. Minimum order $10.
  PC.
Discount prices on first quality fabrics
and notions.

Ethnic Accessories
Box 250
Forestville, CA 95436
(707) 887-2909
32-page catalog $1.50; overseas $2.50.
  MO, PC.
The catalog offers patterns for antique
clothing and ethnic folkwear. There are
patterns for blouselike French
cheesemaker's smocks, Syrian dresses,
Japanese kimonos, Afghani nomad
dresses, Egyptian shirts, sarouelles
(pants from Turkey, Africa and India),
Tibetan panel coats, shirts of the
Ukraine, lovely Hong Kong cheongsam
dresses, Austrian dirndls and many
more. Pattern prices range from $4 to
$7.50.

Exotic Thai Silks
252 State St.
Los Altos, CA 94022
(415) 948-8611
4-page brochure, .35¢ U.S. Does not sell
  overseas. MC, V, MO, PC.
Exotic Thai Silks buys natural silks
direct from foreign loomers in China,
India, Thailand, Japan, and Italy. They
offer over 40 different kinds of silks at
discounts of about 30% below retail
prices. There are Indian raw silks (about
$10 a yard), Haboti silk satin stripe ($6
a yard), and Italian Dupionni ($18 a
yard). For swatch samples they require
a small (usually less than one dollar)
deposit, and request samples be
returned in thirty days.

Fabric Cut-Aways
100 Chafen
P.O. Box 292
Glendale, SC 29346
(803) 579-2033
22-page newsalog, $1 refundable U.S.
   Does not sell overseas. MO, PC.
Fabric Cut-Aways is the mail order
division of an outlet store that sells
factory remnants by the pound, in
lengths ranging from six inches to two
yards. They sell velvets, satins, velours,
denims, cottons, and knits. The Quilter's
Special is a six-pound bag (equal to
twenty-four yards) of dress-weight
woven cotton blends (no knits) in
lengths from six inches to one yard, for
$6.95. They also sell manufacturers
samples', patterns, and quilting
supplies.

Fashion Touches
P.O. Box 804
Bridgeport, CT 06601
(203) 333-7738
16-page color brochure, free U.S. Does
   not sell overseas. MO, PC.
Fashion Touches custom covers belts
and buttons from your own fabric. They
also repair worn and frayed belts—and
they sell buckles, too.

The Green Pepper, Inc.
941 Olive St.
Eugene, OR 97401
(503) 345-6665
20-page catalog, $1; overseas $2. MC, V,
   PC.
Green Pepper makes great-looking
sewing kits for ski wear, running gear,
camping attire, rainwear, and bicycle
gear. The kits have been rated according
to their sewing difficulty from one to five
stars. Many novices have successfully
completed difficult kits, the owners say,
but beginners will be faster (and more
likely to have fun) with the one star kits
to start with.

Gutcheon Patchworks, Inc.
611 Broadway
New York, NY 10012
(212) 673-0990
Swatch packet and price list, $1. PC.

Gutcheon patchworks will send a
swatch packet of over 150 swatches of
polished cottons. The minimum order is
one-half yard per color, one yard per
order. Prices range from $3.95 to $4.25
a yard. They also carry over forty-five
quilt book titles at discounts of about
50% of retail price.

Hallie Greer
Cushings Corner Rd.
P.O. Box 165
Freedom, NH 03836
(603) 539-6007
16-page color catalog, free U.S. MC, V.
Hallie Greer offers some very lovely
country fabrics, such as "Bunny Latch"
(in rose or country blue) and "Boy Blue's
Sheep," at $15 a yard. These fabrics are
also available in ready-made curtains,
bedspreads, pillows, and other home
furnishings.

Hearthside
P.O. Box 27
Church Hill Rd.
Charlotte, VT 05445
(800) 451-3533
Vermont (802) 425-2198
16-page color brochure, $2; overseas $3.
Hearthside has a full line of 100%
natural cotton quilt kits, which are
completely pre-cut to save time. With
some of their kits you can pick your own
choice of fabrics from among nearly
seventy colored swatches. There are
many quilt patterns to choose from—
and each has its skill level indicated.

Imaginations
51 Marble at Blandin Ave.
Framingham, MA 01701
(617) 620-1411
Catalog, $10; overseas $14. AE, MC, V,
   MO, PC.
Imaginations sends a catalog of color-
coordinated fabric swatches. From these
fabric groupings it is easy to mix and
match selected fabrics to create a
coordinated outfit, or to plan an entire
wardrobe. The prices are not discount,
but appear to be slightly lower than
going retail prices.

Kieffer's
1625 Hennepin Ave.
Minneapolis, MN 55403
(612) 332-3395
33-page catalog, free U.S. and overseas.
 MO, PC.
Kieffers sells fabrics and trims for
making lingerie: tricot, lingerie elastics,
laces in many styles, widths and colors.
They also carry patterns for all ages and
styles, including men's cotton briefs,
children's undergarments, bras, slips,
peignoirs and girdles.

Knit-Kits, Inc.
216 3rd Ave. No.
Minneapolis, MN 55401
(612) 332-0361
48-page catalog, $1 U.S. and overseas.
 Minimum order $15. MC, V, MO, PC.
Knit-Kits mail orders (and retails to
fabric stores) some excellent fabric
lines—including Carters, Wamsutta,
Concord, Healthtex, Peter Pan, VIP, and
others—at great prices.

Maxine Fabrics Co.
417 Fifth Ave.
New York, NY 10016
(212) 685-1790
Price list and swatch sampler, $3;
 overseas $5. Minimum order $5. MO,
 PC.
Maxine offers over 100 swatches of
imported and domestic fabrics to choose
from at reasonable prices.

Newark Dressmaker Supply, Inc.
P.O. Box 2448 Dept. IS
Lehigh Valley, PA 18001
(215) 837-7500
44-page catalog, free U.S. and overseas.
 MC, V, MO, PC.
Newark sells name-brand sewing
supplies at discounts of 5% to 50% off
retail prices. Quality threads, zippers,
pins, laces, buttons, fasteners,
interfacing, appliqués, measuring tools,
pressing accessories, books, and
patterns.

Nizhonie Fabric, Inc.
East Highway 160 P.O. Box 729
Cortez, CO 81321
(303) 565-7079

6-page color brochure, free U.S.
 Minimum order 3 yards. Does not sell
 overseas. MC, V, MO, PC.
Nizhonie sells traditional fabrics with
handpainted American Indian border
print designs. Fabrics are 100% cotton
or linen, are all 45-in. widths, and are
priced from $12 to $14 a yard.

Past Patterns
2017 Eastern, SE
Grand Rapids, MI 49507
(616) 245-9456
20-page catalog, $5; overseas $10.
"Over 100 years of vintage fashions
available in patterns." There is an 1894
ladies' wrapper (or tea-gown); a 1905
dainty gown with flounced train, corsets,
and petticoats; a gentleman's 1903
round-cornered sack suit; an Edwardian
jacket, some high-neck blouses, a ladies'
promenade suit, and lots of dresses and
hats from the 30s and 40s.

Patterns of History
816 State St.
Madison, WI 53706
(603) 262-0459
6-page brochure, free U.S. and overseas.
 MC, V, MO, PC.
Patterns of History offers about ten
authentic patterns from styles worn
from 1835 to 1896, for men and women.
There's even a pattern for a bustle to
give your finished gown that distinctive
form.

The Pattern People
P.O. Box 11254
Honolulu, HI 96828
(808) 537-4011
32-page catalog, $1; overseas $2. MC, V,
 MO, PC.
Sewing Patterns for Hawaiian and
resort wear including muumuus,
holokuus, many styles of sundresses,
pareaus, Chinese and Japanese wear,
and great wrap-and-tie shorts.

Platypus
P.O. Box 396
Planetarium Station
New York, NY 10024
(212) 874-0753
28-page catalog, $1; overseas $2.
 Minimum order $5. MO, PC.

Original and exclusive patterns and kits for dolls, toys, and quilted items. There are Veronica of the Victorian 1860s, and thirteen-inch-tall Sally and Sebastian, who look like lots of fun to play with.

Quiltwork Patches
430 NW 6th St.
Box 724
Corvallis, OR 97339
(503) 754-1475
32-page catalog, $2, with swatches $3; overseas $3, with swatches $4. MC, V, MO, PC.
Quiltwork Patches manufactures pre-cut quilt kits and also carries a full line of quilting supplies, plus an extensive selection of books, patterns, and quilting stencils.

Richard Adams
29/31 Green St.
Burnley
Lancashire BB10 1UZ England
0282 33462
8-page brochure, free U.S. and overseas. MO, PC.
Richard Adams is located in the center of the Lancashire textile industry and also has excellent resources in Northern Ireland linen manufacture companies. They specialize in the supply of materials and accessories for sewing hobbies: patchwork kits, metal templates, and kits for Teddy Bears and fabric dolls. There are also more than twenty embroidery kits available.

Sew What Fabrics
2431 Eastern SE
Grand Rapids, MI 49507
(606) 245-0834
16-page catalog with fabric swatches, $10 U.S. and overseas. MC, V, PC.

The Silver Thimble Collection
311 Valley Brook Rd.
McMurray, PA 15317
18-page catalog, free U.S. MC, V, PC.
Books on sewing techniques, including Ultrasuede, and tailoring and patterns for more than ten handbag styles.

Stitch 'N Stuff
4900 Winthrop West
Fort Worth, TX 76116
(817) 738-0545
28-page some color brochure, $1 U.S. and overseas. MO, PC.
Stitch 'N Stuff offers unique patterns, from whimsical dolls to elegant candlewicking. There are over 100 patterns, full size and with easy-to-read instructions. You'll see them occasionally in fabric stores.

Sunflower Studios
2851 Road B½
Grand Junction, CO 81503
(303) 242-3883
12-page some color catalog, free U.S. MC, V, MO, PC.
Sunflower Studios offers over 30 traditional fabrics which are handwoven and dyed in their own studios. They do offer swatch sheets for about $3.75. Write for your specific selection.

Taylor's Cut Aways & Stuff
2802 East Washington St.
Urbana, IL 61801-4699
17-page newsalog, $1 refundable U.S. Does not sell overseas. MO, PC.
Fabric sold by the pound and quarter-yard, including velvet, satin, cottons, and polyester. There are also pre-cut squares of lace, craft books, crochet, and doll patterns available.

Utex Trading
710 Ninth Ave.
Niagara Falls, NY 14301
(716) 282-4887
2-page price list, free U.S. and overseas. MO, PC.
Utex is one of the largest suppliers of Chinese silk in the country. They offer colors, textures, and patterns most suitable for contemporary and classic styles. They import directly from China and offer a fabric swatch service.

YLI Corporation
742 Genevieve, Suite L
Solana Beach, CA 92075
(800) 854-1932
(714) 755-4818
10-page brochure, $2; overseas $3. MC, V, PC.
YLI sells three models of Olfa rotary fabric cutters priced from $6.95 to $9.49.

They also wholesale silk embroidery thread, metallic thread, and ribbon.

STAINED GLASS

Coran-Sholes Industries
509 East Second St.
So. Boston, MA 02127
(800) 343-1600
(800) 322-4813
76-page catalog, $3; overseas $5.
    Minimum order $25. MC, V, MO, PC.
Coran-Sholes started in 1961 and distributes stained glass, lead, equipment, and all related supplies to professionals and amateur stained glass hobbyists.

Delphi Stained Glass
2116 E. Michigan Ave.
Lansing, MI 48912
(517) 482-2617
70-page (some color) catalog, $1 U.S. and overseas. Delphi carries over 250 types of glass including both domestic and imported, machine-rolled and mouth-blown sheet glass. In addition there are approximately 1,000 supply items in their line of art glass supplies.

Glassmasters Guild
621 Avenue of the Americas
New York, NY 10011
(212) 924-2868
12-page catalog, free U.S. and overseas.
    Minimum order $15. MC, V, MO, PC.
Glassmasters sells supplies for stained glass artists: cutters, breakers, patterns and pattern aids, routers, soldering irons, and many books on the subject.

H. L. Worden Co., Inc.
118 Main St.
P.O. Box 519
Granger, WA 98932
(509) 854-1557
20-page color catalog, $1.50 U.S. and overseas. Minimum order $15. MC, V, MO, PC.
Worden's sells craft kits for making Tiffany-styled stained glass lampshades. They offer over eleven

different sizes and eighty different designs, sold in semi-kits (additional supplies required to complete the lampshade), with complete instructions.

Hudson Glass
219 N. Division St.
Peekskill, NY 10566
(800) 431-2964
New York (914) 737-2124
96-page catalog, 95¢ U.S. and overseas.
    Minimum order $5. MC, V, MO, PC.
Hudson sells hundreds of stained glass patterns, many how-to-books, and a complete line of stained glass tools and supplies.

Saylescrafts, Inc.
171 Main St.
Nyack, NY 10960
(914) 358-7730
8-page brochure $1 U.S. Does not sell
    overseas. MO, PC.
Saylescrafts offers stained glass supplies at discounts of 5% to 20% below retail prices on glass, lead came, tools, starter kits, copper foil, lampshade forms, and books.

Whittemore-Durgin Glass Co.
P.O. Box 2065
Hanover, MA 02339
80-page catalog. $1 U.S. and overseas.
AE, MC, V, PC.
Whittemore-Durgin's catalog offers hundreds of stained glass window supplies and tools as well as bits of facts and nonsense. Started in 1969, it now has four retail outlets.

RUG MAKING

Braid Aid Fabrics
466 Washington St.
Pembroke, MA 02359
(617) 826-6091
96-page (some color) catalog, $2 U.S. and
    overseas. MC, V, MO, PC.
Braid Aid manufactures Palette 100% wool fabric in thirty-nine colors for making braided rugs. They sell many braided rug kits and tools.

George Wells Rugs, Inc.
565 Cedar Swamp Rd.
Glen Wead, NY 11545
(516) 676-2056
10-page brochure, free U.S. Does not sell
   overseas. MO, PC.
George Wells sells both kits and finished
hand-hooked rugs, tools and supplies.

Shillcraft
500 N. Calvert St.
Baltimore, MD 21202
(800) 638-1544
48-page color catalog, free; overseas $2.
   MC, V, MO, PC.
Shillcraft sells hundreds of latch-hook
rug kits in three yarn qualities: 100%
wool, wool and nylon blend, and 100%
DuPont Acrylic. The exacta-graph color
guide designs are printed on paper in
the exact size of the pattern you use. It
makes it quite simple to follow the color
guide, row by row. There are
picturesque wall hangings and
traditional, modern, Oriental, and floral
designs to choose from.

W. Cushing & Co.
North St.
P.O. Box 351
Kennebunkport, ME 04046
(207) 967-3711
Catalog, prices unavailable, U.S. and
   overseas. PC.
W. Cushing has a very large selection
of hooked rug patterns and supplies.
They also manufacture Cushing's
"Perfection Dyes" for dyeing craft
fabrics.

WOODWORKING

Albert Constantine & Son, Inc.
2050 Eastchester Rd.
Bronx, NY 10461
(212) 792-1600
108-page some color catalog, $1 U.S. and
   overseas. Minimum order $7.50. MC,
   V, MO, PC.
Constantine offers many unique
specialty products for woodworkers and
antique restorers. There are exotic
imported woods and other hard-to-find
tool items. There is the private

Constantine label on many of their fine
products.

Armor Products
P.O. Box 290
Deer Park, NY 11729
(516) 667-3328
56-page catalog, $1; overseas $2.
   Minimum order $5. MC, V, MO, PC.
Hobby supplies for woodworkers:
furniture and toy plans, hardware and
tool items, wooden toy parts, carvings
and moldings.

The Bartley Collection
747 Oakwood Ave.
Lake Forest, IL 60045
(312) 634-9510
24-page color catalog, $1; overseas $2.
   MC, V, MO, PC.
Bartley offers many furniture
reproductions kits, from a Chippendale
console table of cherry or mahogany
($269) to TV and stereo cabinets ($495)
and a Queen Anne Highboy ($990).

Bay Country Crafts
U.S. Route 13
Oak Hall, VA 23416
(800) 368-4410
16-page color catalog. AE, MC, V, PC.
Bay Country offers a wide selection of
"Do-A-Duck Kits"—craft kits for
complete assembly and painting of duck
decoys. Some of these are too pretty to
actually be used as decoys, but they can
be nice home decorator items, book
ends, lamp bases or planters.

Bob Morgan Woodworking Supplies
1123 Bardstown Rd.
Louisville, KY 40204
(502) 456-2545
36-page color catalog, $1 U.S. and
   overseas. MC, V, MO, PC.
Bob Morgan carries a large selection of
wood veneers for home craftsmen and
antique restorers. There's a good variety
of wooden toy parts, plans, books,
patterns, chair caning supplies, and
related woodworkers' items.

Cohasset Colonials
38 Parker Ave.
Cohasset, MA 02025
(617) 383-0110

32-page color catalog, $1; overseas $3. Cohasset Colonials sells American antique reproduction furniture kits: all solid wood and easy-assembly instructions that require no special skills or woodworking tools. Stain, glue, and hardware is included in each kit.

Conover Woodcraft Specialties, Inc.
18125 Madison Rd.
Parkman, OH 44080
(216) 548-3481
30-page catalog, $1; overseas $2.
    Minimum order $15. MC, V, MO, PC.
Conover specializes in woodworking handtools. Many of the tools are modeled from antique tools no longer manufactured, such as the Conover Threadbox ($178.50 for a set of three), which cuts external threads on a wooden dowel.

Craftplans Co.
21801 Industrial Blvd.
Rogers, MN 55374
(612) 428-4101
24-page catalog, 50¢ U.S. and overseas.
    MO, PC.
Craftplans offers over ninety plans and patterns for woodworking, including shadow boxes, dollhouses, decoys, planters, birdhouses, alphabet patterns, cradles, cupboards, and tea carts.

Craftsman Wood Service, Co.
1735 W. Cortland Ct.
Addison, IL 60101
(312) 629-3100
144-page some color catalog, $1;
    overseas $2. Minimum order $10. MC,
    V, MO, PC.
Craftsman has over 4,000 items for the wood hobbyist. They feature hard-to-find tools and supplies, and domestic and imported hardwoods from 1/64 in. to 4 in., depending on the wood.

Dalcraft
600 Hogan St.
Starkville, MS 39759
(601) 324-1314
32-page catalog, $2 U.S. and overseas.
    MC, V, MO, PC.
Dalcraft offers 250 full-size woodworking plans in many categories: grandfather clocks, bookcases, tables,

chairs, beds, dining sets, curios, and more.

Economy Enterprises
P.O. Box 23
Highland, MD 20777
(301) 776-3792
50-page catalog, $2; overseas $3. MO, PC.
Economy Enterprises offers a do-it-yourself catalog of building projects using mostly recycled materials. Their plans include power tools, saws, lathes, antique furniture, toys, and garden tools.

Educational Lumber Co., Inc.
P.O. Box 5373
Asheville, NC 28813-5373
(704) 255-8765
20-page catalog, $1 refundable U.S.
    Limited overseas sales. Minimum
    order $150. PC.
Educational Lumber is a small company specializing in lumber for schools and craftsman. They offer Appalachian hardwood among many others.

Furniture Designs
1425 Sherman Ave.
Evanston, IL 60201
(312) 475-3213
50-page catalog, $2; overseas free. MO,
    PC.
Full-size plans of fine furniture pieces. Each plan contains a bill of materials and an "exploded" perspective drawing which explains how all parts are assembled. There are over 150 plans available.

Garret Wade
161 Avenue of the Americas
New York, NY 10013
(800) 221-2942
(212) 807-1757
268-page color catalog, $3; overseas $5.
    AE, MC, V, MO, PC.
Garret Wade offers one of the largest selections of high quality wood-working tools and supplies. Their beautiful catalog is conveniently arranged into major categories: accessories, books, carving and sculptor's tools, chisels and knives, clamping tools, drilling tools, files, finishing supplies, Inca power tools, Japanese tools, marking tools, planes, plans, saws, scraping tools,

screwdrivers, sharpening tools, turning tools, and workbenches.

Midland Walnut Co.
705 Hwy 71 W.
P.O. Box 262
Savannah, MO 64485
(816) 324-3612
8-page brochure, free U.S. and overseas. Minimum order twenty-five board feet of lumber. MC, V, MO, PC.
Midland Walnut Co. sells wood and wood products. There is kiln-dried hardwood lumber, squares and gun stock blanks, molding (picture and architectural trim), oval frames, bowls, table legs, sconces, cutting boards, and trays. They specialize in walnut but also offer cherry, oak, apple, butternut, and other hardwoods.

Shaker Workshops
P.O. Box 1028
Concord, MA 01742
(617) 646-8985
32-page catalog 50¢; overseas $1.
Shaker Workshops produces wood kits based on the original Shaker pieces found in museums and private collections. Each kit is complete with all the materials needed, including sandpaper, glue, stain, hardware, and instructions, and most require only simple tools (screwdriver and hammer) for completion. Designs include the popular elder chair ($110), trestle table ($310), lowback chair ($60), Mt. Lebanon settee ($200), and rocker ($127).

The Toymaker Supply Co.
2907 Lake Forest Rd.
Box 5459
Tahoe City, CA 95730
24-page newsalog, $1 U.S. Does not sell overseas. MC, V, MO, PC.
Patterns, parts, and books to make wooden toys—from trains, race cars, and dump trucks to push-and-pull toys and jump rope handles. The catalog includes more than 300 full-size, easy-to-make wooden toy designs.

U-Bild Patterns for Better Living
P.O. Box 2383
Van Nuys, CA 91409
(213) 785-6368

112-page (some color) catalog, $1.95 U.S. Does not sell overseas. MO, PC.
The catalog includes over 700 woodworking and handcraft projects. They have plans and guides which contain step-by-step directions, photos, complete materials, lists, and traceable patterns.

Walpole Woodworkers
767 East St.
Walpole, MA 02081
(800) 343-6948
Massachusetts (617) 668-2800
22-page (some color) catalog, AE, MC, V, MO, PC.
Walpole sells complete kits for making cedar lawn and patio furniture. Each kit contains all the hardware, glue, pre-drilled wood, and instructions. An attractive four-piece grouping (including Boothbay rocker, Kennebec arm chair, Penobscot settee, and Wiscasset table) sells for about $400.

Western Reserve Antique Furniture Kit
Box 206A
Bath, OH 44210
12-page catalog, $2; overseas $5. MO, PC.
Western Reserve produces reproduction kits and finished products (in a variety of museum pieces) of New England, Shaker, and Pennsylvania Dutch furniture.

Windsor Classics, Ltd.
15937 Washington St. Dept. L
Gurnee, IL 60031
(312) 249-5558
4-page brochure, $1 U.S. and overseas. MC, V, MO, PC.
Windsor Classics offers furniture kits for butler tray tables, Queen Anne end tables and footstools, chests, and tea tables in mahogany, cherry and black walnut. They are available either finished or unfinished.

Wood Carvers Supply, Inc.
3056 Excelsior Blvd.
Minneapolis, MN 5416–4684
(612) 927-7491
88-page catalog, $2 U.S. and overseas. MC, V, MO, PC. COD.
Wood Carvers Supply carries 3,000 wood carving tools and supplies. They offer

the finest quality tools available and many are manufactured by them.

Woodcraft
41 Atlantic Ave.
Box 4000
Woburn, MA 01888
(800) 225-1153
96-page color catalog, AE, MC, V, MO, PC.
Woodcraft offers a large selection of fine tools and equipment for the wood hobbyist.

The Woodworker's Store
21801 Industrial Blvd.
Rogers, MN 55374
(612) 428-4101
112-page color catalog, $1; overseas $6. Minimum order $7.50.
The Woodworker's Store features veneers, inlays, hardwood lumber, carved and embossed mouldings, wood parts, furniture trim, tools, finishing materials, and a good selection of books.

Yield House
Rte. 16
North Conway, NH 03860
(603) 356-3141
76-page color catalog, free U.S. Does not sell overseas. AE, MC, V, PC.
The Yield House offers over 175 items: desks, files, organizers, music and entertainment consoles, sewing and hobby centers, bath and kitchen accessories—all in solid New England Pine. They were also winners of "The Best in Catalog" award, sponsored by the Maxwell Sroge Publishing Co. of Colorado Springs, Colorado.

ELECTRONICS

SEE ALSO
- Department Stores and Major
  Mail Order Houses
- Gifts
- Housewares-Appliances
- Music
- Photography

CONSUMER ELECTRONICS

Burdex Security Co.
1015 West "O" St.
P.O. Box 82802
Lincoln, NE 68501
(402) 474-4055
40-page catalog, free U.S. AE, MC, V, PC.
Burdex specializes in security systems, including alarm systems for the home and car, TV surveillance systems, smoke and fire detectors, and security lights.

DAK
10845 Vanowen St.
N. Hollywood, CA 91605
(800) 325-0800
64-page color catalog, free U.S.
Minimum order $20. MC, V, PC.

Delta Satellite Corporation
One Echo Plaza
Cedarburg, WI 53012
(800) 558-5582
(414) 375-1000
Delta sells home satellite earth stations for watching television. It is an informative catalog, and offers a good choice of home satellite earth stations and accessories.

ECTO Electronics
Rt. 9N
Plattsburg, NY 12901
(518) 561-8700
112-page newsalog, $1; overseas $3.
Minimum order $10. MC, V, MO, PC.
ECTO specializes in closeouts and cut-price liquidation offers on electronics, video, telephone, electronic parts, and computers. Discounts range from 20% to 90% below retail price. They mail two and one-half million catalogs annually, and ship to over thirty countries worldwide.

Edmund Scientific Company
101 E. Gloucester Pike
Barrington, NJ 08007
(609) 547-3488
48-page color catalog, free; overseas $2.
AE, DC, MC, V, MO, PC.
Edmund Scientific is a major U.S. designer, manufacturer, and retailer of optical equipment, scientific supplies, and kits. Its territory ranges from spyscopes and refractors to otoscopes, spirometers, and blood pressure cuffs. There are also computerized calorie counters, pulse meters, dental aids, and microscopes.

Electron-Kit, Ltd.
388 St. John St.
London EC1V 4NN England
01 278 0109
4-page brochure $1; overseas free. BD, MC, V, MO.

Electron-Kit is one of the leading suppliers of electronic construction kits in England.

Heath Co.
Hilltop Rd.
St. Joseph, MI 49085
(616) 982-3200
96-page color catalog, free U.S. and
  overseas. MC, V, MO, PC.
Electronic products from the fundamentals of electricity to robotics technology, in kit form, are available from Heath Company.

J S & A Group, Inc.
One J S & A Plaza
Northbrook, IL 60062
(312) 564-7000
48-page color catalog, free U.S. and
  overseas. AE, DC, MC, V, MO, PC.
J S & A's catalog is called "Products That Think." This catalog is designed in the catalog-magazine concept, and offers repeats of their best-selling products and a collection of their newest innovations and electronic breakthroughs. It's also loaded with interesting product information. Their products include Fresh Air Bubble air purifier, Magic Stat Thermostat, European halogen headlights, and the Brother EP-20 portable video typewriter. You can bet J S & A's next catalog will have even more unusual and fascinating electronic wonders.

Law Enforcements Associates
135 Main St.
Belleville, NJ 07109
(201) 751-0001
100-page catalog, $10 U.S. and overseas.
  MC, V, MO, PC.
This catalog offers hundreds of innovative crime control, surveillance, and protective devices for the consumer and the professional. There are communication and sound devices, optical surveillance devices, personal defense devices, and much more.

Louisville Lock & Key
3926 Shelbyville Rd.
Louisville, KY 40207
(800) 626-2611
22-page catalog, free U.S.; overseas $3.
  AE, MC, V, MO, PC.
Louisville carries a large line of security products to protect your car from thieves and vandals. The Ungo Box TL-1000 sells for $179 and has a sensitive motion detector that will activate a 107 db electronic siren. There are many other alarm systems available.

Markline Co. Inc.
411 Waverly Oaks Rd.
Waltham, MA 02154
(617) 891-6250
42-page color catalog, free U.S. Does not
  sell overseas. AE, DC, MC, V, MO, PC.
Markline has been a leader in brand-name consumer electronics. They offer unusual, sometimes unique electronic gifts with excellent product introduction. There is Canon's new credit card calculator ($19.95), so slim it fits right next to your American Express card. The Panasonic hairdryer ($19.95) weighs less than nine ounces. The Eagle Scoremaster golf computer ($99.95) stores and recalls all aspects of your game and the scores of other members of your foursome.

Phone City, Inc.
1152 Avenue of the Americas
New York, NY 10036
(212) 869-9898
26-page catalog, $1 U.S. and overseas.
  AE, MC, V, MO, PC.
Phone City offers telephones—decorative, antique, cordless, modern, business systems, and answering systems.

Phone Control Systems
92 Marcus Ave.
New Hyde Park, NY 11040
(516) 746-2794
65-page catalog, $1 U.S. Does not sell
  overseas. MO, PC.
Phone Control Systems carries one of the largest selections of telephone systems at discount prices of about 20% to 25% below retail prices. The catalog provides excellent product descriptions.

The Sharper Image
650 Davis St.
San Francisco, CA 94111
(800) 344-4444
(415) 788-4747
56-page color *The Sharper Image*
    Catalog, 8-page color *The Sharper*
    Image Woman catalog, free U.S. and
    overseas. AE, DC, MC, V, MO, PC.
Unique executive toys, consumer
electronics, conveniences, and personal
products have made *The Sharper Image*
catalog one of the hottest catalogs on the
market. Consider these: Alco Check
($78) is designed in Sweden where it is
used by private citizens and police law
enforcement agencies—you simply blow
into the mouthpiece to check your
alcohol intake level, and a red light
indicates 10% (too much) alcohol in
your blood stream, yellow light means
caution, and green light safety. The
Compuscale ($130) digitally displays the
caloric content of individual portions of
over 700 generic and brand-name foods.
There's a great selection of exercise and
weight machines, phone systems, and
electronic gadgets. Don't miss this
one.

The Shelburne Company
110 Painters Mill Rd.
Owings Mills, MD 21117
(800) 638-6170
28-page color catalog, $2 U.S. AE, DC,
    MC, V, MO, PC.
Shelburne offers electronic products
including the Novus Electronic
bathroom scale ($59.95), which features
a digital readout module that can be
positioned at eye level. Cup Cake
($24.95) is a coaster-size electric coffee
cup warmer. When the coffee cup's
handle is either to the left or right, the
Cup Cake automatically turns on and
when the cup handle faces forward, it's
off. There are many other terrific
electronic items available.

Synchronics
Unique Merchandising Mart
Building 42
Hanover, PA 17333
(800) 621-5199
Illinois (800) 972-5855

31-page color catalog, $2 U.S. and
    overseas. AE, DC, MC, V, MO, PC.
Ingenious electronic products such as
hands-free and cordless phone systems,
a tiny Minox EC spy camera, a five-inch
color portable TV, and others, available
from Synchronics.

Weather Fax Guide
3730 Nautilus Ave.
Brooklyn, NY 11224
(212) 372-0349
30-pages, $1; overseas $2. MC, PC.
Weather Fax sells military surplus and
industrial electronic equipment,
including satellite and weather
recording devices, for both amateur and
commercial use.

COMPUTER

Allco Products International
P.O. Box 43074
Detroit, MI 48243-0074
(519) 258-3738
60-page catalog, $1 refundable U.S. and
    overseas. V, MO, PC.
Allco sells Timex/Sinclair computers
and other hi-tech consumer electronic
items including video games, watches,
and telephones.

Cambridge Digital Systems
Division of Compumart
P.O. Box 568
65 Bent St.
Cambridge, MA 02139
(617) 491-2700
52-page catalog, free U.S. and overseas.
    MO, PC.
Cambridge carries fully supported and
integrated DEC and DEC-compatible
hardware and software operating
systems from over twenty-five
companies, including the NCR Tower
system.

Computer Mail Order
477 E. Third St.
Williamsport, PA 17701
(800) 233-8950
(800) 648-3311
Pennsylvania (717) 327-9575
44-page catalog, free U.S. MC, V, MO,
    PC.

Computers and accessories from Atari, Commodore, Eagle, Hewlett-Packard, Sanyo, Televideo, Amdek, Maxwell, and Epson. There are also about ten pages of software featured.

Computer Shopper
P.O. Box F
407 W. Washington Ave.
Titusville, FL 32796
(800) 327-9926
175-page newsalog, $1.95 U.S. MC, V.
The Computer Shopper is a magazine for buying, using, and selling computer hardware and software.

Elek-Tek, Inc.
6557 N. Lincoln Ave.
Chicago, IL 60645
(800) 621-1269
50-page catalog, free U.S. Does not sell overseas. Minimum order $15. MC, V, MO, PC.
Computers, calculators, and accessories by Hewlett-Packard, Texas-Instruments, Atari, Sharp, Canon, Casio, Star, Epson, and Comrex.

Hardware, Software, Anywhere
10 Cones St.
Brooklyn, NY 11231
(212) 596-3592
Price list, free U.S. and overseas. MO, PC.
Hardware, Software, Anywhere carries home computers, peripheral accessories, and software items at low prices—"We beat all competition." They will provide a price list on request for each line they carry.

The Home Software Guide
P.O. Box 2031
Nashua, NH 03061-2031
(800) 227-1929
(603) 882-1455
64-page color catalog, free U.S. AE, MC, V, PC.
The guide to software programs includes IBM, Atari, Vic-20, Apple, Commodore 64, and accessories. The catalog is color coded to each computer company. Each software program is fully described and includes a simple code section indicating format(s) offered and accessories required.

MISCO, Inc.
Holmdel, NJ 07733
(800) 631-2227
99-page color catalog, free U.S. and overseas. MC, V, MO.
MISCO offers one-stop shopping for all computer and word processing supplies: flexible disks, magnetic tapes, paper, ribbons, print wheels, cleaning kits, computer disks, and accessories. The catalog features over 1,000 products from all the major brands.

Olympic Sales Company
216 S. Oxford Ave.
Los Angeles, CA 90004
(213) 739-1100
130-page catalog, $2; overseas $5.
    Minimum order $10. MC, V, MO, PC.
Olympic Sales operates seven retail stores and a large mail order business of top name-brand electronic calculators, personal computers, and electronic office equipment at competitive prices.

Pace Micro Software Centers
Lock Box 328
Bensenville, IL 60106
(312) 595-0238
150-page newsalog, $3; overseas $5. MC, V, MO, PC.
Pace carries a complete selection of software books and accessories for all popular micro computer brands, such as Atari, Apple, Commodore, Radio Shack, Timex/Sinclair, and Texas Instruments. Prices on most items are at discounts of 20% to 30% below retail prices.

Pan American Electronics, Inc.
1117 Conway Ave.
Mission, TX 78572
(800) 531-7466
8-page brochure, free U.S. and overseas. AE, MC, V, MO, PC.
Pan American Electronics is a Radio Shack authorized sales center, offering discounts on Radio Shack merchandise from 10% to 50% below retail prices. Especially popular is the Radio Shack TRS-80 computer line.

Power Up
125 Main St.
Half Moon Bay, CA 94019
(800) 227-6703

California (800) 632-7979
16-page color catalog, free U.S. AE,
  MC, V.
Software programs for IBM and Apple
computer systems, for all members of
the family.

Strom
P.O. Box 197
Plymouth, MI 48170
(313) 455-8022
24-page newsalog, free U.S. PC.
Strom's catalog offers hundreds of
educational software programs from
leading firms. Each program listing is
described, age or grade level rated, and
computer compatibility indicated. This
is an excellent source, especially if
you're a parent seeking some pre-school
level computer programs for reading or
math readiness. There are many to
choose from.

MOVIE

Blackhawk Films
1235 W. 5th St.
Box 3990
Davenport, IA 52808
(319) 323-9736
64-page newsalog, free U.S. and
  overseas. MC, V, MO, PC.
Blackhawk Films are the largest
distributors of motion pictures from the
silent era, as well as offering a large
selection of current studio releases.

Canyon Cinema
2535 3rd St. #338
San Francisco, CA 94107
(415) 626-2255
300-page catalog, $5 U.S. and overseas.
  MO, PC.
Canyon Cinema rents the finest avant-
garde films, animation, documentaries,
erotic, cultural, and expressionistic
films. Most films are 16mm format,
although they distribute 8mm and super
8mm also.

Film Classic Exchange
P.O. Box 77568 Dockweiler Station
Los Angeles, CA 90007
(213) 731-3854
Brochure, free U.S. and overseas. MO.

Film Classic Exchange specializes in
new prints of motion pictures made
between 1895 and 1940. They sell mainly
to film archives, film and TV producers,
and serious collectors. Film prints are
available in 8mm standard, super 8mm,
16mm, and video cassette.

Manbeck Pictures Corp.
3621 Wakonda Dr.
Des Moines, IA 50321
(515) 285-8345
30-page brochure, free U.S. Does not sell
  overseas. MO, PC.
Manbeck distributes 16mm sound and
silent film classics. There's "The Heart
of Texas Ryan," starring Tom Mix; the
1923 "Hunchback of Notre Dame,"
starring Lon Chaney; "The Eagle,"
starring Rudolf Valentino; the first
screen version of "Dracula," starring
Max Schreck; "Flying Deuces," starring
Stan Laurel and Oliver Hardy; and a few
memorable films by W. C. Fields.

Movie Newsreels
P.O. Box 2589
Hollywood, CA 90028
(213) 467-2448
7-page brochure, 25¢; overseas 50¢
Movie Newsreels offers an extensive list
of color slides, videotapes, and films of
the NASA Space Program. They include
the John Glenn flight, Gemini flights,
Apollo moon landings, Skylab, and the
Space Shuttle.

Reel Images, Inc.
Box C
Sandy Hook, CT 06482
(800) 243-0987
Connecticut (203) 426-2574
64-page catalog, $1 U.S. and overseas.
  AE, DC, MC, V, MO, PC.
Reel Images offers over 1,000 different
movie titles. Their specialty is nostalgia
movies, and they also have feature-
length classics, cartoons, musical
comedies, documentaries, theatrical
trailers, movie highlights, and movies
on Hollywood personalities.

Super 8 Sound
95 Harvey St.
Cambridge, MA 02140
(617) 876-5876

Catalog, $3; overseas $5. MC, V, MO, PC. Super 8 Sound manufactures and sells a very comprehensive list of Super 8 filmmaking products, from splicers to the most advanced cameras and single and double system sound equipment.

Wolfe Worldwide Films
1541J Parkway Loop
Tustin, CA 92680
(714) 544-0622
126-page catalog, $1.50; overseas $1.
   Minimum order $5. MC, V, MO, PC.
Wolfe stocks 15,000 color slide duplicates of foreign countries, United States travel sites, and nature. They offer sets of slides with scripts on Holy Land travel, specific country travel sets, and animals and their environments. Used primarily by schools, churches and travel agencies.

Zipporah Films, Inc.
54 Lewis Wharf
Boston, MA 02110
(617) 742-6680
12-page newsalog, free U.S. and
   overseas. MO.
Zipporah Films distributes fifteen documentary films by Frederick Wiseman, including "Seraphita's Diary."

STEREO, AUDIO AND VIDEO

Annex Outlet
43 Warren St.
New York, NY 10007
(212) 964-8661
4-page brochure, free U.S. Does not sell
   overseas. MO.
Annex Outlet carries a full line of recording products and videotapes at low prices, including Maxell, TDK, Scotch Sony, RCA, Fuji, and Panasonic.

Audio Advisor
Box 6202
Grand Rapids, MI 49506
(616) 451-3968
18-page brochure, free U.S. and
   overseas. AE, MC, V, MO.
Audio Advisor carries over 200 product lines of stereo and audio equipment.

Crutchfield Corporation
1 Crutchfield Park
Charlottesville, VA 22906
(800) 446-1640
82-page color catalog, free U.S. Does not
   sell overseas AE, DC, MC, V, MO, PC.
Crutchfield is one of the leaders in car stereo equipment. Their catalog (they mail over two million annually) also carries a good selection of phone systems, answering machines, and computer accessories. Prices range from 10% to 40% below manufacturers' list price. A technical staff will answer questions and assist you with car installations, and home computer questions are fielded at their toll free number.

Illinois Audio, Inc.
12 E. Delaware Place
Chicago, IL 60611
(312) 664-0020
Price list, free U.S. Does not sell
   overseas. MC, V, MO, PC.
Illinois Audio has a large selection of name-brand stereo equipment and accessories at prices 2% to 5% over dealers' cost prices. Call or write (with model numbers) for a price quote.

International Hi Fi District
Moravia Center Industrial Park
Baltimore, MD 21206
(301) 488-9600
6-page brochure, free; overseas $2. MC,
   V, MO, PC.
Nationally advertised brands of high fidelity and video equipment, and accessories, at discounts of up to 45% below retail price.

Intersonics
P.O. Box 113
Toyohasi 440
Japan
0532 88–4773
Price list, free U.S. and overseas. BD,
   MO.
Intersonics manufactures high fidelity audio components and accessories including tone arms, speaker cables, interconnecting cords, and related products.

The Millers/Soundstage
1896 Maywood Rd.
South Euclid, OH 44121
(216) 291-9832
10-page brochure, free U.S. Does not sell
  overseas. MO, PC.
Miller's Soundstage sells tape/slide
synchronizers, dissolve units, and
related products.

Sound Reproduction, Inc.
7 Industrial Rd.
Fairfield, NJ 07006
(201) 227-6720
40-page catalog, $1; overseas free. DC,
  MC, V, MO, PC.
Sound Reproduction carries over forty
brands of stereo components such as
Sony, Pioneer, Technics, Akai, and
others. Since 1956.

Speakerlab, Inc.
P.O. Box C 30325
Wallingford Station
Seattle, WA 98103
(800) 426-7736
(206) 633-5020
30-page catalog, free; overseas 2
  International Reply Coupons.
Speaker lab sells high fidelity speakers
for home and car use, both assembled
and in kit form.

Stereo Equipment Sales
6730 Santa Barbra Court
Baltimore, MD 21227
(800) 638-3920

112-page catalog, free U.S. Does not sell
  overseas AE, DC, MC, V, MO, PC.
Stereo offers home and car stereos,
amps, tuners, turntables, cassette decks,
blank tapes, microphones, speakers,
audio, and computer furniture.

Video Playground
3001 Malmo Rd.
Arlington Heights, IL 60005
(800) 323-3478
36-page color catalog, free U.S. and
  overseas. AE, DC, MC, V, MO, PC.
Video Playground offers a good selection
of video accessories and video-tape
movies.

Walt Disney Films
6904 Tujunga Ave.
No. Hollywood, CA 91605
(800) 423-2200
48-page color film rental catalog, 30-
  page color video rental catalog, free
  U.S. Does not sell overseas. MC, V, MO,
  PC.
The best of Walt Disney's movies are
available for home entertainment in
both 16mm and video formats. Here are
the classics: "Alice in Wonderland,"
"Mary Poppins," "Swiss Family
Robinson," "Old Yeller," "20,000
Leagues Under the Sea," "The Legend
of Sleepy Hollow," and "Treasure
Island."

FOOD & DRINK

SEE ALSO
- Beauty and Health
- Gifts

GOURMET

Dean & DeLuca
121 Prince St.
New York, NY 10012
(212) 254-7774
20-page brochure, free U.S. and
   overseas. AE, MO, PC.
Dean & DeLuca offers some of the finest
imported foods. There is Pesto from
Crespi, Sherry and Balsamic vinegars,
Martelli and Fini Italian pasta, and
extra virgin cold-pressed olive oils. They
also offer excellent kitchenware items,
including all-porcelain dinner and
cookware by Pillivuyt of France, and
heavy gauge stainless steel cookware by
Paderno of Italy.

Fauchon
26-28 de la Madeleine
Paris 75008 France
742 60 11
45 page catalog, free U.S. and overseas.
   Prices in French francs. AE, DC, MC,
   V, PC.
Fauchon, on Place de la Madeleine, is
a luxury "épicerie" specializing
exclusively in French foods. Each day
the twenty chefs cook dishes that can
be bought from the Gastronomy
Department—hot, or ready to cook.
Twenty pastry cooks make over seventy
different and delicious cakes, which
may be eaten "sur place" or carry out.
To mail order customers, Fauchon lists
(in French) hundreds of their wonderful
foods: teas, coffees, preserves, nuts,
condiments, canned soups, foie gras,
spices, vinegars, brandied fruits, and
confectioneries. It's always a delight to
look at Fauchon's Import section where
American delicacies are featured. One
such item was Aunt Jemima's pancake
mix.

Fortnum and Mason
Piccadilly
London W1A 1ER England
01 734 8040
60-page color catalog, free U.S. and
   overseas. Price in British pounds. AE,
   CB, DC, V, PC.
For twenty-seven decades Fortnum's
has been purveyors of fine foods to the
British upper crust and to worldwide
celebrities. Shopping on the ground
floor, under the famous crystal
chandeliers, you'll find exquisite
displays of caviar, smoked salmon,
pâtés, and champagne truffles. You may

select your own groceries or a morning-coated attendant will take your order and wrap your goods. Fortnum's is renowned for their food hampers packed with delicious soups, Stiltons, smoked salmon, assorted biscuits, Akbar coffee, Fortnum and Mason Christmas pudding, ox tongue, and Dijon mustard. The catalog displays these hampers well, in addition to items from their department store—men's and women's clothing and gifts. This catalog is a must for every gourmet.

Fraser Morris
931 Madison Ave.
New York, NY 10021
(212) 988-6700
90-page catalog, $2 U.S. and overseas.
    AE, DC, MC, V, MO, PC.
"Distinguished first families of New York . . . have, decade after decade, chosen Fraser Morris as their purveyor for the finest foods, rare condiments, and the superb delicacies to give glamour and grace to their elegant tables," states the catalog. They carry imported chocolates that would delight any chocophile: Bendicks from England, Lindt and Tobler from Switzerland, Droste from Holland, and chocolate from Belgium. You will easily find your special brand of delicacies listed by categories: cookies and biscuits, vinegars and oils, sauces and seasonings, coffees and honeys, teas and cocoas, and nuts and dried fruits, to name a few.

Maison Glass
52 East 58th St.
New York, NY 10022
(212) 755-3316
116-page color catalog, $5 U.S.; overseas $10. AE, DC, MC, V, MO, PC.
Maison Glass is the Fortnum and Mason or Fauchon of America. Their catalog is the finest and most comprehensive food catalog available. Both the catalog and food items are expensive, but the selection is unsurpassed. Offering "tout bien de rien" (the best of everything): caviar, foie gras, truffles, Smithfield hams, concentrated meat and fish stocks, delicious imported cheeses,

green and pink peppercorns, balsamic and sherry wine vinegars, extra virgin olive oils, fine chocolates, and more.

GENERAL

Balducci's
424 Sixth Ave.
New York, NY 10011
(212) 673-2600
2-page brochure, free U.S. Does not sell overseas. AE, MO, PC.
Balducci's is a famous importer of fine Italian foods. It is here that you will find a wonderful holiday assortment of Lazzaroni and Amaretti cookies, and Torrone (3.7 lbs. for $40), a nougat confection imported from Cremona. Torrone comes in four flavors—Tenero, Tropic, Grand Mariner and Bianco Nero. The International Sausage Basket ($185) includes twelve assorted salamis and sausages representing six countries—Rumania, Germany, Italy, Switzerland, Denmark, and Hungary. They will mail order other items (such as coffees, teas, and olive oils) upon request.

California Seasons
625 Cannery Row
P.O. Box 1350
Monterey, CA 93942–1350
(408) 372-5868
16-page color catalog, free U.S. Does not sell overseas. MC, V, MO, PC.
California Seasons presents a fine collection of California products. Monterey Jack cheese (originated on the Monterey Peninsula in the late 1890's) is available in plain, hot, garlic, and dill. Vintage wines from Beaulieu and Mirrasou are delivered only in California. Also available are San Francisco-style salami, marinated artichoke hearts and mushrooms, date walnut cake, almonds and pistachio nuts. They are available in attractive gift boxes—with discounts on ten or more gift packs ordered.

Callaway Gardens
Pine Mountain, GA 31822
(800) 537-5353

16-page color catalog, free U.S. and
overseas. AE, MC, V, MO, PC.
Calloway Gardens, the famous vacation
spot in Pine Mountain, Georgia, now
offers some of their unique products
through the country store catalog.
Special favorites are the Muscadine
preserves, jellies, and sauces made from
the Muscadine grape (native to eastern
and southern United States). The aroma
of Georgia-cured bacon is sure to wake
the household up. The Southern
Breakfast ($24.95), attractively
packaged in a wooden box, includes 2
to 3 lbs. of Georgia-cured bacon, 2 lbs.
of Speckled Heart grits, plus syrup and
muscadine jelly and sauce. (All you have
to do is buy the eggs.)

Chalet Suzanne Foods
P.O. Box AC
Lake Wales, FL 33859–9003
(813) 676-6011
6-page newsalog, free U.S. and overseas.
AE, DC, MC, V, MO, PC.
Chalet Suzanne offers over twenty-five
canned gourmet soups and sauces:
cream of romaine, New England clam
chowder, vichyssoise, gazpacho, cream
of watercress, cucumber, chicken
michon, seafood newburg and more.
(These very soups, they say, were served
aboard Apollo 15 and Apollo 16 trips to
the moon.) It's so hard to decide; better
try the six soup sampler for $12.50.

Conte D. Savoia
555 W. Roosevelt Rd.
Chicago, IL 60607
(312) 666-3471
Color catalog, free U.S. and overseas.
MC, V, MO, PC.
Conte D. Savoia sells bulk products—
spices, beans, pasta, and coffee beans.
They also carry a complete line of
cooking utensils, bowls, and pans. A
variety of imported canned goods are
available from France, Germany,
England, Italy, India, Japan, and
U.S.S.R.

Creole Delicacies Co.
533 Saint Ann St.
New Orleans, LA 70116
(504) 525-9508

6-page brochure, 50¢; overseas $1. AE,
DC, MC, V, MO, PC.
Located in the heart of New Orleans'
French Quarter, Kenneth Verlander and
his sister, Lisette Verlander Sutton, have
helped visitors from around the world
select delicious Louisiana food items:
creamy pecan pralines, made fresh in
their patio kitchen; creole seasonings
and sauces; and canned soups (turtle
soup, gumbo, crayfish bisque, and
shrimp creole).

Figi's
630 South Central Ave.
Marshfield, WI 54449
(715) 387-1771
80-page color catalog, free U.S. Does not
sell overseas. AE, DC, MC, V, MO, PC.
Figi's catalog is subheaded "Gifts in
Good Taste." Indeed, in a recent catalog,
forty-four pages were devoted to
marvelous-looking cheeses, sausages,
and hams. The rest of the catalog would
satisfy even the biggest sweet tooth: fruit
and nut cakes, tortes, Danish Kringles,
brownies, Pffernuesse, fudge, and
Chocolate Pickles. (Relax—Chocolate
Pickles are just sweet milk chocolate,
molded to look like pickles and
disguised in bright green foil.)

Gazin's
2910 Toulouse St.
New Orleans, LA 70179
(504) 482-0302
32-page catalog, 50¢ U.S.; overseas $1.
MC, V, MO, PC.
Gazin's specializes in ingredients and
products for Creole cooking, the
traditional cuisine of the early settlers
in southern Louisiana: jambalaya
mixes, Creole sauce, spices, and seafood
gumbo. Thick Creole praline sauce,
brimming with luscious pecans, makes
a perfect topping for cakes, waffles, and
parfaits. Pralines are available too, at
$7.95 for a fourteen-ounce box. Many
cookbooks are available including
Brennan's, a collection of recipes from
the famous Brennan's restaurant, for
$11.95.

The Gift Factory
4210 S. W. Cedar Hills Blvd.
Beaverton, OR 97005
(503) 643-7634
14-page catalog, free U.S. Does not sell
    overseas. MC, V, MO, PC.
This gift shop features famous Oregon
gourmet food products in custom gift
packing. Probably the most well known
is Beaver Horseradish, hot to the taste
and beautifully white. Also under the
Beaver label are over twenty varieties
of mustards that range from hot to
sweet. Other Oregon products include
Cap'n Chunks canned smoked Salmon,
Carmine's Vintage Wine Jelly,
Tillamook Cheese, Oregon filberts, and
Inglehoffer spices. Gift packs start at
$2.18.

H. Roth & Son
1577 First Ave.
New York, NY 10028
(212) 734-1111
52-page catalog, free U.S. and overseas.
    Minimum order $10. AE, DC, MC, V,
    MO, PC.
Don't miss this catalog of wonderful and
unusual cookware from Europe, plus
pungent spices and ingredients for your
gourmet cooking. There are baking
moulds, fancy cookie cutters, cookbooks,
coffee mills, cutlery, gadgets, grinders,
graters, and spaetzle makers. There is
also woodenware—implements, rolling
pins, and cutting boards. You'll find
dough, fruit fillings, decorations and, of
course, an order form.

Le Gourmand
Box 433 Route 22
Peru, NY 12972
(514) 483-1609
8-page brochure, free U.S. Does not sell
    overseas. MC, V, MO, PC.
Le Gourmand's brochure is an
interesting combination of recipes and
gourmet foods: Paul Corcellet Lime
Vinegar, Sanchez Romate Sherry
Vinegar, Monari Federzoni Balsamic
Vinegar, Suchard Express Cocoa, Van
Houten Cocoa, and Lindt Chocolates, to
name a few. Le Gourmand claims its

products range from 10% to 50% less
expensive than those of other
companies.

Ray's Brand Products
1920 South 13th
P.O. Box 1000
Springfield, IL 62705
(217) 523-2777
Price list, free U.S. Does not sell
    overseas. PC.
Ray's offers delicious canned chili and
coney sauce. They do not contain any
fillers—just meat, spices (lots of them)
powdered onion, garlic, and beans.
Minimum order is one case (two 6-packs
of seven and one-half ounce cans) of
chili.

S. E. Rykoff & Co.
P.O. Box 21467
Market Street Station
Los Angeles, CA 90021
(800) 421-9873
48-page color catalog, free U.S. Does not
    sell overseas. AE, MC, V, MO, PC.
S. E. Rykoff features an unusual and
delicious selection of foods, paper
products, and cookware. A few items
formerly available only to restaurants
and hotels (and many items that are
specially packaged for S. E. Rykoff) are
offered. Delicate Vol-au-Vent and
Barquettes (puff pastry cases) can be
filled with tiny spring vegetables,
creamed seafoods, or your own creation.
Imported Dutch chocolate "doilies" in
four distinctive patterns are a delicious
crowning touch for a mousse or fancy
ice cream. There's nothing finer than
French pâté de foie gras; accompany
this with French imported cornichons
(tiny pickles) and tangy cocktail onions
for special hors d'oeuvres.

Sey-Co Products Co., Inc.
7651 Densmore Ave.
Van Nuys, CA 91409
(800) 423-2942
California (213) 785-0421
24-page catalog, free U.S. and overseas.
    AE, MC, V, MO, PC.
Sey-Co Products offers a complete line
of gourmet non-perishable food

products, from appetizers to desserts. Their sweet pickled fruits have been highly praised by gourmets. They are made in small batches with a fine syrup and rich spices. There are sweet pickled melonaires, peaches, watermelon rind, grapefruit peel, honeydew, and cantaloupe. Rumcots (apricots in rum) are only one of their many "spirited" fruits available.

A Taste of Philadelphia
622 Milmot Ave.
Swarthmore, PA 19081
(215) 328-5060
8-page brochure, $1 U.S. Does not sell
    overseas. MC, V, MO, PC.
Fred Catona mail orders "foods that made Philadelphia famous" by express mail or airfreight. He specializes in "Hoagies to Go"—long split rolls with cheese, smoked meat, tomato and lettuce, olive oil and oregano. Displaced Philadelphians will be thrilled to know he also offers other Philly favorites such as cinnamon buns, Bookbinder's soups, cheesesteak, soft pretzels, and scrapple (a brown-and-serve loaf made from pork scraps, eaten with eggs and warm syrup). He has sent hoagies to forty-nine states and many foreign countries, starting at $17.50 for a seven-inch hoagie delivered.

Those Green Bros.
P.O. Box 5284
Denver, CO 80217
(303) 296-3555
16-page brochure free U.S. Limited
    overseas sales. MO, PC.
This produce company features famous Colorado pascal celery. Pascal celery is grown at high altitudes and is appreciated for its big, crisp, cream-white stalks. Wrapped in parchment and packed in a waterproof flight box, they will ship pascal celery anywhere in the U.S. Eight selected stalks for $18.95. Those Green Bros. also offer tempting smoked turkeys, cheeses, clover honey, jellies, smoked pheasants, and chickens.

IMPORTED

China Bowl Trading Co.
169 Lackawanna Ave.
Parsippany, NJ 07054
(201) 335-1000
Price list, free U.S. Does not sell
    overseas. MO, PC.
China Bowls sells authentic Chinese cooking ingredients including spices and herbs, sauces and flavorings, noodles, dried mushrooms, and other dried specialty products. They also offer tea, fortune cookies, and chopsticks.

The Chinese Kitchen
P.O. Box 218
Stirling, NJ 07980
(201) 665-2234
32-page catalog, $1 U.S. and overseas.
    Minimum order $10. MC, V, MO, PC.
From the Chinese Kitchen catalog you'll find authentic spices, sauces, condiments, utensils, and ingredients used in Oriental cooking. Many exotic hard-to-find food items, chinese porcelain dinnerware, gift items, cookbooks, teas, dessert and snack items. The Mushroom Assortment pack ($14.95) is a superb way to sample the different varieties of Oriental mushrooms; it contains dried black mushrooms, wood ears, lily flowers (not a fungus, but used in many of the same ways), straw mushrooms, and oyster mushrooms (with a flavor reminiscent of abalone). Other assortment packs are available for spices and condiments.

Ferrara Foods & Confections
195 Grand St.
New York, NY 10013
(800) 235-3515
New York (212) 226-6150
6-page color catalog, free U.S. and
    overseas. AE, MC, V, MO, PC.
Antonio Ferrara opened his pasticceria in 1892 and the demand for his Italian goodies grew. Ferrara packages and ships its own brands of coffee (both espresso and cappuccino), petit rhum babas (delizioso!), candies (Torrone and the Ferrara Kiss), and hundreds of other Italian delicacies all over the world. Cannoli shells (six shells for $2) are

ready for any filling—cannoli cream, pudding custard, or whipped cream.

Gourmail
816 Newton Rd. Drawer 516
Berwyn, PA 19312
(215) 296-4620
8-page brochure, free U.S. and overseas.
MC, V, MO, PC.
The art of Indian cooking is well presented in this brochure—and the canned gourmet food items and recipes make it simple. Chhole (curried chickpeas) is a popular dish from Punjab. Its thick, hot sauce is spiced with onion, tamarind, and ginger. Madhur Jaffrey's cookbook, *An Invitation to Indian Cooking* $12.95 is available with an assortment of spices (coriander, fennel, garam masala, cumin, turmeric, and fenugreek).

House of Spices
76–17 Broadway
Jackson Heights, NY 11373
(212) 476-1577
8-page brochure, free U.S. and overseas.
MO, PC.
House of Spices offers the largest selection of Indian spices, condiments, canned vegetables, Dalls, beans, flours and kitchen utensils. There are pickles: Chhunda (shredded mango), Kerda, and God-Keri (Mango Dry Date Gunda). And there are flours: Besan, Moong, Urid, Bajeri, and Chappati. There are also utensils for the kitchen: dettol, iron tava, and a brass sev machine.

J. A. Demonchaux Co.
827 North Kansas
P.O. Box 8330
Topeka, KS 66608
6-page brochure, price unavailable. PC.
J. A. Demonchaux imports gourmet food products from France. Crystallized flowers (violets and mimosa) used for cake decorations are available, starting at $7.45 for a three and one-half ounce box. Cherries in cognac, truffled goose liver pâté, and Belgian baby carrots are also offered.

Manganaro Foods
488 Ninth Ave.
New York, NY 10018
(212) 563-5331
4-page brochure, free U.S. Does not sell overseas. Minimum order $15. MO, PC.
Gourmet imported Italian food. The Pasta-Plus Gift Box ($35) includes pasta, canned plum tomatoes, grated parmesan cheese, olive oil, wine vinegar, espresso coffee, and a box of Amaretti (almond flavored cookies). Individual imported items are also available: Olio Sasso (a North Italian pure olive oil), Filli DeCecco packaged pasta, and Perugina Torrone (a traditional hard nougat candy studded with almonds).

Mrs. De Wildt
R.D. 3
Bangor, PA 18013
(215) 588-1042
7-page price list, free U.S. and overseas.
MO, PC.
Mrs. De Wildt specializes in spices, ingredients, and prepared foods for Indonesian cooking. If you plan on making Rijstaffel for your guests, you'll find the necessary ingredients for that "rice table" from Mrs. De Wildt. Gado Gado and Serundeng may sound strange, but they are delicious—spiced peanut paste, and fried spiced coconut with peanuts. Tempeh products (cultured soy foods) are also available.

Pacific Trader
19 Central Square
Chatham, NY 12037
(518) 392-2125
9-page brochure, $1 U.S. Does not sell overseas. MC, V, MO, PC.
Pacific Trader is an Oriental grocery and import store. They carry just about everything you would need for making sumptuous Chinese or Middle Eastern meals: Melizanes Imam, Alphonso olives, Harrisa, Conimex spices, oyster sauce, tahini, and peach chutney.

Paprikas Weiss
1546 Second Ave.
New York, NY 10028
(212) 288-6117
32-page some color catalog, $1. MC, V.
Imported Szaloncukor, a traditional
Hungarian Christmas chocolate candy,
is but one of the hundreds of wonderful
food, cookware, and gift items stocked
by Paprikas Weiss. There are many
imported herbs and spices in attractive
apothecary jars, priced at $14 for a
choice of six.

Tia Mia
720 N. Walnut St.
El Paso, TX 79903
(915) 533-0464
16-page newsalog, $2 U.S. and overseas.
    Minimum order $25. AE, MC, V, MO,
    PC.
Here's a terrific source for all the
ingredients you'll need to fix those
delicious Mexican dishes: antojitos
(appetizers), gazpachos, tacos,
enchiladas, tamales, flautas, burros,
tostadas, chiles rellenos, and
chimichangas. You can buy many spicy
ready-made salsas and chilies, from
mild to hot. Now you can serve the
dessert Sopapillas at home; they are
golden, deep-fried triangles of puffy
bread served drizzled in honey. The mix
is available in a gift basket which sells
for $9.95.

Tsang and Ma
P.O. Box 294
Belmont, CA 94002
(415) 595-2270
6-page brochure, free U.S. and overseas.
    MC, V, MO, PC.
Tsang and Ma presents a large selection
of Oriental vegetable seeds for the home
gardener: Bok Choy (Chinese white
cabbage), Hinn Choy (Chinese spinach),
Dai Gai Choy (broadleaf mustard
cabbage), Doan Gwa, Gow Choy, snow
peas, and others. Regional seasonings,
oils, and kitchen items (clay pots,
steamers, cleavers, dinnerware and
utensils) are also available.

Vander Vilets
Westdale Food Company
3245 West 11th ST.
Chicago, IL 60655
48-page catalog, $1 U.S. Does not sell
    overseas. MO, PC.
Vander Vilets imports food and gift
items from Holland: Klene licorice,
Patria biscuits, Droste chocolates,
Tonnema Roll candies, Vandewal cakes,
Holland herring, and (of course) wooden
shoes.

FISH

Atlantis Caviar
714 Sea Mountain Hwy.
North Myrtle Beach, SC 29582
(803) 249-3711
Price list, free. MC, V, PC.
Sturgeon Caviar is available in four-
ounce and seven-ounce jars. A free
eight-page brochure of gourmet caviar
recipes is sent with your order.

Briggs-Way Co.
Ptramigan Trail
Ugashik, AK 99683
Briggs-Way offers glass-canned Alaska
salmon. Within minutes of catching
them, the king, red, and medium red
salmon are iced and processed. The firm
fleshed, glass-canned salmon is
delicious and bears little taste
resemblance to salmon canned-in-tin.
The salmon is available either lightly
salted or no salt added, and there is a
minimum order of twelve five-ounce
jars. Their new product, Hickory
Smoked Salmon Caviar Spread, is
excellent for hors d'oeuvres or just plain
good snacks. For those who are
nutrition-conscious, the caviar contains
nearly 30% protein.

Caviarteria, Inc.
29 East 60th St.
New York, NY 10022
(212) 759-7410
16-page brochure, free U.S. and
    overseas. AE, MC, V, MO, PC.
This catalog is titled *Treasury of
Magnificent Caviar* for good reason.
Caviarteria is the country's largest

supplier of caviar. If you have acquired a fine taste for those glittering little fish eggs, and have a pocketbook to match, you can indulge in Caspian Imperial for about $100 per three and one-half ounces. For starters you might be interested in a four-jar, six-ounce sampler for $29.95. They also carry pâté de foie gras, truffles, exotic dried mushrooms, and Scotch smoked salmon.

Crawford Lobster Co.
62 Badgers Island
Kittery, ME 03904
(207) 439-0920
16-page color catalog, free U.S. and
    overseas. AE, MC, V, MO, PC.
Live Maine lobsters and clams direct to you by Air Freight. Only the choicest hardshelled lobsters are shipped live, direct to you, states the catalog. Six live lobsters for only $42.95 (add $35 to $45 for Air Freight charges), but what a meal! Or what a surprising gift! They also offer fresh oysters, cherrystone and littleneck clams, Irish smoked salmon from Dublin, imported caviar, and attractive gift boxes of chowders, pâtés, Indian pudding, and canned lobster meat.

George Campbell and Sons
    (Fishmongers) Ltd.
18 Stafford St.
Edinburg WH3 7BE Scotland
031 225 7507
Price list, free U.S. and overseas. MO,
    PC.
Founded in 1872, George Campbell sells the finest fish and game. They were granted the Royal Warrant in 1962, and supply fish, poultry and game to Her Majesty the Queen in Edinburgh. Scotch salmon is sold in either sides or slices. There are also smoked haddock fillets, kippers, and many other choice selections.

Hegg & Hegg
Smoked Salmon, Inc.
801 Marine Drive
Port Angeles, WA 98362
6-page brochure, free U.S. and overseas.
    MO, PC.
Fred Hegg has a thriving Port Angeles business of selling Alder Smoked Red

Salmon. Salmon from the Puget Sound waters are smoked over native Alder wood by a technique used for centuries by the Pacific Northwest Indians. The salmon arrives at your door deliciously moist in vacuum-sealed plastic, with a special recipe folder included. Enjoying worldwide fame, Hegg & Hegg supplies smoked salmon to some of the nation's finest stores and mail order companies. Whole smoked salmon ($30) or half smoked salmon ($16.50), with prices slightly higher east of the Rocky Mountains.

Josephson's Smokehouse & Dock
106 Marine Dr.
P.O. Box 412
Astoria, OR 97103
(505) 325-2190
Price list, free U.S. and overseas. MC,
    V, MO, PC.
Josephson's offers a variety of Pacific Northwest smoked salmon. There is traditional Scandinavian-style smoked salmon, which comes in moist, medium, or dry and pickled. Smoked sockeye salmon—deep red in color, moist and delicate in flavor—is sold by the side. Premium lox, made from the highest quality Chinook salmon—light red in color, moist and oily in texture—is available November through March. Prices start at $20 for one pound of smoked salmon, and go up from there.

Murray's Sturgeon Shop
2429 Broadway
New York, NY 10024
(212) 724-2650
Price list, free U.S. Does not sell
    overseas. Minimum order $50. PC.
One of Manhattan's best purveyors of smoked fish and caviar, Murray's sells Norwegian salmon and Atlantic salmon caught from the waters of Nova Scotia. There is lake sturgeon ($30 per lb.), which is expensive as well as smoked, and white fish ($7.95 per lb.), which many people agree is just as tasty. Especially tempting are the homemade pickled salmon and herring sauces. Fresh Russian and Iranian Malossol (meaning very little salt) Caviar is also available.

Ritchies of Rothesay
37 Watergate
Rothesay
PA20 9AD Isle of Bute
Scotland
0700 3012
Brochure, free U.S. and overseas. MO,
PC.
As a family business for over thirty
years, Ritchies is well known for their
smoked Scotch salmon. Caught from the
estuaries of the Highland rivers in the
county of Argyll, where the pure waters
come from the Scottish mountains, a
two-pound side costs $35, postpaid.

Specialty Seafood
1719 13th St.
Anacortes, WA 98221
(206) 293-4661
12-page color catalog, free U.S. and
    overseas. No shipments made to Post
    Office Box addresses. AE, DC, MC, V,
    MO, PC.
Specialty Seafood company started
twenty-five years ago, selling smoked
salmon and oysters. They are winners
of many national graphic design and
marketing awards, and you will see
their distinctively wrapped, delicious
salmon in many fine department stores
and mail order catalogs. A one and one-
half pound smoked salmon (in a
beautiful gift box) is especially suitable
for gift-giving for $29.95 postpaid. No
refrigeration is necessary for these
specially sealed vacuum packages. (The
catalog states you can store these
unopened packages up to a year.)

Wisconsin Fishing Co.
1112 N. McDonald St.
P.O. Box 965
Green Bay, WI 54305
(414) 437-3582
12-page brochure, free U.S. Does not sell
    overseas. MC, V, MO, PC.
Wisconsin Fishing Company sells a full
line of fish and seafoods: cod, haddock,
sole, trout, salmon, shrimp, crab, lobster,
scallops, octopus, squid, and smoked
fish. They pride themselves on
procuring the finest fish and seafood
from around the globe: Japan, India,
Brazil, New Zealand, the Eastern and
Western Seaboards, and the Southern

Coast. Fresh fish orders are carefully
packaged in insulated cartons and dry
ice. Shipments get to you in 24-48 hours
by either Greyhound bus express or by
Parcel Post (December through Easter
only).

MEATS

Amana Society Meat Shop
Amana, IA 52203
(319) 622-3113
14-page color brochure, free U.S.;
    overseas limited sales. PC.
Amana sells fine smoked ham, sausage,
and bacon. The story of Amana goes
back 250 years to Germany, where a
group seeking religious freedom
migrated to America. Today the name
has earned recognition for its tradition
of excellent craftsmanship and
excellent meats. Amana's meat
processing is an old-fashioned method
based on the Amana conviction that
time itself is a vital ingredient. Meats
hang in the century-old smokehouse
tower, soaking up the aroma of the
woodsy smoke.

Broadbent's
B. & B. Food Products
Route 1
Cadiz, KY 42211
(502) 235-5294
16-page color catalog, price unavailable.
    Does not sell overseas. AE, MC, V, PC.
For over 70 years Broadbent Farm of
southwestern Kentucky has been
providing people with delicious hams,
bacon, and sausage. These hams have
won the Grand Champion Country Ham
Award at the Kentucky State Fair many
times. A nine-pound ham starts at
$46.50, and serves more than 20 people—
generously.

Czimer
Route 7, Box 285
Lockport, IL 60441
(312) 460-2210
2-page brochure. MO.
Hard-to-find game and game birds.
"Make your next dinner an adventure,"
says the brochure—and it undoubtedly
would be an adventure if you offered

zebra, hippopotamus, lion, caribou, mountain sheep, llama, kangaroo, rattlesnake, or beaver. John Czimer's complete list is most unusual—most meats are available in ground meat, steaks, and chops. (Rattlesnake steaks might appear odd, so the meat is simply sold by the pound.)

Dutchess Farms
Old Indian Rd.
Milton, NY 12547–9735
(914) 795-2175
10-page brochure, free U.S. and
    overseas. MC, V, MO.
Dutchess Farms has for over thirty years proudly offered delectable turkey and ham. The Dutchess turkey ($1.60 per lb.), an all-American favorite, has been praised by gourmets as "the thorough-bred of turkeys." It's available in your choice of weights from eight to twenty-five pounds. The Dutchess triple-smoked ham ($3 per lb.) is a mild hickory-smoked, tender and juicy ham available in nine-to sixteen-pound weights. Dutchess Farms also provides a unique idea—a complete holiday banquet featuring either the Dutchess turkey or triple smoked Ham. Banquets come in two sizes, serving four to six, and six to twelve people. Write them for the mouth-watering details.

Early's Honey Stand
Rural Route 2
Spring Hill, TN 37174
(615) 486-2230
32-page color catalog, free U.S. Does not
    sell overseas. AE, DC, MC, V, MO, PC.
Early's Honey Stand ships native Tennessee foods all over America: country smoked bacon, tangy sausage, hams, and home-canned items—honey, sorghum, jams, relishes, and sparkling cider. Started in 1925 as a roadside stand, selling honey and country fixings, both their business and fine reputation have grown. Mentioned in *Bon Appetit*, Early's offers a great selection of gift boxes for plenty of good country eatin', starting with the Just Right Box for $13.95, postpaid.

Fin 'N Feather
Route 25
Dundee, IL 60118
(312) 742-5040
16-page color catalog, free U.S. AE, MC,
    V, MO, PC.
For over 45 years Fin 'n Feather has refined the art of smoking and curing birds, hams, and meats. Special gift ideas include smoked pheasant (a two-pound gift box, $19.95), and eight sweet and tender smoked quail for $24.95. Smoked turkeys start at $26.95, and there's a good variety of gift packs available, including the Turkey Delight—a four-pound hickory-smoked turkey breast, stuffed olives, horseradish, and two kinds of cheese for $29. Gift Club Plans are a thoughtful way of keeping your remembrances coming all during the year; Fin 'n Feather offers four plans that start at $49. The prices are so reasonable, and the variety so extensive, you probably could complete your entire gift shopping list here.

The Forsts
C.P.O. Box 1000P
Kingston, NY 12401
(914) 331-3500
12-page brochure, free U.S. Limited
    overseas sales. Minimum order $9
    Candy; $7 Fruit. MO, PC.
From the heart of the Catskill mountains comes smoked delicacies: turkey, ham, bacon, and pheasant. The cherished family smoking and curing recipes have been handed down from the original shop started in 1880. The Forsts Picnic Pak contains six pounds of assorted palate-pleasing meats and cheeses. Give it as a special gift, or keep it handy so you're ready for unexpected guests. For you last minute shoppers, Forsts has same-day shipping on all these wonderful items.

Four Oaks Farm
Rt. 5 Box 36
Lexington, SC 29072
(803) 356-3194
6-page brochure, free U.S. Does not sell
    overseas. MC, V, MO, PC.

"Old timey country pork products," country store items, jams, jellies, pickles and relishes, states the brochure. The country-styled bacon is hickory-smoked to perfection and aged to create that taste-tempting Old South favorite ($25.45 for a nine pound slab). Hams are available all year in your choice of sugar-cured, or sugar-cured and hickory-smoked, starting at $32. A little more expensive than the whole hams are the boneless ham slices, but many think the extra convenience offsets the additional cost (box of five 12-ounce packages, $21.95). All are shipped in special gift boxes by Parcel Post or United Parcel Service, depending on your locality.

Fred Usinger
1030 N. Third St.
Milwaukee, WI 53203
(414) 276-9100
4-page price list, free U.S. Does not sell
    overseas. MO, PC.
"American's Finest Sausage" is more than Usinger's slogan; it is a promise kept since 1880. To mention only a few of their savory offerings: tongue, head cheese, braunschweiger, mortadella, mosaic, Gothaer Cervelat, Landjaeger, Thueringer, Polish, Teawurst, and Yachtwurst. This specialty sausage company was described by the *Milwaukee Journal* as "a 100 year quest for the best of the wurst." You'll pay a few pennies more for the best, but it will be worth it.

Gaspar's Sausage Co.
P.O. Box 436
N. Dartmouth, MA k02747
(617) 998-2012
3-page mostly color price list, free U.S.
    Does not sell overseas. MC, V, MO, PC.
Gaspar's sells the finest Portuguese sausages. Linguica, a mild sausage, is their most popular, and Chourico, a spicier brand of sausage, is also available. Assorted gift packs start at $13.95 for a four-pound box.

Golden Trophy Steaks
3548 N. Kostner
Chicago, IL 60641
(312) 282-2900
16-page color catalog, free U.S. Does not
    sell overseas. AE, MC, V, PC.
Gourmet beef, veal, and lamb. The catalog will surely whet your appetite with these delicious-looking main entrees: T-bones, sirloin butt steaks, rib eyes, and London broils. There are Chateaubriands, eye of the rib, prime lamb loin chops, and filet mignons. For those who like to entertain on the spur of the moment, you can let Golden Trophy do the preparation: Rock Cornish hen stuffed with rice, Roast Duckling Montmorency, and Beef Wellington are shipped frozen and ready for the oven. What could be more simple?

Gould's Country Smokehouse
River Rd.
P.O. Box 145
Piermont, NH 03779
(603) 272-5856
8-page brochure. Does not sell overseas.
    MC, V, MO, PC.
Corn cob smoked ham, bacon, and trout. Back in the '20s people used to drive for miles to Piermont Village where, in front of the store, hams would smolder over a barrel of hot corn cobs. The demand for Gould's corn cob smoked hams increased, and the barrel soon became outdated. Today the in-plant smoker provides the same fine products. Half hams start at $29.95, four-pound sliced ham at $24.95, and two pounds of sliced bacon for $10.95.

Gwaltney of Smithfield
P.O. Box 489
Smithfield, VA 23430
(804) 357-3131
4-page color brochure, free U.S. and
    overseas. AE, MC, V, MO, PC.
It is here you'll find those hams of legend, Smithfield hams. From the little Virginia town on the Pagan River, Gwaltney Smokehouses offers Smithfield hams, the traditional favorites of those who enjoy the robust flavor of a fully aged, dry-cured ham ($43.95 for a fourteen-pound ham). The Williamsburg ham is called a young Smithfield; it is cured for a shorter time, and the flavor is milder ($32.95 for a fourteen-pound ham). Health

enthusiasts will appreciate a no-nitrite bacon—with the rich salt-cured flavor of true colonial cooking, but without added nitrites.

Harrington's
618 Main St.
Richmond, VT 05477
(802) 434-3411
32-page color catalog, price unavailable U.S. Does not sell overseas. AE, MC, V, MO, PC.
Vermont cob-smoked ham, bacon, and turkey are favorites at Harrington's, but they also offer country sausage, loin chops, steaks, smoked pheasant, wild rice, sugar-cured beef, and Scottish-style smoked salmon. Available all year.

High Valley Farm
14 Alsace Way
Colorado Springs, CO 80906
8-page color brochure, free U.S. Does not sell overseas. MO, PC.
Well known for their own line of pâtés, High Valley Farm also sells smoked meats, including turkey, ham, and bacon. Smoked rainbow trout pâté, mentioned in *Gourmet,* is a product from their own hand-raised trout. They also carry Pheasant pâté, pâté of smoked turkey, cocktail pâté of turkey livers, and chopped chicken liver pâté. You may want to give them as gifts (a five-can assorted pâté gift pack, $12.95), or have some on hand to offer your guests—something way beyond the usual hors d'oeuvre pâtés.

Jugtown Mountain Smokehouse
P.O. Box 366
Flemington, NJ 08822
(201) 782-2421
Smoked over hickory and sassafras logs, Jugtown Mountain Smokehouse offers nine kinds of sausage, five kinds of bacon (including meaty and flavorful Irish Bacon), seven kinds of smoked cheese, thirty-two spreading cheeses, three types of ham, and eight kinds of smoked poultry. Whew! There's a lot of Jugtown specials!

Lawrence's Smokehouse
Rt. 30
Newfane, VT 05345
(802) 365-7751
8-page brochure, free U.S. and overseas. MC, V, MO, PC.
Gourmet smoked meat and poultry. Lawrence's uses corn cobs to gently cold smoke a full range of pork products, turkey, trout and salmon. They also sell eighteen cheeses, including low cholesterol varieties.

Manchester Farms
P.O. Box 97
Dalzell, SC 29040
(803) 469-2588
2-page color brochure, free U.S. Does not sell overseas. MC, V, MO, PC.
Manchester Farms has offered quail to supermarkets, restaurants, and mail order customers for years. Winner of the 1982–83 Small Business of the Year award for the state of South Carolina, their farm-raised and grain-fed quail are fresh frozen and oven ready. Prices start at $45 for sixteen fresh frozen or smoked quail.

McArthur's Smokehouse
Main St.
Millerton, NY 12546
(518) 789-3722
16-page color catalog, free U.S. and overseas. AE, MC, V, MO, PC.
"Victualler since 1876," McArthur's hickory-smoked hams are not as dry or salty as the Southern variety. Their traditional curing method is the rare New England cure, where the meat is marinated in molasses and salt water, then soaked in fresh water to take out the saltiness. Packed and shipped in old-fashioned, handcrafted wooden boxes (if you like). They also offer hickory-smoked bacon, sausage, smoked salmon and trout, pork, beef and lamb. A choice selection of wild game birds will please discriminating gourmets: quail, chuckar partridge, ringneck pheasant, muscovy duck, and wild turkey.

Meadow Farms Country Smokehouse
P.O. Box 1387
Bishop, CA 93514
(619) 873-5311
2-page color brochure, free U.S. Does not sell overseas. MC, V, MO, PC.
"The taste and aroma that mahogany produces is what made this little

smokehouse famous," states the brochure. Try their mahogany-smoked bacon and give it a comparison taste test with your favorite bacon. It's their best seller, and it's delicious! Meadow Farms claims it is the best in the country, and it would be difficult to dispute. Jerky Stick, Landjager (which means hunter sausage), smoked ham, and Italian salami are also available.

Menuchah Farms Smoke House
Route 22
Salem, NY 12865
(518) 854-9279
Price list, free U.S. and overseas.
    Minimum order $20. MO, PC.
Apple-smoked meats and poultry, including chicken, turkey, duck, Cornish game hen, goose, filet mignon, leg of lamb, and pork loin. Their fruit-wood-smoked items do not contain additives, preservatives, or chemicals. Orders received by November 15th will receive a 10% discount.

Omaha Steaks International
4400 South 96th St.
P.O. Box 3300 Dept. 1502
Omaha, NE 68103
(800) 228-2778
30-page color catalog, $1 U.S. Does not sell overseas. AE, CB, DC, MC, V, MO, PC.
Omaha Steaks is one of the leading suppliers of steaks to the nation's restaurants and mail order buyers. Filet Mignons with seasoned butter sauce start at $49, for six 6-ounce filets. They also have sirloins cut from the heart of the short loin, and a variety of steak combination packages. Thick juicy Porterhouse steaks, T-bone steaks, Ranch club steaks, and filets of prime rib (also called rib eye steaks) are available.

Ozark Mountain Smoke House
P.O. Box 37
Farmington, AR 72730
(501) 267-3567
14-page color catalog, free U.S. Does not sell overseas. MC, V, MO, PC.
"We sugar cure and hickory smoke hams, bacon, sausage, poultry and cheese, bake our own breads, cookies

and pastry, and make our own pickles. Reasonably priced sandwiches, washed down with real apple cider, make the Ozark Mountain Smokehouse a popular place at meal times," states the brochure. Well, since you may not be able to visit Ozark Mountain Smoke House, you should know that, in addition to the above mentioned, they also offer a great gift pack. The Breakfast gift pack, $14.75, recaptures the flavors of a real old-fashioned Ozark Mountain breakfast: a pound of sliced Arkansas bacon, which is ready to fry (the drippings make "red eye gravy"), a pint of strawberry preserves, and about two pounds of hominy grits. Now *that's* something to wake up to.

Pfaelzer Brothers
4501 W. District Blvd.
Chicago, IL 60632
(312) 927-7100
12-page color catalog, $2 U.S. Does not sell overseas. AE, DC, MC, V, MO, PC.
Over 60 years ago three brothers named Pfaelzer traveled to Chicago neighborhoods, selling meat from a horse-drawn wagon. Today a multimillion dollar business has evolved that has become synonymous with direct mail marketing of meats—with consistently superior quality. Filet mignon, Chateaubriand (5 lbs. for $63.95), rib eye steaks, Porterhouse steaks, and T-bones are available. Fully cooked ribs are finger-licking good at $49.95 (for a six-pound slab). Other pre-browned items include lots of chicken: à la Kiev, Cordon Bleu, à la Pfaelzer, Marco Polo, and Romanoff.

The Sausage Maker
177 Military Rd.
Buffalo, NY 14207
(716) 876-5521
72-page newsalog, price unavailable U.S. and overseas. MC, V, MO.
"The Sausage Maker is a complete one-stop shopping center for sausage making and meat curing supplies," says Rytek Kutas, owner of the Sausage Maker. His book, *Great Sausage Recipes and Meat Curing* ($8.95), was mentioned by Craig Claiborne, food editor for *The New York Times*. The

catalog contains casings, cures, spices, tools, and kits you'll need for sausage stuffing.

Signature Prime
143 South Water Market
Chicago, IL 60608
(800) 621-0397
Illinois (312) 829-0900
6-page color brochure, free U.S. and
  overseas. MC, V, MO, PC.
Signature Prime has an established reputation (since 1884) for supplying the better American clubs, hotels, and restaurants with the highest quality of meat products. Corn-fed beef is carefully aged, flash frozen, and shipped to you in dry ice packaging. They also offer a distinctive gourmet selection of dock-fresh seafood and other delicacies: shrimp, double loin lamb chops, veal, and turkey (roasted, uncooked, or smoked).

The Smithfield Packing Co.
P.O. Box 447
Smithfield, VA 23430
(804) 357-4321
2-page color price list, free U.S. and
  overseas. AE, MC, V, MO.
Fully cooked hams, prized by gourmets, are made from an old family recipe: dry-cured, heavily smoked, aged, browned with their special coating flame process, and ready to serve. The approximately 10-pound ham comes bone-in for $49.95, or boneless for $54.95. Half-slab bacon is salt dry-cured; hickory-smoked bacon is $12.95 for five pounds.

Sugardale Foods
Box 8440
Canton, OH 44711
(216) 455-5253
20-page color catalog, free U.S. Does not
  sell overseas. MC, V, MO, PC.
Sugardale offers carefully selected and hand-trimmed steaks: Filet Mignon, Boneless Strip Steak, Top Sirloin, Porterhouse, Rib Eye, Prime Rib Roast, and Chateaubriand. This tempting catalog shows thick juicy steaks at their finest. Everyone remembers a delicious food gift, and Sugardale food gifts say "You're someone special" to customers, employees, or businesses, states the

catalog. Gift givers will find Sugardale has a variety of gift packs available—cheese, snack packs, chocolates, jams and preserves, and nuts. One page is devoted to honey jars with clever labels: "It's sweet doing business with you," and "For your honey of a loan/Piscataqua Savings Bank," and like that.

Summer Isles Foods
The Smokehouse
Achiltibuie, Ullapoll
Ross-Shire Scotland IV26 2YG
085 482 353
4-page brochure, free U.S. and overseas.
  Price in Scottish pounds. MO, PC.
Fine traditional foods from the local fishermen, crofters, and stalkers of the Scottish highlands: salmon, trout, chicken, turkey, ham, sausage, fine pâtés, venison, and seafoods. The salmon is cured in a brine with rum, treacle, and a special brew of juniper berries, peppercorns, and a little garlic. It is then smoked in a mixture of oak wood, gathered from a cooperage which produces whicky casks of juniper wood. The unique technique gives foods a distinctive fragrant aroma. Smoked fish include juniper-smoked salmon, Summer Isles trout, and Highland eel. Oak-smoked chicken, turkey, and venison are also available. The ham is specially cured in a brine of molasses, black peppers, juniper berries, and five gallons of home brewed beer. Perfection is reached after more smoking in oak, and gentle cooking.

Teel Mountain Farm
Rt. 1, Box 130
Stanardsville, VA 22973
(804) 985-7746
6-page brochure. AE, DC, MC, V.
Organically grown beef, veal, and chicken. On 350 acres of rolling pastures and woodlands of the Blue Ridge Mountains of Virginia, two very special products are raised: Baby Beef, the stage between young veal and older, heavier, beef weighing 200 pounds; and Teel Veal, the young 13-week-old calves weighing 100 pounds. Both are raised without insecticides, medications, growth stimulants, or antibiotics, and their grazing lands are free of pesticides

or herbicides. The animals are free to roam the pastures at their mothers' sides, and their diet sounds like a gourmet health food orgy. A special fifteen-pound sampler of assorted cuts is available for $79, and is shipped to you in dry ice by UPS or Air Parcel Post Special Delivery.

Wimmer's Meat Products
126 W. Grant St.
West Point, NE 68788
(402) 372-2437
24-page color catalog, free U.S. Does not sell overseas. AE, MC, V, MO, PC.
Wimmer's offers over 100 varieties of European-styled sausages and cured meats. All are processed with natural spices and natural casings and do not contain fillers. All the meats are so beautifully displayed that one would almost expect to smell the spicy aroma just looking at the catalog. Wimmers quality sausage is matched by quality gift service; enclosed gift cards (of course), order acknowledgment card to the sender, and a notice of safe arrival from the receiver to Wimmers. Now that is pretty thoughtful, but Wimmer's goes one step farthur (as number one companies usually do): those customer response cards are then forwarded to the sender—so you can appreciate the gift recipient's delighted comments. Nice going, fellas.

CHEESE

Avalon Cheese Company
Red Road
McMinnville, TN 37110
(800) 262-6827
16-page color catalog, free U.S. Does not sell overseas. MC, V, MO, PC.
Avalon Mountain cheddar cheese is made by hand in the hills of Tennessee, using old English cheddaring recipes. Winner of the Tennessee Governor's Trophy seven times, signifying that Avalon cheddar is the best in the state, should surely entice cheese lovers to bite. The catalog displays attractive gift packs and a few yummy recipes.

Calef's Country Store
Rt. 9 P.O. Box 57
Barrington, NH 03825
(603) 664-9551
2-page price list, free U.S. and overseas. MO, PC.
Calef's Country Store is not much different than it was when Mary Calef opened it 115 years ago. Browsing through Calef's, you'll still find crackers in barrels, Barbados molasses, flour, boots and shoes, enamelware, china, ammunition, seeds, and poultry feed. From their mail order list be sure to order some Calef Cheese ($3.99 per lb.). It's something more than cheddar. "It's snappy," says father Austin. "Makes a man sit up and take notice."

Cheese Junction
1 West Ridgewood Ave.
Ridgewood, NJ 07450
(800) 631-0353
Cheese Junction's catalog brings you more than 100 varieties of gourmet cheese from around the world. Nine assorted cheeses are available in the Executive Gift Assortment for $25.95: luscious imported Camembert, its Danish cousin Cream Dania, and the ever popular Danish Blue Cheese are accompanied by Butter Cheese, Gouda-like Klein-Kase, and Garlic & Herb Danube Spread, not to mention Smoked Gruyère Log from Austria, and Shrimp Grunland and Walnut Grunland from Germany. New York State Cheddar, aged twelve months, starts at $4.29 per pound. All orders are shipped immediately on receipt, guaranteed to arrive in perfect condition or your money back.

The Cheese 'N More Store
8100 Hwy. K South
Merrill, WI 54452
(715) 675-6145
4-page color brochure, free U.S. Does not sell overseas. MO, PC.
The Cheese 'N More Store features fine cheese by the pound and in attractive gift packs. Some of the favorites are Colby (an original from Colby, Wisconsin), Jarlsburg, Rondele, Baby Swiss, Brick, Gouda from Holland, and cheddar. You can't miss their store

located five miles north of Wausau, Wisconsin: it is a giant fifty-foot cheddar with a wedge cut out for the entrance, painted cheddar cheese yellow.

Cheese of All Nations
153 Chambers St.
New York, NY 10007
(212) 732-0752
68-page catalog, AE, MC, V.
Over 1,000 varieties of imported and domestic cheeses.

Crowley Cheese
Healdville, VT 05758
(802) 259-2340
4-page brochure, free U.S. and overseas. MC, V, MO, PC.
Crowley is the only New England cheesemaker producing true farm-style Colby cheese with its rich, soft texture and full flavor, states the brochure. Located in Healdville since 1824, the factory is believed to be the oldest cheese factory in the Western Hemisphere, and has been designated a National Historic Place. Though mechanization has taken over some factories, at Crowley's the curds are still "cut" and "raked" by hand, using the familiar tools of the last century. Colby cheese is a little softer and smoother textured than cheddar and is available in three sizes: two and one-half, five, and twenty-five pound wheels.

Daisyfresh Dairy Cultures
P.O. Box 36
Santa Cruz, CA 95062
(408) 476-5390
2-page brochure, free U.S. and overseas. MO, PC.
Daisyfresh Dairy Cultures sells four different dairy cultures for making your own homemade buttermilk, sour cream, yogurt, and Swiss acidophilus (an extra mild yogurt-tasting dairy product). Each culture packet includes "how-to" helpful hints, and some unusual recipes. The cost is about $2 per packet, or about 20% less than charged in most health food stores.

Dakin Farm
Route 7
Ferrisburg, VT 05456
(802) 877-2936
16-page some color catalog, free U.S. and overseas. MC, V, MO, PC.
The original farm was founded in 1792 by Timothy Dakin, then sold to the Cutter family who have created a tradition of offering the finest quality Vermont products. They select the finest cheddar cheese Vermont has to offer, age it to maturity, then cut and wax it for fresh keeping. (A pint of Dakin's 100% pure maple syrup starts at $8.40.)

Eichten's Hidden Acres
16705 310th St.
Center City, MN 55012
(612) 257-4752
8-page brochure, free U.S. Limited
   overseas sales. MO, PC.
Joe and Mary Eichten specialize in Dutch Gouda made from their own farm-produced milk. The natural cheese is aged 60 days and made without additives, preservatives, artificial flavoring or coloring. The Eichten's have taken many honors at the Minnesota State Fair for both their Gouda and Baby Swiss. Their mild Gouda starts at $2.85 per pound.

Ferris Fine Foods
P.O. Box 5412
Madison, WI 53705
8-page color catalog, free U.S. Does not
   sell overseas. MO, PC.
Ferris Fine Foods are purveyors of Wisconsin's finest cheese. Superb Baby Swiss has a soft, creamy smooth, white texture and the well-known "eyes" that characterize Swiss cheese. Swiss Baby Cheese ($9.50 for a two-pound block) was their most popular cheese last year. The high quality and mellow body of this cheese also makes it a wonderful cooking cheese. Also popular is their excellent Beef Summer Sausage, made with high quality lean beef (no filler) and hickory smoked to achieve a tangy flavor.

Gethsemani Farms
Trappist, KY 40073
6-page brochure, free U.S. Limited
   overseas sales. MO, PC.

Food & Drink

Gethsemani Farms is owned and operated by the Trappist monks. It was the first of sixteen Trappist-Cistercian monasteries in the U.S. Today the Trappist monks make their own cheese and fruit cakes and sell them mail order to help meet their modest living needs. Trappist Cheese is made from an old world formula developed in the tradition of the Cistercian order. It is a Port Sault type of cheese and comes in mild, aged, and smoky varieties for about $7.25 for one and a half pounds. Their delicious two and one half pound fruit cakes are $11.75.

Harman's Cheese & Country Store
Sugar Hill, NH 03585
(603) 823-8000
John Harman's Country Store sells aged New York Cheddar Cheese. New York is noted for great cheddar, and at Harman's (in New Jersey) it's even better—aged two years before they put it on the market. They buy ten tons of "aged cheddar" when it is only six months old, then store it in their cooled-to-forty-degrees cellar for an additional eighteen months before bringing it to their store. They offer you cheddar at the peak of perfection at $11.15 for a two-pound block.

Ideal Cheese Shop
1205 2nd Ave.
New York, NY 10021
(212) 688-7579
Price list, free U.S. Does not sell overseas. Minimum order $25. MC, V, MO, PC.
Ideal Cheese Shop is responsible for introducing many new cheeses to the U.S. over the years. Boule de Perigord, for one, is a French chèvre studded with truffles. Other special cheeses include St. André (a French triple crème), Granduca (Italy's white mold), Jarlsberg from Norway, Boursault, Caprice de Dieux, Corolle, Explorateur, and Cream Dania (plain and with chives). Ideal Cheese Shop offers about 250 cheeses—possibly the largest variety available.

Kolb Lena Cheese Co.
301 W. Railroad St.
Lena, IL 61048
(815) 369-4577
8-page color brochure, free U.S. Does not sell overseas. MO, PC.
Kolb Lena Cheese Co. makes over a dozen different all-natural, all-American-made specialty cheeses including Brie, Feta, Baby Swiss, Camembert, Alpendeler, Sno Belle, Cheddar, low-salt Swiss, Colby, Monterey Jack, Fruit Cheese, and more. Kolb's Delico brand cheeses have been acclaimed by many food editors and famous chefs for their excellence.

Maytag Dairy Farms
RR #1, Box 806
Newton, IA 50208
(800) 247-2458
Iowa (515) 792-1133
20-page color catalog, free U.S. and overseas. MC, V, MO, PC.
Since 1941 Maytag Dairy Farms has been making quality blue cheese. As the finest American blue, 80 percent of Maytag blue cheese is sold by mail order. Two 8-ounce foil-wrapped wedges sell for $8.60.

Morningland Dairy
Rt. 1 Box 188B
Mt. View, MO 65548
(417) 469-3817
Price list, self-addressed stamped envelope U.S. MO, PC.
Morningland Dairy has grown over the last two years and now produces ten varieties and 6,500 pounds of cheese per month. Sold by the pound or in boxes, or in random cuts weighing six to ten ounces. Their cheese is made from the raw milk of Holstein cows, using no artificial coloring or preservatives. Cheddar (mild, medium sharp, and sharp), Colby, Monterey Jack, Caraway Seed Jack, and Hot Pepper Jack are a few of their varieties.

New England Cheesemaking Supply Co.
Box 85241
Ashfield, MA 01330
(423) 628-3808
24-page catalog, free U.S. and overseas. MC, V, MO, PC.
Here is where you can find kits, equipment, cultures, tools, and books for making your own cheese at home. Many of these items are not readily available

in the stores. Cottage cheese, cheddar, Gouda, ricotta, feta, camembert and even blue and Swiss Cheese can be made at home. Cheese vats, cheese presses, molds, and other related equipment are available for those interested in larger scale cheesemaking. Mozzarella is one of the most exciting cheeses to make—the kit is available for $7.95 and includes everything you will need, except the milk. The Introductory Cheese kit ($15.95) would make a unique gift; it includes a polyethylene mold (to hold up to a pound and a half of cheese), cheese starter, culture, cheese rennet tablets, a packet of herbs, a thermometer, one yard of cheese cloth, a plastic curd cutter, and a sixteen-page illustrated recipe booklet. From this starter kit you can make a variety of cheeses, including herbal, whey, cottage, and several delicious lightly pressed cheeses. This catalog may start you off on an interesting new hobby.

Plymouth Cheese Corp.
Box 1
Plymouth, VT 05056
(802) 672-3650
Price list, free U.S. MO, PC.
Plymouth Cheese is an old-fashioned Vermont granular curd cheese, carefully aged and naturally cured. It is an original cheese of New England, going back to colonial days, and features a rich, open-bodied texture. Three pound wheels are available (in mild or medium sharp) for about $11.50.

Sonoma Cheese Factory
2 Spain St.
Sonoma, CA 95476
(707) 938-5232
8-page brochure, free. AE, MC, V, MO, PC.
Sonoma Jack Cheese is a mild cheese, excellent in sandwiches, omelettes, soufflés, fondues, lasagne, enchiladas, or for just plain snacking. Sold by the wedge, or in gift packs in many varieties: Traditional style, Garlic, Onion, Carraway, Hot Pepper, Lite, and No Salt Added.

The Swiss Cheese Shops
P.O. Box 429
Monroe, WI 53566–0429
(608) 325-3493
8-page catalog, free U.S. Does not sell overseas. MC, V, MO, PC.
The Swiss Cheese Shops started in 1938 as a roadside cheese store, and have been mail ordering special aged Alpine Brand cheeses since 1940. One of the more interesting gift packs is a combination of Wisconsin Cheddar curds and Mozzarella String cheese; priced at $8.95, it would be great for parties as hors d'oeuvres, or for snacking (as Miss Muffet apparently found out).

The Swiss Colony
1112 7th Ave.
Monroe, WI 53566
(606) 246-2000
152-page color catalog, free U.S. AE, CB, DC, MC, V, MO, PC.
The Swiss Colony, famous for their fine cheese selection, also carries delicious meats, fruits and sweets.

Tillamook Cheese
P.O. Box 313
Tillamook, OR 97141
(503) 842-4481
8-page brochure, free U.S. Does not sell overseas. V.
Tillamook Cheese is a style of cheddar originally developed in England, brought to Tillamook from Canada, and perfected by cheesemakers in Tillamook over a seventy-year period. Available in low sodium, medium, and sharp. Prices start at $8.75 for a two-pound loaf, delivered. Tillamook Cheese is a real pleaser.

The Village Cheese Shop
507 E. Silver Spring Dr.
Whitefish Bay, WI 53217
(414) 962-3110
24-page color catalog, $1 U.S. Does not sell overseas. MC, V, MO, PC.
The Village Cheese Shop mails fine Wisconsin cheeses (cut to order), cookware, and gourmet gifts throughout the United States.

Win Schuler Foods
P.O. Box 119
Clinton, CT 06413
(203) 669-4131
24-page color catalog, free U.S. Does not
  sell overseas. AE, DC, MC, V, MO, PC.
Over 30 years ago Win Schuler created
Bar-Scheeze, a zesty cheddar spread
which is creamy smooth and
spreadable. Available in attractive
crocks and earthenware mugs, or in
family size fourteen-ounce cups. Prices
start at $8.95 for two 14-ounce cups of
Bar-Scheeze. Serve with Bar-Schips and
your favorite beverage for Monday night
football. Other snackables are available:
Lanzi's Cashew Nut and Rice Crunch,
Jalapeno and Herb Cream Cheese
Spreads, and one pound of California
Pistachios, all for $12.50.

HERBS AND SPICES

Cathay of Bournemouth Ltd.
32 Cleveland Rd.
Bournemouth, BH1 4QG England
0202 37178
68-page color catalog, $4 U.S. and
  overseas. V, MO, PC.
Cathay is the largest retail herbalist in
Great Britain. The catalog offers
informative descriptions of traditional,
tested, and effective medicinal herbal
treatments. The reading is delightfully
different than the usual American
health catalog. You'll find Excel
Embrocation liniments to apply to
Lumbago, and discover Slippery Elm is
used to clear up "wind" and eructation
from flatulence. They also carry
cosmetics (which is listed in another
section of this book).

Charles Loeb Mr. Spiceman
615 Palmer Rd.
Yonkers, NY 10701
(914) 961-7776
24-page catalog, free; overseas $2. MC,
  V, MO, PC.
Over 120 varieties of spices and herbs,
from small jars to bulk sizes, are offered.
Prices are 40% to 60% off retail prices
when you buy by bulk, they say. Their
salt-free line is in the process of being
expanded. They also sell candy items

including Finland licorice, rock candy,
crystallized ginger, gold foil-wrapped
coins, and cakewriter gels.

Country Herbs
Rt. 7
Stockbridge, MA 01262
(413) 298-3054
16-page catalog, free; overseas 2
  International Reply Coupons. MO, PC.
  C. O. D.
Country Herb potpourris are made by
Country Herbs from aromatic herbs,
spices, and flowers. They also carry
sachets and pomanders and Norfolk
Lavender products from England, and
a lovely English wild rose soap. An
original needlepoint design kit ($45),
and a lovely soft grey-colored Artemisia
dried wreath ($20), would make lovely
gifts. The catalog is illustrated in line
drawings.

Culpepper Ltd.
Hadstock Rd. Linton
Cambridge CB1 6NJ England
233 891196
10-page price list, $1 U.S. and overseas.
  AE, CB, MC, V.
The aim of the Culpepper House is "to
provide the public with simple herbal
remedies, pure cosmetics and natural
perfumes, and to create a taste for the
wholesome and beautiful products of
the earth." They offer medicinal herbs
from Agar Agarto Wormwood, and
virtually everything in between.
Attractive printed cotton bags of herbs
and spices can hang in the kitchen, or
you can purchase ground herbs in glass
jars with cork stoppers.

Faith Mountain Herb
P.O. Box 199
Sperryville, VA 22740
(703) 987-8824
16-page catalog, $2; overseas $3. AE, MC,
  V, MO, PC.
Cherry Faith Woodward offers a lovely
variety of dried herb creations made in
their own workshop: wreaths, brooms,
herb bundles, and hats. Many of the
items are handcrafted by local Blue
Ridge artisans—rugs hard-to-find
Virginia white oak baskets, sachets, and
potpourris.

The Herb Patch
P.O. Box 583
Boulder City, NV 89005
(702) 293-2416
32-page catalog, free U.S. and overseas.
  MO, PC.
Since 1977, The Herb Patch deals mostly in bulk herbs and spices. There are many herbal blends listed, with a brief description of the healthful effects of each. Nutra-Bio products are blends of herbs used for homeopathic therapeutics. Traditional brands of teas are also available.

Hilltop Herb Farm
P.O. Box 1734
Cleveland, TX 77327
(713) 592-5859
4-page brochure, 50¢ U.S. and overseas.
  AE, MC, V, MO, PC.
More than 2,000 varieties of herbs, scented geraniums, and other green things are grown in Hilltop Herb Farm and restaurant. Their famous Tranquil-tea is a blend of 19 herbs and teas, gentle and relaxing ($3 for 3 ozs.). At the other end of the taste spectrum is a sampler of two popular relishes (Hellfire and Damnation, and Fire and Brimstone) which, of course, would spice up your favorite Mexican dish.

Indiana Botanic Gardens
P.O. Box 5
Hammond, IN 46325
(219) 931-2480
64-page catalog, 25¢ U.S. and overseas.
  MC, V, MO, PC.
Indiana Botanic Gardens are the oldest and largest suppliers of herbs and herbal products in the U.S. Founded in 1910 by Joseph E. Meyer, it is owned and operated by his descendants. The current inventory contains over 1,000 different forms of herbs, teas, and other natural ingredient products. The most common way to use herbs is in the form of herbal teas, sometimes called infusions. But there are suggestions for making herbal medicines and poultices, too.

Kalfon Spice, Tea & Coffee
Rt. 1 Box 252
Pelion, SC 29123
(803) 894-4211

4-page brochure, free U.S. and overseas.
  MC, V, MO, PC.
Kalfon sells natural whole spices and herbs in disposable grinders. You just twist the top and grind the amount of spice needed. Kalfon seems to have developed the better mouse trap—now you won't have to throw away half full jars and cans of stale, pre-ground spices. (Take a look at your spice racks; some of them probably date back into ancient times.) Spices are sold individually ($2.50) or in attractive wooden racks of ten ($28) and thirty ($78). Country theme spice sets are also available for Mexican, Chinese, and Greek Cooking.

Le Jardin Du Gourmet
West Danville, Vt 05873
16-page catalog, 50¢ U.S. and overseas.
  MO, PC.
Raymond Saufroy sells inexpensive seed packets for about 250 different kinds of herbs and vegetables. His .20¢ seed packet offer has been a tremendous success—the small seed packets only contain twenty to thirty seeds, some less. For those with small gardens, or who would like to experiment with different plants, this is a terrific opportunity. Besides the .20¢ seed packets, he also carries seeds from France, Holland, Germany, Africa, Holland, Russia and Roumania.

Lifespice
Sansel, Inc.
60 West 15 St.
New York, NY 10011
(212) 929-2106
4-page brochure, free U.S. Does not sell
  overseas. PC.
Lifespice sells salt-free spices, condiments, and dressings. If you're one of those wise people restricting your sodium intake, you'll enjoy the zippy blends Lifespice has developed. Tomato Velvet tastes like delicious old-fashioned catsup, or it could be used as a tomato base with your favorite poultry, meat, and pasta dishes. Sweet Heat Chutney is a surprising blend of hot spices and sweet apricots. Lemon Sesame Mustard Sauce, Green Peppercorn Sauce, Our House Salad

Dressing, and Hot Shot Barbeque Sauce are packed in distinctive glass jars.

Magic Garden Herb Co.
P.O. Box 332
Fairfax, CA 94950
(415) 663-8565
8-page brochure, 25¢; overseas $1. MO, PC.
Magic Garden carries over 200 herbs and spices, some of which are hard to find in the U.S. They will also special order any herbs that are available but not listed in the catalog. Smokers who are trying to quit might enjoy the herbal alternative to cigarettes—Ginseng cigarettes, "aromatic and satisfying."

Nature's Herb Company
281 Ellis St.
San Francisco, CA 94102
(415) 474-2756
36-page brochure, 50¢ U.S. and overseas. MO, PC.
Domestic and imported herbs and spices. A very handy alphabetical index of over 400 herbs and spices lists each price per pound. The catalog is then designed by sections identifying remedies for general dysfunctions.

The Rosemary House
120 S. Market St.
Mechanicsburg, PA 17055
(717) 697-0511
28-page catalog, $1; overseas $2. MO, PC.
The Rosemary House has hundreds of herbs, spices, plants, seeds, oils, sachets, soaps, teas, candles, books, notepapers, kitchen gadgets, and baskets—all with an herb or plant theme. They further encourage would-be herbal gardeners with a tempting offer. For $25, you send them the details of your garden—its size and location, and your particular interest in herbs. They will send you an herb garden design and a full credit towards your plants. Pretty good idea.

San Francisco Herb Co.
250 14th St.
San Francisco, CA 94103
(800) 227-4530
California (415) 861-7174
4-page brochure, free U.S. Does not sell overseas. Minimum order $40. PC.

The San Francisco Herb Company wholesales the finest quality herbs, spices, teas, and natural foods in machine-packaged one-pound units for health food stores, co-ops, and restaurants. These wholesale prices are available to you if the minimum order is met. Pricing out a 1-ounce jar of whole cloves in the supermarket is $1.89; from the catalog it is 50¢.

Well-Sweep Herb Farm
317 Mt. Bethel Rd.
Port Murray, NJ 07865
(201) 852-5390
38-page catalog, 75¢ U.S. Does not sell overseas. Minimum order $5. MO, PC.
Over 500 varieties of herb plants are listed. Dried flowers are sold by the individual bunch or in color-coordinated mixtures. The shipping season for the plants extends from April 15th through October 15th by UPS. The plants are shipped in two- or three-inch pots, properly labeled and well rooted. All other items are available the year round.

Wide World of Herbs, Ltd.
11 St. Catherine Street East
Montreal 129, Canada H2X 1K3
1 514 842 1838
The herbal emporium was founded by Jacob Thuna, a local herbalist. Today Wide World of Herbs offers an extensive array of fine herbs and spices from around the world. There are many delicious sounding herbal teas—Lemon Grass served hot with a clove, and Fenugreek Seed, often used in place of tea or coffee. There are many tips on natural hair coloring for blondes, brunettes, and redheads. You'll also find herbs for insect repellents, beers, smoking mixtures, natural dyes, and mordants.

HEALTH FOODS

Bolton Farms
780 N. Clinton Ave.
Trenton, NJ 08638
(609) 989-8753
6-page brochure, $1 U.S. Does not sell overseas. MC, V, MO, PC.

Bolton Farms offers a full range of dehydrated and freeze-dried foods designed for long-term storage. They offer complete dinner entrees, vegetables, soups, gravies, fruits, beverages, desserts, and snacks—all nitrogen-packed in family-sized cans. All you do is add the water and cook if necessary. Foods can be purchased individually or in one-person unit supplies for thirty-five days, six months, or one year.

General Nutrition Corp.
418 Wood St.
Pittsburgh, PA 15222
(800) 245-6562
Pennsylvania (412) 288-4600
48-page catalog, free U.S. and overseas. MC, V.
General Nutrition Corporation is a large vitamin and mineral mail order house. They offer over two thousand products, many of which they manufacture themselves. From the vitamin A to the mineral zinc, and with many health products in between. They have weight-gaining formulas, weight-losing formulas, and Siberian Ginseng.

International Yogurt Company
628 North Doheny Dr.
Los Angeles, CA 90069
(213) 274-9917
4-page brochure, free U.S. and overseas. MO, PC.
International Yogurt Company sells freeze-dried yogurt products for making yogurt at home. Yogurt culture, Kefir culture, acidophilus milk culture, incubators, dairy thermometers, and rennet tablets. Yogurt Shampoo and Creme Rinse is also available.

Jaffe Bros.
P.O. Box 636
Valley Center, CA 92082–0636
(619) 749-1133
8-page brochure, free U.S. and overseas. MC, V, MO, PC.
Jaffe Bros. offers an excellent selection of organically grown dried fruits, nuts, seeds, oils, and grains. "Organically grown" is defined in the brochure as those plants and trees that have been cultivated by natural methods, thereby excluding chemical fertilizers, insecticides, and fumigants. The dried fruits are unsulphured, including apples, apricots, Black Mission figs, Calimyrna Figs, peaches, pears, prunes, Thompson seedless raisins, and Monukka raisins. There are about twenty seeds and nuts, and twenty more grains and grain products.

Martens Health & Survival
P.O. Box 725
Carlsbad, CA 92008
(619) 438-0866
30-page newsalog, free U.S. Does not sell overseas. AE, MC, MO, PC.
JoAnn and Norvel Martens sells Neo-Life, an excellent line of dehydrated foods especially packaged and prepared for long-term storage. Neo-Life has an expanded product line that now includes nutritional supplements, weight control products, skin care products, and household cleaners. This firm has been recommended by Howard Ruff, economist and author of *How to Prosper During The Coming Bad Years.*

Northern Health Foods
13 South 4 Box 66
Moorhead, MN 56560
(218) 236-5999
Price list, free U.S. and overseas. Minimum order $4. MO, PC.
Since 1965, Northern Health Foods has been in the bulk health food mail order business. Most of the products listed are grown naturally in the Red River Valley of North Dakota and Minnesota. They ship to every state in the U.S. and many foreign countries.

Pure Planet Products
1025 N. 48th St.
Phoenix, AZ 85008
(602) 267-1000
18-page catalog, 25¢ U.S. Does not sell overseas. MC, V, MO, PC, C.O.D.
Pure Planet Products sells health care products, foods, teas, and spices. Name brands include Dr. Bronner, Finn, Barth, De Souza, and Viva Vera Aloe. You can also save money by custom mixing and encapsulating your own powdered herbs and vitamins with the

Capsule Machine ($9.95, with empty capsules).

S. I. Equipment, Ltd.
17019 Kingsview Ave.
Carson, CA 90746
(213) 631-6197
48-page newsalog, $2 U.S. Does not sell
    overseas. AE, MC, V, MO, PC.
S. I. Equipment is one of the largest
suppliers of survival foods and
equipment. Mountain House dehydrated
foods, packed in #10 cans with nitrogen
atmosphere, have a ten-year-plus
storage life. They also sell survival
equipment such as first aid kits,
kerosene lamps, heaters, water
purifiers, grains and mills, radiation
detection equipment, and small tools.
There are eleven pages on survival
manuals and reference books.

Stow-A-Way Sports Inc.
166 Cushing Hwy.
Cohasset, MA 02025
(617) 383-9116
32-page catalog, free U.S. and overseas.
    MC, V, MO, PC.
Stow-A-Way offers lightweight,
nonperishable foods for recreational use
and expedition outfitting. Name brands
include Stow-Lite, Mountain House, Dri-
Lite, and Richmoor at a discount of up
to 10% to 30% off retail prices.
Backpackers and hikers can arrange to
have Stow-A-Way leave food at pick-up
points along the way (at designated Post
Offices) along the Appalachian Trail.
Imagine forgoing through wilderness
trails, then dining on quiche!

Stur-Dee
Island Park, NY 11558
(800) 645-2638
New York (800) 632-2592
88-page catalog. Minimum order $20 on
    toll free calls. MC, V, PC.
Stur-Dee is a famous mail order
company of health products, cosmetics,
vitamins and minerals with their own
label. There are good savings to be found
by comparing your health food store's
products with the prices (and half-price
sales) from Stur-Dee.

Survival Center
5555 Newton Falls Rd.
Ravenna, OH 44266
(216) 678-4000
40-page brochure, $1 U.S. and overseas.
    AE, MC, V, MO, PC.
"Quality food storage and supplies for
self-reliant living." They offer their own
exclusive brand of survival foods,
Hanna Mills nitrogen-packed grains,
and freeze-dried foods. They also carry
Mountain House freeze-dried foods,
grain mills, food dehydrators, solar
panels, wind generators, cross-bows,
water purifiers, survival shelters, and
lots of "how-to" books.

Trail Foods Co.
P.O. Box 9309
North Hollywood, CA 91609
(213) 897-4370
8-page brochure, 50¢ U.S.; overseas
    $1.20. Minimum order $20. MC, V, MO,
    PC.
Trail Foods sells freeze-dried foods from
Mountain House, Dri-Lite, and
Richmoor. Up to a 30% discount is
available for quantity orders. Backpacks
from Eureka, Centuri, Orion, and Astral
are also listed.

Walnut Acres
Penns Creek, PA 17862
(717) 837-0601
42-page color catalog, free U.S. and
    overseas. MC, V, MO, PC.
Walnut Acres offers about 500 different
organically grown foods. Many of the
delicious foods are grown on their 500-
acre farm which, they claim, has been
chemically free since 1946. They offer
a huge selection of granolas, cereals,
cookies, flours, canned soups, peanut
butters, cheeses, jams and jellies, dried
fruits, honeys, dressings, and vegetarian
products. A terrific catalog with much
to offer.

FRUIT

Barfield Groves
P.O. Box 68
Polk City, FL 33868
(813) 984-1316

16-page color catalog, free U.S. Does not sell overseas. MC, V, MO, PC.
Fresh tree-ripened pink seedless grapefruits, honey tangerines, and navel, temple, and seedless Valencia oranges from Florida. Every box of fruit is picked and packed fresh, the same day the fruit leaves Barfield Groves.

Benech Farms
20250 McKean Rd.
P.O. Box 6387
San Jose, CA 95150
(408) 298-9789
16-page color catalog. MC, V, PC.
Sun-dried apricots are the specialty at Benech Farms. They also sell dried Bing cherries, dates, pears, peaches, prunes, apple rings, raisins, nectarines, and figs.

Blue Heron Fruit Shippers
7440 N. Trail
Sarasota, FL 33508
(800) 237-3920
4-page brochure, free U.S. and overseas. MC, V, MO, PC.
Tree-ripened Florida oranges and grapefruit. The Mineola Tangelos (difficult to find on grocery shelves due to their perishability) are one of their mail order specialties—"Its taste is more Tangerine, the size more Grapefruit—seedless and so juicy that we tell people that they're best eaten in the bathtub!" Other popular fruits are temple, navel, and Valencia oranges, Orlando tangelos, and pink seedless grapefruit.

Hadley Fruit Orchards
48980 Seminole Dr.
Cabazon, CA 92230
(714) 849-4668
16-page color catalog, free U.S.
   Minimum order $10. MC, V, MO, PC.
Driving east from Los Angeles on Interstate 10, a few miles before you reach Palm Springs is an institution of Southern California: Hadley's. It's a "must stop" for all travelers wishing to select fine fruits and nuts, or cool off with a date milk shake. Now, with this colorful mail order catalog you can purchase beautiful fruit gift packs displaying a mosaic of apricots, prunes, pineapple, walnut-stuffed figs, glazed cherries, and date candies. Crunchy

nuts, too, are available in a variety of colored tins. They also offer miniature fruit cakes, nibbles, trail mixes, and honey.

Harry and David
Bear Creek Orchards
Medford, OR 97501
(503) 776-2121
32-page color catalog, free U.S. and overseas. MC, V, MO, PC.
Harry and David are the creators of the original Fruit-of-the-Month Club. They offer delicious fresh fruit, preserves, bakery goods, and living plants. Fruit varieties grown in their own Bear Creek Orchards include Royal Riviera pears, Royal Beurre bosc pears, and Oregold peaches. They also buy other varieties of superior fruits from selected growers. Started in 1934, Harry and David are a unique mail order success story; their catalog is a "must" for all gift-givers.

Lee's Fruit Company
P.O. Box 450
Leesburg, FL 32748
(904) 753-2064
Price list, free U.S. Does not sell overseas. MO, PC.
Lee's grows and sells organically grown oranges and grapefruit. Without using insecticides or poisonous sprays, Lee McComb fertilizes his groves with natural rock minerals and sea solids. The sea-solid micronutrients aid the groves' natural balance and helps to maintain their disease-resistance levels.

Mission Orchards
2296 Senter Rd.
P.O. Box 6947
San Jose, CA 95150
(408) 297-5056
32-page color catalog, free U.S. Does not sell overseas. AE, CB, DC, MC, V, MO, PC.
Mission Orchards has been in the fruit gift-packing service for almost fifty years. They are well known for their large and juicy Crown Comice pears. You can always be proud of giving a gift from Mission Orchards.

Pinnacle Orchards
441 South Fir St.
P.O. Box 1068
Medford, OR 97501
(503) 772-6271
32-page color catalog, free U.S. Does not
   sell overseas. AE, MC, V, MO, PC.
Located in the Rogue River Valley of
Oregon (along with another well-known
mail order fruit company), Pinnacle
offers attractive fresh fruit gifts,
processed fruits, nuts, preserves, and
candy. The Pick-A-Peck Basket (about
$21.95) is a one-peck harvest basket
containing their popular Comice pears,
sometimes known as "christmas pears"
because they peak at the holiday season.

Pioneer-Seminole Groves
326 W. Merritt
Merritt Island, FL 32952
(800) 327-2853
Florida (305) 452-3833
16-page color catalog, free U.S. and
   overseas. AE, DC, MC, V, MO, PC.
Pioneer-Seminole Groves sells boxes of
fruit—Crown Comice pears, seedless
navel oranges, Red Delicious apples,
temple oranges, honey tangerines, pink
seedless grapefruit, Valencia oranges,
mangos, sun-dried fruit, Persian limes,
and Green Goddess avocados. They also
have a nice selection of candy and, for
the holidays, a Christmas Amaryllis and
a miniature Christmas Spruce Tree.

Pittman & Davis
P.O. Box 2227
Harlingen, TX 78551
(512) 423-2154
16-page color catalog, free U.S. and
   overseas.
Pittman & Davis offers gift packages of
Texas oranges and grapefruits. They
ship mid-November to mid-March, with
your payment due the 10th of the month
following shipment. If you order
oranges, all November and December
shipments will be sweet seedless navel
oranges. Sometime in January or
February, Mother Nature will oblige
Pittman & Davis to switch to late-
maturing Valencia oranges. Valencias
are not as large or as sweet as navels,
but they are the finest juice oranges.

Zeys of Texas
P.O. Box 1048
Mission, TX 78572
(512) 585-8383
12-page color catalog, free U.S. MC, V,
   MO, PC.
Texas Ruby Red grapefruit, pecans, and
country kitchen meats. These big, juicy
grapefruits are fully tree-ripened and
hand-selected for quality and
appearance. Gift packs are available in
boxes or attractive Mexican baskets.

NUTS

Almond Plaza
California Almond Growers Exchange
1802 C. Street
Sacramento, CA 95814
(916) 446-8402
24-page color catalog, free U.S. and
   overseas. MC, V, MO, PC.
Almond Plaza products, famous since
1949 for premium quality and delicious
good taste, offer plenty of almonds:
roasted, blanched, slivered, salted,
unsalted, barbecued, and flavored.
There is also almond candy (nougats,
almond brittle, Jordan almonds, and
almond popcorn crunch). A new
product, almond butter, is a delicious
alternative for people who would like
a nut spread with more subtlety of
flavor. Try their gift pack assortment
containing four 12-ounce jars—one each
of almond butter smooth, almond butter
crunchy, almond butter honey
cinnamon, and almond butter crunchy
honey cinnamon ($16, delivered).

Berrenda Mesa Farms
Irvine Recreation Park
3415 Michelson Dr.
Irvine, CA 92715
(800) 626-6887
California (800) 628-6887
16-page color catalog, free U.S. AE, MC,
   V, PC.
Pistachio nuts in economy bags,
decorator tins, and gift packs are offered
by Berenda Mesa Farms—as well as
almonds in many styles.

Calhoun Pecan Shelling Co.
P.O. Box 784
Mansfield, LA 71052
(318) 872-2921
4-page color brochure
Pecans, and nothing but! This small pecan-shelling plant is a family-run business offering high quality nuts. A three-pound economy box of halves is $16.75, and pecan pieces $13.50. The five-pound box, $27.45, is ideal for the holiday baker. The one-pound four-ounce gift tin sells for $9.50, and is a great gift for special friends or deserving clients.

Fiesta Nut Corp.
75 Harbor Rd.
Port Washington, NY 11050
(800) 645-3318
New York (516) 883-1400
16-page color catalog, $1 U.S.; overseas
   $2. AE, MC, V, MO, PC.
Fiesta Nut Corporation sells raw or roasted, salted or unsalted nuts. They carry both domestic and imported nuts, including pistachios, cashews, walnuts, almonds, Brazil nuts, pecans, filberts, and macadamias. They also carry about nine varieties of dried fruits.

Goodbee Pecan Plantation
P.O. Box 3650
Albany, GA 31708
(912) 883-1365
16-page color brochure, free U.S. and
   overseas. DC, MC, V, MO, PC.
From Dougherty County, Georgia, Goodbee Pecan Plantation offers rich and flavorful pecans. Only the top grade pecans (fancy Mammoth whole halves) and the finest gourmet milk chocolate (from Ambrosia Chocolate Co. of Milwaukee) are used. Gift packs of pecan clusters and chocolate-covered pecan halves are available, as well as pecans roasted, unroasted, and pieces (for cooking).

Gourmet Nut Center
1430 Railroad Ave.
Orland, CA 95963
(916) 865-5511
10-page color catalog, free U.S. Does not
   sell overseas. MO, PC.

These gourmet nuts, grown in the central valleys of California, are great for cooking, baking, salads, desserts, and for crunchy, delicious snacks. "The Gourmet Nut Center is the retail division of the T. M. Duche Nut Co., one of the oldest and largest processors and distributors of California nuts," states the catalog. Almonds are available whole, sliced and slivered, roasted, unroasted, salted and unsalted. Flavored almond varieties include smoked barbeque, cheese, garlic and onion, and sour cream and onion.

House of Almonds
5300 District Blvd.
Bakersfield, CA 93309
(805) 835-6561
24-page color catalog, free U.S. Does not
   sell overseas. AE, MC, V, MO, PC.
Gourmet quality almonds, pistachios, and cashews are offered. More than fifty years ago, Frank Slate and his son planted almond trees that were the beginning of House of Almonds in the San Joaquin Valley. Today they have a worldwide mailing of over two million catalogs a year. They are deserving leaders in fine gift foods.

Joe C. Williams
P.O. Box 640
Camden, AL 36726
(205) 682-4559
3-page brochure, free U.S. Does not sell
   overseas. PC.
Fresh shelled pecan halves in three-pound tin pails are about $17.95. They are available November through August.

Koinonia Partners
Rt. 2
Americus, GA 31709
(912) 924-0391
16-page brochure, free U.S. and
   overseas. MO, PC.
Koinonia sells pecan and peanut products, including granola, smoked pecans, spiced pecans, pecan bark, carob peanut crunch, and fruitcake. Koinonia Farm is an international Christian community started in 1942, dedicated to providing a ministry to their community and neighbors. Some

of the efforts they are involved in are building low-income housing, farming, schooling, and handcrafts.

Mauna Loa Macadamia Nut Corp.
S. R. Box 3, Volcano Hwy.
Hilo, Hawaii 96720
(808) 966-8612
16-page color brochure, free U.S. Does not sell overseas. AE, MC, V, MO, PC.
Mauna Loa is the largest grower in the world of those rare butter-sweet nuts, macadamias. Delicious plain, they also lend themselves to many delectable varieties: roasted in coconut oil, coated in essence of Kona coffee, glazed in butter candy, brittled or coated with caramel and chocolate. Two 12-ounce tins of macadamia nuts are priced at $19.95, delivered.

Sternberg Pecan Company
P.O. Box 193
Jackson, MS 39205
(601) 366-6310
Price list, free U.S. Does not sell overseas. MO, PC.
Sternberg's sells shelled pecans of top quality grade, including Fancy Mammoth halves, that are perfect for baking or gift giving. They also include a wonderful recipe booklet which includes a melt-in-your-mouth recipe for Southern Pralines.

Sunnyland Farms
Albany, GA 31703
(912) 883-3085
48-page color catalog. Does not sell overseas. MC, V, PC.
Sunnyland Farms offers pecans in bulk, in gift packs, and in candies. They offer both Schley and Stuart pecans in the shell, and many choices of shelled packs: a three-pound economy pack ($20.30), a three-pound package of pecan pieces for cooking ($20.50), and Jiffy Gifts—a case of nine 14-ounce polybags priced at $52.25. Candies include Sugar 'n Spice, orange-frosted, pecan logs, pralines, brittle, brickle, toffee, date nut cake, clusters, choco-nuts, chocolate bark, and nut delights.

BAKED GOODS

Baldwin Hill Bakery
Baldwin Hill Road
Phillipston, MA 01002
(617) 249-4691
3-page brochure, free U.S. Does not sell overseas. MO, PC.
Baldwin Hill bread is 100% whole wheat bread. Hy Lerner and Paul Petrofsky make this bread using organic stoneground flour and pure well water, leavened with natural sourdough and baked over a wood fire in a traditional brick oven. There is a minimum order of twelve loaves.

Bent's
7 Pleasant St.
Milton, MA 02186
(617) 698-5945
4-page brochure.
Bent's ("Bakery Specialties Since 1801") sells common crackers and water crackers. The water cracker is made with flour and cold water, no salt. The result: a very hearty cracker. Bent's famous common cracker completes a bowl of chowder, or is great for dunking and dipping. It seems a shame to use them as crumb toppings for casseroles, but you could. Two 14-ounce packages of either kind start at $5.

The Birkett Mills
163 Main St.
Penn Yan, NY 14527
(315) 536-3311
Price list, free U.S. PC.
Birkett Mills sells buckwheat products— flour, pancake mixes, and groats. Quantities are available in two, four, and five-pound sacks.

Collin Street Bakery
401 West 7th
Corsicana, TX 75110
(214) 872-3951
6-page brochure, free U.S. and overseas. AE, DC, MC, V, MO, PC.
Last year DeLuxe Fruit Cakes were shipped to all fifty states and 192 foreign countries. Collin Street Bakery, honored by the New York Gourmet Society, sells fruit cakes starting at $9.35 for a two-pound cake. Prime harvest cherries and

fruits are blended into a rich batter, crunchy with native pecans. Following the original recipe, every DeLuxe Fruit Cake is hand-decorated and custom-baked.

Eilenberger's Butter Nut Baking Co.
P.O. Box 710
Palestine, TX 75801–0710
(214) 729-2176
4-page color price list, U.S. and overseas. AE, MC, V, MO, PC.
Eilenberger's features fruit cakes, hand-prepared with real creamery butter and selected Texas pecans. They also make a very popular Texas Pecan Cake, made with one-third Texas pecans, dates, pineapple and cherries, and moistened with honey. One of their newer items made a smashing debut: Australian Apricot Cake, made with big rich Australian apricots, baked in a light butter batter with a touch of juicy pineapple and brandy. Two-pound cakes start at $10.

Elisabeth The Chef
St. Mary's Rd.
Sydenham Estate
Leamington Spa CV31 1JP
Warwickshire England
10-page color catalog, free U.S. and overseas. Prices in British pounds. MO, PC.
"Celebration cakes for Easter, Mother's Day, and all sorts of occasions through the post from Elizabeth the Chef," states the catalog. Incredibly delicious-looking cakes include the Dundee Cake, made with currants and sultanas macerated in fresh lemon juice to give it moistness, then decorated with whole almonds. The Royal Warwick Cake, made with fruit soaked in rum, brandy and lemon juice, is baked with a thick layer of almond paste in the center and crowned with split almonds. The Rembrandt is a triangular section of almond sponge cake, moistened with rum syrup, interleaved with vertical layers of buttercream and nibbed almonds, wrapped in marzipan, and finally coated with chocolate. The keeping time on fruit cakes is approximately three months, but the Rembrandt (for one) is best eaten within a week of receipt. Prices start at $10.

E. Otto Schmidt
Zollhausstrabe 30
8500 Nurnberg 50
Germany
01149 911 80141
12-page color brochure in German, free U.S. and overseas. Prices in German marks. MO.
E. Otto Schmidt specializes in Lebkuchen, traditional German cookies rich in spices and honey. Though the tempting brochure is in German you'll have not trouble selecting an assorted gift pack of Lebkuchen favorites. Shipped in a decorative tin, Christmas just wouldn't seem right without them.

Fantasia Confections
3465 California St.
San Francisco, CA 94118
4-page color brochure, free U.S. Does not sell overseas. MC, V.
Family-owned and family-run, Fantasia is said to be the place San Francisco gourmets go when they prefer more elegant desserts than they can create themselves. Their customers include the finest hotels and restaurants and a growing number of mail order customers. One of Fantasia's specialties is Baumkuchen (log cake), originated by the gypsies of Rumania. This cake consists of fifteen to twenty-five thin layers of buttery batter poured over a "baking log." Each layer is a delicate toasty shade, and fine-textured. Baumkuchen is cooked in three- to four-foot lengths (you order by the inch). An eight-inch hollow section, standing on end, offers some creative opportunities for a grand dessert.

Forgione
International Confections, Ltd.
2105 Lakeland Ave.
Ronkonkoma, NY 11779
(800) 292-9660
27-page color catalog.
Forgione collects some of the best goodies worldwide to display in tempting gift packs in their catalog. There are Grifo tins from Italy filled

with Perugina's finest chocolates ($15.50), sauces from Fortnum and Mason, Lindt truffles from Switzerland, Virginia hams, Droste Pastilles from Holland—and much more.

The Great Valley Mills
Rt. 309
Quakertown, Bucks County PA 18951
(215) 536-3990
16-page catalog, free U.S. and overseas. MC, V, MO, PC.
The Great Valley Mills have been a mail order house since 1898, offering stone ground flours, whole grains, triple-smoked corn grain-fed hams, and smoked turkeys. They grind their own flours as orders are received and ship them the next day. Stone ground flours are available in buckwheat, brown rice, soy bean, graham, rye, and oatmeal to name a few.

Heartymix Co.
1231 Madison Hill Rd.
Rahway, NJ 07065
(201) 382-2432
8-page brochure, free U.S. Does not sell overseas. MO, PC.
Heartymix offers a line of thirty-one quick and easy deluxe baking mixes. These mixes can be used for breads, rolls, English muffins, bagels, biscuits, waffles, muffins, croissants, pizza crust, pie crusts, and cookies. There are also salt-free and wheatless mixes for those people with allergies. All mixes are made from natural ingredients, naturally fortified, low in cholesterol and saturated fats, and containing no artificial preservatives. Each mix is packed in a one and one-half pound plastic bag with detailed nutritional information and recipe ideas included.

Hills of Westchester, Inc.
3400 Windom Rd.
Brentwood, MD 20722
(301) 864-4421
24-page color catalog, free; overseas $1. AE, DC, MC, V, MO.
This confectionery enterprise specializes in petits fours and butter cookies, available boxed or tinned. Four catalog pages are devoted to varieties of fruit cakes, including a lovely tin of

miniatures. Pastel and chocolate petits fours are also offered in assorted gift packs with the tasty butter cookies. There is much to choose from.

Matthews 1812 House
Whitcomb Hill Rd.
Cornwall Bridge, CT 06754
(203) 672-0149
8-page color brochure, free U.S. and overseas. AE, MC, V, MO, PC.
Deanna Matthews started this mail order business from her home in Cornwall Bridge, Connecticut, selling fruit cake from her mother's adapted recipes. Deanna's fruit cakes do not contain candied fruit, rinds, peels, or preservatives. Her Fruit and Nut Cake has a honey and brown sugar batter, and is full of crisp pecans, moist dates, raisins, and apricots. She also has done well with her Brandied Apricot Cake— a little tart, but still sweet enough, with lots of apricots.

Moravian Sugar Crisp Co.
Route 2
Clemmons, NC 27012
(919) 764-1402
4-page brochure, free U.S. and overseas. MO, PC.
Moravian Sugar Crisp Company makes homemade cookies in five flavors: Moravian Ginger Crisps, Sugar Crisps, Chocolate Crisps, Lemon Crisps, and Butterscotch Crisps. Each cookie is rolled paper-thin, cut by hand, and wrapped in individual stacks to insure arrival in excellent condition.

Pepperidge Farm Mail Order Co.
P.O. Box 119 Route 145
Clinton, CT 06413
(800) 243-9314
Connecticut (203) 669-4131
20-page color catalog, free U.S. and overseas. AE, DC, MC, V, MO, PC.
Pepperidge Farm mail orders a collection of products too "special" for supermarket shelves. These include the confectionery intoxicant, Irish Whiskey Cake ($29.92), made from fresh walnuts with generous portions of butter, eggs and milk—and soaked in ten ounces of the finest imported Irish Whiskey. Imported from the Nobo bakery of

Holland is the Dutch Butter Almond Ring ($8.95), a ring of tender, flaky butter crust with a scrumptious almond filling. Godiva chocolates are also featured.

Wolferman's Good Things to Eat
2820 W. 53rd St.
Fairway, KS 66205
(800) 255-0169
(913) 432-6131
12-page color catalog, free U.S. Does not sell overseas. AE, MC, V, MO, PC.
Wolferman's was founded in 1888 as a specialty food store, and became famous for its English muffins. Their unique size, texture, and flavor have made them a true Kansas City tradition. In addition to English muffins they also sell fine food items (all excellent accompaniments to the English muffin): Nelson's of Aintree preserves, Twining's Tea, Tiffin Room coffee, and Honey Acres Apricot Honey.

SWEETS AND SNACKS

The Backman Company
P.O. Box 898
Reading, PA 19603
(215) 320-7800
12-page color catalog, free U.S. Does not sell overseas. MC, V, MO, PC.
The Backman Company specializes in pretzels. They also sell a variety of cheese sticks and popcorn (cheese and white), packed in decorative tins and gift boxes. A ten-year-old child of Reading, Pennsylvania, once defined a pretzel as "a strip of dough that has a nervous condition. You know, it's all tied up in knots." The Centennial Drum Collection $19.95 is a snacker's delight with four varieties of pretzels—cheese sticks, individually wrapped Dutch Pretzels, Thin Twist Pretzels, and Crunchy Nutzels.

Butterfield Farms
330 Washington St.
Marina Del Rey, CA 90291
(213) 822-0700
8-page color brochure. U.S. and overseas. MC, V, MO, PCL

Butterfield Farms offers Bavarian Mints, California Pistachios, almonds, and fruit cake. Bavarian-style pretzels are available in a giant three and one-half gallon tin decorated with graphics and funny facts—"How many pretzels would it take to connect all four bases on a baseball diamond?" and other such fun nonsense. Great gift idea for kids at summer camp.

Clark Hill Sugary
Dept. B
Canaan, NH 03741
(603) 523-7752
4-page brochure, free U.S. and overseas. MC, V, MO, PC.
Clark's sells old-fashioned 100% pure maple syrup from the sap of New Hampshire maple trees, and bottled in attractive little jugs. Nothing extra is added to the syrup—no additives, sugars or preservatives. One pint, $6; one quart, $10; one-half gallon, $17.

Culpeppers Popcorn
14000 Dinard Ave.
Santa Fe Springs, CA 90670
(213) 921-7961
4-page color brochure, free U.S. Does not sell overseas. MO, PC.
Over 32 flavors of popcorn. Oh sure, there is the usual salted and candy-coated with nuts. But imagine reaching into a bag of blue colored popcorn and crunching down on the taste of blueberry! The current list of some of these amazing popcorn flavors includes: cheddar cheese, chocolate, butter-flavored, peanut butter, eggnog, blueberry, cinnamon, strawberry, taco, coconutty corn, pineapple-coconut, sour cream and onion, root beer, wild cherry, licorice, and green apple. Surprise someone with a twelve-flavor sampler ($11.95).

Desoto Confectionery and Nut Co.
P.O. Box 75
Desoto, GA 31743
(912) 874-1200
17-page color brochure. Does not sell overseas. MC, V, MO, PC.
Desoto Confectionery and Nut Company sells chocolate candies and nuts. They are best known for their "Crickle," a

light and delicate brittle, in six flavors: peanut, pecan, cashew, almond, coffee, and coconut. Shipped the very day it is made, a Crickle Six Pak ($15.95) contains six assorted half-pound bags.

Green Mountain Sugar House
R. F. D. #1
Ludlow, VT 05149
(802) 228-7151
16-page catalog, free U.S. and overseas. AE, MC, V, MO.
The Harlow family sells pure maple syrup, maple candy, and a good selection of other Vermont products such as cheese, honey, and smoked meats.

Henry and Cornelia Swayze
Brookside Farm
Turnbridge, VT 05077
(802) 889-3738
4-page price list, free U.S. and overseas. MO, PC.
Henry and Cornelia Swayze have been making maple syrup for twenty years. They offer three strengths: medium amber, dark amber (with a deeper caramel-maple flavor), and cooking syrup (a very dark maple syrup with a pronounced caramel flavor). Maple syrup production is as much a phenomenon as honey production; it takes forty quarts of sap to produce one quart of maple syrup. And that takes one maple tree (twelve inches in diameter) an entire sugaring season to produce. Enjoy mother nature's sweetness. One-pint jugs start at about $6.

Perugina
636 Lexington Ave.
New York, NY 10022
(212) 688-2490
22-page color catalog, free U.S. Does not sell overseas. Minimum order $10. AE, MC, V.
Through their tempting catalog, Perugina now offers classic Italian chocolates, hard candies, and cookies made in Perugina, Italy. You'll find Bluette, Cinzia, Panettone, Giandjua, and the very rich Rossana.

Plumbridge
30 East 67th St.
New York, NY 10021
(212) 371-0608

10-page brochure, free U.S. and overseas. AE, MC, V, MO, PC.
Plumbridge, founded in 1883, offers fine confections made according to old family recipes. Plumbridge caters to the carriage trade, and offers their delicacies in a variety of elegant gift containers, including antique Oriental porcelains.

The Popcorn Factory
13970 W. Laurel Dr.
Lake Forest, IL 60045
(800) 621-5559
Illinois (800) 972-5858
8-page color catalog, free U.S. and overseas. AE, MC, V, MO, PC.
The Popcorn Factory sells gourmet popcorn flavored with genuine cheddar cheese, homemade caramel, and rich creamery butter. Available in one, two, four, and six and one-half gallon decorator cans. Prices start at $8. (The Cretors family has been in the popcorn business for almost a century.)

Senor Murphy, Candymaker
P.O. Box 2505
Santa Fe, NM 87501
(505) 988-4311
Senor Murphy features candy made with piñon nuts (brittle, toffee, tortugas, caramels, rolls, and clusters). Piñon Brittle is $8 for a fourteen-ounce box. A specialty of the shop is their homemade Red or Green Chili Jelly, spooned over Cream Cheese or Brie—it's a delicious and unusual cracker spread. Gracias, Senor Murphy.

Sugarbush Farms
RFD 7
Woodstock, VT 05901
(802) 457-1757
4-page brochure, free U.S. Does not sell overseas. AE, DC, MC, V, MO, PC.
In early March, Jack and Marion Ayers harness up their team of work horses and begin hanging more than 2,000 sap buckets on different trails through the woods. From this they produce pure maple syrup unrivaled in flavor by your supermarket brand. Also available are delicious cheeses: rich and creamy Green Mt. Bleu, Sage Bar (a mellow

cheddar with flecks of sage), and Hickory and Maple Smoked Cheese.

Wileswood Country Store
P.O. Box 328
Huron, OH 44839
(419) 433-3355
4-page newsalog, 25¢ U.S. Limited
   overseas sales. MC, V, MO, PC.
Unpopped popcorn gift packs, plus old-fashioned candies and private label jellies and relishes, are offered from Wileswood. Wileswood Country Store popcorn is so popular people have been known to travel way out of their way to buy it at the Huron, Ohio store. The Country Store Popcorn Sampler Kit ($8.95 prepaid) contains a 30-ounce cloth bag of Country Store Popcorn, a 13-ounce jar of popping oil, a shaker of salt, and popping instructions.

PRESERVES

Alaska Wild Berry Products
Box 374
Homer, AK 99603
(907) 235-8858
16-page brochure, free U.S. and
   overseas. MC, V, MO, PC.
Alaska Wild Berry Products, as the name implies, produces jams, jellies, sauces, and syrups. Alaskan wild berries are hand-picked on the Kenai Peninsula and go into unique jellies including: Salmon Berry, Highbush Cranberry, Rosehips, Lingenberry, Wild Raspberry, Mossberry, and Elderberry. A gift box of nine 4-ounce assorted jars of jelly is priced at $24.50. Sourdough sauce is a blend of wild Lowbush Cranberries, applesauce, sugar, vinegar, onions, and spices. It is a delicious condiment for meat—or a tasty dip with salmon or fresh vegetables.

Crabtree & Evelyn
Box 167
Woodstock, CT 06281
(203) 928-2766
24-page color catalog, $3 U.S. and
   overseas. Minimum order $7.50. PC.
Crabtree & Evelyn offers delectable preserves, mustards, chutneys, herbs, and spices in antique decorator packaging. With the exception of one or two mustards, all of their products are free of artificial colors and synthetic flavors. There are many cookies and gingerbread men, marmalades, fruit preserves, fruit vinegars, and syrups to choose from.

Hickin's Mountain Mowings Farm
RFD 1 Black Mountain Rd.
Brattleboro, VT 05301
(802) 254-2146
12-page brochure, .25¢ U.S. and overseas.
   MO, PC.
On Black Mountain in Dummerston, Vermont, fruits and vegetables are grown to produce fine homemade jellies, jams, preserves, butters, pickles, and relishes. Some of the more unusual offerings include Dill Carrots, Corn Relish, Pepper Relish, Unsweetened Raspberry Jam (pucker up!), Pear Butter, and ten fruit butters. Add a pretty bow to one of these, and it makes a lovely hostess gift.

Knott's Berry Farm
8039 Beach Blvd.
Buena Park, CA 92670
(714) 827-1776
24-page color catalog. U.S. and overseas.
   AE, MC, V, MO, PC.
Knott's Berry Farm is famous for their delicious jams, jellies, and preserves—especially Boysenberry, a hybrid berry they developed. Every tourist in Southern California has Knott's Berry Farm on his sightseeing list. It is the nation's oldest and largest independent theme amusement park with 135 rides, shows, shops, and attractions celebrating the Old West. It began in 1920, when Walter Knott rented some farmland and set up a small roadside stand. When the Depression hit, Mrs. Knott started selling chicken dinners and homemade jams. But the lines soon grew long, so Walter Knott brought in the first Ghost Town buildings to entertain the waiting guests. The rest is history. By mail order they feature the Holiday Hostess gift pack, which contains six of their finest half-pound jars of Boysenberry, Strawberry, Apricot, Pineapple, Peach, Plum Preserves, and Orange Marmalade for

$11.50, delivered. If you should be so lucky as to visit Knott's Berry Farm, don't leave without having tried their Boysenberry pie.

The Silver Palate
274 Columbus Ave.
New York, NY 10023
(212) 799-6340
Color catalog. $2 U.S.; overseas $4. AE, MC, V, MO, PC.
Sheila Lukins and Julie Rosso opened the Silver Palate in 1977, offering scrumptious takeout foods—similar to shops you'd find on European street corners. Customers loved their homemade food, including preserves, salads, and even whole dinners. Today they offer (under the Silver Palate label) sweet sauces, Raspberry Fudge Sauce, Carmel Pecan Sauce, Fudge Sauce Grand Marnier, Vanilla Clementines, and Fruit Melange in Cognac. Other specialties of this successful business include Blueberry Chutney, Green peppercorn oil, and Jalapeño Chili Chutney. To indulge in the Silver Palate will require some silver in your pocket.

Thousand Island Apiaries
RD 2 Box 212
Clayton, NY 13624
(315) 654-2741
Price list, free U.S. and overseas. MO, PC.
They offer delicious honey made from the flowers of the Thousand Islands regions of the St. Lawrence River. You'll pay more for this honey than for your favorite supermarket variety, but sometimes only the best will do. Honey processing at low temperatures (120°) ensures the preservation of natural nutrients and essential oils, which gives Thousand Islands Apiaries honey its unique aroma and flavor. A three-pound can is priced at $7.50.

Wood's Cider Jelly
RFD 2 Box 266
Springfield, VT 05156
(802) 263-5547
Price list, free U.S. Does not sell overseas. MO, PC.
"We make our own cider jelly, unsweetened, by boiling fresh cider

down until it will jell. It is a very dark, rich jelly that goes well with meats and donuts," says Willis Wood. This used to be a common New England product; nowadays very few places make this natural jelly. Four 8-ounce jars are priced at $7. Be sure to include your street address as they ship by UPS.

CHOCOLATES

André Bollier
5018 Main St.
Kansas City, MO 64112
(816) 516-3440
8-page brochure, free U.S. Does not sell overseas. MC, V, MO, PC.
Chocolate candies and other confiserie items are offered by Master Confiseur-Conditor, André Bollier. Truffles, "the Queen of the chocolate candies," are prepared weekly to insure freshness as well as smoothness and softness of texture. Very reasonably priced.

Bissinger's
205 West Fourth St.
Cincinnati, OH 45202
(513) 241-8182
Bissinger's is considered by many to represent the finest chocolates in this country. Chocolate Nut Balls (a two-pound box for $11.95) have been a virtual trademark through the years. They are made from freshly ground almond paste packed between plump pecans and walnuts, then dipped in fondant and chocolate. Bissinger's famous assortment box ($9.95 per pound) contains a sampling of just about everything they make. Started in 1863 by Karl Bissinger, former Confiseur Imperial to Emperor Louis Napoleon.

Charbonnel et Walker
1 Royal Arcade
Old Bond St.
London W1X 4BT England
01 629 4396
6-page color brochure, free U.S. and overseas. AE, DC, MC, V.
If you want to express your affection, try saying it with chocolates from Charbonnel et Walker. The lovely flowered gift boxes are tied with a pink

cord wire, originally designed in Victorian times to avoid the noisy rustling of paper wrappings in the theater. A key list inside every box identifies the different centers: creams, marzipans, pralines, truffles, caramels, and fudges. A Charbonnel et Walker specialty is Les Bôites Blanches, an assorted gift box containing a few ingeniously moulded chocolate letters covered in gold foil. You can send a special someone a significant message— or just a telephone number.

Filbertreats
356 North West 1st Ave.
Canby, OR 97013
(503) 266-8172
10-page color brochure, free U.S. and
    overseas. MO, PC.
Filbertreats offers delightfully different candy made with Oregon-grown Filberts. The beautiful northwest Willamette Valley is an ideal spot for growing Filberts, commonly called Hazelnuts. Oregon Filberts have a snow white meat and a thin skin that makes them suitable for salted or confectionary treats. The one and one-quarter pound Quadrapaks contain an assortment of four candy-coated jumbo Filberts, including chocolate, vanilla, butterscotch, and sherried (which is a spiced nut). Other Filbert candies are toffee, turtles, brittle, and many choices of creams.

Fudge Factory
Box 1142 Rt. 7A
Manchester Center, VT 05255
10-page brochure, free U.S. and
    overseas. MC; V, MO, PC.
Ronald Mancini operates the Fudge Factory at an old fashioned ice cream parlor named Mother Myricks. For those who are too far away to sidle up to the marbletopped soda fountain counter, Ronald offers his chocolate confectioneries in a tempting brochure that even a reformed chocoholic couldn't resist. The two-pound Fudge Sampler ($12.95) is most popular, with smooth, creamy fudge favorites (chocolate walnut, old fashioned penuche, real maple walnut, and freshly ground peanut butter fudge).

Godiva
P.O. Box 4116
Huntington Station
New York, NY 11746
(800) 223-6005
8-page color catalog, free U.S. AE, MC,
    V.
Godiva is one of the most famous chocolatiers in the country. Their chocolate perfections are sold in Godiva's distinctive gold ballotins and other elegant wrappings. They are always received as "presents with presence."

Harbor Sweets
Box 150
Marblehead, MA 01945
(617) 745-7648
14-page color catalog, free U.S. and
    overseas. MC, V, PC.
Don't miss this clever catalog of imaginative chocolate candies with a nautical theme. Sweet Sloops are sailboat shaped almond butter crunch. The mainsail and jib are made of white milk coating, floating in rich, dark chocolate with pecan spindrift washing her sides. A 13-ounce gift box of thirty or more pieces sells for $13, postpaid. Marblehead Mints are thin chocolate wafers, with a tiny sailboat embossed on a sea of bittersweet chocolate, for about the same price as Sweet Sloops. For beachcombers there are Sandollars, pecan halves hidden in soft creamy butter caramel and covered with a chocolate sand dollar.

Hershey's Chocolate World
Park Blvd. Box 800
Hershey, PA 17033
(717) 534-4990
16-page color catalog, free U.S. Does not
    sell overseas. MC, V, MO, PC.
If American Chocoholics united and formed a headquarters, it would be located in Hershey, Pennsylvania. This catalog is a collection of all those Hershey Chocolate goodies America has been delightfully devouring since 1895. The famous chocolate creations— Chocolate Kiss, Milk Chocolate Bar, Miniature, Rolo, Kit Kat, Mr. Goodbar, and Whatchamacallit (that is actually

the name of a candy bar)—are featured in about forty-five chocolate gift packages. Most of the gift packs are in attractive tins and mugs designed from old Hershey labels and advertising themes.

Kron Chocolatier
764 Madison Ave.
New York, NY 10021
(212) 472-1234
10-page color catalog, $1 U.S.; overseas $2. AE, MC, V, MO, PC.
"Our reputation for creating the ultimate in chocolate is known around the world," states the catalog. What the catalog shows are the unique custom chocolate molds that Kron has become famous for. Resembling dismembered manikins, you can order a life-size body part for $60 and up. (Know anyone who'd get a kick out of receiving a life-size leg $75, complete with garter?) The "lista chocolate" also offers molds of a telephone, phonograph, tennis racquet, Kron bear, magnum of Kron, and a ruler of chocolate presented in an old fashioned sliding top box. The list is full of exciting chocolate forms, including escargots (hollow snail shells you could fill with ice-cream or mousse). Maybe you'd like to custom create your own chocolate greeting card?

Li-Lac Chocolates
120 Christopher St.
New York, NY 10014
(212) 242-7374
4-page brochure, free U.S. Does not sell overseas. AE, DC, MC, V, MO.
Li-Lac chocolates, a Greenwich Village tradition since 1923, still handmakes and hand dips chocolates fresh daily in small batches. In addition to their fine assortment of filled centers, bark, butter crunch, and nut chews, Li-Lac also has a good selection of moulded chocolates if you're trying to find an unusual gift. Chocolate Jewel Box is $18.50 empty, and filled is $21.50. The preppy alligator ($2.25), Seven-piece tool set ($6.75), and foil-wrapped butterflies ($1.50 each) all look wonderful.

Madame Chocolate
1940-C Lehigh Ave.
Glenview, IL 60025
(312) 729-3330
16-page brochure, free U.S. Does not sell overseas. MC, V, MO, PC.
Madame Chocolate offers quality chocolate and related equipment for home cooks, bakers, and candymakers. In unsweetened, bittersweet, semi-sweet, milk chocolate (America's favorite), and "white chocolate," some of the finest chocolate name brands are available: Wilbur, World's Finest, Tobler, Lindt, Surfin, Poulaine, Feodora, Ghirardelli, Verkade, Guittard, Nestlé, and that Belgian favorite, Callebaut. Chocolate is available in bars, chips, sprinkles, cocoa beans, and coatings. Candy-making supplies include sticks, wrappers, molds, oils, flavors, fillings, colors, thermometers, and related utensils. Don't miss this catalog.

Maud Borup Candies
20 West Fifth St.
St. Paul, MN 55102
(612) 293-0530
10-page catalog, free U.S. and overseas. MC, V, MO, PC.
Maud Borup, founded in 1907, offers over 100 varieties of hand-dipped chocolates. Their Fudge Wreath ($13.95), gift tied on a holiday tray, is especially suitable for holiday gifts.

Milton York Candy Co.
P.O. Box 416
Long Beach, WA 98631
(206) 642-4466
4-page brochure, free U.S. Does not sell overseas. MC, V, MO, PC.
All fine chocolates are hand-dipped in milk or dark chocolate. Chocolate dipped fruits ($7.50 per pound) include orange sticks, sweet prunes, honey-glazed Australian apricots, and pineapple, ginger and cranberry jells—just right for Thanksgiving or Christmas.

Portland Puddles
11207 SW Capitol Hwy.
Portland, OR 97219
Price list, free U.S. Does not sell overseas. MO, PC.

Portland Puddles are unique puddle-shaped chocolate candies that come in two 2-ounce pieces to a box. Imprinted with "Portland," these novelty candies have created a smiling image for the frequently damp Oregon climate. They are $3.95, postpaid.

Schatz-Konditorei
A-5020 Salzburg
Getreidegasse 3
Schatz-Durchhaus
A-5020 Salzburg Austria
0 62 22 42792
Price list, free U.S. and overseas.
Schatz-Konditorei mail orders genuine Salzburger Mozartkugeln. This specialty is made from pistachio marchpane, hazelnut, and nougat, and is dipped in rich chocolate. Orders are arranged in different-sized boxes, which show an old engraving of Salzburg. The mini-package, containing fifteen pieces, is priced at $14.20 air mail (packaging and postage included), and are tax free. Wunder(candy)bar!

Standard Candy Company
P.O. Box 101025
Nashville, TN 37210
(615) 889-6360
Price list, free U.S. Does not sell
   overseas. MO, PC.
For years a special blend of chocolate peanuts, caramel, and marshmallows has been well known in Nashville as "Goo Goo Clusters." Word has spread, and now you can find them in many chic stores and theaters throughout the country. A box of twenty-four Goo Goo Clusters will cost you about $17.25 (and 5,800 calories).

Sweet Revenge
Grand Hyatt Hotel
109 E. 42nd St.
New York, NY 10017
(212) 986-2595
16-page color catalog, free U.S. AE, MO,
   PC.
Sweet Revenge has some very tempting Fruits de Mer, imported sculptured chocolate sea shells filled with a delicious hazelnut praline ($15 for twelve ounces). There are many cute chocolate molds: Teddy Bear ($24),

Calculator ($6.95), Gold Bars (imported, of course, from Switzerland, $10.50), and a fun assortment of nursery rhyme characters.

Teuscher Chocolates of Switzerland
620 Fifth Ave.
New York, NY 10020
(212) 246-4416
4-page color brochure, free U.S. and
   overseas. Minimum order $12.50. AE,
   MC, V, MO.
Teuscher Chocolates of Switzerland offers handmade Swiss imported chocolates. Once a week chocolates are flown in by jet, fresh from Zurich in a temperature-controlled compartment. Switzerland is recognized for its superior skill in producing the finest chocolates. Truffles are their specialty; the fourteen-ounce Sampler Box sells for $21. Diabetic chocolates, made without sugar or artificial sweeteners, are also available.

Van Duyn Chocolate Shops
5603 S. W. Hood Ave.
Portland, OR 97201
10-page color catalog, free U.S. and
   overseas. AE, MC, V, MO, PC.
Van Duyn's carries an exquisite assortment of dark and delicious chocolates—chocolate butter creams, whipped truffles, caramels, almond butter toffee, and nut clusters. Chocolate lovers will appreciate a logo T-shirt ("I take Chocolate bribes"), and coffee bugs that carry slogans ("Chocolate Makes the World Go Round").

COFFEE AND TEA

Cheese Coffee Center
2115 Allston Way
Berkeley, CA 94704
(415) 848-7115
12-page brochure, free U.S. and
   overseas. MC, V, MO, PC.
This brochure offers a good selection of cheese, coffees, and teas. Bagged tea brands include: Wagners, Typhoo Tea from England, Bushells and Billy Tea from Australia, Pompador Teas from Holland, and Celestial Seasonings. Over fifty different loose teas are available;

over forty different coffees, from Aged Arabica to Zimbabwe, are available in bulk. Over 100 cheeses are also available, including many kinds of Blue, Cheddar, Swiss, and French. They ship UPS, so be sure to include a street address.

The Coffee Connection
342 Western Ave.
Brighton, MA 02135
(617) 254-1451
Brochure, free U.S. Does not sell
    overseas. MC, V, PC.
The Coffee Connection stocks over twenty varieties of coffee (from the Americas, Africa, and Indonesia) that they roast themselves twice a week. They also buy teas by the chest from the country of origin, and offer over thirty varieties of the finest black, green oolong, scented, blended, and herbal teas. The Coffee Connection sells only top grade authentic coffees; Mocha Java, for example, is made with Yemen Mocha Mattari (extremely rare) and Java—not "Mocha Java Style," which some stores will occasionally try to sell.

Maria's
111 Stratford Rd.
Winston-Salem, NC 27104
8-page catalog, free U.S. and overseas.
    MC, V, PC.
Maria's offers twenty-nine varieties and blends of coffee, shipped the same day they are roasted. They also have extensive lists of teas, spices, herbs, cheeses, fruits, and nuts. An interesting gift (only $3.50) is the Vanilla Bottle, seven-inches tall with cork stopper. They put in a Mexican vanilla bean, you put in Vodka or brandy—and be patient for a month. You'll have a delicious pure vanilla extract.

Northwestern Coffee Mills
217 North Broadway
Milwaukee, WI 53202
(414) 276-1031
12-page catalog, 50¢ U.S. and overseas.
    MC, V, MO, PC.
Northwestern Coffee Mills slow roasts their own coffee beans in their vintage 1914 roasting ovens. They offer a good variety of coffees, both whole bean and

ground. Their catalog is very informative, providing descriptions on taste and strength, and excellent tips on decaffeinated coffees.

The Pannikin
645 "G" St.
San Diego, CA 92101
(619) 239-1257
20-page catalog, free U.S. and overseas.
    MC, V, MO, PC.
Bob and Gay Sinclair carry an extensive variety of coffee and tea accessories, from preparation to serving. They offer over twenty types of fresh roasted coffee, and 80 types of bulk tea. Their coffees are roasted twice a week to ensure freshness. They have an interesting selection of coffee makers, including the elegant French Melior Chambord: the stainless plunger presses the flavor out while holding the grounds firmly to the bottom of the hand-blown glass-and-chrome beaker. They also carry grinders, Espresso pots, Samovars, tea pots, cups, and warmers.

Porto Rico Importing Company
201 Bleecker St.
New York, NY 10012
(212) 474-5421
4-page brochure, free U.S. and overseas.
    MC, V, MO, PC.
Porto Rico offers a selection of thirty freshly roasted coffees, seventy-five teas, forty herbal teas, decaffeinated coffees, teas, and coffee pots. Swiss water-decaffeinated coffees (decaffeinated without chemicals) are available in Colombian, Espresso, and Chocolate Almond. Decaffeinated teas are available in Orange Spice, English Breakfast, and Earl Grey.

Schapira Coffee Co.
117 W. 10th St.
New York, NY 10011
(212) 675-3733
4-page brochure, free U.S. MO, PC.
Since 1903 Schapira has offered fine coffees blended and unblended. Maracaibo from Venezuela, Djimmah from Ethiopia, and Ethiopian Mocha (known for being a light and flavory cup). For a brisk, hearty flavor try Flavor Cup Tea, which is their own private

blend of rare Indian and China teas. In addition to their good variety of coffees and teas, they sell tricolettes, hand grinders, espresso pots, Melitta pots, and imported Moulinex electric coffee mills. Ask for their special order form.

Simpson & Vail
38 Clinton St.
P.O. Box 309
Pleasantville, NY 10570
(914) 747-1336
12-page catalog, free U.S. and overseas.
  MC, V, MO, PC.
Importer of specialty coffees and rare teas. It may be time to venture away from the lookalike coffee cans that load the supermarket shelves and try something special. A good bet might be a coffee blend Simpson and Vail calls Extra Rich Special Blend (at $4.55 per pound), or a lighter blend, American Roast (at $4.45 per pound). With a little more courage you might try Tanzania Peaberry—a uniquely shaped Arabica coffee bean which brews a light and flavorful cup with an influence of wine.

Sir Thomas Lipton's
800 Sylvan Ave.
Englewood Cliffs, NJ 07632
(800) 526-0359
New Jersey (201) 894-7522
32-page color catalog. Does not sell
  overseas. AE, MC, V, MO, PC.
This catalog offers a regal selection of Sir Thomas Lipton Connoisseur Teas. There are tea services by Royal Doulton and Royal Worcester, and beautiful Wedgewood teapots and silver to accompany the ceremony known as afternoon tea. Fine teas include Darjeeling from the foothills of the Himalayan Mountains, Uva Ceylon, English Breakfast, Earl Grey, Yunnan, and many others. Pure butter Walkers Shortbread Fingers come in a decorative tin, and fancy Oregon Red Raspberry preserves in reusable French canning jars.

Stash Tea Company
P.O. Box 610
Portland, OR 97207
(503) 227-5077

16-page catalog, free U.S. and overseas.
  MC, V, MO, PC.
Whether you brew by the cup or pot, prefer tea bags or loose tea, you can select from over twenty tea flavors in Stash's catalog. All the tea-brewing implements are also available: canisters, tins, jars, kettles, infusers, teapots, and mugs. They buy all their tea in whole leaves, and cut it into teabag form right before it is blended to assure freshness.

Temple T Tea Bags
P.O. Box 6104
Philadelphia, PA 19115
(215) 728-5818
Price list, free U.S. and overseas.
  Minimum order one case. MO, PC.
Since 1952, Temple T Tea Bags has been supplying churches and organizations with tea bags for fund-raising projects. Stock labels identify your organization on each box of tea bags. Your organization profits about 40% on the resale of each box of tea bags.

Whittard & Co., Ltd.
111 Fulham Rd.
London SW3 6RP England
01 589 4261
4-page price list, free U.S. and overseas.
  Prices in British pounds. AE, DC, MC,
  V, MO.
Since 1886, Whittard & Co. has offered possibly the largest selection of teas and coffees available. Many customers request their own special blends— which Whittard's dutifully records in the shop's recipe book for safekeeping. Coffees are roasted on the premises daily to ensure freshness—"There is no substitute for freshly roasted coffee, ground just before it is required."

WINE AND LIQUOR

Laws vary from state to state regarding the interstate sale and shipment of wine. When ordering a wine catalog, inquire about the regulations of wine transport to your state, or of the state to which you wish to send a gift of wine.

Cutter and Robinson
1333 Sunnyslope
Belmont, CA 94002
2-page brochure, Self-addressed
stamped envelope; overseas 2
International Reply Coupons. MO, PC.
Cutter and Robinson offer many
different styles of wine and beer label
designs. They will also custom print a
label of your own design. The labels are
lettered in calligraphy, and are printed
in black ink on buff-colored paper with
gummed backing. Blank labels are
available in four different styles. Good
idea for all those liqueur recipes you've
been meaning to make up for holiday
gifts.

Napa Valley Connection
1121 Hunt Ave.
St. Helena, CA 94574
(707) 963-1111
California (800) 422-1111
16-page color catalog, $1; overseas $5.
AE, MC, V, MO, PC.
Over ninety carefully selected Napa
Valley wines, gift packs, and wine-
related products are offered in this
sharp catalog. "Our commitment is to
present wines that exemplify the finest
varietal achievements from the long-
established and new wineries of this
renowned valley," states the catalog.
They offer Monticello Cellars, Raymond,
Burgess Cellars, Chappellet, Mt. Veeder,
and Heitz, to name a few. You may select
one of their wine gift packs, or create
one of your own.

Nationwide Gift Liquor Service
2201 E. Thomas Rd.
Phoenix, AZ 85016
(800) 528-6148
Arizona (602) 957-4923
6-page color brochure, free U.S. and
overseas. AE, DC, MC, V, MO.
Nationwide Gift Liquor Service does not
sell or mail wines or liquor. They are
a service company and will send gifts
of liquor, liqueur, champagne, or wine
anywhere in the country through a
cooperative network of over 1,000

quality dealers. From the catalog you
may select from over 35 quality brands,
have your order gift wrapped with your
personal message attached, and
delivered—all by phone. The Directory
of brands includes Jack Daniel's,
Seagram's Crown Royal, Tanqueray
Gin, Hennessey, Grand Marnier, and
Dom Perignon, to mention a few of the
finest. Service charges range from $10
to $15. Certain states have laws
prohibiting this service.

Morrell & Co.
307 East 53rd St.
New York, NY 10022
(212) 688-9370
72-page newsalog, free U.S. and
overseas. Minimum order $50 in New
York City, $75 in New York State, and
five cases outside of New York State.
PC.
This catalog is a wine encyclopedia,
beginning with Alsace and ending with
Wine Wares. Included is a two-page
article by Peter Morrell, titled, "An
Intelligent Wine Buying Strategy for the
Year." He advises that there are great
French red and white burgundies in a
spring sale, and suggests champagne
lovers should buy cases of Brut Royal,
a 100% French Chardonnay Sparkling
wine.

Windsor Vineyards
P.O. Box 368
Windsor, CA 95492
(707) 433-6511
(800) 862-4910
18-page color catalog, free U.S. Does not
sell overseas. AE, DC, MC, V, MO, PC.
Windsor Vineyards offers a fine
selection of quality California wines and
estate-grown vintage champagnes. The
catalog is a fine salute to California
wines. These fine wines will make an
impressive gift. Windsor Vineyards also
offers a variety of personalized wine
labels on each gift bottle, such as
"Chosen to celebrate the birth of . . . ,"
"From all of us at . . . ," and "Selected
expressly to say. . .".

GARDEN

SEE ALSO
- Beauty and Health—Health
- Food and Drink—Health
- Tools

EQUIPMENT AND SUPPLIES

A. M. Leonard, Inc.
6665 Spiker Rd.
Piqua, OH 45356
(513) 773-2694
80-page newsalog, free; overseas 2
   International Reply Coupons.
   Minimum order $15. MC, MO, PC.
A. M. Leonard sells quality professional
gardening hand tools and equipment.

Aqua-Ponics
17221 E. 19th St.
Santa Ana, CA 92701
(714) 541-5169
16-page color brochure, $2; overseas
   free. MC, V, MO, PC.
Hydroponic garden planter and
supplies.

Erkins Studios
14 E. 41st St.
New York, NY 10017
(212) 679-8804
30-page catalog, $3; overseas free. MO,
   PC.
Erkins sells elegant garden statuary and
fountains. There are lead statues
imported from England and hand-cut
stone statues from Italy.

Florentine Craftsmen
654 First Ave.
New York, NY 10016
(212) 532-3926
56-page catalog, free U.S.
Florentine Craftsmen features
ornamental sculptured fountains,
gazebos, statues, vases, and benches to
decorate your interior or exterior garden
settings.

Gardenwork
Catherine de Barnes
Solihull B92 ODE England
021 705 5131
4-page brochure, $1.50 U.S. and
   overseas. AE, DC, V, MO, PC.
Gardenwork specializes in traditional
garden tools and hard-to-find functional
tools.

Gothard
P.O. Box 370
Canutillo, TX 79835
3-page brochure, free U.S. and overseas.
   MC, V, MO, PC.
Gothard sells insecticide-free
alternatives for pest control:
Trichogramma bugs! These insects
control harmful insects and worms
when used regularly on ornamental and
commercial crops.

Greenhouse Specialties
9849 Kimker Lane
St. Louis, MO 63127
2-page brochure, $1 refundable U.S.
   Does not sell overseas. MO, PC.
Greenhouse Specialties sells Crystalite,

a fiberglass (Lascolite) Fortified Acrylic, specially made for greenhouses. They also sell fans, shutters, and small heaters for greenhouse construction.

Hammond Barns
Box 584
3130 Hardacre Ct.
New Castle, IN 47362
(317) 529-7822
6-page brochure, $1 U.S. and overseas. MO, PC.
Hammond Barns sells plans and blueprints for constructing a barn. Barns range in size from doghouse and toolshed to single-car garage and horse barn size.

Lilypons Water Gardens
995 International Rd.
Lilypons, MD 21717
(301) 874-5133
52-page color catalog, $3; overseas $5. AE, MC, V, MO, PC.
Lilypons is one of American's largest water garden specialists, with 40 acres of ponds devoted to water lilies and other aquatic plants. Once a luxury of the wealthy ponds are now available to many, with easy-to-install low-cost pool liners and fiberglass pools. Lilypons sells water lilies, aquatic plants, ornamental pool fish, fiberglass pools, pool liners, pumps, filters, and all the accessories related to garden pools.

Lord & Burnham
Box 255
Irvington, NY 10533
(914) 591-8800
35-page color catalog, $2; overseas, free. Minimum order $25. AE, MC, V, MO, PC, C.O.D.
Lord & Burnham's catalog is actually more like a planning and buyer's guide to solariums and greenhouses. They display many homes designed or redecorated with beautiful solariums, in many great designs.

McGregor Greenhouses
1195 Thompson Ave.
Santa Cruz, CA 95062
(408) 476-5390
6-page brochure, $1 refundable U.S. Does not sell overseas. Minimum order $10. MC, V, MO, PC.

McGregor sells six models of greenhouses, plus greenhouse extensions and accessories, at factory direct prices. McGregor stands by their product and will supply prospective customers with a list of McGregor greenhouse owners in your climate area, to check customer satisfaction.

Moultrie Manufacturing Co.
P.O. Drawer 1179
Moultrie, GA 31768
(800) 841-8674
32-page color catalog, $1; overseas $3. MC, V, MO.
Moultrie's catalog features elegant Old South reproductions of cast iron lawn furniture—in cast aluminum. They are far lighter and less expensive than cast iron, but still feature the gracious designs of the past. There are lawn furniture, urns, benches, fountains, columns, and an impressive collection of gates and fences.

Necessary Trading Co.
328 Main St.
New Castle, VA 24127
(703) 864-5103
40-page catalog, $2 refundable U.S.; overseas free. BD, MC, V, MO, PC.
Necessary Trading Company specializes in organic gardening supplies. They offer over 600 different natural products for pest control, plant nutrition, and soil improvement.

Slocum Water Gardens
1101 Cypress Gardens Blvd.
Winter Haven, FL 33880
(813) 293-7151
32-page color catalog, $2; overseas $4. MO, PC, C.O.D.
Slocum sells "everything for the lily pool"—water lilies, lotus-flowering plants, aquatic and fountain supplies, goldfish, Koi, and scavenger fish.

Smith and Hawkins
68 Homer
Palo Alto, CA 94301
(415) 324-1587
32-page color catalog, free U.S. Does not sell overseas. AE, MC, V, MO, PC.

Smith and Hawkins are well known for their fine hand tools for woodworking and gardening. There are fine imported tools from many countries, including forks, spades, shovels, watering cans, pruners, shears, machetes, hoes, and axes.

Struck-Kit
Dept MOSG
Cedarsburg, WI 53012
(414) 377-3300
12-page brochure, $1 U.S.; overseas free. MC, V, MO.
Struck-Kit sells crawler tractor kits for home, ranch, and small farm use.

Troy Bilt
Garden Way Manufacturing Co.
102nd Street & Ninth Ave.
Troy, NY 12180
(800) 833-6990
(518) 235-6010
16-page color catalog, free U.S. MC, V, MO, PC.
Troy Bilt offers fine garden equipment, including the expandable rake ($10.75), eight styles of tillers, and the handy Garden Way Cart (from $76.95 to $140.95).

Turner Greenhouses
Highway 117 South
P.O. Box 1260
Goldsboro, NC 27530
(919) 734-8345
14-page color brochure, free U.S. Does not sell overseas. MC, V, MO, PC.
Turner offers hobby greenhouses made of Galalume framework and a choice of two coverings, Lascolite fiberglass or polyethylene.

Twin Oaks Hammocks
Rt. 4 Box 169
Louisa, VA 23093
(703) 894-5125
6-page color brochure, free U.S. and overseas. MC, V, MO, PC.
The Twin Oaks hammocks are traditional Southern-style rope and oak construction. They are available in three sizes, and range in price from $59 to $69.

William Tricker
74 Allendale Ave.
Saddle River, NJ 07458
(201) 327-0721
32-page color catalog, $1 U.S. and overseas. MC, V, MO, PC.
A complete line of aquatic supplies for lily ponds.

York Mountain Mailbox
3729 N. Claremont
Fresno, CA 93727
(209) 291-2878
1-page brochure, free U.S. Does not sell overseas. MO, PC.
York Mountain sells handcrafted Mail Box "houses," complete with cedar shake roofs, ranging in price from $20 to $40. Guy McConnell, owner, will also take your ideas, blueprints and pictures, and custom make a mail box for you.

PLANTS

The African Violet Co.
100 Floral Ave.
Greenwood, SC 29647
(803) 374-3316
15-page color catalog, free U.S. AE, MC, V, PC.

Beahm Epiphyllum Gardens
2686 Paloma St.
Pasadena, CA 91107
(213) 792-6533
18-page brochure, 50¢ U.S. and overseas. MO, PC.
Beahm carries over 3,000 different varieties of Epiphyllums (flowering succulents) in their nursery. They list over 250 varieties in their mail order brochure, as well as some Hoyas and Rhipsalis. Many of the Epiphyllum varieties are a result of their own hybridization program.

Bodnant Garden Nursery
Tal Y Cafn
Colwyn Bay
Clwyd LL28 5RE
Wales
0492 67 460
24-page brochure, free U.S. and overseas. MO, PC.

Ornamental trees and shrubs propagated at the Bodnant Garden.

Bountiful Ridge Nursery
P.O. Box 250
Princess Anne, MD 21853
(301) 651-0400
55-page color catalog, free U.S. and
  overseas. AE, MC, V, MO, PC.
Their nursery stock is primarily fruit trees, berry plants, grapevines, and nut trees. They offer a complete line of all these: peaches, apples, apricots, nectarines, plum pears, raspberries, strawberries, blackberries, table grapes, wine grapes, Tay berries, and more. Presently they are growing 500,000 to one million apple trees, and another million peach trees, and can handle large overseas orders.

Brownell Holly Farms
P.O. Box 22025
Milwaukee, OR 97222
(503) 631-7475
12-page color catalog. MC, V, MO, PC.
Brownell sells holly wreaths, arrangements, sprays, corsages and berried tips all year long.

Buell's Greenhouses, Inc.
P.O. Box 218IM
Weeks Rd.
Eastford, CT 06242
(203) 974-0623
32-page price list, 25¢ and self-addressed
  stamped envelope; overseas 2
  Internation Reply Coupons.
Buell's offers over 200 varieties of African violets, plus Buell's Hybrid Gloxinias, Columneas, Episcias, Terrarium plants, tubers, Rhizomes, and other exotic plants.

Caprilands Herb Farm
Silver St.
Coventry, CT 06238
(203) 742-7244
4-page brochure, self-addressed
  stamped envelope. Does not sell
  overseas. PC.
Caprilands sells over 300 varieties of herbs and scented geraniums. Plants will not be shipped between November 1st and March 1st.

Cordon Bleu Farms
418 Buena Creek Rd.
P.O. Box 2033
San Marcos, CA 92069
(619) 744-3851
18-page price list, free U.S. and overseas.
  MC, V.
Cordon Bleu Farm specializes in day lilies.

Country Hills Greenhouses
Route 2
Corning, OH 43730
96-page price list, $2.50 U.S. Does not sell
  overseas. Minimum order $10.
A large variety of both rare and common houseplants.

Dutch Mountain Nursery
7984 N. 48th St.
Augusta, MI 49012
(616) 731-5232
6-page brochure, 25¢; overseas 50¢.
  Minimum order $10. MO, PC.
Dutch Mountain sells native plants that attract birds. Most of the plants have berries or flowers that attract birds for food, nectar, or nuts.

Emlong Nurseries
2671 W. Marquette Woods Rd.
Stevensville, MI 49127
(616) 429-3612
56-page catalog, free U.S. Does not sell
  overseas. MC, V, MO, PC.
Emlong offers an excellent line of fruit trees including semi-dwarf apples, dwarf peaches, northern cherry, plums, nectarines, and apricots. There are also standard apples, peaches, cherries, plums and pears, strawberries, and flowering trees.

Endangered Species
12571 Redhill Ave.
Tustin, CA 92680
(714) 730-6323
24-page newsalog, $4; overseas free.
  Minimum order $15. MC, V, MO, PC.
Endangered species specializes in rare and exotic plants. There are Dracaenas, Philodendrons, and many varieties of succulents.

Fischer Greenhouse
Oak Ave.
Linwood, NJ 08221
(609) 927-3399
16-page color brochure, 25¢; overseas $1.
    Minimum order $6.95. MC, V, MO, PC.
Fischer Greenhouses operates about
four acres of greenhouses that grow
African Violets and other flowering and
foliage ornamentals. (The catalog lists
only African Violets.)

Fisks Clematis Nursery
Westleton, N. Saxmundham
Suffolk, England
072873
40-page color catalog, $1; overseas $1.50.
    MO, PC.
Fisks sells Clematis to many parts of the
world and offers over 140 different
varieties. They exhibit each year at the
Chelsea Flower show in London.

Flickerings Nursery
Box 245
Sagamore, PA 16250
12-page brochure, free U.S. Does not sell
    overseas. MO, PC.
Flickerings sells evergreen bareroot
seedlings and transplants, including
Scotch Pine, White Pine, Austrian Pine,
White Spruce, Norway Spruce, Douglas
Fir, Hemlock, and others.

The Garden Spot
4032 Rosewood Dr.
Columbia, SC 29205
(803) 787-7463
Price list, self-addressed stamped
    envelope U.S. Does not sell overseas.
    MO, PC.
The Garden Spot sells over 150 ivies,
including some rare and novelty
varieties.

Gilbert H. Wild & Son, Inc.
1110 Joplin St.
P.O. Box 338
Sarcoxie, MO 64862
(417) 548-3514
96-page color catalog, $2; overseas free.
    Minimum order $10. MO, PC.
Hundreds of varieties of iris, day lilies,
and peonies are available.

Gossler Farms Nursery
1200 Weaver Rd.
Springfield, OR 97477
(503) 746-3922
16-page brochure, $1; overseas $2. MO,
PC.
Gossler Farms offers over 60 varieties
of Magnolias as well as companion
ornamental trees and shrubs. They ship
in late November through December,
and February through March when the
plants are dormant.

Hastings Southern Garden Guide
P.O. Box 4274
Atlanta, GA 30302
(404) 524-8861
80-page color catalog, free U.S. and
    overseas. Minimum order $5. MC, V,
    MO, PC.
Hastings specializes in garden stock
especially suitable for the Southern
states. There are hundreds of varieties
of Southern vegetable crops, such as
greens, okra and cow peas, muscadines,
pecans, persimmons, pomegranates and
kiwi fruit.

Henrietta's Nursery
1345 N. Brawley
Fresno, CA 93711
(209) 275-2166
48-page newsalog, $1 U.S. and overseas.
    MO, PC. Minimum order $15. MO, PC.
There are over 1,000 varieties of
succulents and cactus, with some
unusual and rare varieties from around
the world. There are over 700 varieties
of Epithicicactus, to desert-type cactus,
and bulb-like succulents native to South
Africa and Madagascar.

Henry Field Seed & Nursery Co.
407 Sycamore St.
Shenandoah, IA 51602
(712) 246-2110
100-page color catalog, free U.S. Does
    not sell overseas. Minimum order $10.
    MC, V, MO, PC.
Henry Field's is a well known nursery
carrying a full line of stock (bareroot
deciduous stock and some potted
houseplants). They also have an
extensive line of garden seeds and

gardening supplies. They recently introduced the Turnbull Giant Pear Tree, which bears three-pound fruit resembling an apple in shape, and a pear in color, taste, and texture.

Holly Gate Cactus Nursery
Billingshurst Lane
Ashington, Pulborough
West Sussex RH20 3BA England
0903 892930
80-page catalog, $2; overseas $1.
    Minimum order $5. MC, V, MO, PC.
Holly Gate sells thousands of different cacti and succulent plants, and even features a lovely cactus garden that visitors to their nursery can enjoy.

Huff's Garden Mums
Box 187
Burlington, KS 66839
(316) 364-2933
34-page catalog, free U.S. Does not sell
    overseas. Minimum order $5. MO, PC.
Huff's offers over 800 varieties of Chrysanthemums, many of which no other nursery carries. There are many tupes and bloom dates. There are also low prices for special groupings of ten popular varieties.

Inter-State Nurseries
504 "E" St.
Hamburg, IA 51640
(800) 831-4104
(712) 382-2411
56-page color catalog, free U.S. Does not
    sell overseas. MC, V, MO, PC.
Well known for their large selection of ornamental plants, fruit trees, and roscs.

Jackson and Perkins
1 Rose Lane
Medford, OR 97501
(503) 776-2000
40-page color catalog, free U.S. and
    overseas. MC, V, MO, PC.
Jackson and Perkins owns more rose patents than any other firm in the U.S., and is recognized as the world's largest rose growers and nurserymen. In addition to roses they also offer bulbs, seeds, nursery plants, and products for the gardener. Jackson & Perkins says, "We offer only one grade, the finest."

Kordonowy's Dahlias
401 Quick Rd.
Castle Rock, WA 98611
32-page price list, 40¢ U.S. Does not sell
    overseas. AE, MO, PC.
The Kordonowys grow and import lots of Dahlias.

Krider Nurseries
P.O. Box 29
Middlebury, IN 46540
(219) 825-5714
32-page color catalog, free U.S. Does not
    sell overseas. MC, V, MO, PC.
Krider carries a large and diversified selection for the home, yard, and garden: rose bushes, shade and ornamental trees, flowering shrubs, and fruit and nut trees.

Lakeland Nurseries
340 Popular St.
Hanover, PA 17331
(717) 637-6000
40-page color catalog, free U.S. Does not
    sell overseas. AE, DC, MC, V, MO, PC.

Legg Dahlia Gardens
Hastings Rd.
R. D. #4 Box 168
Geneva, NY 14456
8-page price list, free U.S. Does not sell
    overseas. MO, PC.

The Lehman Gardens
420 10th St. S.W.
Fairibault, MN 55021
(507) 334-8404
3-page price list, free U.S. Does not sell
    overseas. MO, PC.
Lehman's lists over 120 varieties of Northern-grown garden mums.

Lyndon Lyon Greenhouses
14 Mutchler St.
Dodgeville, NY 13329
(315) 429-8291
10-page color brochure, 50¢ U.S. Does
    not sell overseas. MO, PC.
Lyndon's specializes in African Violets, unusual houseplants, and miniature roses. They originated the first double pink violets in the late 1940s.

Mellinger's, Inc.
2310 West South Range Rd.
North Lima, OH 44452
(216) 549-9861
108-page catalog, free; overseas $4. MC,
V, MO, PC.
Mellinger's since 1927 has been
supplying horticultural products (seeds,
plants, and supplies) worldwide.

Merry Gardens
P.O. Box 595
Camden, ME 04843
8-page brochure, 50¢ U.S. Does not sell
overseas. MO, PC.
Merry Gardens offers many house plants
and herbs.

Mini-Roses
P.O. Box 4255
Dallas, TX 75208
(214) 946-3487
16-page brochure, free U.S. Does not sell
overseas. MO, PC.
Over 150 varieties of outdoor-grown
miniature rose bushes available as bush
types, climbers, trailers, and hanging
baskets.

Moore Miniature Roses
2519 Noble Ave.
Visalia, CA 93277
(209) 732-0190
8-page color brochure, free U.S. Does not
sell overseas. MO, PC.
Many varieties of miniature roses—good
quality and disease-resistant.

Musser Forests, Inc.
Box 340
Indiana, PA 15701
(412) 465-5686
40-page color catalog, free U.S. and
overseas. Minimum order $10. MC, V,
MO, PC.
Musser sells evergreen and hardwood
seedlings and transplants. They also
offer a variety of ground covers and
ornamental shrubs.

Nor'East Miniature Roses, Inc.
58 Hammond St.
Rowley, MA 01969
(617) 948-2408

16-page color catalog, free U.S. and
overseas. MO, PC.
Nor'East offers over 100 varieties of
miniature roses.

Orchids by Hausermann
2N 134 Addison Rd.
Villa Park, IL 60181
(312) 543-6855
52-page color catalog, $1.25 U.S. and
overseas. Minimum order $10. AE,
MC, V, MO, PC.
Hausermann grows and sells orchids
exclusively. There are hundreds of types
to choose from, varying from large
showy varieties that anyone can grow
to the unusual and unique varieties for
the connoisseur.

Peter Pauls Nurseries
R. D. #2
Canandaigua, NY 14424
(716) 394-7397
4-page price list, 25¢; overseas 2
International Reply Coupons.
Minimum order $5. MC, V, MO, PC.
Peter Pauls offers over 75 species of
carnivorous or insectivorous plants,
seeds, and supplies.

Shady Hill Gardens
805 Walnut St.
Batavia, IL 60510
32-page price list, $1 refundable. Does
not sell overseas. MO, PC.
Shady Hill has one of the largest
commercial collections of Geraniums in
the U.S. They offer over 700 varieties
including scented (herb) geraniums,
rosebud geraniums, dwarf and
miniature geraniums, stellar, fancy leaf,
Regal, and many others.

P. Kolhi & Co.
Park Rd.
Srinager, Kashmir
190009 India
15-page price list, 5 International Reply
Coupons. Minimum order $20. BD,
MO.
P. Kolhi offers wild, alpine, and
temperate climate tree, shrub and
perennial seeds and flower bulbs. They
specialize in winter- and spring-
blooming bulbs—Himalayan Allium,

Arisaemas, Colchicum Luetuem, Corydalis Diphylla, and Crocus Sativus.

Powell's Gardens
Route 2, Hwy 70
Princeton, NC 27569
(919) 936-4421
26-page price list, $1.50; overseas free. MO, PC.
Powell's is a large grower of perennials, irises, day lilies, rock garden plants, and dwarf evergreens.

Prentiss Court Groundcovers
P.O. Box 8662
Greenville, SC 29607
(803) 277-4037
2-page brochure, 25¢ U.S. Does not sell overseas. MC, V, MO, PC.
Prentiss offers over seventy varieties of groundcovers (including vinca, liriope, ivy, pachysandra, and ajuga) at low bulk-order prices.

R. Harkness & Co. Ltd.
The Rose Gardens
Hitchen, Herts
SG4 OJT England
0466 34027
40-page color catalog, $1; overseas free. V, MO, PC.
R. Harkness grows nearly 300 different rose varieties, "the cream of the new and the best of the old." Many of their hybrids have won international acclaim. They will also send import information with your catalog.

Rod McLellan Co.
1450 El Camino Real
So. San Francisco, CA 94080
(415) 871-5655
24-page color catalog, 50¢; overseas $1.50. Minimum order $10. MC, V, MO, PC.
Rod McLellan offers many varieties of orchids including Sophros, Cattleyas, Phalaenopsis, and many more.

Roses of Yesterday and Today
802 Brown's Valley Road
Watsonville, CA 95067–0398
(408) 724-3537
80-page catalog, $2; overseas free. MC, V, MO, PC.

They list approximately 250 varieties of old, rare, and unusual roses: damasks, albas, mosses, hybrid perpetuals, gallicas, bourbon, centifolias, and some newer roses.

Savage Farm Nursery
P.O. Box 125 PW
McMinnville, TN 37110
(615) 668-8902
24-page color catalog, free U.S. Does not sell overseas. MO, PC.
Savage carries a general line of over 250 varieties of nursery stock.

Singers Growing Things
17806 Plummer St.
Northridge, CA 91325
(213) 993-1903
31-page catalog, $1.50; overseas $2. Minimum order $15, overseas $35. MC, V, MO, PC.
Singers offers rare and unusual succulents. They grow specimen plants, cycads, cactus, plumerias, and sansevierias.

Siskiyou Rare Plant Nursery
2825 Cummings Rd.
Medford, OR 97501
(503) 772-6846
52-page catalog, $1.50. Does not sell overseas. MO, PC.
Siskiyou offers a large selection of alpine rock and woodland plants, and wildflowers for the rock garden. They also carry dwarf conifers, dwarf hardy ferns, dwarf maples, and alpine rhododendrons.

Stark Bros. Nurseries & Orchards
Louisiana, MO 63353
(314) 754-5511
60-page color catalog, free U.S. Limited overseas sales. MC, V, MO, PC.
Stark offers a wide selection of dwarf, semi-dwarf, and standard fruit trees. They also carry nut trees, small fruits, roses, shrubs, and ornamentals.

Tranquil Lake Nursery
45 River St.
Rehoboth, MA 02769
(617) 252-4310
22-page brochure, 25¢; overseas free. Minimum order $10. MO, PC.

Tranquil Lake carries day lilies, Siberian iris, Japanese iris, and perennials.

Volkmann Bros. Greenhouses
2714 Minert St.
Dallas, TX 75219
(214) 526-3484
22-page color catalog, 35¢ plus self-addressed stamped envelope. Does not sell overseas. MO, PC.
Volkmann's carries many varieties of African violets, and a few models of lighted plant stands.

White Flower Farm
Litchfield, CT 06759
(800) 243-2853
(203) 567-0801
100-page color catalog, $5 U.S. Does not sell overseas. MC, V.
White Flower provides excellent information on plants and gardening in addition to over 1,200 varieties of perennials and 600 varieties of bulbs.

Wildlife Nurseries
P.O. Box 2724
Oshkosh, WI 54903
(414) 231-3780
35-page catalog, $1; overseas free. Minimum order $10. MO, PC.
Wildlife Nurseries sells natural aquatic planting materials for wild ducks, fish, and other wildlife. They are experienced in the specific game foods to be planted throughout the U.S. to both attract and hold waterfowl and game. They sell giant wild rice, Sago Pond plants, Duck Potatoes, Bur Reed, and others.

SEEDS AND BULBS

Burpee, W. Atlee
300 Park Ave.
Warminster, PA 18974
184-page color catalog, free U.S. Does not sell overseas. AE, MC, V, MO, PC.
Founded in Philadelphia in 1876 by W. Atlee Burpee, this company is currently one of the largest and best known mail order seed companies in the world. They offer over 1,800 different varieties of

high quality flowers, and vegetables created for the home gardener.

Allwood Bros. Ltd.
Hassocks, Sussex
BN6 9LX England
4229
24-page catalog, free U.S. and overseas. MC, V, PC.
Allwood specializes in carnation seeds and plants; only seed are exported, however.

The Banana Tree
715 Northampton St.
Easton, PA 18042
10-page brochure, 25¢; overseas free. MO, PC.
The Banana Tree specializes in uncommon and rare seeds and bulbs, and offers over forty varieties of banana trees.

Borchelt Herb Gardens
474 Carriage Shop Rd.
East Falmouth, MA 02536
(617) 548-4571
2-page price list, self addressed stamped envelope. Does not sell overseas. MO, PC.
Organically grown herb seeds by mail order. Locally they offer 300 varieties of herb plants in a one-half acre display garden (which customers enjoy).

Breck's
6523 N. Galena Rd.
Peoria, IL 61632
58-page color catalog. MC, V, PC.

Butterbrooke Farm
78 Barry Rd.
Oxford, CT 06483–1598
(203) 888-2000
4-page brochure, free U.S. and overseas. MO, PC.
Butterbrooke sells common vegetable seeds in standard packets for 30¢ per packet. All seeds are untreated, high germination, and pure strains.

Clyde Robin Seed Co.
4233 Heyer Ave.
Castro Valley, CA 94546
(415) 581-3467

80-page color catalog, $2; overseas $4.
 Minimum order $3. MC, V, MO, PC.
There are wild flower seeds, grass seeds,
tree seeds, and lentil and alfalfa seeds
for sprouting. (There are gopher control
seeds available, too.)

The Daffodil Mart
Rt. 3 Box 794
Gloucester, VA 23061
(804) 693-3966
15-page brochure, free U.S. and
 overseas. Minimum order $15. MO,
 PC.
The Daffodil Mart grows and sells about
500 varieties of daffodil bulbs, and has
a large selection of miniature daffodils.

DeGiorgi Company, Inc.
1409 Third St.
P.O. Box 413
Council Bluffs, IA 51502
(712) 323-2372
120-page catalog, $1 U.S. and overseas.
 MO, PC.
Vegetable and flower seed growers,
importers, and suppliers. Their catalog
is extensive and very informative.

Franz Roozen
Vogelenzangseweg 49
2114 BB Vogelenzang
Holland
02502 7245
18-page color catalog, free U.S. and
 overseas. Minimum order $19. BD,
 MO, PC.
Franz Roozen's nursery was established
in 1789. Specializing in new and
unusual tulip bulbs, they offer many
exclusive varieties.

George Park Seed Co.
Box 31
Greenwood, SC 29647
(803) 374-3341
124-page color catalog, free U.S. Does
 not sell overseas. AE, MC, V, PC.
George Park's offers over 3,000 seed
varieties as well as bulbs, plants, herbs,
exotic plants, and gardener's aids.

Gurney's Seed and Nursery
2nd & Capitol
Yankton, SD 57079

65-page color catalog, free U.S. Does not
 sell overseas. MC, V, MO, PC.
"Today a gardener can find virtually
everything necessary to grow a garden—
except the land—in Gurney's catalog."
Established in 1866, Gurney's mails
millions of catalogs a year that include
over 4,000 items—seed, nursery stock,
and gardening aids.

Harris Seeds
3670 Buffalo Rd.
Rochester, NY 14624
96-page color catalog, free U.S. Does not
 sell overseas. MC, V, MO, PC.
Flower and vegetable seeds, including
many hybrids and many Harris-
exclusive flower and vegetable varieties.

Horticultural Enterprises
P.O. Box 810082
Dallas, TX 75381-0082
2-page brochure, free U.S. Does not sell
 overseas. MO, PC.
Horticultural Enterprises sells over
thirty varieties of chili seeds—from
Aconcagua to Yung Ko, and from very
hot to mild.

J. B. Wijs & Zoon
Aalsmeerderweg 436
Holland
02977 29411
4-page color brochure, free U.S. and
 overseas. PC.
Flower bulbs, including tulips, crocus,
narcissi, hyacinth, and anemone.

J. L. Hudson, Seedsman
P.O. Box 1058
Redwood City, CA 94064
111-page catalog, $1; overseas $3. BD,
 MO, PC.
Established in 1911, J. L. Hudson
specializes in offering rare and
uncommon species of seeds. Collected
from all parts of the world, they span
the plant kingdom from the most
primitive land plants (such as lichens,
club mosses and ferns) to conifers and
orchids.

Johnny's Selected Seeds
Foss Hill Rd.
Albion, ME 04910
(207) 437-9294

72-page catalog, free U.S. and overseas.
AE, MC, MO, PC.
Johnny's sells vegetable seeds—with a
special emphasis on areas with short
and/or cool growing seasons. (They also
carry modern and heirloom varieties.)

Kester's Wild Game Food Nurseries
P.O. Box V-I
Omro, WI 54963
(414) 685-2929
34-page catalog, $2 U.S. Does not sell
overseas. MC, V, PC.
Kester's has a good variety of aquatic
plants and a wide variety of seeds to
provide food and nesting cover for
wildlife.

Lockhart Seeds
P.O. Box 1361
Stockton, CA 95201
64-page catalog, $1 U.S. and overseas.
Minimum order $2.99. MC, V, MO, PC.
Lockhart's offers a good assortment of
vegetable seeds including Lockhart's
own onion varieties. There are Oriental
vegetables, lawn and ground cover
seeds, old favorites, and the latest
hybrids. (They also sell seeders,
spreaders and sprayers.)

Michigan Bulb Co.
1950 Waldorf NW
Grand Rapids, MI 49550
(616) 453-5401
4-page color brochure, free U.S. AE, MC,
V, MO, PC.
Michigan Bulb Company sends out over
three and one-half million packages of
bulbs (mostly from Holland), trees,
shrubs, plants, and seeds each year.

Mrs. J. Abel Smith
Orchard House, Lettygreen
Hertford, SG14 2N2
England
07072 61274
Price list, free U.S. and overseas. MO,
PC.
Mrs. Abel Smith, a daffodil grower and
hybridiser, has developed quite a few
exclusive varieties—which are sold
mainly to those who buy for exhibition
or breeding stock.

Old Seeds Catalog
2901 Packers Ave.
P.O. Box 7790
Madison, WI 53707
(608) 249-9291
80-page newsalog, free; overseas $4.50.
Old Seeds, established in 1888, supplies
seeds, nursery stock, and garden
supplies. All seed varieties are
germination-tested by their own
registered seed technologist.

P. de Jager & Sons
P.O. Box 100
Brewster, NY 10509
(800) 343-1059
32-page color catalog, free U.S. MC, V,
MO, PC.
A complete selection of bulbs.

Pinetree Garden Seeds
P.O. Box 1399
Portland, ME 04104
(207) 772-1669
64-page catalog, free U.S. and overseas.
MC, V, MO, PC.
Pinetree specializes in vegetable, flower,
and herb seeds for gardeners with
limited space. They offer Tom Thumb
lettuce, Gypsy pepper, Sugar Snap peas,
and many others.

Rex Bulb Farms
P.O. Box 774
Port Townsend, WA 98368
(206) 385-4280
72-page color catalog, 10¢; overseas $2.
MC, V, MO, PC.
Rex Bulb Farms is a well-known
supplier of lily bulbs. They offer a large
selection of world-famous varieties.

Richters
Box 26
Goodwood, Ontario
LOC 1AO Canada
(416) 640-6677
64-page catalog, $2 U.S. and overseas.
MC, V, MO, PC.
Richters is a well-known supplier of
herb seeds, gourmet vegetable seeds,
alpine and wildflower seeds, dried herbs
and spices, oils, herbal gifts, and
potpourris.

Robert Bolton & Son
Birdbrook, Halstead
Essex England
44085246
12-page color catalog, free U.S. and
  overseas. V, MO.
Bolton's sells about forty types of sweet
pea seeds. Since 1901.

Sanctuary Seeds
2388 W. 4th Ave.
Vancouver, B.C.
U6K 1P1 Canada
(604) 733-4724
34-page catalog, $1 U.S. Does not sell
  overseas. Minimum order $10. MO,
  PC.
Sanctuary sells over 250 varieties of rare
and unusual culinary and medicinal
garden seeds, and non-hybrid vegetable
seeds.

Stokes Seeds
Box 548
Buffalo, NY 14240
160-page (some color) catalog, free U.S.
  and overseas. MC, V, MO, PC.
A complete line of garden seeds is
available.

Thompson & Morgan
P.O. Box 100
Farmingdale, NJ 07727
(201) 363-2225
196-page color catalog, free U.S. and
  overseas. MC, V, MO, PC.
Thompson & Morgan produces one of
the largest seed catalogs in the world,
distributed to nearly 130 different
countries. Founded in 1855, they offer
over 4,000 vegetable and garden seeds.

Twilley Seeds Co.
P.O. Box 6J
Trevose, PA 18901
(215) 639-8800

88-page color catalog, free U.S. and
  overseas. MC, V, MO, PC.
A complete line of vegetable and flower
seeds, and garden merchandise.

Van Bourgondien Bros.
P.O. Box A, Route 109
Babylon, NY 11702
(516) 669-3523
64-page color catalog, free U.S. Does not
  sell overseas. AE, MC, V, MO, PC.
Van Bourgondien offers one of the
largest listings of Holland flower bulbs
available in the U.S. Also they offer a
complete listing of hardy perrenials,
fruit trees, flowering plants, and other
garden-related items. This is a family-
owned business with offices and
growing fields in the town of Hillegom,
near Amsterdam.

Vermont Bean Seed Company
Garden Lane
Bomoseen, VT 05732
(802) 265-4212
96-page catalog, free U.S. and overseas.
  Minimum order $5. AE, MC, V, MO,
  PC.
Vermont offers one of the larger
selections of bean seeds in the U.S. Also,
large vegetable and flower seed
selections.

Watkins Seeds
P.O. Box 468
New Plymouth, 4600
New Zealand
067 86800
40-page color catalog, $2 surface, $2.50
  air mail U.S. and overseas.
  Minimum order $15, New Zealand $3.
  MC, V, MO.
Founded in 1921, Watkins is a well
known mail order seed firm. They offer
a good variety of vegetable and flower
seeds.

GIFTS

SEE ALSO
- Clothing
- Department Stores and Major Mail Order Houses
- Electronics-Consumer
- Handcrafts
- Housewares

ELEGANT

Alfred Dunhill of London
620 Fifth Avenue
New York, NY 10010
(212) 481-6950
40-page color gift catalog, $2; overseas free AE, MC, V, PC.

With the same sense of distinctive quality and excellent service that prompted Alfred Dunhill to open his tobacco shop in London's Duke Street over seventy years ago, Dunhill's today prevails as the purveyor of the finest gentlemen's merchandise. Today there are seventeen Dunhill retail shops, seven of which are America. Dunhill is one of the leading names in personal luxury items. The elegant black crocodile attaché case features solid 18-karat gold locks. Included in the case is a business card compartment with Oriental cabochon, gemlight lighter, fountain pen, two ballpoint pens and a pencil in 18-karat gold. This Dunhill exclusive is priced at $25,000. The catalog includes many fine gifts for gentlemen—"You will find all you need to embrace the essence of what English elegance is all about."

American Express Company
125 Broad St.
New York, NY 10004
(212) 323-2000
40-page color gift catalog, 33-page color *American Express Means Business* catalog, free U.S. Does not sell overseas. AE.

American Express offers sophisticated electronics such as the Workstate ($895): as powerful as most desk top computers, and loaded with extras—but weighing just over three pounds, and only the size of a piece of paper. It's a technological wonder, in the office or on the road. There are luxurious furs: ranch mink, coyote parka (for him) and a blue fox jacket (for her). There is lovely artwork, jewelry, and many "objects of desire." Unique and extravagant is the Firefly Hot Air Balloon ($14,000). This majestic balloon (77,000 cubic foot envelope) is available in your choice of fifteen colors and graphics, and includes burner, fuel cylinders, gondola, instrumentation panel, inflator fan, and pack-up bag. The new *American Express Means Business* catalog is aimed at the executive and features the latest electronic gadgets, computer accessories, travel accessories, and terrific "executive tools." Note: payment is by American Express card only.

Brielle Galleries
707 Union Ave.
Brielle, NJ 08730
(201) 628-8400

32-page color catalog, free U.S. and
 overseas. AE, MC, V, MO, PC.
Brielle Galleries caters to a
sophisticated clientele whose interests
include porcelain art sculpture, gems,
exquisite jewelry, and European and
American crystal and art glass. They
offer gift items in wood, bronze, brass
and pewter, and have a lovely selection
of fine china, sterling, and table
accessories. Since 1949.

Camalier & Buckley
1141 Connecticut Ave. NW
Washington D.C. 20036
(202) 347-9500
32-page color catalog, free U.S. Does not
 sell overseas. AE, MC, V, PC.
Camalier & Buckley are renowned for
fine leather goods and luggage. Their
latest collection offers fine leathers and
gift items including Italian hand-tooled
leather desk appointment folders,
scrolled in 24-karat gold Florentine with
soft moire linings. The desk blotter is
priced at about $350, picture frame $140,
and pair of bookends $125. There is
Gladstone's English kit bag, Bordeaux
leather jewel box, and office sets by
Gold-Pfeil.

The Edbury Collection
115 Powdermill Road Box 65
Maynard, MA 01754
(617) 897-8010
24-page color catalog, free U.S. and
 overseas. AE, DC, MC, V, MO, PC.
The Edbury Collection offers collectors
items and gifts from the United
Kingdom and Europe. They come from
the historic past, reproductions of
British museum pieces, art galleries,
workshops, and potteries. The
handmade walnut-and-brown leather
telescope and tripod is an exact copy of
the original by Peter Dolland, master
instrument maker of the eighteenth
century, except for the superior
magnification of the five lenses. Crafted
by Malcolm King in Sussex, it is priced
at $3,380. There are graceful Ashmolean
lead crystal candleholders ($60), and a
framed collection of "Bullets that
shaped American History," by Albert
Warren, who collected the original
molds of lead bullets used in the great

battles of American history. Perhaps
you'd prefer a red Rolls-Royce Corniche,
priced at $750. That's right—it's a
battery-powered accurate scale replica
for children (or the young at heart).

Eximious, Ltd.
10 West Halkin St.
London, SW1X 8JL England
01 235 7222
32-page color catalog, $2; overseas free.
 AE, DC, MC, V.
Eximious has designed and collected an
elegant variety of items suitable for
presents for special occasions, ranging
from a weekend thank-you present to a
100th birthday gift. Many of the classic
gifts are personalized: leather photo
albums, silver-plated playing card
holders, gallery trays, jardinieres,
dressing table accessories, luggage,
crystal decanters and tumblers, stud
boxes, and embroidered guest towels.

Mappin & Webb
170 Regent St.
London W1R 6BQ England
8-page color catalog. AE, DC, V, PC.
For over 200 years Mappin and Webb
has supplied quality jewelry, silver,
giftware, watches, and clocks to royalty
and distinguished gentry. This lovely
catalog features only the best.

Neiman–Marcus
P.O. Box 2968
Dallas, TX 75221
(800) 634-6267
134-page color *Christmas Catalog,* $3.
 MO, PC.
Renowned for their fabulous gifts, furs,
precious jewels, and fashions, Neiman–
Marcus is in a class of its own. Each year
Neiman–Marcus presents a matching
His and Her gift—such as two Chinese
Shar-Pei puppies, complete with an
Oriental pagoda dog house—in their
spectacular Christmas catalog. For
serious mail order catalog shoppers, this
catalog is the one they look forward to
the most.

Willoughby and Taylor
2912 Iron Ridge
Dallas, TX 75247
(800) 323-1718
(800) 942-8881

Willoughby and Taylor's catalog presents elegant gifts and fashions for men and women in rich, dramatic color photograph spreads. There are French Limoges porcelain plates, an exquisite malachite jade pendant watch ($175), a full-length ranch mink coat ($3,500), cloisonne candlesticks, and many more beautiful pieces.

OVER $25

Abercrombie & Fitch
400 South Edward St.
Mount Prospect, IL 60057
(800) 228-5566
(800) 642-8777
36-page color catalog. AE, DC, MC, V, MO, PC.
Abercrombie & Fitch offers his-and-her safari outfits, complete with rabbit's fur felt safari hats trimmed with a zebra leather band. There are many gifts to please the hunter; Leica binoculars; superbly crafted decoys by Tom Taber and Hersey Kyle; and handsome men's sportswear.

America's Wineland Crafts
Box J
Rolling Hills Estates, CA 90274
(213) 539-5005
32-page color catalog, $2 U.S. and overseas. AE, DC, MC, V, MO, PC.
Over 200 wine-related items for wine service, storage, and gifts.

The Armchair Emporium, Ltd.
825 Surrey Lane
Algonquin, IL 60102
(312) 658-8111
14-page color catalog. U.S. MO, PC.

Barbra George
17 Progress St.
Edison, NJ 08820
(201) 561-7890
32-page color catalog, free U.S. Does not sell overseas. AE, MC, V, PC.

Best Impressions
P.O. Box 720187
Atlanta, GA 30358
(404) 394-6003
32-page color catalog, free U.S. and overseas. AE, DC, MC, V, MO, PC.

Bleecker Street Gallery of Gifts
Suite 104
6 Koger Executive Center
P.O. Box 13066
Norfolk, VA 23506
(800) 424-2733
16-page color catalog, free U.S. MC, V, MO, PC.
Bleecker's features gift items made in America: exquisite porcelain Christmas ornaments by Margaret Furlong, brass trivets from Virginia Metalcrafters, nautical limited edition serigraphs, and cat and dog figures from Sandicast.

Casual Living
Kent Rd.
P.O. Box 1078
New Milford, CT 06776
(203) 355-3128
48-page color catalog, free U.S. and overseas. AE, DC, MC, V, MO, PC.
Some of the more unusual gifts from Casual Living include bookends formed from interesting gargoyle-looking building fragments—from houses on New York City's upper West Side ($48 for the pair). And a solid brass ice chest, made from a true replica of a British Admiralty porthole.

Comfortably Yours
51–1G West Hunter Ave.
Maywood, NJ 07607
(201) 368-0400
40-page color catalog, $1 U.S. Does not sell overseas. AE, DC, MC, V, MO, PC.
"Our catalog is about comforts, filled with usual and unusual products that make life more pleasant, safer, and more convenient for everyone." The items include specially designed shovels and garden tools, backsaving cushions, aids for the eyes and ears, for bed and bath. Touchables ($8.50) is an enlarged dialing keyboard that fits over your standard desk touch tone phone. The Talking Scale ($125) is a digital weight scale and more—a clear male voice also announces your weight correctly.

Cream O' The Crop, Inc.
1113 Del Nido Court
Ojai, CA 93023
(800) 421-6726
(805) 646-2601
16-page color catalog, free U.S. AE, MC, V, MO, PC.
Contemporary craft and folk art items.

David Kay
26055-D Emery Rd.
Warrensville Heights, OH 44128
(216) 464-5125
28-page color catalog, free U.S. and overseas. AE, DC, MC, V, MO, PC.
Over 145 wonderful gifts with nature themes, outdoor and indoor garden tools, and gardening aids: sun dial, door mats, distinctive bird feeder, barbeque charcoal keeper, space saver folding utility cart, pool and lawn games, rain gauge, convenient composter, and patio accessories.

Delta Flightline
3825 West Green Tree Rd.
P.O. Box 17001
Milwaukee, WI 53217
(800) 558-8990
Wisconsin (414) 352-0425
24-page color catalog, free U.S. AE, CB, DC, MC, V, MO, PC.
Delta Airlines' gift catalog, *Flightline,* offers many gift items to make traveling more enjoyable or, when you get there, vacation more relaxing. Priv-A-Sea Cabana (about $70) is a portable eight-sided canvas cabana, two-feet-tall, that can be used as a wind break, for privacy, or as a safe playing area for children. There are travel bags of many styles (featuring the Delta Airlines logo) and popular electronic gifts.

Dimensions Unlimited
400 S. Edward St.
Mt. Prospect, IL 60056
(800) 323-6959
Illinois (800) 942-0596
32-page color catalog, free U.S. AE, CB, DC, MC, V, MO, PC.
Dimensions offers good-looking luggage sets by Kluge, St. Moritz, St. Ives, and Lark. There are many elegant travel accessories, leather wallets, and clever electronic gift items.

Distinctive Designs
7047 B Greenville Ave.
Dallas, TX 75231
(800) 527-6829
Texas (214) 987-1852
22-page color catalog, free U.S. AE, DC, MC, V.
There are stylish personalized gifts for children including bright yellow lunch boxes, belts, sweater, lace panties, barettes, chairs, duffel bags, toothbrushes, and Christmas ornaments. There are also personalized tote bags, aprons, luggage, and stationery for adults. Don't miss this catalog.

Enticements
777 Irvington Place
Thornwood, NY 10594
(914) 747-1411
24-page color catalog, free U.S. Does not sell overseas. AE, MC, V, MO, PC.

Famous Barr
601 Olive St.
St. Louis, MO 63101
(800) 325-7656
Missouri (800) 392-7796
55-page color catalog, free U.S. MO, PC.
Famous Barr of St. Louis, Missouri, offers lovely gifts and fashions for the whole family. There are also jewelry, perfume, china, crystal and silver, and toys to be treasured.

Features
2575 Chantilly Dr.
Atlanta, GA 30324
(800) 241-5056
32-page color catalog, free U.S. Does not sell overseas. AE, DC, MC, V, MO, PC
Elegant gifts from $12 to $495 for the whole family, friends, and even the boss.

The Gallery
Wallins Corners Rd.
Amsterdam, NY 12010-1893
(800) 833-2008
New York (800) 342-6116
39-page color catalog, free U.S. AE, MC, V, MO, PC.
Beautiful objets d'art in glass, brass, crystal and cloisonne, plus many lovely gift and decorator items.

Geary's
351 North Beverly Drive
Beverly Hills, CA 90210–4794
(800) 421-0566
(800) 252-0013
78-page color catalog, $1. AE, MC, V, MO,
  PC.
Geary's of Beverly Hills offers crystal by
Baccarat and Lalique, sterling silver
and a lovely selection of fine gifts. Not
all gift items are expensive. The
menagerie birthday candle set by Reed
and Barton features six miniature
silverplate animals for $12. And they
sometimes devote a few pages to special
sale items.

The Great American Gift Catalog
American Airlines
P.O. Box 2001
Milwaukee, WI 53201-9728
Color Catalog, free U.S. AE, CB, DC, MC,
  V, MO, PC.
American Airlines' gift catalog features
travel cases for skis, ski boots, golf clubs
(with American Airline logo), plus
travel accessories, jewelry, and popular
electronic gadgets.

Hamakor Judaica, Inc.
6112 N. Lincoln Ave.
Chicago, IL 60659
(312) 463-6186
48-page color catalog, $2; overseas $4.
  AE, DC, MC, V, MO, PC.
A Judaica collection of items including
objets d'art, Shabbat and holiday
essentials, books, records, family games,
and toys.

Hammacher Schlemmer
147 East 57th St.
New York, NY 10022
(800) 368-3584
(800) 572-2803
62-page color catalog, free U.S. and
  overseas. AE, MC, V, MO, PC.
Founded in 1848, Hammacher
Schlemmer has been called "New York's
most famous store since before the Civil
War." They claim to be the first to
introduce the steam iron, portable radio,
electric razor, pop-up toaster, Mr. Coffee,
microwave ovens, blenders, and electric
can openers. They offer the submersible
Aqua Scooter ($389.50), Computer

Scrabble Master (plays at four skill
levels and has a 12,000 world
vocabulary, priced at $149.50), English
heated towel stand ($159.50), jet-
propelled surfboard ($2,450), and many
more great items.

Hog Wild
Faneuil Hall Market
280 Friend St.
Boston, MA 02114
Gift and clothing items, all featuring
pigs! The catalog cover boasts "The Pork
Avenue Collection." There are sweaters,
soft sculptures, shirts and sports clothes
with hog pictures and logos. There are
(of course) piggy banks, too.

Horchow Collection
P.O. Box 340257
Dallas, TX 75234
(800) 527-0303
(800) 442-5006
32-page color catalog, $3; overseas $10.
  AE, MC, V, MO, PC.
Roger Horchow is said to be the father
of the glossy specialty catalog aimed at
the affluent mail order shopper. He
started in 1971, and set the trend for
those fabulous, well-designed catalogs
full of objets d'art carefully mixed with
elegant dresses, men's fashions, and gift
items. Horchow offers gifts priced from
$7 to $490. There are the clear glass
dessert sets ($20) imported from France
which have always been a favorite, as
well as Oriental porcelain, children's
toys, holiday decorations, and table
accessories.

Kaplan's Ben Hur
2125 Yale St.
Houston, TX 77008
(713) 861-2121
48-page color catalog, $1 U.S. Does not
  sell overseas. AE, MC, V, MO, PC.
There are over 200 gift items of china,
crystal, and silver from names such as
Baccarat, Lalique, Lladro, Boehm, and
Waterford.

Luxe
Unique Merchandising Mart
Building 44
Hanover, PA 17333
(800) 621-5199

51-page color catalog. AE, DC, MC, V, PC.

Markline
P.O. Box C-5
Belmont, MA 02178
(800) 225-8493
Massachusetts (617) 891-6495
42-page color catalog, free U.S. AE, CB, DC, MC, V, MO, PC.
Markline features the latest, most technologically advanced products from top manufacturers. The Canon credit-card-thin calculator is one-tenth of an inch thick ($19.95). Casio's large-screen mini TV weighs less than twelve ounces, measures 4 × 5 in., and is only about an inch thick ($299.95). There are micro electronic greeting cards which look like regular greeting cards on the outside; when opened, the cards play a special tune (four cards for $24.95). You may select Birthday, Seasons Greetings, or mixed assortment packs.

Michael C. Fina
580 Fifth Ave.
New York, NY 10036
(212) 757-2530
208-page color catalog, free U.S. MC, V, MO, PC.
Michael C. Fina offers jewelry, watches (including Rolex and La Cloche), sterling and silver plate, china, crystal, cutlery, clocks, luggage, leather goods, pens, binoculars, and radios at discount prices.

The Nature Company
P.O. Box 7137
Berkeley, CA 94707
(800) 227-1114
California (415) 524-8340
36-page color catalog, free U.S. and overseas. AE, V, PC.
Here is a collection of many handmade gifts inspired by nature, or items to allow you to enjoy nature more. There is a graceful cast bronze sculptured antelope by Loet Vanderveen ($700), amber necklace imported from Northern Europe ($184), furry stuffed penguins ($23.25), and telescopes to gaze at the stars or at nature up close.

Nauticalia, Ltd.
121 High St.
Shepperton-on-Thames
Middlesex TW17 9BL England
09322 44396
16-page catalog, $1 U.S. and overseas. V, MO, PC.
Nauticalia is a leading manufacturer and distributor of marine artifacts. They make bosun's whistles for the world's navies; as gifts they make them in gold and silverplate. They also make great-looking ship's bells. Both whistles and bells can be engraved with a house, pub, or ship's name.

Northwest Orient Skyshop
3825 West Green Tree Rd.
P.O. Box 17001
Milwaukee, WI 53217
(800) 558-8990
20-page color catalog, free U.S. Does not sell overseas. AE, CB, DC, MC, V, MO, PC.
From the Northwest Airline gift catalog there are many personal accessories in compact travel sizes: water pic, electric toothbrush, rechargeable shavers, clothes iron, alarm clock, hair dryer, and electric rollers. There are also great gift items for exercise enthusiasts.

Oar House
P.O. Box 1285
Erie, PA 16512
(814) 455-2987
8-page catalog. MC, V, PC.
Oar House sells nautical gifts and accessories: four schooner mugs, brass porthole mirror ($39.95) and clock ($125), brass lanterns, and furniture.

Port O' Call Pasadena
906 Granite Dr.
Pasadena, CA 21101
(213) 796-7113
22-page color catalog, 20¢ U.S. Does not sell overseas. AE, MC, V, PC.

Preston's
Greenport
Long Island, NY 11944
(516) 477-1990

112-page mostly color, free U.S. and overseas. AE, MC, MO, PC.
Preston's offers a large selection of wooden ship models (already built or in kit form), marine paintings, ships wheels, clocks, nautical lamps, and other items for home decorating.

The Price of His Toys
9559 Santa Monica Blvd.
Beverly Hills, CA 90210
(213) 274-9955
14-page catalog, free U.S. Does not sell overseas. AE, MC, V, MO, PC.

Richard Kihl Ltd.
164 Regents Park Rd.
London NW1 8XN England
586 3838/0873
Color brochure, free U.S. and overseas. AE, DC, MC, V, MO, PC.
Richard Kihl's internationally known shop specializes in antique and modern wine accessories. He offers a large selection of antique glasses, decanters, silver and silver plate coasters, wine funnels, tastevins, labels, corkscrews, Port tongs, and good-looking brass and mahogany wine racks.

Russell's
799 Bush St.
San Francisco, CA 94108
(800) 227-3416
(415) 543-6620
32-page color catalog. AE, DC, MC, V, MO, PC.

San Francisco Paper World
50 Maiden Lane
San Francisco, CA 94108
(415) 421-0209
16-page color catalog, $1 U.S. and overseas. AE, MC, V, PC.
Selected antique and contemporary gift items and exclusive stationery collections. There are paperweights, crystal sculptures, Russian lacquer boxes, and Bliston & Battersea-style enameled bibelots. There are gifts for children and the young at heart, including an ingenious wall hanging— an M & M candy dispenser for $28.50.

Sculley & Sculley, Inc.
506 Park Ave.
New York, NY 10022
(800) 223-3717
(212) 755-2590
48-page color catalog, $2 U.S.; overseas free. AE, DC, MC, V, MO, PC.
Sculley & Sculley offers handpainted porcelain figurines by Herend, an eighteenth-century reproduction mahogany chest, a beautiful Oriental handpainted umbrella stand, and other fine pieces.

Smyth
25 W. Aylesbury
Timonium, MD 21093
(800) 638-3333
30-page color catalog, free U.S. and overseas. AE, DC, MC, V, MO, PC.
Smyth's offers a fine collection of china by leading manufacturers, beautiful giftware, diamond and 14-karat gold jewelry, top name-brand watches-all at prices 20% to 40% below retail.

Sointu
20 East 69th St.
New York, NY 10021
(212) 570-9449
20-page catalog, $2; overseas $6. AE, MC, V, MO, PC.
Sointu, in French, means harmony and balance. The Sointu catalog features well-selected items for special design, quality and appeal. There are wristwatches designed by Sointu and Porche, futuristic Scotch tape dispensers from Tokyo, a minimal linear fireplace tool set from Holland, ivory and obsidian chopsticks, pens and lighters from Italy, and toys from all over the world.

Trifles
P.O. Box 819075
Dallas, TX 75381–9075
(800) 527-0277
(800) 442-5801
62-page color catalog, $2 refundable U.S. and overseas.
Fine gifts for every occasion in the tested tradition of Horchow—from the Candle Tower, a traditional European-

style Christmas decoration, to Lindt truffles, to an elegant caviar server $20, to fashions for men and women.

The Unicorn Gallery
P.O. Box 4405
New Hampshire Ave.
Colesville, MD 20904
(800) 638-2616
32-page color catalog, $1 U.S. and
   overseas. AE, CB, DC, MC, V, MO, PC.
The Unicorn Gallery offers women's fashions (and many gifts) with a unicorn theme: needlepoint pillows, jewelry cases, bisque vases, and boxed note cards. There are gifts for all occasions, starting at $10 and up.

The Wine Enthusiast
P.O. Box 63
Chappaqua, NY 10514
(800) 228-2028
Nebraska (800) 642-8300
   32-page color catalog, $1 U.S. Does not
   sell overseas. AE, MC, V, MO, PC.
The Wine Enthusiast sells items for the enjoyment of wining and entertaining. The wine hobbyist will find wine storage systems, from 1,940 bottle (capacity) temperature-controlled units to decorative table top wine racks. There are corkscrews, decanters, carriers, and chillers.

UNDER $25

Abbey Press
78 Hill Dr.
St. Meinrad, IN 47577
(812) 357-8011
48-page color catalog, $1 U.S. Does not
   sell overseas. MC, V, MO, PC.
The Abbey Press Christian Family catalog offers specially selected gift items (ranging from $5 to $30) to help you celebrate Christmas, Easter, and other family occasions. There is something for everyone—newlyweds, new arrivals, grandparents, children, parents, and friends. There are nativity scenes, advent wreaths, sculptured items, and Christmas cards.

The Added Touch
132 Trafalgar Rd.
Oakville, Ontario
L6J 929 Canada
(416) 845-5032
36-page catalog, free U.S. and overseas.
   MC, V, MO, PC.

*Alaska Airlines/Goldcoast Gift
   Boutique*
P.O. Box 2001
Milwaukee, WI 53201–9728
20-page color catalog, free U.S. Does not
   sell overseas. AE, CB, DC, MC, V, MO,
   PC.
Travel accessories include leather accessories kit ($24.95), featherweight nylon luggage, a model of an Alaskan airlines 727 jet, and Alaska Airline destination posters.

Another Cat-A-Log
P.O. Box 22054
Cleveland, OH 44122
(800) 222-4700
(800) 222-4800
20-page color catalog, $1 U.S. and
   overseas. MC, V.
Many personalized gifts to choose from and many original gift ideas not found in other catalogs. Colorful kites ($25) are available hand painted with your name, club, or college. White stretch tights in sizes 6 month through 14 are personalized and hand painted with designs at $25 for a set of two.

Aristera, The Left Hand People, Inc.
P.O. Box 2224
Woburn, MA 01888
(617) 944-6729
16-page catalog, $1 U.S. and overseas.
   MC, V, MO, PC.
Products for left-handers: scissors, pruners, ink stamps, T-shirts, rulers, pens, kitchen helpers and coffee mugs.

Artisan Galleries
2100 N. Haskell Ave.
Dallas, TX 75204
(214) 827-2191
32-page catalog, free U.S. Does not sell
   overseas. AE, MC, V, MO, PC.

Aztech
P.O. Box 10167 GS
Springfield, MO 65808
(800) 641-6508
Missouri (417) 882-0002
30-page color catalog, free U.S. AE, DC,
   MC, V, MO, PC.
Aztech offers a good sampling of the
latest electronic items on the market.
There's a small five-pound electronic
portable typewriter for about $180, desk
top copiers by 3M for $149.95, and many
phone systems.

Baby Safe
1729 Superior Ave.
Cleveland, OH 44114
(216) 781-1650
16-page color catalog, 25¢ U.S. Does not
   sell overseas. MC, V.
Baby safe has collected some of the
newest and most trusted baby products
on the market today for their catalog.
There are car seats by Century, baby
bath tubs, locking diaper pails, walkers,
strollers, play pens, and high chairs.

Bo-Tree Productions
205 South McKemy St.
Chandler, AZ 85224
(602) 961-0168
30-page color catalog, free U.S. MC, V,
   PC.
There are calendars, datebooks, and gift
items, all with animal or nature themes.

Carefree House
711 W. Broadway
Tempe, AZ 85282
(602) 968-4411
48-page color catalog, U.S. Does not sell
   overseas. AE, DC, MC, V, MO, PC.

Chatco Collection
P.O. Box 62-PR
Wilmette, IL 60091
(312) 475-3049
12-page catalog, $1; overseas $2. MO, PC.
Practical gift items for people who love
cats. All the gift items bear cat motifs
or designs. There are door knockers,
jewelry, cookie tins, mugs, wooden
cutting boards, and more.

Chris Craft
Route #7
Manchester Center, VT 05255
(800) 528-6050
(802) 362-3141
39-page color catalog. AE, DC, MC, V.

Crispin Jones, Ltd.
138 El Camino Real
Box 83
Monticello, IA 52310
(319) 465-5104
6-page brochure, free U.S. Does not sell
   overseas. MO, PC.
Crispin Jones features lovely gifts
imported from England, Scotland, and
Wales. There are charming tea cozies,
egg cups from Aboty Pottery of Wales,
and a great book—*English Desserts,
Pudding, Cakes and Scones,* which
includes 110 delicious recipes.

Darby Creek
128 Coulter Ave.
P.O. Box 431
Ardmore, PA 19003
(800) 345-8501
Pennsylvania (800) 662-5180
32-page color catalog, free U.S. AE, DC,
   MC, V, MO, PC.

Deluxe Saddlery
1817 Whitehead Rd.
Baltimore, MD 21207
(301) 265-6975
80-page color catalog. AE, MC, V, MO,
   PC.
Gift items featuring animal themes,
especially horses. Stuffed animals,
figurines, tote bags, and items for the
home.

Feminist Horizons
965 Elizabeth St.
Pasadena, CA 91104
(213) 798-6259
24-page catalog, $1 U.S. and overseas.
   MC, V, MO, PC.
T-shirts, bumper stickers, and books
with feminist themes.

Figi's
630 S. Central Ave.
Marshfield, WI 54449
(715) 387-1771

32-page color catalog, free U.S. Does not sell overseas. AE, MC, V, MO, PC.
Figi's catalog offers a selection of fine quality specialty items (in luxurious color photographs) for the home, office, and travel. The prices are surprisingly low: Pierre Cardin writing pen $27, leather monogrammed money clip $10.95, monogrammed solid brass corkscrew $19.95, and nylon shopping tote bag $13.

Friends of Animals
One Pine St.
Neptune, NJ 07753–9988
24-page color catalog, $1 U.S. V, MC, MO, PC.
Gift items for all kinds of animal lovers.

Gentle Giants
2100 M. Street N.W.
Washington D.C. 20037
(800) 228-2606
(800) 642-8777
46-page color catalog, free U.S. AE, MC, V, MO, PC.
Gifts with whale themes include knitted sweaters, tree ornaments, jewelry, home decorator items, men's ties, pool inflatables, and more. Gentle Giants will donate a portion of the net proceeds from the sale of any item to help the international campaign to "Save the Whales."

Giggletree
Winterbrook Way
Meredith, NH 03253
(603) 279-7011
100-page color catalog, free U.S. Does not sell overseas. AE, MC, V, MO, PC.

The Good Idea Store
P.O. Box 2226
15072 NE 40th St.
Redmond, WA 98052
(206) 882-0887
32-page color catalog, free U.S. MC, V, MO, PC.
The Good Idea has selected some of the better gift ideas for their catalog. They include many innovative time- and space-saving ideas.

Grand Finale
P.O. Box 819027
Farmers Branch, TX 75381–9027
(214) 934-9777
The Grand Finale features all the close-outs from famous companies at reduced prices. China, crystal, silver, fashions, jewelry, and great gifts that you may have seen elsewhere are now featured in Grand Finale at discounts of up to 50%. (Both the original and sale price are shown.) Don't miss this catalog.

Griffith Pottery House, Ltd.
37 Edison Rd.
Aylesbury
Buckinghamshire England

Griffith Pottery House
100 Lorraine Ave.
Oreland, PA 19075
(215) 887-2222
32-page color catalog, free U.S. and overseas. MC, V, MO, PC.
Specially selected gifts for your favorite firefighter: mugs, cookie cutters, Christmas ornaments, and many other gift items.

House of David
5 W. Summit Avenue
P.O. Box 777
Lakewood, NY 14750
(716) 763-1347
32-page catalog, free U.S. Does not sell overseas. MC, V, MO, PC.
Israeli imports, books, Bibles, and accessories that help people to express their Hebraic faith.

The James Company
3200 SE 14 Ave.
Ft. Lauderdale, FL 33316
(800) 327-3799
36-page color catalog, AE, MC, V, PC.
Delicious-looking food items (Dundee cake, shortbread, and Jenners traditional Scotch Bun), kitchen items, table accessories, and children's toys.

Joan Cook
3200 SE 14th Ave.
Ft. Lauderdale, FL 33316
(305) 761-1600

112-page color catalog, free U.S. and overseas. AE, MC, V, MO, PC.

J. Rushton's, Inc.
P.O. Box 5510
Sanford, FL 32772
(800) 327-7175
Florida (305) 339-1126
32-page color catalog. MC, V, MO, PC.

Left Hand Plus
P.O. Box 1204
Aurora, IL 60507
10-page catalog. PC.
Aids, gadgets, and T-shirts for the left-handed person.

Left Hand World
P.O. Box 26316
San Francisco, CA 94126
15-page catalog, MC, V, MO, PC.
Watches, kitchen aids, scissors, playing cards, and writing aids designed for left-handed persons.

Lillian Vernon
510 South Fulton Ave.
Mount Vernon, NY 10550
(914) 699-4131
152-page color catalog, free U.S. Does not sell overseas. AE, CB, DC, MC, V, MO, PC.
Lillian Vernon is a well known gift catalog offering a great selection of products, ranging from household items to specialty gifts, all at affordable prices. Many of their products are imported from the Far East and Europe; they include practical items for the kitchen, bathroom, bedroom, entertaining, children's toys, and stationery.

Mail Order Oregon
P.O. Box 29112
Portland, OR 97229
(503) 223-1790
10-page newsalog, free U.S. and overseas. AE, MC, V, MO, PC.
Mail Order Oregon features terrific products manufactured or processed in the State of Oregon. There are sculptures from Myrtlewood, chocolates, gift assortments of tea from Stash Tea Company, cheese from Bandon, and delicious sausage from Verboort.

Mystic Seaport Museum Stores
Mystic, CT 06355
(203) 536-9688
36-page color catalog, $1; overseas $3. AE, MC, V, MO, PC.
Nautical gifts for the yachtsman, boat owner, and lover of the sea. The leather-bound Yacht Log ($29.95) can be personalized in embossed gold. There are boating belts for the crew ($14.95), a humorous fog-cutting knife ($12.95), slip cases for bunk pillows ($18.95), and ship-shaped cookie cutters ($12.95).

The National Canine Defense League
10 Seymour St.
London W1H 5WB England
20-page color catalog, free U.S. and overseas. MO, PC.

New York Botanical Garden
Bronx, NY 10458
(212) 220-8720
24-page color catalog. MC, V, PC.
Posters, mugs, ceramics, pillows, stationery, calendars, toiletries, and small garden planters—all with colorful floral designs.

The Paragon
Tom Harvey Rd.
Westerly, RI 02891
(401) 596-0134
68-page color catalog, $1 U.S. Does not sell overseas. AE, MC, V, MO, PC.

P'Chelle
1115 Sunset
P.O. Box 260
Richland, WA 99352
4-page brochure, free U.S. MC, V, MO, PC.

Pier 1 Imports
800 Forest Park Blvd.
Ft. Worth, TX 76102–5899
(800) 972-1000
48-page color catalog, free U.S. AE, MC, V.
Imported gifts from around the world include children's canvas director's

chairs ($19.95), rattan shelves, nesting dolls from Poland (about $6), five-tiered bamboo birdcage ($20), and a handcrafted walnut-and-beech wood chess set from Belgrade ($35).

Potpourri
Department P119
204 Worchester St.
Wellesley, MA 02181
(800) 225-4127
(617) 237-7755
64-page color catalog. AE, MC, V, MO, PC.

The Private I
P.O. Box 18093
Spartanburg, SC 29318
(803) 579-3522
14-page color catalog, free U.S. and overseas. MC, V, PC.

Propinquity
6158 Santa Monica
Los Angeles, CA 90038
(213) 461-3096
30-page color catalog, $1 U.S. Does not sell overseas. AE, DC, MC, V, MO, PC.
Trendy and flashy gifts inspired by Hollywood. You can even have your name in neon lights—starting at $190 for one to seven letters, up to $240 for sixteen letters. (No kidding.)

Rainbow of Gifts
Unique Merchandising Mart
Building 30
Hanover, PA 17333
(800) 821-5800
40-page color catalog, $2 U.S. and overscas. AE, CB, DC, MC, V, MO, PC.

Regal Greetings & Gifts, Inc.
2221 Niagara Falls Blvd.
Niagara Falls, NY 14304
88-page color catalog, free U.S. MC, V, PC.
Regal Greeting has gifts for all—and a terrific selection of greeting cards, wrapping paper, ribbons and labels—at very low prices. There are many excellent children's gifts (for under $3), handy kitchen items, and organizers for the home and office.

Sierra Club
205 South McKemy
Chandler, AZ 85224
(602) 961-0333
48-page color catalog, U.S. and overseas. AE, MC, V, MO, PC.
There are apparel, gifts, and gear that sport the Sierra Club logo. (They are an organization dedicated to the safeguard of the environment.) There are lovely photos, prints, and stationery with beautiful nature scenes. A 10% discount is available for Sierra Club members.

Signatures
3163 Redhill Ave.
Costa Mesa, CA 92626
(714) 966-0184
64 color pages, free U.S. AE, MC, V, PC.

The Silvers
1201 Boston Post Road
Milford, CT 06460–2794
(800) 243-9280
(203) 874-3881
32-page color catalog, free U.S. AE, MC, V.

Sports Gift Digest
1020 Church St.
Evanston, IL 60201
(312) 491-6440
36-page newsalog, free U.S. and overseas. MC, V, MO, PC.
Sports Gift Digest offers an extensive selection of sports books, biographies of superstars, team histories, and manuals and guides for improving your game. They also sell logo items (licensed by the NFL, NBA, and NHL): T-shirts, caps, jackets, and jewelry.

Store 64
3159 Redhill Ave.
Costa Mesa, CA 92626
(714) 557-4289
52 color pages, free U.S. Minimum order $15. AE, MC, V.

Svenska Stuga Butik
322 N. Milwaukee
Libertyville, IL 60048
(312) 362-8890
24-page color catalog, free U.S. and overseas. AE, DC, MC, V, MO, PC.

Scandinavian imports, some exclusive to Svenska Stuga Butik. There are crystal, jewelry, Christmas table top decorations, gifts, mobiles, and music boxes.

Tapestry
Unique Merchandising Mart
Building 46
Hanover, PA 17333
(800) 621-5199
32-page color catalog, $2 U.S. and overseas. AE, CB, DC, MC, V, MO, PC.

Texas Dry Goods, Inc.
2461 E. Long
Ft. Worth, TX 76106
(817) 625-6379
10-page color catalog, free U.S. and overseas. AE, MC, V, MO, PC.
From Billy Bob's World's Largest Honky Tonk, located in Fort Worth, Texas, comes a catalog of their unique souvenirs. Some are unusual and some are simply tasteless. Most items are T-shirts, unusual mugs, etc., with Billy Bob's logo. Then there is the Cow Chip Pen set ($10) which, sterilized and lacquered, is a one-of-a-kind desk pen holder. Bullie Bags can be used as car litter bags or golf ball holders ($19.95); they are made from genuine bull scrotums.

Tidewater Specialties
U.S. Rt. 50 Box 158
Wye Mills, MD 21679
(301) 820-2076
38-page color catalog, free U.S. and overseas. AE, MC, V, MO, PC.
Tidewater Specialties catalog features gifts, clothing, and accessories inspired by hunting, field dog training, the world of waterfowl, and outdoor living.

Touch of Class
Huntingburg, IN 47542
(800) 457-7456
Indiana (812) 683-3707
32-page color catalog, AE, CB, DC, MC, V.
Bed linens by Martex, Utica, Perry Ellis, Laura Ashley, Dan River, and Marimekko. There are also great gift items and decorator items.

Travelife
P.O. Box 1692
3825 W. Green Tree Rd.
Milwaukee, WI 53201
(800) 558-8990
24-page color catalog, free U.S. AE, DC, MC, V, PC.
Travelife is a collection of many thoughtful gift items in compact travel sizes, including a collapsable travel umbrella ($27.50), and a pocket alarm clock ($34.90). There is a handy ballpoint pen ($14.95) that features a mini scissors and nail file hidden in the cap—great for clipping newspaper coupons. Framed U.S. and world maps ($21.95 each) come with marking kits to chart the miles you've traveled. The leather attaché case ($70) features a detachable purse; it's both good-looking and convenient.

Valerie's Choice
Linwood Square
Linwood, NJ 08221
(800) 222-0053
New Jersey (800) 222-0252
80-page color catalog, free U.S. AE, DC, MC, V, PC.

Waggin' Tails
2001 Holland Ave.
Port Huron, MI 48060
(800) 882-1273
Michigan (313) 987-2264
32-page color catalog, U.S. and overseas. MC, V, MO, PC.
Gifts for animal lovers—and for the animals, too: coffee mugs that read "I Love My . . . ", and then your choice of various breeds pictured ($4.49); kitty litters (and even a commode adaptation) to potty train your cat ($29.99); and (of course) the all-important super scoops, door gates, and pet doors.

Wireless
45 East Eight St.
St. Paul, MN 55101
(800) 824-7888
(800) 852-7777
16-page color catalog, free U.S. Does not sell overseas. MC, V, MO, PC.
Records, books, T-shirts, and gift items chosen to appeal to listeners of public radio—particularly the popular

program from Minnesota, "A Prairie Home Companion."

SOMETHING FOR EVERYONE

Bruce Bolind
P.O. Box 9751
Boulder, CO 80301
(303) 443-3143
80-page color catalog, $1 U.S. Does not sell overseas. AE, MC, V, MO, PC.

Carol Wright
3601 NW 1st St.
Lincoln, NE 68521
(402) 474-2018
64 pages, free U.S. AE, MC, V, MO, PC.

The Ferry House
554 North State Road
Briarcliff Manor, NY 10510
(914) 762-1496
64-page color catalog. AE, MC, V, MO, PC.

Hanover House
Unique Merchandising Mart
Building 2
Hanover, PA 17333
80-page color catalog, $1 U.S. and overseas. AE, CB, DC, MC, V, MO, PC.
The offer a 10% senior citizen discount.

Happy Things
48 Millgate
Newark, Nottinghamshire
England
0636 72624
47-page color catalog, 2 International Reply Coupons; overseas free.
Minimum order $7.50. MC, V, PC.

Harriet Carter
Stump Rd.
Montgomeryville, PA 18936
(215) 368-3367
112-page color catalog, free U.S. Does not sell overseas. AE, MC, V, MO, PC.

Jean Stuart
Stuart Building
Pleasantville, NJ 08232
(800) 222-0053
New Jersey (800) 222-0252

96-page color catalog. AE, MC, V, MO, PC.

The Lighter Side
Mt. Clemens, MI 48043
(313) 791-2800
40-page color catalog. MC, V, PC.

Lincoln House
2015 Grand Ave.
Kansas City, MO 64108
(816) 842-3319
64-page color catalog, free U.S. Does not sell overseas. MC, V, MO, PC.

Mature Wisdom
Unique Merchandising Mart
Building 28
Hanover, PA 17333
(800) 621-5800
Illinois (800) 972-5858
48-page color catalog, $1 U.S. and overseas. PC.

Miles Kimball
41 West Eighth Ave.
Oshkosh, WI 54906
194-page color catalog. PC.

The Music Stand
Norwich, VT 05055
(802) 649-1004
64-page color catalog. MC, V, MO, PC.
Gifts with the theme of music and dance.

New Hampton
Unique Merchandising Mart
Building 10
Hanover, PA 17333
(800) 621-5800
Illinois (800) 972-5858
64-page color catalog, $1 U.S. and overseas. AE, CB, DC, MC, V, MO, PC.

Old Village Shop
Unique Merchandising Mart
Building 8
Hanover, PA 17333
(800) 621-5800
96-page color catalog, $1 U.S. and overseas. AE, CB, DC, MC, V, PC.

Popular Products
451 Maethy S.E.
Grand Rapids, MI 49508
(616) 452-0459

24-page newsalog, free U.S. Does not sell overseas. MO, PC.

Sleepy Hollow Gifts
6651 Arlington Blvd.
Falls Church, VA 22042
(703) 534-0921
72-page color catalog, free U.S. PC.

Spencer
Spencer Bldg.
Atlantic City, NJ 08411
112-page color catalog, free U.S. AE, MC, V, PC.

Starcrest of California
3159 Redhill Ave.
Costa Mesa, CA 92626
66 color pages. Minimum order $5. MC, V, MO, PC.

Taylor Gifts
Box 206
Wayne, PA 19087
(215) 688-3046
112-page color catalog, free U.S. and overseas. AE, MC, V, MO, PC.

Walter Drake & Sons
Drake Bldg.
Colorado Springs, CO 80940
104-page color catalog. MC, V, PC.

York Gifts
400 Rayon Dr.
Parkesburg, NV 26102
(304) 422-7144

INTERNATIONAL

Amazing Grace Elephant Company
P.O. Box 97857, TST
Kowloon, Hong Kong
3 699357
32-page color catalog, $2 surface, $3 air mail refundable U.S. and overseas.
A great selection of old and new Asian crafts and clothing at terrific prices. There are charming sunshade umbrellas ($6.45), handpainted wooden "palace combs" ($4.90), velvet-lined brass evening bags ($29.60), traditional Chinese junk compass ($6.60), and cloisonne slip-over lighter cases ($7.50). This is a great catalog for nice but inexpensive gift shopping.

Amsterdam Airport Shopping
1118 ZG Schiphol Airport
P.O. Box 7501
Holland
020 5179111
50-page color catalog. U.S. and overseas. Prices in Dutch guilders. AE, DC, MC, V, MO.
Amsterdam Airport Schiphol's gift shop is one of the largest. They produce an excellent mail order catalog. The prices are listed in Dutch guilders, with indications of U.S. dollar equivalents also listed. (The exact price, of course, must be determined at the time the order is placed.) Watches, luggage, cameras and electronics, binoculars, and many other products are offered.

Brown Thomas & Co., Ltd.
Grafton St.
Dublin 2 Ireland
776861
32-page color catalog, $2; overseas free. AE, CB, DC, MC, V, MO, PC.
Brown Thomas is an exclusive department store located in the heart of Dublin. In their catalog they offer a nice selection of Irish craftmanship: crystal glassware and other items from famous Irish companies like Donegal, Aran, and Waterford, not to mention world-famous Wedgewood, Cashmere, and Royal Worcester.

Cashs
St. Patricks St.
Cork, Ireland
021 964411
40-page color catalog, $2; overseas free. AE, MC, V, PC.
Cashs carries most of the best known brand names of Ireland, England, and Europe in fine china, glassware, and gifts. They also carry many lovely traditional Irish garments. Their prices are competitive with U.S. retail prices— even after mailing charges and customs duties.

Cuckoobird Productions
Peckham Bush Tunbridge
Kent England
812368

8-page color brochure, $2; overseas, a self-addressed stamped envelope. Minimum order $50. MO, PC.
Cuckoobird Productions is a cottage industry making several cotton-printed kitchen coordinates: pot holders, placemats, aprons, jam jar covers, tray cloths, tea cosies and egg cosies. The items are usually individually printed to form a theme, such as Strawberry Garden or Market Town, in bright and cheery colors.

Den Permanente
8 Vesterbrogade
DK-1620 Copenhagen V
Denmark
12 44 88
63-page color catalog, $2 surface, $3 air mail; U.S. and overseas. Prices in Danish kroner. AE, DC, MC, V, MO, PC.
Den Permanente offers an extensive collection of Danish arts, crafts, jewelry, toys, Christmas ornaments, dinnerware, fashions, glassware, and furniture. This fine selection of Danish-designed products features products characteristically unpretentious and functionally styled.

Egertons
Lyme St.
Axminster, Devon
EX13 5DB England
0297 32742
56-page catalog, free surface, $2 air mail; overseas free. AE, DC, MC, V, MO, PC.
A nice variety of gifts—from food and wine hampers (filled with gourmet foods) to perfumery, fashions, jewelry, lingerie, knitwear, and toys. There are Scottish tartans, bonsai from Wales, collector's dolls from England, and bakery products from Ireland.

El Mercado Mexican Imports
P.O. Box 12196
San Antonio, TX 78212
(512) 824-0212
32-page catalog, $2 U.S. and overseas. MC, V, MO, PC.
Carefully selected, finer quality Mexican imports representing items from many regions. Baskets, clothing,

decorator items of brass, copper, onyx and glass, furniture, and rugs are offered. Mexican onyx backgammon set (12 × 10 in.) is priced at $54. Brass candlesticks are $27 a pair, and a hand-hammered copper-framed mirror (22 × 18 in.) is $73.50.

Finn Port Co.
4944 Xerxes Ave. S.
Minneapolis, MN 55420
16-page color catalog. MC, V, PC.
Finn Port features Scandinavian gifts including straw and wooden Christmas ornaments and decorations, ceramic tiles, table cloths (with pretty Dala horse and Swedish Kurbits designs), and many lovely painted and decorated candlesticks.

House of Tyrol
P.O. Box 909
Gateway Plaza
Cleveland, GA 30528
(404) 865-5115
48-page color catalog, $1 U.S. Minimum order $10. AE, DC, MC, V, MO, PC.
House of Tyrol offers Alpine gift novelties, dinnerware, decorative items, and toys. There is also German music (on LPs and cassettes), Alpine fashions, and jewelry.

Kilkenny Design
Castle Yard Parade
Kilkenny Ireland
056 22118
16-page color catalog, $1; overseas free. AE, DC, MC, V, MO, PC.
Kilkenny offers handblown glassware and distinctive ceramics, as well as handwoven pure wool bedspreads, knee rugs, blankets and stable blankets. They feature the traditional Aran knit bedspread and the handwoven pure wool Wicklow bedspread with the soft brushed finish, both priced from about $116 to $158.

Klod Hans
Hans Jensensstraede 34
DK 5000 Odense C
Denmark

14-page brochure, $1 U.S. and overseas. MO, PC.

Klod Hans is located across the street from Hans Christian Andersen's house on a narrow street in Denmark. Klod Hans is visited by many and sells its Danish gifts by mail order. There are brightly painted Christmas ornaments and decorations, advent calendars (with little pockets for small gifts), candlesticks in many sizes, mobiles, bell pulls, and a nice variety of Royal Copenhagen porcelain.

Naturally British
13 New Row
Covent Garden
London WC2 England
01 240 0551
28-page catalog, $1; overseas free. AE, DC, MC, V, MO, PC.
Naturally British prides themselves in selling goods that are handmade by British craftsmen, not mass produced. Started in Covent Garden in 1978, today they offer jewelry, furniture, pottery, sweaters, toys, and glassware through their fine catalog.

Nepal Craft Emporium
G.P.O. Box 1443
Kathmandu, Nepal
12500
24-page catalog, $5 U.S. and overseas. AE, MO.
Nepal Craft Emporium features metal handcrafts in brass, copper, and zinc. Nepalese art forms are highly decorative metal forms, made from the traditional lost wax process, and often finished with silver or gold wash. There are studded filigree forms such as animals, birds, boxes, and jewelry. There are also beautifully carved wood boxes and chests.

Scotch House
187 Post St.
San Francisco, CA 94108
(415) 391-1264
32-page color catalog, free U.S. and overseas. AE, DC, MC, V, MO, PC.
There are Scottish kilts in toddlers sizes, and sweaters by Pringle, Lyle & Scott, Coxmoore, and Ballantyne. There are fashions by Highland Queen, hats by

Jonathan Richard, and kilts made-to-measure. Edinburgh crystal, Buchan stoneware, books, flags, plaques, and tapes are available.

Scotland Direct Limited
The Bell Tower
New Lanark
Lanark ML11 7BR Scotland
2574
A variety of small brochures, free U.S. and overseas. AE, MC, V, MO, PC.
Scotland Direct will send brochures if you write requesting a specific category, such as jewelry, gifts, crystal, or collectibles.

Scottish Lion
Rt. 16 Box 560
North Conway, NH 03860
(603) 356-6381
48-page color catalog, $1 U.S. and overseas. AE, DC, MC, V, MO, PC.
The Scottish Lion carries everything from kilts and ties, to Harris tweed blazers and wool sweaters, to clan badges and jewelry. They carry the finest quality merchandise mainly from England, Ireland, Scotland, and Wales.

Shannon Mail Order
Shannon Free Airport
Ireland
06161444
52-page color catalog, $1; overseas free. AE, MC, V, MO, PC.
Shannon Mail Order carries top quality European merchandise such as Spode, Roual Doulton, Wedgewood and Beleek china, plus renowned Irish linen, and Waterford and Cavan crystal—all available at very attractive prices.

Surma
11 E. 7th St.
New York, NY 10003
(212) 477-0729
20-page catalog, free U.S. and overseas. MO, PC.
Surma specializes in Slavic gift and import items. There are Ukranian Easter egg-decorating kits, nesting dolls, embroidered aprons, and blouses. There are also Rumanian blouses, folk dance records, music boxes, and spices.

Taiwan Handicraft Promotion Center
1 Hsu Chow Rd.
Taipei, Taiwan
936-5741
12-page color catalog, free U.S. and
    overseas. AE, MC, V, MO, PC.
The Taiwan Handicraft Promotion
Center is devoted to the promotion of
Chinese artistic handcrafts. Located in
downtown Taipei, The Chinese
Handicraft Mart is a group of three
stores including The Gift Store, Jewelry,
and Home Furnishings. Through the
catalog they offer beautiful jade
pendants, bracelets and necklaces,
cloisonne, Tang tricolored glazed
ceramic ware, hand-carved jewelry
boxes, and ginger jar lamps.

Tesoros del Sol
7910 Ivanhoe Ave. Suite 234
LaJolla, CA 92037
(714) 298-3229
20-page color catalog. MC, V, MO, PC.
"Treasures of the Sun" offers colorful
handcrafted gifts from Mexico. There
are many ceramic items, famous
Equipal chairs, and tables made from
cedar splits and pigskin that naturally
darken with age. From Tonala, they
offer ceramics with the Brunida (or
burnished) glaze. There are also
Mexican tin Christmas ornaments,
dresses, and woven wall hangings.

True Tartans
18 W. 262 Kirland
Villa Park, IL 60181
(312) 495-1510
17-page catalog. PC.
True Tartans offers clan crest items,
kilts, doublets, lace jabots and cuffs.
They carry all registered tartans and
clan crest items in all existent badges.

COUNTRY

Buffalo Peddler
Box 110
135 Norwood Dr.
West Seneca, NY 14224
(716) 675-4856
24-page (some color) catalog, $1 U.S. and
    overseas. MC, V, MO, PC.

Buffalo Peddler features useful and
decorative items for the home: hand-
sewn Eight Point Star Quilts (queen size,
$675), Country Fair Stoneware,
enamelware coffee pots ($12.95), wooden
toys, colorful ceramic switchplates, and
hand mirrors framed in hardwood
maple ($13.50).

Clymer's of Bucks County
Canal St.
Nashua, NH 03061
(800) 258-1791
48-page color catalog. AE, MC, V, MO,
    PC.
Country gift items include handmade
gingham-covered stools ($19.95),
Hutch's carved goose ($375), and a
handpainted goose box ($65) that could
be used for a magazine rack or kindling
box. There are popover pans, old-
fashioned tin canisters ($12.95), and
many great gift ideas for children.

The Country Loft
South Shore Park
Hingham, MA 02043
(800) 225-5408
Massachusetts (617) 749-7766
48-page color catalog, $5 U.S.
    refundable; overseas free. AE, DC,
    MC, V, MO, PC.
The Country Loft features "everything
for the country home." There are high
quality pieces of antique reproduction
furniture (made especially for the
Country Loft) and a charming collection
of handcrafted country decorative
accessories—braided rugs, quilt stands,
and a schoolhouse slate board, framed
in oak, for writing down important
messages.

Country Manor
Mail Order Dept. Route 211
Sperryville, VA 22740
40-page catalog, free U.S. AE, MC, V, PC.
There is English Staffordshire ironstone
dinnerware in blue calico, canister sets
in cobalt blue glass, "mountain
homespun" tablecloths, and
handpainted piggy banks, cornshuck
dolls, potpourri, and baskets.

Country Notebook
1730 Butter Rd.
Dover, PA 17315
(800) 528-6050
32-page color catalog. AE, DC, MC, V,
    MO, PC.
Country notebook offers some of the best
(and more unusual) types of country
gifts. The beautiful appliquéd fireplace
screen, framed in wood with a fabric
background, is priced at $159. There are
also authentic European cookie molds,
and terrific kid's toys, and much more.

The Country Store and Farm
Route 2 Box 304
Vashon, WA 98070
(206) 463-3655
50-page newsalog, free U.S. AE, MC, V,
    MO, PC.
The catalog presents (in line drawings
and some photographs) a wide variety
of country gifts. There are food items,
kitchenware, lamps and lighting
accessories, beauty products (wooden
mirror and combs), gardening supplies,
and clothing.

Country Traditions
9000 Stub Rd.
East Orwell, OH 44034
(216) 422-3531
20-page catalog, free U.S. Does not sell
    overseas. MO, PC.
All the lovely items offered are
handmade by crafts people dedicated to
careful design and quality
workmanship. They offer many patch
work items—pillows, wreaths, crib
quilts, and wall hangings. Stacey P.
Small, President, says she works closely
with the crafts people to accommodate
special orders, including color selection,
size, and materials.

Craftsmen's Workshop
P.O. Box 1776
Plainfield, NJ 07060–1776
16-page catalog, $1; overseas $2.50
    surface $4 air mail. MC, V, MO, PC.
Craftsmen's Workshop has gathered
craft goods from almost every state (and
many foreign countries) to offer in their
catalog. There are colorful appliquéd
home and kitchen accessories, pottery,

and a lovely selection of functional and
decorative brassware.

Jennifer House
New Marlboro Stage
Great Barrington, MA 01230
(413) 528-1500
96-page some color catalog, 25¢ U.S. and
    overseas. AE, MC, V, MO, PC.
"New England Americana
Marketplace." There are gifts,
traditional decorative accessories,
flatware, homespun tablecloths, rugs,
and country clothes, all designed
exclusively for Aunt Abigail's Attic, and
available only from Jennifer House.

Lynchburg Hardware and General Store
East Side of Square
Lynchburg, TN 37352
(615) 759-7184
32-page color catalog, free U.S. and
    overseas. AE, DC, MC, V, MO, PC.
Lynchburg's catalog is full of down
home humor, descriptive narratives,
and lots of American products. There
are Gee Haw Whimmey Diddles and
Coon Hound pups under the same roof
as the most complete selection of Jack
Daniel Distillery merchandise to be
found. There's the complete collection
of the famous Foxfire books, plus
wooden games (Skittles and Nine Men's
Morris), popping corn and fixings,
Tennessee cast iron cookware, and a big
(3 × 5 ft.) nylon American flag ($25).
"Founded in 1912 and doing honest and
reliable business ever since."

North Shore Farmhouse
Box A
Greenhurst, NY 14742
32-page some color catalog, $1 U.S. Does
    not sell overseas. AE, MC, V, MO, PC.
The North Shore Farmhouse catalog is
a mixture of color photographs and
interesting line drawings of their
country colonial craft kits and ready-
made hand goods. The spice wreath kit
($8.95) features nineteen different
spices and easy instructions. There are
hand-dipped candles, farm bells, soft
Christmas ornaments, and ice cream
makers.

The Old House Gifts
294 Head of the Bay Road
Buzzards Bay, MA 02532
(617) 759-4942
16-page newsalog, 25¢ U.S. Limited
    overseas sales. MO, PC.

Old South Country Kindlin'
P.O. Box 872
Brewton, AL 36427
(205) 867-2981
2-page brochure, free U.S. Does not sell
    overseas. MO, PC.
Old Country Kindlin' is real kindling
wood in gift bundles or economy boxes,
priced at about $11 for a five-pound
bundle. This kindling is from Virgin
Long Leaf Pine timber, grown along the
Gulf coast. It has an unusually large
amount of natural resin and ignites so
easily that, with only two or three
broken splinters, you can start a roaring
fire in just seconds.

Paddle Wheel Shop
P.O. Box 12429
St. Louis, MO 63132
(800) 325-4268
40-page color catalog, $1 U.S. Does not
    sell overseas. MC, V, MO, PC.
Gifts, collectibles, clothing, and
novelties reminiscent of the classic Old
South: riverboat gambler's hat, brass
Southern Comfort ice bucket ($40), and
citronella candle ($9.95). The lemon-
scented candle wax, in a galvanized
steel bucket, is used outdoors to keep
insects away.

Perkins Country Collection
Village Rd.
Jackson, NJ 03846
(603) 383-9612
32-page color catalog, free U.S. AE, CB,
    DC, BC, V, MO, PC.
Perkins Country Collection offers
beautifully crafted solid pine and oak
furniture, brass beds, fabrics and wall
papers, and accessories—all with the
country look. There are Braided Rugs
(up to a 12 × 15 ft. size), roll-top desks,
wing chairs ($475), and a small dropleaf

Pine Table just right for a small dining
area or kitchen ($275). There are
traditional and whimsical quilted pieces
and ceramics.

The Plow & Hearth
560 Main St.
Madison, WI 22727
(703) 948-7010
32-page catalog. AE, MC, V, PC.
The Plow & Hearth offers a great choice
of useful items for the home. The
flameproof Oriental-design hearth rugs
range from $39.95 to $44.95, and the
guard screen (to keep pets and children
away from hot wood stoves) are two of
the many fireplace and woodcutting
accessories offered. There are some
great old-fashioned items, like the
Apple-Corer-Peeler-Slicer for $19.95.
This gadget is a terrific gift for those
people you thought had everything—it
clamps onto the table top and, in about
ten rotations of the handle, it finishes
the job the name implies!

Sturbridge Yankee Workshop
Blueberry Rd.
Westbrook, ME 04092
(800) 343-1144
Maine (207) 774-9045
Lovely country decorator items for the
home. The solid pine Steeple clock
($119), solid brass candlestick wall
lamps ($160), and authentic
reproduction maple Bow Back writing
chair ($279) are some of the larger items
they offer. There is a good selection of
small gift items and collectibles, too.

Vermont Country Store
Rt. 100
Weston, VT 05161
(802) 824-3184
96-page catalog, 25¢; overseas 1
    International Reply Coupon.
    Minimum order $5. MC, V, MO, PC.
Amongst the Calico aprons, English
ironstone dinnerware, and Vermont
baskets are bits of Yankee editorial
wisdom, poetry, and woodcuts. A
delightful and most practical catalog.

HANDCRAFTS

SEE ALSO
- Collectibles
- Crafts
- Gifts
- Hobby

INTERNATIONAL

African Heritage, Ltd.
P.O. Box 41730
Nairobi, Kenya
554378
36-page catalog, $5; overseas free. AE, DC, V, MO, PC.
African Heritage is Africa's largest Pan-African Gallery, located on Nairobi's main thoroughfare, Kenyatta Avenue. It includes a gallery, Pan-African restaurant, and garden craft center. The catalog offers traditional and contemporary handcrafts and art from East, West, Central, and Southern Africa. There is stunning African jewelry (designed by Alan Donovan), and Bombolulu jewelry fashioned from copper, seed pods, and coconut shells. There is also African beadwork, carved art, batik, calabash art, and Kisii stone art.

Bethlehem Training Centre
P.O. Box 6558
Addis Ababa, Ethiopia
18 41 97
3-page brochure, $1; overseas free.
Bethlehem Training Center offers lovely handwoven tapestries of Ethiopian scenes, made of natural colored yarns from local highland sheep. They are available in two sizes (17 × 24 in. and 17 × 43 in.) and are in natural colors of black, grey, browns, beige, and off-white. They are priced from $55 to $95 postpaid.

Elizabeth Best
89 Palmerston Rd.
London N 22 England
01 888 6122
No catalog available. U.S. and overseas. BD.
Elizabeth Best personally designs and sews commemorative Victorian pincushions made to your requirements. Pincushions were a traditional gift for the newborn from the sixteenth to the nineteenth century. But they can be ordered for any occasion—weddings, birthdays, Christmas, Valentine's Day, anniversaries, births and christenings. Made of voile, lace, ribbon, and beads, they are truly a sentimental and romantic gift.

Folklore Olga Fisch
P.O. Box 64
Avencia Colon #260
Quito, Ecuador
231-767
Catalog, $4; overseas $6. MO, PC.
Folklore offers an interesting collection of the finest handcrafts Ecuador has to offer: beautiful rugs designed by Olga Fisch, and high fashion designed by Gogo Anhalzer. Olga's thick-napped rugs of primarily earth tones all have

"O. Fisch" woven into the lower right corner, and have adorned floors at Lincoln Center, the United Nations, and other notable places. Gogo's fashions are drawn from Indian designs adapted to high fashion, and are stunning. She offers dresses, capes, tunics, coats, and ponchos.

The Friends of Finnish Handicraft
Meilathi 700250
Helsinki 25, Finland
90 418 530
5-page color brochure, $5 U.S. and
  overseas. MO.
The Friends of Finnish Handicraft was founded in 1879 with the intention of collecting and preserving old and traditional designs and patterns of Finnish textiles. Today they sell all kinds of rijijy tapestries in colorful and beautiful designs.

Gg. Lang sel. Erben
Dorfstrasse 20
P.O. Box 28
8103 Oberammergau Germany
08822 508
183-page catalog, $14 U.S. and overseas.
  MO, PC.
This company is well known for their woodcarvings of saints, madonnas, profane figures, wall plaques and crèches.

Good Shepherd's Store
Ahu Aita Brothers
Bethlehem, Israel
02 742249
16-page brochure, $3 U.S. and overseas. Good Shepherd's Store catalog features religious items carved from mother-of-pearl and olive wood. They have been exporters since 1958 and are well equipped to handle mail order requests.

Handart Embroideries
Room #106 Hing Wai Building
36 Queen's Road Central
Hong Kong
5 235744
10-page brochure, free U.S. and
  overseas. AE, MC, V, MO, PC.

Handart Embroideries sells hand-crocheted tablecloths (72 × 90 in. for $38), and hand-embroidered tablecloths (72 × 90 in., plus eight napkins, for $30 to $50). There are many place mats and napkins to choose from. Jewelry includes cloisonne bracelets ($20), pendants ($10), jade bracelets ($25) and beaded necklaces ($25), and many ivory pendants, bracelets, and earrings. Popular cotton velvet slippers in black, red, or blue.

Iroqrafts
RR7H
Ohsweken Six Nations Reserve
Ontario NOA IMO Canada
(416) 765-4026
50-page catalog, $2 refundable; overseas
  $3 refundable. MO.
Iroqrafts catalog offers many traditional and ceremonial Iroquois crafts and arts from the Six Nations Indian Reservation.

Kainuun Pirtti Oy
Varastokatu 2
87100 Kajaani 10
Finland
986 38800
8 color pages, $5 U.S. and overseas. PC.
There are many beautiful Finnish traditional raanus (tapestries), linen table runners and tablecloths, poppana shopping bags, and aprons available from Kainuun Pirtti Oy.

Puzzleplex, Ltd.
Stubbs Walden
Doncaster, South Yorkshire
DN6 9BY England
0302 700997
4-page brochure, $2 U.S. and overseas.
  MC, MO, PC.
Peter Stocken handcrafts three-dimensional wooden jigsaw puzzles from fine woods: yew, walnut, cherry, holly, rosewood, palisander and olive. Because each puzzle is made by hand from a single piece of wood, each is unique. There are round and oval puzzles as well as special shapes, dragons, and crocodiles. These fine puzzles are acquired as objets d'art, and

special commissions are always welcomed.

Ryijypalvelu
Kasarmikatu 34 A2
Helsinki, Finland
20-page color catalog, $5 U.S. and
    overseas. MO.
Ryijypalvelu offers over 100 beautiful
Finnish wall rugs, ready-made and in
kits. There are both modern and
traditional designs.

Sauna Shop
Mannerheimintie 22–24
Helsinki, Finland
90 602 536
6-page brochure, free U.S. and overseas.
    AE, MC, V.
Located in the heart of Helsinki, the
Sauna Shop sells kitchen towels, large
bath towels, slippers, and bathrobes in
Finnish fabrics and designs. There are
many wooden items—pails and dippers
(for use in your sauna), racks, and door
plates.

Treasure House of Wordly Wares
P.O. Box 127
Calistoga, CA 94515–0127
(707) 942-9976
8-page brochure, self-addressed
    stamped envelope; overseas 70¢. AE,
    MC, V, MO, PC.
Treasure House offers an interesting
collection of folk art, artifacts, dolls,
American Indian goods, and gifts from
around the world. The brochure has
simple line drawings and descriptions;
For $1 they will send you a photo of any
item, for you to have a closer look. There
are brass cricket boxes from India,
menorahs from Israel, and sea life wood
sculptures handcrafted by Seri Indians
of Northern Mexico.

Tropicrafts
P.O. Box 97
Roseau Dominica
West Indies
2747
10-page brochure, free U.S. and
    overseas. MO, PC.
Tropicrafts sells many designs of
handmade straw floor mats (for about

$1.70 per square foot). There are straw
hats ($5), and a large selection of purses
and beach bags with colorful appliqués.
All items are made by local women of
the community.

AMERICAN

Adobe Gallery
413 Romero N.W.
Albuquerque, NM 87104
(505) 243-8485
16-page catalog, $3 U.S. Does not sell
    overseas. AE, MC, V, MO, PC.
Adobe Gallery primarily stocks
authentic handmade pottery, Kachina
dolls, weavings, rugs and baskets, and
original art and graphics by Southwest
Indian artists.

Arrowcraft Shop
P.O. Box 567
Gatlinburg, TN 37738
(615) 436-4604
The Arrowmont school of arts and crafts
was established in 1912 by the Pi Beta
Phi sorority, a national organization for
college women. The Arrowcraft Shop
sells handweaving, regional crafts, and
contemporary gifts. There are delightful
children's wooden and quilted toys,
handwoven place mats, towels and baby
blankets, and the distinctive Pi Beta Phi
tote bags.

Arctic Trading Company
P.O. Box 910
Churchill, Manitoba
ROB OEO, Canada
(204) 675-8804
72-page catalog, $10 U.S. and overseas.
    AE, MC, V, MO, PC.
The Arctic Trading Company's catalog
won the recent Canadian award for Best
Catalog and Mailing Campaign. The
catalog features traditional Canadian
Eskimo and Indian art. There are bright
colored beadwork framed on tanned
hides, and other traditional artforms of
the north—birch bark biting, porcupine
quillwork, and Inuit tapestries.
Beautiful flowers are created from
caribou and moosehair tuftings and sold
in wooden frames. There are many

---

handmade fur parkas and mukluks for men and women.

Artisan's Cooperative
P.O. Box 216
Chadds Ford, PA 19317
(215) 388-1436
24-page color catalog, $2; overseas free. AE, MC, V, MO, PC.
Their cooperative is a non-profit corporation organized to represent rural artisans and provide them with a marketplace, and with marketing assistance to enable them to produce their craftwork. All the items are handmade in rural parts of America and often reflect the traditional hand skills of each region. Their great collection includes handmade quilts from Appalachia and the Deep South, original clothing, handwoven rugs and place mats, handmade pottery, glass, jewelry, metalwork, wood and folk toys. An excellent catalog.

Berea College Student Craft Industries
CPO 2347
Berea, KY 40404
(606) 986-9341
24-page color catalog, free; overseas 2 International Reply Coupons. AE, MC, V, MO, PC.
The lovely crafts in this catalog are made by the full-time students at the four-year Berea College. The profits from these handcrafts are the college's primary form of financial aid, and the meaningful labor brings pride in work well done for the students. There are children's soft toys, candles, ceramics, handwoven shawls, crib and carriage covers, and place mats.

Country Accents
R.D. 2 Box 293
Stockton, NJ 08559
44-page catalog. PC.
Janus and Marie Plaotas make pierced tin panels of their own original designs or adapted from American and European folk art. These panels are suitable for framing, for setting in kitchen cabinets or cupboard doors, or many other creative and decorative applications. They also handmake weather vane silhouette replicas of the early eighteenth and nineteenth centuries.

The Country House
851-D U.S. 41 South
Inverness, FL 32650
(904) 726-4400
10 pages, free U.S. MC, V, MO, PC.
There are over ten gift items offered by the Country House, all handcrafted from Florida pine cones. The Scarecrow ($15.95) is a wreath featuring a raffia-haired scarecrow face, and might be used as a wall decoration to celebrate the autumn holidays.

Dorothy H. Becker
1378 E. 8 St.
Brooklyn, NY 11230
(212) 339-4789
1-page color brochure, free U.S. and overseas. MO, PC.
Linen calendars in eight lovely designs of birds, nature, and cats are priced at $4 each.

Four Winds Trading Post
Rt. 93
St. Ignatius, MT 59865
(406) 745-4336
12-page brochure, $1 U.S. and overseas. MO, PC.
The Four Winds Trading Post catalog features Indian crafts and goods from the Rocky Mountains and prairies of Montana. Moccasins are Indian-made from tanned buckskin and moosehide.

Grey Owl Indian Craft Co.
113–15 Springfield Blvd.
Queens Village, NY 11429
(212) 464-9300
176-page catalog, $1; overseas $2 MC, V, MO, PC.
The Grey Owl catalog features over 4,000 Indian craft items. There are costume kits available for the beginner and advanced sewer. They sell ready-made war bonnets and beaded novelties as well as raw supplies, bulk supplies, and many books and records.

Martha Wetherbee Basketmaker
Star Rt. Box 35
Sanbornton, NH 03269
(603) 286-8927

50-page catalog, $3.50; overseas $4. MO,
PC.

Martha Wetherbee handcrafts baskets
made from the brown ash tree, native
to New England. There are laundry
baskets, market baskets, and baskets for
the garden in exact reproductions of
original Shaker baskets made over 100
years ago. Museums throughout the
country have loaned Martha the Shaker
basket molds, and through her years of
research she has rediscovered many of
the methods and systems used by the
Shakers in basket weaving. Prices range
from about $60 to $600 for a nesting set.

'Ol Salty's Quarterboards
28 J. H. Sears Rd., Box 45
East Dennis, MA 02641
(617) 385-3143
1-page color brochure, free U.S. Does not
sell overseas. MC, V, MO, PC.

Quarterboards were originally
displayed on every sailing vessel,
proudly displaying the ship's name. 'Ol
Salty's creates six by thirty-inch
mahogany quarterboards with your
name (or company name) carved and
painted in your choice of attractive
letter styles. Prices per letter range from
$6 to $18, depending on the size, and
there are fifteen mahogany board
designs to choose from. It's a great gift
idea for a housewarming or business.

Patchwork Sampler
9735 Clayton Rd.
St. Louis, MO 63124
(314) 997-6116
Four catalogs: *Patchwork Sampler
Antique Basket, Quilt, Decoy,* and
Folk Art catalogs, $2 each U.S. MC, V,
PC.

The Patchwork Sampler has selected
some of the best American antique
crafts to present in each of four catalogs.
All items have the same fine quality of
hand workmanship, including children's snow sled, hobby horse, Amish
bakery cupboard, pineapple log cabin
quilt, Maine berry basket, and lots more.

Pipestone Indian Shrine Association
P.O. Box 727
Pipestone National Monument
Pipestone, MN 56164
(507) 825-5463

6-page brochure, free; overseas $1 BD,
MC, V, MO, PC.

The brochure features Indian
handcrafted items made from the
pipestone quarries of Pipestone
National Monument. Pipestone is a
reddish stone that Indians have used to
carve their ceremonial objects for
centuries. Most famous are their pipes,
but other objects—such as the turtle, a
sign of fertility for the Sioux—are also
available.

Prairie Edge
P.O. Box 8303
Rapid City, SD 57701
(605) 341-4525
32-page color catalog, free U.S. and
overseas. AE, MC, V, MO, PC.

Handmade artifacts of the Northern
Plains Indian tribes tell of the culture
it represents. The Hoop of Life is a brass-
inlaid mounted buffalo skull,
representing all the various aspects of
life. There are early war shields, such
as the Turtle Shield, which were
capable of repelling some early musket
balls, and hunt records displayed on elk
hide.

Supernaw's Oklahoma Indian Supply
Box 216
Skiatook, OK 74070
(800) 331-3069
(918) 396-1713
32-page newsalog, $1; overseas free. MC,
V, MO.

Supernaw's Oklahoma Indian Supply is
a major supplier of craft materials and
ready-made items. There are supplies
and materials for making Indian
costumes, including beads (made of
many materials), feathers, and bells.

West Rindge Baskets
Main St.
West Rindge, NH 03461
(603) 899-2231
4-page color brochure, free U.S. and
overseas. PC.

Handwoven New England baskets are
offered in over twenty-five styles, from
small nut baskets to laundry and picnic
hampers. Priced from $9 to $23.

HOBBY

SEE ALSO
- Books
- Collectibles
- Crafts
- Electronics
- Garden
- Tools

GENERAL

Glen L. Marine Designs
9152 Rosecrans
Bellflower, CA 90706
(213) 630-6258
144-page catalog, $2; overseas $4. MC, V, MO, PC.
Glen L. Marine sells plans, patterns, and kits for making full-scale boats, from dinghys to forty-nine foot cruisers.

Kalem Glove Manufacturer
2557 N. Dubonnet Ave.
Rosemead, CA 91770
(213) 280-4305
2-page brochure, free; overseas 50¢. MO.
Kalem manufactures and sells falconer's gear: gloves, falconer's bags, swivels, jesses, leashes, perches, and leather lures.

Occult Digest
Box 2010
Toluca Lake, CA 91602
(213) 763-2992
190-page catalog, free U.S. and overseas. Minimum order $5. MO, PC.
Occult Digest offers over 5,000 occult, metaphysical, and religious items. There are symbolic jewelry, oils, herbs, incense, Tarot, the I Ching, and books on astrology, magic and voodoo.

BEEKEEPING

Glorybee Honey, Inc.
1006 Arrowsmith
Eugene, OR 97402
(800) 228-2008
(503) 485-1649
16-page catalog, free U.S. and overseas. MC, V, MO, PC.
Glorybee is a large supplier of beekeeping supplies: hive bodies, supers, frames, smokers, veils, pollen traps, and extracting equipment. They also sell honey bottled and in bulk (drums and 60-lb. buckets), pollen, pollen tablets, royal jelly, and molasses.

Walter T. Kelley Co.
Clarkson, KY 42726
(502) 242-2012
64-page catalog, free U.S. PC.
Walter T. Kelley is a manufacturer and distributor of beekeeper's supplies. Since 1924.

MODEL AIRPLANES

Cleveland Model & Supply Co.
10303 Detroit Ave.
Cleveland, OH 44102
(216) 961-3600
32-page brochure, $1.50 U.S. and overseas. Minimum order $10. MO, PC.

Cleveland has one of the world's largest lines of plans for proportionately scaled aircraft—of museum quality and capable of flying. They range from miniatures to one-quarter full size, and from static to rubber, both gas-powered and radio-controlled. Since 1919.

Sig Manufacturing Co.
Montezuma, IA 50171
(800) 247-5008
120-page color catalog, $2 U.S. and
  overseas. MC, V, MO, PC.
Sig carries a wide range of model airplane kits, accessories, and supplies. The Kadet Mark II ($50.95) is a very popular trainer for beginners. The Piper J-3 Cub ($59.95 and $174.95) is available in two sizes, one-quarter or one-sixteenth the size of a full-scale aircraft.

MODEL SHIPS

Authentic Shipmodels Amsterdam
Bloemstraat 191
Amsterdam 1016 LA
Netherlands
20 246601
128-page *Ship Model Kit* catalog, 28-
  page color *Completed Ship Model*
  catalog, $8 each U.S. and overseas. AE,
  DC, MC, V, MO.
Authentic Shipmodels offers shipmodels in both finished and kit forms. The fully finished scale models are made from authentic materials of the old sailing vessels, built in limited series or one-of-a-kind models according to authentic museum plans. In addition to ship models they also feature scale models of early inventions, such as the Gutenberg Printing Press, da Vinci inventions, a 1766 Dutch Windmill, and functioning sundials.

Dromedary Ship Modeler's Center
6324 Belton Dr.
El Paso, TX 79912
(915) 584-2445
72-page catalog, $6; overseas $7.
  Minimum order $10. MC, V, MO, PC.
Dromedary sells everything required to build ship models—except talent, says the owner, Dr. Milton Roth. There are

tools, fittings, and kits. Books on the subjects include modeling techniques and ship history.

Model Expo Inc.
23 Just Rd.
Fairfield, NJ 07006
(201) 575-6253
72-page color catalog, $3; overseas free.
  Minimum order $15. AE, MC, V, MO,
  PC.
Model Expo sells historic ship model kits made of hardwoods and brass. There are many pages of tools, fittings, and accessories.

MODEL TRAINS

Cherry's
62 Sheen Rd.
Richmond
Surrey TW9 1UF England
48-page catalog, $4 U.S. and overseas.
  PC.
Cherry's is one of the leading suppliers of live steam models including working steam locomotives, traction engines, stationary engines, and steam plants.

Hambling's
29 Cecil Court
Charing Cross Rd.
London WC2N 4EZ England
01 836 4704
No catalog available. AE, MC, V, MO,
  PC.
Hambling's are specialists in railway modeling. They carry ready-to-run and kit forms of mostly British railroad locomotives and railways. To those interested in British railways, write with your special interests and they will supply you with manufacturers catalogs, if available.

Little Engines
P.O. Box 7
2135 W. 250th St.
Lomita, CA 90717
(213) 326-2434
100-page catalog, free U.S. and overseas.
  MO, PC.
Live steam locomotive kits are available in five scales, from ¼ in. to 1½ in. scale.

The assembly kits have already had the lathe and milling work, drilling, and tapping done. The catalog introduction gives a good description of how much labor and skill is required to complete their kits.

MODELS—GENERAL

America's Hobby Center
146 West 22nd St.
New York, NY 10011–2466
(212) 675-8922
160-page newsalog, $2; overseas free.
    BD, MO, PC.
America's Hobby Center stocks thousands of hobby supplies and parts from virtually every brand-name manufacturer. Established in 1931, America's Hobby Center is nationally and internationally recognized.

Empire Models
P.O. Box 42287
Tucson, AZ 85733
(602) 881-1257
60-page catalog, $2; overseas $3. MC, V, MO, PC.
Empire sells radio-controlled model aircraft, boats (both r/c and static), racing cars, and accessories worldwide. Their prices are discounted 10% to 50% below retail prices. Advertisements state "We speak boats," and they offer building hints, tips, and help by mail or telephone.

Hobby Surplus Sales
P.O. Box 2170 IM
New Britain, CT 06050
(203) 229-9069
128-page newsalog, $1; overseas $2. MC, V, MO, PC.
A great selection of model-building hobby supplies for railroad, planes, and cars.

Northeastern Scale Models, Inc.
99 Cross St.
P.O. Box 425
Methuen, MA 01844
(617) 688-6019
16-page catalog, $1 U.S. and overseas.
    Minimum order $10. MC, V, MO, PC.
Northeastern manufactures scale moldings, strip wood and sheet wood, siding and structural shapes, and hardware for doll house and miniature builders and architects.

Richardi's Auto Models
26 Diamond Spring Rd.
Denville, NJ 07834
(201) 625-0997
16-page catalog, $2 U.S. and overseas.
    AE, BD, MC, V, MO, PC.
Richardi's specializes in miniature car collections, offering a large selection of authentic miniature cars. Many of the models are scaled from the original car blueprints, and are offered in authentic car colors.

Space Age Distributing Co.
421 Fontenelle S.E.
Grand Rapids, MI 49508
(616) 455-3323
4-page brochure. 50¢ U.S. Does not sell overseas. MO, PC.
Space Age offers four sizes of flying model hot air balloons, from six- to twelve-feet-tall and ranging in price from $5.95 to $10.95.

Tower Hobbies, Inc.
P.O. Box 778
Champaign, IL 61820
(800) 637-6050
(800) 252-1113
180-page catalog, $2; overseas surface $3.50, air mail $6.50. MC, V, MO, PC, C.O.D.
Tower stocks between two and three million radio-controlled models, plus parts and accessories from over 180 manufacturers. They also sell their own private label products of model airplanes, boats, cars and radios. Prices are discounted up to 50% below retail price.

WINE AND BEERMAKING

Duane Imports
P.O. Box 433
Hershey, PA 17033
(717) 566-0368

28-page handbook, $1 U.S. and overseas.
  MC, V, MO, PC.
Duane Imports sells some excellent
home-brewing kits, starting at about
$19.95. The handbook contains the
interesting history of brewing and
brewing guidelines. Not only is it a fun
hobby, but it is an inexpensive means
to enjoying good returns: beer made
with Duane's premium Brewing Packs
costs less than twelve cents a bottle.

Milan Home Wine & Beers
57 Spring St.
New York, NY 10012
(212) 226-4780
24-page catalog, $3; overseas $4.
  Minimum order $15. MO, PC.
Milan offers home beer and
winemaking supplies including
flavoring extracts, spices, and herbs, all
blended and packed by them. (They also
have testing facilities for spoiled wines.)

Presque Isle Wine Cellars
9440 Buffalo Rd.
North East, PA 16428
(814) 725-1314

48-page catalog, free U.S. Does not sell
  overseas. MC, V, PC.
Presque Isle sells supplies for the home
winemaker (including many
authorative books on the subject):
chemicals, rinsers, bottles, corks, caps,
hose and tubing, presses, glasses, filters,
and labels.

Semplex of U.S.A.
4805 Lyndale Ave. North
Minneapolis, MN 55430
(612) 522-0500
24-page catalog, free U.S. and overseas.
  MC, V, MO, PC.
Semplex, founded in 1962, ships
worldwide everything needed for the
production of home wine and beer.

The Village Store
999 Main Rd.
Box C51
Westport, MA 02790
(617) 636-2572
14-page brochure, free U.S. and
  overseas. MC, V, MO, PC.
The Village Store offers a complete line
of home-brewing and winemaking
supplies, plus herbs and how-to books.

HOUSEWARES

SEE ALSO
- Antiques
- Art
- Crafts
- Electronics
- Gifts
- Large Department Stores and Mail Order Houses

APPLIANCES

AAA-All Factory
241 Cedar
Abilene, TX 79601
(915) 677-1311
8-page brochure, $1 refundable U.S. MC, V, PC.
AAA-All Factory sells vacuum cleaners, ceiling fans, and floor care products at discounts of up to 75% off retail prices.

Bernie's Discount Center, Inc.
821–6th Ave.
New York, NY 10001
16-page catalog, free U.S. Does not sell overseas. MO, PC.
Bernie's sells the latest products in top name-brand appliances on a cost-plus basis (which is usually wholesale cost plus 15% on appliances, and 10% on electronics). They quickly drop companies and products that indicate quality problems, or poor service and replacement problems. There are kitchen appliances galore, portable TVs, telephone answering systems, irons, electric rollers, electric shavers, and many more.

Bondy Export Co.
40 Canal St.
New York, NY 10002
(212) 925-7785

No catalog available. U.S. and overseas. AE, MC, V, MO, PC.
Bondy does not carry a catalog, but they do carry all major brand cameras, movie and slide projectors, film video recorders, microwave ovens, vacuum cleaners, typewriters, calculators, mixers, food processors, telephone and answering machines, and most small appliances—everything at discounts of 30% to 50% off retail prices. Before you make your next small appliance purchase, write Bondy's (with a model number and self-addressed stamped envelope) for a price quote.

Ecotech, Inc.
P.O. Box 9649 Dept. IM
Washington D.C. 20016
(202) 244-3858
70-page catalog, $1; overseas $2. MC, V, MO, PC.
Ecotech's catalog features many of the alternative energy products available today—active and passive solar systems, wood stoves, furnaces, boilers, and energy conservation appliances and accessories.

European Water Works
711 W. 17th St. Suite G-8
Costa Mesa, CA 92627
(714) 631-7340
Brochure, free U.S. and overseas. MC, V, MO, PC.

European Water Works sells the Swiss Showerbrush ($59.95), which dispenses oils and gels, Biotherm Hydro Massage for your bathtub, and Massator Pedio Foot Massager ($179) to massage your tired feet, calves, legs, or back.

Health Energy & Survival Catalog
P.O. Box 151067
Salt Lake City, UT 84115
(801) 572-1433
40-page newsalog, $1; overseas $5. MC, V, MO, PC.
Name-brand health and survival appliances: wheat grinders, flour mills, juicers, cherry stoners, sausage stuffers, mixers, and food dehydrators are available.

Lehman Hardware & Appliances, Inc.
Box 41
Kidron, OH 44636
(216) 857-5441
80-page catalog, free U.S. Minimum order $5. MC, V, MO, PC.
Lehman's catalog features over 400 non-electric items directed toward serving the Amish and Swiss Mennonite communities. There are grist mills, kerosene lamps, refrigerators run by kerosene, fruit presses and dryers, food mills, carbide lamps, copper wash boilers, windmills, sausage stuffers, cream separators, and much more.

LVT Price Quote Hotline, Inc.
Box 444
Commack, NY 11754
(800) 645-5010
New York (516) 234-8884
4-page brochure, free U.S. Does not sell overseas. MO, PC.
LVT sells over 200 name brands of major appliances, TVs, microwave ovens, video recorders, telephone answering machines, computers, calculators, digital watches, kerosene heaters, cash registers, and air conditioners at discounts of up to 40% off retail prices. Call or write with model number for a price quote. Don't miss the opportunity of calling their toll-free number for a price quote—their prices are terrific.

Sewin' in Vermont
84 Concord Ave.
St. Johnsbury, VT 05819
(800) 451-5124
Vermont (802) 748-3893
Price list, free U.S. Does not sell overseas. MC, V, MO, PC.
There are over fifteen models of sewing machines by Viking, Pfaff, and Singer, at discounts of 20% to 30% off retail prices, available here.

BED AND BATH

Agatha's Cozy Corner
Woodbury Plaza
Portsmouth, NH 03801
(800) 258-0857
36-page color catalog, free U.S. AE, MC, V.
Agatha's offers one of the nicest selections of 100% cotton flannel sheets—not your usual solid colors, but flannel sheets in attractive prints, geometrics, and stripes. There are also lovely percales, cute children's sheets, and Martex towels.

Annie Cole
4 St. Simon's Ave.
London SW15 6DU England
01 788 8786
4-page brochure, $2; overseas free.
    Prices in British pounds. V, MO, PC.
Annie Cole, recently honored in being selected by the Design Council, offers beautiful traditional handknitted bedspreads and cushions both finished and in kits. Some of these designs are 200 years old and are knitted in fine cotton with small needles—tomorrow's heirlooms. Prices range from $207 to $468.

Brook Hill Linens, Inc.
698 Madison Ave.
New York, NY 10021
(212) 688-1113
5-page brochure, free U.S. Does not sell overseas. AE, MO, PC.
Brook Hill features elegant bed linens with elaborate hand embroidery, hand crochet, intricate openwork, and lined lace, at prices that match their elegance.

Cabin Creek Quilts
Box 383
Cabin Creek, WV 25035
(304) 595-3928
24-page catalog, free U.S. and overseas.
  MC, V, MO, PC.
Cabin Creek Quilts is a West Virginian
Cooperative of 100 women. They handmake quilts in ten styles and from a
choice of many fabric swatches. They
also will take custom quilt orders and
match fabric swatches, wallpaper, or
photographs. Prices for these beautiful
quilts range from $200 for a double size
quilt, to $750 for a king size, flower
garden-style quilt.

The Company Store
1205 South Seventh St.
Lacrosse, WI 54601
(800) 356-9367
16-page color catalog, free U.S. and
  overseas. AE, MC, V, MO, PC.
The Company Store is one of the largest
manufacturers of top quality down
products in the country. They offer down
robes by Gloria Vanderbilt, jackets and
coats by Bill Blass, and many styles of
down comforters and pillows. The
prices are at least 50% below normal
retail prices. A queen size, channel-style
down comforter is priced at $99. The
ladies' full-length diagonal quilt coat
(by Bill Blass) is $120.

Cuddledown
106 Main St.
Yarmouth, ME 04096
(207) 846-9781
36-page color catalog. AE, MC, V, MO,
  PC.
Down comforters, comforter covers (in
many fabric choices), flannel sheets,
and pillows are available from
Cuddledown. There are also wool or
cotton underwear for men and women
in many styles.

Down Home Comforts
Box 281
W. Brattleboro, VT 05301
8-page brochure, $1. Does not sell
  overseas. MO, PC.
Em Eisenhauer is the owner of this one-
person company. She makes custom

down comforters of all weights. She will
also make featherbeds (with your choice
of amount of fill and size) at most
reasonable prices.

Down Town
P.O. Box 271
Kenilworth, IL 60043
(800) 942-6345
Illinois (800) 323-6556
2-page brochure, free U.S. and overseas.
  MC, V, MO, PC.
Down Town offers great buys on down-
filled products. Standard-sized pillows
(20 × 36 in.) filled with 100% down are
priced at $30. Full-sized comforters (76
× 86 in.) are priced at $99. They also
feature cozy cotton flannel sheets,
imported from Portugal.

Feathered Friends
2130 First Avenue
Seattle, WA 98121
(206) 622-0974
20-page catalog, $1 U.S. and overseas.
  MC, V, MO, PC.
Feathered Friends specializes in down
comforters, sewn with Egyptian cotton
imported from West Germany, and top
quality goose down. They also carry
bedding accessories with the emphasis
on natural fibers, such as all-cotton
flannel sheets and comforter sheet
covers. Feathered Friends will also
custom-make a comforter cover for you;
just send them two flat sheets and the
dimensions of your comforter. (Prices
range from $20 to $27 for this service.)
For $5 they will send *you* a kit and
pattern, if you prefer to make your own
down comforter cover.

The Goodwin Family Weavers
P.O. Box 314
W. Cornish Rd.
Blowing Rock, NC 28605
(704) 295-3577
6-page some color brochure, $1 U.S. Does
  not mail overseas. MC, V, MO, PC.
The Goodwin Family offers 100% wool
afghans, cotton coverlets or wool-and-
cotton coverlets, place mats and
tablecloths. "Using the same looms that
were powered by waterwheels over a
hundred years ago, the Goodwins have

steadfastly held on to the old ways of weaving, making just one concession to advancing technology—the use of electricity to run the antique looms."

Harris Levy, Inc.
278 Grand St.
New York, NY 10002
(212) 226-3102
No catalog. Minimum order $15. AE, MC, V.
Harris Levy is an importer of high quality bed linens, table linens, blankets, bath towels, comforters, curtains, and kitchen towels. They carry selected domestic brands of sheets, pillow cases, shams, bed ruffles, blanket and duvet covers, all kinds of towels, robes, and shower room accessories. Their inventory is very large and their prices are great—discounts of about 20% to 40% below retail price. Call or write for a price quote.

Homespun Crafts
P.O. Box 1776 Dept. C-4
Blacksburg, SC 29702
(800) 438-7939
(800) 458-3491
22-page color catalog. AE, MC, V, MO.
Cotton thermal blankets, patchwork quilts, bedspreads, curtains, tablecloths, and bath towels are available from Homespun Crafts.

Laura Copenhaver Industries, Inc.
P.O. Box 149
Marion, VA 24354
(703) 783-4663
35-page brochure, $1 U.S. and overseas.
Laura Copenhaver offers beautiful handmade canopies in four styles, all authentic copies of very old designs for tester beds. She also makes woven coverlets in many styles, colors, and antique designs, and custom-made curtains with handmade fringes.

Leron
745 Fifth Ave.
New York, NY 10151
(212) 753-6700
8-page color brochure, free U.S. AE, MC, V, MO, PC.

This small brochure is just a sampling of the exclusive linen collection—everything from boudoir pillows and monogrammed handkerchiefs to embroidered ruffled bed linen sets—that Leron's Fifth Avenue shop has to offer.

Lucy Stewart's Private Stock
Rte. 16 Main St.
North Conway, NH 03860
(800) 227-1617
(800) 772-3545
24-page color catalog, free U.S. AE, DC, C, V, MO, PC.
Lucy Stewart's offers many printed and stripped flannel sheets, cotton bedspreads, and handcrafted quilts.

Moseley's
738 Lincoln Rd.
Miami Beach, FL 33139
22-page color catalog, free U.S. AE, DC, MC, V.
Beautiful monogrammed satin sheets, linen tablecloths, and monogrammed satin-trimmed terry towels by Martex are a few of the fine offerings from Moseley's.

The Original Bed
P.O. Box 23453
Minneapolis, MN 55423
(617) 922-1777
1-page brochure, $2 U.S. and overseas. MC, V, MO, PC.
The Original Bed manufactures futons—cotton-filled, muslin-covered portable mattresses used by the Japanese for thousands of years. Prices range from $75 for a twin size to $105 for a king size. They also offer Obi's slat beds—the hardwood frames to support the futons ($130 to $190).

Pembroke Squares
28 Westmoreland Place
London SW1 England
01 834-9739
6-page brochure, $1; overseas free. MO, PC.
Pembroke Squares makes hand-crocheted bedspreads in twelve traditional Victorian designs. They are beautifully made of pure cotton (in

white or oatmeal shades) and are machine washable. Each is made individually for each customer.

The Quiltery
Box 337 RD4
Boyertown, PA 19512
(215) 845-3129
8-color pages, $1 U.S. and overseas. MO, PC.
The "plain people" (Amish and Mennonite) have always made fine quilts. The Quiltery is a cottage industry (employing forty women), producing handmade quilts in traditional patterns. They specialize in custom colors and sizes to coordinate with or match the client's requirements. Prices range from $275 to $400.

Rubin & Green, Inc.
290 Grand St.
New York, NY 10002
Brochure, free; overseas $1. MC, V, PC.
Sheets, towels, and comforters at discounts of 20% to 50% off retail.

Russell's Quilt Co.
1173 W. Central Ave.
Brea, CA 92621
(213) 691-3005
8-page some color brochure, $1; overseas $2. AE, MC, V, MO, PC.
Russell's specializes in custom-designed prime quality goose down-filled comforters. You may select from their fabrics or supply your own. They make bed pillows, pillow shams, and dust skirts. They also have a comforter recovery and renovation service. Comforter prices range from $99 to $379, depending on size and fill.

St. Patrick's Down
St. Patrick's Mill
Douglas, Cork Ireland
021 931110
14-page some color catalog, free U.S. and overseas. AE, BD, DC, MC, V, MO.
St. Patrick's Down manufactures down comforters and comforter cases in many lovely colors. Various grades of down fill are explained, and the prices are very

reasonable. A log cabin down patchwork quilt is also available.

Scintilla Satin Shop
4802 N. Broadway
Chicago, IL 60640
(800) 621-5138
8-page color catalog. AE, DC, MC, V, MO, PC.
Satin sheets are available in many colors, priced at about $28 for a double sheet and $17.50 for a pair of pillowcases.

The Stevens Catalogue
7 Commercial Dr.
Greenville, SC 29607
(800) 845-8793
32-page color catalog. AE, MC, V, MO, PC.
The Stevens Catalogue is many people's favorite. They offer a terrific selection of bed linens, from contemporary to early American, from easy to muted plaid. There are sheets, pillow cases, shams, and comforters in coordinating colors.

Warm Things, Inc.
180 Paul Dr.
San Rafael, CA 94903
(415) 472-2154
12-page color catalog, free U.S. and overseas. MC, V, MO, PC.
Warm Things makes baffle-constructed down comforters in four choices of fill. There are lovely duvets and down pillows, too.

Wethersfield Station
211 Maple St.
Wethersfield, CT 06109
(800) 852-5000
(203) 529-1330
10 color pages, free U.S. Does not sell overseas. MC, V, MO, PC.
Wethersfield Station offers 100% cotton flannel sheets in some very attractive patterns: tattersall check, box check, stripe, print, and solid. A double size sheet is priced at about $25.95, and a single pillowcase at $6.50.

CHINA AND CRYSTAL

A. B. Shou
4 Ny Ostergade
Copenhagen, Denmark 1101
1 13 80 95
120-page catalog, free U.S. and overseas.
  MO, PC.
A. B. Shou is located in the heart of
Copenhagen and offers the finest crystal
and porcelain from top brand names:
Waterford, Lalique, Lladro, Hummel,
Herend, Royal Copenhagen, and many
others.

Bennington Potters, Inc.
324 County St.
P.O. Box 199
Bennington, VT 05201
(802) 447-7531
10-page color brochure. $1 U.S. and
  overseas. MC, V, MO, PC.
Bennington Potters sells over 240 items
of stoneware, porcelain, and terra cotta
cookware.

Brugskunst
Nytorv 1
Aalborg 9000
Denmark
24-page color catalog, free U.S. and
  overseas. AE, DC, MC, V, MO, PC.
Brugskunst has some of the finest
Danish collector's porcelains and gifts—
at about 40% below normal U.S. retail
prices. There are Bing & Grondahl
porcelain, faience, stoneware, Royal
Copenhagen and Holmegaard
glassware, Danish cutlery, and articles
of wood, brass, pewter, and crystal. (The
very distinctive "Peru" stoneware
pattern, by Bing & Grondahl, is a good
buy at $37 for a five-piece place setting.)

China Pottery
11 Ta Tu Rd.
Peitou Taipei
Taiwan
891 5111
166-page color catalog, $6 U.S. and
  overseas. AE, DC, MC, V, MO, PC.
China Pottery specializes in making
imitation Chinese classical potteries,
porcelain figures, and objets d'art.

Collinsworth
109 N. Broad St.
Lancaster, OH 43132
(800) 228-5000
23-page color catalog. AE, DC, MC, V,
  MO, PC.
Collinsworth specializes in
monogrammed glassware in many
styles—brandy snifters, beer mugs, wine
decanters, and many types of glasses
and ashtrays.

Emerald
Ballingeary
County Cork Ireland
40-page color catalog, free surface, $1
  air mail; overseas $2.
Established in 1963, Emerald has grown
steadily over the years to become the
third largest Irish export mail order
company. They offer lovely china,
porcelain, and crystal. There are Anri
wood sculptures by Ferrandiz,
Waterford crystal, Coalport's character
collections, Royal Worcester China,
Belleek china, and Spode Christmas
Tree earthenware.

Fallers
Mervue
Galway, Ireland
091 61226
52-page color catalog, $1 U.S. and
  overseas. AE, MC, V, MO, PC.
Founded in Galway in 1879, Fallers is
one of the foremost firms carrying
crystal china, silver, porcelain, and
linen. They carry handmade
woodcarvings by Anri, china by Belleek
and Spode, crystal by Tyrone and
Waterford, and porcelains by Lladro,
Royal Doulton, and Goebel.

Frosig
9 Norrebrogade
DK-2200 Copenhagen N
Denmark
32-page color catalog, free surface, $2
  air mail; overseas free. PC.
Frosig offers a large collection of
dinnerware, plates, and figurines by
Royal Copenhagen and Bing &
Grondahl. Since 1889.

Gered
173/174 Piccadilly
London S1V OPD
01 734 7262
12-page color catalog, free U.S. and
  overseas.
Gered sells Wedgwood and Spode china
at prices up to 50% less than U.S. retail
prices (even after postage, insurance,
and duty). They offer a fine selection
(pictured in the catalogs) and an even
larger price list. This is the best source
if you're looking to purchase Wedgwood
or Spode china.

Graham Jackson, Ltd.
48 Beauchamp Place
London SW3 1NX England
01 584 9128
14-page brochure free U.S. and overseas.
  MC, V, MO.
Graham Jackson offers a full line of
English silverplate patterns including
Kings, Harley, Queens, and Old English.

Greater New York Trading Co.
81 Canal St.
New York, NY 10002
(212) 226-2808
No catalog available. MO, PC.
Greater New York Trading Co. does not
carry a catalog, but they do carry all
standard brands of silver, silverplate
(both hollowware and flatware), and
stainless. They also carry standard
brands of china, crystal and major
appliances, and video systems. They sell
at discount prices of 30% to 60% below
retail prices. (That's probably why
they've been in business since 1929.)

John Sinclair
266 Glossop Rd.
Sheffield Yorkshire
S10 2HS England
0742 750333
10-page color brochure, free U.S. and
  overseas. AE, MC, V, MO, PC.
John Sinclair is one of the leading mail
order companies in Britain, specializing
in commemorative and annual plates,
fine china, oven-to-tableware, crystal
stemware, and porcelain figurines.
(Their catalog is mostly
commemorative plates and figurines;

ask for price information on all other
items.)

Joseph Knox, Ltd.
3 & 4 Barronstrand St.
Waterford, Ireland
051 75307
6-page color brochure, free U.S. and
  overseas. AE, DC, MC, V, MO, PC.
Joseph Knox is world famous for mail
ordering Waterford crystal; they stock
the complete line. They also carry
Belleek china, Irish Dresden, Llado
porcelain, Spode, Beohm, Aynsley,
Minton, Royal Crown Derby, Royal
Worcester, Royal Doulton, Wedgwood,
Coalport and other famous chinas.

Limoges-Unic
12 Rue de Paris
Paris 75010 France
24-page color catalog, free U.S. and
  overseas. Minimum order $150.
Limoges-Unic carries fine china by
Limoges, crystal by Baccarat, and silver
by Christofle.

Pottenbakkerij 't Spinnewiel
Zwanenburgwal 62
1011 JG Amsterdam
Netherlands
020 240578
1-page brochure, free U.S. and overseas.
  AE, MO.
Special monogrammed baby cups and
saucers, banks, and commemorative
plates are featured in Pottenbakkerij 't
Spinnewiel's catalog.

Robin Importers
510 Madison Ave.
New York, NY 10022
(212) 753-6475
6-page color brochure, free U.S. Does not
  sell overseas. AE, CB, DC, MC, V, MO,
  PC.
Robin Importers sells most major lines
of crystal, china, stoneware, stainless
flatware, and kitchen cutlery at
discounts of 20% to 60% below retail
prices. (They do produce a catalog, but
if you don't see what you want, write
for a price quote.)

Rogers & Rosenthal, Inc.
105 Canal St.
New York, NY 10002
(212) 925-7557
No Catalog available. MO, PC.
Rogers and Rosenthal will give you a price quote on sterling silver, china, and crystal. Their prices are discounted by 20% to 60% below retail price.

Rowland Ward
P.O. Box 40991
Nairobi, Kenya
25509
8-page color catalog, free U.S. and
    overseas. AE, DC, V, MO, PC.
Rowland Ward is known for their hand-blown crystal, engraved with big game scenes and animals. There are also handpainted china, enamel boxes, and scarves.

Saxkjaers
53 Kobmagergade
1150 Copenhagen Denmark
01 110777
30-page catalog, free U.S. and overseas.
    AE, DC, MC, V, MO, PC.
Saxkjaers is a family-owned business specializing in Bing & Grondahl and Royal Copenhagen porcelain.

CUTLERY

A. G. Russell
1705 Hwy. 71 North
Springdale, AR 72764
(800) 255-9034
24-page newsalog, $1 U.S. and overseas.
    MC, V, MO, PC.
A. G. Russell specializes in hunting knives and made-to-order hunting knives.

Arlene's
303 Dillingham Ave.
Falmouth, MA 02540
(617) 548-6188
32-page color catalog, free U.S. AE, MC,
    V, MO, PC.
Arlene's offers an excellent selection of cutlery including Henckles professional knives, scissors in many shapes and sizes, grooming kits, pocket knives, gardener's shears and many personal grooming aids.

Aycock Knives
2515 Commercial St. N.E.
Salem, OR 97303
(503) 378-0774
6-page brochure, free U.S. PC.
Aycock manufactures distinctive-looking knives with high-carbon stainless steel blades and solid metal handles, and die-cast of lyanite (an aluminum alloy). They are great knives and very reasonably priced; a four-piece knife set is priced at about $12.95.

Hoffritz
515 West 24th St.
New York, NY 10114–0041
(800) 972-1000
40-page color catalog. AE, CB, DC, MC,
    V, MO, PC.
Hoffritz offers an outstanding collection of fine cutlery, grooming sets, pocket knives, shears, scissors, and clippers, as well as many lovely gift items.

Maher & Grosh Cutlery Co.
P.O. Box 120
315 E. Mapel St.
Clyde, OH 43410
(419) 547-0345
10-page brochure, free U.S. Does not sell
    overseas. MO, PC.
Maher & Grosh sell hunting, kitchen, and pocket knives.

Omni Scissors
P.O. Box 2176
Orange, CA 92669
(714) 997-1651
1-page brochure, free U.S. PC.
Omni Scissors are constructed from fine high-carbon steel, producing an extra strong multi-function cutting tool (priced at $31.90, including postage and handling).

Precision Techniques, Inc.
4976 N. E. 122nd
P.O. Box 30151
Portland, OR 97230
(503) 253-7597
2-page color brochure, self-addressed
    stamped envelope; overseas 2
    International Reply Coupons. MO, PC.

Precision Techniques offers Super Snips, 24-karat gold-plated foldable, pocket-size scissors, for $12.95. It's an elegant stocking-stuffer, or a smart accessory for the business person clipping newspaper articles. (There are also chrome styles available for $4.50.) This handy safety scissor can be used by everyone for sewing, crafts, first aid kits, trimming, coupon clipping, camping, fishing, or to keep in the glove box of your car. (Some great gifts don't have to be expensive.)

Taylor Cutlery
P.O. Box 1638
806 E. Center St.
Kingsport, TN 37662
(800) 251-0254
(800) 251-0255
38-page catalog, $2 U.S. Does not sell overseas. Minimum order $25. MO, PC.
Taylor offers an extensive line of pocket knives, sharpening devices, and cases.

FURNITURE

A. Gargiulo & Jannuzzi
Piazza Tasso
Sorrento 80067 Italy
081 8781041
3 color brochures totaling 10 pages, free U.S. and overseas.
The artisans of Gargiulo & Jannuzzi create beautiful inlaid wood furniture pieces. In the museum of Sorrento you will find several beautiful pieces by Gargiulo's grandfather. There are small jewelry boxes, gaming tables, tea carts, chests, and even dining room sets.

American Hotel Register
2775 Shermer Rd.
Northbrook, IL 60062
(800) 323-5686
Illinois (800) 323-4342
1100-page color catalog, $5 U.S. Does not sell overseas. Minimum order $25. MC, V, MO, PC.
American Hotel Register sells institutional furniture and supplies at discounts of 20% to 40% below retail price. You can find excellent buys on soap and toilet paper by the case,

hideabeds, pillows and linens, towels, vacuuming aids, and lawn chairs.

Ashley Furniture Workshops
3A Dawson Place
London S2 4TD England
01 289 1731
16-page color catalog, $1 surface; $3 air mail U.S. and overseas. MO, PC.
Ashley handmakes beautiful classic eighteenth- and nineteenth-century reproduction leather furniture. Each piece is custom-made with your choice of over 100 leathers available. Ashley specializes in hair-stuffed tufted (deep-buttoned) Victorian Chesterfield sofas and wing chairs. A three-seat Chesterfield sofa sells for about $1,995, and a Queen Anne Wing chair about $1,130.

The Biggs Company
105 East Grace St.
Richmond, VA 23219
(804) 644-2891
60-page catalog, $5; overseas $8. MO, PC.
The Biggs company offers a beautiful selection of handmade famous reproduction pieces of furniture. They make exact replicas of many of the pieces found in Independence Hall, Thomas Jefferson's home (Monticello), and Old Sturbridge Village. (Former U.S. presidents have bought furniture reproductions from Biggs.)

Blackwelder's Industries
Hwy 21 N RR12–390
Statesville, NC 28677
(800) 438-0201
(704) 872-4491
120-page color catalog, $5 U.S. and overseas. MO, PC.
Established in 1938, Blackwelder's is located in the heart of the furniture industry in America. The large color catalog gives complete ordering information on top brand names of furniture, at discounts of 40% below retail price. They can also supply manufacturers catalogs free on request. You can get a great buy on furniture from Blackwelder's—they are well-experienced in exporting furniture overseas and can handle any request, from Oriental rugs and pianos to desks,

bedroom and dining sets, and elegant living room furniture. (Their leather catalog ($3) features chairs and couches in many luxurious styles.) Furniture is shipped via North American Van Lines, and Blackwelder's will be happy to supply example freight rates. Don't miss this catalog.

Cannondale's
Cannondale Buildings
Rt. 113 South
PO Drawer 1107
Berlin, MD 21811
(301) 641-4477
6-page color brochure, free U.S. AE, MC, V, MO, PC.
Brass beds and cribs in many styles are available from the Cannondale catalog.

Charles Webb
7 Thorndike St.
Cambridge, MA 02141
(617) 491-2390
28-page catalog, $2 U.S. and overseas. MO, PC.
Charles Webb, designer and woodworker, handcrafts distinctive contemporary-designed oak, walnut, and cherry wood furniture. There are beds, cribs, chests, night tables, armoires, desks, chairs, and tables.

Conran's
145 Hugenot St.
New Rochelle, NY 10801
16-page color catalog, free U.S. AE, CB, DC, MC, V, MO, PC.
There are contemporary designs from Europe (including desk accessories, attaché cases, stereo and video storage units, and chairs) in the colorful catalog from Conran's. The simple line of the Marlowe bed (from Vermont) coordinates with the duvet bed covers available in many great fabric designs.

Country Workshop
95 Rome St.
Newark, NJ 07105
(800) 526-8001
New Jersey (800) 252-0936
12-page catalog, $1; overseas $2. MC, V, MO, PC.
Beds, chests, cabinets, tables, bookcases and cribs, all made in solid maple, oak

or walnut, finished or unfinished, and available in many sizes.

Die Alpenwerkstatten
263 East Gore Creek Dr.
Vail, CO 81657
(303) 476-2294
32-page color catalog. AE, DC, MC, V, PC.
Die Alpenwerkstatten offers German-styled furnishings, handcrafted in a small Alpine village. It's a delightful catalog.

E. J. Evans
P.O. Box 988
Venice, CA 90291
(213) 821-6400
3-page brochure with fabric samples, .50¢ U.S. and overseas.
E. J. Evans is the U.S. distributor for Fagas brand straps, cushions, and covers for Danish chairs and sofas.

Gerald Curry
Pound Hill Rd.
Union, ME 04862
(207) 785-4633
20-page catalog, $2 U.S. and overseas. MO, PC.
Gerald Curry is an artisan who recreates eighteenth-century furniture with the precision of an old master. He works on custom orders, in any wood and any style—as long as his standards of design and construction can be upheld.

Huddle
3416 Wesley St.
Culver City, CA 90230
7 color pages, free U.S. PC.
Colorful and contemporary-designed baby cribs and children's furniture are available from Huddle.

James Roy, Inc.
15 East 32nd St.
New York, NY 10016
(212) 679-2565
3-page price list, free U.S. and overseas. MC, V, MO, PC.
James Roy advertises "one-third off the manufacturers suggested retail price," on all leading brand names of furniture. In fact, send him the furniture price tag

from another store and he will guarantee his discount.

J & D Brauner
11–15 49th Ave.
Long Island City, NY 11101
49-page catalog. AE, MC, V.
J & D Brauner specializes in butcher block furniture: chopping blocks, tables of all kinds, and many styles of chairs.

Leathercrafter
303 E 51 St.
New York, NY 10022
(212) 759-1955
34-page catalog, $1; overseas $2.50. MC, V, MO, PC.
Leathercrafters manufactures leather chairs, sofas, and ottomans in both contemporary and classic designs.

The Lennox Shop
Rt. 179 Box 64
Lambertville, NJ 08530
(609) 397-1880
46-page catalog, $2 U.S. Does not sell overseas. MC, V, MO, PC.
The Lennox Shop makes their own line of pine furniture plus many decorator accessories—sconces, wall shelves, plaques, and pictures.

Lewis of London
72–17 Austin St.
Forest Hills, NY 11375
(212) 544-8003
10-page color catalog, free U.S.
Lewis of London will send you their baby furniture and crib catalog. Most of the cribs are European-crafted and are, as they say, "beautiful things for beautiful babies." There are contemporary-designed cribs (ranging from $325 to $1,250) with coordinating furniture in many special designs.

Murrow Furniture Galleries, Inc.
3514 S. College Rd.
P.O. Box 4337
Wilmington, NC 28406
(919) 799-4010
130-page catalog, $5; overseas $10. MC, V, MO, PC.
Murrow sells all major furniture lines—such as Drexel, Heritage, Henredon, Baker, Karges, Davis, and many others—

at discounts of 30% to 40% below retail prices.

Nite Furniture Co. Inc.
P.O. Box 246
611 S. Green St.
Morganton, NC 28655
(704) 437-1491
Catalogs on major manufacturers. U.S. and overseas. MO, PC.
Nite Furniture carries over 200 furniture lines. For $25, they will send you a large twenty-five pound box of manufacturers catalogs—a heavy idea. The $25 fee will be applied to your first purchase.

Outer Banks Pine Products
Box 9003
Lester, PA 19113
(215) 534-1234
2-page brochure. 50¢ U.S. and overseas. AE, MC, V, MO, PC.
Outer Banks makes solid pine corner cabinets in Early American and Colonial designs, either fully assembled or kit form.

Plexi-Craft
514 West 24th St.
New York, NY 10011
(212) 924-3244
16-page catalog, $2; overseas $3. MC, V, MO, PC.
Plexi-craft offers elegant lucite furniture at discounts of up to 50% below retail prices. There are tables (in many designs), pedestals, shelves, desks, and desk accessories.

Richard B. Zarbin
225 West Hubbard St.
Chicago, IL 60610
(312) 527-1570
No catalog available. MO, PC.
Richard Zarbin carries over 100 national brands of furniture and sells them at discounts of up to 40% below retail price. To receive a price quote, send them a letter with the manufacturer's name and style numbers and as much descriptive information as possible (size, fabric, etc.). This is a wonderful place to shop for furniture at discount prices.

Rose Furniture, Co.
214 S. Elm St.
High Point, NC 27261
(800) 334-1045
(919) 882-6871
4-page brochure, free U.S. and overseas.
  MO, PC.
Rose Furniture sells over 300 furniture
manufacturers' lines at discounts of
30% to 40% below retail price.

School Days Equipment Co.
973 North Main St.
Los Angeles, CA 90012
60-page catalog, free U.S. and overseas.
  MC, V, MO, PC.
School Days stocks over 8,000 business,
school, and church furniture products.
They are an excellent source for used
lockers, children's chairs and desks, and
used office desks and chairs.

The Seraph
P.O. Box 500
Route 20
Sturbridge, MA 01566
(617) 347-2241
10-page catalog with swatch samples,
  free U.S. AE, MC, V, PC.
Wing chairs and country Chippendale
sofas are available in your choice of
almost 100 fabrics from the Seraph.

Shaker Shops West
5 Iverness Way
Iverness, CA 94937
(415) 669-7256
36-page catalog with fabric samples,
  $2.50 U.S. Does not sell overseas. MC,
  V, MO, PC.
Thomas and Barbara Williams
specialize in authentic reproductions of
furniture and home items of classic
Shaker design. There are finished
pieces, ready-to-finish pieces, and kits
available for tables, chairs, baskets,
carriers, benches, rockers, and foot
stools.

Sion-fuk Enterprises
60 Ta-Hsen 3rd Rd.
Kaohsiung Taiwan
07 751-5648
18-page color catalog, $8; overseas free.
  AE, MC, V, MO, PC.

From Sion-fuk there are beautiful
handcarved wooden screens ($280),
rosewood dining room tables and eight
cushioned chairs ($3,400), a beautifully
carved cocktail bar with brass rails
($450), and many styles of inexpensive
rattan furniture.

Sobol House
Richardson Blvd.
Black Mountain, NC
(704) 669-8031
22 catalogs available at prices ranging
  from .50¢ to $5.
Furniture by leading brand names at
discounts of up to 40% below retail
prices. Write with a price quote, or send
for catalog of the manufacturer you're
interested in.

Thos. Moser Cabinet Makers
Four Cobbs Bridge Rd.
New Gloucester, ME 04260
(207) 926-4446
42-page catalog, $3; overseas $5. MC, V,
  MO, PC.
Thos. Moser handcrafts solid hardwood
furniture, built one piece at a time to
customer's order. (Each piece is signed
and dated.) There are a variety of chairs,
tables, and cabinets available in cherry,
walnut, mahogany, ash, and maple.

Vermont Tubbs
Forestdale, VT 05745
(802) 247-3414
8-page color brochure, free U.S. and
  overseas. MC, V, MO, PC.
Vermont Tubbs is a well-known
snowshoe manufacturer that has
diversified into the furniture market.
They produce very attractive bentwood
furniture utilizing rawhide as the
seating medium. There are chairs,
chaises, beds, tables, and even a home
computer desk.

Wayside Interiors, Inc.
PO Box 207
High Point, NC 27261
(800) 334-8153
North Carolina (919) 885-6717
  Brochures available, free on request.
  MO, PC.
Wayside Interiors carries all the top
furniture manufacturers' lines plus

large selections of accessories. Write for a specific manufacturer's current brochure, or price quote on a specific item.

Yesterday's Yankee
Lover's Lane
Lakeville, CT 06039
(203) 435-9539
14-page newsalog, free with stamped self-addressed envelope. Does not sell overseas. MO, PC.
R. W. Alexander runs a one-man craft shop creating custom cabinetry and furniture from the past. There is a North Shore dresser ($485), a seventeenth-century coved cupboard ($380), an eighteenth-century Dutch Settle table ($187), and a 1760 Raleigh Hutch table ($246).

Yield House
Dept. 8400
North Conway, NH 03860
(800) 258-4720
New Hampshire (800) 552-0320
76-page color catalog, free U.S. AE, MC, V, MO, PC.
"Manufacturer of quality pine furniture for over thirty-five years." There are many styles to choose from.

Young's Furniture & Rug Co., Inc.
1706 N. Main St.
P.O. Box 5005
High Point, NC 27262
(919) 883-4111
Manufacturers' brochures sent free on request. U.S. and overseas. MO, PC.
Young's features furniture from over 100 manufacturers. Popular lines include Henredon, Baker, and Drexel. Prices are discounted by 48% below manufacturer's suggested retail price.

HARDWARE

A. Ball Plumbing
1703 W. Burnside
Portland, OR 97209
(503) 228-0026
31-page catalog. MC, V, MO, PC. C.O.D.
A. Ball offers fine plumbing fixtures manufactured in America and West Germany. They offer everything from

high tank toilets and claw-footed tubs to faucets, grab bars, and tubcote. They sell especially to people doing restoration work on historic landmarks and homes, and they are able to make custom fixtures to meet aesthetic needs and plumbing codes.

Ball and Ball
463 W. Lincoln Hwy.
Exton, PA 19341
(215) 365-7330
108-page catalog. Minimum order $10. AE, MC, V, MO, PC.
Ball and Ball features over 1,500 antique brass reproduction hardware items. They include furniture and cabinet hardware, brass door knockers, fireplace accessories, cast iron and brass butt hinges, seventeenth- and eighteenth-century house hardware, and eighteenth-century lighting fixtures.

Bedlam Brass
19–21 Fair Lawn Ave.
Fair Lawn, NJ 07410
(201) 796-7200
4-page color brochure, $1; overseas $2.
Bedlam Brass sells solid brass component parts for bar railings and hand railing systems: foot and hand rails, decorative castings, gates, brackets, mitres, and bends.

Blaine Window Hardware, Inc.
1919 Blaine Dr. Dept I84
Hagerstown, MD 21740
(301) 797-6500
32-page catalog, $2.50; overseas free. MC, V, MO, PC.
Blaine is one of the largest firms specializing in obsolete and hard-to-find replacement hardware for windows, screens, closet doors, patio and storm doors, lockers, and lavatory partitions.

Cape Cod Cupola Co.
78 State Rd.
No. Dartmouth, MA 02747
42-page catalog, free U.S. MC, V, MO, PC.
Cape Cod sells weather vanes and cupolas on which to mount them. (There are many styles of weather vanes, in both copper and cast aluminum.) They also sell Old English chimney letters.

Crawford's Old House Store
301 McCall
Waukesha, WI 53186
(414) 542-0685
34-page catalog, free U.S. MC, V, MO.
Crawford's Old House is a good source
for preservation, restoration, and
renovation supplies. They offer
reproduction hardware, wood moldings,
lighting, plumbing, and many books on
the subject.

Dovetail, Inc.
P.O. Box 1569
Lowell, MA 01853–2769
(617) 454-2944
15-page color catalog, free U.S. MC, V,
    PC.
Dovetail designs, manufactures, and
installs ornamental plaster. The catalog
features over seventy items for ceiling
medallions, cornices, and friezes.

Furniture Revival
580 S.W. Twin Oaks Circle
Corvallis, OR 97333
(503) 754-6323
30-page catalog, $2 U.S. Minimum order
    $15. MC, V, PC.
Furniture and cabinet restoration
hardware (including brass hooks and
pulls, trunk parts, chair cane, and chair
replacement seats) are offered.

Kayne & Son Custom Forged Hardware
Route 4 Box 275A
Candler, NC 28715
(704) 667-8868
24-page *Hand Forged Hardware* catalog,
    12-page *Colonial Hardware* catalog,
    $2 each or $3.50 for both; overseas
    $3.50 each or $6 for both. MO, PC.
Steve Kane will hand-forge hardware to
your specifications. There is no
production run; each order is filled from
customers' descriptions or sketches. The
catalog shows some of Steve's own
designs, which are also available.

Mendicino Millwork
P.O. Box 669
Mendicino, CA 95410
(707) 937-4410
8-page catalog, $2 U.S. and overseas.
    MO, PC.

Mendicino creates Victorian
gingerbread trims including authentic
molding, sawn brackets, corbels, porch
railings, quality doors, sashes, and
shingles. Manufactured in Mendicino
from Northern California Redwood, all
wood is paint grade or better.

Nomaco, Inc.
Hershey Dr.
Ansonia, CT 06401
(203) 735-4628
10-page color catalog, free U.S. and
    overseas. MO, PC.
Nomaco manufactures reproductions,
medallions, and moldings made of
lightweight plastic. They are easily
installed with the adhesives, filler, and
trimming devices available from
Nomaco. Moldings are available in
three styles—crown, cove, and scallop—
and there are rosettes, which range in
size from a two and one-half inch button
(used to decorate doorways or mantels)
to a twenty-seven inch circle (that can
surround a chandelier).

The Renovator's Supply
Renovator's Old Mill
Millers Falls, MA 01349
(413) 659-3152
48-page color catalog, $2 U.S. Does not
    sell overseas. MC, V, MO, PC.
The Renovator's Supply specializes in
Victorian and Colombian hard-to-find
home decorator items. There are door
and cabinet hardware, plumbing,
lighting, wrought iron, curtains,
weathervanes, bathroom accessories,
brass, and porcelain. Although they are
not a discount business, they do offer
items sold directly from their factories—
which can range from 20% to 70% below
retail price.

Restoration Hardware
438 Second St.
Eureka, CA 95501
(707) 443-3152
36-page catalog, $3 refundable U.S. and
    overseas. AE, MC, V, MO, PC.
From Restoration there are fine quality
brass and bronze hardware, bath
fittings, plumbing, lighting, moldings,
millwork, unusual fittings for the
kitchen, woodworking tools, and books.

Scotty's
5300 N. Recker Hwy.
P.O. Box 939
Winter Haven, FL 33882–9990
192-page catalog. MC, V.
Over 10,000 items for building, home repairs, and remodeling—from aluminum siding and ceiling fans, to shelving and windows.

Williamsburg Blacksmiths, Inc.
Buttonshop Rd.
Williamsburg, MA 01096–0778
(413) 268-7341
22-page catalog, $2.50 U.S. Minimum order $25. Does not sell overseas.
Williamsburg offers reproduction wrought-iron hardware, ranging from door latches and strap hinges, to window hardware and large cabinet hardware.

INTERIOR DECORATING

Andy H. Weaver Company
16891 Farmington Rd.
W. Farmington, OH 44491
(216) 548-8799
16-page brochure, free; overseas $1. MC, V, MO, PC.
Weaver's specializes in clocks of all kinds—17-jewel lever pocket watches, wood reproductions, original keywind, and quartz battery-operated clocks. Since 1958.

Artesanos Imports Co., Inc.
P.O. Drawer G
Santa Fe, NM 87501
(505) 983-5563
12-page color catalog, $1 U.S. Does not sell overseas. MC, V, MO, PC.
Artesanos features antique and modern Mexican furniture, and Talavera tile. There is the handsome Equipales furniture of pigskin and cedar whose design dates back to the days of the Mexican Conquest. There are wrought-iron plaza benches, brass lamp bases, and five pages of beautiful Talavera tile designs.

Bachmaier & Klemmer
P.O. Box 2220
Berchtesgaden West Germany D-8240
08652 5079

5-page color brochure, $2; overseas free. Six styles of Black Forest cuckoo clocks with prices ranging from $30 to $195.

Canadiana Curtains
Box 833
205 Dunlop St. East
Barrie, Ontario
LYM 4Y6 Canada
(705) 737-3940
10-page brochure with fabric swatches, free U.S. and overseas. MC, V, MO, PC.
Canadiana is Canada's oldest specialized mail order curtain company. They sew regular lengths and widths as well as fill custom orders.

Country Curtains
At the Red Lion Inn
Stockbridge, MA 01262
(413) 298-3921
56-page color brochure, free U.S. and overseas. MC, V, MO, PC.
Country Curtains are available in cotton muslin and permanent press, many with ruffles and others with fringe or lace trim. There are also bedspreads, canopy covers, pillow shams, kitchen and dining room accessories, and pillows.

Creative Murals
P.O. Box 1437
Covina, CA 91722
70-page catalog, $1 U.S. Does not sell overseas. MO, PC.
Creative Murals offers a selection of over seventy paint-by-number wall mural kits for interior or exterior decoration. Available in many sizes, colors, and designs.

Fernandez Angulo
Toledo, N. 4
Madrid 12 Spain
18-page color *Tapestry* catalog, 40-page color *Bedspread and Carpet* catalog.
Beautiful handwoven bedspreads, rugs, and wall tapestries from Fernandez Angulo of Spain.

Foreign Traders, Inc.
P.O. Box 1967
Santa Fe, NM 87504–1967
(505) 983-6441

28 color pages, $2; overseas 2
   International Reply Coupons. MC, V,
   MO, PC.
Foreign Traders, established in 1927, is
a recognized supplier of fine
handcrafted furniture, folk art, and
designer items from around the world.
They specialize in Spanish Colonial
furniture, tile, and folk art. There are
one-of-a kind old carved doors. Equipale
furniture, chairs from Mexico, lanterns
and chandeliers, mirror frames of brass
and tin, primitive Haitian metal
sculpture, and imported Berber textiles.

Heritage Clock Co.
P.O. Drawer 1577
I-85 & Clark Rd.
Lexington, NC 27293–2577
(704) 956-2113
40-page color catalog, $1; overseas, free.
   Minimum order $5. AE, DC, MC, V,
   MO, PC.
Heritage specializes in all types of
clocks—grandfather, wall, mantel,
cuckoo, carriage, anniversary, kitchen,
and map clocks—at discounts of 30% to
50% below regular retail prices.

Hippo Hall
65 Pimlico Rd.
London SW1 England
7307710
8-page color brochure, $4; overseas free.
   AE, DC, MC, V, MO.
Hippo Hall offers a delightful collection
of coordinated children's furnishings,
fabrics, wallpapers, and bed linens.
There are happy red clowns in
wallpaper-and-duvet coverings, and red
hearts in wallpaper with matching
quilted bedspreads.

Home Organizers
1259 El Camino Real
Menlo Park, CA 94025
(415) 322-8044
32-page color catalog, $1 U.S. and
   overseas. AE, MC, V, MO, PC.
Home organizers sells storage aids,
space-saving products, and home
organizers for closets, kitchen, bath,
home or office. Products include
everything from small desk accessories
to complete kitchen work centers. Since
1980.

Homespun Fabrics and Draperies
10115 Washington Blvd.
Culver City, CA 90230
(213) 839-6984
7-page brochure, $1.25; overseas $2.50.
Homespun makes 100% woven cotton
draperies and fabrics. These natural
fibers are great for people with allergies.

Laura Ashley
55 Triangle Blvd.
Carlstadt, NJ 07072
104-page color Home Furnishings
   catalog, $4 U.S. Does not sell overseas.
   AE, MC, V, MO, PC.
Laura Ashley is renowned for
exquisitely colored prints blended with
florals or geometrics, or for coordinating
print fabrics with decorator wallpapers.
The first section of the catalog shows
wallpaper and fabric collections, all
pictured in lovely room groupings. The
second section shows separately the
available furnishing fabrics, borders,
paints, bed and table linens, rugs, and
lampshades. Don't miss this catalog.

Lovelia Enterprises, Inc.
356 East 41st St.
New York, NY 10017
(212) 490-0930
20-page color catalog, $4 U.S. and
   overseas. MO, PC.
Lovelia is one of the largest American
importers of machine-woven tapestries
from France, Belgium, and Italy. Many
of their tapestries are woven
reproductions of originals that hang in
American and European Museums—in
sizes ten inches to ten feet. The Gobelin
and Aubusson tapestries are woven on
old looms (from the original jacquards)
in either wool or 100% cotton.
"Gathering the Grapes" ($325) is a 35
× 50 in. reproduction of the late
fifteenth-century original which
currently hangs in the Cluny Museum
in Paris.

The Masterworks
165 West 91st St.
New York, NY 10024
6-page color brochure, $2 U.S. Does not
   sell overseas. MO, PC.
The Masterworks creates original
sculptures with an old-world flavor in

a variety of materials, from cold-cast metals to marble-like Carazini and terra cotta stone. Their brochure shows some of their pieces, and they invite custom orders.

Placewares
351 Congress St.
Boston, MA 02210
(617) 451-2074
22-page catalog, $1 U.S. Does not sell
  overseas. AE, MC, V, MO, PC.
Placewares "specializes in places to put things." They stock over 1,400 products to help you get organized. Elfa, the original wire basket storage system from Sweden, is terrific for closets and work spaces. If you're thinking of building, remodeling, or just reorganizing, the owners (Lu and Maynard Lyndon) also provide five terrific planning guides for kitchens, closets, bathrooms, children's and laundry rooms.

Plan-It-Kit, Inc.
Box 429
Westport, CT 06881
(203) 259-8896
4-page brochure, .25¢; overseas 1
  International Reply Coupon. MC, V,
  MO, PC.
These two- and three-dimensional furniture arranging kits allow you to arrange movable miniature furniture on a scaled floor design model. An ingenious planning aid for interior design layouts.

Reinhart Design Center, Inc.
5225 N. Greene St.
Philadelphia, PA 19144
(215) 849-5500
4-page color brochure, .25¢ U.S. and
  overseas. MC, V, MO, PC.
Reinhart features do-it-yourself closet storage kits. Each kit is designed to provide the proper storage for particular garments—for men, women, or children. As children grow or needs change, the closet can easily be rearranged.

Robert Compton, Ltd.
Star Route Box 6
Bristol, VT 05443
(802) 453-3778

8-page brochure, $2; overseas $4. MO,
  PC.
Robert Compton designs impressive stoneware fountains suitable for indoor or outdoor use. There are also some imaginative stoneware aquariums offered.

Robinson's Wallcoverings
225 W. Spring St.
Titusville, PA 16354
(814) 827-1893
6-page color catalog with samples, $1
  U.S. Does not sell overseas. Minimum
  order $10. AE, MC, V, MO, PC.
Robinson's sells wallpaper (with many matching and coordinating fabrics) for curtains, comforters, pillows, shams, and table covers.

Rollerwall
P.O. Box 757
Silver Spring, MD 20901
(301) 649-4422
8-page brochure, free U.S. and overseas.
  MC, V, MO, PC.
Design painting created by textured roller painting is inexpensive and requires no experience. There are 100 rollerwall designs to choose from.

Shibui Wallcoverings
P.O. Box 1638
Rohmert Park, CA 94928
(800) 824-3030
(707) 526-6170
4-page color brochure.
Many Designer wallpapers—including jute fibers, grasscloth, foliage, genuine cork, textured weaves, rush cloth and bamboo-design linen—are featured in Shibui Wallcoverings catalog.

Svenskt Tenn
Strandvagen 5A
114 51 Stockholm
Sweden
08 63 52 10
6-page color brochure, $1 U.S. and
  overseas. Minimum order $25. AE, BD,
  DC, MC, V.
Svenskt Tenn is one of the most exclusive shops in Scandinavia for interior decoration and gift items. The catalog also includes furniture, lamps, shelves, and fabrics.

Wild Wood Gallery, Inc.
Box 300
4001 South Salina St.
Syracuse, NY 13205
(315) 469-5078
32-page color catalog, $1 U.S. Does not
    sell overseas. AE, MC, V, MO, PC.
Wild Wood carries inexpensive home
decorator accessories, especially wall
plaques, pictures, and ornaments.

KITCHEN

Ad Hoc Softwares
410 West Broadway at Spring
New York, NY 10012
(212) 925-2652
6-page brochure, free U.S. MC, V, MO,
    PC.
Ad Hoc features attractive kitchen
textiles—towels, placemats, linens, and
napkins.

American Barbecue Tradition
18731 Pintail Lane
Gaithersburg, MD 20879
(301) 963-8276
8-page brochure, free U.S. Does not sell
    overseas. MO, PC.
The Smoke N' Pit ($69.99) is a sturdy
heavy metal self-basting outdoor
smoker. There is a larger capacity unit,
and even one electrical model available.

Berarducci Brothers Manufacturing Co.
1900 Fifth Avenue
McKeesport, PA 15132
29-page catalog, free U.S. PC.
Berarducci sells Automatic Dolce
electric Pizzelle Bakers to make those
delicious crispy treats and Altea noodle
machines with many available
attachments. For wine makers, there are
fruit crushers, bottle corkers, cork
stoppers, barrels and kegs, and barrel
faucets.

Brookstone
127 Vose Farm Rd.
Peterborough, NH 03458
(800) 341-2600
48-page color catalog, free U.S. AE, MC,
    V, MO, PC.
Brookstone offers hundreds of some of
the finest gourmet cooking utensils and

kitchen accessories. There are extra
large cooking racks, ice cream bombe
molds, whipped cream makers, twelve-
inch glass pie plates, aged vanilla
extract, Belgian waffle irons, and
croissant cutters. (There are also many
handy items for the TV dinner home.)

The Chef's Catalog
3915 Commercial Ave.
Northbrook, IL 60062
(800) 331-1750
(312) 480-9400
36-page color catalog, free U.S. AE, MC,
    V, MO, PC.
The Chef's catalog cover says
"Professional restaurant equipment for
the home chef." There is Calaphon
cookware, copper pans in many styles,
restaurant syrup dispensers, heavy-
gauge aluminum bake pans, French
Sabatier knives, tempting sauces by
Narsai, and preserves by the Silver
Palate.

Clothcrafters, Inc.
P.O. Box 176
Elkhart Lake, WI 53020
(414) 876-2112
4-page brochure, free U.S. and overseas.
    MC, V, MO, PC.
Clothcrafters is a small company which
began as a manufacturer of press cloths
for Wisconsin cheesemakers in 1936.
They now offer a mail order line of
quality cloth products for the kitchen
and home: chef's aprons ($6), chef's hats
($6.50), cotton dish towels (three for
$4.50), napkins, table cloths, and
cheesecloth salad and jelly bags.

Colonial Gardens Kitchen
270 West Merrick Rd.
Valley Stream, NY 11582
(800) 228-5656
Nebraska (800) 642-8777
110-page color catalog, free U.S. AE, MC,
    V, PC.
Hundreds of terrific and inexpensive
kitchen and home accessories for
making cooking and entertaining easier.

Community Kitchens
P.O. Box 3778
Baton Rouge, LA 70821–3778
(800) 535-9901

48-page color catalog, $1 U.S. Does not sell overseas. AE, MC, V, MO, PC.
Community Kitchens sells many types of ground coffee and coffee beans. Especially nice are all the great accessories they offer—home grinders, Bee House ceramic canisters, coffeemakers, and many styles of thermal carafes, (including the elegant Alfi Thermal carafe, $95, of polished chrome.)

Copco
2240 West 75th St.
Woodridge, IL 60517
(312) 963-7100
10-page color brochure, free U.S. and overseas. MC, V.
Copco offers fashion kitchenware, including handsomely designed porcelain-enameled teakettles ($29.99), Bistro coffeemakers from Europe ($14.99 to $29.99), and Copco iron cookware.

Coppershop
48 Neal St.
London SC2H 9PA England
836 2986
32-page catalog, $5; overseas free. MO, PC.
There is a complete line of solid copper cooking utensils and decorative household objects. All items are solid copper, not plated. This is a great catalog.

The Countryside General Store
103 North Monroe St.
Waterloo, WI 53594
(414) 478-2115
62-page newsalog, free U.S. MC, V, MO, PC. C.O.D.
The Countryside General Store features old-fashioned merchandise still popular today: Salad Maid Food & Vegetable Cutter ($36.95), cherry pitters, hand corn-shellers, steamers, strainers, juicers, and much more.

Crate & Barrel
190 Northfield Rd.
Northfield, IL 60093
(312) 466-9300
32-page color catalog, $2 U.S. Does not sell overseas.

Crate & Barrel is an exciting catalog of contemporary cookware, glassware, tableware, bedding, fashions, and contemporary home furnishing accessories. Most of the items are brightly colored imports from Europe. There are red-and-white striped French deck chairs, insulated beverage coolers, ingenious levered bottle stoppers, bright picnic tableware, and practical terra cotta patio lights (scented with citronella to discourage unwanted flying guests).

Cross Imports
P.O. Box 128
Newton Highlands, MA 02161
46-page newsalog, AE, MC, V, MO, PC.
Imported cookware and kitchen utensils from around the world.

David Mellor
4 Sloane Square
London SW1W 8EE England
01 730 4259
100-page catalog, $2.30 surface; $4.42 air mail; overseas free. MO, PC.
David Mellor's collection of professional-quality kitchen equipment is probably the best in England. He has chosen the very best of each kind of equipment to add to his line. They emphasize handmade products from small craft workshops throughout Britain, including functional pottery, woodenware, and basketware. A wonderful catalog—fun to read.

E. Dehillerin
18 and 20 Rue Coquilliere
Paris 75001 France
236 5313
12-page (some color) catalog.
An excellent source of quality French cookware, including copper cookware, bakeware, tableware, choppers, grinders, pasta machines, molds, and cutlery, to name a few.

Epicure
65 E. Southwater
Chicago, IL 60601
(312) 977-3740
32-page color catalog, free U.S. Does not sell overseas. AE, MC, V, MO, PC.

Over 160 great utensils and accessories for cooking, serving, and entertaining.

Figi's
630 Central Ave.
Marshfield, WI 54449
(715) 387-1771
68-page color catalog, free U.S. Does not sell overseas. AE, MC, V, MO, PC.
Figi's offers quality gourmet cookware, from the smallest practical kitchen gadgets to functional butcher block work islands. They feature cookware, bakeware, appliances, serving pieces, and kitchen utensils.

Holland Handicrafts
211 El Cajon Ave.
P.O. Box 792
Davis, CA 95616
(916) 756-3023
2-page brochure, $1 U.S. Does not sell overseas. Minimum order $10. MO, PC.
Adrienne Trouw offers decorative molds for chocolate, butter, candies, and cookies. Imported from Holland, there are many delightful shapes to mold from: an intricately detailed St. Nicholas, an adorable Teddy Bear, a bunny rabbit, and many others. Prices range from $5 to $15.

Judy's Specialties
317 N. Second St.
Lompoc, CA 93436
(805) 735-1777
8 pages, $1 U.S. and overseas. MC, V, MO, PC.
Judy's specializes in candy making supplies—molds, hard candy flavorings, pastel coatings, tartlet tins, candy boxes, and labels.

Imoco
P.O. Box 2052
2201 Parkside
Irving, TX 75061
(800) 527-2525
16-page color catalog, free U.S. AE, MX, C, MO, PC.
Imoco sells top-quality housewares at terrific prices. Consider these offerings: A twenty-piece set of French White Corning Wear for 60% below retail price and a Corelle 45-piece Livingware collection for 45% below retail price. They also carry Samsonite luggage, Cannon towels, and stainless steel cookware.

Kartell U.S.A.
P.O. Box 1000 Liberty Hwy.
Easley, SC 29640
(800) 845-2517
South Carolina (803) 859-1236
14-page brochure, free U.S.
Contemporary-designed tableware by Kartell.

Kitchen Bazaar
4455 Connecticut Ave. N.W.
Washington D.C. 20008
(202) 363-4600
32-page catalog, $2; overseas $3. AE, MC, V, MO, PC.
Kitchen Bazaar offers hundreds of useful kitchen items: pans, wooden utensils, knives, spice grinders, Krupp Brewmaster coffeemaker, Chinese bowls and spoons, and soufflé dishes.

Kroin
14 Story St.
Cambridge, MA 02138
(617) 492-4000
8-page color brochure, free U.S. PC.
Kroin offers distinctive European-designed kitchen fixtures, such as a self-rimming basin in ten color choices, with cutting board and draining board accessories.

The Little Old Bread Man
500 Independence Ave. S.E.
Washington, D.C. 20003
(202) 544-6858
4-page brochure, free U.S. and overseas. PC.
Clyde Brooks not only sells great bread pans (for Paris Baguette French Bread and San Francisco Sour Dough bread); he gives you the delicious recipes, too.

Maid of Scandinavia Co.
3244 Raleigh Ave.
Minneapolis, MN 55416
(800) 328-6722
Minnesota (612) 925-9256
240-page (mostly color) catalog, $1 U.S. and overseas.

One of the largest specialty cooking and baking catalogs offers a huge variety of items: cake molds of all shapes, hundreds of cookie cutters (including all 50 United States for 70¢ each), specialty cooking tools and gadgets, electrical kitchen appliances, and a complete line of cake decorating supplies. If you're looking for some extra special cooking utensil or decorating item, you'll probably find it here.

Mehu-Maija Products
Podunk Rd.
Tramansburg, NY 14886
(607) 387-6716
Brochure, free U.S. Does not sell
    overseas. MC, V, MO, PC.
The Mehu-Maiju is a juice-extractor steam cooker.

The Microwave Gallery
P.O. Box 1271
Burnsville, MN 55337
(800) 328-2846
16-page color catalog, MC, V, MO, PC.
Handy kitchen aids for microwave cooking, plus lots of cookbooks.

Patti Deer
5620 Bonnie
San Bernardino, CA 92404
(714) 874-1396
12-page brochure, $1 U.S.; overseas free.
    MO, PC.
Over 100 handmade, heavy metal cookie cutters are featured here. They will also design special cookie cutters to order.

Preston Distributing Company
Lowell, MA 01852
9-page catalog, free U.S. and overseas.
    MC, V, MO.
Cast iron cookware and accessories, including many styles of tea kettles.

Quick Cook, Inc.
439 Central Ave.
Rochester, NY 14605
(800) 334-0854
(716) 546-7663
24-page color catalog, free; overseas $2.
    MC, V, MO, PC.
Quick Cook offers difficult-to-find microwave cooking accessories: micro bacon presses, omelet pans, micro

barbecue grills, and ground beef cookers. There are cooking tips and microwave recipes (Burgundy Meat Balls) throughout the catalog. (This catalog gives hope to those who would like to venture beyond the baked potato.)

R & R Mill Company
45 West 1st North
Smithfield, CT 84335
(801) 563-3333
8-page brochure, free U.S. and overseas.
    AE, DC, MC, V, MO, PC.
R & R Mill specializes in home flour mills, both electric and hand-operated. There are dehydrators, kerosene lamps, canners, and juicers.

The Silo
Upland Rd.
New Milford, CT 06776
(203) 355-0300
24-page catalog, free U.S. and overseas.
    AE, MC, V, MO, PC.
The Silo offers culinary equipment and useful table and cookware gifts. There are handmade (and signed) earthenware dishes, and glass by Priscilla Manning.

Weston Bowl Mill
Main St.
Weston, VT 05161
(802) 824-6219
10-page brochure, 50¢ U.S. Does not sell
    overseas. Minimum order $5. MC, V,
    MO, PC.
Over 100 wooden items, made primarily by Weston Bowl Mill. There are bowls, lazy susans, cutting boards, plates, trays, sconces, spoon racks, shelves, and wall and kitchen accessories and toys.

Williams Sonoma
P.O. Box 7456
San Francisco, CA 94120
(415) 652-1555
64-page color catalog, $1 U.S. Does not
    sell overseas. AE, DC, MC, V, MO, PC.
Williams Sonoma is the favorite cookware catalog among many. They offer the finest in quality kitchenwares, each item tested personally by Chuck Williams, founder of the company. Many items are imported, such as Callebaut bittersweet chocolate from

Belgium, and the rolling cookie cutter from West Germany that creates those all-time favorites, animal cookies. Some items are made exclusively for Williams Sonoma. And if the catalog isn't terrific enough, they always add some tempting new recipes, like Chocolate Cheesecake, Creme Brulee, and Ginger Cake. Don't miss this catalog.

Wilton Enterprises, Inc.
2240 West 75th St.
Woodridge, IL 60517
(312) 963-7100
192-page color catalog, $3.50 U.S. and
    overseas. MC, V.
Wilton's offers over 1,000 varieties of cake decorating and candy making equipment and supplies. There are bags and tips, tools and sets, colors, mixes, cutters, patterns, cake toppings, wedding ornaments, and baking pans. There are many pages of recipes, hints, and decoration ideas that make this one terrific catalog. Good buys on plastic cookie cutters from Hong Kong, a set of 26 alphabet cookie cutters ($6.95), and a numerical set plus mathematical signs ($4.95).

The Wooden Spoon
Route 6
Mahopac, NY 10541
(800) 431-2207
62-page color catalog, $1 U.S. Does not
    sell overseas.
The catalog advertises "cooking tools and gourmet gadgets." They have some unusual items, such as Shish-Ka-Basket ($11.95), which makes grilling tender vegetables simple and serves scoops in three great sizes, from one and one-quarter to two and three-quarters inches. There are lattice pie crust cutters ($3.50), stainless steel mesh colanders, natural scallop shells, and stoneware custard cups.

Zabar's
2245 Broadway
New York, NY 10024
(800) 221-3347
(212) 787-2000
32-page color catalog, free U.S. Does not
    sell overseas. AE, DC, MC, V, MO, PC.

Zabar's is a New York experience few people miss. 35,000 people pass through their doors a week—lines are long. By mail order you can enjoy some of the excitement of Zabar's; they offer some of the best quality kitchenware at low prices. (They aren't "discount," but some of their low prices are hard to beat.) They offer durable Calaphon cookware, the Cremina Olympia Espresso machine ($298), Krupps 10-cup Brewmaster ($52.95), and a great selection of copper pots by Mauviel and Cohr.

LIGHTING

Arcman Corporation
807 Center St.
Throop, PA 18512
(717) 489-6402
16-page (some color) catalog, free U.S.
    and overseas. AE, MC, V, MO, PC.
Arcman sells unique lamps made from old electric watt hour meters and encased in glass domes. When the lamp is turned on the meter gears turn and dials rotate, recording the energy used by the lamp bulb. They are suitable for engraving and would make great gifts.

Authentic Designs, Inc.
The Mill Rd.
W. Ruppert, VT 05776
(802) 394-7713
64-page catalog, $3; overseas free. MO,
    PC.
Authentic Designs sells handcrafted Early American reproduction lighting fixtures. There are about sixty chandeliers and over twenty-five wall lamps to choose from.

The Brass Lantern
353 Franklin St.
Duxbury, MA 02332
(617) 837-2591
12-page catalog, 50¢ U.S. and overseas.
    MO, PC.
The Brass Lantern designs and manufactures original lanterns, and reproduces some of the finest Colonial brass lamps. There are also lanterns for outdoors, swags, indoor table lights, and chandeliers.

Brasslight, Inc.
90 Main St.
Nyack, NY 10960
(914) 353-0567
12-page catalog, $2 refundable U.S. Does
   not sell overseas. PC.
Brasslight features a variety of lamps
at discounts 50% below retail prices.

Designer Collections by Cerbini
P.O. Drawer V Dept IMO
Merrick, NY 11566
8-page color catalog, $1 U.S. Does not sell
   overseas. MO, PC.
There are authentic reproductions of oil
lamps, candle holders, hurricane lamps,
and wall sconces in solid brass and oak.

Elie Eppstein
PO Box 328
Haifa 31-999 Israel
04 87164
6-page color brochure, $1 U.S. and
   overseas. MO, PC.
Elie Eppstein handcrafts simple,
primitive-shaped hanging lamps. Made
of unglazed pottery, their warm earthy
tones and textures are really quite
lovely.

George Kovacs Lighting
24 West 40th St.
New York, NY 10018
(212) 944-9606
56-page catalog, $2 U.S. and overseas.
   MO.
George Kovacs carries well-designed,
contemporary, and highly styled
lighting and home accessories, ranging
from moderate to high priced.

Hans-Agne Jakobbsen
Box 83
S-28500 Markaryd
Sweden
14-page catalog, $1 U.S. and overseas.
   MO.
Beautiful Swedish candleholders,
kerosene lamps, and electrical
chandeliers.

Hayfields
E. Deering Rd.
Deering, NH 03244
(603) 529-2442

4-page color brochure, $1; overseas free.
   PC.
Reproduction antique lamps. There are
also Vermont sap buckets, and milk cans
decorated in early American folk art.

Heritage Lanterns
Sea Meadown Lane
Yarmouth, ME 04096
(207) 846-3911
48-page (some color) brochure, $2;
   overseas $5. MC, V, PC.
Heritage sells chandeliers, sconces, and
ceiling (and hanging) indoor lights.
Outdoor lights include wall, bracket,
ceiling, and post lights. The lamps are
well made of solid brass or copper (and
pewter finish is also available).

King's Chandelier
P.O. Box 667
Eden, NC 27288
(919) 623-6188
96-page catalog, $2; overseas $4. MC, V,
   MO, PC.
King's designs their own crystal
chandeliers using many components
imported from Europe. There are over
100 to choose from, at prices close to (or
below) wholesale prices.

Lundberg Studios
131 Marine View Ave., Box C
Davenport, CA 95017
(408) 423-2532
6-page color brochure, $3 U.S. and
   overseas. AE, MC, V, MO, PC.
Lundberg's collection of Tiffany
reproduction all-glass lamps is
available in ten contemporary designs,
with prices ranging from $295 to $480.

New Stamp Lighting Co.
227 Bay Rd.
North Easton, MA 02356
(617) 238-7071
28-page catalog, $2; overseas $7. AE, MC,
   V, MO, PC.
There are colonial, early American, and
traditional lighting fixtures made from
solid brass and copper, manufactured by
New Stamp Lighting at very reasonable
prices.

Rainbow Art Glass
49 Shark River Rd.
Neptune, NJ 07753
(201) 922-1090
20-page color catalog, $3; overseas, $4.
  AE, MC, V, MO, PC.
Rainbow art sells stained glass lamp
shades, terrariums, suncatchers, and
decorative items for walls and windows.
Clocks and mirrors are available,
finished or in kits.

St. Louis Antique Lighting Co.
25 N. Sarah
St. Louis, MO 63108
(314) 535-2770
12-page color catalog, $3 U.S. Does not
  sell overseas. MC, V, MO, PC.
There are many beautiful solid brass
pieces, handcrafted chandeliers, wall
sconces, and table lamps. St. Louis
Antique Lighting will also do restoration
work, and take custom design orders.

Victorian Reproductions, Inc.
1601 Park Ave. So.
Minneapolis, MN 55404
(612) 338-3636
35-page catalog, $4 U.S. and overseas.
  MC, V, MO, PC.
Victorian Reproductions makes hand-
built antique reproductions of lighting
chandeliers, wall lamps, table lamps,
and floor lamps. They also do lost wax
casting of old ornate brass hardware and
hard-to-find parts. They offer a good
selection of reproduction glass shades—
and can custom build them from your
drawings.

LINEN

F. Rubbrecht
23 Grand-Place
Brussels B-1000
Belgium
02 512 01 18
13-page catalog, $2 U.S. and overseas.
  AE, DC, MC, V, MO.
F. Rubbrecht is a manufacturer of
handmade Belgian lace. There are
placemats, napkins, tablecloths, aprons,
roll covers, guest towels, coasters, tray
cloths, table centers, wedding veils,

christening gowns, baby bibs and
bonnets. They also sell authentic
antique Brussels lace.

Het Kantenhuis
Kalverstraat 124
Amsterdam 1012 PK Holland
020 248618
No catalog available. AE, DC, MC, V,
  MO.
Het Kantenhuis will answer all written
requests and send photographs of
specific items. They offer beautiful
tablecloths in damask, embroidery on
cotton, linen, cross stitch, appliqué with
lace, and all lace in practically any size.
There are also small doilies (round, oval
or rectangular), handmade lace,
guipure, and embroidery.

Pratesi Linens, Inc.
381 Park Ave. South
New York, NY 10016
16-page color catalog, $2 U.S. and
  overseas. AE, MC, V, MO, PC.
Pratesi is an Italian linen firm founded
in 1927. Pratesi linens are generally
acknowledged to be the most exquisite
in the world, and their price reflects this.
One king size silk sheet is priced at $990.
You can imagine that Pratesi's clientele
is most impressive.

Rue de France
77 Thames St.
Newport, RI 02840
8-page brochure, free U.S. PC.
Beautiful French lace place mats,
aprons, tablecloths, bedspreads, and
pillows are available. (Pillows range
from $27 to $30, and tablecloths from
$52 to $72.)

The White House
51/52 New Bond St.
London W1Y OBY England
01 629–3521
16-page color catalog, free U.S. and
  overseas.
When the White House opened in 1906,
their aim was to provide the finest
quality linens for the more discerning
shoppers. The White House became a
world-famous establishment where
nothing but the best will do. The linen

department offers fine damask cloth, cashmere blankets, Egyptian cotton and Irish linen sheets, embroidered towels, and fine linens by D. Porthault.

The Wholesale House
1319 Broadway
Hewlett, NY 11557
(800) 645-3372
56-page color catalog, $1; overseas $2.
   AE, MC, V, MO, PC.
The Wholesale House features top-of-the-line designer linens and bath accessories at discounts of 30% to 65% below retail prices. They are all first quality, and all fully guaranteed.

RUGS AND TILE

Adams & Swett
380 Dorchester Ave.
Boston, MA 02127
(617) 268-8000
Brochure, $1 U.S. Does not sell overseas.
   V, MO, PC.
Adams & Swett offer braided and rag rugs. Since 1856.

Casa Quintao
Rua Ivens 30
Lisboa 1200
Portugal
36 58 37
13-page color catalog, free U.S. and overseas. PC.
Casa Quintao exports Portuguese needlepoint rugs. These handmade wool rugs feature linen canvases, and are embroidered in pastel colors or in a large range of bright shades. There are contemporary designs as well as beautiful replicas of seventeenth- and eighteenth-century designs.

Helen Williams
12643 Hortense St.
Studio City, CA 91604
(213) 761-2756
4-pages, self-addressed stamped envelope; overseas 1 International Reply Coupon.
Helen Williams sells antique Delft tiles that date from 1650 to 1800. Delft tiles are unmistakable in appearance; they are true faience (tin glazed), best known in colors of (Delft) blue and a warm shade of brown. There are popular Dutch scenes of windmills, ships, houses, and tulip fields (sometimes called "Volendammers," because so many of them were made in the town of Vlendam). Prices range from $17 to $50 for each tile.

National Welfare Organization
6 Ipatias St.
Athens, Greece
3222 718
Color catalog, free U.S. and overseas.
   AE, DC, MC, V, MO, PC.
National Welfare Organization offers rugs in the traditional Greek designs, found in Byzantine and modern folk art as well as contemporary designs. Their handknotted carpets, handwoven rugs (kilimis), needlepoint rugs, cushions, bags, and tapestries are available in many sizes and lovely colors.

Peerless Imported Rugs
3028 North Lincoln Ave.
Chicago, IL 60657
(800) 621-6573
32-page color catalog, free U.S. AE, MC, V, MO, PC.
Peerless's catalog displays many beautiful Oriental rugs. There are Savonnerie and Aubusson; Classic Herz; and Isfahan, Bendarah, and Dhurries from India. There are also the soft-colored, bordered Ravinia from Japan, Sumak from Russia, Beshir from Belgium, and Portuguese Berber rugs.

Terra Designs
211 Jockey Hollow Rd.
Bernardsville, NJ 07924
(201) 766-3577
5-page brochure, $1; overseas $2. MO.
Terra Designs makes handcrafted ceramic tiles. They make their own clay, glazes, and molds, and employ local artisans and potters to produce these old-world styled, hand-painted tiles.

Tibetan Refugee Self Help Center
Havelock Villa
65 Ghandi Rd.
Darjeeling, India
2346

40-page catalog. $1.50 U.S. and overseas. AE, V.

Tibetan Handcrafts includes over thirty beautiful carpets made of wool (from Nepal) in deep, rich colors. Their 6 × 3 ft. rugs are priced around $165.

SILVER AND PEWTER

A. Benjamin & Co., Inc.
82 Bowery
New York, NY 10013
(212) 226-6013
No catalog available. MO, PC.
A. Benjamin does not offer a catalog, but will answer all price quote inquiries that include a self-addressed stamped envelope (or IRCs). They offer most of the top brand names in china, crystal, silver, glassware, and jewelry at discounts of 25% to 50% below retail. They also carry old silver patterns and previously discounted china and crystal patterns. Since 1946.

Colonial Casting Co., Inc.
443 So. Colony St.
Meriden, CT 06450
(203) 235-5189
12-page catalog, .50¢ U.S. Does not sell overseas. MO, PC.
Colonial Casting offers handcrafted lead-free pewter with an antique finish. Made in reproduction and original pieces, the practical designs are available in either Colonial or scalloped patterns.

Denise Poole
Timberland House
Horncastle Rd.
Woodhall Spa, Lincolnshire
LN10 6UZ England
52809
12-page brochure, free U.S. and overseas. BD, MO, PC.
Denise Poole sells antique Georgian and English Silver, and Victorian and Sheffield Plate. There are candlesticks, cigarette boxes, tea services, toast racks, tongs, fish slices, and many other lovely pieces.

Hampshire Pewter Company
Rte. 28 RFD 2
Wolfeboro, NH 03894
(603) 569-4944
8-page catalog, $2 U.S. and overseas. MC, V, MO, PC.
"Our pewter is the only American pewter hand-cast and hand-finished in the 'Queen's Metal' pewter alloy, a five-metal combination, including silver, and manufactured as the colonial American pewterers crafted their pieces."

Mappin & Webb, Ltd.
170 Regent St.
London W1R 6BQ England
01 734 0906
24-page color catalog, free U.S. and overseas. AE, DC, MC, V, MO.
Jonathan Mappin established his silver foundry in 1774; today Mappin silver and silverplate is found in the homes of monarchs the world over. They are also renowned jewelers and offer a fine selection of Spode, Royal Daulton, Royal Worcester, and Stuart crystal.

Pilgrim Pewterers
Stow, MA 01775
(617) 568-8838
3-page, $1 U.S. and overseas. MO, PC.
Lydia Holmes produces pewter from original bronze molds used hundreds of years ago. She received her first pewter mold (which had been in the family for five generations) from her grandfather, Ellis Brewster. Lydia actually produces modern original pewters rather than reproductions.

WOODSTOVES

Ceramic Radiant Heat
8 Pleasant Dr.
Lochmere, NH 03252
(800) 343-0991
(603) 524-9663
10-page color brochure, free U.S.

Consolidated Dutchwest
Box 1019
Plymouth, MA 02360
(800) 225-8277

Massachusetts (617) 747-1963
32-page color brochure, free U.S. MC, V,
   MO, PC.

Neway Distributors, Inc.
P.O. Box 187
East Wakefield, NJ 03830
30-page catalog, $1 U.S. Does not sell
   overseas. MC, V, MO, PC.

Vermont Castings, Inc.
Prince St.
Randolf, VT 05060
(802) 728-3111
8-page brochure, free U.S. MC, V, MO,
   PC.

The Warming Trend
Box 1184
Manchester Center, VT 05255
(802) 362-4111
32-page (some color) catalog, $1 U.S.
   Does not sell overseas. MC, V, MO, PC.
The Warming Trend offers many energy
conservation products for windows and
doors; for water, electrical, heating, and
cooling systems; and for stoves and
fireplaces.

JEWELRY

SEE ALSO
- Antiques
- Clothing
- Gifts
- Handcrafts
- Large Department Stores and Mail Order Houses
- Museums

A. G. A. Correa, Co.
P.O. Box 401
Wiscasset, ME 04578
(800) 341-0788
Maine (207) 882-7873
32-page (mostly color) catalog, free U.S. and overseas. AE, MC, V, MO, PC.
A. G. A. Correa designs unique 14- and 18-karat gold nautical jewelry. There is an exact replica of the Plath micrometer drum sextant, complete in every detail including the moving radius arm. Other designs include the Herreshoff anchor, a center-of-effort symbol, a clinometer, and sailing jewelry. Beautiful diamond constellation brooches (starting at $787) are hand-formed in 14-karat gold settings, with the size of each diamond in proportion to the magnitude of its corresponding star.

Cairncross
18 St. John St.
Perth PH1 5SR Scotland
0738 24367
4-page brochure, free U.S. and overseas. AE, MC, V, MO, PC.
Since 1869, jewelers and goldsmiths from Caincross have been fashioning Scottish pearl jewelry. Mussel pearls (harvested from Scottish river beds) range in color from whites, creams, and greys to silky golds and lilacs. Most of the pins and earrings are set in designs of flowers and plants natural to Scotland (ferns, heather, brambles, and bulrushes). Brooch prices range from $80 for a pearl stick pin, to $790 for four pearls in an 18-karat gold lily of the valley setting.

Carl's
86 West Palisade Ave.
Englewood, NJ 07631
(201) 568-5990
14-page color catalog, free U.S. MC, V, MO, PC.
Fine jewelry is listed with both a suggested retail price, and Carl's discount price—about 30% below retail. There are also a few lovely china, silver, and crystal pieces.

Cartwheels
2500 Grubb Rd.
Wilmington, DE 19810
(302) 475-3600
12-page color brochure, $1 refundable U.S. and overseas. AE, DC, MC, V, MO, PC.
Cartwheels specializes in bi-toned gold coin jewelry: necklaces, clips, cufflinks,

and belt buckles. Bi-tone processing is a gold plating process which highlights the intricate detail on the raised relief of authentic silver coins. (Prices range from about $29 to $129.) Gold coins are also available.

The Craft Shop at Molly's Pond
on U.S. 2
Cabot, VT 05647
16-page brochure, $1 U.S. and overseas. MC, V, MO, PC.
Creating silver jewelry designs inspired by the Vermont countryside, Luella Schroeder transforms nature's seeds, wild strawberries, wood knots, and fossil shells into perfectly captured molds and wax casts. Little creatures (such as polliwogs and salamanders) serve as sculptor's models for silver pins. (Prices range from $10 to $75.)

Deepak's Rokjemperl Products
61 10th Khetwadi
Bombay 400004 India
388031
14-page price list, free U.S. and overseas. AE, BD, MO, PC.
Deepak's exports precious and semi-precious stones, cut and polished or in the rough. Cut stones include cabochons, facetted stones, stars, and cat's-eyes. They also export silver filigree ornaments: carvings of bone ivory, sandal-wood, rosewood, and buffalo horn. They pay postage on all orders over $25. (If you're interested in ornaments of carvings, send $1 by registered mail for their illustrated catalog.)

Fortunoff
Direct Sale Division
P.O. Box 1550
681 5th Ave.
New York, NY 10022
24-page color catalog, $2 U.S. and overseas. AE, CB, DC, MC, V, MO, PC.
"Now you can have the experience previously only New Yorkers could have. Stroll through the aisles of our Fifth Avenue store—by browsing through our catalog," says Fortunoff. In business for over 60 years, Fortunoff is known as "the source" for gold jewelry,

diamonds, pearls, precious gems, silver, and gifts. Fortunoff's spokeswoman, Lauren Bacall, says, "You don't need a special occasion to give a gift. Just a very special person."

H & A Enterprises, Inc.
143-19 25th Ave.
Whitestone, NY 11357
(212) 461-4131
28-page color catalog and brochure, $1.75 U.S. and overseas. AE, MC, V, MO, PC.
H & A Enterprises offers hypoallergenic pierced earrings. The 14-karat gold, sterling silver, and gold-filled hypoallergenic earrings are nickel-free. If you get rashes or infections from pierced earrings—and have already tried medicated creams and frequent changings—you might try the H & A Enterprises catalog. The Micro Drain post earrings are made from surgical-grade stainless steel tubing. The hollow post allows air to circulate and soothe the sensitive tissues, says H & A Enterprises. Reasonably priced.

Holland Jewelry, Inc.
11 West Beauregard Ave.
San Angelo, TX 76903
(915) 655-3135
Holland offers handmade sterling silver and 14-karat gold belt buckle sets. There are hand-chased and engraved buckles featuring leaf designs, and trophy buckles engraved with a saddle bronco rider, steer, calf roper, and barrel racer.

International Import Company
PO Box 747
Stone Mountain, GA 30086
(404) 938-0173
56-page catalog, free U.S. and overseas. MO, PC.
International Import Company carries just about every known stone from A to Z. Their inventory of about 100,000 gems includes cut stones only, with qualities varying from poor to excellent. As members of "Who's Who in the Jewelry Industry," they have served museums, large jewelry chains, and conventions with their speaking, writing, and consulting services. (Three pages of

their catalog describe ordering procedures and policy.)

Itracho Watch Co., Ltd.
P.O. Box 289
8027 Zurich Switzerland
01 720 04 97
32-page color catalog, $3 U.S. and overseas. MO, BD.
Inexpensive novelty Itracho Swiss-made watches, Hudson Swiss-made watches, and timepieces designed as pendants, rings, key rings, pens, lighters, and lipsticks are available. There are many wristwatches for men, women, and children to choose from.

James Avery Craftsman
P.O. Box 137
Kerrville, TX 78028
(800) 513-7198
Texas (800) 292-7059
James Avery Craftsman designs, manufactures, and markets their own 14-karat gold and silver jewelry. Started in 1954, over the years their philosophy to execute a design in its simplest form has come to be recognized as, "the Avery look." The collection includes rings, bracelets, earrings, charms, tie tacks, wedding bands, belt buckles, key chains, pins, bookmarks, and paperweights. They make both secular and religious jewelry as well.

Kenya Division, Day and Frick, Inc.
1760 N. Howard St.
Philadelphia, PA 19122
(215) 739-4080
Kenya Gems offers simulated diamonds (from one-half carat to six carats) at about $75 a carat. You can have a Kenya Gem made to rival the finest blue-white diamond, says Kenya Division. Actually, Kenya sells their simulated diamonds by size, not weight. (To match true diamond size, each 1 carat Kenya Gem actually weighs slightly more than a true diamond.) Have one set in a 14-karat gold setting—and worry no more about theft, loss, and high insurance.

Mappin & Webb
170 Regent St.
London W1R 6BQ England
01 734–3801

8-page color brochure. U.S. and overseas.
This company can trace its days back to King George III when, in 1774, Jonathan Mappin first opened his silver workshops. Mappin & Webb (by appointment to the Queen) sells the finest in silver, jewelry, and gifts. Watch brands include Rolex, Omega, Baume Mercier, and their own high quality Mappin & Webb. Mappin & Webb have established branches in fourteen locations including Paris, Cannes, Cologne, Dusseldorf, and Tokyo.

M & I Haberman, Inc.
112 E. 42nd St.
New York, NY 10168
(212) 697-5270
102-page color catalog, $2 U.S. and overseas. MC, V, MO.
Since 1963, M & I Haberman has sold jewelry and name-brand watches at a discount—up to 30% on watches and about 50% on jewelry.

Nacar
Jaime III, 5
Palma de Mallorca—Baleares
Spain
215848
Price list free U.S. and overseas. Prices in $U.S. MO, PC.
Nacar is a well-established firm selling Majorica (simulated) Pearls by mail. There are different kinds of pearls. Fine pearls are accidentally formed inside an oyster: when an irritant penetrates, to protect itself it builds layers over the irritant and (with luck) years later a perfectly shaped and colored pearl is harvested. Cultured pearls are obtained by artificially inserting beads into oysters, grown in watery breeding fields. The value of either type pearl is based on the years of growth, shape, luster, color, and defects. Both fine pearls and cultured pearls are clearly subject to whims of nature. Then there are simulated pearls, entirely created by man. Majorica Pearls are noted for their excellent reproduction qualities of iridescence, resistance, perfection, and beauty. Single strands start at about $38.

N. Bloom & Son
40 Conduit St.
London W1 England
01 629 5060
8-page color brochure, $3 U.S. and
   overseas. AE, DC, MC, V, MO.
Founded in 1912, by Nathan Bloom, this
company sells carefully selected antique
jewelry and silver. There are beautiful
dinner rings: a Victorian amethyst
surrounded by twelve diamonds, an
emerald-cut diamond, and a 61-carat
star sapphire. Many are one-of-a-kind
items, but N. Bloom will always try to
find a particular piece for you. (Maybe
a diamond encrusted dragonfly? Or a
Etruscan-style cameo locket?)

One Is Silver
Plainfield Pike
Greene, RI 02827
(401) 397-9660
16-page color catalog, $5; overseas $6.
   MC, V, MO, PC.
Uniquely designed animal jewelry in 14-
karat gold and sterling silver. Jim
Yesberger designs charms, rings,
buckles, bracelets, and pendants that
are finished and detailed inside and out.
A few pieces (such as a bronze elephant
letter knife) are limited editions,
numbered and signed. Charms are
priced at about $24, with the most
expensive item being a 14-karat gold
twin bird head ring, at $1,200.

Rama Jewelry
987 Silom Rd.
Bangkok Thailand
234–7521
24-page color brochure, free U.S. and
   overseas. Minimum order $50. BD,
   MO.
Established in 1960, Rama is an
exporter of Thai jewelry, carved teak,
and sterling silver. The catalog displays
elegant dinner rings, brooches,
bracelets, and necklaces. Carved
sterling candelabras, picture frames,
enameled boxes, cocktail and tea sets
are also available. Located across from
the Rama Hotel in downtown Bangkok,
Rama Jewelry is well experienced in
mail order requests.

Razzle Dazzle
310 E. Paces Ferry Rd.
Atlanta, GA 30305
(404) 233-6940
8-page (some color) brochure, $2;
   overseas $3. MC, V, MO, PC.
There are hand-painted enamel
earrings (crafted in china and 18-karat
gold vermeil), sterling silver, and
handwrought foundry-cast brass. Each
earring is handpainted and varies
slightly. (Average price is $28.) Very
different and very pretty.

Rennie Ellen Diamonds
15 West 47th St. #401
New York, NY 10036
12-page catalog, $3 U.S. Does not sell
   overseas. MO, PC.
Rennie Ellen, wholesale diamond cutter
and manufacturer, offers quality
diamonds at a 50% savings from retail
stores. Known as "the mayor of 47th
Street" (the congested block of jewelers
in New York City), Rennie works hard
on improving the reputation of the
diamond dealing trade. If you don't see
exactly what you're looking for in the
catalog, write her explaining what you
want (and can afford), and she will be
most helpful. This is one terrific
place to buy diamonds. (She also sells
cubic zirconias under the name of
Kane Enterprises, at about $10 per
carat.)

Robert M. Glass Co.
530 W. 6th St.
Los Angeles, CA 90014
(213) 626-6666
50-page color catalog, price unavailable
   U.S. Does not sell overseas. AE, DC,
   MC, V, MO, PC.
The Vanity Fair catalog displays
beautiful jewelry at discount prices,
advertised at up to 50% below regular
retail. The catalog displays two prices
for each item, the recommended retail
price and the Vanity Fair selling price.
You'll find diamond rings, chains,
earrings, bracelets, pearls, gold coins,
and watches.

The Sharper Image
406 Jackson St.
San Francisco, CA 94111
(800) 344-4444
28-page color catalog, free. AE, CB, DC, MC, V, MO, PC.
One of Sharper Image's newer catalogs is *Gemstones and Jewelry*. It offers some dazzling items. Blue topaz is featured in beautiful show pieces—14-karat gold pendants, and contemporary rings. An original pendant, featuring a 4-carat cabochon amethyst mounted in 14-karat gold and sterling silver, is about $299. There are blue sapphires and diamonds in many unique combinations.

Tiffany & Co.
Fifth Avenue and 57th St.
New York, NY 10022
(800) 526-0649
(800) 452-9146
57-page color catalog, $5 U.S. and overseas. AE, DC, MC, V, PC.
Tiffany is the Rolls-Royce of jewelry stores. The catalog features elegant and expensive contemporary-designed jewelry. If you really are set on impressing someone with a gift from Tiffany's, you can find a few inexpensive items (such as the sterling silver heart locket for $20). A clever gift idea is Tiffany Money, presented in a drawstring pouch: each coin is redeemable for its designated worth in Tiffany products.

T. Seng & Son
511/ 9–10 Phetchaburi Rd.
Bangkok 4, Thailand
282–9334
48-page color catalog, $5 U.S. and overseas. Prices in $U.S. BD.
T. Seng & Son offers gold and silver jewelry, featuring sapphires, rubies and diamonds. There are mostly rings, with some necklaces, bracelets, and pendants, and inexpensively priced.

Zuni Craftsmen Cooperative Association
P.O. Box 426
Zuni, NM 87327
(505) 782-4425
14-page color catalog, free. MC, V.
Beautiful handcrafted sterling silver and turquoise jewelry, designed by the Zuni craftsmen of New Mexico. There are uniquely styled bracelets, necklaces, earrings, and pins—priced from as little as $12, to more than $1,000.

LARGE DEPARTMENT STORES & MAIL ORDER HOUSES

B. Altman & Co.
361 Fifth Ave.
New York, NY 10016
117-page color catalog, free U.S. AE, DC, MC, V.
B. Altman's catalog is stocked with fashions for the whole family, jewelry, and home accessories. There's such a great selection that you could easily complete your entire Christmas shopping list from this catalog alone.

Best Products
P.O. Box 25031
Richmond, VA 23260
(800) 446-9827
(800) 552-9814
500-page catalog, $1 U.S. Does not sell overseas. MC. V.
Best Products offers over 8,000 general merchandise items at discount prices. They operate 120 catalog showrooms in eleven states. The catalog features suggested retail prices and the discounted Best Products price.

Bloomingdale's
155 E. 60th St.
New York, NY 10022
(212) 705-2059
52-page color *fashions* catalog, 60-page color *home/living* catalog, $3 U.S. and

overseas. Minimum order $10. AE, MC, V, MO, PC.
New York's famous Bloomingdale's offers mostly gorgeous clothes for fashion-conscious women and a few clothes for men. Designers include Ann Klein, Henry Grethel, Naomi Kamali, Calvin Klein, Christian Dior, Liz Claiborne, and Evan-Picone to name a few. The exciting *Home Living* catalog features fine china, crystal, silver, gourmet cookware, linens, luggage, and lighting.

Cumberland General Store
Rt. 3
Crossville, TN 38555
(615) 484 8481
156-page catalog, $3.75; overseas free. MC, V, MO, PC.
Cumberland General Store offers "Goods in endless variety for man and beast." They offer hundreds of quality, practical goods. The catalog pictures and artwork are from the turn of the century, in keeping with the products offered: cast iron teakettles, kitchen utensils for "everyday fixin'," cooking ranges, authentic homestead house plans, parlor lamps, home dairy and poultry equipment, and livestock equipment. Have you been searching for

a goat harness or a wash boiler? Cumberland General Store carries them.

Fingerhut Corporation
4400 Baker Rd.
Minnetonka, MN 55343
(612) 932-3100
100-page color catalog, free U.S. Does not sell overseas. MO, PC.
Fingerhut offers clothing and general merchandise in the low to medium price range. Started in 1948, Fingerhut is a large mail order firm fulfilling eight million orders annually.

Garfinkel's
1401 F. St. N.W.
Washington, D.C. 20004
(202) 628-7730
68-page color catalog, $3 U.S. and overseas. AE, MC, V, MO, PC.
Garfinkel's is one of the most prestigious fashion stores in the nation's capital. They have ten retail stores in the District of Columbia, Maryland, and Virginia. They offer high quality clothing, accessories, and gifts for the entire family. Their catalog emphasizes fashions for the career woman—clothing for business and after hours. Dresses range from about $125 to $525.

Gump's
250 Post St.
San Francisco, CA 94108
(415) 982-1616
82-page color catalog, $3 U.S. Does not sell overseas. AE, DC, MC, V, MO, PC.
Gump's has been a shopping tradition in San Francisco for over 120 years. Their selections emphasize Oriental objets d'art of carved jade, jeweled trees with petals of delicate carnelian, rose quartz and amethyst, and leaves of nephrite jade. There are nineteenth-century Imari porcelains, ranging in price from $165 for a small rectangular dish to $6,500 for a nine-inch-tall hibachi. Many items are made exclusively for Gump's including an obelisk in lapis lazuli for about $600.

Harrods
Knightsbridge SW1 7XL England
01 730 1234
Harrods British Publications, Inc.
11–03 46th Ave.
Long Island City, NY 11101
200-page color Christmas catalog, $5.50; overseas $3. AE, DC, V.
Harrods is probably the world's most famous department store. Their Christmas "magazine" is available in mid-October and contains page after page of gorgeous fashions, perfumes, accessories, gourmet foods, luggage, and toys. The Range Rover is a scale model of a real Rover, with battery-powered engine and radio for about $3,360. There are books, including *The Englishwoman's Kitchen* and *Sloane Ranger Diary*. Fashions range from tuxedos and furs to lace-trimmed negligees.

I. Magnin
Union Square
135 Stockton St.
San Francisco, CA 94108
(415) 362-2100
44-page color catalog, $3; overseas $6. AE, DC, MC, V, MO, PC.
I. Magnin has a reputation for the finest quality merchandise. The catalog is an edited version of their twenty-five stores, and predominantly features women's current fashions and accessories. A very elegant catalog from an equally elegant store.

J. C. Penney Co. Inc.
P.O. Box 2056
Milwaukee, WI 53201
1334-page color catalog, $2 refundable U.S. Does not sell overseas. MC, V, MO, PC.
J. C. Penney distributes two large general catalogs each year (spring and fall), fifteen monthly mailers, and a Christmas and Summer catalog. Like many of the large mail order firms, they have developed smaller catalogs directed at specific consumer groups including Big Men's (hard-to-find sizes for big and tall men), Uniforms (suitable for medical personnel, cosmetologists, pharmacists, and waitresses), Rugged

Work Wear (everything from steel-toed shoes to hard hats), and a collection of Fashion Apparel for Women and Half Sizes.

Jemoli
Case Postale
CH–8088 Zurich
Switzerland
630-page color catalog, $2; overseas free.
   Written in French and prices in Swiss francs. MO.
Jemoli is a large Swiss general merchandise catalog, carrying fashions for the whole family, linens, furniture, kitchenware, athletic equipment, and togs. There is an excellent selection of European duvet covers, and bed linens especially for children. Current fashions are designed for a youthful clientele, from sportswear to evening wear. There are some terrific styles in boots for men and women.

Jenners
48 Princes St.
Edinburgh Scotland
031 225 2442
34-page color catalog, free U.S. and
   overseas. AE, DC, MC, V, MO, PC.
Jenners is one of the oldest department stores in the world. It has been owned by the same family since 1838. The impressive late Victorian store-front opens to the grand hall (and beautiful balconies) where there are over 100 departments from which to select fine merchandise. There are china, glass, gifts, perfumery, audio, linens, dress fabrics, and Scottish food products. The catalog mailed annually in October is but a glimpse of all that Jenners is.

Macy's
Catalog Dept.
151 West 34th St.
New York, NY 10001
(212) 695-4400
3 catalogs mailed over a three-month
   period, $3; overseas $10.
Macy's, the nation's most famous department store, sends out a number of catalogs throughout the year. For those of you who have not been to New York, now you can enjoy Macy's right at home.

Marshall Field's
Box 1165
Chicago, IL 60690
(312) 781-1000
75-page color *Christmas* catalog, $3.
From Chicago's old and reputable department store you'll find men's and women's fashions, jewelry, furs, lingerie and glamorous sleepwear, great gift ideas, and much more . . .

Montgomery Ward
Montgomery Ward Plaza
Chicago, IL 60671
(312) 467-6699
914-page color catalog, $3 refundable
   U.S. and overseas. MC, V, MO, PC.
Montgomery Ward began in 1872, when Aaron Montgomery Ward began printing and distributing to farmers a one-page price list of basic goods. The farmers were delighted to buy from a wide selection of goods, at fair prices, direct from Chicago. In twelve years the price list grew to a 200-page catalog featuring thousands of items. Today Montgomery Ward's catalog is much larger, and aimed at the general public. They also feature major appliances which are not always found in mail order catalogs.

Oy Stockman
P.O. Box 220
SF-00101 Helsinki 10 Finland
90 176 181
No catalog available. Manufacturers
   brochures $5. AE, BD, V, MC.
Oy Stockman offers manufacturers brochures on many foreign items: Ski wear by Luhta, cutlery by Fiskar, china by Arabia, glassware by Iitala, and toys by Brio, Aarikka Oy, and Jukka. Once you've selected an item from the brochures, they will send you a price quote including the transportation cost. The best buys are on purchases under $50; Oy Stockman will send it marked "gift," and most parcels sent to the U.S. (under $50) are received duty free.

Quelle International
P.O. Box 999
Oceanside, NY 11572
(516) 536-4357

970-page color catalog, $10 refundable U.S. Mostly written in German and prices in German marks. MO.

Quelle is Europe's largest mail order house (and very similar to Sears or Penneys). Even if you don't read German, the catalog layout is so familiar that finding the product description, size, and color is quite easy. The order form is in English, which helps quite a bit. Better than half the catalog features fashions for the whole family. (There are some darling children's snowsuits and heavy knit tights in many colors and cute prints.) There is also luggage, jewelry, books, housewares, tools and toys. The address listed here is the U.S. representative for Quelle.

Sakowitz
1111 Main St.
P.O. Box 1431
Houston, TX 77251
(800) 231-2332
(800) 392-2071
40-page color catalog, $3 U.S. and overseas. AE, MC, V, MO, PC.

Glamorous Sakowitz goes all out to offer something special in their holiday catalog. You can order a 1,300-foot-long banner with your own message to be flown over the football field for twenty minutes during the Super Bowl, or have a bust carved (of you) in a two-foot block of bittersweet chocolate by the famous Lenotre of France. Sakowitz offers elegant women's clothes, furs, and jewelry. Also, luggage and men's and children's wear.

Saks Fifth Avenue
449 West 14th St.
New York, NY 10014
(800) 221-3505
New York, NY (212) 940-5333
66-page color catalog, free U.S. Does not sell overseas. AE, DC, MO, PC.

The most famous New York department store promotes glamorous women's fashions and accessories in their catalog. There are also some darling children's clothes and handsome menswear.

Sears, Roebuck and Co.
Sears Tower
Chicago, IL 60684
(312) 875-2500
1,400 page color catalog, $2 from your nearest Sears store, and overseas. MO, PC.

Sears started in 1886 (not long after Ward) and remains today the giant in the mail order business. The catalog includes everything to clothe a family; to repair, build, or furnish a home; and to entertain all ages and interests. In addition to the large general catalog, Sears also prints some forty specialty catalogs—many of them free. They include catalogs for special sizes, office equipment, cookware, sporting goods, and home improvement.

Spiegel, Inc.
1515 West 22nd St.
Oak Brook IL 60521
(800) 523-3100
(800) 345-4500
600-page color catalog, $3 U.S. Does not sell overseas. AE, MC, V, MO, PC.

Spiegel was established in 1905 and, in the mid '70s shifted to merchandising better quality brands. Their target market is women in higher income levels who desire better quality merchandise with the convenience of mail order shopping. Fashions by Carole Little, Pierre Cardin, Ellen Tracy, Evan-Picone, Bill Blass, Adrienne, and Evelyn de Jonge. There are also home furnishings, bed and bath accessories, appliances, and home entertainment items. They also produce specialty catalogs priced at $2 each: Home Decor (furniture and accessories from Karastan, Century, Frederick Cooper), Liz Claiborne (terrific women's fashions), For You (fashions for the larger woman), Shoes and Accessories (by Anne Klein, Charles Jourdan, and Gloria Vanderbilt), Here's Lookin' At You Kid (fashions by Esprit Lee and Levi in sizes infant to teens), Norma Kamali, and Proportion: Petites.

Unity Buying Service
P.O. Box 3004
Hicksville, NY 11802
(800) 645-7222
(800) 632-7577
340-page color catalog, $6 U.S. Does not
    sell overseas. MC, V, MO, PC.
Unity Buying Service operates
exclusively as a mail order firm (with
one outlet store in Schaumburg,
Illinois). The general merchandise
items are priced at 10% above factory
prices and include jewelry, home
entertainment, home furnishings, and
hardware.

Wenz
P.O. Box 30
D-75 30 Pforzhiem 100
West Germany
532-page color catalog, $3; overseas free.
    Written mostly in German and prices
    in German marks. MO.
Wenz of Germany carries fashions for
men, women, and (some) children.

There are also fashion accessories,
jewelry and watches, and housewares.

Whole Earth Access
2990 7th St.
Berkeley, CA 94710
(415) 845-3000
280-page catalog, $3; overseas $6. MC, V,
    MO, PC.
Whole Earth Access features many
products for basic living at discounts of
10% to 60% off retail. The items are
functional—general housewares, hand
and power tools, woodstoves, clothing,
and books. Each product features an
excellent description and either a photo
or drawing. Everything is very basic;
clothing consists of overalls for the
whole family, ragg sweaters, and flannel
night shirts. Kitchenware includes
juicers, fruit presses, canners, and
crockery bowls. There are some great
buys here.

MUSEUMS

SEE ALSO
* Art
* Handcrafts

Albright Knox Gallery
The Gallery Shop
1285 Elmwood Ave.
Buffalo, NY 14222
(716) 882-8700
4-page color brochure, 50¢; overseas $1.
  MC, V, MO, PC.
Albright Knox Gallery is the third oldest
public art museum in the U.S. The
Gallery Shop catalog features some of
the museum's contemporary-inspired
products: sculptures, posters, note cards
and artists' quote T-shirts.

Alexandria Lyceum Museum Shop
201 W. Washington St.
Alexandria, VA 22314
(703) 548-1812
2-page brochure, free U.S. Does not sell
  overseas. PC.
Located in the historic Lyceum building
in the George Washington Bicentennial
Center, the Alexandria Lyceum
Museum Shop is currently expanding
their brochure to include a wider
selection of their gifts. They offer a
replica of the collapsible Thomas
Jefferson Ladder ($140). The original
was given to George Mason and is on
display in Gunston Hall. There are other
fine historical reproduction pieces.

*American Museum of Science and
  Energy*
300 Tulane Ave.
Oak Ridge, TN 37830

12-page color catalog, free U.S. PC.
The American Museum features many
gift items—from T-shirts, emblems, and
souvenirs to books, science activity kits,
and posters.

The Art Institute of Chicago
The Museum Store
Michigan Avenue at Adams St.
Chicago, IL 60603
(800) 323-1717
Illinois (800) 942–8881
31-page color catalog, free U.S.
The Art Institute offers jewelry, cards,
and some beautiful reproduction pieces
from the Vatican Museum, including
the ninth-century Cross from the Altar
of the Oratory of San Lorenzo. This
beautiful 24-karat gold electroplate
reproduction is eleven and one-quarter
inches tall ($178).

Birmingham Museum and Art Gallery
Chamberlain Square
Birmingham B3 3DH England
021 235 4051
12-page color catalog, free U.S. and
  overseas. MO.
Birmingham Museum offers top quality
stationery items, featuring
reproductions from the collections of
the Birmingham Art Gallery. The
emphasis is on pre-Raphaelite posters
and William Morris textiles (sold as
notebooks, clipboards, and a lovely four-

drawer cabinet for storing papers). There are replicas and full color reproductions of favorite paintings, such as Warwick Castle, by Canaletto.

British Museum Publications
46 Bloomsbury St.
London WC1B 3QQ England
01 323 1234
24-page (mostly color) catalog, free U.S. and overseas. AE, DC, V, MO, PC.
The British Museum has selected some of the finest treasures of their museum for the production of replicas. There are exquisite jewels, sculptures, ivories, reliefs, and seals. Each piece is stamped (as a guarantee of authenticity) and comes with a descriptive card. One of the most interesting pieces is the only authentic replica available of the famous Lewis Chess set ($144), found on the Isle of Lewis in 1831. The original pieces were made of walrus ivory, of British or Scandinavian origin (from the mid to late twelfth century).

The Brooklyn Museum Gallery Shop
Eastern Parkway
Brooklyn, NY 11238
16-page color brochure, free U.S. MC, V, MOK, PC.
The Brooklyn Museum offers many gift items including Russian nesting dolls ($11.25), tree ornaments from Ecuador ($7), a small hammered brass-and-copper evening bag from India ($38), and many fine porcelains (with decorations adapted from works in the permanent collection of the museum).

Buten Museum
The Buten Museum Shop
246 North Bowman Ave.
Merion, PA 19066
(215) 664-6601
20-page catalog, free U.S. and overseas. MC, V, PC.
Buten offers unique and often hard-to-find Wedgwood ceramics in pink, blue, taupe, lilac jasper, and some out-of-production colors (and imperfect pieces).

Colonial Williamsburg
P.O. Box CH
Williamsburg, VA 23187
(800) 446-9240
(804) 229-1000
40-page color catalog, free U.S. AE, MC, V, MO, PC.
The Colonial Williamsburg Foundation comprises numerous reproduction programs and historical buildings, including the 1773 Public Hospital, the Wallace Decorative Arts Gallery, and the Crafts House. Available in the Colonial Williamsburg catalog are many beautiful reproduction pieces. The eighteenth-century terrestrial telescope ($1,600) is an exact replica of the original (now displayed in the George Wythe House). There is a sterling silver reproduction of a sucker fork ($53), a pewter humidor ($147), brass andirons ($225), and many lovely brass candlesticks.

The Computer Museum Store
300 Congress St.
Boston, MA 02110
(617) 426-7190
16-page color catalog, free U.S. Does not sell overseas. MC, V, MO, PC.
The Computer Museum (located on the Museum Wharf in Boston) is dedicated to preserving the history of information processing, through their exhibits, publications, and archives. Their gift catalog celebrates this historical evolution by offering everything from an abacus to a silicon chip-carrying tie pin. There are one-of-a-kind computer drawings by renowned artist Harold Cohen; men's ties featuring a subtle core planet pattern; and a solid chocolate personal computer for $6.50.

Cooper-Hewitt Museum
2 East 91st St.
New York, NY 10028
6-page brochure, free U.S. MC, V, PC.
The Cooper-Hewitt Museum is the Smithsonian Institution's National Museum of Design. They feature posters, including a cut-away view of the oceanliner Normandie ($2), and books on the design and history of antiques.

Country Music Hall of Fame & Museum
4 Music Square East
Nashville, TN 37203
18-page color catalog, free U.S. AE,
MC, V.
Gift items with the theme of Nashville,
the "Country Music Capital of the
World," are available. There are many
photographs of some of the top vocalists
in country music, posters, bumper
stickers, emblems, and T-shirts. For
those of you who have not sampled
Nashville's chocolate concoctions, "Goo
Goo Clusters" (a chewy combination of
chocolate, marshmallow, caramel, and
peanuts), they go (two boxes of six each)
for $6.25.

Fogg Art Museum
Harvard University
32 Quincy St.
Cambridge, MA 02141
24-page catalog, free U.S. and overseas.
PC.
The Fogg Art Museum is one of three
teaching museums used by Harvard
students. Together with the Busch-
Reisinger and Arthur M. Sackler
Museums, they house one of the finest
university art collections in the world
and represent almost all artistically
important periods and nationalities.
Available by mail order catalog are art
books, note cards, reproductions, and
posters.

Folger Shakespeare Library
201 East Capitol Street SE
Washington, D.C. 20003
(202) 546-2626
48-page color catalog, $2; overseas $3.
Minimum order $15.
The Folger Shakespeare Library catalog
is described as "a renaissance of gifts
and books." The items reflect the Folger
collection: Shakespeare and the
Renaissance period. From elegant to
humorous and from scholarly to
contemporary, there are many areas of
interest. There are ceramic and papier-
maché masks, jester puppet wands,
games on Shakespeare quotations,
Wedgwood plates in jasper ware and
Queens ware, and books on architecture,
literature, history, music, and theater.

Freer Gallery of Art
12th and Jefferson Dr.
Washington D.C. 20560
(202) 357-1432
75-page (some color) catalog, $1;
overseas free. MO, PC.
The Freer Gallery of Art catalog offers
a fine selection of Oriental and Near
Eastern art reproductions. There are
prints, notepaper, jewelry, desk
accessories, and needlework kits—all
made exclusively for the Freer Gallery
of art.

The Huntington Library
1151 Oxford Rd.
San Marion, CA 91108
(213) 792-6141
24-page catalog, $1; overseas free. MO,
PC.
The Huntington Library, Art Gallery
and Botanical Garden catalog features
exclusive facsimiles of historic and
literary works in the Library collections.
Notecards, posters, and slides are also
available.

International Center of Photography
1130 Fifth Avenue
New York, NY 10028
(212) 860-1767
4-page brochure, $1 U.S. and overseas.
AE, MC, V, MO, PC.
The museum shop reflects the
exhibitions of the International Center
of Photography. The catalog features all
new photography published each year,
listings of educational and critical
books, and exhibition catalogs and
posters.

McCalls at Old City Park
1717 Gano St.
Dallas, TX 75215
(214) 421-0901
Many of the items in the museum gift
shop are reminiscent of the
merchandise found in North Central
Texas from about 1840 to 1910. There
are handcrafted wooden dominoes
($31.95), old-fashioned wooden tops
($4.98), sock dolls, and tin
candleholders.

Metropolitan Museum of Art
Fifth Avenue and 82nd St.
New York, NY 10028
(212) 879-5500
116-page color catalog, $1 U.S. and
    overseas. AE, MC, V, MO, PC.
One of the world's greatest museums
offers over 1,000 pieces of silver (ware),
crystals, porcelains, sculptures, jewelry,
scarves, prints, books, and cards—all
reproductions of their fine exhibits.
There are lovely engagement calendars
($6.95), stars ($28.50) and snowflakes
($28.50) for Christmas ornaments, and
reproductions of early nineteenth-
century bottles and flasks.

Metropolitan Opera Gift Collection
1865 Broadway
New York, NY 10023
(800) 223-7585
(212) 582-6713
16-page color catalog, free; overseas $1.
    AE, MC, V, MO, PC.
The Metropolitan Opera Gift catalog
contains opera-related gift items. The
Met Classics Library Series offers a
novelization of each opera, including a
full libretto plus articles and photos.
There are limited edition porcelain
sculptures ($500) honoring immortal
operatic roles (such as the famous
clown, Canio, in Pagliacci). Records of
the great artists ($9.98) are available.
Also, a great album of sixteen Christmas
carols ($9.98) sung by some of the
current Met stars, including Pavarotti,
Price, Sutherland, and Tebaldi.

The Minneapolis Institute of Arts
2400 Third Avenue South
Minneapolis, MN 55404
9-page color catalog, free U.S. PC.
A selection of poster reproductions (of
paintings) and books on art are
available from the Minneapolis
Institute of Arts.

Museum of the American Indian
Broadway at 155th St.
New York, NY 10032
(212) 283-2421
62-page catalog, $2 U.S. and overseas.
    AE, MC, V, MO, PC.
The catalog features many books
devoted to the collection, preservation,
and study of all things concerned with
the anthropology of the native peoples
of the Americas. For their contemporary
crafts, postcards, research reports, and
biographies, there is no catalog
currently available—but inquiries are
welcome.

Museum of the City of New York
Museum Shop
1220 Fifth Ave.
New York, NY 10029
(212) 534-1672
6-page catalog, $1 U.S. and overseas. AE,
    MC, V, MO, PC.
The Museum Shop's selection is
centered on New York City and its
history in the eighteenth and nineteenth
centuries. Many items are reproductions
of antique books, silverware, and
children's toys. The *Country Diary of
an Edwardian Lady* ($20), handcrafted
wooden Jack-In-The-Boxes ($15 to $35),
and a tea tray ($40) detailed with
fashion illustrations from the 1912–1914
Paris Gazette, are a few of their
offerings.

Museum of Fine Arts, Boston
479 Huntington Ave.
Boston, MA 02135
(617) 267-9300
48-page color catalog, $1; overseas $3.
    AE, MC, V, MO, PC.
The Museum of Fine Arts offers jewelry,
fashion accessories, prints, books,
musical instruments, home furnishings,
and educational toys that are
reproductions or adaptations of the
museum's many works of art.
Needlepoint kits for mahogany side
tables ($55), and a five-piece silver plate
tea service ($780, adapted from an
original by Paul Revere) are two lovely
items. There is an illustrated book-and-
record set of Peter and the Wolf, by
Sergei Prokofiev, for about $24.

Museums & Galleries of Great Britain
Gift Selection
24 St. Charles Square
London W10 6EE England
01 960 1650
16-page color catalog, $1; overseas free.
    V, MO, PC.

The gift selection available in this catalog includes replicas of art treasures from major museums and reproductions from art galleries in Great Britain. Stationery, cards, and gift wrap (based on periods of art), and games, puzzles, jewelry reproductions, and books are available. Some of the replicas are from priceless treasures (and hoards) of kings and princes. Some are from tiny museums not on the usual tourist routes. The catalog is a lovely collection in itself.

National Trust for Historic Preservation
Preservation Shops
1600 H. Street NW
Washington D.C. 20006
(202) 673-4200
24-page color catalog, free U.S. and overseas. AE, MC, V, MO, PC.
The National Trust is a non-profit organization that encourages public participation in the saving of America's heritage and cultural resources. They operate house museums, and each has a retail outlet. Most of the catalog products are reproductions and adaptations of pieces in the National Trust's collections, or replicas of actual houses. There are paper houses filled with potpourri ($16.95). Drayton Hall, the only pre-Revolutionary mansion remaining on the historic Ashley River in Charleston, South Carolina, is detailed in miniature on a lovely lacquered box ($685). Also available are memo pads (featuring historical sketches), plates, and key and mug racks.

Nostalgia Station
901 W. Pratt St.
Baltimore, MD 21223
(301) 237-3746
24-page catalog, $1.50 U.S. Does not sell overseas. DC, MC, V, MO, PC.
Nostalgia Station, the catalog produced by the B & O Railroad Museum, offers an extensive collection of railroadiana. From elegant B & O blue china to inelegant T-shirts, and through the *Dinner in the Diner Cookbook,* there are gifts (men's ties) and collectibles for everyone.

Oceanic Society Gifts
Stamford Marine Center
Magee Ave.
Stamford, CT 06902
(203) 327-9786
16-page color catalog, free U.S. and overseas. MC, V, MO, PC.
The Oceanic Society works to protect and preserve marine ecology, from San Francisco Bay to Long Island Sound. The catalog features gifts that encourage appreciation for the marine environment. Wooden Salad Servers ($20) are hand-carved with a duck design on the handle; a cuddly stuffed Puffin ($13) is designed by R. Dakin; and a beautiful calendar ($5.95) features underwater photographs of coral reefs around the world, by Foster Bam.

Old Sturbridge Village
Museum Gift Shop
Sturbridge, MA 01566
(617) 347-9843
8-page color brochure, free U.S. and overseas. AE, MC, V, MO, PC.
Each item in this catalog is a reproduction of selected Old Sturbridge Village museum pieces. Nine-inch solid cast brass candlesticks are an exact copy of a Louis XIV. The Herend candy dish ($42) has a delicate open weave of porcelain strands, with the Rothschild bird painted on the bottom of the dish. And, true to New England history, there is a 1776 Fife-and-Drum set ($7.75) that includes drum, drum sticks (of course), drub sling, plastic fife and a U.S. flag.

Rijksmuseum-Stichting
Hobbemastraat 21
1071 X2 Amsterdam
Netherlands
02 732121
13-page catalog, free U.S. and overseas. The Rijksmuseum- Stichting catalog features reproductions of paintings, applied arts, toys, books, canvas reproductions, and posters of the museum's collections.

Smithsonian Institution
P.O. Box 2456
Washington, D.C. 20013
59-page color catalog, free U.S. AE, MC, V.

The Smithsonian celebrates America, from past to present, with a collection of fine replicas from their museum. There are replicas of Civil War carpet bags (from $110 to $165) and a miniature pewter Parrott cannon and limber ($21). There are even Christmas cards with Santa and his group aboard the Space Shuttle ($7). There are jewelry, needlepoint, furniture art, collectibles, and children's toys.

Winterthur Museum and Gardens
Winterthur, DE 19735
(302) 656-8591

32-page color catalog, $1 U.S. and overseas. AE, DC, MV, C, MO, PC. Winterthur Museum, originally the estate of Henry Francis du Pont, became a museum in 1951. It now boasts the largest American decorative arts collection of fine items made or used in America, from 1650 to 1850. Their excellent reproductions program features a (limited edition) sterling silver Paul Revere tankard ($1,400), and a Chippendale lowboy ($3,800). The selection of furniture, textiles, glass, ceramics, prints, and silver is excellent.

MUSIC

SEE ALSO
- Books
- Electronics: Stereo, Audio and Video

INSTRUMENTS

Alas Accordion Co.
16 W. 19th St.
New York, NY 10011
(212) 675-9089
10-page brochure, free U.S. and
    overseas. MC, V, MO, PC.
Alas Accordion sells and repairs all
types of accordions, concertinas, button
accordions, and electronic accordions.
They carry the top-of-the-line Cordovox,
Farfisa, Accorgan, and Crumar. (Prices
start at $375.)

Appalachian Dulcimers
232 W. Frederick St.
Staunton, VA 24401
(703) 886-1122
4-page brochure, free U.S. and overseas.
    MO, PC.
A. W. Jeffreys sells handcrafted three-
and four-string dulcimers, in either
walnut or cherry wood, with a spruce
soundboard and rosewood tuning pegs.
The Appalachian dulcimer is for the
most part a simple three-string folk
musical instrument with historical
origins in Norway and Sweden. It is the
easiest of all stringed instruments to
learn to play. The first string (melody)
is fretted with the left hand, and the
other strings sound a constant drone
when strummed by the right hand. With
the dulcimer you receive a noter and

pick, and a booklet with instructions for
tuning and playing plus illustrative
songs for each technique.

Berg Musical Instruments
Rt. 1 Box 31
Equality, IL 62934
(618) 276-4824
2-page brochure, free U.S. PC.
Dulcimers handmade by Bill and Lora
Berg.

Bold Strummer
1 Webb Rd.
Westport, CT 06880
(203) 226-8230
72-page catalog, $1 refundable U.S.;
    overseas free. MC, V, MO, PC.
Bold Strummer is one of the leading
guitar book suppliers of both classical
and electric guitar in the U.S. and
overseas. A well-respected firm, their
ads read, "Anything and everything for
and about the guitar."

B. W. M. Benn Harpsichords
4424 Judson Lane
Minneapolis, MN 55435
(612) 922-2280
8-page catalog, .50¢; overseas $1. MO, PC.
B. W. M. Benn custom makes beautifully
detailed harpsichords and music stands.
The harpsichord's elegant cabinet is
made of rich oiled walnut and inlaid
designs, delicate trim moldings, and

burled veneer. The stand may have turned legs, based on historical examples. The finely crafted and carefully finished music stands can be custom-inlaid, incorporating the design of your choice.

Capritaurus Music
P.O. Box 153
Felton, CA 95018
(408) 335-4478
66-page catalog, $4.50 U.S. Does not sell overseas. MC, V, MO, PC.
An interesting catalog of domestic and exotic folk instruments. They carry harps, hammered dulcimers, auto harps, psalteries, hurdy-gurdies, zithers, ukuleles, mandolins, fipple flutes and more, much more. The catalog is nicely written, with photographs of the instruments and descriptions of their specifications and some historical references. The Panpipes look interesting—they come from a family of Andean pipes known as Zamponas of Sikus. Each Panpipe consists of two rows of cane pipes, which can be played by one or two people in a most unusual duet.

Dulcimer Shoppe
P.O. Drawer E
Hwy 9 North
Mountain View, AR 72560
(501) 269-4313
16-page catalog, $1.25 U.S. and overseas. 4-page color brochure, free. MC, V, MO, PC.
The Dulcimer Shoppe offers twelve models of finished mountain dulcimers, all handcrafted of fine black walnut wood. Each dulcimer comes with an instruction book written by the Dulcimer Shoppe craftsmen. They also sell two models of dulcimer kits (both made of walnut wood), for those who wish to make their own. These fine McSpadden dulcimers are given prizes each year in the National Mountain Dulcimer contest.

Elderly Instruments
1100 N. Washington
P.O. Box 14210
Lansing, MI 48901
(517) 372-7890

Three newsalogs; 78-page *Instruments,* 87-page *Records,* 128-page *Music Books,* all free U.S.; overseas $2 each. Minimum order $5. MO, PC.
Elderly's carries a large stock of standard folk instruments, accessories, building materials, instruction and song books, all at 10% to 50% off list price, says the catalog. They carry thousands of small- and big-label hard-to-find record albums in bluegrass, blues, folk, calypso, rockabilly, and international categories.

Fred's Music Shop
140 North Ninth St.
Reading, PA 19601
(215) 373-4545
44-page catalog, free U.S. and overseas. MC, V, MO, PC.
Fred's claims to carry the largest selection of strings for stringed musical instruments to be found anywhere, at up to 40% off retail. If you're looking for strings for unusual instruments, you'll probably have good luck finding it here. There are over eighty different brand names of stringed instruments listed.

Freeport Music
144 Wolf Hill Rd.
Melville, NY 11747
(516) 549-4108
24-page newsalog, $1 U.S. and overseas. Minimum order $10. MC, V, MO, PC.
Name-brand musical merchandise and instruments offered at discounts up to 60% off of manufacturers suggested list price. Brand names include Gibson, Ovation, Guild, Tama Ludwig, Hohner, Ibanez, and many others. Trumpets, saxophones, guitars, amplifiers, keyboards, violins, drums and their accessories are also available. They also carry musical saws, for those so inclined.

Hubbard Harpsichords
144 Moody St.
Waltham, MA 02154
(617) 894-3238
21-page catalog, $1 U.S. and overseas. PC.
In the eighteenth-century carriage house on the grounds of the historic Lyman Estate, workers devote their

efforts entirely to custom crafting historical keyboard instruments based on antique prototypes. They make beautiful harpsichords, clavichords, spinets, virginals, and fortepianos of the sixteenth, seventeenth and eighteenth centuries. Delivery time of custom-built instruments is approximately one year.

Hughes Dulcimer Company
4419 West Colfax
Denver, CO 80204
(303) 572-3753
8-page brochure, free U.S. and overseas. MC, V, MO, PC.
A full line of stringed musical instrument kits including Dulcimers,Hammered Dulcimers, Banjos, Guitars, Lutes, Mandolins, Folk Harps, Lyres, Balalaikas, Kalimbas, and Harpsichords. Kits are available in three kinds of woods: walnut, spruce, and Philippine mahogany. Your assembly time varies—from six to ten hours to construct a small dulcimer, to thirty or forty hours for a guitar. And only common hand tools are needed to assemble the instruments: knife file, plane, coping saw, drill, sandpaper, and paint brush. No special clamps or skills are required (so the brochure states). Basic dulcimer kits start at about $25; for those truly unskilled, there are completed instruments for sale. They're easy to learn to play (the brochure says). You can learn in ten minutes—fifteen minutes if you're left-handed.

International Violin Company, Ltd.
4026 West Belvedere Ave.
Baltimore, MD 21215–5587
(301) 542-3535
56-page catalog, free U.S. and overseas. MO, PC.
International Violin Company offers an extensive variety of stringed instrument bows, cases, accessories, parts, strings, tonewood, and tools—both domestic and imported at a 20% discount price. Violins are available in sizes from 1/8 to 4/4, and half-size cellos through full-size. Bows are available in fiberglass, brazilwood, and pernambuco (including master bows with exquisite sterling silver trimmings). Started in 1933, they are dedicated to serving the needs of the stringed instrument maker, repairer, dealer, player, teacher and student in America and many foreign countries.

Koch Recorder
Haverhill, NH 03765
(603) 989-5620
2-page brochure, free U.S. AE, MO, PC.
William F. Koch, Senior, was the first maker of recorders in America, and now the tradition is carried on by his son, William F. Koch, Jr. The recorders are made from either cherry, maple or cocobolo wood, with English (baroque) fingering. They are available in soprano, alto, and tenor. Prices start at about $31, and include a cleaning swab, fingering chart, instructions for care, and a sturdy box.

Ledford's Musical Instruments
125 Sunset Heights
Winchester, KY 40391
(606) 744-3974
4-page brochure, free U.S. Does not sell overseas. MO, PC.
Ledford's hand crafts dulcimers—the Appalachian Dulcimer, the Sweetheart Dulcimer, and the Dulcitar, all carved from the finest native black walnut. The Sweetheart ("courtin' ") Dulcimer is played with two people facing each other—each with his or her own set of strings. (The story was that the couple needed no chaperone as long as tunes from the dulcimer were heard.) The Dulcitar has a beautiful classic guitar-like tone; it was invented in 1971, by Homer C. Ledford. It was chosen by the Smithsonian Institute as part of its world tour exhibit. The Dulcitar's six nylon strings and five chromatic frets allow you to play in any key, like a classic guitar. The remaining frets are played like the dulcimer, with all six strings tuned in open chord. The Dulcitar is good for accompanying folk singing or other musical instruments. The Dulcitar is $595, and Dulcimers start at $125.

Magnamusic Distributors, Inc.
Rt. 41
Sharon, CT 06069
(203) 364-5431

20-page catalog, $2 U.S. and overseas. PC.

Magnamusic sells an excellent selection of recorders and recorder music for school children and concert musicians. There are fine recorders made by Moeck, Adler, Heinrich, and Zen-on. Sheet music published by Moeck, Baerenreiter, Pelikan Pan, Anfor, Muses Gardin, Marlborough, Consort, Sweet Pipes, and Magnamusic is also available.

Mandolin Brothers
629 Forest Ave.
Staten Island, NY 10310
(212) 981–3226
80-page catalog, free U.S. and overseas. MC, V, MO, PC.

Mandolin Brothers sells the finest vintage guitars, banjos, and mandolins made in America from 1833 to 1969. They are especially well known for offering vintage Gibson and E F Martin instruments. They offer only the finest (new and used) fretted instruments plus modern accessories: multitrack recording equipment, strings, amps, appraisal and repair services, instruction books, electronic tuners and more. The Martin HD-28 guitar, with fiberglass hard shell case, is priced at $1,035. And the popular Stelling handmade banjos (from Spring Valley, California) range from $1,100 to $5,300.

National Educational Music Co.
1181 Rt. 22
PO Box 1130
Mountainside, NJ 07092
(800) 526-4593
New Jersey (201) 232-6700
22-page catalog, free U.S. and overseas. AE, MC, V, MO.

NEMC is the largest distributor of band and orchestra instruments in the U.S. Since 1956, they have sold at discount prices (ranging from 30% to 50% off manufacturers' list prices) brand-name instruments to schools and government agencies both in America and overseas. They have also provided musical instruments over the past few years to military bands in all four branches of the service.

PAIA Electronics
1020 W. Wilshire
Oklahoma City, OK 73116
(405) 843-9626
16-page color catalog, free U.S. and overseas. MC, V, MO, PC.

PAIA sells electronic kits to construct devices for musical special effects. There are a variety of synthesizers, recording studio devices, and guitar amplifiers. You can enjoy substantial savings by constructing your own musical electronic effects.

Player Piano Co.
704 E. Douglas
Wichita, KS 67202
(316) 263–3241
160-page catalog, $3.50 U.S. and overseas. MC, V, MO, PC.

A complete line of materials and accessories for restoration of player pianos, old and new, as well as a complete stock of music rolls at discount prices. Player pianos were popular from 1910 to 1930, when over 2 million were made. Today the interest has revived, and Durrell Armstrong, owner, has contributed towards the preservation of many player pianos. His catalog is an informative guide on repairing player pianos, in addition to providing a mail order source for every replacement part—bellows cloth, piano roll, valve, pouch, and more.

Precision Drum Co.
151 California Rd.
Yorktown Hts. NY 10598
(914) 962-4985
6-page brochure with sample finishes, $1 U.S. and overseas. MO, PC.

Precision Drum Co. sells do-it-yourself kits for modernizing your old drums— by re-covering them with decorative plastic coverings. The plastic is identical to that used by the major drum manufacturers, and is available in pearl, sparkle, satin flame, and wood grains. (Recovering your old drum set with these simple kits costs about one-tenth the price of buying new drums.)

Rhythm Band Inc.
P.O. Box 126
Fort Worth, TX 76101
(817) 335-2561

40-page color catalog, free U.S. and
overseas. MC, V, MO, PC.
This colorful catalog displays an
extensive variety of quality elementary
rhythm instruments for school use.
Started in 1961, Rhythm Band sells
beginners' musical instruments to all
fifty states and over sixty foreign
countries. There is no minimum order,
so it's an excellent place to select a
musical instrument for your child:
many kinds of drums, chromaharps,
flutophones, recorders, diatonic bell
sets, chromatic bell sets, guitars,
ukuleles, and dulcimers. There are two
pages of fun board games, flash cards,
and bingo games—all with musical
themes.

Robinson's Harp Shop
33908 Mount Laguna Drive.
P.O. Box 161
Mount Laguna, CA 92048
(619) 473-8556
8-page brochure, free U.S. and overseas.
MO, PC.
Robinson's sells materials for making
folk harps: blueprints, strings, and
hardware. They also carry books,
records, and cassettes, and they publish
a quarterly newsletter—Folk Harp
Journal.

Sam Ash Music Corp.
124 Fulton Ave.
Hempstead, NY 11550
(800) 645-3518
New York (212) 347-7757
Telephone and written requests.
Minimum order $15. AE, MC, V, MO,
PC.
This family-operated business, now in
its 60th year, is the largest discount
musical equipment dealer in the U.S.
They operate seven large stores in the
New York City area, plus a large mail
order department. They list their
discount prices from 30% to 40% off
manufacturers list price—and often
their special sales are closer to a 50%
discount. They carry a complete line of
musical instruments for the
professional, hobbyist, and student,
including band and orchestral
instruments, electronic keyboards
(synthesizers and electric pianos),

electric and acoustic guitars, drum
corps equipment, folk instruments—in
fact, almost anything except pianos and
home organs. (Although they don't offer
a catalog or brochure, they gladly accept
telephone and written inquiries.)

Shar Products Company
2465 S. Industrial
P.O. Box 1411
Ann Arbor, MI 48106
(800) 521-0791
Michigan (800) 482-1086
32-page catalog, free U.S. and overseas.
MC, V, MO, PC.
Shar is the oldest and largest stringed
instrument (and accessory) discount
mail order house in the U.S. They offer
a 20% discount off list price, and carry
over 10,000 items in stock (along with
7,500 sheet and chamber music titles).
Most orders are shipped within twenty-
four hours. As one customer wrote,
"Shar, you're fantastic! Prompt service,
good selection of merchandise, and the
most friendly personnel."

Silver & Horland, Inc.
170 W. 48th St.
New York, NY 10036
(212) 869-3870
Catalog, free U.S. and overseas.
Minimum order $15. AE, MC, V, MO,
PC.
Silver & Horland offer a complete line
of musical instruments, except
percussion and home pianos. They
specialize in vintage and older
instruments, and cater to musicians,
would-be musicians, and collectors.
Since 1930.

Stewart-MacDonald
21 N. Shafer St.
P.O. Box 900
Athens, OH 45701
(800) 848-2273
33-page catalog, $1 U.S. and overseas.
MC, V, MO, PC. .C.O.D.
Stewart-MacDonald sells kits for
making banjos and mandolins. Most kits
require doing the final sanding,
applying the finish, and assembling the
instrument; Stewart-MacDonald has
already done all the major work on the
neck and body of each instrument. The

kits include completely detailed and illustrated assembly instructions. The mandolin kit is slightly more involved, but the basic process is still relatively simple. The Curly Maple Diamond Eagle banjo kit is about $567.

PRINTED MUSIC

The Boston Music Company
116 Boylston St.
Boston, MA 02116
(617) 426-5100
48-page catalog, free U.S. and overseas.
  Minimum order $5. AE, DC, MC, V,
  MO, PC.
The Boston Music Company offers some of the best selling music books and sheet music from General Music Publishing Company, G. Henle, and Williamson Music. The catalog is categorized by instrument: piano (books, ensembles, and solos), organ (organ and choral), vocal, holiday music, instrumental, concert band, orchestra, and instructional books.

G. Schirmer Music Mail Order
48–02 48th Ave.
Woodside, NY 11377
(212) 784-8520
400-page catalog, $5 U.S. and overseas.
  AE, MC, V, MO, PC.
G. Schirmer's is the nation's premier music store. The 123-year-old firm encompasses the entire spectrum of music in this excellent catalog. There are over 30,000 works, including classic and contemporary music, for solo instrument, vocal, ensemble, orchestra and band, secular music for solo and chorus, jazz, pop, and folk. There are collections of orchestral scores and libretti of the great operas and ballets. Through the Schirmer Performance Department, larger works are available for rent.

Keyboard Workshop
Box 700
Medford, OR 97501
(503) 664–2317
24-page brochure, free U.S. and
  overseas. MC, V, MO, PC.
Duane Shinn offers over 100 cassette courses in piano instruction. The

courses cover all aspects of keyboard music, from beginner to advanced, and each course comes complete with cassette and coordinated printed literature. Some courses include summary sheets, sheet music, and books, but each course is complete in itself. There are several courses for around $13—in chord, improvising, style and technique, reading music, gospel and evangelistic playing, and harmony—to name a few.

Mail Order Music
P.O. Box 310
New Berlin, WI 53151
(800) 558-0912
Wisconsin (414) 784-2223
28-page catalog, free U.S. and overseas.
  MC, V, MO, PC.
Mail Order Music sells instruction and song books for organs, mini-organs, pianos, guitars, and vocals. They offer a good selection for beginners—and feature an Easy-To-Play Speed Music series.

William Elkin Music Services
Station Rd. Industrial Estate,
Salhouse, Norwich
Norfolk NR13 6NY England
0603 721302
Many catalogs available on request, free
  U.S. and overseas. Monthly news
  sheets, free U.S. and overseas. MO, PC.
William Elkin Music Services supplies music from any and all publishers from around the world, they say. The newsletters will give you some idea of the music publishers that they represent. If you're looking for something specific, write and they will send you ordering information. A few of the publishers whom they represent include Trinity College of Music (London), XYZ (Dutch), Deacon House (England), Chappell (England), and Edwin Ashdown.

RECORDS AND TAPES

Andy's Front Hall
P.O. Drawer A
Voorheesville, NY 12186
(518) 765-4193

40-page catalog, free U.S. and overseas. MC, V, MO, PC.

Bill and Andy Spence offer an excellent collection of hard-to-find records, books and tapes (and instruments) of classical, jazz, bluegrass, vintage, folk, traditional, and ethnic music. Just reading the titles and descriptions makes for an interesting time: American Folksongs for Children, Seasons of the Year, Whoever Shall Have Some Peanuts, and This Side of the Ocean.

Chesterfield Music Shops
226 Washington St.
Mt. Vernon, NY 10553
(914) 667-6200
32-page newsalog, free U.S. and overseas. AE, DC, MC, V, MO, PC.

Chesterfield is one of the oldest and largest mail order record suppliers in America. They carry a wide variety of records—classics, popular, spoken word, shows—at prices up to 70% to 80% off manufacturers retail. Mailings about four times a year will keep you informed on the latest bargains. Music for Twos and Threes is a special activity and game album for the very young, for $5.39.

Colon Records
Treinta y Tres Orientales 955.57
1236 Buenos Aires, Argentina
922-5323
80-page catalog, $2 U.S. and overseas. Prices in $U.S. MO, PC.

Colon Records specializes in old gramophone records: opera, classical, vocals, instrumentals, bands, and tango. They also have old opera theater programs, and photographs of operatic singers and personalities.

County Sales
P.O. Box 191
Floyd, VA 24091
(703) 745-2001
Six brochures, 4-page *Old Time Music*, 4-page *Modern and Progressive Bluegrass*, 4-page *Country Music Books*, 4-page *Fiddle Music*, 4-page *Gospel Records*, all free U.S. and overseas. MO, PC.

County Sales is known as "the source" for a fine selection of traditional/rural bluegrass, mountain fiddle, and Cajun music. Their inventory includes over 3,000 different LP titles, and they supply to all fifty states and over 18 foreign countries.

Down Home Music
10341 San Pablo Ave.
El Cerrito, CA 94530
(415) 525-1494
64-page newsalog *Blues*, $2; overseas 2 International Reply Coupons. 96-page newsalog *Vintage Rock 'N Roll*, $3; overseas 2 International Reply Coupons. 16-page newsletter, free U.S. and overseas. AE, MC, V, MO, PC.

Down Home carries over 15,000 different records in the following categories: blues, gospel, bluegrass, country, American folk music, jazz (from its beginnings to about 1960), and 50s rock 'n roll. They also carry ethnic music—English, Irish, Scottish and European folk. The catalogs offer informative reviews of all their offerings.

Francesco Bongiovanni
28 Rizzoli St.
40125 Bologna, Italy
051 225722
14-page color brochure, free U.S. and overseas. MO, PC.

Giancarlo Bongiovanni offers Bongiovanni label records of operatic arias recorded live in concert: Pedro Lavirgen, Giorgio Merighi, Renato Brusoni, Leo Nucci, Katia Ricciarelli, Mirella Freni, and Ruggiero Raimondi, to name a few. There are also famous records from the past, including Rigoletto (with Lina Pagliughi).

Global Records
3009 Faulkner Dr.
Rowlett, TX 75088
(214) 475-0607
2-page price list, free U.S. and overseas. MO, PC.

Global offers selections of LPs in classical, Latin, Country, Jazz, pop, and inspirational. They are mostly priced at $8.98.

House of Oldies
35 Carmine St.
New York, NY 10014
(212) 243-0500
32-page catalog, $3 U.S.; overseas $4
    surface, $8 air mail. MO, PC.
House of Oldies specializes in rare and
out-of-print forty-fives and LP records
(rock 'n roll, pop, jazz, and rhythm and
blues). They also have a mail order
search service. The catalog does not list
prices; you send them your want list
(even if your choice is not listed) and
they will return the list to you with the
prices indicated. Some golden oldies
include Louie Louie, Little Old Lady
from Pasadena, Gloria, Shimmy
Shimmy, Go Away Little Girl, The Jerk,
and Barbara Ann.

Indian House
P.O. Box 472
Taos, NM 87571
(505) 776-2953
8-page (some color) brochure, free U.S.
    and overseas. AE, MC, V, MO, PC.
Indian House has over 75 different high-
fidelity recordings of traditional
American Indian music from tribes in
the Southwest, Southern Plains,
Northern Plains, Southeast, and
Canada. Indian House specializes in in-
depth recordings of a selected song type;
one album might contain 10 Yeibichei
songs or twenty-four peyote songs
(heavy) by one group of singers. This
permits a deeper study and
understanding of that song type. Most
other sources of Indian recordings offer
survey albums, which contain many
different types of songs on one album.

In Sync Laboratories
2211 Broadway
New York, NY 10024
(212) 873-6769
6-page brochure, free U.S. and overseas.
    MC, V, MO, PC.
In Sync Laboratories offers superior
classical music cassette recordings.
Alan Silver, owner, has developed
superb individually calibrated,
prerecorded cassettes, duplicated in real
time on premium quality high bias tape
from uncompressed studio masters. The
result is a realistic tone, wide in range

and void of hiss or other background
noise. The cassette retail list price is
$17.98; the mail order price is $13.98.

Lyle Cartridges
365 Dahill Rd.
Brooklyn, NY 11218
(800) 221-0906
New York (212) 871-3303
8-page brochure, self-addressed
    stamped envelope U.S.; overseas 1
    International Reply Coupon.
    Minimum order $15. MO, PC.
Lyle offers ten different lines of
magnetic cartridges, replacement
styluses, and many record care
accessories. Their main attraction is the
availability of factory original
replacement styli, including the oddball
types (such as those needed to play the
old 78 recordings).

Lyrichord Discs
141 Perry St.
New York, NY 10014
(212) 929–8234
6-page brochure, free U.S. and overseas.
    Minimum order of two records. MO,
    PC.
Lyrichord offers a good variety of ethnic
records and cassettes from around the
world: Chinese, Japanese folk and
religious music, Tibet, Iran,
Afghanistan, India, Korea, the Middle
East, Africa, South America, Australia,
and Europe. Titles include Persian Love
Songs, Chinese Opera, Sexual Dances of
the Indians of Gran Chaco (Argentina),
and other fascinating titles.

Maildisc and Company
280 Central Park Rd.
London E6 3AD England
01 472 8969
400-page *Gramophone Classical*
    catalog, 66-page *Pop and Jazz* catalog,
    U.S. and overseas. BD, V, MO, PC.
Maildisc offers over 19,000 classical,
pop, and jazz records currently available
in Britain exclusively by mail order.

The Merry Music Box
20 McKown St.
Boothbay Harbor, ME 04538
(207) 633-2210
16-page brochure, free U.S.

The Merry Music Box features a unique offering of records and tapes of recorded musical box melodies. The album Christmas Joy features a beautiful selection of Christmas recordings from antique musical boxes including Silent Night, Adeste Fideles, Ave Maria, Babes in Toyland, The Messiah, and other favorites. The albums and cassettes range in price from $9 to $10.

Moby Music
14410 Ventura Blvd.
Sherman Oaks, CA 91423
(213) 881-9908
48-page catalog, $1 U.S. and overseas. MC, V, MO, PC.
There is a complete selection of domestic LPs and cassettes, at good discount prices, from Moby's. They also carry audiophile albums, Japanese pressings, and some limited edition issue LP's, deletions and cut-outs. Their service is fast and "it's like having a great record store at your mailbox wherever you are."

Monitor Records
156 Fifth Ave.
New York, NY 10010
(212) 989-2323
4-page price list, free U.S. and overseas. MO, PC.
Monitor specializes in "Music of the World"—folk and popular recordings from foreign countries. Many of the records come complete with texts. There are many belly dancing records listed.

Parnassus Records
2188 Stoll Rd.
Saugerties, NY 12477
(914) 246-3332
44-page brochure, free; overseas $8 air mail. MO, PC.
Parnassus Records catalog varies from 1,000 to as many as 1,700 listings of rare records. They offer only LPs and 45s, and indicate the condition of the record by grading (m) mint, (a) used but showing no signs of wear, (b) showing wear, and (c) showing scratches but playable. They also offer an extensive search service.

Peter Russell's Hot Record Store, Ltd.
58 New George St.
Plymouth PL1 1PJ England
0752 669511
12-page price list, $1 U.S. and overseas. MC, V, MO, PC.
Peter Russell is recognized locally and internationally for jazz and blues records, tapes, and books. They will also order anything available in England, and carry a large turnover in deletions and second-hand records. Since 1959.

The Quality Connection
18653 Ventura Blvd. Suite 314
Tarzana, CA 91356
(800) 423-0688
(800) 228-2028
28-page catalog, free U.S. and overseas. AE, MC, V, MO, PC.
The Quality Connection offers hard-to-find high technology recordings—records, tapes and compact discs, and audio accessories. The recordings are limited editions made from the recording artist's original master tape. Prices range from $7.95, to $350 for collections. Artists include the Beatles, Frank Sinatra, The Chicago Symphony, the Rolling Stones, Chuck Mangione, Luciano Pavarotti, and hundreds of other well-known performing artists.

Rashid Sales Co.
191 Atlantic Ave.
Brooklyn, NY 11201
(212) 852-3295
100-page catalog, free U.S. Does not sell overseas. Minimum order $10. MC, V, MO, PC.
Rashid sells imported Arabic and Greek language and music records, videotapes, and books.

The Record Hunter
507 5th Ave.
New York, NY 10017
(212) 697-8970
20-page catalog, free U.S. and overseas. AE, DC, MC, V, MO, PC.
The Record Hunter sells a large selection of records, tapes, and cassettes in many categories: popular, jazz, Broadway, classical, opera, and international. All selections are factory-sealed (no seconds) at good sale prices.

Records International
P.O. Box 1140
Goleta, CA 93116–1140
(805) 687-0327
16-page catalog, free U.S. and overseas.
  MO, PC.
Records International specializes in
imported records of classical music not
generally available in America: rare
symphonic, instrumental, chamber,
operatic, and vocal music from the
seventeenth to the twentieth centuries.
More than 150 labels are imported from
Western and Eastern Europe, Britain,
Scandinavia, USSR, the Orient,
Australia, and Latin America. Since
1975 they have been serving private
collectors, universities, libraries, and
radio stations both in America and
overseas. The knowledgeable staff can
respond to requests in English, French,
Spanish, Portuguese, and Swedish.

Rose's Collectors Records
300 Chelsea Rd.
Louisville, KY 40207
(502) 896-6233
64-page catalog, free U.S. and overseas.
  MC, V, MO.
Rose's specializes in records that are
hard-to-find, rare, no longer made, or
collectors items. They have a
particularly good selection of nostalgic
performances from the 20s, 30s and 40s.

Valentino Inc.
151 W. 46th St.
New York, NY 10036
(212) 246-4675
12-page price list, free U.S. and overseas.
  MO, PC.
Valentino provides sound effects on LP
records. Their company slogan is,
"From a cat's meow to a lion's roar—
from a pistol shot to a world war." They
have supplied such sound effects for
Broadway plays, movies, television, and
radio since 1932. Bacon frying, cash
register drawer opening, cattle
stampede, earthquake rumbling,
turkeys gobbling, bear attacking and
other sounds. (might make an
interesting parlor game of "name that
noise.")

Worldtone Music
230 7th Ave.
New York, NY 10011
(212) 691-1934
14-page dance record catalog, free U.S.
  and overseas. Minimum order $10.
  MO, PC.
Worldtone caters to the dance world,
offering a large supply of dance records
including folk, square, round, line,
ballroom, belly, ballet, modern, tap, and
aerobic dances. They also have a catalog
on dance shoes, books, and accessory
items.

PHOTOGRAPHY

SEE ALSO
• Electronics
• Large Department Stores and
Mail Order Houses

GIFTS

Albert White and Company
K.P.O. Box K-70202
Kowloon, Hong Kong
3 673168
70-page catalog, $1 U.S. and overseas.
MO, PC.
Albert White and Company carries
photographic equipment, audio
equipment, and watches.

Dale Laboratories
2960 Simms Street
Hollywood, FL 33020–0900
(800) 327-1776
Dale Laboratories offers 35 mm film
processing services. Unlike many local
photo finishing laboratories, Dale offers
a special service on Eastman Kodak's
type 5247 film, Kodacolor VR, and other
color negative films: they offer the
customer a choice of receiving slides,
prints, or both slides and prints, from
a single roll of film.

Far East Company
P.O. Box 97335 TST
Kowloon, Hong Kong
3 666647
60-page catalog, free by sea mail, $1.50
airmail U.S. and overseas. BD, PC.
The Far East Company sells cameras
and Seiko watches. There are 35mm
cameras by Minolta, Konica, Mamiya,
Nikon, Olympus, and Pentax. There are
over 120 film cameras including
Bronica, Mamiya and Pentax, and
Nikonos Underwater camera.
Binoculars from Nikon, Pentax, Carl
Zeiss, and Leica are also available.

47th Street Photo
32 E. 19th St.
New York, NY 10003
(800) 221-5858
(800) 221-7774
New York (212) 260-4410
148-page catalog, $1 U.S. and overseas.
Minimum order $25. AE, MC, V, MO,
PC.
A terrific store offering the widest range
of top name-brand cameras, electronics,
audio, video, computers, and darkroom
accessories at very low prices. They offer
up to 70% discount, and frequently
advertise sales in the *New York Times*
and *Wall Street Journal.* This is a "don't
miss" catalog, well worth the $1
ordering fee.

Garden Camera
135 W. 29th St.
New York, NY 10001
(212) 868-1420
128-page catalog, free U.S. and overseas.
Minimum order $5. MC, V, MO, PC.
In 1969 Garden Camera was one of the
pioneers in discount camera equipment
by mail order. It has since branched out

into home electronics, video, and personal computers. They sell leading brands of photography equipment at discounts from 30% to 60% off list price. Cameras, lenses, darkroom equipment, video recorders, televisions, telephones, calculators, and answering machines are available.

The Lab
Box 15100
St. Louis, MO 63110
(314) 371-0059
16-page catalog, free U.S. Does not sell overseas. Minimum order $3. MC, V, MO, PC.
The Lab sells and processes color film. Four print grades are available—machine, analyzed machine, custom, and exhibition. They also offer reprints, enlargements, mounting and framing, and special services: (cropping, dodging, burn-in, edge burning, and vignetting).

The Lens and Repro Equipment Corp.
33 W. 17th St.
New York, NY 10011
(212) 675-1900
Information sheet, free U.S. and overseas, MC, V, MO, PC.
They buy, sell, rent, and trade new, used, and demo photographic and reproduction equipment. This includes cameras, lenses, enlargers, darkroom equipment, lighting, finishing equipment, sinks and tanks. (This is a good opportunity for photographers to trade in their surplus equipment and update their systems.) They are also an outlet for Kotiner archival washers and multi-purpose easels.

Master Color Labs
G.P.O. Box 30
Newark, NJ 07101 .
(201) 385-9553
Master Color Labs has been in the color film-processing business for over thirty years and was one of the first to offer direct mail order film-processing services, both in America and overseas.

Modernage Photographic Services
1150 Ave. of the Americas
New York, NY 10036
(212) 997-1800
22-page catalog, free U.S. Does not sell overseas. Minimum order $4.50. MC, V, MO.
Modernage is an internationally renowned film-processing lab serving amateurs and professionals. This is the photographic lab used by photojournalists, museums, public relations executives, exhibit designers, and professional photographers for the finest printing and developing. But, remember—for this quality service you wouldn't expect the same prices available at your supermarket's photo drop box.

Negafile Systems
3069 Edison - Furlong Rd.
P.O. Box 78
Furlong, PA 18925
(215) 348-2356
36-page catalog, free U.S. and overseas. MC, V, MO, PC.
Negafile Systems manufactures photo files constructed of wood for archival storage. They also sell glassine envelopes, acetate sleeves, polyethelene tabbing, and kraft envelopes for long-term storage of photographic products. Since 1939.

Norman Camera Co.
3602 S. Westwedge
Kalamazoo, MI 49008
(616) 345-0164
88-page catalog, free U.S. Does not sell overseas. Minimum order $10. MC, V, MO.
Norman Camera Company is a large midwest photo store carrying all authorized imported and first quality domestic photography equipment.

Pentagon Camera
2900 Washington Blvd.
Arlington, VA 22201
(703) 524-5865
20-page catalog, free U.S. and overseas. Minimum order $10. MC, V, MO, PC.
Pentagon offers a complete line of cameras and accessories at good prices. Pentagon will also provide trade or cash values on your used camera equipment. A reputable mail order firm since 1955.

Photo Weber
Pilatusstrasse 1.18
CH 6003 Luzern, Switzerland
041 23 35 35
Price list, free U.S. and overseas. MO.
Photo Weber, founded in 1948, is an
internationally known and respected
photo dealership. They do not publish
a catalog but will be happy to supply a
price list on request. They carry many
name brands of cameras and specialize
in Leica, Contax, and Hasselblad. (They
also carry popular Swiss brand watches,
including the Swatch (49.90 Sfr.), a
quartz watch.)

Porter's Camera Store
Box 628
Cedar Falls, IA 50613
(319) 268-0104
112-page catalog, free U.S. Does not sell
   overseas. MC, V, MO, PC.
Porter's offers thousands of cameras and
photographic supplies. Started in 1914,
they advertise in leading photo
magazines and have a mailing list of
over 100,000 customers.

Sierra Visions
85 N. Edison Way, Suite 2
Reno, NV 89502
(800) 648-4862
26-page catalog, free U.S. Does not sell
   overseas. MC, V, MO, PC.
Sierra Visions sells cameras and hard-
to-find accessories for outdoor
photography. Bruce Clancy, owner, says,
"All products are carefully designed or
selected to provide the utmost quality
and function for outdoor
photographers." The photographers vest
($59.95) allows you to have your
equipment at your fingertips and to
shoot in comfort. The vest has a total
of twenty-two pockets designed to carry
the camera body plus a variety of lenses,
filters, film, flashes and light meters.

The Solar Cine Products
4247 S. Kedize Ave.
Chicago, IL 60632
(800) 621-8796
Illinois (312) 254-8310
55-page catalog, 50¢ U.S. Does not sell
   overseas. Minimum order $5. MC, V,
   MO, PC.

Solar Cine started in 1937 as a mail order
film-processing service. Today, their
business has expanded to include
photographic equipment and supplies to
a mailing list of over 250,000. (A twenty-
four exposure, 35 mm, color print film
processing on borderless lustre paper
costs $5.36.)

Spiratone
136–06 Northern Blvd.
Flushing, NY 11354
(212) 886-2000
40-page catalog, 75¢; overseas $3. AE,
   DC, MC, V, MO, PC.
Spiratone sells photographic
accessories (no cameras) for the
amateur and professional. Since 1941.

T. M. Chan and Co.
P.O. Box 33881
Sheung Wan Post Office #1C
Hong Kong
450 875
86-page catalog, free U.S. and overseas.
   Price in U.S. dollars. MO, PC.
An extensive offering of still cameras,
binoculars, cassette recorders, and
watches. Cameras by Asahi Pentax,
Canon, Mamiya, Minolta, Nikon,
Olympus, and Rollei. Lenses by Soligor,
Tokina, Tamron, and Vivitar.
Binoculars by Asahi, Carl Zeiss, and
Nikon. Watches by Seiko and Rolex.

Wall Street Camera Exchange
82 Wall Street
New York, NY 10005–3699
(212) 344-0011
304-page catalog, free U.S. MC, V, PC.
Wall Street sells everything in cameras,
photographic equipment, and
accessories. (They also offer an
electronic section offering phones and
answering machines, recorders,
calculators, radios and radar detectors,
televisions, and watches.)

Zone V
291 Buckminster Rd.
Brookline, MA 02146
(017) 731-3178
Price list, free U.S. and overseas. MC,
   V, MO, PC.

Zone V sells complete kits to prepare your own darkroom solutions for film and paper developing. The Black and White Photo Chemicals Kit will make over twenty-five quarts of classic D–76 formula, and includes chemicals, instruction manual, formulas, chart, and measuring spoons. The kits are designed with simple instructions; the measuring spoons are for mixing small quantities. Mixing your own can mean big savings over packaged products. Other kits include Jumbo Negative Kit, Slides from Negative Kit, Direct Positive Kit, Color Print Kit, E–6 Chrome Kit, Color Negative Kit, and 2203 Color Print Kit.

Zone VI Studios
Newfane, VT 05345
(802) 257-5161
32-page catalog, free U.S. and overseas.
   AE, MC, V, MO, PC.
Zone VI designs, manufactures and sells specialized photographic equipment: tripods, dry mount jigs, printing frames, archival film and print washers, focusing cloths, cold light heads, stabilizers, viewing filters, and paper. The Zone VI field camera is made of fine cherry or rosewood with brass fittings. Not available from any other supplier, this camera is a classic—"beautiful to look at and a pleasure to use."

REPAIR & REPLACEMENT SERVICES

ANTIQUES

Antique Trunk Co.
3706 West 169th St.
Cleveland, OH 44111
(216) 941-8618
Price list, 50¢; overseas $1. MO, PC.
Antique Trunk Company carries a complete line of antique trunk restoration parts: locks, handles, square nails, rivets, corners, trunk coverings, and embossed metals. They sell a "how-to repair manual" for $3.50 postpaid, as well as plans for full-sized trunks.

Bradywicks
709 E. Gutierrez
Santa Barbara, CA 93103
(805) 963–0320
Brochure, U.S. and overseas. MO, PC.
Bradywicks is one of the leading firms specializing in restoration and conservation of art objects and antiques. They conserve and restore period furniture including Chinese and European, fine quality modern furniture, gilded and faux finishes, and lacquers (including coromandel and cinnabar). They are also well known for their restoration of ceramics and porcelains, ivory and shell, hardstones and cloisonne. There is no consulting fee.

BOOK BINDING

Henry Sotheran Ltd.
2,3,4, & 5 Sackville St.
Piccadilly
London W1X 2DP England
01 734 1150
Sotheran's of Sackville Street is one of London's oldest and most famous bookshops. Their Binding and Restoration Service has been in existence for over 100 years and uses the fine methods and materials employed by the world's leading museum laboratories. An estimate is given either on receipt of the given volume, or by detailed description of the size, binding, and general state of the volume.

Sky Meadow Bindery, Inc.
20 Sky Meadow Rd.
Suffern, NY 10901
(914) 354-7101
1-page information sheet, free U.S. and overseas. PC.
Sky Meadow specializes in hand bookbinding and book restoration. There is a $50 minimum for book binding. Write for specific information on restoration services and fees.

CHINA REPLACEMENT

The following companies specialize in a variety of china replacement services. Some companies offer a china matching service, buying and selling used china and keeping requests on file for hard-to-find items. Other companies deal strictly in locating discontinued china patterns, or second quality china, direct from the manufacturers. A few companies offer the matching service in crystal, silver, silver plate, and flatware as well as china.

Only Reject China company offers a catalog. When contacting the other companies, compile a list of the patterns and pieces you wish to buy or sell. Be sure to enclose a self-addressed stamped envelope; most of the companies will not respond if you don't. If the company can't find a match they will generally keep your inquiry on file until they can locate the desired buyer or merchandise.

Fran Jay Popkorn
Rte. 202 RD7 Box 710
Flemington, NJ 08822
(201) 782-9631

Harrison's Antiques
480 N. Orange Ave.
Orlando, FL 32801
(305) 425-6481

Hoffman's Patterns of the Past
513 S. Main
Princeton, IL 61356
(815) 875-1944

The Jewel Box, Inc.
Corner Main & Broad
Albertville, AL 35950
(205) 878-3301
Offers a discontinued china matching service.

Locators, Inc.
P.O. Box 1259
908 Rock St.
Little Rock, AR 72202
(501) 371-0858

Pattern Finders
P.O. Box 206
Port Jefferson Station, NY 11776
(516) 928-5158

Patterns Unlimited
P.O. Box 15238
Seattle, WA 98115
(206) 523-9710

Reject China Shops
34 and 56/57 Beauchamp Place
London SW3 England
581 0733
16-page color catalog, $3 U.S. and overseas.
Reject China Shop sells first quality and second china, crystal, and giftware at prices up to 50% off U.S. retail prices.

Replacements, Ltd.
1510 Holbrook St.
Greensboro, NC 27403
(919) 275-7224

Topex Co.
Tiffin Ohio Pattern Exchange
58 Linda Lane
Tiffin, OH 44883
(419) 447-7939
Discontinued matching service for crystal, china, and silver.

The Saints' House of Crystal
475 E. Second St.
Richland Center, WI 53581
(608) 647-3340
The Saints' House offers a crystal matching service.

CLOCKS AND MUSIC BOXES

Keith Harding
93 Hornsey Rd.
London N7 6D5 England
607 6181
10-page catalog, $10; overseas $5. AE, DC, MC, V, MO, PC.
Keith Harding is internationally recognized as a leading authority on the restoration of antique music boxes and clocks. Write with your specific requests for repair or restoration.

DOLLS

Doll Repair Parts
9918 Lorain Ave.
Cleveland, OH 44102
(216) 961-3545
10-page brochure, 50¢; overseas free.
  MO, PC.
Doll Repair Parts sells doll parts for
antique dolls including wigs, socks,
shoes, dresses, patterns, and glass eyes.
They also repair modern and antique
dolls.

New York Doll Hospital
787 Lexington Ave.
New York, NY 10021
(212) 838-7527
New York Doll hospital is well known
for antique doll restoration. They also
buy, sell, and appraise antique dolls.
Estimates for doll restoration work are
free.

Paradise Doll Part Supply
576 Roberts Rd.
Paradise, CA 95969
(916) 877-1670
4-page brochure, 25¢ U.S. Does not sell
  overseas. MO, PC.
Paradise sells porcelain doll parts and
muslin bodies for antique dolls.

Recollect Doll Supplies
83A Trafalgar St.
Brighton, E. Sussex
BN1 4EB England
  16-page (some color) catalog, $3.50;
  overseas free. MC, MO, PC.
Recollect offers one of the largest
selections of antique doll parts for doll
making and repairing. There are wigs
in many styles and colors, all-bisque
bodies, arms, legs, and clothes.

METALS

Hiles
Precious Metal Plating and Silversmiths
2028 Broadway
Kansas City, MO 64108
Hiles can perform just about any plating
and metal repair service you might
need. They repair sterling, silver plate,
pewter, coin silver, copper, and brass.
They plate in silver, gold, brass, nickel
and copper—polish and refinish, too.
Lost or broken pieces of silver, wood,
and ivory can also be reproduced. To
plate a square silver tray, measuring 14
× 10 in., costs about $63.

Thome Silversmiths Inc.
328 East 59 St.
New York, NY 10022
(212) 758-0655
Thome Silversmiths repairs silver—and
also pewter, brass, bronze and copper.
They do silver and gold plating, metal
polishing, and removal of engravings.

SHOES

Ken-Kap, Inc.
5155 Rio Vista Ave.
Tampa, FL 33614
(813) 886-7573
6-page brochure, free U.S. and overseas.
  MO, PC.
Ken-Kap completely resoles, rebuilds
and restores all types of worn-out
athletic shoes, including upper and
inside repairs. They also fill orthopedic
prescriptions for people who require
custom work. Resoling "runs" about
$13.95 to $17.95.

TOYS

During the rugged lifetime of a toy,
parts may get lost or damaged. Each
of the major toy companies listed below will provide you with a price
list of replacement parts for their
major toys.

Fisher-Price
Consumer Affairs Replacement
Parts Sales
Consumer Affairs Department
East Aurora, NY 14052

Johnson&Johnson
Child Development Toys
Replacement Parts Department
Grandview Road
Skillman, NJ 08558

Kenner Products
Consumer Relations
1014 Vine Street
Cincinnati, OH 45202

Mattel, Inc.
P.O. Box 30801
Terminal Annex
Los Angeles, CA 90038

Playskool, Inc.
Customer Service
4501 W. Augusta Blvd.
Chicago, IL 60651

Schaper Mfg. Co.
P.O. Box 1426
Minneapolis, MN 55440

Tomy Toys
P.O. Box 6252
Carson, CA 90749

SPORTS & RECREATION

SEE ALSO
- Clothing - Sportswear
- College and Prep School Gift Catalogs
- Large Department Stores and Mail Order Houses

GENERAL

Continental Air Sports
113 S. Monroe Siding Rd.
Xenia, OH 45385
(513) 376-4344
Telex 288368
56-page catalog, $2; overseas $6. AE, MC, V, MO, PC.
Continental Air Sports sells parachuting systems and accessories for sport enthusiasts, paratroops, and emergency services. They offer altimeters, jumpsuits, boots, books, patches, decals, posters, helmets, flotation equipment, and parachute construction materials. Popular recreational para-sails are available in many bright colors.

Jayfro Corporation
P.O. Box 400
Waterford, CT 06385
20-page color catalog, free U.S. and overseas. MO.
Jafro's Funstuff catalog is loaded with popular exercise and recreation games and equipment. There is volleyball, basketball, tetherball, tennis, golf, soccer, croquet, baseball, swing sets, bike racks, water sport, and pool accessories, balance beams, mats, bean bag games, scooters, ping-pong, foam shapes, jump ropes, chin-up bars, weight benches, and exercise bikes.

Leslie's Swimming Pool Supplies
20222 Plummer St.
Chatsworth, CA 91311
(800) 423-5345
California (800) 382-5611
33-page color catalog, prices unavailable, U.S. MC, V, MO.
Swimming pool owners will find all their pool accessories and maintenance supplies in this descriptive catalog: water treatment aids, pool covers, solar covers, filters, pumps, cleaners, pool sweeps, chemicals, and winterizing kits. They also sell *Leslie's Swimming Pool Maintenance Manual* (101 pages), a good reference book for $6.99.

Ocean Hockey Supply Co.
Chambers Ridge Rd.
Bricktown, NJ 08723
(800) 631-2159
29-page color catalog, $1 U.S. MC, V, MO, PC.
A complete line of ice hockey equipment and accessories, including gloves, hats, coveralls, helmets, guards, pads, jerseys,

sticks, goalie gloves and pads. They also offer street hockey equipment.

Rainbo Sport Shop
4836 N. Clark St.
Chicago, IL 60640
(312) 275-5500
36-page catalog free, U.S. and overseas. MC, V, MO, PC, COD.
Rainbo's carries everything for ice skating—from boots and blades to practice and show dresses, bags, jewelry, and stationery. Boots by SP-Teri, Riddell, Oberhamer, and Hyde (and Polar Sport's new nylon leotards), are just a few of their items.

Soccer International
P.O. Box 7222 Dept. P.W.W.
Arlington, VA 22207
(703) 524-4333
8-page color brochure, $2 U.S. Does not sell overseas.
Soccer International sells soccer balls (in three sizes, according to the age and skill of the players) as well as a variety of uniforms, training aids, and gifts for players, officials, and coaches. Prices for balls range from about $14 to $70. (A lighted soccer ball is designed with an insertable light stick for nighttime play, priced at $18.50.)

Soloflex
Hawthorne Farm Industrial Park
Hillsboro, OR 97124
(800) 453-9000
24-page color catalog, free U.S. Does not sell overseas. AE, MC, V, MO, PC.
Soloflex has developed one of the most popular home weightlifting machines in recent years. Soloflex provides traditional iron-pumping exercises (with 380 pounds of resistance) in four sizes: 5, 10, 25 and 50 pounders. Soloflex measures 6 feet by 4 feet, and is priced at $565, plus $60 shipping.

Sub 4
2620 Temple Heights Dr.
Oceanside, CA 92056
(800) 782-4444
23-page color catalog, free U.S. and overseas. AE, MC, V, MO.

A classic line of running apparel for both top athletes and weekend joggers alike.

Ultimate Performance Products
P.O. Box 2688
Alameda, CA 94501
(415) 530-0618
Brochure, free U.S. and overseas. MC, V, MO, PC.
For exercise and sport enthusiasts, Ultimate Performance Products markets Music in Motion's "synchronized high performance music" cassette tapes designed to accompany sports and fitness activities on personal headset stereos. Ski Tunes' Cruising 1 incorporates a visualizing exercise which takes you on an imaginary run (good for listening on the ski lift) and music to schuss by. Separate tapes are available with music tempos for powder and mogul skiing. Music in Motion's tapes also include joggercise, running, weightless aerobics, cycling, and stress control. Tapes sell for $10.95 with discounts available on two or more tapes. They also sell cassette players, bounce free carriers, headphones, and rechargeable battery kits.

BIKING

Bicycling Lighting Systems
P.O. Box 1457
Falls Church, VA 22041
(703) 941-0666
4-page brochure, free U.S. and overseas. MC, V, MO, PC.
Ed Kearney designs, manufactures and sells bicycle lights that are far superior to any other system on the market. He has been making them (since 1975) because he was dissatisfied with lights sold in stores and, out of necessity, decided to manufacture a better lighting system. These lights are not inexpensive, but nothing else matches the breadth and brightness of his lights (according to the brochure).

Bike Nashbar
215 Main St.
New Middletown, OH 44442
(800) 345-2453
Ohio (216) 542-3671

56-page catalog, 50¢ U.S. and overseas. MC, V, MO, PC.

Bike Nashbar offers bicycle products suited for touring, racing, and commuting. They advertise prices 20% to 40% lower than bike shops, and have a "guaranteed lowest price" offer. There are companion sidecars, bike camping gear, parts, tools, helmets, hats, and clothing.

Cycle Goods Corp.
2735 Hennepin Ave., S.
Minneapolis, MN 55408
(800) 328-5213
Minnesota (612) 872-7600
179-page catalog, $3; overseas $4, refundable with first $30 purchase. AC, DC, MC, V, MO, PC.

This is a catalog of bicycle equipment and parts the whole family can use. They offer parts for the single-speed and three-speeds, as well as the specialty bikes. Started in 1979, it offers one of the largest selections of bicycle parts, accessories, tools, and clothing. The prices are low, and they are known internationally for quick service.

Palo Alto Bicycles
P.O. Box 1276
171 University Ave.
Palo Alto, CA 94302
(415) 328-0128
50-page catalog, $1 U.S. and overseas. MC, V, MO, PC.

Here is an extensive range of bicycle components and accessories for racing and touring. They also manufacture their own line of Palo Alto bicycle products.

The Third Hand
Hwy. 89 & Manzanita Lane
P.O. Box 456
Markleeville, CA 96120
(916) 694-2334
The Third Hand sells tools for bicycle maintenance and repairs. There are brake tools, crank extractors, chain tools, lubricants and sealers, repair stands, and much more. There is an excellent selection of books and publications on bicycle mechanics and cycling.

Touring Cyclist Shop
P.O. Box 4009
Boulder, CO 80306
(303) 449-4067
48-page brochure, $1 U.S. and overseas, refundable with first purchase. MC, V, MO, PC.

This company started out in 1970 manufacturing their own brand of lightweight bicycle bags—Touring Cyclist Brand Panniers. They have expanded, and now design, manufacture, and sell other gear for bicycle tourists: front and rear panniers, daytrippers, spare tire bags, super shopping bags, carriers, and supports. You'll find their gear listed in many sports mail order catalogs.

BOATING

Andries DeJong
Muntplein 8
1012 WR Amsterdam Holland
020 245251
12-page brochure, $1 U.S. and overseas. Printed in Dutch. Minimum order $100. MO, PC.

Andries De Jong is best known for their beautiful brass bell-striking ship's clocks with quartz movements. Founded in 1787 (and still located at the same address), they offer finely crafted brass lanterns, barometers, bars and handlerods. There are also many national and international flags available.

Bacon & Associates
P.O. Box 3150
Annapolis, MD 21403
(301) 263-4880
14-page brochure, free U.S. AE, MC, V, MO.

Bacon & Associates is a brokerage firm buying and selling second-hand sailboat sails. Sails range in size from small sailboat, seventy-foot yachts, and vary in quality from much used to new. (All sails are one-of-a-kind, so it is probably best that you list your second and third choices when ordering.) There is a ten-day examination period on all purchases.

C. Plath, North America
222 Severn Ave.
Annapolis, MD 21403
(301) 263-6700
68-page color catalog, free U.S. and
  overseas. Minimum order $10. AE,
  MC, V, MO, PC.

C. Plath has specialized in fine nautical instruments and navigational aids for fifty-two years. They are famous for their sextants, brass clocks, and lamps. Binoculars, navigation computers, plotting tools, books, compasses, and emergency lights are available. This company for the first fifty years was known as "Weems and Plath"—started by the same people who developed some of today's navigational standards.

Defender Industries
255 Main St.
P.O. Box 820
New Rochelle, NY 10802–0820
(914) 632-3001
200-page catalog, free U.S. and overseas.
  MO, PC.

Defender Industries catalog is subheaded "Complete Marine Catalog." It covers everything from almanacs to wire rigging, and everything in between. The alphabetical index at the back is most helpful in searching through this volume for a specific item. Defender guarantees a "lowest price offer," which means they will honor a lower price if you include a tear sheet from the cheaper source.

Goldbergs' Marine
202 Market St.
Philadelphia, PA 19106
(215) 627-3700
112-page (some color) catalog, free;
  overseas $5. Minimum order $25. AE,
  MC, V, MO, PC.

Goldbergs' offers a unique line of pleasure boating and fishing equipment. You'll find all the big name brands here—plus many hard-to-find items at discount prices (at least 20% and sometimes 30% to 40% off retail). There are clothing, boating bags, depth finders, shower systems, marine clocks, flags, water skis, compasses, sailboat hardware, fishing harnesses and rods, and much more. Goldbergs' is a family business, operating three retail stores and processing over 1,000 mail orders daily.

Harrison Hoge Industries
104 Arlington Ave.
St. James, NY 11780
(516) 724-8900
24-page color catalog, $1 U.S. and
  overseas. AE, DC, MC, V, MO, PC.

Importers, designers, and manufacturers of inflatable boats since 1968. They are currently one of the largest sellers of inflatable boats in America, with their popular Sea Eagles (available with mounted motors), explorer canoes, sailing rigs, floating island rafts, Sea Eagle surfers, and variety of inflatable lounges for pool and beach fun. When ordering the catalog, be sure to specify the *Sea Eagle* number, as they also make a *Fishing Lure* catalog.

Marinetics Corporation
1638 Placentia Ave.
Costa Mesa, CA 92627
(800) 854-4601
(714) 646-8889
17-page brochure, $3 U.S. and overseas.
  MO, PC.

Marinetics sells electrical products used by pleasure boats, racing sailboats, luxurious power cruisers, and even utilitarian fishing boats. Since 1967 they have designed and distributed marine electrical power systems controls, instruments, and distribution panels.

M & E Marine Supply Co.
P.O. Box 601
Camden, NJ 08101
(609) 858-1010
340-page catalog, $2; overseas $5.
  Minimum order $10. MC, V, MO, PC.

This catalog offers one of the country's most complete listings of boating supplies, at prices 10% to 40% below retail. The catalog is an excellent guide to all that is available in boating equipment: pages of boating hardware, tools, lights, boarding ladders, signal kits, galley equipment, fishing chairs, and more.

Overton's Inc.
P.O. Box 8228
211 Jarvis St.
Greenville, NC 27834
(800) 334-6541
(800) 682-8263
80-page color catalog, free U.S. and
  overseas. MC, V, MO, PC, COD.
Overton's is probably the largest mail-
order ski dealer in the world. They carry
skis, sporting goods, and marine
accessories from all the top brand-name
manufacturers: Connelly, Master Craft,
Jobe, Kidder, Ebonite, Casad, Pro Line,
plus their own brand, Overton. Don't
miss this one.

Stokes Marine Supply
45 Water St.
East Providence, RI 02914
(517) 278-2614
52-page catalog, free U.S. V, PC.
Stokes Marine Supply sells marine
engines and equipment, offering same-
day shipping on most orders. They also
buy used marine engines.

Thomas Foulkes
100 Landsdowne Rd.
Leytonstone
London E11 3HB England
01 539 5084
24-page catalog, $1 U.S. and overseas.
  AE, DC, MC, V, MO, PC.
Thomas Foulkes is a well-established
firm offering "everything for boats."
Over 90% of their boating equipment is
British-made.

Tugon Chemical Corporation
Box 31
Cross River, NY 10518
(203) 762-3953
6-page brochure, free U.S. and overseas.
  MO, PC.
A complete line of marine epoxy
products. They are used by shops,
manufacturers, and owners to construct
and maintain wooden boats. There are
many other nonmarine applications for
epoxy products, too. Since 1967.

Universal Hovercraft
Box 281
1204–3rd St.
Cordova, IL 61242
(309) 654-2588

24-page catalog, $1; overseas $2. MO, PC.
Universal sells plans for making your
own hovercraft: ride on a ten-inch
cushion of air and travel over water,
land, snow, ice, and sand. Plans for
hovercrafts are available, from the 10-
foot vehicle powered by lawn mower
engines to a 26-foot craft capable of
carrying fifteen persons. Plans start at
about $10.

Wind in The Rigging
125 E. Main Street
Port Washington, WI 53074
(414) 284-3494
20-page (some color) catalog, free U.S.
  MC, V, MO, PC.
There are many practical items any
sailor would use and enjoy: no-spill
sputnik-shaped coffee mugs,
personalized sail ties, folding boat
ladder, and sailing gloves and belts
featuring coded flags on a navy
background.

Yachtmail Co., Ltd.
5–7 Cornwall Crescent
London W11 1PH England
01 727 7273
29-page catalog, free U.S. and overseas.
  MC, MO, PC.
Yachtmail sells a comprehensive range
of boating equipment for cruiser yachts.
They sell at tempting prices, with
discounts ranging from 5% to 20%.
There are autopilots, Carl Zeiss sextants
and binoculars, and depth sounders by
Seafarer.

CAMPING AND OUTDOORS

Brigade Quartermasters, Ltd.
266 Roswell St.
Marietta, GA 30060
(404) 428-1234
80-page color catalog, free U.S. and
  overseas. AE, MC, V, MO, PC.
Brigade carries all types of items for
outdoors, camping, hunting, rappelling,
and survival. They are probably best
known for their military-like
sportswear—field and mission packs,
carrying equipment, field uniforms,
headwear, and military boots. (Some of
the items are army surplus, but Brigade

also makes their own line.) There are a few tents, sleeping bags, and first aid kits, and also some pathfinding equipment.

Cabela's
812–13th Ave.
Sidney, NE 69160
(308) 254-5505
130-page color catalog, free U.S. and
   overseas. MC, V, MO, PC.
Cabela's offers hundreds of items for the outdoor enthusiast: fishing, hunting, camping, boating, clothing, footwear, gifts, archery, optics, and plenty more. If you are currently receiving a sports mail order catalog, chances are that it is Cabela's; they currently have over 375,000 customers who regularly buy from them by mail. The catalog appropriately reads "World's foremost outfitter—fishing, hunting, and outdoor gear." Don't miss this catalog.

Colorado Tent Co.
2228 Blake St.
Denver, CO 80205
(303) 294-0924
24-page catalog, free U.S. Does not sell
   overseas. AE, DC, MC, V, MO, PC.
Colorado Tent designs and sells large wall tents—the traditional canvas tent chosen by hunters, guides and outfitters. Chosen for its versatility and spaciousness, the tent provides ample head room and full utilization of floor space. The tents are available in eight sizes and start at about $383, for an eight by ten model. They also sell canvas saddle bags, slickers, woodburning stoves for sportsmen, and an interesting canvas creel designed to keep the fish cool.

Don Gleason's Campers Supply
90 Pearl St.
P.O. Box 87S
Northampton, MA 01061–0087
80-page (some color) catalog, free;
   overseas $1 surface, $4 airmail. MC,
   V, MO, PC.
Don Gleason's carries an extensive selection of equipment for camping, backpacking, and mountaineering. (They carry all the small items along with the major items, too.) There are

sixteen pages of tents and backpacks by Camp Trails, Jan Sport, North Face, Kelty, Coleman, and Kirtland. There are plenty of equipment and utensils for campfire cooking and, of course, a small but essential selection of bug repellent.

Dunns
Hwy. 57
Grand Junction, TN 38039
(901) 764-6901
72-page color catalog, free U.S. and
   overseas. AE, DC, MC, V, MO, PC.
Dunns offers brand name merchandise for hunters at discounts of up to 25% below retail. There are insulated and camouflage clothing by Duxbak, and Wing 'N Shot hunters coats in safety orange. There are hats, gloves, shoes, warm underwear, and waders. The waterfowl hunter will find decoys, duck and goose calls, blinds, slings, and traveling dog kennels.

Early Winters
110 Prefontaine Place South
Seattle, WA 98104
(201) 624-5599
56-page color catalog, free U.S. and
   overseas. AE, DC, MC, V, MO, PC.
The catalog features hard-to-find items for outdoor uses: knives, flashlights, tents, backpacks, cooking gear, clothing, and parkas. Early Winter designs and sells Gore-Tex tents, outerwear, jogging suits, and other items. This company is a "tents-to-riches" success story, having started in 1976 with the Light Dimension tent—the first outdoor application of waterproof breathable Gore-Tex. Today they are leaders in supplying quality outdoor equipment, featuring garments made with Silver Lining fabric—a radiant heat barrier developed by NASA for use in spacecraft.

Gander Mountain
P.O. Box 128
Wilmot, WI 53192
(414) 862-2331
100-page color catalog, free; overseas
   MC, V, MO, PC.
Gander carries a large selection of outdoorsman's supplies for hunting and fishing. Camouflage clothing is

available in many styles and degrees of insulation. They also offer knives, gun cases, accessories, reloading equipment, and archery equipment.

Indiana Camp Supply
405 Osborne Ave.
Pittsboro, IN 46167
(317) 892-3310
72-page catalog, free U.S. Does not sell
    overseas. AE, MC, V, MO, PC.
Indiana Camp Supply offers one of the best selections of medical kits for the outdoorsman. They have pocket first aid kits ($6.30), advanced medical kits ($125), and many others to choose from in between. Some kits are designed to be carried by each member of an outing, while others will supply first aid to a large group. They also stock about 150 outdoor-oriented books, and over 600 items in their Trail Food section. This is a unique catalog for the outdoorsman.

Inward Bound
378 Webster St.
Manchester, NH 03104
(603) 668-8573
6-page brochure, free U.S. and overseas.
    MO, PC.
Whether you shoot white water rapids, dive to explore caves and wrecks, windsurf or just enjoy the water, Inward Bound provides wet suits, and neoprene accessories to make it more enjoyable. Wet suits by Parkway, Omni, Henderson, and Jetsuit.

Johnson Camping, Inc.
One Marine Midland Plaza
P.O. Box 966
Binghamton, NY 13902
(607) 723-7546
rq. questionnaire 10/4/83
23-page color catalog, free U.S. MO, PC.
Johnson Camping features backpacking, expedition and family tents, and backpacks by Eureka and Camp Trails.

Kirkham's Outdoor Products
3125 S. State St.
Salt Lake City, UT 84117
(801) 486-4161
38-page color catalog, free U.S. and
    overseas. AE, MC, V, MO, PC.

Kirkham's manufactures tents, sleeping bags, backpacks, cartop luggage carriers, and luggage. The Springbar tent is one of their finest products, designed with nearly vertical sidewalls for more useable interior space and made from 100% cotton army duck. They are available in many dimensions and styles.

Laacke & Joys Co.
1433 N. Water St.
Milwaukee, WI 53202
(414) 271-7885
16-page catalog, free U.S. Does not sell
    overseas. AE, MC, V, MO, PC.
Laacke & Joys dates back to 1844, when it was founded as a ship chandler and sailmaker serving the sailing vessels on the Great Lakes. The company no longer makes sails, but continues to manufacture a fine line of 100% canvas tents and other products under the trade mark "Wildwood." Canvas tents are great family tents because the material has the strength and body to span the large area, yet is light enough to breathe. Their tents start at about $349.

Mountain Safety Research
P.O. Box 3978
Terminal Station
Seattle, WA 98124
(201) 624-7048
10-page color brochure, free. PC.
Mountain Safety Research has researched, designed, and manufactured some excellent outdoor equipment. The MSR Bicycling Helmet, made with a Lexan shell and polystyrene foam liner, is priced at about $46, and the MSR Climbing Helmet is about $49. The MSR X-GK stove system has passed many rigorous high altitude expedition tests and has also proven to be versatile and maintainable in extreme conditions.

Northwest River Supplies
P.O. Box 9186
430 West 3rd St.
Moscow, ID 83843
(208) 882-2383
32-page color catalog, free; overseas $1.
    MC, V, MO, PC.

Since 1976, this company has supplied whitewater enthusiasts with river rafts, canoeing accessories, and kayak supplies. They also feature cartop carriers, camping supplies, and books. Their specialty is watertight bags (chosen as the gear bags for the 1981 American Himalayan Whitewater Expedition), available in Bills Bags (3.8 cubic foot capacity) or in small and handy Stuff and Tuff Sacks, and ranging in price from $8.95 to $45.

P & S Sales
P.O. Box 1500
Chapel Hill, NC 27515
(919) 929-2183
64-page catalog, free U.S. Does not sell
   overseas. MC, V, MO, PC.
P & S Sales offers men's outdoor clothing and equipment for hunting and camping.

REI
P.O. Box C-88126
Seattle, WA 98188
(800) 426-4840
98-page color catalog, free U.S. and
   overseas. MC, V, MO, PC.
REI is a Seattle, Washington,-based consumer cooperative, organized to provide a variety of outdoor recreation products. They offer a superb selection of clothing and equipment for outdoors. There are accessories for backpacking, climbing, bicycling, skiing, and water sports (canoes, kayaks, and board sailing). Membership is not required, but for a $5 fee members are entitled to a yearly dividend based on their purchases.

Sims Stoves
P.O. Box 21405
Billings, MT 59104
(406) 259-5644
4-page color brochure, free U.S. and
   overseas. MC, V, MO, PC.
Graham Sims's father invented the woodburning Sims Stoves in the late 1940s. This stove (with attached shelf and oven) provides a work space for the camp cook and an oven that will bake anything from cookies to a wild turkey, while coffee perks on the stove top. Sims Stoves have been reviewed in *Mechanics*

Illustrated and *Back Country Cooking*, and are priced at about $216.

Stephensons
RFD 4 Box 145
Gilford, NH 03246
(603) 293-8526
48-page color catalog, $3 U.S. and
   overseas. MO, PC.
The Stephensons catalog of excellent backpacking, mountaineering, and camping equipment is one-of-a-kind. There is a direct marketing statistic that states that the average person takes a three-second glance to decide if he is going to toss out the latest mail order catalog. Jack Stephenson, owner, has greatly extended the life of his catalog: all the male and female models lounging by their tents and carrying backpacks are nude. (Well, there are a few Arctic scenes where the models are insulated.) The other striking aspect is that the catalog format is part catalog, part book. It is most informative, and fun to read.

The Yak Works
2030 Westlake Ave.
Seattle, WA 98121
(800) 426-9935
Washington (206) 623-8053
60-page color catalog, free U.S. and
   overseas. AE, V.
Yak Works started in 1972 as a tiny outfit that built "Yakpaks"—frameless backpacks with a patented suspension system. The company has since expanded and now manufactures high-quality packs, sleeping bag systems, Gore-Tex raingear, and other outdoor recreation clothing. They also carry a wide selection of outdoor adventure gear, from kayaks to solar battery rechargers.

DIVING

Central Skindivers of Nassau
2608 Merrick Rd.
Bellmore, NY 11710
(516) 826-8888
40-page catalog, $U.S. and overseas. MC,
   V, MO, PC.

All major brands of equipment for skin and scuba diving (including spearfishing, treasure hunting, and photography) are offered. "We sell, service, teach, repair, custom design and manufacture." Prices are 15% to 40% below retail prices (they say).

New England Divers
131 Rantoul St.
Beverly, MA 01915
(800) 343-8132
Massachusetts (617) 922-6951
32-page catalog, free U.S. and overseas. Minimum order $15. AE, MC, V, MO, PC.
Established in 1951, New England Divers is the largest retailer of diving equipment in the U.S. They have eight retail stores and a large mail order division. There are cylinders, tank accessories, regulators, buoyancy compensators, pressure and depth gauges, and dry suits.

FISHING

Bass Pro Shops
P.O. Box 4046
Springfield, MO 65808
(808) 227-7776
Missouri (417) 883-4960
386-page color catalog. MC, V.
An outstanding sporting goods store for the fisherman. There are Bass tracker boats and hundreds of fishing and camping accessories. Don't miss this catalog.

Bud Lilly's
Box 698
39 Madison Ave.
West Yellowstone, MT 59758
(406) 646-7801
70-page catalog, free U.S. and overseas. MC, V, MO, PC.
This catalog specializes in fly fishing equipment for western trout fishing. Bud Lilly's is especially well known for their custom hand-tied and commercially tied flies. New patterns are constantly being added, including some new steelhead flies for fishing in the Pacific Northwest.

Dan Bailey
P.O. Box 1019
Livingston, MT 59047
(406) 222-1673
78-page (some color) catalog, free U.S. and overseas. MC, V, MO, PC.
Dan Bailey's is a manufacturer of fishing flies. They are one of the leading fly tackle mail order houses in the U.S. The catalog shows many color pages of the flies, lines, and reels available. There are also assortment packages (for specific areas and fishing conditions) available.

E. Hille
The Angler's Supply House, Inc.
P.O. Box 996
Williamsport, PA 17703
(717) 323-7564
59-page catalog, $1 U.S. and overseas. AE, MC, V.
E. Hille sells kits and materials for making your own fishing flies, lures, and fishing rods. They also sell many books on the subject, plus related tools and materials. Their fly tying kits are custom designed for the novice, and contain the correct materials needed. Four kits are available: a very basic kit, a deluxe trout and panfish kit, a kit for bass and trout flies, and a kit for cork bugs. They start at about $22. Hille's Lamiflex graphite rods (blanks and kits) are also available.

Kaufmann's Streamborn
P.O. Box 23032
Portland, OR 97223
(503) 639-6400
90-page (mostly color) catalog, free; overseas $3. AE, MC, V, MO, PC.
Kaufmann's carries everything for the fly fisherman and fly tying. Kaufmann's offers worldwide guide services and information (and even schools) in fly fishing.

Harrison Hoge Industries
104 Arlington Ave.
St. James, NY 11780
(516) 724-8900
24-page color catalog, $1 U.S. and overseas. AE, DC, MC, V, MO, PC.
Harrison Hoge Industries sells Panther Martin sonic spinner and other fine

lures: Superfrog, Weedwing, Rocky, and Minken.

Limit Manufacturing Corporation
451 N. Central Expressway
Box 359
Richardson, TX 75080
(214) 231-5982
128-page catalog, $2 U.S. and overseas. Minimum order $10. MC, V, MO, PC.
Sporting goods for the fisherman—rods by Fenwick, Lamiglas, and Lew. Spinning rod assembly kits and fly typing materials and tools are also available.

Normark Corporation
1710 E. 78th St.
Minneapolis, MN 55423
(612) 869-3291
2-page brochure, free U.S. Does not sell overseas. MO, PC.
Normark is the exclusive distributor of Rapala Fishing lures, those lures that resemble the "stricken wobble of a doomed minnow."

Okiebug Distributing Co.
3501 S. Sheridan
Tulsa, OK 74145
(918) 622-2657
40-page catalog, free U.S. and overseas. MC, V, MO, PC.
Okiebug carries a wide variety of all bass fishing materials, plus fly fishing gear and other bait fish products.

Orvis
10 River Rd.
Manchester, VT 05254
(802) 362-1300
80-page color catalog, free U.S. and overseas. AE, MC, V, MQ, PC.
The Orvis company sells a complete line of fly fishing tackle, mostly exclusive products, as well as custom shotguns, hunting accessories, a distinctive line of classic sporting gifts, and traditional clothing. They claim to be the only company in the world to make fly rods from all four types of raw materials: bamboo, graphite, fiberglass, and boron. They also produce some excellent books, pamphlets, and videotapes for fly fishermen (and students in their fly fishing and shooting schools) each year. Since 1856.

The Tackle Box
303 Dillingham Ave.
Talmouth, Cape Cod, MA 02540
112-page (some color) catalog, free U.S. and overseas. MC, V, MO, PC.
The Tackle Box offers over 5,000 items for the fisherman.

Thos. D. Robinson & Son, Ltd.
321 Central Ave.
White Plains, NY 10606
(800) 431-0200
New York (914) 948-8488
62-page newsalog, free U.S. Does not sell overseas. MC, V, MO, PC.
A very large selection of fresh and salt water fishing tackle from leading name brands, with discounts up to 40% below retail. There are also catalogs available for camping and hunting gear.

Thomas & Thomas Rodmakers, Ltd.
22 Third St.
P.O. Box 32
Turners Falls, MA 01376
(413) 863-9727
90-page (some color) catalog, $2; overseas $5. Minimum order $5. AE, MC, V, MO, PC.
Thomas & Thomas fly fishing rods are considered the finest ever made; their work sets the standard for their industry. (President Reagan once gave a matched brace of salmon rods to Prince Charles and Lady Diana.) The Thomas & Thomas product list is thorough and extensive, covering nearly every aspect of the sport of fly fishing. Many products are unique to Thomas & Thomas, and available through no other supplier.

Tom C. Saville, Ltd.
Unit 7 Salisbury Square
Nottingham NG7 2AB England
0602 784248
128-page catalog, $2 U.S. and overseas. MC, V, MO, PC.
Established in 1950, Tom C. Saville is among the leading suppliers of fresh water game fishing equipment in England. They have been recommended in fishing books and magazines for their quality fly fishing tackle.

GOLF AND TENNIS

Austad's
4500 E. 10th St.
P.O. Box 1428
Sioux Falls, SD 57101
(605) 336-3135
50-page color catalog, free U.S. and
    overseas. AE, MC, V, MO, PC.
Austad's is one of the largest non-
manufacturing distributors of golf
equipment in the world. About 90
percent of the business stems from
orders from a mailing list of over 800,000
people. You'll find most every brand of
balls, clubs, shoes, bags, and accessories
in the catalog. Fast service is assured;
their company warehouse stocks over
6,500 golf carts, 80,000 sets of clubs,
150,000 dozen golf balls, and eight
million golf tees. But the best part is:
some of their prices appear to be
considerably below retail prices.

Conquest Sports West, Inc.
1015 Gayley Ave. - Suite 215
Los Angeles, CA 90024
(213) 393-1032
3 pages, free. PC.
Conquest sells repair supplies for tennis
rackets: gut, grips, grip tacker, and grip
sprays.

Custom Golf Clubs
10206 N. Interregional Hwy.
Austin, TX 78753
(513) 837-4810
80-page color catalog, free U.S.; overseas
    $2 surface mail, $10 airmail. MC, V,
    MO, PC.
Custom Golf Clubs sells a large supply
of golf equipment worldwide. They are
best known for manufacturing custom
woods and irons under the name
"Golfsmith." Every Golfsmith club is
made to the precise specifications of the
customer. Just send them the exact
specifications—length, weight, color,
grip size, and flex.

Edwin Watts Golf Shops
187A Greenacres Rd.
Ft. Walton Beach, FL 32549
(800) 874-0146
Florida (800) 342-7103

There is a large selection of professional
golf equipment (at discounts from 20%
to 50% off retail): clubs by Taylor, Lynx,
Spalding, Wilson, Power Bilt,
Northwestern, and MacGregor. They
carry an electric golf cart, Kangaroo
Katty, for about $320, as well as others.

Golf Day
3015 Commercial
Northbrook, IL 60062
(312) 433-4653
48-page catalog, 50¢ U.S. Does not sell
    overseas. Minimum order $20. AE,
    MC, V, MO, PC.
Golf Day features a lot of do-it-yourself
golf supplies not always available in the
stores: refinishing, repairing, and
customizing materials. They say they
"ship orders to golfers on all continents
except Antarctica."

Golf Haus
700 N. Pennsylvania
Lansing, MI 48906
(517) 482-8842
5-pages, free U.S. and overseas. MC, V,
    MO, PC.
Golf equipment and supplies—clubs,
bags, balls, head covers, umbrellas,
shoes, and more.

The Golfworks
4820 Jacksontown Rd.
P.O. Box 3008
Neward, OH 43055–7199
(800) 848-8358
Ohio (800) 762-1831
124-page catalog, free U.S. and overseas.
    MC, V, MO, PC.
Golfworks has an extensive list of
machines, gauges, tools, clubs, heads,
components, and supplies for whoever
needs them: repair shops,
manufacturers, custom club makers,
and do-it-yourselfers.

Hills' Court
Manchester, VT 05254
(802) 362-1200
32-page color catalog, free U.S. AE, MC,
    V, MO, PC.
Hills' Court features a wide selection of
men's and women's tennis clothes.
There are many cute tennis dresses
(including a maternity tennis dress),

---

warm-up outfits, sweaters, hats, shoes, and socks. Also available are accessory court items: ball bags, racquet rack, and ball hopper.

Holabird Sports Discounters
Holabird Industrial Park
644 Beckley St.
Baltimore, MD 21224
(301) 633-3333
2-page brochure, prices unavailable.
  U.S. and overseas. MC, V, MO.
Holabird offers leading name-brand tennis racquets at very reasonable prices. (Call for price quotes. And compare.)

Kassal Enterprises
P.O. Box 92
Hasbrouck Heights, NJ 07604
(201) 288-3671
8-page brochure free U.S. and overseas.
  MO, PC.
Tennis Partner, manufactured in Sweden, is distributed in the U.S. by Kassal Enterprises. The Tennis Partner is an inclined "playing court," designed to be an effective aid for improving stroke technique for all levels of tennis players. The area needed for use is approximately 2 × 3 × 5 meters (which includes swinging room for the player). It's a great device for training and warming up, and can be used inside or (weather permitting) outside.

Las Vegas Discount Golf and Tennis
4813 Paradise Rd.
Las Vegas, NV 89109
(800) 634-6743
Nevada (702) 798-6300
16-page catalog. U.S. and overseas. AE,
  DC, MC, V, MO, PC.
Name-brand golf and tennis equipment, at discounts of 25% to 40% off retail: clubs by Lynx, MacGregor, Wilson, Northwestern, and Spalding; golf shoes by Foot-Joy; and athletic shoes by Nike, Adidas, K-Swiss, and Asahi.

Lombard's
1861 NE 163 St.
N. Miami Beach, FL 33162
(305) 944-1166

16-page brochure. $1 U.S. and overseas.
  MO, PC.
Lombard's sells golf and tennis equipment at discounts of 30% to 60% off retail. It is no accident that Lombard's sells over 10,000 tennis racquets a month; their prices are consistently lower than other companies' "discount" prices. They carry Bard, Fischer, Yonex, Yamaha, Donnay, Kennix, Head, Bancroft, Spalding, Dunlop, Snauwaert, Rossignol, and others. They have a good selection of children's tennis racquets and carry Ping golf bags, Prince ball machines, racquetball racquets, and all the accessories.

National Golf Center
Division of Bost Enterprises Inc.
18 Lois St.
Norwalk, CT 06851
(203) 847-1231
21-page color brochure, free U.S. and
  overseas. AE, DC, MC, V, MO, PC.
National Golf Center sells specialty golf equipment. The Sof-Spike golf shoe features soles with thirteen durable soft spikes (replacing the traditional eleven steel spike golf shoes). The golf shoes are light and comfortable, and eliminate the need for changing shoes to go indoors. Sof-Spike golf shoes are also less expensive (about $40 a pair). Trav-L-Golf bag ($124.95) is a slim lightweight and water-repellent nylon golf bag, featuring a damage-resistant top that locks on for travel.

Nevada Bob's Pro Shops
Golf and Tennis
4701 Maryland Pkwy.
Las Vegas, NV 89109
(800) 634-6202
Nevada (702) 736-3686
6-page brochure, free U.S. and overseas.
  AE, DC, MC, V, MO, PC.
Name-brand tennis and golf equipment at terrific prices. Tennis racquets, racquetball racquets, balls, eye guards, strings, golf clubs, bags and balls, and golf shoes. (Call the 800 telephone number to confirm stock availability— and these terrific prices.)

Players Tennis Shop
490 Westport Ave.
Norwalk, CT 06851
(800) 243-5033
6-page brochure. AE, MC, V, MO.
Tennis Racquets, strings, grips, and
accessories are available.

Professional Golf and Tennis Suppliers
2086 N. University Dr.
Pembroke Pines, FL 33024
(305) 432-6636
4-page brochure, free U.S. and overseas.
  AE, DC, MC, V, MO, PC.
This brochure features tennis, golf,
racquetball, and jogging equipment in
an easy-to-read price list format. This
is one of the best selections of tennis and
jogging shoes (and tennis bags)
attainable by mail order.

Rayco Tennis Products
1436 University Ave.
San Diego, CA 92103
(800) 854-6692
California (714) 295-4777
2-page price list, free U.S. and overseas.
  MC, V, MO, PC.
Rayco Tennis Products specializes in
strings for tennis racquets at discounts
of 50% off retail. They also carry
racquets and grips.

Royal Golf Corporation
10100 S. Dixie Hwy.
P.O. Box A
Clarkston, MI 48016
(800) 521-8072
Michigan (800) 482-9274
31-page color catalog, prices available
  U.S. and overseas. AE, BD, DC, MC,
  V, MO, PC.
Over 70 pages are devoted to the latest
styles of golf clothes and shoes for men
and women. Royal's rubber spike golf
shoe for women ($38) features multi-
spiked rubber soles that grip firmly and
provide cushioned support on the
hardest surfaces. The leather Royal
Kiltie pack ($9.95) includes three kilties
in colors of tan, red, and navy to
compliment all your outfits.

Tee-Off Co.
5610 Flagstone St.
Long Beach, CA 90808
(213) 425-4128
2-page brochure, free U.S. and overseas.
  MO, PC.
Tee-Off Co. has developed a unique
device for practicing golf indoors or
out—anyplace there is space to swing a
golf club. When the practice ball is hit,
the ball orbits around a metal arm (from
which it is suspended by an unbreakable
nylon cord). The swivel action shows
how you hit. A straight shot orbits
straight out; hooks and slices orbit at a
telltale angle. It automatically tees itself
up again when the ball comes to a rest.
The outdoor model ($12.95) or the indoor
platform model ($18.95) would make a
terrific gift for a golfer.

Tennis Lady
P.O. Box 7106
Dallas, TX 75209
(800) 527-7523
Texas (214) 353-9631
32-page color catalog. AE, MC, V, MO,
  PC.
Terrific tennis togs for men and women.
Name brands include Ellesse of Italy,
Whims, Quantums, Fila, Pierre Cardin,
Head, and Ultrasport. There are velour
warm-ups, tennis dresses and skirts,
maternity wear, and sweaters—for
playing hard or sitting fashionably on
the sidelines.

HORSEBACK RIDING

Deluxe Saddlery Co.
1817 Whitehead Rd.
Baltimore, MD 21207
(800) 638-2470
(301) 265-6975
96-page catalog free; overseas $2. AE,
  MC, V, MO, PC.
There are fine English and Western
saddlery, riding apparel, sportswear,
and excellent gifts for the horse lover.
Eighteen pages are devoted to riding
clothes, many made in England.

Eiser's
1304 N. Broad St.
Hillside, NJ 07205
(800) 526-6987
103-page catalog, free U.S. and overseas.
  AE, MC, V.
"Everything for the horse and rider for over 80 years," says the catalog cover. Eiser's is one of the oldest riding equipment institutions in the U.S. Both English and Western gear are available. Boots from Northampton and saddles by Hartley, G. Passier & John, and Stubben are featured. There are clothing, Western hats, roping saddles, and riding crops. (They offer several custom items, including chaps and boots.)

Hall Saddlery
Div. of Laacke & Joys
1433 N. Water St.
P.O. Box 92912
Milwaukee, WI 53202
(414) 271-7885
16-page catalog, free U.S. Does not sell
  overseas. MC, V, MO, PC.
Another source of English riding apparel, bridles, bits, stirrups, Western saddles, spurs, and horse-grooming products.

H. Kaufman & Sons Saddlery Co.
139–141 E. 24th St.
New York, NY 10010
(212) MU4-6060
80-page catalog, free. AE, CB, DC, MC,
  V, MO, PC.
An excellent selection of English and Western boots, clothing, saddles, equipment, books, and gifts. Be sure to write if you don't find a particular item listed in the catalog—Kaufman's saddlemakers, bootmakers, and custom tailors can supply almost any item known to the horse world.

Libertyville Saddle Shop
P.O. Box M
Libertyville, IL 60048
(312) 362-0570
191-page catalog, $3 U.S. and overseas.
  AE, DC, MC, V, MO, PC.
Libertyville is internationally known as a supplier of quality equestrian merchandise. The catalog offers

thousands of products—many difficult to find elsewhere. English saddles by Crosby, Whippy, Gold Medal, Hermes, Passier and Felsbach of Switzerland, and more. There are also English pads, bridles, reins, martingales, bits, whips and crops, clothing, boots, hats, training equipment, and Western saddles for show and roping.

Miller's
235 Murray Hill Pkwy.
E. Rutherford, NJ 07073
(201) 460-1200
104-page catalog, $2 U.S. and overseas.
  Minimum order $10. AE, DC, MC, V,
  MO, PC.
Miller's specializes in English-style horseback riding outfits and equipment, doeskin riding jodphurs, and boots by Wembley, Elan, Griffin, and Marlborough. There are many pages devoted to horse care and stable equipment.

HUNTING

Anderson Archery Corporation
Box 130
Grand Ledge, MI 48837
(517) 617-3251
68-page catalog, free U.S. and overseas.
  Minimum order $25. MC, V, MO, PC,
  COD.
This excellent catalog offers a fine selection of archery items available from Anderson's: camouflage clothing, leading brand-name bows, quivers, bow sights, targets, arrows, arm guards, broadheads, tracking devices, and tools and accessories.

Bianchi Leather Products
1000 Calle Cortez
Temecula, CA 92390
(800) 854-8545
California (717) 676-5621
61-page color catalog, $3 U.S. and
  overseas. MC, V, MO, PC.
Bianchi's provides high quality leather holsters, gun belts, and shooter's accessories for sportsmen, law enforcement officers, and the military. Started in 1957 by John E. Bianchi, a

former policeman in suburban Los Angeles.

Bob's Gun Shop
P.O. Box 2332
Hot Springs, AR 71913
(501) 623-6785
90-page catalog, $4 U.S.; overseas $6.
  MO.
Bob's Gun Shop is a large supplier of gun parts. They stock repair parts for over 160 models of guns, firing pins for 1075 models, and magazines for 600 models.

Decoys Unlimited
Box 69
Clinton, IA 52732
(319) 243-3948
8-page brochure, $1 U.S. Does not sell
  overseas. MC, V, PC.
Decoys Unlimited develops and markets cast aluminum molds for making your own inexpensive plastic waterfowl decoys. The molds start at about $75 (for a Diver Body mold), and are filled with a medium weight polystyrene.

Dixie Gun Works
Reel Foot Ave.
Union City, TN 38261
(800) 238-6785
550-page catalog, $3 U.S. and overseas.
  AE, MC, V, MO, PC.
They claim to offer the world's most complete selection of black powder guns and accessories and antique gun parts. They also feature the Tennessee Squirrel Rifle and the Dixie Tennessee Mountain Rifle, in both finished models and kits.

Freeland's Scope Stands
3737–14 Ave.
Rock Island, IL 61201
(800) 447-1666
Illinois (309) 788-7449
184-page catalog, $2.50 refundable U.S.
  and overseas. MC, V, PC.
Freeland is noted for their own line of target shooting accessories and fine scope stands, as well as excellent imported items for hunting.

George Lawrence
306 S.W. First Ave.
Portland, OR 97204
(503) 228-8244
19-page color catalog, $2 U.S. and
  overseas. MC, V, MO, PC.
The George Lawrence Company is well known for their fine workmanship of leather holsters, cartridge belts, and related leather accessories. They started in 1857 making saddles and harnesses, and still operate today as a family business—in the original building in Portland, Oregon.

Golden Age Arms Co.
14 W. Winter St.
Delaware, OH 43015
(614) 369-6513
Golden Age Arms specializes in high quality muzzle-loading rifles, pistols, and parts for both the professional and amateur gun builder. They also offer a choice selection of books on the subject, including the encyclopedic *Firearms, Traps, and Tools of the Mountainmen,* by Carl Russell.

Nite Lite Co.
P.O. Box 1
Clarksville, AR 72830
(501) 754-2146
96-page catalog, free U.S. Does not sell
  overseas. MC, V, MO, PC, COD.
Nite Lite offers sporting goods and supplies for the hunter and for sporting dogs.

Numrich Arms Corporation
Williams Lane
West Hurley, NY 12491
(914) 679-2417
432-page catalog $4.95; overseas $5.95
  surface, $12 airmail. Minimum order
  $5. DC. MC, V, MO, PC, COD.
Numrich specializes in hard-to-find gun parts for obsolete guns, as well as replacement parts for current production guns. They carry spare parts for Enfield and Springfield, as well as many others. They advertise over 200 million parts in stock, and will quote prices for written requests.

Reinhart Fajen
P.O. Box 338
Warsaw, MO 65355
(816) 438-5111
52-page (mostly color) catalog, $4 U.S.
and overseas. MO, PC.
Reinhart's offers a variety of quality
gunstocks of many designs for hundreds
of different gun actions. They are
available in several kinds of woods:
walnut, fancy figured walnut, maple,
myrtlewood, mesquite, and laminated
woods. There are also many finishing
materials and tools available.

The Shotgun News
Box 669
Hastings, NE 68901
244-page tri-monthly publication. $15
for one year's subscription.
Shotgun News is an excellent source for
buying or selling guns. The cover states
"The trading post for anything that
shoots: shot guns, rifles, hand guns,
accessories, modern and antique."

Southeastern Outdoor Supplies
Route 3, Box 503
Bassett, VA 24055
(703) 638-4698
88-page catalog, 25¢ U.S. and overseas.
MC, V, MO, PC.
A complete line of trapping supplies.
Traps are available for most animals,
including rat, fox, squirrel, weasel,
muskrat, mink, beaver, and bear. There
are also lures and callers for elk, turkey,
and many others. Fur stretchers by
Victor and Peerless are offered.

Sport Shop
110 Gordon St.
Grifton, NC 28530
(800) 682-6264
(800) 334-5778
52-page catalog, free U.S. and overseas.
MC, V, MO, PC.
Sport Shop maintains a large computer-
controlled inventory of archery and bow
hunting supplies. In addition to bows by
Bear, Ben Pearson, Browning and Hoyt,
they also offer custom arrows, vanes and
feathers, shafts and arrow accessories.

Tidewater Specialties
U.S. Rt. 50, Box 158
WYE Mills, MD 21679
(800) 638-3696
Maryland (820-2076)
54-page color catalog, free U.S. AE, MC,
V, MO, PC.
Tidewater offers many gift items with
a duck or hunting theme, including
calendars, pillows, bath towels, snack
table sets, glasses and mugs, money
clips, and sport clothes for men and
women.

Timberwolf Cutlery
P.O. Box 757
Clanton, AL 35045
(800) 633-4266
46-page newsalog, free U.S. MC, V, MO,
PC.
There are many leading name-brand
hunting knives and sheathes. There are
also binoculars, tents, backpacks, and
camping accessories.

MOUNTAINEERING

Beck Outdoor Projects
P.O. Box 2223
Santa Barbara, CA 93120
6-page brochure, .20¢; overseas free. MO,
PC.
Bruce Beck specializes in carefully
handmade bindings (or straps) to hold
on crampons and snowshoes. The straps
are made from neoprene-nylon, nickel-
plated steel buckles, and copper belt
rivets. These are superior to the leather
variety as they will not stretch when
wet, or collect ice build-up. Accessory
straps are also available for attaching
items to a pack, and come in lengths
from fifteen to forty-eight inches.
Snowshoe bindings start at about $10.50.

Forrest Mountaineering
1517 Platte Street
Denver, CO 80202
(303) 433-3372
24-page catalog, free U.S. and overseas.
AE, MC, V, MO, PC.
Forrest designs and sells equipment for
climbing. Their product line includes
outdoor clothing, climbing harnesses,

and other soft gear. Ice and rock axes, hammers, and protection nuts for climbing are also available. Here you'll find quality products designed for people risking their lives every time they do a climb or approach a summit. One item Forrest Mountaineering has developed is the unique Fall Arrest—a shock absorber deployed as a link between the protection point in the rock and the climbing rope. The Fall Arrest has the capability to absorb energy without recoil, and sells for about $30.

SKIING

Akers Ski
Andover, ME 04216
(207) 392-4582
32-page newsalog, free U.S. Does not sell overseas. MC, V, MO, PC, COD.
Akers is a small family-run business specializing in Nordic (cross-country) skiing equipment and accessories. They feature the Trak Nowax Esprit Ski (about $105), good for the casual weekend skier. There is also a good selection of skis for advanced skiers and children, for touring and racing. There is an excellent selection of hard-to-find items such as cross-country ski waxes, cable bindings, roller skis, and children's clothes. Since 1978.

Foot Research Group
10240 SW Nimbus L-14
Portland, OR 97223
Brochure, free.
Foot Research Group offers a special computer-programmed ski boot selection service. For $19.95, you receive a detailed questionnaire which you fill out and return. The Foot Research Group then analyzes this information and informs you about which ski boots on the market are most likely to fit your foot—and skiing performance—needs. You will need to supply accurate foot measurements, a special pressure-sensitive foot imprint, and information on your height, weight, and (truthful) skiing ability.

Gorsuch, Ltd.
263 E. Gore Creek Dr.
Vail, CO 81657
(800) 525-9808
Colorado (303) 949-4005
32-page color catalog, prices unavailable. U.S. and overseas, AE, DC, MC, V, MO, PC.
Gorsuch offers a terrific selection of ski and sportswear clothing. One-piece ski suits and separates by Bogner are shown in flashy colors and designer styles. One hundred percent wool ski sweaters, by Demeter, come in the beautiful colors of lilac, pink, and soft blue, and in lovely patterns with coordinating hats. There are a few pages of men's and children's clothing (and aprés-ski boots, too).

The North Face
P.O. Box 2399, Station A
Berkeley, CA 94702
(415) 527-9700
16-page color catalog, free; overseas $4. AE, MC, V, MO, PC.
The North Face manufactures top-of-the-line clothing and equipment for backpackers, skiers, and other outdoor enthusiasts. "Quality, high performance and functionalism are our watchwords, and we can outfit anyone from the weekend hiker to the serious mountaineer or downhill skier." The ski wear catalog features durable ski parkas, vests, and ski pants, using a variety of tested insulating materials and construction techniques. The prices are most reasonable.

Powder Hounders
706 Brumback St.
Boise, ID 83707
(208) 343-8351
4-page brochure, free U.S. and overseas. MC, V, MO, PC.
Powder Hounders has developed a unique electronic ski locator device called "Ski Hummers," used for locating lost skis in powder snow. The battery-powered noisemakers (weighing less than one ounce) are attached to each binding. When your skis are released from their bindings, a constant humming sound is emitted that allows you to find your lost skis in up to four

feet of powder snow. Priced at about $39 per pair.

Powder House
311 SW Century Dr.
Bend, OR 97702
(800) 221-2019
Oregon (503) 389-6234
31-page color catalog, free U.S. AE, MC, V, MO, PC.
Power House features some great ski wear for men and women by CB Sports, Serac, Head, and Mistral. There are ski boots by Solomon and Lange, and active wear by New Balance and Dolfin.

Reliable Racing Supply
624 Glen St.
Glen Falls, NY 12801
(518) 793-5677
32-page color catalog, $1 U.S. and overseas. AE, MC, V, MO.
Specialty ski equipment and clothing. Panaja boot muffs ($46 a pair), made from Cordura nylon and foam insulation, are designed to keep ski boots dry, warm, and pliable. Reliable offers a selection of Alpine skis by Fischer and Spaulding, and cross-country skis by Fischer, Karhu, Rossignol, and Sundins. There are many ski racing accessories including racing bibs, banners, slalom poles, helmets, and clothing. They also feature training devices such as Road Ski ($139.50), designed to simulate cross-country skiing on snow, and Techni-Ski ($150), a no-snow training device for Alpine skiing (complete with rubber stoppers for ski poles).

Sno Craft
Tannery St.
Norway, ME 04268
(207) 743-7053
2-page brochure, free U.S. and overseas. MC, V, MO, PC.
Sno Craft has been one of the leading developers and manufacturers of fine snowshoes for over seventy-five years. Whether for work or recreation, Sno Craft features refined styles and fine workmanship for many snowshoeing conditions, snowmobiling, speed, all-purpose, and working and hunting in brush. Prices range from about $48 to $86.

STATIONERY & SUPPLIES

```
┌─────────────────────────────────────┐
│             SEE ALSO                 │
│         • Art/Supplies               │
│           • Books                    │
│            • Gifts                   │
│    • Large Department Stores and     │
│        Mail Order Houses             │
└─────────────────────────────────────┘
```

CARDS AND STATIONERY

American Stationery Co.
100 Park Ave.
Peru, IN 46970
(317) 473-4438
16-page color catalog, free U.S. Does not
    sell overseas. MC, V, MO, PC.
American Stationery offers high quality
personalized stationery, address labels,
and embossers at prices up to 35% below
retail. They have a wide range of paper
to suit every need from consumer to
business, from traditional to
contemporary. Postcards with colored
borders and personalized (with name
and address on one line), are priced at
$3.50 for a box of fifty.

Anita Beck Cards
Reindeer House
3409 W. 44th St.
Minneapolis, MN 55410
(612) 920-4741
32-page color catalog, $1 U.S. Does not
    sell overseas. MC, V, MO, PC.
Anita Beck is renowned for her brightly
colored cheerful note cards, stationery,
and calendars. The note cards are

mostly gay flowers and some charming
animals. They are plain on the inside,
ready for your personal greeting. The
boxed note cards are $3 (for ten cards),
and make delightful gifts. There are
also keep-books, unique recipe cards,
postcards, and Christmas cards.

Ars Femina
1937 Chestnut St.
Philadelphia, PA 19103
(215) 922-4403
4-page color brochure, free U.S. PC.
Calendars of flowers, still lifes, and
abstract designs in brilliant colors by
Sara Steele, and priced at about $8.

Baby Lines
P.O. Box 82
Hastings-on-Hudson, NY 10706
(914) 478-0121
32-page catalog, free U.S. and overseas.
    Minimum order 25 announcements.
    MC, V, MO, PC.
A large selection of custom-printed
birth announcements. From the most
correct and traditional to the unique,
such as the "Theater Ticket"
announcement (which cleverly

announces the new billing). There are also announcements for adoptions and christenings.

Birth-O-Gram
1825 Ponce de Leon Blvd.
Coral Gables, FL 33134
(305) 446-6015
68-page pamphlet, $1 U.S. Does not sell overseas, MC, V, MO, PC.
Birth-O-Gram sells birth announcements that tie in with your work, sport, or hobby. Announcements featuring the parents' special interest include professions (legal, teaching, accounting, firefighter, banker, medical and dental) and sports (fishing, hunting, golf, and football). One card (in the shape of an airplane) announces a happy landing by the birth of . . .

Cahill and Co.
145 Palisade St.
Dobbs Ferry, NY 10522
(914) 693-3600
64-page catalog, $2 U.S. and overseas. AE, MC, V, MO.
Cahill offers a variety of fine stationery and note cards. Shakespearean Note Cards display a calligraphic Shakespearean quotation, with the initial capital letter in Wedgewood blue and flowerets of yellow and green. The Cathedral Note Cards show a dozen dramatic photographs of the great Norman cathedrals of England and France. They also sell personal stationery (on laid paper), prints, bumper stickers, and books. Other catalogs on books and stationery are available.

Chadwicks
9765 Deering Ave.
Chatsworth, CA 91311
(213) 882-8776
8-page color brochure, free U.S. MC, V, PC.
Many styles of photo albums for 35mm, Instamatic, and Instant print photos.

Conservation Books
228 London Rd.
Reading, Berkshire
RG6 1AH England
0734 663281
2-page brochure, free U.S. and overseas. MC, V, MO, PC.
High quality personal stationery made from 100% recycled paper. The beautifully textured Woodland Wove recycled paper has the weight and finish comparable to the best paper. Consider the owner, John Treble's, opening catalog statement: "It takes 175 million trees . . . to supply us in Britain with paper every year . . . and over two-thirds of this paper is either dumped or burnt after being used only once."

Current
The Current Blvd.
Colorado Springs, CO 80941
(303) 471-4910
64-page color catalog, free U.S. Does not sell overseas. MO, PC.
Current is a family-owned company offering stationery featuring original Current designs: greeting cards, note paper, stationery sets and note pads, craft kits, craft books, cookbooks, and recipe cards. There are also exciting children's toys and games, useful organizers for the home and office, and gifts and gift wrap. There are good price discounts on quantity orders.

Foreign Cards
Box 123P
Guilford, CT 06437
4-page color brochure, free U.S. and overseas. MO, PC.
You'll find a large assortment of international postcards in this brochure. There are hundreds of picture postcards of American and international historic sites, viewpoints, cities, and famous places. Postcard collectors will find this an excellent source to buy from. Travelers who ruined some crucial pictures (discovered only when they returned home) might enjoy the opportunity to complete their photo albums from Foreign Cards.

Gemini Studio
21 West 17th St.
New York, NY 10011
(212) 924-6547
4-page brochure, 40¢; overseas $1. Minimum order $6. MO, PC.

Gemini Studio sells postcards, note paper, and posters of some of today's ballet superstars as photographed by internationally renowned dance and theater photographer, Max Aldman. Dramatically reproduced in black and white, there are several images of Mikhail Baryshnikov and Natalia Makarova. There are also some excellent photo postcards of the grand mime artist, Marcel Marceau. Postcards are priced at about 60¢; note paper 75¢.

Impress
Slough Farm, Westhall
Halesworth, Suffolk
IP19 8RN England
4-page brochure, free surface, $1 airmail; free overseas. Minimum order $5. MC, V, MO.
Impress sells blank cards, pressed and dried flowers, and feathers to individuals wishing to create their own unique handmade greeting cards. There is a large range of sizes, colors, and qualities of blank cards, from expensive and elaborate to plain and simple (and inexpensive).

Library of Congress
Card and Gift Catalog
Information Office, Box A
Washington D.C. 20540
32-page color catalog, free U.S. and overseas. MO, PC.
Beautiful greeting cards for Christmas, Hannukah, Valentine's Day, and general use. A brief description of the original work appears on the back of each card. There are many lovely cards including a floral design by Walter Crane, a winter photograph of a small town in Vermont by Marion Post Wolcott, and an engraving by Paul Revere. There are also many lovely reproductions, maps, books, music and records.

Merrimade
27 S. Canal St.
Lawerence, MA 01843
16-page color catalog, free U.S. and overseas. $1 for catalog and samples. Minimum order $5. MO, PC.

Merrimade offers a large selection of personalized stationery and unusual accessories. There are monogrammed tissue napkins, towels, placemats, and place cards. Personalized products include bridge score pads, cards, postcards, luggage tags, all-occasion gift ribbon, matchbooks, and a number of different types of address labels.

The Newburyport Printmaker
7 Park St.
Newburyport, MA 01950
(617) 462-6021
32-page catalog $1 U.S.; overseas $2. MC, V, MO, PC.
There are pen-and-ink prints and note cards with scenes from the farmlands, mountains, seacoast, and villages of New England. Blake Hughes, artist and owner of Newburyport Printmaker, offers these lovely pieces at excellent prices—$3 for a box of ten note cards and envelopes.

Posty Cards
2100 Grand Ave.
Kansas City, MO 64108
(800) 821-7968
4-page color brochure, free U.S. and overseas. Minimum order of 75 cards. MC, V.
Posty Cards is a family-owned manufacturer of greeting cards. Posty Cards are especially well known for their conservative and very attractive business greeting cards. There are many lines to choose from, all in good taste.

The Printery House of Conception Abbey
P.O. Box 2
Conception, MO 64433
(816) 944-2331
32-page color catalog, free U.S. Limited sales overseas, MC, V, MO, PC.
The Printery House offers high quality greeting cards, Christmas and holiday cards, and calendars with religious artwork and sentiments. They are also the sole U.S. distributors of icons produced by the Benedictine Monastery in West Germany. The unique "Family Book of Life" is a special book for recording and appreciating the religious events of members of the family.

Renaissance Greeting Cards
P.O. Box 126
Springvale, ME 04083
(800) 341-0375
Maine (207) 324-4153
60-page color catalog, $1 U.S. Does not
sell overseas. MO, PC.
Renaissance sells greeting cards for all
occasions and seasons including
complete Valentine, Christmas,
Halloween, Thanksgiving, and Jewish
New Year collections. The artwork is in
vibrant colors and the sentiments are
usually one or two cheerful lines. The
catalog beautifully presents each card
with the greeting displayed in the actual
print type. These fun cards are about 75¢
each. (A good example of how much fun
mail order shopping can be.)

Sormani Calendars
P.O. Box 403
Greenwich, CT 06836
(203) 531-7400
16-page color catalog, free U.S. and
    overseas. AE, DC, MC, V, MO, PC.
Sormani sells full color calendars of
many descriptions, including the
beautiful calendars from Korch of
Munich. There are fine art
reproductions, sports, special interest,
scenic, nature, and foreign country
calendars. Many are suitable for
framing. Prices range from about $4.95
to about $25.

Tide-Mark Press
P.O. Box 813
Hartford, CT 06142
(203) 289-0363
Brochure, free U.S.
Calendars aimed at people with special
interests. These calendars are filled with
facts and information, which make
interesting reading throughout the year.
The theme photographs are
outstanding: baseball, opera, bread-
baking, and the sea. Prices around $7
to $8.

Tree
242 Park Avenue South
New York, NY 10003
(212) 533-3896
8-page color brochure. MC, V, MO, PC.

Tree offers keep-books and albums for
recording photographs, memories, and
funny things children say. The Old
Fashioned Country Diary ($9.95) is a
lovely combination of appointment book
and diary to remember mustn't-forget
dates—and to remember each day years
later.

Valerie Harper
1 Worthy Lane
Winchester S021 2AT England
56 207
2-page price list, $1 U.S. and overseas.
    Minimum order 200 printed sheets
    and envelopes. AE, DC, MC, V, MO,
    PC.
Valerie Harper sketches detailed pen-
and-ink drawings of your home for your
uniquely personalized letterhead
stationery. All you do is provide her with
a photograph of your house for her to
work from, and (of course) the
payment—about $65, for 200 headed
sheets, 100 plain sheets and 200
matching envelopes. It would be a super
gift for anyone setting up home.

GRAPHIC ARTS

Alvin & Co.
P.O. Box 188
Windsor, CT 06095
(203) 243-8991
224-page catalog, free U.S. and overseas.
    Minimum order. MO, PC.
Alvin & Co. offer a complete line of
drafting, engineering, and graphic art
supplies. The catalog is large and well
organized, and features a selection of
products used in the commercial,
industrial, scientific, graphic arts, and
educational fields. There are superb
technical pens (the Reform Refograph,
at a good price), brushes, drawing sets,
drafting machines and scales, art tables,
lamps, and much more.

Bizzaro Inc.
P.O. Box 126, Annex Station
Providence, RI 02901
(401) 521-1305
36-page catalog, $1 refundable, U.S. and
    overseas. MC, V, MO, PC.

Kenn and Madeleine Speiser design the actual images (and fabricate the rubber matrices and pads) for the delightful rubber stamps which they mail order. They offer a catalog of over 2,000 rubber stamps and an inventory of funny faces, characters, animals, and unusual forms that is constantly changing. The average price of most single stamps is about $5, and sets are also available.

Elbow Grease
P.O. Box 25056
Richmond, VA 23260
18-page catalog, free U.S. MO, PC.
Elbow Grease specializes in very unusual rubber stamp images. There are zany characters, and many images that will make you laugh. The average price is around $6, but the stamps are also a little larger than the "usual."

Graphic Chemical & Ink Co.
728 N. Yale Ave.
P.O. Box 27
Villa Park, IL 60181
(312) 832-6004
52-page catalog, free U.S. and overseas. MO, PC.
Graphic Chemical & Ink is a major source for printmaking supplies and inks for etching, block print, stone lithography, and silkscreen. They manufacture their own fine inks as well as sell other lines, including Handschy Chemical (Hanco).

Martin Yale Industries
500 N. Spaulding Ave.
Chicago, IL 60624
(312) 826-4444
12-page color catalog, free U.S. and overseas. Minimum order $20. MO, PC.
Martin Yale offers a full line of bindery-type graphic arts equipment. There are auto folders, hydraulic cutters, high speed letter openers, collators, and check signer imprinters. There are over twenty models of paper trimmers.

100 Proof Press
P.O. Box 34 I
Eaton, NY 13334
(315) 684-3547

28-page catalog, $1 U.S. and overseas. PC.
100 Proof Press produces 848 different pictorial rubber stamps. They are mounted on hardwood blocks without handles and are proofed before shipping. There are many different alphabet styles, and an excellent selection of cartoon type characters, animals, old advertisements, military insignia, and greetings. Prices range from $1 to $5.

T. N. Lawrence & Son
2–4 Bleeding Heart Yard
Greville St., Hatton Garden
London ECIN 8SL England
01 242 3534
8-page catalog, free U.S. and overseas. Minimum order $15. MO, PC.
T. N. Lawrence is a well-known manufacturer of engravers' boxwood blocks and wood-cutting blocks. They carry blocks, tools, and materials for wood engraving, wood and lino cutting, etching, and handmade papers. Papers include English handmade papers (barcham green), R.W.S. handmade water color paper, waterleaf, imitation Japanese vellum, hand-marbled papers, and genuine Whatman papers.

NOVELTY

Badge-A-Minit
Box 800
Civic Industrial Park
LaSalle, IL 61301
(815) 224-2090
56-page color catalog, free U.S. Does not sell overseas. AE, DC, MC, V, MO, PC.
Malcolm Roebuck manufactures and sells Badge-A-Minit kits, an inexpensive tool (plus materials) for making badges. These novelty buttons, badges, and pendants are about 2-1/4″ in diameter and come with a choice of backings— pin-on, sticky back, and magnetic back. There are simple starter kits and more professional models for making badges as a hobby or a fund-raising enterprise. The starter kit sells for around $25, and has enough parts for making ten buttons. There are many creative ways

for the whole family to enjoy them: make a badge of the new baby's picture for proud grandpa to wear, or a badge for mom to proudly display her child's artwork.

Equality Products
1554 Bardstown Rd.
Louisville, KY 40205
(502) 459-8755
32-page catalog, free U.S. and overseas. MC, V, MO, PC.
Equality Products offers a variety of goods such as buttons, bumper stickers, posters, mugs, notepads, postcards, pens, pencils, T-shirts, and matchbooks imprinted with slogans that take a light-hearted approach to the very serious issue of women's rights. The catalog contains over 240 slogans on forty-three different items.

The Hug Factory
P.O. Box 4353
Louisville, KY 40204
(502) 459-9398
12-page catalog, free U.S. and overseas. MC, V, MO, PC.
Judith Steer calls what she markets "hugging paraphenalia"—T-shirts, buttons, bumper stickers, stationery pads, and stickers, all with her logo: a bear hugging itself. There is usually a word or phrase (on each item) encouraging hugging, and feeling good about oneself.

Johnson Smith Co.
35075 Automation Dr.
Mt. Clemens, MI 48043
(313) 791-2800
48-page catalog, free U.S. Does not sell overseas. MC, V, MO, PC.
Most people are familiar with the name of Johnson Smith, the mail order catalog of practical jokes, light-hearted gifts, and humorous things that make everybody laugh. Zipper bananas, wall-walking spider, electronic music Christmas cards, squirting toilet seats, giant sunglasses, mammoth real cigars (10–1/2″ long), round dice that roll up legitimate numbers, and of course the 'ol whoopee cushion. Since 1914.

Lakeside Products Co.
6646 N. Western Ave.
Chicago, IL 60645
(312) 761-5495
24-page catalog, 50¢ U.S. and overseas. MC, V, MO, PC.
Housewares and novelty items, including automatic needle threader, personal burglar alarms, trick playing cards, and miniature flashlights. There are also many safety items: blinking safety lights and emergency auto lights.

Morris Costume Co.
3108 Monroe Rd.
Charlotte, NC 28205
(704) 332-3304
200-page catalog, $5 U.S. and overseas. MC, V, MO, PC.
Morris is best known for their huge selection of rubber masks. The horror masks (says the catalog) are professionally hand-crafted works of art. There are many gruesome categories of masks: aliens, distortions, nightmares, creepshows, and all the major characters from the latest space movies. Morris Fantasie Faces kits are high quality latex prosthetics, designed like those in Hollywood, complete with make-up. They also offer numerous magic tricks, jokes, gags, hats, costumes, make-up, and special effects.

OFFICE SUPPLIES

Associated Bag Co.
160 S. Second St.
Milwaukee, WI 53204
(414) 272-2380
64-page catalog, free U.S. MC, V, MO, PC.
Associated Bag Co. offers polyethylene bags in hundreds of sizes, gauges, and styles. They also sell anti-rust and anti-static flexible packaging. There are bags for hazardous waste, lab sampling, cushioned bubble-packing, shipping, and large furniture and equipment bag covers.

The Bill-A-Pack Co.
3440 Winnetka Ave., N.
Minneapolis, MN 55427
(800) 328-5668
(612) 545-3200
62-page color catalog. PC.
The Bill-A-Pak Co. offers a complete line of quality printing and office supplies.

Buy Direct, Inc.
216 W. 18th St.
New York, NY 10011
(800) 221-5332
(212) 255-4424
32-page catalog, free U.S. Does not sell overseas. MC, V, MO, PC.
Buy Direct offers stock and custom computer forms, letterheads and envelopes on a carrier, computer supplies and furniture at discounts of 10% to 40% below manufacturer's list prices.

Caddylak Systems
201 Montrose Rd.
Westbury, NY 11590
(516) 333-8221
32-page catalog, free U.S. and overseas. Minimum order $10. AE, DC, MC, V, MO.
Caddylak is the largest manufacturer and marketer of scheduling boards. These magnetic visual control boards are aids to help businesses run efficiently by scheduling meetings, personnel assignments, creating budgets, and scheduling computer time better.

CMC
110 W. Washington
Lisbon, OH 44432
(216) 424-5363
48-page catalog, free to businesses, $1.50 to individuals U.S. Does not sell overseas. MC, V, MO, PC.
There is a large variety of office products at prices 30% to 70% off list price: printed and unprinted envelopes, purchase orders, invoices and correspondence forms, and name-brand office supplies. Started in 1954 as a manufacturer of envelopes, they have continued to expand in the office products line. Each catalog contains discount coupons, good for additional savings.

Day-Timers
P.O. Box 2368
Allentown, PA 18001
(215) 395-5884
112-page color catalog, free U.S. Limited overseas sales. AE, DC, MC, MO, PC.
Time-Planner Diaries help busy people keep organized. These handbooks are great for organizing appointments, errands, financial records, and for general record keeping. You can choose the size (desk or pocket) and page format that is best suited to your schedule and personal needs. Day-Timers also carries stationery, office forms, custom-printed binders and office products.

Demco
P.O. Box 7488
Madison, WI 53707
(800) 356-1200
Wisconsin (608) 241-1201
200-page color catalog, free U.S. and overseas. Minimum order $30. AE, MC, V, MO, PC.
With over 6,000 items in stock, Demco is one of the leading national manufacturers of office and library supplies and equipment—with over seventy-five years of service. There are lots of molded plastic magazine storage cases, racks, and shelves. If you have just purchased a computer, there are some good personal computer desks, storage and supply items sold here.

The Drawing Board
256 Regal Row
P.O. Box 220505
Dallas, TX 75222
(800) 527-9530
78-page color catalog. AE, MC, V.
The Drawing Board offers business forms and office supplies, business cards, computer supplies, stationery, labels, note pads, and typewriter supplies.

Fiberbilt Cases
601 W. 26th St.
New York, NY 10001
(800) 847-4176
16-page color catalog, free U.S. and
overseas. AE, MC, V, MO, PC.
They stock over 5,000 different sizes and
styles of carrying and shipping cases for
equipment. Custom sizes can also be
ordered, in quantities of one to
thousands. Ask for the specific brochure
that would fit your interests: audio-
visual, sales aids, jewelry sales,
computer hardware, photographic,
animal carriers. (They all look very
sturdy.)

Fidelity Products Co.
5601 International Parkway
New Hope, MN 55428
(800) 328-3034
Variety of catalogs, free U.S. Does not
sell overseas. AE, DC, MC, V.
Fidelity's 128-page *Supplies and
Equipment for Office and Industry* is
full of storage units and organizers,
industrial bins and desks. The 55-page
*Catalog of Data & Word Processing
Products* includes many name-brand
computer diskettes, diskette library files,
and computer stock forms. They also
offer most brands of mini-computer and
word processing printer ribbons (and
printwheels). The 32-page *Fidelity
Home Shopper Catalog* offers many
solutions for storage problems in the
home.

Frank Eastern Co.
625 Broadway
New York, NY 10012
(212) 677-9100
56-page catalog free U.S. Does not sell
overseas. Minimum order $40. MC, V,
MO, PC.
Frank Eastern carries everything you
need for your business or home office
at discounts of up to 60%: bookcases in
wood and steel, executive and clerical
desks, calculators and copy machines,
and many small desk supplies. Since
1946.

Grayarc
P.O. Box 2944
Hartford, CT 06104
(800) 243-5250
62-page catalog, free U.S. MC, V, PC.
Grayarc offers a large selection of labels,
forms, office and shipping supplies.
There are handy personalized memos
with duplicate copies to avoid inter-
office confusion, and many other forms
designed to make your business run
smoother. There are shipping and
mailing labels, bills of lading forms,
general purpose forms, invoices, and a
very large selection of envelopes.

IBM Direct
One Culver Rd.
Dayton, NJ 08810
(800) 426-2468
57-page color catalog, free U.S. MC, V,
PC.
IBM sells typewriter ribbons, and
elements and supplies for computers
and office equipment.

Jesse Jones
P.O. Box 5120
Philadelphia, PA 19141
(800) 621-5809
Illinois (800) 972-5858
31-page color catalog. AE, MC, V.
Jesse Jones specializes in handy
organizers for the home or office,
magazine cases for specific magazines
(or custom size), and slip cases for
dustproof storage. There are also record
and tape cases, and letter file cases.

Light Impressions Corp.
P.O. Box 940
Rochester, NY 14603
(800) 828-6216
92-page catalog, $2 U.S. and overseas.
AE, MC, V, MO, PC.
Light Impressions supplies archival
products for storage and display to
photographers, artists, historical
societies, hospitals, business, and
industry. They are used for the storage
and display of valuable negatives,
documents, prints, mat boards, and
works of art on paper and fabric. Their
archival products include portfolio

boxes, archival albums, and enclosure materials for negatives.

Medical Arts Press
3440 Winnetka Ave., N.
Minneapolis, MN 55427
(612) 545-3200
126-page color catalog. PC.
Office forms, professional stationery, and related accessories for the medical office. There are end-tab file folders and color-coded labels, appointment logs, insurance record logs, and more.

Memindex
149 Carter St.
Rochester, NY 14601
(800) 828-5885
(716) 342-7990
23-page color catalog, free U.S. AE, MC, V, PC.
Memindex sells desk organizers, wall planning guides, and desk accessories. They also carry many "Photowalls"— floor-to-ceiling, wall-to-wall decorator murals showing beautiful outdoor scenes.

National Business Furniture
222 E. Michigan St.
Milwaukee, WI 53202
(414) 276-8511
48-page color catalog, free U.S. Does not sell overseas. MC, V, MO, PC.
National Business Furniture offers quality office furniture at discount prices of 25% to 40% off retail. The catalog features wood and steel office desks, chairs, files, bookcases, reception furniture, conference furniture, storage cabinets, and computer furniture. They feature top brand names including Samsonite, Hon, La-Z-Boy, Dolly Madison, Indiana Desk, and others.

New England Business Service
500 Main Street
Groton, MA 01471
(800) 225-6380
(800) 252-9226
64-page color catalog, free U.S. PC.
New England Business Service is a leading supplier of standardized business forms (and other printed products) to small businesses in the U.S.

and Canada. There is a wide selection of business stationary, cards, sales forms, mailing containers, and supplies.

Quill
100 S. Schelter Rd.
Lincolnshire, IL 60069
(312) 634-4850
240-page catalog, free U.S. Does not sell overseas. Sells only to businesses on an open account.
Quill is one of the major mail order distributors of general office supplies and equipment in America with over 300,000 customers. Since 1956.

Rapidforms
501 Benigno Blvd.
Bellmawr, NJ 08031
(609) 933-0480
70-page color catalog, free U.S. Does not sell overseas. PC.
Rapidforms sells plain or imprinted business forms, letterheads, envelopes, price-marking labels and guns, one-write systems, labels, bags, registers and register forms, and various other office supplies.

The Reliable Corporation
1001 West VanBuren St.
Chicago, IL 60607
(800) 621-4344
Illinois (312) 666-1800
48-page color catalog, free U.S. Does not sell overseas. Minimum order $10. AE, MC, V.
Office supplies, machines and equipment. The 48-page *Office Supplies Machines and Furniture Catalog* offers many pages of pens, pencils, markers, and related desk supplies. The 46-page *Computer Supplies Sale Catalog* offers good buys on diskettes, word processor ribbons, and computer furniture. (There is also continuous letterhead stationery at very reasonable prices.) The 24-page *Business Electronics Sale Catalog* offers typewriters, transcribers, calculators and telephones.

South Shore Systems
685 Washington St.
Hanover, MA 02339
(617) 826-6366

100-page catalog, $5 U.S. Does not sell overseas. MO.
Basic office supplies and furniture. They also have a good selection of accounting systems for single writing entry and data processing supplies.

Spear
P.O. Box 7025
Colorado, Springs, CO 80933–7025
(303) 471-9850
6-page brochure, free U.S. MC, V, PC.
Desk and door nameplates in about thirty different styles.

V. W. Emicke Associates
P.O. Box 160
Bronxville, NY 10708
(914) 337-1900
72-page color catalog, free U.S. Does not sell overseas. MO, PC.
V. W. Emicke specializes in internationally copyrighted personnel and office forms currently in use by over 300,000 organizations in the U.S., Canada, and Europe. There are forms to streamline every aspect of personnel management, from the selection process through exit interview.

Wilcox International
2737 Shermer Rd.
Northbrook, IL 60062–7798
Illinois (800) 942-5144
311-page color catalog. MC, V.
Suppliers of stationery, office supplies, and furniture for hotels. They have some great prices and selections on lawn chairs and tables, bedroom sets, folding tables, lamps, chairs, desks, and linens (for home use—why not?)

Xerox Corporation
Route 303 and Bradley Rd.
Blauvelt, NY 10913
(800) 431-1666
New York (800) 942-1200
58-page color catalog. PC.
Office supplies, including: typing and word processor supplies, copiers, computers, furniture, and management aids.

PENS

Good Service Pen Shop
1079 Forest Hills Dr., S.W.
Rochester, MN 55901
(509) 281-1988
Catalog, free; overseas $3. MO, PC.
There are both antique fountain pens and new fountain pens by Lamy, Pilot, Waterman, and Mont Blanc. There are also old pens by Parker, Sheaffer, Eversharp, Waterman, and Conklin, plus mechanical pencils. The beautiful hand-painted lacquer pens by Pilot have tips of 18K gold, and are available in both fine and medium points. If you have an old favorite fountain pen that needs rejuvenating, the Good Service Pen Shop will happily make the repairs for you.

International Pen Shop
2 West 46 St.
New York, NY 11215
(212) 575-555
40-color catalog, free U.S. and overseas. AE, DC, MC, V, MO, PC.
International Pen Shop claims to carry the largest selection of fine writing instruments in the world. They carry over forty-six different brands from around the world. There are one-of-a-kind pens crafted for them by master jewelers (some in solid gold), technical pens, music writing pens, antique pens, and pens for artists, calligraphers, and cartographers. There are elegant pens from Dupont, Elysee, Dunhill, and Mont Blanc. The Mont Blanc Diplomat in 18K solid gold (with 18K gold nib) can be yours for around $6,500 (postpaid). Paraphernalia (from Italy) offers strikingly original pens they describe as "beyond the contemporary."

National Pen Corporation
9395 Cabot Dr.
San Diego, CA 92126
(800) 854-1000
California (619) 566-7800
16-page catalog, $3 U.S. Does not sell overseas. MC, V, MO, PC.
National Pen Corporation has been manufacturing and supplying the nation's businesses and consumers with

quality writing instruments for over eighteen years. They offer many kinds of pens, from non-retractable ledger pens to various retractable pens, and their newest item is the liquid ink Fun Machine pen.

WEDDING AND HOLIDAY SUPPLIES

Ann's Wedding Stationery
P.O. Box 326
Carrollton, MO 64633
(800) 821-7011
Ann's Wedding Stationery offers an excellent selection of wedding stationery—and all the accessories to plan a beautiful wedding.

Cordon Bleu
3010 Bailey Ave.
Buffalo, NY 14215
(716) 836-4100
36-page color catalog, free U.S. and overseas. MC, V, MO, PC.
Wedding invitations and accessories. Wedding invitations are available both printed and novographed (raised print) in many lovely styles. The invitations or announcements are furnished with inside and outside envelopes and tissues on quality paper at very reasonable prices. The catalog design makes it easy to price and compare.

Emgee
3210 Koapaka St.
Honolulu, HI 96819
(800) 367-2666
Hawaii (808) 836-0988
16-page catalog, $2 U.S. and overseas. MC, V, PC.
There are approximately 400 designs of Christmas ornaments and table pieces manufactured in Honolulu. They are handcrafted in wood in Hawaiian or traditional motifs. (Religious, sports and hobby themes, too.) Easter and baby nursery ornaments are also available.

Fortress
Church Supply Stores
2900 Queen Lane
Philadelphia, PA 19129
(800) 367-8737
32-page color catalog, free U.S. and overseas. Minimum order $10. V, MC, PC.
Fortress Church Supply stores offers Advent wreaths and calendars, music boxes, candles, and Nativity scenes.

Holiday House
P.O. Box 791
Upper Montclair, NJ 07043
(201) 256-0901
6-page brochure, free U.S. Does not sell overseas. MO, PC.
Gifts for the wedding couple might include their invitation—permanently displayed. Invitations (birth, wedding, graduation, Bar Mitzvah, or even newspaper clippings) can be copied exactly on the sterling silver tops of a small wood box, or etched on a clear glass hurricane globe. The actual invitation can be fixed on a tray, plaque, bookend, or desk basket, and then be lacquered for permanence.

Rexcraft
Rexburg, ID 83440
(800) 635-3898
(800) 635-4653
50-page catalog, free; overseas $4. MC, V, MO, PC.
There are formal and informal designs for wedding invitations offered by Rexcraft. Various kinds of stocks and colors of paper are available. Rexcraft also has a good selection of personalized and non-personalized items: napkins, scrolls, ribbons, reception and wedding merchandise.

Wedding Stationery by Dawn
Box 100
Lumberton, NJ 08048
(800) 257-9567
44-page color catalog, free U.S. Does not sell overseas. MC, V, MO, PC.
Dawn offers a beautiful collection of wedding stationery, accessories, and gifts for the bridal party. Their prices are advertised at a discount of 20% to 50% off retail. (The low prices don't mean you are sacrificing selection; this is an excellent catalog to plan your wedding by.

TOBACCO, CIGARS, & PIPES

```
SEE ALSO
• Clothing- Men
• Gifts
```

Alfred Dunhill of London
620 Fifth Ave.
New York, NY 10010
(212) 481-6950
40-page color catalog, $2; overseas free.
  AE, MC, C, PC.
Recognized for their excellence in
gentleman's accessories and smoking
accoutrements, the Dunhill signature is
synonymous with traditional elegance.
In 1910 the Dunhill Briar pipe was first
introduced. It was the first to carry the
now legendary white spot, the Dunhill
hallmark. The catalog features
handmade humidors and cigars by
Montecruz, H. Upmann, Ramon Allones,
Flor de A. Allones and a nice selection
of pipes and smoking accessories.

Andrew Marks Pipemaker
Frog Hollow
Middlebury, VT 05753
(802) 462-2112
8-page brochure, $1. Does not sell
  overseas. V, MO, PC.
Andrew Marks handcrafts pipes from
briar root, carefully selected for its
beauty, strength of grain, and
exceptional smoking qualities. The
finest vulcanite stem is handcut to
complement each pipe design. Andrew

Marks's pipes are all signed and dated.
He is an artisan, seeking perfection in
the pipe's sculptured form and smoking
elegance.

Connoisseur
51 W. 46th St.
New York, NY 10036
(212) 247-6054
14-page catalog. AE, MC, V, MO, PC.
If Sherlock Holmes were on assignment
in the streets of New York City, he might
very well discover The Connoisseur and
stop to browse. They design and
manufacture all their own pipes and
blend their own tobaccos. Algerian,
Calabrian, and Grecian Briar is selected
and cured to produce cool, dry smoking
pipes. Standard shapes start at $12.50,
classic and Danish-styled start at $40.
One-of-a-kind and custom-made pipes
are yours for $350—or maybe you'd
rather send in your old favorite for
repairs. (All repairs are done in their
own shop and returned to you in two
weeks.)

Dean Swift
P.O. Box 2009
San Francisco, CA 94126
(415) 982-7990

Information on request. MO, PC.
Fancy sniffing snuff is becoming a popular alternative to cigarette smoking. The English-type nasal snuffs are usually a blend of briar-cured burley and dark-fired tobaccos. The tobaccos are put into a machine known as "three pestles and mortars," and ground into a coarse powder. A little aging, moisture, essential oils, and scents are added to produce Dean Swift's fine snuffs. Their introductory offer of $5 U.S. ($6 overseas) includes three assorted snuff tins and written instructions. You may never have to heed a "No Smoking" sign again.

Famous Smoke Shop
1450 Broadway
New York, NY 10018
(800) 847-4062
16-page catalog, free U.S. and overseas. MO, PC.
Famous Smoke Shop features an extensive selection of some of the world's finest cigars and tobaccos at very reasonable prices. They offer Partagas, Macanudo, Montecruz, Famous Dominican cigars, Primo del Cristo, and other excellent brands.

Georgetown Tobacco and Pipe Store, Inc.
3144 M St., NW
Washington D.C. 20007
(202) 338-5100
16-page catalog, 50¢ U.S. and overseas. AE, MC, V, MO, PC.
Georgetown stocks quality pipe and tobacco products from around the world as well as their own exclusive brands. There are tinned European pipe tobaccos and briar pipes from England, Denmark, Ireland and Italy; lighters by Dunhill, Dupont, Zippo, and Colibri; all-tobacco cigars, predominately handmade, from Central America, the Caribbean, Europe, and the Pacific Islands. Phone customers will find friendly and knowledgeable assistance from the catalog sales department.

G. Smith and Sons
Smith the Snuff Blender
74 Charing Cross Rd.
London WC2H ONG
01 836 7422

6-page brochure, free. AE, DC, MC, V, MO, BD.
For over 100 years, Smith the Snuff Blender has blended choice tobaccos with rare perfumes of aromatic herbs and spices. Since Victorian days, generations have been delighting in sniffing a pinch now and then. If you're a beginner, G. Smith and Sons suggests selecting a medium mixture: while offering all the pleasures of snuff-taking, medium does not have the pungency and penetrating effect of the very coarse, dark types or the very fine, light varieties. Are you up to snuff? (Sorry.)

Hayim Pinhas
Tahtakale, Kristal Han 312-ist
Istanbul, Turkey
26-page catalog, free. Minimum order of two pipes. PC.
Meerschaum is a white stone found and mined in Asia Minor. It is organic in origin, lightweight and very porous. Meerschaum pipes are hand-carved and waxed, which gives them their distinctive velvety finish. Tobacco absorbed in the Meerschaum will gradually color the bowl from the bottom up, taking on a rick brown tone after years of smoking. Plain bowled pipes start at $10. Buying direct from Hayim Pinhas is your best buy for meerschaum pipes.

J R Tobacco Corp.
100 Sterling Mine Rd.
Sloatsburg, NY 10974
(800) 431-2380
New York (914) 753-2745
60-page catalog, free U.S. Does not sell overseas. Minimum order $10. AE, MC, V, MO, PC. COD.
Cigar smokers are often pictured as successful businessmen, hotshot lawyers, or backroom deal-makers. To most most cigar smokers, buying and smoking cigars is a luxury and an image enhancer. Lew Rothman claims to sell over 3,000 varieties of cigars, with prices to fit every pocketbook. (His prices are 20% to 60% lower than retail.) Lew Rothman also offers the J R Alternative cigars—reasonably priced quality cigars

in lieu of the very expensive brand-name cigars.

Nat Sherman
711 Fifth Ave.
New York, NY 10022
(800) 972-1000
New York (212) 751-9100
50-page color catalog, free U.S. and
   overseas. Minimum order $10. AE, CB,
   DC, MC, V, MO, PC.
Nat Sherman is known as the
"tobacconist to the world." Using only
pure tobacco, they offer a large selection
of cigars, tobaccos, cigarettes, pipes,
humidors, cutters, lighters, and pens.

Nurhan Cevahir
Istaklal Caddesi Bekar Sokak No 12/4
Beyoglu Istanbul
Turkey
444123
From a white, lightweight block of
meerschaum, Turkish artisans can
carve the heavily etched Laughing
Bacchus, the delicate Tulip, or the
unpretentious Trapeze pipes. There are
pipes to fit many characters and moods.
(Some of these carved heads are
ferocious enough to give pipe dreamers
nightmares.) Prices start at $15.

Wilke Pipe Shop, Inc.
400 Madison Ave.
New York, NY 10017
(212) 755-1118
10-page brochure, free. Minimum order
   overseas $35. AE, MC, V, MO.
This small, friendly staff offers
unpainted, handcrafted, briar root
pipes—which they originated in 1872.
There is a large selection of fine
imported cigars from Brazil, Holland,
Switzerland and Germany, and popular
"baked cigars" from Brazil. You can also
roll your own from Wilke cigarette
blends.

TOOLS

SEE ALSO
- Crafts/Woodworking
- Gardening/Equipment
- Housewares/Hardware
- Large Department Stores and Mail Order Houses

Abbeon Cal, Inc.
123–116A Gray Ave.
Santa Barbra, CA 93101
(905) 996-0810
992-page catalog,
Abbeon offers 992 pages of instruments, engineering and drafting tools, graphic arts devices, furnaces, furniture, and tools of all types. Excellent product descriptions provide sizes and specifications for each item.

Airborne Sales Co., Inc.
8501 Steller Dr.
PO Box 2727
Culver City, CA 90230
(213) 870-4687
92-page catalog, $1 refundable, U.S. and overseas. $10 minimum order. AE, MC, V, MO, PC.
Since 1947, Airborne Sales Co. has been offering large discounts on aircraft, marine, automotive, and industrial items including magnets, winches, pumps, hydraulics, motors, relays, tools, valves, and gauges. They sell new, used, and surplus items manufactured by Airborne, items which they distribute, and items for which Airborne is the dealer.

American Machine & Tool Co.
4th Ave. & Spring St.
Royersford, PA 19468
(215) 948-3800
16-page catalog, free U.S. and overseas. MC, V, MO, PC.
American machine manufacturers bench-type home workshop power tools and accessories at very reasonable prices. The accessory line includes such items as lathe tools, measuring tools, lathe chucks, tool cases, specialty vises, drill-sharpening devices, and special cutting tools.

Bailey's, Inc.
P.O. Box 550
Laytonville, CA 95454
(707) 984-6133
68-page catalog, $1 U.S. and overseas. MC, V, MO, PC.
Bailey's sells logging, forestry, and safety equipment. There are Alaskan Sawmills, hydraulic vertical wood-splitters, wedges, chain saws and parts, logging clothes, and other essentials for woodcutters.

Brookstone Company
127 Vose Farm Rd.
Peterborough, NH 03458
(603) 924-9511
Brookstone is famous for providing household, workshop, and garden gadgets. Advertising "hard-to-find tools and other fine things," the catalog is a good shopping source for handy and useable gifts including the no-stoop dustpan/sweeper, lamp timer,

inconspicuous safes, and jumper cables. The hobbyist and professional putterer will find fold-away table legs to create your own inexpensive workshop table, and a cushioned mat to soften and insulate your workshop floor.

By Hand and Foot, Ltd.
P.O. Box 611
Brattleboro, VT 05301
(802) 254-2101
20-page catalog, free U.S. MC, V, MO, PC.
By Hand and Foot imports and manufacturers quality human-powered tools for gardening, farming, and forestry.

Centaur Forge Ltd.
P.O. Box 340
117 N. Spring St.
Burlington, WI 53105
(414) 763-9175
88-page catalog, $2; overseas $4.
  Minimum order, $35. MC, V, MO.
Centaur Forge claims to carry the world's largest and most varied line of blacksmithing and horseshoeing equipment and supplies. Same-day shipping is available on all merchandise including anvils, forges, horseshoes and nails, and hoof pads. Books and supplies on blacksmithing, metalworking, and welding are available.

Direct Safety
7815 S. 46th St.
Phoenix, AZ 85040
(800) 528-7405
(602) 968-7009
66-page color catalog. MC, V, MO, PC.
Safety products, protective clothing, and equipment for businesses and industrial use.

D.R.I. Industries, Inc.
11105 Hampshire Ave. South
Bloomington, MN 55438
(612) 944-3530
104-page some color catalog, free. Does not sell overseas. AE, CB, DC, MC, V, MO, PC.
The home handyman will find fasteners, tools, and organizers of high quality and low cost. The Dream Shop ($399.99) is D.R.I.'s most expensive item. It contains over 13,500 pieces of hardware, organized and labeled in more than seventy bins and cabinets. (Paul Harmon, owner, claims that buying those parts at a retail store would cost more than $1,000.) The Nut and Bolt Shop ($19.95) is a set of 2,101 of the most-used sizes of nuts, bolts, screws, washers, and cotter pins—now organized in a 25-drawer, fifty-five bin, labeled cabinet. These handyman-type products will appeal to both craftsmen and small businesses.

The Fine Tool Shops, Inc.
20 Backus Ave.
Danbury, CT 06810
(800) 243-1037
32-100 page color catalog, free U.S. and overseas. AE, DC, MC, V, MO, PC.
Fine Tools sells a huge range of quality woodworking tools—European workbenches, carving tools from England, Makita power tools from Japan, and tool chests from America. Those orange-handled garden pruners (by Saboten of Japan) are designed with a special blade pivot mechanism to reduce friction, and will delight both weekend gardeners and hardware junkies.

Forestry Suppliers, Inc.
205 W. Rankin St.
P.O. Box 8397
Jackson, MS 39204–9987
(800) 647-5368
Mississippi (800) 682-5397
480-page some color catalog, U.S. and overseas. MC, V, PC.
Over 8,000 professional products for use in forestry, surveying, engineering, drafting, agriculture, geology, and parks and recreation.

Fox Maple Tools
Snowville Rd.
West Brownfield, ME 04010
(207) 935-3720
24-page catalog, $1; overseas $2.
  Minimum order $10. MC, V, MO, PC, COD.

Steve Chappell is the U.S. distributor for Ashley Iles Tools. Woodworking enthusiasts will recognize him as the English craftsman who hand-forges chisels and other fine carving and turning tools. In addition to many kinds of woodworking tools (including finish sanders for cabinet makers), Fox Maple Tools also specializes in timber frame construction tools. Using squared off pine beams, Fox Maple has become a source of materials and know-how for the traditional framing methods inherent in New England's 200-year-old houses.

Frog Tool Co.
700 W. Jackson Blvd.
Chicago, IL 60606
(312) 648-1270
Over 5,000 varieties of fine hand woodworking tools, workbenches, chisels, gouges, rasps, files, lathes, vises, hammers, and kits are listed in this catalog. Thirty-four pages are devoted to an extensive coverage of books on woodworking, including toys, blacksmithing, log cabins, woodcarving, furniture, carpentry, and repairs. If you're thinking of just getting started, there are some great step-by-step books.

Gilliom Manufacturing Inc.
1700 Scherer Parkway
St. Charles, MO 63301
(314) 724-1812
8-page brochure, $1; overseas $2. MC, V, MO, PC.
Gillom sells build-it-yourself power tools: lathe-drill presses, belt sanders, table and band saws, wood shapers, and circular saw tables. The plans and kits are designed for the average home craftsman to build. Using household carpenter tools (they say), "If you can build a square wood box, you can build an accurate, durable power tool."

The Goldak Co.
547 W. Arden Ave.
Glendale, CA 91203
(213) 240-2666
4-page brochure, $3; $5 overseas. MO, PC.

Founded in 1933, Goldak Co. designed and sold metal locators and pipe detectors used by the public for locating underground metals, pipes, and cables. They still supply the utility companies, but also have customers among modern-day treasure hunters. Using a metal detector while beachcombing, or treasure hunting in old Ghost Towns, can unearth coins, rings, and artifacts.

J. Cheap & Sons
Cheaps Pond Park
Box 7199
Warrensville, OH 44128
(800) 821-4142
Ohio (216) 292-1090
38-page catalog, free U.S. MC, V, MO, PC.
Tools for home, craft, car gardening, woodworking, and hobby use—"Rarely undersold."

Jerry co Inc.
601 Linden Pl.
Evanston, IL 60202
(312) 475-8440
48-page newsalog, free U.S. Does not sell overseas. MC, V, MO, PC.
Jerry co offers surplus mechanical instruments and small electrical parts.

Shopsmith, Inc.
750 Center Dr.
Vandalia, OH 45377
(800) 543-7586
(513) 898-6070
56-page catalog, free U.S. Does not sell overseas. Minimum order $10. MC, V, MO, PC.
Shopsmith is a manufacturer and direct marketer of woodworking power tools and accessories. There are layout and measuring tools, clamping tools, and many types of saws and finishing tools. All Shopsmith tools must meet rigid evaluation tests before being listed in the catalog, and all tools are supported with excellent instructional material.

Surplus Center
P.O. Box 82209
Lincoln, NE 68501
(402) 474-4366
124-page catalog, $1; $2 overseas. AE, MC, V, MO, PC.

Many of these new and used tools are purchased as surplus—and can save you up to 85% of what the item originally cost, or what you would have to pay through regular retail. There are generators, tools, jacks, lights, pumps, hydraulic equipment, motor parts, and more. Started more than fifty years ago, Surplus Center remains a family business offering a large variety of tools at great prices.

U. S. General
100 Commercial St.
Plainview, NY 11803
(800) 645-7077
196-page catalog, MC, V, PC.

"Over 600 late-model hand and power tools for the homeowner, mechanic, and industrial user."

Zip Penn, Inc.
P.O. Box 15129
Sacramento, CA 95851
(800) 824-8521
(800) 952-5535
30-page catalog, free U.S. MC, V, MO,
   PC, COD.
Zip Penn sells chain saws, lawn mowers and small engine parts. They have parts to fit about eighteen name-brand saws: David Bradley, Dolmar, Echo, Frontier, Jobu, Pioneer, Jonsereds, Lombard, and Massey Ferguson to name a few.

TOYS & FUN

SEE ALSO
- Books
- Electronics/Computer
- Gifts
- Large Department Stores and Mail Order Houses
- Museums

Animal Town Game Co.
P.O. Box 2002
Santa Barbara, CA 93120
(805) 962-8368
32-page annual newsalog, free. MO, PC.
Ken and Jan Kosbun have created board games that blend the spirit of fair competition with the spirit of cooperation. The fun of these games is in the process: helping each other, making decisions together, trusting, and doing your best (not just being the winner). Save the Whales ($23) challenges the players to work together to save eight whales from extinction. Misjudgements or bad luck will cause the catcher ship to catch a whale—a sad event for everyone! Madison Avenue ($17) requires role-playing in a game contrasting the advertising industry of Madison Avenue—and the environmental goods and ideas of Briar Patch. Ken Kosbun has a monthly drawing for a free board game for those people on his mailing list.

Ann Watson
54 Nunda Blvd.
Rochester, NY 14610
(716) 244-0808
4-page brochure, free U.S. PC.
Ann Watson makes unique soft-sculptured dolls, made to resemble a particular person. She works from photographs, or descriptions of the person's coloring and favorite clothing. The fourteen-inch basic doll in the buff starts at $80; clothing and accessories are extra. Can you think of a special person you'd like to honor, or a celebrity you'd like to cuddle?

Baron Bridge Supplies
151 Thierman Lane
Louisville, KY 40207
(502) 895-1354
32-page catalog, free $2 overseas. MC, V, MO, PC.
Baron is one of the leading bridge supply houses in the world. They supply books, cards, gift items, and supplies for bridge games at clubs and at home. With catalog items such as Killing Defense ($5.95), Slam Bidding ($11.95) and Defend With Your Life ($16.50), you might think that bridge is a violent card game. (True, bridge is the only game that has more shin injuries than soccer.)

Bear Creek Co.
Sugar Pine Rd.
Medford, OR 97501
24-page color catalog, free. Printed
    spring and fall. MC, V, MO, PC.
This catalog offers a delightful
collection of toys, stuffed animals, books,
and clothing for children. Bear Creek
exclusives include Hippo Bath Puppet
($7.65), and a space-saving corner
playhouse of nylon cloth ($39.75). For
children eight years or older, the
Weather Station ($23.65) includes more
than ten different meterologic studies.
In addition to great toys, Bear Creek
offers you many extras, such as batteries
included in toys requiring them, gift
wrapping, and a flat shipping charge of
$2 for any number of gifts shipped in
America.

Bear-In-Mind
73 Indian Pipe Lane
Concord, MA 01742
(617) 369-5987
48-page (some color) catalog, $1;
    overseas $2. AE, MC, V, MO, PC.
Bear-In-Mind started in 1978 when two
housewives decided to start a business
that would complement their roles as
wives and mothers. Fran Lewis claims
her company is the first, oldest, and
largest bear mail order company in the
world. Arctophiles (bear lovers) will
recognize Teddy Bear designers Gund,
Vanderbear, Steiff, Hermann, Alresfor,
Littlefolk, Avanti, Kinser and Clemens.
There are over 150 soft and furry
companions in this catalog, including a
twelve and one-half inch Richard Steiff
limited edition bear ($90), and a seven-
inch Original Teddy $12.

The Bear Necessities
BN Mail Order Inc.
P.O. Box C-10
Belmont, MA 02178
(800) 543-3450
Massachusetts (617) 647-9365
24-page color catalog. AE, MC, V, MO,
    PC.
This catalog offers a large selection of
bears and "bearaphernalia": calendars,
Christmas stockings, music boxes,
luggage, and chocolate—all with the
bear theme.

Big Toys
2601 South Hood St.
Tacoma, WA 98409
(206) 572-7611
12-page catalog, $1. MC, V, MO.
In 1970 Chuck Kirby and Barney Minger
formed the Big Toys Company,
specializing in outdoor play equipment.
Using heavy log framework, slide
chutes, steering wheels, belt swings,
cargo nets, and fireman's poles, they've
designed outdoor play equipment that
is both safe and durable. The modular
system enables a family to build a
variety of safe and imaginative play
structures for children of all ages.
Starting at $205, it's nice to know this
investment can be added to—or even
dismantled and reassembled if you
move.

Bits & Pieces
125 Walnut St.
Watertown, MA 02172
(800) 544-7295
32-page color catalog, free. AE, MC, V.
Bits and Pieces features over a hundred
colorful and challenging puzzles. There
are jigsaw puzzles, including the clever
Hay in the Needle Stack ($6.95), a one-
thousand-piece Dungeons and Dragons
($10.95), and Jelly Beans (ten thousand
pieces, totaling 3,000 calories). There
are puzzle rings, wooden animal
puzzles, rhombic puzzles, and tangle
sculptures to boggle your brains.

B. J. Alan Company, Inc.
P. O. Box 3
Columbiana, OH 4408
(800) 321-9071
Ohio (800) 362-1034
24-page color catalog, $2. Does not sell
    overseas. Minimum order $25. MC, V,
    MO, PC.
B. J. Alan Co. states they are the largest
importer and distributor of fireworks in
America. You'll find them all here—
ladyfingers, rockets, aerials, ground
spinners, parachutes, sparklers, and
snakes. The biggest pop listed here is
an M-60 firecracker. There are also
Roman candles with ten repeating
colorful shots (priced at one dozen for
$6.99), and bottle rockets with report,
shooting 200 feet in the air ($12.99 a

gross). Read the order form carefully for legal and liability statements.

Boards and Bees Pro Shop
1942 Alba SW
Wyoming, MI 49509
(616) 452-7031
Price list, self-addressed stamped
   envelope. MO, PC.
"When a ball dreams, it dreams that it is a flying disc," says Tom Poll, owner of Board and Bees Pro Shop, the largest flying disc and frisbee mail order company. Tom offers many collectors and discontinued items, including Wham-O, Whirley, Discraft, and Webb. You might consider retiring your old Pluto Platter of the 60s, and buying a new one!

The Boomerang Man
311 Park Ave.
Monroe, LA 71201
(318) 323-2356
24-page newsalog, free; overseas 3
   International Reply Coupons. MO, PC.
This catalog specializes in boomerangs, also known as Bs, booms, and sticks. Boomerangs come in many shapes. There are some shaped like the letters "E" and "F", called E-rangs and F-rangs. The Crosstick ($3.50) is great for younger children who want to throw and haven't yet developed the touch. All boomerangs are accompanied by detailed throwing instructions. With a light touch and a flick of the wrist you, too, can learn to fly one of these wooden, double-winged, aerodynamic wonders. A little more practice in this growing sport and you may want to compete in the "Now You See It, Now You Don't See It" boomerang tournament held each June, in Washington, D.C. Al Gerhard holds the record with a 123-yard throw with a hickory boom. And he never even had to chase it.

Charlotte Weibulls Dockcenter
Gustav Adolfs Torg 45
S-211 39 Malmo Sweden
040 23 03 65
What once was a dress shop for Swedish national costumes in Malmo is now one of Sweden's most popular souvenir shops. There are many lovely dolls dressed in costumes of every Swedish district, from Lappland to Skane. There are also dolls from fairy tales, holidays, and foreign countries. Lucia doll ($11) and Lace-Making Lady ($25) are both priced well.

Cherry Tree Toys
P.O. Box 369
Belmont, OH 43718
(614) 484-1746
16-page catalog, $1; overseas $2.
   Minimum order $10. Discount
   available on orders over $50. MO, PC,
   COD.
Cherry Tree Toys is located in a turn-of-the-century cigar factory in the rolling hills of southeast Ohio. They offer a complete selection of plans, kits, and finished cherry wood toys. Kits contain everything needed to build the toys, using your own simple hand tools. The individually handcrafted finished toys have animals with animated features and vehicles with moving parts. These durable toys have been featured in over thirty national magazines and sold throughout the world.

Childcraft
20 Kilmer Rd.
P.O. Box 500
Edison, NJ 08818
(800) 631-5657
New Jersey (201) 572-6100
52-page color catalog, prices
   unavailable. AE, MC, V, MO, PC.
Childcraft is well known for their fine selection of sturdy toys, children's furniture, building blocks, and teaching devices. Many of the toys are imported from Britain, Germany, Italy, France, Sweden, Spain, and the Far East. Sinkadink ($22.95) is a novel molded sink that attaches to the side of a standard bathtub. It is convenient place to keep a cup, toothbrush, soap, and wash cloth; the splashes drip to the inside of the tub. See-Saw Rocker ($39.95), used indoors or out, is a durable, curved polyethylene mold that will teach a child balance in a fun experience.

Clarkpoint Croquet Co.
P.O. Box 457
Southwest Harbor, ME 04679
(207) 244-9284
4-page brochure, free. MO, PC.
Clarkpoint Croquet Company is located
in the Claremont Hotel, Southwest
Harbor, Maine. The 100-year-old hotel
is the home of the prestigious croquet
tournament, The Claremont Croquet
Classic. Croquet equipment usually falls
into two categories, the backyard variety
and the very expensive. Alan Madeira,
hoping to increase the popularity of the
sport, has developed a high quality
product, reasonably priced. The
Claremont Classic Set ($145) features
hardwood mallets and balls.
Professional sets and custom mallets are
also available. The Lignum Vitae mallet
is $80.

The Compleat Strategist, Inc.
11 East 33 St.
New York, NY 10016
(800) 225-4344
New York (212) 685-3880
24-page brochure, free. AE, MC, V, MO,
    BD, PC.
The Compleat Strategist deals
exclusively in war games and games of
strategy, adventure, and fantasy. They
offer the popular Dungeon and Dragons
(basic set $12), and all the supplements.
Wargaming is a serious hobby for some,
with involved games governed by
complicated rules and games that
sometimes last for days. (Occasional
breaks are taken for fortification and
necessities, such as going to work.)
Started in 1976, they now operate ten
retail stores.

Constructive Playthings
2008 West 103rd Terrace
Leawood, KS 66206
(913) 642-8244
16-page color *Home* catalog, free. 200-
    page color *School* catalog, free on
    letterhead stationery requests. MC, V,
    MO, PC.
For almost 30 years, Constructive
Playthings has provided quality play
equipment, educational toys, and
creative materials for the education of
children. Many products are
manufactured by them from solid hard
maple. Counting Hands ($8) is a wooden
puzzle with numerals of fingers and dots
underneath for counting and matching.
Mini-Motor Mat ($9.95) is a complete
miniature village on a 4 × 5 ft. heavy
duty vinyl screen. Small drivers learn
about traffic lights and safety rules
while manipulating their little cars
through "town." (It might even be a good
gift idea for a 16-year-old.)

Conquest Games
1122 W. Burbank Blvd.
Burbank, CA 91506
(213) 849-7847
2-page brochure, free. MO, PC.
Conquest is a 2-player ($16.50) and 4-
player ($32) strategy game. The board
consists of four islands connected by
bridges and sea passages. It is strictly
a game of skill, using 26 medieval pieces
(including chariots, knights, galleons,
and elephants). Two soldiers can mount
an elephant which, in turn, can board
a galleon and launch an amphibious
attack. The object of the game is to
maneuver (on land and sea) to capture
your opponents pieces and territory.
Unlike most war games, there are only
two pages of rules and they are simple
to comprehend. (Instructions are also
available in French, Spanish and
German.) The inventor, Donald Benge,
says its like playing chess on a map. The
advantage over chess is that the *first*
game of Conquest is fun to play. In fact,
even if you don't like chess, this game
is fun.

Cuisenaire
12 Church St., Box 0
New Rochelle, NY 10805
(914) 235-0900
48-page color catalog, free U.S. and
    overseas. MO, PC.
Cuisenaire has developed mathematics
learning materials for ages 4 through
16. There are the Cuisenaire rods,
Powers of Ten, and problem-solving
materials. Used by many schools as
exciting manipulative math exercises,
they are also available for fun learning
at home.

Different Drummer Workshop
Eaton Hill Rd.
Solon, ME 04979
(207) 643-2572
6-page brochure, $1. MO, PC.
More than fifty wooden toys are made from native Maine pine and hardwoods, smoothly sanded and simply designed. A doll's high chair ($14.50) is adapted from a Shaker design and completely doweled. Ducky pull toy ($5.50) and Battue, an ancient Oriental puzzle ($8), offer fun for all ages.

Discovery Corner
Lawerence Hall of Science
University of California
Berkely, CA 94720
(415) 642-1016
10-page annual color catalog, free; overseas $1. Minimum order $10 on charge card. MC, V, MO, BD.
The Lawrence Hall of Science is a center where the public attends classes, special events, exhibits, and a research center helping to develop science curricula. They also have developed an excellent catalog of gifts that encourage science play and investigation. Nasa Space Shuttle ($8.95) and Space Freighter ($8.95) are two realistic model kits designed in cooperation with NASA. Sky Challenger ($4.95) offers a cosmic adventure in stellar mapping. A miniature solar radio ($14.95) has the solar panel attached to a visor.

Dollsville Dolls and Bearsville Bears
373 S. Palm Canyon Dr.
Palm Springs, CA 92262
(619) 325-2241
20-page catalog, free if you mention this book. AE, MC, V, MO.
Dollsville Dolls and Bearsville Bears new catalog shows about 200 Teddy Bears, including Humphrey Beargart, Queen Elizabear, and Lord Tedward (who sports a .25 kt. diamond pin in his cravat). They offer a $2 coupon with the order form, and discounts for quantity orders: 10% off for three or more bears, 20% off for six, and 30% off for twelve or more bears.

Education Station
1645 Downs Drive
West Chicago, IL 60185
(800) 228-2626
(312) 231-2980
32-page color catalog, free U.S. AE, DC, MC, V, MO, PC.
In its catalog Education Station presents some of the best toys in each of its categories: electronic toys, science discovery, building blocks and modules, books, collecting, toddler toys, arts and crafts, and imagination. Don't miss this one.

The Enchanted Doll House
Rt. 7
Manchester Center, VT 05225
(802) 362-3030
80-page color catalog, $2 U.S. and overseas. AE, MC, V, MO, PC.
"We try to offer toys that are not only fun, but grow with the children and hold interest over time," says Barbara Haviland, President of the Enchanted Doll House. The catalog is divided equally between dolls, toys, and children's interests, and miniature workshop material. Dolls range from play dolls to the most sought-after collectibles, including dolls from Madame Alexander, Effanbee, Marjorie Spangler, and Gail Ann Duggan. Handcrafted Southern mansions, Victorian manors, and townhouses can be furnished from over 1,200 miniatures and room settings. Do-it-yourself enthusiasts will find kits and a complete selection of finishing materials. If you get the chance, stop to visit the actual Enchanted Dollhouse, located in an 1850 Southern Vermont farmhouse.

Family Pastimes
RR # 4
Perth, Ontario
Canada, K7H 3C6
(613) 267-4819
16-page newsalog, .25¢. MO, PC.
Ruth Deacove's family, has developed over 30 games that foster the spirit of cooperation rather than competition. Lay down your arms, warriors! Slide up to the family table for a friendly game of Mountaineering $8.95, Earth Game

$10.50, or Choices $2.25. You all win together in Community $14.50, if you can develop a community village by helping one another.

F. A. O. Schwartz
5th Avenue at 58th St.
New York, NY 10151
(212) 644-9400
24-page color catalog, free. AE, DC, MC, V.
To be locked inside F. A. O. Schwartz overnight might be many a child's fantasy come true. The catalog, chock full of delights for the young at heart, is just a sampling of America's most famous toy store. The Laredo Jeep $2,195, by Sila of Italy, is battery powered and reaches 7–8 mph. A Horse and Sulky $595, by Trupa of Italy, is kid powered with the range of speed varying on the child's intake of breakfast Wheaties. The Sounds Like Home Dollhouse $450, is a two-storied, furnished, country home electronically recreating sounds of doorbell ringing, firelogs crackling, birds chirping, clock ticking, teapot whistling, eggs frying on the stove and water running- a few homey sounds were discretely left out.

Flying Buffalo
P.O. Box 1467
Scottsdale, AZ 8525–1467
(602) 966-4727
8-page brochure. U.S. and overseas. PC.
Flying Buffalo moderates multi-player, play-by-mail games. Starweb is a game of stellar empires clashing over different worlds, and Heroic Fantasy is a game of warriors exploring a multi-level labyrinth filled with treasures (and guarded by monsters). Write Flying Buffalo for more information on play-by-mail games.

Galt Toys
P.O. Box 230
Guilford, CT 06437
(203) 265-7222
64-page color catalog, free. MC, V, PC.
Every year hundreds of new toys of every size, shape, and color are put on the market. Father marvels at the design and mother loves the concept—but not many survive the test of Junior. Galt

Toys was founded 147 years ago in Manchester, England. They have been developing and selling toys that children will play with, over and over again. Available from the American subsidiary are high quality toys whose range spans infant, preschool, arts and crafts, puzzles, imaginative play, outdoor play, games, stocking stuffers, and science. Seen in many toy stores and catalogs are the Alphabet Frieze ($8.95) and Geometric Sorting Board ($16.95). Picture Board ($9.95) is a puzzle with each lift-out piece hiding an interesting picture underneath it.

Go Fly A Kite
1201 Lexington Ave.
New York, NY 10028
(212) 472-2623
24-page color catalog, $2. Does not sell overseas. AE, MC, V, MO, PC.
With over 100 kites, winders, and air toys pictured, this is the most colorful catalog in the book. Both imported and manufactured by Go Fly A Kite, this twenty-year-old company offers them all. Some of the most suitable kites for children are the 3 × 3 ft. Sky Gypsies. Made of nylon and hand appliquéd (teddy bear, clown, boat, unicorn), the kites sell for $17. One thousand feet of 30-pound test string is $2.50. Both the large Jalbert Parafoil ($165) and the award-winning Rainbow Stunt Kite ($100) are magnificent to view. No wind today? Why not hang a wind sock from the porch, or drape a serpent kite from your child's bedroom ceiling?

The Great American Toy Company
12530 E. Bryce Circle
Cerritos, CA 90701
(213) 865-3045
7-page catalog, $1 refundable with purchase. MO, PC.
The Great American Toy Company sells handmade wooden toys finished in a non-toxic mineral oil. No two are exactly alike. The Company staff is made up of teachers who work part time during the school year and full time during the summer months.(It's probably good therapy for them.) Some of the more unusual wooden toys are a jointed bear ($11.95) that stands, sits,

and balances in any number of positions. Nine small pieces of furniture fit into one block of wood for $4.95.

Growing Child
P.O. Box 620
22N. Second St.
Lafayette, IN 47902
(317) 423-2624
52-page color Christmas catalog, 24-page Baby catalog, $1; free to newsletter subscribers. Monthly newsletter, $8.95 for a year subscription. Does not sell overseas. AE, MC, V, MO, PC.
Growing Child is a child development newsletter that is available to parents on a subscription basis. The monthly newsletter is age-graded from birth through age six. For example, when your child is one month old, you will receive the issue that tells all about the growth, development, and behavior (sleep, eat, sleep) of a one-month old, etc. In addition to your newsletter you will receive the toy catalog, offering special toys, books, and records from the best manufacturers in Europe and America. With most of the items they send "toy cards"—little suggestions on how to maximize the learning value and enjoyment of that item for your child.

G. Wilikers
1345 Diversey Parkway
Chicago, IL 60614
(312) 528-4700
32-page color catalog, free U.S. MC, V, MO, PC.
G. Wilikers offers arts and crafts for children: papier maché kits, Reeves magic brush paints, and a weaving loom by Brio. There are musical toys, building modules, games, and science toys.

Hamley's
Regent St.
London W1 St.
London W1 England
120-page color catalog, U.S. and overseas. AE, DC, V, MO.
Founded in 1760, Hamley's is one of the world's best loved toy shops. There are loads of traditional toys, as well as the popular electronic games. There are imaginative costumes: space suits,

Spider Man, Superman, and Commando. Hamley's always seems to offer a few exciting pages devoted to stocking fillers, magic, books, games, puzzles, models, and dolls. A delightful catalog.

Hank Lee's Magic Factory
24 Lincoln St.
Boston, MA 02111
(617) 482-8749
200-page catalog, $4. AE, MC, V, MO, PC. Hank Lee carries everything—well, probably everything in magic: tricks for the beginner, sophisticated stage illusions, close-up magic, coin and card tricks, mentalism, kidshow magic, and accessories. They can also fill requests for custom effects in their large production facility. The only disappointment with this excellent catalog is that the secrets of the illusions . . . are still secret.

Into The Wind
1729-SG Spruce St.
Boulder, CO 80302
(303) 449-5356
16-page some color catalog, $1; overseas $2. MC, V, MO, PC.
Check this catalog for some great prices on kites, from space age ripstop nylon airfoils to traditional silk butterflies. Do you have childhood memories of making paper kites with tails fashioned from bits of rags? They usually took sudden nose-dives, or became tangled in the only tree in the field. Modern technology has changed kiting styles and materials. And the combinations of color and applications of aerodynamics has made kite flying a form of kinetic art. The frighteningly realistic Windy Bat, imported from England, is $21. The Trilby stunt kite has a forty-five foot tubular tail for skywriting. Priced at $15, or a triple pack for $36.

The Juggling Arts
612 Calpella Dr.
San Jose, CA 95136
(408) 267-8237
10-page catalog, $1 U.S. and overseas. MO, PC.
The Juggling Arts has props for both the beginner and the professional juggler:

juggling balls, clubs, spinning plates, and cylinders. Fire torches ($10.50) are for the brave or foolhardy. To get your act started there are also books on instruction and comedy routines.

Just For Kids
Winterbrook Way
Meredith, NH 03253
(603) 279-7011
98-page color catalog, free U.S. Does not
    sell overseas. AE, MC, V, MO, PC.
Just For Kids offers some bright and fanciful toys for kids of all ages. There are soft rattles for baby, tub toys, and the latest toy creations from Europe. Not only are there toys, but you'll find darling crib linen sets, car seat covers, wall hangings, and play equipment. This is a great catalog!

Kinderparadies Hamburg
Neuer Wall 7
2000 Hamburg 6
West Germany
250-page color catalog, $2 surface, $3 air
    mail. Written in German and prices
    in German marks. DC, MC, V, MO.
Kinderparadies' catalog is written in German, but it is very easy to order from—the order number and price are clearly marked. They feature many of the top name-brand German and European toys, including stuffed animals by Stieff, and trains and railroad accessories by Marklin.

La Piñata
#2 Patio Market Old Town
Albuquerque, NM 87104
(505) 242-2400
Price list, free. MC, V, MO.
Quick, get your bat and blindfold ready. No wait, these piñatas are so pretty— maybe you should use them as a party table centerpiece, or a children's room decoration. La Piñata has the largest selection in the Southwest. They come in three sizes: miniature ($3.50), medium fancy ($6.95), and fancy large ($9.98 to $12.98). There are piñata superheros to choose from (Batman, Spiderman, and Superman). Seasonal piñata figures include hearts, pumpkins, turkeys, witches and Santas. There are, of course, many animals and story book

characters, too (Pooh Bear, Raggedy Ann and Humpty Dumpty). An enclosed card provides the history of the piñata, and they will gladly enclose a special message and/or signature specified by you. Good gift idea.

Learning World
500 Westlake Avenue North
Seattle, WA 98109
(206) 464-1600
300-page color catalog, $2. U.S. and
    overseas. MC, V, MO, PC.
Learning World offers toys, teaching aids, parental help material, school supplies, and educational materials for young children. The catalog features everything from Big Dippers (large primary pencils) to stadium bleachers. They offer a terrific selection especially for pre-school and grade school children: educational wall posters, workbooks, lacing and tying cards, construction paper, puzzles, art easels, economy jars of paste, and much more.

Maher Ventriloquist Studios
P.O. Box 420
Littleton, CO 80160
(303) 798-6830
16-page catalog. MC, V, MO, PC.
Teaching a dummy to talk looks easy— with all the books, cassettes, and accessories available from Maher's. There are books on learning ventriloquism, and developing comedy routines for school and church groups. Clinton Detweiler personally builds ventriloquial figures from years of tested experience. Each wood composition dummy is given a distinct personality by hand-carving the features. These dummies command a price of $455. There are extra options available. Wiggling ears will be an additional $40, and a raising arm $35. Want your dummy to spit? $20. Stop right there, please.

Mountain Craft Shop
American Ridge Rd., Rt. 1
New Martinsville, WV 26155
(304) 455-3570
8-page newsalog, free. Minimum order
    $10. MO, PC.

What do Whimmydiddle, Bull-Roarer and Flipper Dinger have in common? They all are strange names for traditional American toys. About fifty West Virginian artisans work in Dick Schnacke's Mountain Craft Shop to produce the best available source of American folk toys. Carried in many of America's most famous museum shops, they are listed here with an average price of $5.

Mountain Toy Makers
Box 51M
Long Lake, NY 12847
(518) 624-6175
(518) 624-6157
10-page catalog, 50¢; $1 overseas. MO, PC.
Mountain Toy Makers features wooden trucks, trains, cars, and toys made from white pine, cut from the local Adirondack Mountains. The smoothly sanded helicopter ($6), is equipped for I.F.R. (Imaginary Flight Rules). The Dump Truck ($30), Pusher ($20), and Grader ($14.50) will survive most youthful engineering projects. The best buy must be the Doll Cradle ($25.50), that will accommodate up to an eighteen-inch doll.

The Mouse Hole Workshop
524 Kinderkamack Rd.
Westwood, NJ 07675
(201) 666-1263
2-page brochure and price list, 25¢; overseas 40¢. MO, PC.
"In the time of swords and periwigs and full-skirted coats . . . there lived a tailor in Gloucester." *The Tailor of Gloucester,* by Beatrix Potter, inspired Kathleen Maseychik to create her character mice. There are more than 87 varieties of four-inch felt mice, each handcrafted and carefully fitted with a special personality. Sold in some large U.S. toy stores and famous gift catalogs, they are priced at $10.

North American Bear Co., Inc.
645 North Michigan Ave. RM. 810
Chicago, IL 60611
(312) 943-1061
4-page color brochure.

Imagine a Teddy Bear picnic with Bjorn Bearg, Zsa Zsa Gabear, Scarlett O'Beara, and Douglas Bearbanks. Can you bear it? Bjorn Bearg ($38) is wearing a white tennis outfit complete with racquet and headband (all undressable). Bearishnikov ($38) is in dancer togs. All bears are twenty-inches-tall, surface washable, and very snuggable.

Old Time Teddy Bears
304 SE 87th Ave.
Portland, OR 97216
(503) 256-4563
1-page color picture and price list, with self addressed stamped envelope. MO, PC.
Add a contemporary name to the list of notable Teddy Bear designers: Karen Walter. Karen's Teddy Bears resemble those turn-of-the-century bears— humpbacked, fully jointed, and with pretty black shoe-button eyes. The first Teddy Bear was the result of a too-cute-to-shoot cartoon, depicting President Teddy Roosevelt on a hunting trip in Mississippi. It's newest manufacturer has virtually launched a newly famous toy company: Karen's $10 to $25 bears are far less than collectors are paying for other originals.

Paradise Products, Inc.
P.O. Box 568
El Cerrito, CA 94530
(415) 524-8300
72-page color catalog, $3; overseas $3 surface, $7 air mail. Minimum order $30. MC, V, MO.
Paradise Products sells all the party supplies and decorations to make your next party a success. Next time transform your party room into a corner of Las Vegas, Waikiki, Paris, San Francisco, or Rome. Seasonal, Holiday, Ethnic, and Theme party kits available, including Safari Caribbean, Winter Carnival, Patriotic, California Dreamin', and Dixieland. Merrymaking items for an Oktoberfest party could include beer steins (you provide the beer), Tyrolean hats, German flag pennants, bunting, Kurfursten-damm street sign, balloons, posters, and table decorations.

Pentangle
Salisbury Lane
Over Wallop Hants
S020 8HT England
0264 781833
14-page color catalog, $1 U.S. and
    overseas. MO, PC.
Pentangle started a craze by loosing
upon the world the Rubik's Magic Cube.
The world record-selling puzzle (with
43,252,033,274,489,856,000
combinations) has also engendered
nearly as many copyright infringement
lawsuits, says Pentangle. If you have
recovered from the Rubik's Cube mania
and are ready for another mental
mystifier, Pentangle offers over fifty
different puzzles. Rotascope is a circular
version of the simple sliding square
puzzle that's been around for over 100
years. The prices are listed in British
pounds. (Let's face it: if you can tackle
a Pentangle puzzle, you can surely figure
out how many dollars there are in a
pound.)

Play-By-Mail
P.O. Box 21484
Sacramento, CA 95821
(916) 487-5722
35-page catalog, free. MC, V, MO, PC.
Play-By-Mail gaming is a fast-growing
area of the fantasy and wargaming
hobbyists. The company, Schubel & Son,
acts as the gamemaster and referees the
rules and combat determinations. The
player enjoys the excitement and
adventure of playing and meeting other
players through the mail. Both small
games (where ten to fifty people
participate) and a single giant game
(with 2,000 players from all over the
world) are available. Science Fiction
games are staged in the high technology
world of super robots. Fantasy games
have themes where magic forces and
barbarian warriors do battle.

Playper Corporation
P.O. Box 312
Teaneck, NJ 07666
(201) 836-7300
3-page color price list, free; overseas 1
    International Reply Coupon. MO, PC
    from the U.S.

"Mom, there's nothing to do!" It's time
to pull out the Funcovers by Playper
Corporation, Mom. Funcovers are
colorful paper wrappers for half-gallon
milk cartons that transform the cartons
into big building-block toys. There are
six perforated and scored wrappers to
a package. Packages are available in
Bricks, Trucks, Big City, Downtown,
Words/Animals, and Numbers for $3.50
each. Developed by Marjorie Weinberg
as a low-cost, high quality construction
kit, they are suitable for one child or the
entire neighborhood, for ages 3 through
10. If you start saving those empty milk
cartons today, by the time you've sent
for your price list and received your
order you'll have enough to build quite
a "town."

Pollock's Toy Museum
1 Scala St.
London W1P 1LT England
636-3452
6-page brochure, free U.S. and overseas.
    MO, PC.
Pollock's offers toy theaters. Published
in book form, each book includes a
theater printed on cardboard, plus
scenery, characters, and text for one
play. The backcloths measure seven and
one-half inches by six inches and the
characters are about three-inches-tall.
Scissors and glue are required for
assembly, and each theater set sells for
about $3. Theater productions include
Cinderella, Ali Baba and the Forty
Thieves, The Sleeping Beauty, and The
First of Twelfth Night, to name a few.

Red Balloon
1073 Wisconsin Ave. NW
Washington D.C. 20007
(202) 965-1200
18-page catalog, free U.S. Does not sell
    overseas. Minimum order $10. AE,
    MC, V, MO, PC.
This catalog shows line drawings of
children's toys ranging from the old-
fashioned and traditional pogo sticks
and carpenter's tool sets to the electronic
age, including Gyrobots and water
rockets. And then there is a collection
of toys you just don't find everywhere
that makes this catalog special: double-
runner ice skates, musical spoon

(percussion) instruments, Together Time Cards (wonderful activities to combat boredom), coin changer (the real thing, great for learning to count money), and a balloon animal kit (all the balloons and instructions for twisting balloon animals).

Resources for the Gifted
3421 North 44th St.
Phoenix, AZ 85018
(602) 840-9770
24-page color catalog, free. Minimum
   order $20. MC, V, MO, PC.
There are plenty of mind motivators and thinking cap activities here for the talented and gifted child, pre-school to 12th grade. Analyze ($7.95), Create-A-Code ($9.95), and The Great Brain ($29.95) reveal the fun of problem-solving using logic and creative thought processes. Kathy Kolbe offers books, games, and kits that encourage children to analyze and mentally stretch. Recently, Kathy polled kids nationwide asking them their favorite items from the catalog. She then grouped these games, and sells them for a package discount price of $99.50.

Spielzeug-Rasch
Gerhart-Hauptmann-Platz 1
2000 Hamburg 1
West Germany
250-page color catalog. $2.50. Written in
   German and prices in German marks.
   MO, PC.
Juguete! Spielzeug! Giocattolo! Jouets! No matter what language you mention the word "toys" in, children will understand. Spielzeug-Rasch and Kinderparadies work off the same general catalog. They offer stuffed animals by Stieff, trains and railroad accessories by Marklin, and many other popular German brand-name toys.

Spinning Fool Top
P.O. Box 158
Sparta, TN 38583
(615) 484-8862
2-page brochure and price list, free. MO,
   PC.
The Spinning Fool top has been hand-carved in the Southern Appalachians for more than 100 years. The story of

the history of this specially designed top is worth sending away for. Now with speed-increasing refinements (and a patent to boot), this handle-type top ($4.10) has a reported record spinning time of twelve minutes. (Try to top that one.)

Stocking Fillas
Tennant House
The Village, Prestbury
Cheshire SK10 4EL England
32-page color catalog, 1 International
   Reply Coupon U.S. and overseas. V,
   MO, PC.
Over 150 smaller and inexpensive toys and gifts. There are many toys that would make terrific party favors, stocking or piñata stuffers, or Halloween trinkets. There's a good selection priced between $1 and $3 (and many toys not found in America.)

Toy Balloon Corporation
204 East 38th St.
New York, NY 10016
(212) 682-3803
4-page brochure, free, PC.
Balloons of every size, shape and color. There are round balloons from six inches in diameter to giant display balloons six feet in diameter. There are special shape balloons—heart, doll, rabbit face, airship, and doggy. Balloons come in stripes, polka dots, marbleized, and in special fashion colors of brown, purple, lavendar, burgundy, black, clear, and peach. Trademarks and slogans can be imprinted in a variety of colors. There are also balloon accessories such as blow pumps, shower nets, cello sticks, strings, and easy clip-on balloon fasteners.

Toys To Grow On
PO Box 17
Long Beach, CA 90801
(800) 421-5354
34-page color catalog, $1 U.S. and
   overseas. AE, MC, V, MO, PC.
There are balls to kick, stickers to lick, and sticks and paints to . . . well, you know. This is a catalog you shouldn't miss. The classic Jack-In-The-Box ($16.95) is Italian-crafted from polished hardwood. Safety Stilts ($5) are actually

five-inch buckets the child holds on to with hand cords. Tennis Anywhere (usually means it's fairly safe indoors) comes complete with two rackets, portable net, and foam rubber balls. There are several free booklets available: *Ten Tips on Choosing Toys for Children, Toys for Sick Children,* and *Toys To Take on an Airplane.*

Tryon Toymakers
Rt. 3 Box 148
Campobello, SC 29322
(803) 457-2017
14-page color catalog, $1; overseas $2. PC.
There's not a single toy requiring a battery—just timeless wooden toys painted in bright primary colors. The company began around the turn of the century, and today the same handcrafted toys are sold in fine galleries, museum shops, and specialty shops throughout the U.S. What would you put in your dream box? Tryon Toymaker's brightly painted dream box holds a wolf, princess, cowboy, lollipop, magic wand, ice cream cone, spotted cat, flying unicorn monster, and a flower—wonderful things for story telling or just fun fantasy.

Tully Toys
4606 Warrenton Rd.
Vicksburg, MS 39180
(601) 638-1724
1-page pictured price list, free. Does not sell overseas. MO, PC.
Rocking horses have been around for a few hundred years. Their simple concept has given birth to many childhood fantasies. Tully Hall has created a menagerie of rocking creatures: Ride on a Dinosaur, Rhinoceros, or long-necked Giraffe. If you'd like a more unusual mount, try a chicken or a shrimp. All rocking toys are priced at $40, except the tall Giraffe (who has a slightly taller price).

U.S. Chess Federation
186 Rtd. 9W
New Windsor, NY 12550
(914) 562-8350
8-page catalog, free MC, V, MO, PC.
Chess Life magazine subscription $14. Masters and novices alike can join the U.S. Chess Federation. This national organization offers national tournaments, rating system, *Chess Life* Magazine, and a membership organization. The free U.S. Chess Federation catalog sells chess boards and sets, cassettes, tournament and club supplies, and postal play. For you blitz buffs, there are chess clocks imported from Germany and Japan. There are many books, several specializing in openings, middle games and combinations, and endgames. Check this one out, mate. (Sorry).

U. S. Games Systems, Inc.
38 East 32nd St.
New York, NY 10016
(212) 685-4300
48-page color catalog. $1; overseas $5. MO, PC.
U.S. Games offers over 100 different decks and books on tarot and cartomancy. When the mysterious Tarot cards are spread on the table, they are reputed to have wonderful powers of foretelling fate and the future. "Reading" the 78 tarot cards must be learned. The cards have different meanings, according to their placement and order.

Wff'N Poof
1490-FB South Blvd.
Ann Arbor, MI 48104
(313) 665-2269
Price list, free. MO.
What game is drawing kids to a Chicago grade school an hour earlier every day for scrimmages? Football might be your likely guess; Equations would be the correct answer. Equations is a pre-algebra game that can be as simple or complex as the players make it, depending on their math knowledge level. Kids love it, and it makes learning fun. Wiff 'N Poof makes other "games for thinkers," all priced around $12. Games of logic, creative math, science, word structures, strategy, and set-theory will challenge all ages.

Wonders
P.O. Box 1348
Beaufort, SC 29902
(800) 845-8248
South Carolina (803) 846-8155
32-page color catalog. U.S. and overseas.
   AE, MC, V, MO, PC.
Children's toys for all ages. Nautilus is
a big one-piece molded plastic mountain
for climbing fun. It offers a cave to hide
in, and a slide, all in a 3 × 4 ft. space.
Farm Fences and Farm Families
(combined) contain twenty-four heavy
plastic fence sections and farm animals,
created in meticulously handpainted
detail. There's even a farm couple, and
a decorative storage tin.

The Wooden Soldier
North Conway, NH 03860
(603) 356-6343
32-page color catalog, free U.S. AE, MC,
   V, MO, PC.
The Wooden Soldier offers a delightful
mixture of children's toys and clothes.
There are delicate porcelain Christmas
dolls and ornaments, including a few
special treetop angels. Jack-In-The-Box
($24) features a bear popping out of a
beautifully découpaged wooden box.
Quilted and appliquéd snow suits,
jumpers, and overalls are available in
sizes 12 months to 4T. If you haven't seen
Stieff's Fawn, it's here and priced at $64.

Wooden Swing Company
45 New York Avenue Dept. IM
Framingham, MA 01701
(617) 620-1909
11-page color brochure, free U.S. and
   overseas. MC, V, PC.
The Wooden Swing Company sells
quality backyard wooden playground
equipment, manufactured by Swing
Design. There are swing sets, gyms,
slides, climbing ropes, playhouses, and
sandboxes. Prices range from $20 for
some swing set accessories, to as high
as $1,000 for some swing set designs.

World Wide Games, Inc.
3527 West S.R. 37
PO Box 450
Delaware, OH 43015
(614) 369-9631
24-page catalog, free U.S.; overseas $2,
   refundable. MC, V, MO, PC.
Anyone for a quick game of Gomoku,
Skittles, Pooff, or Yoot? Though the
names sound strange they are all
handcrafted wooden games, with
origins from around the world. There
are action, skill, and strategy games for
all ages, including Dutch Shuffleboard
($106), French Table Cricket ($88),
Chinese Tangram ($25), and American
Indian Pommawonga ($7.50). Skittles is
a fascinating game that originated in
China and was taken by sailors back to
England, where it acquired the English
name of skittles. Each player sends a
spinning top traveling through a box,
scoring as it knocks down pins.

Yards of Fun
P.O. Box 119
N. Manchester, IN 46962
(800) 348-5400
12-page color catalog, free U.S. and
   overseas. MC, V, MO, PC.
Yards of Fun manufactures fine
residential wooden playground
equipment in six major units. The major
swing and climbing units can be
remodeled (with a variety of
accessories) to accommodate a growing
family's needs. They are pressure-
treated and warranted for twenty years
against rot and insects.

Yesteryear Toy Co.
P.O. Box 3283
Charleston, WV 25332
(304) 744-2152
6-page color catalog. AE, MC, V, MO, PC.
Yesteryear Toys offers you an
alternative to plastic, micro chips, and
battery-operated toys. There are over 80
different old-fashioned toys, all
handcrafted and painted. Start a toy
soldier collection, including a guard
house, cannon and drum . . . The
beautifully detailed Davis Creek
Railroad is a seven-piece train set
($300). Each car is approximately three
and one-half inches tall by four inches
long. An engine, tender with logs, boat
car, sleeper, baggage car, mail car, and
caboose (complete with politician),
make up the rest.

TRAVEL

American River Touring Association
445 High St.
Oakland, CA 94601
(415) 465-9355
24-page catalog, free. MO, PC.
American River Touring Association offers exciting white-water river trips throughout the world. Licensed professional guides enrich your experience with their knowledge of geology and history of the river environments. You can choose from a four-day trip on the Rogue River in Oregon ($315), to a more adventurous tour of the Amazon headwaters in Peru ($1,285). Churning rapids, serene still waters, and passages through canyon walls offer the photographer and explorer alike a unique vacation. As campsite chefs, the guides treat you to gourmet roughage by night.

Aventours Travel, Ltd.
801 Second Ave.
New York, NY 10017
(212) 807-8770
24-page color catalog, free MC, V, MO, PC.
Aventours says, ". . . the only way to really enjoy your American adventure is to get out there and live it." Participants (ages eighteen through thirty) from all over the world experience the natural wonders and big cities of America on Adventours. Traveling in deluxe air-conditioned motor coaches, Aventours are a combination camping and motor tour. The nineteen-day Southeast Circle Tour ($629) visits New York, stops along the eastern Seaboard, and Orlando's Disney World. On the northbound leg stops include Memphis, Nashville, Winston-Salem, and Washington.

Bike Vermont
P.O. Box 75
Grafton, VT 05146
(802) 843-2259
4-page brochure, free MO, PC.
Bike Vermont offers weekend and five-day midweek guided bike tours in Vermont. Staying in small and unique country inns, you'll find cozy bedrooms, friendly innkeepers, and hearty meals. The weekend tours ($145) feature both nights at the same country inn. A basic loop of twenty to twenty-five miles can be lengthened with other routes, depending on your skill, energy, and enthusiasm. The midweek tours ($365) start on Sunday evening and finish back at the same inn the following Friday. (A different inn is visited each night.) Vermont does have hills, which they don't apologize for; after all, it wouldn't be Vermont without them. Two experienced leaders and a support van accompanies each group of fifteen to twenty bikers. Children (starting at age 10) accompanied by their parent(s) are welcomed.

Bradt Enterprises, Inc.
95 Harvey Street
Cambridge, MA 02140
(617) 492-8776
16-page catalog, .50; overseas $1. AE, MC, V, MO, PC.
Bradt Enterprises publishes guidebooks for backpackers interested in hiking in third-world countries. There are guidebooks for backpacking in Latin America, Africa, Greece, and river travel in many parts of the world. Adventure seekers will find *Africa: The Nile Route* a good guide for surface traveling in North Africa from Cairo to Nairobi. Those wishing to explore beyond the usual European tourist traps will enjoy the *French Farm & Village Holiday Guide,* an interesting annual edition listing over 1,500 inexpensive French farm houses (or Gites). Most of the guidebooks are in the $6 to $9 price range.

Council on International Education Exchange
Student Travel Catalog
205 East 42nd St.
New York, NY 10017
65-page some color catalog, free.
The Student Travel Catalog has the most complete coverage of student travel information available. The catalog "helps you decide where to go and how to get there, as well as how to get around and what to do once you're there." It provides information on passports, student I.D. cards, American Youth Hostel cards, Railpasses, tours, work or study-abroad programs, exchange programs, and travel fares. If you're a young person interested in international education and/or travel, advanced planning with this catalog can make your trip a success.

Echo: The Wilderness
6529 Telegraph Ave.
Oakland, CA 94609
(415) 652-1600
14-page color catalog, free U.S. and
    overseas. MC, V, MO, PC.
Echo runs white water raft trips throughout the West and in Alaska. Trips range from float trips through the Birds of Prey Natural Area (on the Snake River in Idaho) to very challenging white water trips on such greats as the Tuolumne and Middle Fork of the Salmon River. What started in 1971 as a one-river guide company has now grown to 70 guides running fifteen rivers throughout the Western U.S.

Ford's Travel Guide
Box 505
22151 Calrendon St.
Woodland Hills, CA 91365
(213) 347-1677
137-page *Freighter Guide* subscription
    printed semi-annually, $12; 160-page
    International Cruise Guide
    subscription printed quarterly, $28.
    MO, PC.
Ford's *Freighter Travel Guide* is the best on the market for information on cargo-passenger ships. The illustrated guide lists all popular freighter cruises, and describes ships and accommodations.

Rates are listed both one-way and round-trip. Ford's *International Cruise Guide* is a worldwide directory of cruises by geographic area. Each review lists sailing dates, minimum fares, ports of call, and length of cruise. For your vacation planning convenience the directory is cross-indexed by steam line, ship, sailing date, point of embarkation, destination, and ports of call.

Forsyth Travel Library, Inc.
P.O. Box 2975
Shawnee Mission, KS 66201
(913) 384-0496
8-page catalog, 25¢; overseas 2
    International Reply Coupons. MC, V,
    MO, PC.
Forsyth Travel Library is a leading distributor of travel books and maps for travelers and travel agents in North America. They are the sole distributors in North American for the Thomas Cook Continental Timetable ($15.95), which contains over 800 detailed tables of current rail schedules for every major British and European Passenger rail route. Travel guides by Ford, Fielding, Fodor, Michelin, Berlitz, Baedeker, and Frommer are available.

Michelin Tire Corporation
Guides and Maps Division
2500 Marchus Ave.
Lake Success, NY 11042
10-page brochure, free U.S. and
    overseas. AE, MC, V, PC.
Today Michelin is one of the largest publishers of travel guides and maps to over 150 cities and countries around the world. The famous Red Guides rate hotels and restaurants and provide facts about scenic views, average meal costs, and maps. The Green Guides provide information on sightseeing, culture, suggested itineraries, attractions, and maps. Few people remember that the first pneumatic bicycle tire was invented in 1891 by the Michelin brothers. Once car manufactures recognized their advantages and applied them to automobiles, it wasn't long before people were inspired to travel by car. Michelin produced the first motorist's and cyclist's guide in

1900; now it has grown to over 400 pages of useful advice on where to eat, sleep, and buy fuel and spare parts.

New Age Travel
International Spare Room
839 Second St., Suite 3
Encitas, CA 92024
(619) 436-9977
20-page catalog, $4; overseas $5. MO, PC.
Looking for sleeping accomodations has always been a challenge; motels are located so that you seem to go by the best ones between 9:00 AM and noon. New Age Travel offers bed-and-breakfast information services for many popular tourist spots as well as off-the-beaten-track locations. Recently expanded services include information on home exchange listings, and car and rail transportation information.

Ocean Voyages, Inc.
1709 Bridgeway
Sausalito, CA 94965
(415) 332-4681
48-page catalog, $1; overseas $2. MO, PC.
Mary Crowley has organized a worldwide network of over sixty schooners, yawls and sloops for hire, offering sailing charters in places like Hong Kong, the Caribbean, the Seychelles, Tahiti, and the Aegean Islands. Ocean Voyages offers planned sailing adventours, where small groups have the sense of their own yacht and take an active part. Mary says whether there are just four people wishing to discover the wonders of the Galapagos, or an alumni group yacht dockside in an exotic area, it need not be expensive. Seven days on a 50-foot sloop in the Hawaiian Islands starts around $550.

Quester Tours
257 Park Ave. South
New York, NY 10010
(212) 673-3120
32-page catalog, free. PC.
Quester Tours offers unusual natural wildlife explorations of national parks and nature reserves. The experience is broadened as other aspects of natural history are explored (art, architecture and archeology). For example, if you select the Machu Picchu (Peru) tour, the focus is on the Incan city as well as flora and fauna. (Endemic birds of that tour include Cock of the Rock and the Cinnamon Flycatcher.) Although the Temple of the Tooth in Kandy sounds like an ideal location for this year's Dental Association convention, it is actually an excursion available on the Sri Lanka (Ceylon) tour ($3,006). The price includes first class accommodations, meals, and land and air fare from New York.

Traveler's Checklist
Cornwall Bridge Road
Sharon, CT 06069
(203) 364-0144
8-page catalog, free. MC, V, MO, PC.
If you have ever searched from store to store for the travel accessories you need for your trip, you'll find a terrific selection offered by Traveler's Checklist in its new catalog. Included are such basics as foreign voltage converters, adapter plugs, personal appliances, money belts, wheels for luggage, toiletry kits, travel clocks, and pocket flashlights. Travel necessities include a money convertor ($4), a Film Shield Pouch for protecting film from airport security screens ($8.95), and a luggage caddy ($22). The 5-Way Personal Security System sounds an eighty-five decibel warning against fire, smoke, and break-ins, and also acts as an emergency signal and safety light ($49.95).

Travelore Report
225 South 15th St.
Philadelphia, PA 19102
(215) 545-0616
6-page newsletter. One year
   subscription $25; overseas $30. MC, V, MO, PC.
This newsletter is an insider's guide and source reference to worldwide vacationing destinations. It offers helpful advice on the best ways to travel, what to see and do, and what to avoid. There are good tips on planning, hotels, shopping, dining, car rentals, tours, and cruises. Started in 1971, it is a well-respected, tell-it-like-it-is traveler's guide.

Travel Smart
Dobbs Ferry, NY
(914) 693-8300
8-page newsletter. One year
  subscription, $37. AE, MC, V, MO, PC.
Travel Smart is one of the best traveler's
newsletters. Features include a roundup
of unusual tours, charter facts, discount
air fares, money tips abroad, cruises,
current conditions in a country, and
travel notices. Get the nitty-gritty facts
about Taipei, or the latest price on
sleeper trains in Egypt.

Unique and Exotic Travel Reporter
P.O. Box 98833
Tacoma, WA 98499
(206) 582-0339
8-page newsletter. One year
  subscription $24; overseas $32. MC, V,
  MO, PC.
This monthly newsletter is "written for
those who have done the usual already."
These unique tours and cruises offer
some very special travel opportunities.
Highlights from recent newsletters
include running on the Inca Trail,
sunken ships in Australia, trans-
Siberian Railway tour, schooner cruises
from Maine, and an opera cruise to
Scandinavia. (In many cases these
exotic tours are less expensive than the
"grand tour" trips offered by travel
companies.) A twenty-one day
photography tour in Peru is $1,985 (land
only). Traveling by Douglas or Boeing
will seem boring compared to the
sampling of transportation modes
described in this unique newsletter:
dogsled, camel, Concorde, balloon, and
log raft.

The Y's Way
356 W. 34th St.
New York, NY 10001
(212) 760-5856
12-page catalog, free. MO, PC.
The Y's Way provides a network of
21,000 clean and comfortable rooms at
YMCAs in the center of town—at an
average cost of $16.40 a night (single)
or $12.60 per person (double). With 95
overnight lodging centers in 64 North
American cities, Y's Way is the nearest
counterpart to the European youth
hostel system existing in America. Also
available are many packaged tours to
Y vacation centers in the Blue Ridge,
Adirondacks, Berkshires, and Rocky
Mountains. Packages from three to eight
days (to New York, San Francisco, New
Orleans, and the Hudson River Valley)
are also available.

UNUSUAL

American Asian Worldwide Services
P.O. Box 2777
Orcutt, CA 93455:0777
(805) 937-5230
16-page brochure, free U.S. MC, V, PC.
Mail order brides is an old business in
the U.S. The Western homesteaders used
to contact East Coast marriage brokers
who specialized in matchmaking.
Usually, coach fare was all that was
required for East to meet West. Today
the mail order bride business is much
more sophisticated. American Asian
Worldwide Services (AAWS) offers
professional assistance in introducing,
interviewing, and marrying Asian
ladies to American men. The women are
mostly from Maylasia and the
Philippines, and have a variety of
educational backgrounds and interests.
AAWS offers information on how to
utilize their search service, tips for
effective correspondence, interviewing
guides, travel and immigration
information, and (of course) a dignified
Las Vegas Wedding package (free
witnesses). To find out more about
AAWS, simply write and request their
information package. To be active in
their matchmaking services requires a
fee for a six-month club membership.
There are also subscriptions to the
monthly club bulletins and consultation
services available.

Barrett Side by Side Bicycles, Inc.
Angola, NY 14006
(716) 549-4157
Brochure, free U.S. and overseas.
Barrett is the world's only manufacturer
of a two-wheeled side-by-side bicycle
built for two. Uniquely designed, two
riders of matched or unmatched
weights ride close to each other. One
rider is the controller and the other need
not even know how to ride a bicycle.
Built mostly by hand (at the rate of about
fifty bicycles per year), Barrett bikes are

strictly a mail order business. There are
two models available—a folding
lightweight model for $1,140, and the
standard model for $840.

Big League Cards
121 Cedar Lane
Teaneck, NJ 07666
(201) 692-8228
Price list, free U.S. Does not sell
    overseas. AE, DC, MO, V, MO, PC.
Jim Bouton has created a terrific
novelty—Big League Cards. These are
authentic-looking baseball cards with
pictures of (look again) yourself, or
anyone interested in immortalizing
themselves. For about $25 you can
receive your picture and statistics on a
full color, regulation size, 50-card pack
of baseball cards. These might be used
as business cards, birth announcements,
or just to tell someone "you're Big
League."

Brookfield Nursery and Tree Plantation
844 Hutcheson Drive
Blacksburg, VA 24606
(703) 552-8733
Price list free U.S. MC, V, PC.
UPS delivers a lot of wonderful
Christmas goodies to peoples' doors
every year, but a boxed Christmas tree?
Yes, Brookfield Nursery will mail order
a White Pine Christmas tree (the thick
bushy kind) for $24.95 (and $29.95 west
of the Mississippi). The trees are packed
by a special machine in a wax-lined
carton designed by the owner, Mr.
Larson.

Bynamics Corporation
109 Railside Rd.
Don Mills, Ontario
M3A 3PA Canada
(416) 449-2490
Bynamics Corporation offers the
advanced EDO 600 System. This slim,
multi-function, leather-bound desk top

console allows you to perform many complex tasks with pushbutton ease. It is advertised as "a synergistic composite of executive desk top needs." A few of the EDO's functions are: an intelligent one or ten phone line telephone with LED display, a multi-memory calculator, and a calendar, clock, and alarm. The telephone itself is an electronic wonder, with storage memory of 112 telephone numbers—and the hands-free feature allows you to talk from anywhere in the room without the usual echo chamber sound. There is also automatic redial, a muting device which allows your caller to continue his monologue while you make private remarks in your office, and a pre-dial feature which allows you to view the telephone number—and correct a wrong one before the call goes through. The single line EDO 600 system sells for $895, and the multi-line is $1,395.

C'est Croissant
P.O. Box 1987
Allentown, PA 18105
(215) 821-5511
2-page brochure, free U.S. Does not sell
    overseas. AE, MC, V, MO, PC.
Imagine UPS delivering to your door (or office) a dozen oven-fresh croissants and three jars of delicious preserves, elegantly wrapped with a red-and-white striped tea towel and bright red ribbon. Creative gift-givers have proclaimed this "the gift of the year." The flaky croissants arrive beautifully boxed, and enclosed are simple warming instructions that ensure bakery freshness. The Croissant Gift Pack includes one dozen croissants (all butter, all almond, or half-and-half), preserves, tea towel, and special handwritten gift card, and is priced at $18. What a thoughtful thank-you gift, or a wonderful brunch invitation—"You provide the croissants and I'll supply the rest."

Chocolate Photos
200 West 57th Street, Suite 1105
New York, NY 10019
(212) 977-4340
2-page color brochure, free U.S. Does not
    sell overseas. AE, MC, V, MO, PC.

"Have your favorite face captured in chocolate!" All that's needed is a photo from which staff artists create a line drawing. The image is transferred to a mold, then filled with the finest imported chocolate. The embossed image and name is then wrapped in gold foil and is available in twelve or twenty-four piece boxes. (They can also produce your business logo from a business card, not to mention your pet, house, car, or your holiday or personal message. The Box of twelve sells for about $22.50.

Christmas Letters
2930 Pearl Street
P.O. Box 1560
Boulder, CO 80306
(303) 442-7927
3-page brochure $1 U.S. and overseas.
    Minimum order 50 copies. MO, PC.
Christmas Letters offers a creative way to wish your friends a Merry Christmas. You can share a favorite photo and news about your family on specially selected letterheads, cards, or postcards. You create the design and send in your photograph; Christmas Letters sends back to you Christmas letters that are really special.

Elegance in Wood
230 Pinehurst Ave.
Los Gatos, CA 95030
(408) 358-1100
John Linstrum has revolutionized the art form of business cards. Handmade from thin slices of fragrant wood veneers, these distinctive business cards are sure to make an impression on clients. There are over 100 species of wood available, ranging from pine to walnut, and the name of each wood is embossed on the back. The basic price is about $20 for 1,000 cards, plus a one-time engraving plate charge.

Facemakers, Inc.
140 Fifth St.
Savanna, IL 61074
(815) 273-3944
4-page some color catalog, $5; overseas
    $7. MO, PC.
Facemakers specializes in reproducing their clients' portraits in the styles of significant old masters of the past. You

can be painted as one of your ancestors, or a general from the Civil War, or a coquette from the court of Louis XV. Any historical or legendary character is possible. One of Facemaker's clients was so pleased with her first Fragonard-style ceiling painting that she commissioned twenty-two more paintings—one for each room in her mansion and each in a different style, from Flemish Renaissance to a ten-by-thirty-foot mural depicting her as Venus in Wagner's "Tannhauser." Prices start at $500.

Feartek Productions
7 East 20th Street, 11th floor
New York, NY 10003
(212) 741-0253
60-page color catalog, $17.50 U.S. and
    overseas. MO, PC.
Feartek creates scary apparitions, poltergeists, and other frightening figures for dark rides and haunted houses in Amusement Parks. Previously only the most prominent families could afford skeletons in their closets. Now (for $795) you can have one, too. There is a tortured corpse impaled on a spiked rack, there are gruesome decapitated heads, and a ghastly apparition complete with blood-curdling screams. (Lighting effects available.) There are over fifty humanoid figures, eighteen fantasy figures, and more than forty-five display accessories available. Prices for humanoid figures range from $46 (for a plastic hand on an arm stump) to $2,995 (for four whispering half-human, half-stone figures). Jim Goodman, president, also has a separate and unique line of visual merchandising displays, under the trademark of Canthus.

Flying Foods International
43–43 Ninth St.
Long Island City, NY 11101
(212) 706-0825
10-page brochure, free U.S. and
    overseas.
Three young men successfully ventured into the food import business in a unique way: they fly in the finest fresh foods the whole world has to offer, and sell to famous restaurants and the most

discriminating epicures. Fresh Dover Sole from the North Sea arrives in New York within twenty-four hours after it is caught. They offer such extraordinary specialities as Italian Radicchio (wild chicory), rare Maché (a buttery-textured lettuce from France), Scallops from the Isle of Man, Blue Hawaiian Shrimp, fresh Foie Gras from France, and Italian sun-dried tomatoes. They have opened offices in Houston, Dallas, Philadelphia, Boston, Seattle, and Los Angeles. And they have recently begun exporting hard-to-find American foods, including Shiitake (wild American black forest mushrooms), chili peppers, fresh Louisiana Shrimp, and mesquite charcoal from Texas (a six-pound bag sells for $15.95). Call them to cater your next gala event.

Gargoyles, Ltd.
512 South Third St.
Philadelphia, PA 19147
(215) 629-1700
32-page some color catalog, $5; overseas
    free. AE, MO,
Gargoyles specializes in architectural antiques and reproductions for restaurant interior designs. They offer package restaurant decor and interiors. When you consider all the catalog has to offer, there are items that would be great for home decorating, too, especially the den. There are pub mirrors, framed prints and wall sculptures, ceiling fans and tin ceilings. There are many colorful plaques, as well as brass and copper accessories. There are some terrific antique carved mantels, gingerbread trim, and bolsters that could be incorporated in a remodeling or new construction home project.

International Star Registry
1821 Willow Road
Northfield, IL 60093
(800) 282-3333
(312) 441-8520
Price list, free U.S. MC, V, PC.
What's better (and less expensive) than having an impressive building named in your honor? A star, that's what. International Star Registry will name a star in the constellation of your choice

for $35. You will receive a certificate and two sky charts which show the location of your star. The star will be in the Northern Hemisphere and visible with the aid of a small telescope. The star names will be filed in the Registry's Swiss vaults, and will be listed in a forthcoming book. Now there's something to put in your sweetheart's Christmas stocking.

In Touch Networks, Inc.
322 W. 48th St.
New York, NY 10036
(212) 586-5588
8-page brochure, free U.S.
In Touch Networks, Inc. is a closed circuit radio reading service for the blind. They have recently introduced the "In Touch Mail Order Shopper," a weekly half hour radio program which describes (and provides ordering information on) articles from a wide variety of catalogs. The program is distributed to over 100 other radio reading services, and is available directly from In Touch at a cost of $3.50 for a tape or cassette.

Le Nez du Vin
68 Lockwood Rd.
Riverside, CT 06878
(203) 637-9106
4-page brochure, free U.S. and overseas. MO, PC.
"Le Nez du Vin," by Jean Lenoir, is literally an encyclopedia of aromas, an innovative tool and self-educating system to learn to recognize and memorize the fifty-four most commonly found scents in wine. The handsome case comes with fifty-four vials of essence and their reference cards. Can you pick out the scent of mown hay in Sauvignon Blancs, the smell of cloves in Chardonnays, or the odor of hazelnut in a good Meursault? This is a great work aid for amateur tasting enthusiasts and wine professionals. It sells for $250 including shipping charges.

Miya Epoch
1635 Crenshaw Blvd.
Torrance, CA 90501
(213) 320-1172
8-page brochure, free U.S. and overseas. MC, V, MO, PC.

Miya Epoch introduced the first electric fishing reel eleven years ago, and now has the latest computerized fishing reel model available—the Miya Epoch 1000, priced at about $1,300 (about 30% to 40% below retail price). From shallow to extremely deep ocean floors, this computerized fishing reel has big memory banks for programming your own fishing techniques. A few of the amazing things the reel does include: frees spool and releases line, memorizes depth of line released, memorizes space and cycles of each jig, auto-winds, gives warning signals when load becomes excessive, and many more.

Nomadic Tipi Maker
17671 Snow Creek Rd.
Bend, OR 97701
(503) 389-3980
14-page brochure, $1; overseas $2. MO, PC.
Jeb Barton creates made-to-order tipis (or tepees). Made from 100% cotton duck, the basic designs are those outlined in the book, *The Indian Tipi,* by Reginald and Gladys Laubin (Sioux Indians). Jeb's company has simply added greater reinforcing, more durable weather resistant fabrics, and design variations including the Blackfoot lift pole flap and the Cheyenne extensions of smoke flaps. *The Indian Tipi* book, an excellent reference source, is sent with each tipi, or is available without a tipi for $5.

Previews
51 Weaver St.
Greenwich, CT 06830
(203) 622-8600
380-page color catalog, $18 U.S. and overseas. AE, MO, PC.
Previews is the world's leading international real estate firm specializing in the marketing of luxury properties. Their list of clients includes Jimmy Stewart, Dean Martin, Kim Novak, and Presidents Ronald Reagan, Gerald Ford and Jimmy Carter, and Kings and Queens of Europe. The annual catalog, *Previews Guide to the World's Finest Real Estate,* features a manor house on a private island in Bermuda, a villa in Marrakesh once

owned by the King of Morocco, a dude ranch in New York, and lovely Southern mansions. Previews began in 1933 (you can imagine what some of those properties sold for then) and was unique in offering 16mm motion pictures of the estates they were marketing. Today they continue their lucrative marketing strategy with a glamorous catalog, color brochures on specific properties (by request), and video cassette tours of all major properties. Now you can go house shopping (or villa, mansion, castle, ranch, and island shopping) without ever leaving your armchair.

Robert D. Grimm Marketing, Inc.
305 East 46th St.
New York, NY 10017
(212) 838-5115
4-page color brochure, free U.S. AE, MC, V.
Robert Grimm offers some fun gift ideas—two helium filled mylar balloons in a gift box ($20.95). For an additional charge a music box can be added. Opening the box triggers the tune of your choice to play. They also sell giant chocolate chip cookies (sixteen inches in diameter for $24.95) and special occasion cakes complete with plates, forks, and candles ($23.95). How they keep the cake from arriving as an upside-down cake . . . is their secret.

Robot Shack
P.O. Box 583
El Toro, CA 92630
28-page brochure, $3; overseas $7. MO, PC.
Robot Shack manufactures personal robot kits and parts for those who want to design and construct robots from scratch. Only minimal skills are needed to assemble the kits (so they claim). Robots can be controlled either by the on-board controller, remote radio control, or by interfacing with a home computer. Robot kits range from $29.95 to $499.95. (Robots can perform guard duty by sounding a chirping alarm when people approach.) Other optional robot functions include acting as a night light in the house, reacting to sounds, moving android-like arms, blinking lights (and eyes and heart), telling time,

blowing up balloons, and squirting water.

Stromberg's
Pine River, MN 56474
(218) 543-4223
56-page color catalog, free U.S. MC, V, PC.
Stromberg's is nationally recognized as "the source" for unusual pets. For a mere $4,750 you can own a zebra; for $450, a pair of swans will grace your lake; and for $100 a peacock will add a little color to your estate grounds. There are also llamas, bobcats, bear cubs, timber wolves, buffalo, cougar cubs, and ostriches. Their fowl collection is almost limitless.

Think Big
390 West Broadway
New York, NY 10012
(800) 221-7019
(212) 925-7300
6-page color brochure, free U.S. and overseas. AE, MC, V, PC.
Think Big has taken everyday household items—pencils, crayons, toothbrushes, matches, coffee cups, can openers, tennis rackets, safety pins, wisks, coat hangers, screws, and stamps—and made them BIG. Each sculpture is duplicated down to the finest detail. The Ticonderoga yellow pencil is seventy inches tall, and is priced at $90.

Wilderness Log Homes
Route 2
Plymouth, WI 53073
(414) 893-8416
50-page some color brochure, $6. U.S. and overseas. MC, V, MO, PC.
Wilderness Log Homes sells Insulog and Full Log pre-cut home kits. They offer a selection of over 40 models of cozy-looking log homes. Although these homes have always been popular as lake and mountain cottages, they are now recognized by builders as excellent choices for primary dwellings. These comfortable log homes can be built for less, and are energy-efficient. Prices range from $25,000 to $50,000 (for standard packages) and include all the materials except plumbing, electricity, and heating.

APPENDIXES

CLOTHING SIZE CHART

Women
Dresses and Sweaters

	XS	S	M	L	XL				
United States	6	8/10	12/14	16/18	20				
British	8	10/12	14/16	18/20	22				
Continental	36	38/40	42/44	46/48	50				

Shoes

United States	5	5½	6	6½	7	7½	8	8½	9	9½	10
British	3½	4	4½	5	5½	6	6½	7	7½	8	8½
Continental	36		37		38		39		40		41

Stockings

United States	8	8½	9	9½	10	10½
British	8	8½	9	9½	10	10½
Continental	0	1	2	3	4	5

Men
Suits and Sweaters

	S	M	L	XL
United States	36	38/40	42	44
British	36	38/40	42	44
Continental	46	48/50	52/54	56

Shirts

United States	14	14½	14	15½	16	16½	17
British	14	14½	15	15½	16	16½	17
Continental	36	37	38	39	41	42	43

MAIL ORDER SHOPPING RECORD

Name and Address of Company	Name of Item	Product Number	Catalog Date and Page Number	Price	Shipping and Extra Charges	Date Ordered	Form of Payment	Date Received

U.S. CUSTOMS DUTY

Alcoholic Beverages

	Int. Rev. Tax (per proof gal.)	Customs Duty (per proof gal.)	
Distilled Spirits:			
Brandy	$10.50	35¢ to $3.40	($8.88)
Gin	$10.50	50¢	($7.52)
Liqueurs	$10.50	50¢	($11.64)
Rum	$10.50	$1.57	($7.52)
Tequila	$10.50	$1.25 to $2.27	($6.34)
Vodka	$10.50	87¢ to $2.56	($6.72)
Whiskey			
Scotch or Irish	$10.50	35¢	($7.52)
Other	$10.50	43¢	($5.00)
Wine*			
Sparkling	$2.40–$3.40	$1.17	($6.00)
Still	17¢–$10.50	31½¢–$1	($1.25)
Beer*	$9 bbl. (31 gal.)	6¢	(50¢)

* *Per gallon (128 fluid ounces).*

Antiques produced prior to 100 years before the date of entry—Free (Free) (Have proof of antiquity obtained from seller.)

Automobiles, passenger—2.8% (10%)

Bags, hand leather—6.9 to 10%

Bamboo, manufactures of—9.6 to 13% (45 to 50%)

Beads: Imitation precious and semi-precious stones—
4.7 to 9.9% (20 to 80%)
Ivory—7% (45%)

Binoculars, prism—Free (60%)
Opera and field glasses—Free (45%)

Books, foreign author or foreign language—Free (Free)

Cameras:
Motion picture, over $50 each—5.3% (20%)
Still, over $10 each—5.3% (20%)
Cases, leather—9.0% (35%)
Lenses, mounted photographic—9.6% (45%)

Candy:
Sweetened chocolate bars—5% (40%)
Other—7% (40%)

Chess sets—7.9% (50%)

China, other than tableware
Bone—9.6% (70%)
Nonbone—2.8 to 15.8% (25 to 70%)

China tableware, household, available in 77-piece sets
Bone—12.8% (75%)
Nonbone—
Valued not over $56 per set—32.3% (75%)
Valued over $56 per set—13.2% (75%)

Cigarette Lighters:
Pocket, valued at over 42¢ each—11.1 to 15.8% (110%)
Table—8.4% (60%)

Clocks:
Valued over $5 but not over $10 each—52 + 11.2% + 4.3¢ for each jewel ($3 each + 65% + 25¢ for each jewel)
Valued over $10 each—78 each + 11.2% + 4.3¢ for each jewel ($4.50 each + 65% + 25¢ for each jewel)

Cork, manufactures of—18% (45%)

Dolls and parts—14.8% (70%)

Drawings done entirely by hand-Free (Free)

Earthenware tableware, household, available in 77-piece sets
Valued not over $38 per set—17.5% (55%)
Valued over $38—8% (55%)

Figurines, china—3.1 to 19.1% (20 to 70%)
Film, imported, not qualifying for free entry is dutiable as follows:
Exposed motion-picture film in any form on which pictures or sound and pictures have been recorded, developed or not developed, is dutiable at 0.24¢ per linear foot. (3¢ per linear foot)
Other exposed or exposed and developed film would be classifiable as photographs, dutiable at 3.6% of their value. (25%)
Unexposed film—4.4% (25%)
Flowers, artificial—6 to 31.2% (60%)
Fruit, prepared—Free to 35% (Free to 35%)
Fur:
Wearing apparel—6.9 to 13% (35 to 50%)
Other manufactures of—3.4 to 7.4% (50%)
Furniture:
Wood, chairs—6 to 6.9% (40%)
Wood, other than chairs—3.8% (40%)
Bentwood—9.6%

Glass tableware—8.3 to 44% (60%)
Gloves:
Not lace or net, plain vegetable fibers, woven—25% (25%)
Wool, over $4 per dozen—30¢ lb. + 14.8% (50¢ lb. + 50¢%)
Fur—7% (50%)
Horsehide or cowhide—15% (25%)
Golf balls—4.2% (30%)

Handkerchiefs:
Cotton, ornamented—3.2¢ each + 36.3% (54%)
Cotton, plain 21.3% to 4¢ lb. + 29% (37 to 67.5%)
Linen, machine hemmed—7.8% (50%)

Iron, travel type, electric—39% (35%)
Ivory, manufactures of—5.1% (35%)

Jade:
Cut, but not set and suitable for use in the manufacture of jewelry—2.3% (10%)
Other articles of jade—21% (50%)

Jewelry, precious metal or stone:
Silver chief value, valued not over $18 per dozen—27½% (110%)
Other—9.3% (80%)

Knives, forks, flatware:
Silver—2¢ ea. + 7% (16¢ each + 45%)
Stainless steel—½¢ each + 6% to 1¢ each + 17½% (2 to 8¢ + 45%)
Spoons, tableware
Silver—9.6% (65%)
Stainless steel—6 to 17% (40%)

Leather:
Flatgoods, wallets—5.9 to 8% (35%)
Other manufactures of —2.8 to 7.9% (35%)

Mah-Joncg sets—7.9% (50%)
Motorcycles—4.4% (10%)
Mushrooms, dried—2.2¢ lb. + 7% (10¢ lb. + 45%)
Musical instruments:
Music boxes—5.6% (40%)
Woodwind, except bagpipes—6.2% (40%)
Bagpipes—Free (40%)

Paintings done entirely by hand—Free (Free)
Paper, manufactures of 6.9% (35%)
Pearls:
Loose or temporarily strung and without clasp:
Genuine—Free (10%)
Cultured—2.3% (10%)
Imitation—14% (60%)
Temporarily or permanently strung (with clasp attached or separated) 9.3% to 19.3% (45 to 110%)
Perfume—4¢ lb. + 6.3% (40¢ lb. + 75%)
Postage Stamps—Free (Free)
Printed Matter—Free to 7% (Free to 45%)

Radios:
Transistor—8.2 to 9.2% (35%)
Other—6% (35%)
Rattan:
Furniture—14.9% (60%)
Other manufactures of —9.6% 9 (45%)
Rubber, natural manufactures of—5.1% (35%)

Shaver, electric—5.5% (35%)
Shell, manufactures of—3.4% (35%)
Shoes, leather —2½ to 20% (10 to 30%)
Skis and ski equipment—5.8 to 7.3% (33.3 to 45%)
  Ski boots—Free to 8.5% (20 to 35%)
Sound recordings:
  Records, phonograph—4.4% (30%)
  Tapes—0.9¢ per square foot
Stereo Equipment:
  Depending on components—5.1 to 7.8% (35%)
Stones, cut but not set:
  Diamonds not over one-half carat—Free (10%)
  Diamonds over one-half carat—Free (10%)
  Other—Free to 2.5% (10 to 20%)
Sweaters, of wool, over $5 per lb.—25¢ + 19% (54.5%)

Tape recorders—4.7% (35%)
Televisions—5% (35%)
Toilet preparations;
  Not containing alcohol—6.2% (75%)
  Containing alcohol—6.5¢ + 6% (40¢ lb. + 75%)
Toys—12.3% (70%)
Truffles—Free (Free)

Vegetables, prepared—Free to 17.5% (up to 50%)

Watches, on $100 watch, duty varies from $2 to $5.37 ($14 to $52) plus 9.3% on gold case or bracelet

Wearing apparel:
  Embroidered or ornamented—15 to 40% (90%)
  Not embroidered, not ornamented
    cotton, not, knit—8 to 21% (37½ to 45%)
    cotton, knit—16.7–21% (45%)
    linen, not knit—6% (35%)
    manmade fiber, knit—17¢ lb. + 28.1–21¢ lb. + 32.5%
    manmade fiber, not knit—17¢ lb. + 24–21¢ lb. + 27.5 (76%)
    silk, knit—8.7% (60%)
    silk, not knit—133.2% (65%)
    wool, knit—25¢ lb + 12.8–25¢ + 27.7% (52 to 63%)
    wool, not knit—25¢ lb. + 17.2–33¢ lb. + 21 (58–58.5%)

Wood:
  Carvings and articles of—6.6% (33.3%)

INDEX